# Cross-Cultural Psychology

# Cross-Cultural Psychology

*Contemporary Themes and Perspectives*

Edited by

Kenneth D. Keith

WILEY-BLACKWELL

A John Wiley & Sons, Ltd., Publication

This edition first published 2011

© 2011 Blackwell Publishing Ltd except for editorial material and organization © 2011 Kenneth D. Keith

Blackwell Publishing was acquired by John Wiley & Sons in February 2007. Blackwell's publishing program has been merged with Wiley's global Scientific, Technical, and Medical business to form Wiley-Blackwell.

*Registered Office*
John Wiley & Sons Ltd, The Atrium, Southern Gate, Chichester, West Sussex, PO19 8SQ, United Kingdom

*Editorial Offices*
350 Main Street, Malden, MA 02148–5020, USA
9600 Garsington Road, Oxford, OX4 2DQ, UK
The Atrium, Southern Gate, Chichester, West Sussex, PO19 8SQ, UK

For details of our global editorial offices, for customer services, and for information about how to apply for permission to reuse the copyright material in this book please see our website at www.wiley.com/wiley-blackwell.

The right of Kenneth D. Keith to be identified as the author of the editorial material in this work has been asserted in accordance with the UK Copyright, Designs and Patents Act 1988.

*Library of Congress Cataloging-in-Publication Data*

Cross-cultural psychology : contemporary themes and perspectives / edited by Kenneth D. Keith.
    p.   cm.
  Includes bibliographical references and index.
  ISBN 978-1-4051-9804-2 (hardback)
  ISBN 978-1-4051-9805-9 (paperback)
1. Ethnopsychology–Cross-cultural studies.   I. Keith, Kenneth D. (Kenneth Dwight), 1946–
  GN502.C75 2011
  155.8'2–dc22
                                          2010016194

A catalogue record for this book is available from the British Library.

Set in 11/13pt Dante by SPi Publisher Services, Pondicherry, India.
Printed in Singapore by Ho Printing Singapore Pte Ltd

01   2011

*For Connie and for Sam, Sophie, and Jamie with the hope that you will contribute to a world more peaceful, civil, and beautiful than the one my generation will leave you*

# Contents

# Contributors

**Stephanie L. Anderson**
Central Community College
550 S. Technical Blvd.
P. O. Box 1024
Hastings, NE 68902–1024
sanderson@cccneb.edu

**Bernard C. Beins**
Department of Psychology
Ithaca College
953 Danby Road
Ithaca, NY 14850–7290
beins@ithaca.edu

**Allison Christian**
Department of Psychology
Central Michigan University
101 Sloan Hall
Mt. Pleasant, MI 48859

**Leeva C. Chung**
Department of Communication
Studies
University of San Diego
5998 Alcalá Park
San Diego, CA 92110–2492
leeva@sandiego.edu

**Michael Cole**
Department of Communication

University of California, San Diego
LaJolla, CA 92093
mcole@weber.ucsd.edu

**Robert A. Cummins**
School of Psychology
Deakin University
221 Burwood Highway
Burwood, VIC 3125
Australia
robert.cummins@deakin.edu.au

**Kristy K. Dean**
Department of Psychology
Grand Valley State University
1 Campus Drive
Allendale, MI 49401–9403
deankr@gvsu.edu

**Howard T. Everson**
Center for Advanced Study in
Education
Graduate School & University Center
City University of New York
365 Fifth Avenue
New York, New York 10016
howard.everson@gmail.com

**Peter J. Giordano**
Department of Psychological Science

Belmont University
1900 Belmont Boulevard
Nashville, TN 37212
pete.giordano@belmont.edu

**James T. Gire**
Department of Psychology &
Philosophy
Carroll Hall
Virginia Military Institute
Lexington, VA 24450
GireJT@vmi.edu

**Regan A. R. Gurung**
Department of Human
Development
2420 Nicolet Drive
Mary Ann Cofrin C309
University of Wisconsin, Green Bay
Green Bay, WI 54311
gurungr@uwgb.edu

**Hui-Chin Hsu**
McPaul Center
Department of Child and Family
Development
University of Georgia
Athens, GA 30602
hchin@uga.edu

**Michael R. Hulsizer**
Behavioral and Social Sciences
Webster University
470 East Lockwood
St. Louis, MO 63119
hulsizer@webster.edu

**Hyi Sung Hwang**
Department of Psychology
San Francisco State University
1800 Holloway Ave.
San Francisco, CA 94132
hyisungh@gmail.com

**Noriyuki Inoue**
School of Leadership & Education
Sciences
University of San Diego
5998 Alcalá Park
San Diego, CA 92110–2492
inoue@sandiego.edu

**Terence Jackson**
Middlesex University Business School
Hendon Campus
The Burroughs
London NW4 4BT
United Kingdom
T.Jackson@mdx.ac.uk

**Kenneth D. Keith**
Department of Psychological
Sciences
University of San Diego
5998 Alcalá Park
San Diego, CA 92110–2492
kkeith@sandiego.edu

**Mary E. Kite**
Department of Psychological
Science
Ball State University
Muncie, IN 47306
mkite@bsu.edu

**Anne M. Koenig**
Department of Psychological
Sciences
University of San Diego
5998 Alcalá Park
San Diego, CA 92110–2492
akoenig@sandiego.edu

**David S. Kreiner**
Department of Psychology
Lovinger 1111
University of Central Missouri

Warrensburg, MO 64093–5089
kreiner@ucmo.edu

**Anna L. D. Lau**
School of Psychology
Deakin University
221 Burwood Hwy., Melbourne
Victoria 3125, Australia
anna.lau@deakin.edu.au

**Katie Lawson**
Psychology Department
Radford University
Radford, VA 24142
kmlawson@radford.edu

**Hilary M. Lips**
Psychology Department
Radford University
Radford, VA 24142
hlips@radford.edu

**Linh Nguyen Littleford**
Department of Psychological
Science
Ball State University
Muncie, IN 47306
lnlittleford@bsu.edu

**David Matsumoto**
Department of Psychology
San Francisco State University
1800 Holloway Ave.
San Francisco, CA 94132
dm@sfsu.edu

**Kristen McCabe**
Department of Psychological
Sciences
University of San Diego
5998 Alcalá Park
San Diego, CA 92110–2492
kmccabe@sandiego.edu

**Richard L. Miller**
Department of Psychology
University of Nebraska at Kearney
905 West 25th Street
Kearney, NE 68849–1280
millerrl@unk.edu

**Adriana Molitor**
Department of Psychological
Sciences
University of San Diego
5998 Alcala Park
San Diego, CA 92110–2492
amolitor@sandiego.edu

**Yozan Dirk Mosig**
Department of Psychology
University of Nebraska at Kearney
905 West 25th Street
Kearney, NE 68849–1280
mosigy@unk.edu

**Martin Packer**
Psychology Department
Duquesne University
Pittsburgh, PA 15282
Department of Psychology
University of the Andes, Bogota
packer@duq.edu

**William L. Phillips**
Department of Psychology
Dominican University of California
50 Acacia Avenue
San Rafael, CA 94901
wphillips@dominican.edu

**Loreto R. Prieto**
Department of Psychology
W218 Lagomarcino Hall
Iowa State University
Ames, IA 50011–3180
lprieto@iastate.edu

**Robert L. Schalock**
Department of Psychology
Hastings College
P. O. Box 285
Chewelah, WA 99109
rschalock@ultraplix.com

**Sara Schwatken**
Department of Psychology
W283 Lagomarcino Hall
Iowa State University
Ames, Iowa 50011–3180
saraschw@iastate.edu

**Junko Tanaka-Matsumi**
Department of Integrated
Psychological Sciences
Kwansei Gakuin University

Uegahara, Nishinomiya
Hyogo 662–8501
Japan
Jmatsumi@kwansei.ac.jp

**Linda M. Woolf**
Behavioral and Social Sciences
Webster University
470 East Lockwood
St. Louis, MO 63119
woolflm@webster.edu

**Jennifer Zwolinski**
Department of Psychological Sciences
University of San Diego
5998 Alcalá Park
San Diego, CA 92110–2492
jzwolinski@sandiego.edu

# Preface

Psychology is one of the areas of study currently enjoying great popularity among college and university students. The field is increasingly scientific in its methods, and we are more and more often able to approach what we consider truth in our findings. Or are we? Much of our work is very good, but it may be limited in ways we have often failed to realize.

Until recent times, psychology as it is taught in the United States has been largely a North American psychology. North Americans have conducted most of our research, using North Americans (usually European American students) as research subjects, and too often failing to ask critical questions. Some of those questions are these: Can our knowledge be generalized to people from other backgrounds—cultural, national, ethnic, or racial? Do people of differing backgrounds experience basic psychological processes (development, learning, emotion, social interaction, disorders, sexuality) in the same way? Are there basic psychological principles or truths that transcend culture? Are some psychological principles and processes tied closely only to the cultures in which they arise? These questions, and others like them, must be asked, and it is one of the purposes of this book to guide you in asking them.

The authors of the chapters in this book are not only researchers, but also accomplished teachers. They share with me the conviction that our investment in the students of today is crucial to the future of the cultures of the world. As today's students you are preparing for your roles as tomorrow's leaders. The world has far too much poverty, illness, environmental danger, and intercultural strife. I hope you will play a role in confronting these challenges, and that your background in psychology will help you along the way.

You are perhaps reading this book in a course in cross-cultural psychology. Let us hope that one day, cross-cultural psychology will not be a separate offering—because cross-cultural psychology is not so much an area of content as it is an approach, a method, or a mindset that should pervade our study of human behavior. I hope you will see a day when culture will be an integral part of the mainstream curricula of psychology departments, not just in specialized courses, but as an accepted aspect of all our courses. Then we will truly have a psychology of all people.

Each author represented in this book attempts, in his or her own way, to further the aim of a comprehensive study of human behavior. Their perspectives vary fairly widely, but all bring an inclusive, open attitude to the study of the relation between psychology and culture. I hope, in your study of their work, that you will thoughtfully and deliberately construct your own perspective and take it with you as you embark upon your own career and your role as a responsible citizen of planet Earth.

Kenneth D. Keith
San Diego

# Acknowledgments

I am grateful to the contributors to this volume, whose investment of time and effort reflects their commitment, both to broadening the scope of psychology and to the education of the students of today. Barney Beins and Anne Koenig deserve thanks for editorial assistance and support, and I could not have completed the book without the editorial and technical help of Connie Keith.

I also owe thanks to the reviewers who provided valuable insight and counsel at various points along the way. They include: K. Robert Bridges of The Pennsylvania State University; Catherine Caldwell-Harris of Boston University; Allison S. Carson of Manhattanville College; Stephen F. Davis of Morningside College; William K. Gabrenya, Jr., of Florida Institute of Technology; Salvador Macias, III, of the University of South Carolina Sumter; Edward Orehek of the University of Maryland; Valerie Whittlesey of Kennesaw State University; and Yueping Zhang of Lewis and Clark College. And I extend my appreciation for generous support to the University of San Diego, Kwansei Gakuin University, and St. Clare's College, Oxford.

Finally, three individuals deserve special acknowledgement. Constance Adler at Wiley-Blackwell, with quiet competence and consistency, kept me on schedule and saw the project through to completion. Annie Jackson's diligent and patient editing made the book far better than it might otherwise have been. And I would not have undertaken this task but for the encouragement, persistence, faith, and support of Christine Cardone.

# Part I

# Basic Concepts

The first section of this book includes two chapters intended to provide an introduction to the field of cross-cultural psychology and some of the basic issues and principles that we encounter when we embark upon study of the field. Thus, Part I deals with the construct of *culture*—what it is and some of the key characteristics that define culture. We will see that cross-cultural interest in psychological phenomena is by no means new, but that the nature of that interest has evolved in interesting ways, from the ancient Greeks to the early twentieth century, and now to the twenty-first century.

As modern psychologists have undertaken systematic study of culture, the field of cross-cultural psychology has emerged, but not without some disagreements about how psychologists should understand and use cultural constructs. Among the perspectives arising from these differing viewpoints are cultural psychology, indigenous psychology, and cross-cultural psychology. Cross-cultural psychologists are interested in how culture influences behavior, and in how researchers integrate key cultural variables into their work. These variables include a number of critical dimensions of culture. Best known among these is the individualism-collectivism (IC) dimension, but, as we will see, other dimensions may well be more important than past research has suggested.

Individuals of course become enculturated in the environments into which they are born and in which they develop. This process results, almost inevitably, in a predictable tendency to view other cultures from the perspective of our own. Such ethnocentric tendencies often result in psychological barriers between cultures; we are likely to view cultures different from our own as less desirable and perhaps even threatening. Researchers have undertaken a number of approaches, not only to understanding ethnocentrism, but also to attempting to reduce it; we will review some of these efforts in this section of the book.

Early work in cross-cultural psychology emphasized identifying and measuring differences between cultures. This was perhaps understandable in the early days of the science. In fact, we could make the argument that every science began with description before moving to efforts to explain its subject matter. It seems clear now that the time for obsession with difference is behind us. Cross-cultural psychology today is moving toward not only a more sophisticated understanding of our differences, but also recognition that, despite cultural differences, human beings across cultures share many more commonalities than differences. Part I will prepare us for the many approaches that follow as the authors of the remaining chapters explore various aspects of those differences and similarities.

# 1

# Introduction
# to Cross-Cultural Psychology

## Kenneth D. Keith

In this book we attempt to provide the reader with a wide-ranging introduction to the relation between culture and a number of core subjects in the field of psychology. This aim requires that we begin by defining culture and the intersection between culture and psychology—the discipline we know today as cross-cultural psychology. Although all psychological research takes place in a cultural context, psychological scientists have not always taken account of the influence of culture on psychological processes, or the generalizability of those processes across cultures. This chapter provides a brief overview of these ideas as an introduction to the varied topics that follow in the remainder of the book.

## Culture

Many writers, including anthropologists, sociologists, and psychologists, have written about culture, providing a variety of definitions and descriptions. Heine (2008) described a two-part definition of culture: (a) information (e.g., beliefs, habits, ideas), learned from others, that is capable of influencing behavior; and (b) a group of people who share context and experience. Matsumoto (2009) offered a comprehensive definition, calling culture

> a unique meaning and information system, shared by a group and transmitted across generations, that allows the group to meet basic needs of survival, by coordinating social behavior to achieve a viable existence, to transmit successful social behaviors, to pursue happiness and well-being, and to derive meaning from life. (p. 5)

Matsumoto's (2009) definition shares key characteristics with that of Triandis, Kurowski, Tecktiel, and Chan (1993), who defined culture in terms of objective and subjective characteristics that increase the odds of survival, provide satisfaction for people sharing an environmental context, and are shared via language. Objective elements of culture, as identified by Triandis et al., are the tangible objects of culture (architecture, food, manufactured products), whereas subjective culture comprises such human elements as social, economic, political, and religious practices. It is of course the subjective human elements that are of most interest to psychologists. Recently, Cohen (2009) advocated extension of the notion of culture to a variety of constellations of human groups, including religion, socioeconomic status, and region (within a country). Finally, Berry, Poortinga, Segall, and Dasen (2002) perhaps put it most succinctly, when they called culture simply "the shared way of life of a group of people" (p. 2). Common features of virtually all definitions of culture include the notion of *a group with shared behaviors, values, and beliefs that are passed from generation to generation.* Cultures may vary in their complexity (Triandis, 1980); and some embody significant diversity (i.e., are multicultural), with many subcultures (Miller, 2008), while other cultures are much more homogenous, or "tight" (Triandis, 1977).

It is also important to note what culture is *not*. Perhaps most importantly, culture is not synonymous with nationality or race. We need look only at such diverse nations as the United States or the United Kingdom to see that a nation may include many cultural and subcultural groups—thus making almost pointless a discussion of, for example, "the" American culture. And genetic research has suggested that the biological differences among races are relatively superficial, leading to the conclusion that race is largely psychosocially constructed (Mio, Barker-Hackett, & Tumambing, 2006) and, in the words of Segall, Dasen, Berry, and Poortinga (1999) an "illusion" (p. 20). This does not mean, of course, that biology has no role to play. Behavior is a product of the complex interplay among heredity, environment, and individual skills and knowledge; and the field of evolutionary psychology has sought to explain how evolution has led to the development of the human brain and the capacity to learn, giving rise to the knowledge and values that constitute culture (Pinker, 1994). Culture evolved because it contributed to human survival and reproduction (Baumeister, 2005).

Finally, culture can be construed as a characteristic residing *within* the person, and thus related to all the psychological processes associated with the person; or culture can be viewed as *outside* the person, making it more like a research variable or manipulation (e.g., Triandis, 2000). In the following sections we will discuss the implications of these perspectives for research in the field.

## Why Cross-Cultural Psychology?

Arnett (2008) asserted that the conclusions of research conducted by American psychologists "are based not on a broad cross-section of humanity but on a small corner of the human population—mainly, persons living in the United States"

(p. 602). In his analysis of six prestigious journals of the American Psychological Association, Arnett found that the large majority of authors were from American universities, and that a similar majority of the research participants were Americans—most of them European Americans (the latter state of affairs prompted Guthrie, 1998, to famously observe, in the title of a book on the role of African American psychologists, that *Even the Rat was White*). Further, in those cases in which the authors reported by Arnett were not affiliated with American institutions, they were predominantly from Western and English-speaking universities. It is not, Arnett argued, scientifically sound to believe that studies focused on 5% of the world's population can be generalized to the whole of humanity. In a follow-up to Arnett's study, Webster, Nichols, and Schember (2009) studied a different (but overlapping) group of journals; although they reported an encouraging trend over a 30-year period, they too found a majority of American researchers in the journals they studied. Similarly, Quinones-Vidal, Lopez-Garcia, Penaranda-Ortega, and Tortosa-Gil (2004) found more than 90% of the studies appearing in the *Journal of Personality and Social Psychology* were North American.

Arnett (2008) attributed the lack of cross-cultural research in American psychology at least in part to a philosophy of science dedicated to identifying universal principles. This approach, Sue (1999) contended, has included a focus on internal validity (demonstration of causal connections) at the expense of external validity (generalizability). However, LoSchiavo and Shatz (2009) saw the problem in a different light, acknowledging the lack of cultural diversity in psychological research, but arguing that many American psychologists simply do not have convenient, affordable access to international samples. Nevertheless, North American psychology has been limited in its scope, and American psychologists have tended to treat their findings as if they were universal truths, even when researchers did not test findings in diverse cultures. Psychologists interested in culture, however, have sought to move from assumptions about universal principles to empirical testing across cultures (Heine & Norenzayan, 2006). Whatever the reasons, these concerns about the need to understand the role of culture in psychology are significant, and they extend to the challenges of teaching in psychology as well (e.g., Bronstein & Quina, 1988; Goldstein, 1995; Hill, 2002).

## Teaching About Culture:
## How Have Our Textbooks Changed?

My first experience as a teacher came more than four decades ago when, as a beginning graduate student, I taught introductory psychology. I can still remember the excitement I felt when the department chair offered me the job, and the passion with which I undertook to prepare and present the class. I chose one of the mainstream textbooks of that time (Morgan & King, 1966) and went to work.

When I compare that textbook to those of today, there are many superficial differences. The book was printed on a kind of off-white paper, and all but three of more than 800 pages were printed in black, white, or shades of gray; the only exceptions were illustrations of the color spectrum, the function of cones, and negative afterimages. Strangely, a color wheel illustrating the complementarity of colors actually appeared in black, white, and gray, with pure red portrayed as black!

Today's introductory psychology textbooks are, of course, filled with four-color illustrations, color photographs, and a variety of colorful computer-generated images. But these are only differences of style. The important question we should ask is this: To what extent has the content of the psychology we teach changed over the years? And, more specifically, are we teaching a more inclusive psychology than that of a few decades ago, or a century or more ago? In the context of these questions, we will review some developments in the field as we have attempted to encompass the role of culture in our understanding of psychological concepts and phenomena.

My 1960s textbook (Morgan & King, 1966) had a very brief (three-paragraph) section on cultural influences on personality, and little more than a page on intelligence differences associated with culture—in this case rural vs. urban and "Negroes" vs. Whites. Today, of course, we know that race cannot be equated with culture, and to their credit, Morgan and King concluded that "We are not required to make decisions about groups; instead, the problem is to make decisions about individuals" (p. 441). Nevertheless, in the realm of personality and intelligence, culture got little attention. Elsewhere, in a chapter on social influences, Morgan and King devoted about four pages to a discussion of culture; they defined culture, similarly to today's researchers, in terms of groups sharing behaviors, attitudes, and values. Anthropology rose to the fore in their treatment of culture, with the observation that most such work had been done with cultures deemed "primitive" or "backward" (p. 567). Except for brief references to American culture, the focus was on work in cultural anthropology, including that of Margaret Mead (1935).

Despite mention of cultural differences and the potential for international conflict and communication failure as a result of differential cultural experience, Morgan and King cited few examples in accounting for such differences. The emphasis was on differences involving Native Americans, Samoans, and "primitive" cultures of New Guinea. Within the U.S., Morgan and King noted a couple of rather isolated religious sects, but did not discuss the notion of cultural diversity. Although not using the word "ethnocentrism" (see chapter 2 in this volume), Morgan and King did acknowledge the tendency for people to take for granted the stereotypes and attitudes that characterize their own culture. Nevertheless, the book's index contained only seven entries for "culture" or "cultural," all referring to the personality, intelligence, or social sections of the book. The Morgan and King treatment of culture was typical for the era, and perhaps more comprehensive than some other textbooks of the time. It was certainly more comprehensive than earlier general psychology books. Ladd (1894), for example, made no reference to the concept of culture, and William James (1892/1961) did not mention culture in his widely used *Psychology: The briefer course*.

We might logically ask whether introductory or general psychology books of the twenty-first century are more likely to acknowledge the role of culture than these earlier authors. Happily, the answer is yes. For example, typical introductory books of today (e.g., Bernstein, Penner, Clarke-Stewart, & Roy, 2008; Myers, 2007; Weiten, 2008) may include 30 to 50 index entries dealing with culture, and the books integrate the concept of culture in such mainstream sections as abnormality, achievement motivation, alcohol, altered states, attachment, attitudes, attractiveness, attribution, cognitive development, communication, gender roles, parenting, perception, personality, prejudice, self-esteem, sleep, temperament, testing, and more. Clearly, coverage of culture in the teaching of psychology has come a long way, not only since the 1960s, but also since the 1980s, when Cole (1984) acknowledged the presence of international psychology in the American curriculum, but nevertheless lamented that "cross-cultural work is ghettoized" (p. 1000), leaving students with little knowledge of the psychological characteristics of other cultures.

Today, many student readers may know that people around the world recognize basic emotional expressions, and that cultural display rules regulate these expressions; that there is a complex interplay among genetics, culture, and intelligence; that North American methods of IQ assessment are culturally limited; or that cultural experience with two-dimensional depictions of three-dimensional objects influences recognition and interpretation of photographs or drawings. Students may also know that one person's schizophrenia may be another's vision, or that cultural sensitivity is essential to successful therapy. We are beginning to see recognition of the integral role that culture plays in the ways that psychological principles play out across cultures. But, as always in the evolution of our knowledge and our science, there is plenty of room for improvement, and the field remains haunted by the findings and views of such writers as Arnett (2008) and Sue (1999) about its cultural limitations.

## Cross-Cultural Psychology: What It is and Where It Has Come From

The field of cross-cultural psychology finds itself today in somewhat the same position as the discipline of psychology soon after the turn of the twentieth century, when Hermann Ebbinghaus (1908/1973) observed that "psychology has a long past, yet its real history is short" (p. 3). Just as there was widespread interest in the subjects we now call psychology long before the field was given a name, so it was that many writers were interested in culture and cultural relationships long before the modern concern with the connection between culture and psychology.

Some reports are ancient; thus, as early as five centuries BCE, Hecataeus of Miletus proposed division of the world into Asia and Europe, and observed that "the traditions of the Greeks seem to me many and ridiculous" (Durant, 1939, p. 140). Herodutus, at about the same time, looked down upon those who did not speak Greek or live in Greek city states (Klineberg, 1980). Other reports, often taken as the beginning point for cross-cultural psychology, date from the early twentieth century. W. H. R. Rivers (1905), for example, conducted research comparing visual perception across cultures, and W. G. Sumner (1906), in his study of various cultures, coined the term *ethnocentrism* to denote the tendency of people to elevate their own cultures and to denigrate the cultures of others. At about the same time, Wilhelm Wundt (1916) was engaged in developing his multi-volume folk psychology. Subsequently, although a variety of anecdotal reports appeared, several decades passed before an explosion of cross-cultural work appeared early in the second half of the twentieth century (Lonner, 1974). And cross-cultural psychologists have had major influence in the past two decades (Matsumoto & Juang, 2008) as cross-cultural research has proliferated. For example, a recent PsychINFO© search using "cross-cultural psychology" as the subject returned 1,823 titles published from 1915 to 2009; a similar search for "cultural psychology" produced 1,966 titles. The development of the field has not, however, always progressed smoothly and without the emergence of divergent points of view. Chief among these have been the perspectives known as *cross-cultural psychology, cultural psychology,* and *indigenous psychology.*

## Cross-cultural psychology

Kagitçibaşi and Berry (1989) defined cross-cultural psychology as the "study of similarities and differences in individual psychological and social functioning in various cultures and ethnic groups" (p. 494). Cross-cultural psychologists originally set out to seek universal principles that would apply across cultures (Sinha, 2002). Thus, cross-cultural psychology traditionally involved testing Western theories in other cultures (Laungani, 2002; Yang, 2000), with the notion that culture was independent of the individual and separable from psychological activities and principles (Greenfield, 2000). Cross-cultural psychologists often collect data across multiple cultures, comparing and contrasting effects in an effort to produce knowledge about phenomena that are universal and those that are culture-specific (Triandis, 2000), and attempting to determine how different cultures influence behavior (Brislin, 2000).

Cross-cultural psychologists have conducted much of their research using the research designs and methods of mainstream Western psychology. Although this may allow for the possibility of identification of psychological universals, the cross-cultural approach has received criticism on several fronts. For example, the use of culture as an independent variable, and the associated failure to identify specific aspects of culture that may influence dependent measures, has long been a problem (Lonner, 1974), resulting in flawed conclusions about the causal role of cultural attributes (Ratner & Hui, 2003).

Further, studies have sometimes employed research materials (e.g., tests, apparatus, stimulus arrays) that are unfamiliar or ecologically invalid for people in some cultures (Ratner & Hui, 2003), with the result that conclusions or comparisons may be meaningless. For instance, if we make assumptions about the individualistic or collectivistic (IC) nature of cultures, and then attribute other observed differences between the cultures to our assumptions about the IC dimension, we may go wrong in at least two possible ways: First, the assumptions of individualism and collectivism (if not measured in individual research participants) may be erroneous; and second, reliance on differences in this single cultural dimension as an explanation for differences in outcome measures may mask other, more precise explanatory possibilities. Malpass (1977) summarized the fundamental problem of cultural comparisons in this way:

> No matter what attribute of culture the investigator prefers to focus upon or to interpret as the causative variable, any other variable correlated with the alleged causative variable could potentially serve in an alternative explanation of a mean difference between two or more local populations. (p. 1071)

Clearly, exploring underlying psychological mechanisms in cross-cultural research will be essential to understanding the role of multiple variables (Matsumoto & Yoo, 2006).

## Cultural psychology

Researchers identified as cultural psychologists are less likely than cross-cultural psychologists to be interested in traditional experimental or quasi-experimental approaches, and more likely to see culture as internal to the person (Triandis, 2000). Cultural psychology uses methods and studies problems arising from the everyday activities of particular cultures, with less emphasis on cross-cultural comparison (Greenfield, 2000). Therefore, the methods of cultural psychologists are often ethnographic in nature—meaning they involve extensive observation and rich description of a culture (Heine, 2008). The focus is on finding relationships between a culture and the psychological characteristics of people living in the culture, with the corresponding view that psychological processes derive from the interplay between the person and his or her culture (Shiraev & Levy, 2010).

Cultural psychologists tend to study cultures quite different from their own, are interested in natural (non-contrived) settings and situations, and focus on context (i.e., they are less likely to be interested in psychological principles independent of the context in which they arise) (Triandis, 2000). According to Ratner (2006), in a discussion of cultural psychology, aspects of culture provide the foundations and predictors of psychological processes more effectively than do personal factors. Thus, some writers (e.g., Yang, 2000) have characterized cultural psychology as a hybrid of psychology and anthropology that prefers to define psychology in terms of context-bound concepts. Cultural psychology sees culture as essential to understanding all psychological processes, and is interested in principles derived from culture, rather than imposed upon it (Segall, Lonner, & Berry, 1998).

## Indigenous psychologies

Arising as a reaction to so-called mainstream psychology, indigenous psychology represents the efforts of researchers in many (mainly non-Western) cultures to develop a "science that more closely reflects their own social and cultural premises" (Allwood & Berry, 2006, p. 244). Indigenous psychologies are ways of thinking psychologically that grow out of individual cultures, developing scientific perspectives consistent with the cultural realities of the particular settings (Berry et al., 2002). One consequence of the development of indigenous psychologies has been a movement from investigation of psychological universals to study of culture as a psychological system (Sinha, 2002).

The focus of indigenous psychologies, unlike the comparative focus of cross-cultural psychology and the anthropological tendencies of cultural psychology, revolves around psychological understandings built upon their own unique cultural resources (Allwood & Berry, 2006). Further, indigenous psychologists are interested in studying the particular problems and challenges (e.g., economy, poverty, religion) of their particular cultures. This emphasis on the primary role of culture leads to a specificity that results in a focus on cultural differences and unique aspects of societies, rather than cross-cultural similarities or universal principles (Poortinga, 2005). However, the question remains whether indigenous psychologies will contribute to a broader understanding of global psychology.

## Is there a common ground?

Although the perspective known as cross-cultural psychology has received criticism for placing more emphasis on scientific methodology than on understanding of culture (Laungani, 2002), cross-cultural psychologists have, in recent years, become more sensitive to the need to examine both universal and culture-specific phenomena (e.g., Triandis, 1999). And all of the approaches noted above—cross-cultural, cultural, and indigenous psychologies—have made significant contributions to the so-called cultural revolution in psychology (Ng & Liu, 2000; Yang, 2000).

Despite the limitations various writers have noted in mainstream scientific psychology, it seems unlikely that cultural approaches will unseat the powerful scientific findings of traditional psychology (Ng & Liu, 2000). However, it is also true that the past several decades have seen a dramatic increase in the development of psychological research and theory placing culture in a central position (Segall et al., 1998). Researchers investigating the relationship between culture and psychology have shown the role of culture as a significant influence in many traditional fields of psychological study (e.g., perception, cognition, social behavior, development, education), leading to the conclusion that "Nothing transpires in a cultural vacuum" (Lehman, Chiu, & Schaller, 2004, p. 704).

In an effort to articulate the importance of cross-cultural research, Kim (2007) proposed four perspectives that might be found among researchers:

1   the "pre-encounter research" culture: "I'm not interested,"
2   the "initial encounter" research culture: "Culture is a nuisance,"
3   the "Captain Cook" research culture: "Let's explore and compare," and
4   the "paradigm shift" research culture: "Beyond ethnocentric paradigms" (p. 280).

Kim's point is that researchers must recognize their own worldviews and the influence of worldview on their work—and that reaching the highest level in his hierarchy requires intercultural sensitivity and a willingness to reconsider one's worldview. Such a true paradigm shift would seem to suggest the integration of traditional scientific psychology with a broadened understanding of and sensitivity to, the importance of cultural context.

In a somewhat similar, but more specific, vein, Matsumoto and Yoo (2006) posited the need for an ongoing evolution in cross-cultural research. The field has moved, they suggested, through cross-cultural comparisons, identification of meaningful cultural dimensions, and cultural studies exploring the role of psychological constructs and variables in differing cultural contexts. Now, Matsumoto and Yoo argued, the field must evolve to develop research empirically investigating specific psychological variables or characteristics and their role in producing cultural differences. This approach would move the field from the tendency to assume global-level cultural characteristics (often stereotypically) to measurement of specific influences at the level of individual research participants. One example would be the design of "unpackaging" studies—the identification and incorporation of context variables (e.g., opinions, norms, values, attitudes) to replace broader cultural notions in explanation of cultural phenomena and differences (Matsumoto & Yoo, 2006).

It seems clear that in the future, cross-cultural studies will continue to move toward better understanding of psychological processes involved in cultural differences and of the basis of psychological processes (e.g., behavior) in culture (Lehman et al., 2004). In the chapters to follow, we will review a wide variety of theory and research, representing cross-cultural, cultural, and indigenous approaches. Our effort will be not to make distinctions among these perspectives, but to achieve a broad current understanding of key aspects of the field. We will thus use the term *cross-cultural psychology* inclusively, to denote the full range of interest in the relationship between culture and psychology.

## Some Basic Principles

A few organizing assumptions may help us to conceptualize the content of coming chapters as this volume's authors present a variety of perspectives and areas of research in cross-cultural psychology. These include the following (Keith, 2008):

1  People view and evaluate other cultures from the perspective of their own.
2  Some psychological principles are universal, and some are culture-specific.
3  Several key cultural dimensions aid our understanding and study of cross-cultural phenomena.
4  Despite the many cultural differences identified by cross-cultural researchers, people in various cultures share more commonalities than differences.

### Seeing other cultures in light of our own

It has been more than a century since Sumner (1906) gave a name to the phenomenon of *ethnocentrism*. Ethnocentrism is the tendency for humans to hold up their own group or culture as a standard, seeing it as superior to others (Berry et al., 2002). We may be suspicious of individuals from other groups (Price & Crapo, 2002), and ethnocentrism may lead to conflict with, and stereotyped views of, other groups (Triandis, 1994). Ethnocentrism is probably universal (LeVine & Campbell, 1972), and may be a natural result of the enculturation that children experience as they are socialized in the customs, practices, and ways of behaving that characterize their cultures.

Although ethnocentrism may well be inevitable, people can learn to become more flexible (Matsumoto & Juang, 2008). Nevertheless, ethnocentrism reflects a limited worldview that develops without individual intention or awareness.

### Etics and emics

Cross-cultural researchers have long sought universal behavioral principles—psychological phenomena that are true or valid across cultures—while at the same time realizing that many psychological findings are significantly influenced or limited by their specific cultural context. Deriving from the writings of Pike (1967), the terms *etic* and *emic* have evolved from linguistic usage to describe these two eventualities. Thus, the term *phonetic* has given rise to *etic* (a universal), in recognition of the fact that phonetics exist in all languages; *phonemics*, on the other hand, are sounds that distinguish languages from one another, leading to the use of *emic* as a term to denote a culture-limited phenomenon (Triandis, 1994). For example, nearly every culture might recognize and value intelligence (an etic), but differ widely in the specific aspects of intelligence (e.g., type or speed of problem solving; Keith, 1996) that are considered important (an emic). Or aggression may be of interest in many cultures, but may play out quite differently across different cultures.

Etic and emic can also characterize *approaches* to cultural research (Berry, 1969; Berry et al., 2002). An emic approach involves the study of a particular culture, usually from within, from the perspective of the members of the culture (i.e., indigenous psychology). Alternatively, an etic approach is likely to investigate one or more characteristics of multiple cultures, often from the outside (i.e., traditional cross-cultural psychology) and imposing external measurement (Price-Williams, 1975). Put another way, the etic approach looks for cross-cultural commonalities, while the emic approach searches for meaningful concepts within a specific culture. Although psychologists are often in search of universals, a danger of the etic approach is that researchers, as products of their own cultural experience, may be tempted to impose their own biases and expectations on other cultures and as a result lose the opportunity for meaningful comparison (Segall et al., 1999).

## Dimensions of culture

As investigators have explored psychological similarities and differences occurring across cultures, they have identified a number of key dimensions that have proven useful in understanding cultural influences. The best known of these dimensions are those identified by Hofstede (1980; Hofstede & Hofstede, 2004): (a) individualism-collectivism (IC); (b) power distance (PD); (c) uncertainty avoidance (UA); (d) masculinity-femininity (MA); and (e) long-term orientation (LTO).

These dimensions can be summarized in the following way: IC is the extent to which the individual feels free from group pressure, or to which the individual's goals are similar to or different from the group's; PD reflects the degree to which group members accept an unequal distribution of power, or the difference in power between more or less powerful members of the group; UA is the degree to which a group develops processes to reduce uncertainty and ambiguity, or to deal with risk and unfamiliarity in everyday life; MA is the extent to which gender roles and distinctions are traditional, and masculine (e.g., aggression) or feminine (e.g., cooperation) traits are viewed favorably; and LTO suggests the level of willingness of members of the culture to forego short-term rewards in the interest of long-term goals (Brislin, 2000; Gannon, 2001).

Although researchers have of course studied all these dimensions, investigators have most often invoked IC in the study of cultural differences and similarities, and we will use IC here as an indicator of some of the characteristic findings and challenges that have emerged in the literature. Despite criticism that IC (as well as the other dimensions) lacks explanatory power to further our understanding of the psychology of cultures (Ratner & Hui, 2003), many studies have produced descriptions of cross-cultural similarities and differences on the IC dimension, and investigators have conducted many comparisons of cultural characteristics associated with individualism and collectivism. Oyserman, Coon, and Kemmelmeier (2002), for example, carried out meta-analyses of more than 80 studies conducted both within the U.S. and across many other cultures. Although they found general support for the widely held notion that European Americans tend to be more individualistic and less collectivistic than many other groups, Oyserman et al. criticized the common practice of researchers "to accept any cross-national difference as evidence of IND-COL processes" (p. 44). The latter observation is consistent with the earlier concern of Segall et al. (1999) that IC is an "overused dichotomy" (p. 217).

One way to attempt to avoid over-generalizations about the IC characteristics of cultures is to measure individualism and collectivism at the level of individual research participants. Triandis (1995; Triandis, Bontempo, Villareal, Asai, & Lucca, 1988) termed the individual-level occurrence of collectivism *allocentrism* and individual-level individualism *idiocentrism*, and a number of researchers (e.g., Alavi & McCormick, 2007; Matsumoto, Weissman, Preston, Brown, & Kupperbusch, 1997) have developed procedures intended to make individual-level IC measurements. Their review of scales measuring individual IC allowed Oyserman et al. (2002) to identify psychological domains typically associated with individualism (independence, goal orientation, competition, uniqueness, privacy, self-knowledge, and directness of communication) or with collectivism (relationship to group, belonging, duty, group harmony, advice from others, importance of social context, hierarchy / status, and preference for group work). Such individual measurement of cultural dimensions allows researchers not only to avoid the tendency to stereotype whole cultures (e.g., Matsumoto, 2002), but also to attempt to account for such occurrences as the existence of idiocentric people in collectivist cultures and allocentric people in individualist cultures.

Despite the concerns about over-generalizing the role of cultural dimensions, Triandis et al. (1988) identified some key differences between collectivist and individualist cultures:

1   People in individualist cultures tend to have more in-groups.
2   Collectivist cultures encourage significant vertical relationships (e.g., parent–child, supervisor–worker), while horizontal relationships (e.g., co-workers, spouses, friends) are more important in individualist cultures.
3   People in individualist cultures may be able to easily make friends, but many may be only acquaintances; collectivist people may be less skillful in making friends, but their friendships are likely to be intimate and long-lasting.
4   In-groups in individualist cultures may provide more rights and fewer obligations, but less security and support than those of collectivist cultures.

5　Collectivist cultures enable more stable in-group relationships, while individualists are more likely to leave an in-group that makes excessive demands.
6　For collectivist cultures, cooperation levels are high within in-groups, and lower with out-groups.

These IC characteristics are consistent with the notion that individualism suggests an independent, decontextualized orientation, in contrast to the contextualized, situation-based, detail-focused orientation of collectivism (Oyserman et al., 2002).

Although the IC dimension has produced a large body of fascinating cultural research, a wide range of other cultural dimensions exists. These dimensions include not only those that Hofstede and Hofstede (2004) have identified, but numerous others as well (Matsumoto & Yoo, 2006), including level of complexity and tightness (number of rules and norms) (Triandis, 1999). Although researchers have certainly studied some of these other dimensions, additional work to increase our understanding of more cultural beliefs, attitudes, and values will no doubt expand not only the available cultural knowledge, but our ability to explain cultural differences and similarities, as well.

## Cultural commonalities

Although cultures may vary widely, they all share a common need to solve similar human problems, such as those associated with health, safety, reproduction, and, ultimately, survival (Matsumoto, 2006). Further, as some writers have argued, culture is not limited only to humans; other species, including chimpanzees, may well possess culture too, with some similarities to that of humans (Kendal, 2008). However, despite commonalities, much cross-cultural research in psychology has focused on identifying and describing the differences between cultures. Many of the studies describing psychological differences have done so without clear attempts to explain potential cultural foundations or causes for the differences (Ratner & Hui, 2003). Unfortunately, even in the absence of clear cultural explanations, researchers have sometimes drawn conclusions about presumed causes of differences, often in terms of dimensions like IC, even when groups also differ in other obvious ways (e.g., Segall et al., 1999).

In fact, even when studies show differences between cultures, statistically significant differences may lack practical significance, and consideration of effect sizes (in lieu of simply reporting *p* values) may result in very different perspectives on such differences (Matsumoto, Grissom, & Dinnel, 2001). And, as world cultures continue to become more intermingled and globalized, our perceptions of the differences and similarities among them may well change (Shiraev & Levy, 2010). In the future, it will be important for researchers to bring together the idiosyncratic findings of local and regional (indigenous) psychologies and a true global (cross-cultural) psychology (Poortinga, 2005).

# Conclusion

In a world with far too much conflict, anger, and violence, increased understanding of culture—our own as well as others'—is perhaps the most pressing need for psychological science. Cross-cultural psychology promises to aid understanding of our differences and clarification of our similarities; but understanding will come only on the strength of sound methodology and accurate data. In the chapters that follow, we will see a variety of approaches to development of methods and knowledge that help to develop that understanding.

Psychological knowledge of culture has improved substantially since the early work of Rivers (1905) and Sumner (1906). And we have much more to offer students than Morgan and King (1966) did when I used their introductory psychology textbook. Cross-cultural psychology is an accepted field of study, one that continues to advance toward the dual aims of meeting the rigorous standards of good science and building a level of credibility that will make it acceptable in the unique contexts of the cultures of the world. An important result will be the ability to think differently about ourselves and others.

# References

Alavi, S. B., & McCormick, J. (2007). Measurement of vertical and horizontal idiocentrism and allocentrism in small groups. *Small Group Research, 38*, 556–564.

Allwood, C. M., & Berry, J. W. (2006). Origins and development of indigenous psychologies: An international analysis. *International Journal of Psychology, 41*, 243–268.

Arnett, J. J. (2008). The neglected 95%: Why American psychology needs to become less American. *American Psychologist, 63*, 602–614.

Baumeister, R. F. (2005). *The cultural animal: Human nature, meaning, and social life*. New York: Oxford University Press.

Bernstein, D. A., Penner, L. A., Clarke-Stewart, A., & Roy, E. J. (2008). *Psychology* (8th ed.). Boston: Houghton Mifflin.

Berry, J. W. (1969). On cross-cultural comparability. *International Journal of Psychology, 4*, 119–128.

Berry, J. W., Poortinga, Y. H., Segall, M. H., & Dasen, P. R. (2002). *Cross-cultural psychology: Research and applications* (2nd ed.). Cambridge, UK: Cambridge University Press.

Brislin, R. (2000). *Understanding culture's influence on behavior* (2nd ed.). Fort Worth, TX: Harcourt College Publishers.

Bronstein, P., & Quina, K. (Eds.) (1988). *Teaching a psychology of people: Resources for gender and sociocultural awareness*. Washington, DC: American Psychological Association.

Cohen, A. B. (2009). Many forms of culture. *American Psychologist, 64*, 194–204.

Cole, M. (1984). The world beyond our borders: What might our students need to know about it? *American Psychologist, 39*, 998–1005.

Durant, W. (1939). *The story of civilization: Part II. The life of Greece*. New York: Simon and Schuster.

Ebbinghaus, H. (1908/1973). *Psychology: An elementary text-book*. New York: Arno Press.

Gannon, M. J. (2001). *Understanding global cultures: Metaphorical journeys through 23 nations* (2nd ed.). Thousand Oaks, CA: Sage Publications, Inc.

Goldstein, S. B. (1995). Cross-cultural psychology as a curriculum transformation resource. *Teaching of Psychology, 22*, 228–232.

Greenfield, P. M. (2000). Three approaches to the psychology of culture: Where do they come from? Where can they go? *Asian Journal of Social Psychology, 3*, 223–240.

Guthrie, R. V. (1998). *Even the rat was white: A historical view of psychology* (2nd ed.). Boston, MA: Allyn & Bacon.

Heine, S. J. (2008). *Cultural psychology*. New York: W. W. Norton.

Heine, S. J., & Norenzayan, A. (2006). Toward a psychological science for a cultural species. *Perspectives on Psychological Science, 1*, 251–269.

Hill, G. W., IV (2002). Incorporating cross-cultural perspectives into the psychology curriculum: Challenges and strategies. In S. F. Davis & W. Buskist (Eds.), *The teaching of psychology: Essays in honor of Wilbert J. McKeachie and Charles L. Brewer* (pp. 431–443). Mahwah, NJ: Lawrence Erlbaum Associates.

Hofstede, G. (1980). *Culture's consequences: International differences in work-related values*. Beverly Hills, CA: Sage.

Hofstede, G., & Hofstede, G.-J. (2004). *Cultures and organizations: Software of the mind*. New York: McGraw-Hill.

James, W. (1892/1961). *Psychology: The briefer course*. New York: Harper & Row.

Kagitçibaşi, Ç., & Berry, J. W. (1989). Cross-cultural psychology: Current research and trends. *Annual Review of Psychology, 40*, 493–531.

Keith, K. D. (1996). Measuring quality of life across cultures: Issues and challenges. In R. L. Schalock (Ed.), *Quality of life: Vol. I. Conceptualization and measurement* (pp. 73–82). Washington, DC: American Association on Mental Retardation.

Keith, K. D. (2008). Cross-cultural psychology and research. In S. F. Davis & W. Buskist (Eds.), *21st century psychology: A reference handbook. Vol. 2* (pp. 483–490). Los Angeles: Sage Publications.

Kendal, R. L. (2008). Animal "culture wars." *The Psychologist, 21*, 312–315.

Kim, M.-S. (2007). The four cultures of cultural research. *Communication Monographs, 74*, 279–285.

Klineberg, O. (1980). Historical perspectives: Cross-cultural psychology before 1960. In H. C. Triandis & W. W. Lambert (Eds.), *Handbook of cross-cultural psychology: Vol. 1, Perspectives* (pp. 31–67). Boston: Allyn and Bacon, Inc.

Ladd, G. T. (1894). *Primer of psychology*. New York: Charles Scribner's Sons.

Laungani, P. (2002). Cross-cultural psychology: A handmaiden to mainstream Western psychology. *Counselling Psychology Quarterly, 15*, 385–397.

Lehman, D. R., Chiu, C.-Y., & Schaller, M. (2004). Psychology and culture. *Annual Review of Psychology, 55*, 689–714.

Levine, R. A., & Campbell, D. T. (1972). *Ethnocentrism: Theories of conflict, ethnic attitudes and group behavior*. New York: Wiley.

Lonner, W. J. (1974, April). *The past, present, and future of cross-cultural psychology*. Paper presented at the annual convention of the Western Psychological Association, San Francisco.

LoSchiavo, F. M., & Shatz, M. A. (2009). Reaching the neglected 95%. *American Psychologist, 64*, 565–566.

Malpass, R. S. (1977). Theory and method in cross-cultural psychology. *American Psychologist, 32*, 1069–1079.

Matsumoto, D. (2002). *The new Japan: Debunking seven cultural stereotypes*. Yarmouth, ME: Intercultural Press, Inc.

Matsumoto, D. (2006, October). *Culture and psychology: Best practices and challenges in teaching international perspectives*. Paper presented at the conference on Reaching Out: Best Practices in Teaching Diversity & International Perspectives Across the Psychology Curriculum, Atlanta, GA.

Matsumoto, D. (2009). Teaching about culture. In R. A. R. Gurung & L. R. Prieto (Eds.), *Getting culture: Incorporating diversity across the curriculum* (pp. 3–10). New York: Stylus.

Matsumoto, D., Grissom, R. J., & Dinnel, D. L. (2001). Do between-culture differences really mean that people are different? A look at some measures of cultural effect size. *Journal of Cross-Cultural Psychology, 32*, 478–490.

Matsumoto, D., & Juang, L. (2008). *Culture and psychology* (4th ed.). Belmont, CA: Thomson/Wadsworth.

Matsumoto, D., Weissman, M. D., Preston, K., Brown, B. R., & Kupperbusch, C. (1997). Context-specific measurement of individualism-collectivism on the individual level: The individualism-collectivism interpersonal assessment inventory. *Journal of Cross-Cultural Psychology, 28*, 743–767.

Matsumoto, D., & Yoo, S. H. (2006). Toward a new generation of cross-cultural research. *Perspectives on Psychological Science, 1*, 234–250.

Mead, M. (1935). *Sex and temperament*. New York: Morrow.

Miller, R. L., (2008). Community psychology. In S. F. Davis & W. Buskist (Eds.), *21st century psychology: A reference handbook* (pp. 395–405). Thousand Oaks, CA: Sage.

Mio, J. S., Barker-Hackett, L., & Tumambing, J. (2006). *Multicultural psychology: Understanding our diverse communities*. Boston: McGraw-Hill.

Morgan, C. T., & King, R. A. (1966). *Introduction to psychology* (3rd ed.). New York: McGraw-Hill.

Myers, D. G. (2007). *Psychology* (8th ed.). New York: Worth.

Ng, S. H., & Liu, J. H. (2000). Cultural revolution in psychology. *Asian Journal of Social Psychology, 3*, 289–293.

Oyserman, D., Coon, H. M., & Kemmelmeier, M. (2002). Rethinking individualism and collectivism: Evaluation of theoretical assumptions and meta-analyses. *Psychological Bulletin, 128*, 3–72.

Pike, K. L. (1967). *Language in relation to a unified theory of the structure of human behavior* (2nd ed.). The Hague: Mouton.

Pinker, S. (1994). *The language instinct: How the mind creates language*. New York: William Morrow and Company, Inc.

Poortinga, Y. H. (2005). The globalization of indigenous psychologies. *Asian Journal of Social Psychology, 8*, 65–74.

Price, W. F., & Crapo, R. H. (2002). *Cross-cultural perspectives in introductory psychology* (4th ed.). Pacific Grove, CA: Wadsworth.

Price-Williams, D. R. (1975). *Explorations in cross-cultural psychology*. San Francisco: Chandler & Sharp Publishers, Inc.

Quinones-Vidal, E., Lopez-Garcia, J. J., Penaranda-Ortega, M., & Tortosa-Gil, F. (2004). The nature of social and personality psychology as reflected in *JPSP*, 1965–2000. *Journal of Personality and Social Psychology, 86*, 435–452.

Ratner, C. (2006). *Cultural psychology: A perspective on psychological functioning and social reform.* Mahwah, NJ: Lawrence Erlbaum Associates.

Ratner, C., & Hui, L. (2003). Theoretical and methodological problems in cross-cultural psychology. *Journal for the Theory of Social Behavior, 33*, 67–94.

Rivers, W. H. R. (1905). Observations on the senses of the Todas. *British Journal of Psychology, 1*, 321–396.

Segall, M. H., Dasen, P. R., Berry, J. W., & Poortinga, Y. H. (1999). *Human behavior in global perspective: An introduction to cross-cultural psychology* (2nd ed.). Boston: Allyn and Bacon.

Segall, M. H., Lonner, W. J., & Berry, J. W. (1998). Cross-cultural psychology as a scholarly discipline: On the flowering of culture in behavioral research. *American Psychologist, 53*, 1101–1110.

Shiraev, E. B., & Levy, D. A. (2010). *Cross-cultural psychology: Critical thinking and contemporary applications* (4th ed.). Boston: Allyn and Bacon.

Sinha, D. (2002). Culture and psychology: Perspective of cross-cultural psychology. *Psychology and Developing Societies, 14*, 11–25.

Sue, S. (1999). Science, ethnicity, and bias: Where have we gone wrong? *American Psychologist, 54*, 1070–1077.

Sumner, W. G. (1906). *Folkways: A study of the sociological importance of usages, manners, customs, mores, and morals.* New York: Ginn and Company.

Triandis, H. C. (1977). Cross-cultural social and personality psychology. *Personality and Social Psychology Bulletin, 3*, 143–158.

Triandis, H. C. (1980). Introduction. In H. C. Triandis & W. W. Lambert (Eds.), *Handbook of cross-cultural psychology: Vol. 1, Perspectives* (pp. 1–14). Boston: Allyn and Bacon, Inc.

Triandis, H. C. (1994). *Culture and social behavior.* New York: McGraw-Hill.

Triandis, H. C. (1995). *Individualism and collectivism.* Boulder, CO: Westview Press.

Triandis, H. C. (1999). Cross-cultural psychology. *Asian Journal of Social Psychology, 2*, 127–143.

Triandis, H. C. (2000). Dialectics between cultural and cross-cultural psychology. *Asian Journal of Social Psychology, 3*, 185–195.

Triandis, H. C., Bontempo, R., Villareal, M. J., Asai, M., & Lucca, N. (1988). Individualism and collectivism: Cross-cultural perspectives on self–ingroup relationships. *Journal of Personality and Social Psychology, 54*, 323–338.

Triandis, H., Kurowski, L., Tecktiel, A., & Chan, D. (1993). Extracting the emics of cultural diversity. *International Journal of Intercultural Relations, 17*, 217–234.

Webster, G. D., Nichols, N. L., & Schember, T. O. (2009). American psychology *is* becoming more international. *American Psychologist, 64*, 566–568.

Weiten, W. (2008). *Psychology: Themes and variations—briefer version* (7th ed.). Belmont, CA: Thomson/Wadsworth.

Wundt, W. (1916). *Elements of folk psychology. Outlines of a psychological history of the development of mankind* (trans. E. L. Schaub). New York: Macmillan.

Yang, K.-S. (2000). Monocultural and cross-cultural indigenous approaches: The royal road to the development of a balanced global psychology. *Asian Journal of Social Psychology, 3*, 241–263.

# 2

# Ethnocentrism

## Seeing the World From Where We Stand

### Kenneth D. Keith

There is an old Asian proverb about the frog that lives in the well. The frog, it seems, is quite happy because, after all, the well is a perfectly good place, and the patch of sky he can see from the bottom of his well is a perfectly nice bit of sky. The frog has no need for, nor any interest in, any place but his own. Like the frog in the well, we are all prone to elevate our own place or our own culture as the standard against which we judge others, and to see our own as superior to others. This tendency is known as ethnocentrism (Berry, Poortinga, Segall, & Dasen, 2002). In this chapter, we discuss the concept of ethnocentrism: Who is ethnocentric, how do we become ethnocentric, and how can we reduce ethnocentrism?

Ethnocentrism is likely universal among humans (LeVine & Campbell, 1972) and first appeared in the literature more than a century ago in the writings of W. G. Sumner (1906), although it was even earlier that Charles Darwin (1874) noted that tribes tended to be more sympathetic to their own groups. Ethnocentrism often serves to create perceptions of cross-cultural difference, with resulting intercultural conflict and negative stereotypes (Triandis, 1994); it is thus important to successful intergroup relationships, and our efforts to improve them, that we develop an understanding of ethnocentrism: its characteristics, causes, and amelioration.

## What are the Characteristics of Ethnocentrism?

### The classic perspective

Ethnocentrism has its roots in words implying feelings and judgments that are centered ("centrism") in an individual's own cultural or ethnic ("ethno") context (Brislin, 2000), and frequently involves: (a) perceiving outsiders with suspicion (Price & Crapo, 2002) and (b) individual tendencies toward group self-centeredness

(Bizumic & Duckitt, 2007). Further, we seem to want to be near others who are like us, and we feel different from, and sometimes fearful of, those who are not like us (Strickland, 2000).

The result, Sumner (1906) suggested, is a division between in-groups and out-groups, in which in-group members consider their own practices the standard against which they measure out-groups. Members of the in-group are likely to see themselves as superior to (Hooghe, 2008), and more possessed of virtue than (Hammond & Axelrod, 2006), out-group members. The traditional Sumnerian view includes not only elevation of one's own group, but also negative attitudes toward the "other," the out-group. The potential for negative assessment increases with greater differences between the groups (Berry et al., 2002). And, as Raden (2003) noted, Sumner concerned himself primarily with unitary, homogeneous groups with clearly external out-groups. This was likely due, at least in part, to the fact that Sumner studied groups that found it necessary to unite against other groups in the interest of survival—an idea consistent with the finding of Pratto and Glasford (2008) that individuals value the lives of their in-group members more than those of an out-group when the groups are in competition. Sumner (1906) pointed out, for example, that Jews divided people between themselves (in-group) and Gentiles (out-group), and that the Greeks and Romans (in-groups) saw all others as barbarians (out-groups).

## A contemporary view

Research today, particularly in cultures as diverse as the U.S., often involves studies in which one racial or ethnic subgroup is the in-group, and other groups, although internal to the country, are out-groups (Raden, 2003); and studies have generally continued to support the notion that positive feelings for the in-group and negative feelings for out-groups bear a reciprocal relationship to each other (Brewer, 1999). However, as Brewer (1999; 2007) reported, data from many groups have shown that, although individuals tend to be differentially positive toward their in-group, these attitudes may be independent of their attitudes toward out-groups. In other words, we can have positive feelings toward members of our in-groups without corresponding attitudes of disdain or hostility toward out-groups—a perspective supported by the work of Khan and Liu (2008), who found, in a study of Indians and Pakistanis, more support for favoring the in-group than for disfavoring the out-group.

Bizumic and Duckitt (2007), in a study of three varieties of group self-centeredness (ethnocentrism, fundamentalism, and anthropocentrism) among Australian university students, found that individuals who strongly favor their own human groups over others also tend to favor humans over other species. Thus, prejudice against animals was related to self-centeredness in relation to human out-groups. However, ethnocentrism, like the other forms of self-centeredness, correlated with negative feelings toward *specific* relevant out-groups, but not toward out-groups in general. Further, although Raden (2003) found classic (Sumnerian) ethnocentrism (i.e., positive attitudes toward the in-group, hostility toward the out-group) among some subgroups of a large probability sample of white Americans, in-group bias (without the implication of unfavorable views of out-groups) was more prevalent in his sample. This finding led Raden to point up the methodological importance of the distinction between the classic form of ethnocentrism and the more common in-group bias, suggesting that the latter may be a midpoint between the extremes of classic ethnocentrism and the absence of ethnocentrism. Such current work indicates that the occurrence of ethnocentrism, in its contemporary incarnation, is more complex and more nuanced than the Sumnerian perspective might suggest.

## Who is ethnocentric?

Many writers have discussed the universal tendency of humans to be ethnocentric (e.g., LeVine & Campbell, 1972; Neuliep, Hintz, & McCroskey, 2005; Shuya, 2007). Researchers have studied ethnocentrism in relation to ethnic minorities within the United States (Gittler, 1972; Hraba, 1972; Mutisya & Ross, 2005; Prothro, 1952; Raden, 2003), across nationalities (Beswick, 1972; Cashdan, 2001; Khan & Liu, 2008; Li & Liu, 1975), in the tendencies of consumers to buy domestic products (Chryssochoidis, Krystallis, & Perreas, 2007; Hsu & Nien, 2008; Nguyen, Nguyen, & Barrett, 2008; Vida, 2008), and toward people with disabilities (Chesler, 1965). Ethnocentrism has also been manifest in perceptions of intercultural attractiveness and competence of individuals from other cultures (Neuliep et al., 2005).

Sumner (1906) recounted a long list of cultural groups (including Lapps, Kiowa, Caribs, Greenlanders, Jews, Seri, and others) that developed terms denoting their respective groups as uniquely "men," "people," "chosen," or otherwise superior.

And of course researchers, being human themselves, are also subject to ethnocentrism (Hofstede, 2007). Thus, ethnocentric bias exists not only at the levels of the individual and intergroup relations, but also at the level of the scientists who study psychological phenomena across cultures (e.g., Berry et al., 2002; Hofstede, 2007). Campbell (1970), among others, has proposed research methodologies designed to ameliorate the contaminating influence of ethnocentrism in social science investigations.

Everyone, it seems, is ethnocentric or at least potentially susceptible to ethnocentrism. It seems clear, as Matsumoto and Juang (2004) suggested, that culture serves much like a lens, or filter, "distorting, rotating, and coloring" (p. 65) our view of the world, leading us inevitably to see it from the only vantage point we know—our own.

# How Does Ethnocentrism Develop?

## Biological perspectives

Ethnocentrism may seem to be "automatic" (LeBaron, 2003), as a part of the enculturation of children within a society; a process in which some see the child learning its culture and its attitudes as a kind of *tabula rasa* (LeVine, 1982). On the other hand, some writers have argued for an evolutionary basis for ethnocentrism. Wilson (1978), for example, raised the possibility that biological advantage might accrue to ethnocentric tribal groups, not only from aggression but also from other associated behaviors. Wilson argued that particular behaviors (e.g., specific forms of aggression) are not genetically transmitted, but that cultural structures supporting them may have been. Thus, successful groups were those that successfully divided the world between "us" and "them." Similarly, Thayer (2004) set forth the proposition that evolution has equipped humans with an affinity for those who are biologically related; thus, this view would suggest, people should be expected to support first their immediate family, then other relatives, then their ethnic group, and finally others. This perspective, Thayer said, does not mean ethnocentrism is not subject to environmental influence (e.g., culture, religion, political beliefs), but it does recognize the natural tendency to favor those who are biologically related, and there is some evidence to suggest that an ethnically homogeneous culture (in which people might be assumed to be more biologically similar) may manifest higher levels of ethnocentrism than a more diverse one (Neuliep, Chaudoir, & McCroskey, 2001).

Perceived vulnerability to disease may give rise to negative attitudes toward out-group members (Faulkner, Schaller, Park, & Duncan, 2004). Navarrette, Fessler, and Eng (2007), in a study testing this disease-threat model for intergroup attitudes, found that pregnant women were most ethnocentric during the first trimester of their pregnancy—a finding consistent with the model and supportive of the role of biological factors as an influence on ethnocentrism. In another investigation, Navarrette and Fessler (2006) gathered data indicating an increase in ethnocentrism in individuals who perceived an increased vulnerability to disease—supporting the notion that, because in-group members may present less risk of disease than out-group contacts, individuals may have mental approach and avoidance mechanisms that predispose them to ethnocentric behaviors (e.g., Faulkner et al., 2004). And, although such cognitive processes might be assumed to be involved in ethnocentrism, there is some evidence simply for an individual predisposition to favor in-groups (Hammond & Axelrod, 2006).

On the other hand, Roberts (1997) did not find a significant correlation between ethnocentrism and reproductive success in a study of two distinct ethnic groups in India—perhaps casting doubt on the presumption of evolutionary advantage of ethnocentrism (although such an advantage may well have once existed for such

groups). Ross (1991), in suggesting the incompleteness of a sociobiological explanation for ethnocentrism, argued instead for the possibility of a cultural evolutionary process. Simon (1980), in discussing the relationship between genetics and
human nature, enumerated several cultural universals and suggested that there is
not sufficient evidence to conclude that they are or are not genetically based.
Ethnocentrism may well be one such universal and, as we will see in chapter 7, it
is likely that biological and psychological influences bear a reciprocal relationship
to each other in the evolution of culture and psychological processes.

## Psychological variables

Scientists have studied a number of psychosocial variables that appear to be related
to the behaviors we call ethnocentrism. Some of these are narcissism, religious
fundamentalism, major personality traits, intolerance for ambiguity, and authoritarianism. Numerous studies have shown that ethnocentrism may decrease over
time, as group members develop experience with both the in-group and out-
groups, and views of out-groups may become more positive with experience (Ryan
& Bogart, 1997). Perhaps more interesting is the fact that researchers have found
ethnocentrism related in various ways to characteristics that we might place on a
continuum of "open-mindedness." For example, Bizumic and Duckitt (2008), in a
sample of university students in New Zealand, found a positive relationship
between narcissism (self-centeredness) and intergroup ethnocentrism, leading the
researchers to suggest that narcissism may predispose individuals to hold ethnocentric attitudes. Similarly, Altemeyer (2003), studying Canadian students, found
significant correlations between religious fundamentalism, Manitoba ethnocentrism (Altemeyer, 1996), and religious ethnocentrism; in other words, those scoring high on religious fundamentalism also tended to be ethnocentric—toward
other religions and other sociocultural groups. Altemeyer's (2003) religious fundamentalist participants reported coming from homes in which religion was a focus
of emphasis from an early age, and, he said, have a "very small 'us' and quite a
large 'them' when it comes to faith" (p. 27). The connection between religion and
ethnocentrism is not limited to Canadians. For example, working in India with
Hindu and Muslim adolescents, and comparing them to nonreligious individuals,
Hasnain (2007) found religious persons in both groups to be significantly more
prejudiced and ethnocentric than the nonreligious participants.

In a study investigating the attitudes of American university students toward
foreign-born and domestic instructors, de Oliveira, Braun, Carlson, and de
Oliveira (2009) measured Big Five personality traits of the students (McCrae &
Costa, 1999) as well as attitudes toward the instructors. Among their findings,
these researchers found an ethnocentric bias against the foreign-born instructors
(whom students apparently saw as out-group members), and the student traits of
agreeableness and conscientiousness were positively correlated with positive

attitudes toward the foreign-born teachers. de Oliveira et al. also reported an inverse relationship between attitudes toward the two instructor conditions (i.e., students who liked one instructor group more tended to like the other instructor group less)—a finding that would seem consistent with the classical version of ethnocentrism.

There is a long history of research investigating the relationship of other personal traits to ethnocentrism. Noting the similarity in descriptions of intolerance for ambiguity and for ethnocentrism, Block and Block (1951) designed research to study the relationship between these characteristics. Using a laboratory task and a sample of American university students, these investigators reported that participants considered intolerant of ambiguity were more ethnocentric than those considered tolerant of ambiguity. Taft (1956) employed a variation on the methods used by Block and Block (1951) to study ethnocentrism and intolerance of ambiguity in an Australian group, with similar conclusions: Those intolerant of ambiguity also scored significantly higher on a measure of ethnocentrism. O'Connor (1952), studying a sample of American students, also found similar results: She reported a significant correlation between intolerance for ambiguity and ethnocentrism; she also noted a significant difference between people assessed as high in ethnocentrism and those low in ethnocentrism on a measure of intolerance of ambiguity (Those high in ethnocentrism scored higher on intolerance of ambiguity.)

Parents, of course, play a role in the development of ethnocentrism in their children, and researchers have studied parental characteristics and parenting styles in this context. Thomas (1975) assessed parents for authoritarianism (the tendency to favor absolute obedience to authority) in seven Pacific Island cultures, finding authoritarian parenting characteristics in three of the groups (Tahiti, Cook Islands, and Samoa). In each of these three cultures, authoritarianism was positively correlated with ethnocentrism. A number of studies have shown a relationship between parental characteristics and behavior and ethnocentrism in their children. Epstein and Komorita (1966), for example, found that childhood ethnocentrism was related to the interaction between parental ethnocentrism and punitiveness. In particular, parents who used moderately punitive disciplinary approaches were more likely to have children who shared their parents' ethnocentric attitudes. Mosher and Scodel (1960), in a study of Midwestern American schoolchildren and their mothers, found that the children's ethnocentrism was correlated with that of their mothers, but not with the mothers' authoritarianism.

Finally, in two Dutch samples, Van IJzendoorn (2001) found significant correlations between ethnocentrism and authoritarianism in both high school and university students. This study also revealed negative correlations, for both groups, between moral judgment and both ethnocentrism and authoritarianism. Likewise, in an investigation measuring ethnocentrism and authoritarianism of adolescents and parents in two Hungarian cities, both groups showed a significant relationship between these two variables (Todosijević & Enyedi, 2002).

## Summary

In summary, we can say that scientists of various points of view have proposed numerous explanations for ethnocentrism. It seems likely that ethnocentrism has evolutionary underpinnings, but it is equally evident that it is linked to a variety of environmental / cultural and personal influences, including parental characteristics and individual traits. Bias favoring the in-group may help individuals to organize their experience and reduce uncertainty (Druckman, 2006)—perhaps contributing to efforts to explain the relationship of highly structured views, in the form of authoritarianism and fundamentalism, to ethnocentrism.

Although ethnocentrism may contribute, via evolutionary mechanisms, to the survival and integrity of groups, there is nevertheless abundant evidence of the challenges and obstacles posed by ethnocentrism at the interpersonal and intercultural levels. This state of affairs of course presents concerns for inter-group understanding and relations (Brewer & Brown, 1998). We might, there-fore, logically ask whether there are ways to overcome the effects of this universal phenomenon.

## Can We Reduce Our Ethnocentrism?

Cross-cultural psychology has made efforts not only to understand the ethnocen-tric limits of our cultural / scientific knowledge (Berry et al., 2002), but also to find ways to decrease ethnocentrism among individuals. Brislin (2000) has pointed out that interaction with people of other cultures is likely to challenge our ethnocen-tric perspectives, and numerous writers have suggested that such contact will reduce ethnocentrism. This is not always the case, however (Brewer & Brown, 1998). In this section, we review the potential effects of education and related vari-ables on the ethnocentrism of individual people.

### Role of education

*Higher education*
Hooghe (2008) reported that high levels of education may reduce ethnocentrism. This assertion was borne out by two studies conducted by Plant (1958a, 1958b) more than a half century ago. In one of these studies, Plant (1958b) administered the ethnocentrism scale from *The authoritarian personality* (Adorno, Frenkel-Brunswick, Levinson, & Sanford, 1950) to a sample of American college students, 755 of whom were still available for testing two years later. Of the 755, 505 had completed two years of college, and showed significantly reduced ethnocentrism

at follow-up. The remaining 250 participants did not continue in college or withdrew before the two-year follow-up; this group showed no significant changes in measured ethnocentrism. In this study, Plant also found a significant sex difference, with men showing higher levels of ethnocentrism than women—a finding consistent with other (Hooghe, 2008) discussions of ethnocentrism.

In the second study, Plant (1958a) used a modified version of the Total Ethnocentrism Scale: Public Opinion Questionnaire E, again from the work of Adorno et al. (1950). Of 1,030 students completing the measure as entering college students, Plant invited 315 to be retested at the end of their four-year college career. Of the 315 eligible students, 271 (86%) completed the retest. Both male and female students produced significantly lower ethnocentrism scores following their four years of college. Scores for men were higher than those for women at the time of both the initial testing and the retesting, and Plant's analysis of the difference in shift scores indicated that female students' scores were reduced significantly more than those of males. We should note that in this study, Plant did not report scores for a non-student control group.

*Specific courses*

In another study, designed to more specifically examine the effects of studying cross-cultural psychology on ethnocentrism, Pettijohn and Naples (2009) conducted a comparative investigation across two undergraduate courses: cross-cultural psychology and introductory psychology. Fifty-nine students in these two courses completed the U.S. Ethnocentrism Scale (Neuliep & McCroskey, 1997) and the revised Generalized Ethnocentrism Scale (Neuliep, 2002) at the beginning and completion of their respective courses. These researchers found a significantly greater decrease in ethnocentrism, on both measures, for the cross-cultural students (who decreased their scores on both tests) than for the introductory psychology students (whose scores did not decrease significantly on either measure). This study had numerous flaws, including a number of pre-existing differences between the groups; nevertheless, it suggests that exposure to the content material of cross-cultural psychology may have the capacity to aid in overcoming ethnocentrism.

Borden (2007) reported another educational effort aimed toward reduction of ethnocentrism. She studied university students in two sections of an intercultural communication course, evaluating effects on ethnocentrism of their experience in service learning projects conducted in community settings serving ethnic minorities and international students. Borden used the Generalized Ethnocentrism Scale (Neuliep, 2002) as a pretest and posttest, administering it to students at the beginning of the course and again at the end. This report was essentially an effort to test the so-called "contact hypothesis"—the notion that contact between groups may reduce tension between them (Allport, 1954). The results indicated a significant reduction in ethnocentrism in students completing the service learning experience, suggesting a possible role for such exposure as a means to reduce ethnocentrism. However, the absence of a comparison group and other standard control measures makes it necessary to interpret this project with caution.

Further, as Brewer and Brown (1998) pointed out, the contact hypothesis has often been contradicted by experience. Specifically, as Brewer and Brown explained, the contact hypothesis, or simple exposure to other groups, is likely to succeed only if certain additional factors (social and institutional support, potential for meaningful relationships, equal status between groups, and intergroup cooperation) are in place.

### Predictive variables

Finally, Dong, Day, and Collaço (2008) investigated the possible role of intercultural communication sensitivity and multiculturalism as predictors of ethnocentrism. They administered the Intercultural Sensitivity Scale (Chen & Starosta, 2000), a multicultural ideology scale (Berry & Kalin, 1995), and the Generalized Ethnocentrism Scale (Neuliep, 2002) to 419 American undergraduate students, most of them Caucasians and Asian Americans.

Dong et al. reported significant correlations between both the intercultural sensitivity and multicultural ideology measures and the Generalized Ethnocentrism Scale, and suggested the possibility that increasing intercultural sensitivity and multicultural appreciation (e.g., through educational advocacy, neighborhood and community education, and one-to-one intercultural experience) might reduce ethnocentrism. However, this correlational study, while perhaps identifying promising variables for future research, did not demonstrate a causal connection among these measures. It may simply be the case that individuals who are more ethnocentric are naturally less interculturally sensitive and less multiculturally ideologic, and that all these traits are the product of some other cause. Dong et al. were correct, however, in observing that few empirical studies have investigated specific variables that could decrease levels of ethnocentrism.

## Summary

Despite the universality of ethnocentrism, we have some evidence that culture and experience may influence its occurrence. Thus, students in different cultures show differing levels of ethnocentrism. Specifically, Japanese students have shown higher levels of ethnocentrism than Americans (Neuliep et al., 2001), as have Chinese students (Li & Liu, 1975; Shuya, 2007). Thus, although the evidence suggests the universality of ethnocentrism, levels seem to vary from culture to culture. And some research findings have indicated tentative relationships between education as a mitigating factor and ethnocentrism, and between ethnocentrism and experience in specific courses. However, although exposure to cultural subgroups may hold promise in the effort to overcome ethnocentrism, we know we must be skeptical of claims that exposure alone will achieve this end. Nevertheless, exposure to people and their diversity is likely to play a contributing role in reducing ethnocentrism.

## Conclusion

Ethnocentrism has appeared in the sociocultural literature for more than a century, and we believe it to be a universal human phenomenon. We have seen that ethnocentrism may take different forms—specifically with or without hostility toward out-groups—but always involving the tendency to elevate one's own group (in-group). Although ethnocentrism may have evolutionary roots, researchers have identified a number of psychological traits and conditions associated with it. Studies investigating these psychological variables have generally been correlational in nature, or have lacked sufficient experimental controls to allow causal inferences; research has nevertheless suggested a connection between ethnocentrism and authoritarianism and between ethnocentrism and fundamentalism.

Although ethnocentrism has sometimes diminished with educational experience and intergroup exposure, the studies demonstrating this have lacked the scientific rigor necessary to show causal connections. Further, intergroup exposure seems to require additional supports and relationships to reliably influence out-group prejudice. The base of empirical research directed toward reducing ethnocentrism is sparse; more work will be needed if we are to fully understand this important cultural phenomenon. Only then perhaps, unlike the proverbial frog, will we get beyond our isolated well and our own little patch of sky.

## References

Adorno, T., Frenkel-Brunswick, E., Levinson, D., & Sanford, N. (1950). *The authoritarian personality*. New York: Harper.

Allport, G. W. (1954). *The nature of prejudice*. Reading, MA: Addison-Wesley.

Altemeyer, B. (1996). *The authoritarian specter*. Cambridge, MA: Harvard University Press.

Altemeyer, B. (2003). Why do religious fundamentalists tend to be prejudiced? *International Journal for the Psychology of Religion, 13*, 17–28.

Berry, J. W., & Kalin, R. (1995). Multicultural and ethnic attitudes in Canada: An overview of the 1991 national survey. *Canadian Journal of Behavioral Science, 27*, 301–320.

Berry, J. W., Poortinga, Y. H., Segall, M. H., & Dasen, P. R. (2002). *Cross-cultural psychology: Research and applications* (2nd ed.). Cambridge, UK: Cambridge University Press.

Beswick, D. G. (1972). A survey of ethnocentrism in Australia. *Australian Journal of Psychology, 24*, 153–163.

Bizumic, B., & Duckitt, J. (2007). Varieties of group self-centeredness and dislike of the specific other. *Basic and Applied Social Psychology, 29*, 195–202.

Bizumic, B., & Duckitt, J. (2008). "My group is not worthy of me": Narcissism and ethnocentrism. *Political Psychology, 29*, 437–453.

Block, J., & Block, J. (1951). An investigation of the relationship between intolerance of ambiguity and ethnocentrism. *Journal of Personality, 19*, 303–311.

Borden, A. W. (2007). The impact of service-learning on ethnocentrism in an intercultural communication course. *Journal of Experiential Education, 30*, 171–183.

Brewer, M. B. (1999). The psychology of prejudice: Ingroup love or outgroup hate? *Journal of Social Issues, 55*, 429–444.

Brewer, M. B. (2007). The importance of being *we*: Human nature and intergroup relations. *American Psychologist, 62*, 728–738.

Brewer, M. B., & Brown, R. J. (1998). Intergroup relations. In D. T. Gilbert, S. T. Fiske, & G. Lindzey (Eds.), *The handbook of social psychology, Vol. 2* (4th ed., pp. 554–594). Boston: McGraw-Hill.

Brislin, R. (2000). *Understanding culture's influence on behavior* (2nd ed.). Fort Worth: Harcourt.

Campbell, D. T. (1970). Natural selection as an epistemological model. In R. Naroll & R. Cohen (Eds.), *A handbook of method in cultural anthropology* (pp. 51–85). New York: Natural History Press.

Cashdan, E. (2001). Ethnocentrism and xenophobia: A cross-cultural study. *Current Anthropology, 42*, 760–765.

Chen, G. M., & Starosta, W. J. (2000). The development and validation of the international communication sensitivity scale. *Human Communication, 3*, 2–14.

Chesler, M. A. (1965). Ethnocentrism and attitudes toward the physically disabled. *Journal of Personality and Social Psychology, 2*, 877–882.

Chryssochoidis, G., Krystallis, A., & Perreas, P. (2007). Ethnocentric beliefs and country-of-origin (COO) effect: Impact of country, product and product attributes on Greek consumers' evaluation of food products. *European Journal of Marketing, 41*, 11–12.

Darwin, C. (1874). *The descent of man and selection in relation to sex* (2nd ed.). New York: A. L. Burt Co.

de Oliveira, E. A., Braun, J. L., Carlson, T. L., & de Oliveira, S. G. (2009). Students' attitudes toward foreign-born and domestic instructors. *Journal of Diversity in Higher Education, 2*, 113–125.

Dong, Q., Day, K. D., & Collaço, C. M. (2008). Overcoming ethnocentrism through developing intercultural communication sensitivity and multiculturalism. *Human Communication, 11*(1), 27–38.

Druckman, D. (2006). *Explaining national identity: From group attachments to collective action*. Occasional Papers Series [online]. Brisbane: The Australian Centre for Peace and Conflict Studies. [add URL?]

Epstein, R., & Komorita, S. S. (1966). Childhood prejudice as a function of parental ethnocentrism, punitiveness, and outgroup characteristics. *Journal of Personality and Social Psychology, 3*, 259–264.

Faulkner, J., Schaller, M., Park, J. H., & Duncan, L. A. (2004). Evolved disease-avoidance mechanisms and contemporary xenophobic attitudes. *Group Processes and Intergroup Relations, 7*, 333–353.

Gittler, J. B. (1972). Jews as an ethnic minority in the United States. *International Journal of Group Tensions, 2*(4), 4–21.

Hammond, R. A., & Axelrod, R. (2006). The evolution of ethnocentrism. *Journal of Conflict Resolution, 50*, 926–936.

Hasnain, N. (2007). Does religiousness promote prejudice and ethnocentrism? *Psychological Studies, 52*, 123–125.

Hofstede, G. (2007). A European in Asia. *Asian Journal of Social Psychology, 10*, 16–21.

Hooghe, M. (2008). Ethnocentrism. *International encyclopedia of the social sciences.* Philadelphia: Macmillan Reference.

Hraba, J. (1972). The doll technique: A measure of racial ethnocentrism? *Social Forces, 50*, 522–527.

Hsu, J. L., & Nien, H. (2008). Who are ethnocentric? Examining consumer ethnocentrism in Chinese societies. *Journal of Consumer Behaviour, 7*, 436–447.

Khan, S. S., & Liu, J. H. (2008). Intergroup attributions and ethnocentrism in the Indian subcontinent: The ultimate attribution error revisited. *Journal of Cross-Cultural Psychology, 39*, 16–36.

LeBaron, M. (2003). *Bridging cultural conflicts: A new approach for a changing world.* San Francisco: Wiley.

LeVine, R. A. (1982). *Culture, behavior, and personality: An introduction to the comparative study of psychosocial adaptation.* New York: Aldine.

LeVine, R. A., & Campbell, D. T. (1972). *Ethnocentrism: Theories of conflict, ethnic attitudes and group behavior.* New York: Wiley.

Li, W. L., & Liu, S. S. (1975). Ethnocentrism among American and Chinese youth. *Journal of Social Psychology, 95*, 277–278.

Matsumoto, D., & Juang, L. (2004). *Culture and psychology* (3rd ed.). Belmont, CA: Thomson-Wadsworth.

McCrae, R. R., & Costa, P. T., Jr. (1999). A five-factor theory of personality. In L. A. Pervin & O. P. John (Eds.), *Handbook of personality: Theory and research* (2nd ed., pp. 139–153). New York: Guilford Press.

Mosher, D. L., & Scodel, A. (1960). Relationships between ethnocentrism in children and the ethnocentrism and authoritarian rearing practices of their mothers. *Child Development, 31*, 369–376.

Mutisya, P. M., & Ross, L. E. (2005). Afrocentricity and racial socialization among African American college students. *Journal of Black Studies, 35*, 235–247.

Navarrette, C. D., & Fessler, D. M. T. (2006). Disease avoidance and ethnocentrism: The effects of disease vulnerability and disgust sensitivity on intergroup attitudes. *Evolution and Human Behavior, 27*, 270–282.

Navarrette, C. D., Fessler, D. M. T., & Eng, S. J. (2007). Elevated ethnocentrism in the first trimester of pregnancy. *Evolution and Human Behavior, 28*, 60–65.

Neuliep, J. W. (2002). Assessing the reliability and validity of the generalized ethnocentrism scale. *Journal of Intercultural Communication Research, 31*, 201–216.

Neuliep, J. W., Chaudoir, M., & McCroskey, J. C. (2001). A cross-cultural comparison of ethnocentrism among Japanese and United States college students. *Communication Research Reports, 18*, 137–146.

Neuliep, J. W., Hintz, S. M., & McCroskey, J. C. (2005). The influence of ethnocentrism in organizational contexts: Perceptions of interviewee and managerial attractiveness, credibility, and effectiveness. *Communication Quarterly, 53*, 41–56.

Neuliep, J. W., & McCroskey, J. C. (1997). The development of a U.S. and generalized ethnocentrism scale. *Communication Research Reports, 14,* 385–398.

Nguyen, T. D., Nguyen, T. T. M., & Barrett, N. J. (2008). Consumer ethnocentrism, cultural sensitivity, and intention to purchase local products—evidence from Vietnam. *Journal of Consumer Behaviour, 7,* 88–100.

O'Connor, P. (1952). Ethnocentrism, "intolerance of ambiguity," and abstract reasoning ability. *Journal of Abnormal and Social Psychology, 47,* 526–530.

Pettijohn II, T. F., & Naples, G. M. (2009). Reducing ethnocentrism in U.S. college students by completing a cross-cultural psychology course. *The Open Social Science Journal, 2,* 1–6.

Plant, W. T. (1958a). Changes in ethnocentrism associated with a four-year college education. *Journal of Educational Psychology, 49,* 162–165.

Plant, W. T. (1958b). Changes in ethnocentrism associated with a two-year college experience. *Journal of Genetic Psychology, 92,* 189–197.

Pratto, F., & Glasford, D. E. (2008). Ethnocentrism and the value of a human life. *Journal of Personality and Social Psychology, 95,* 1411–1428.

Price, W. F., & Crapo, R. H. (2002). *Cross-cultural perspectives in introductory psychology.* Pacific Grove, CA: Wadsworth.

Prothro, E. T. (1952). Ethnocentrism and anti-Negro attitudes in the Deep South. *Journal of Abnormal and Social Psychology, 47,* 105–108.

Raden, D. (2003). Ingroup bias, classic ethnocentrism, and non-ethnocentrism among American Whites. *Political Psychology, 24,* 803–828.

Roberts, J. P. (1997). *A sociobiological examination of ethnocentrism between two ethnic units—Tamils and Guraratis—in the city of Pune, India.* Doctoral dissertation, University of Wisconsin-Milwaukee.

Ross, M. H. (1991). The role of evolution in ethnocentric conflict and its management. *Journal of Social Issues, 47,* 167–185.

Ryan, C. S., & Bogart, L. M. (1997). Development of new group members' in-group and out-group stereotypes: Changes in perceived group variability and ethnocentrism. *Journal of Personality and Social Psychology, 73,* 719–732.

Shuya, P. (2007, November). *Intercultural communication apprehension, ethnocentrism and their relationship with gender: A cross-cultural comparison between the US and China.* Paper presented at the annual convention of the National Communication Association, Chicago.

Simon, M. A. (1980). Biology, sociobiology, and the understanding of human social behavior. In A. Montagu (Ed.), *Sociobiology examined* (pp. 291–310). New York: Oxford University Press.

Strickland, B. S. (2000). Misassumptions, misadventures, and the misuse of psychology. *American Psychologist, 55,* 331–338.

Sumner, W. G. (1906). *Folkways: A study of the sociological importance of usages, manners, customs, mores, and morals.* New York: Ginn & Co.

Taft, R. (1956). Intolerance of ambiguity and ethnocentrism. *Journal of Consulting Psychology, 20,* 153–154.

Thayer, B. A. (2004). *Darwin and international relations: On the evolutionary origins of war and ethnic conflict.* Lexington, KY: The University Press of Kentucky.

Thomas, D. R. (1975). Authoritarianism, child-rearing practices and ethnocentrism in seven Pacific Islands groups. *International Journal of Psychology, 10,* 235–246.

Todosijević, B., & Enyedi, Z. (2002). Authoritarianism vs. cultural pressure. *Journal of Russian and East European Psychology, 40*, 31–54.

Triandis, H. C. (1994). *Culture and social behavior.* New York: McGraw-Hill.

Van IJzendoorn, M. H. (2001). Moral judgment, authoritarianism, and ethnocentrism. *Journal of Social Psychology, 129*, 37–45.

Vida, I. (2008). The role of ethnic affiliation in consumer ethnocentrism. *European Journal of Marketing, 42*, 327–343.

Wilson, E. O. (1978). *On human nature.* Cambridge, MA: Harvard University Press.

# Part II

# Approaches
# to Cross-Cultural Research

For many years, Western psychological research, particularly research originating in North America, presented its work as natural fact, even when the studies included few, if any, participants from other cultures. Further, studies often had the additional limitations associated with homogeneity of race (the subjects were usually white) and age (the subjects were often college undergraduates). In Part II, we will explore some of the limitations of Western research, and we will try to understand some of the reasons why researchers have not considered culture in their work.

Given the amazing diversity of people, not only across cultures around the world, but within such diverse countries as the United States and the United Kingdom, it becomes increasingly important that investigators make efforts to make their research more inclusive. Old assumptions about psychological principles and their universality are giving way to a more sophisticated understanding of the relation between universal and culture-specific truths.

Cross-cultural researchers face a variety of special difficulties as they try to untangle and isolate the many facets and dimensions of culture that may influence behavior, and they must use care to avoid confusing cultural variables with others (like socioeconomic status, population density, age, and education) that may also be determinants of human activity. These efforts to improve research design are critical to the ability of investigators to rule out non-cultural alternative hypotheses and to understand the interplay between culture and other characteristics like language and gender identity.

Increasingly, researchers need a level of cultural competence that they would have rarely considered a few years ago. This means they must have some understanding of the cultures they study and the language issues essential to development of fair and meaningful measures, and sensitivity to their own ideological and value-based biases. Organized psychology has made some strides toward achievement of these aims, but important questions and issues remain.

What, for example, are the special ethical issues associated with cross-cultural research? How can researchers maximize the generalizability of their findings? What do investigators do about populations that may be "hidden" by cultural repression or discrimination? And how should behavioral scientists deal with the construct of race, which is often erroneously equated with culture? These are representative of the issues we will encounter in Part II.

# 3

# Methodological and Conceptual Issues in Cross-Cultural Research

## Bernard C. Beins

Culture exerts a notable impact on virtually every aspect of one's behavior, thought, and attitude. Curiously, though, psychologists lost sight of this proposition for much of the twentieth century. This chapter will identify some of the issues that the current generation of psychologists has rediscovered as being critical in researching and understanding the wide variety of human psychological experience.

Several issues merit attention here. First, psychologists will benefit by understanding the degree to which psychological responses reflect tendencies that are universal as opposed to particular to a given culture. Psychologists have concluded in some cases that they identified universals, but upon closer examination, the certainty has faded.

Second, one's *Weltanschauung* clearly drives one's thought processes. Of specific attention has been the difference in perspective as a function of whether one's origins are within a collectivistic or individualistic culture. Again, what seemed to have been relatively clear distinctions have blurred as psychologists have moved from the level of culture to the level of the individual. A third important element in cultural research involves the very pattern of thought processes in people of different cultures. What is obvious and apparent to one is foreign to another.

Fourth, methodological issues per se have turned out to be of importance in understanding psychological processes. New techniques like neural imaging appear to affect even basic processes that one might assume are impervious to culture. Furthermore, on a larger level, how one categorizes participants from different cultures is a thorny issue that remains unsolved. Finally, ethical issues involved in research lurk in unexpected ways. What might be ethical according to one set of standards may not be in another.

Researchers have identified these various issues, but it would be premature to claim that they have achieved resolution. The discipline has made notable progress, but as with any complex area, more questions remain than have been answered with certainty.

## Historical Elements

Cross-cultural research in psychology is growing in scope and quantity, but it has had only a short history. Consequently, psychology is still grappling with fundamental methodological and conceptual issues pertaining to culturally relevant research. PsycINFO© indicates only 12 articles in peer-reviewed journals with a descriptor of *cross-cultural research* through 1959. In contrast, in 2008, there were 95 peer-reviewed articles listed. Naturally, a single descriptor represents only a minute slice of relevant research, but this datum reveals the trend.

Social researchers used to know that behaviors differed across cultures and that those behaviors were mediated by cultural factors. As Linton (1945) noted, "personalities, cultures and societies are all configurations in which the patterning and organization of the whole is more important than any of the component parts" (p. 2). But for a number of decades, many psychologists forgot this fact. During the heyday of behaviorism, it seemed that there was little need to attend to culture for two important reasons.

First, animals did not have cultures, so researchers studying rats (which themselves were white) did not have to consider this construct. Second, if behaviors resulted from reinforcement contingencies, researchers may have reasoned that they needed only to understand reward and punishment, and culture would not have been particularly germane in many cases.

Even among users of projective tests like the Thematic Apperception Test (TAT), there was some belief that cultural background may not have played a role in responses. For instance, Riess, Schwartz, and Cottingham (1950) administered the TAT to Black and White participants and recorded the lengths of participants' responses; the results revealed that the length of utterances did not relate to race. This reliance on the quite objective and measurable number of words uttered was characteristic of the behavioral approach. Interestingly, the researchers did not attend to the content of those responses.

The lack of attention to culture belies the awareness by earlier psychological researchers and by anthropologists that studying culture was an intrinsic part of studying people. Current students of culture would undoubtedly disagree with some interpretations of differences, but the important issue here is that the researchers recognized the importance of those differences. For example, Tylor (1889) attributed differences across cultures through the perspective of Herbert Spencer's model of cultural evolution, with Western "races" at the pinnacle. However, Thomas's (1937) ideas anticipated current thoughts about differences in culture leading to different behaviors; he did not accord different status to what others called the "higher" and "lower" races.

By the 1930s, psychology had adopted a tone that resembles today's. For example, Herskovits (1935) dismissed the notion that African cultures (of which there were many) were primitive or savage. Rather, he noted that strong family ties, strong adherence to governmental and legal principles, and established religions characterized African cultures of that era. He also distinguished the cultures of Black people in Africa and North America, noting that cultures change as people from one culture come into contact with people from another.

Revisions in the ideas about people of non-Western or of southern and eastern European descent in the 1930s seem to have resulted from the influx of a new type of psychologist. Psychology became populated with people from a wide range of ethnicities, particularly Jewish psychologists, who may have been more sensitized to the different life experiences of minorities, and therefore more aware of the cultural factors that eventuate in particular behaviors (Samelson, 1978).

The current focus in psychology on the importance of culture in affecting behavior may similarly result from the influx of a different set of ethnic minorities. Between 1996 and 2004, there was an increase in doctoral degrees among American minorities of 16.6%, an increase in master's level degrees of 90.8%, and an increase in bachelor's degrees of 36% (American Psychological Association, 2008). In addition, as an organization, the American Psychological Association (APA) has focused on the internationalization of the discipline, as evidenced by its 2008 Education Leadership Conference that focused on international connections in psychology.

The current cultural climate in psychology will pave the way for changes in two important aspects of research—the way psychologists conduct their research and the way they interpret their results. Just as understanding the relation between culture and behavior is complex, so must be the way psychologists develop research questions, identify appropriate methodologies, and interpret their data.

## Universals and Measurements Across Cultures

Cross-cultural research poses difficulties that much other research may not face because, in addition to developing designs that show high levels of internal validity, cross-cultural psychologists have to worry about appropriate external validity. There are also practical issues of generating appropriate participant samples from varied cultures. Furthermore, drawing inferences from data can be difficult because researchers need to understand the intricacies of each culture. Attention to cross-cultural research is relatively new in psychology, thus the methodological and interpretive issues still merit critical scrutiny.

An important component of both the internal and the external validity is the nature of measurements across cultures. As Chen (2008) has noted, measurements across cultures may not be comparable because of factors such as translation issues, failure of items being measured to capture the same construct across cultures, different response styles, and social desirability.

Compounding this dilemma is the fact that some apparently etic traits have emic components in a particular culture that may be irrelevant in another. For instance, in Chinese culture, the etic construct of dependability includes emic components like being gracious to others, truthful, and family oriented (Cheung & Leung, 1998).

Some cross-cultural investigations on universal processes (e.g., Ekman's, 1972, work on recognition of emotions) have attained the status of "classic" research. But conclusions even about the supposed universality of the ability to recognize emotions must be modified to take culture into account. Ekman's (1972) research on how accurately people recognize facial expression of emotions provides an appropriate backdrop with which to begin a discussion of how questions evolve across the various phases of culturally oriented research. Ekman discovered that some emotions are universally recognized. He displayed faces to people in five different cultures and asked them to identify the emotion expressed in the picture. Respondents from the United States, Chile, Brazil, Argentina, and Japan all identified the emotions at well above chance levels, implying that a display of emotion has a universality that transcends individual cultures.

As Elfenbein and Ambady (2003) pointed out, though, cultural factors are not irrelevant to the recognition of emotion. For example, the various groups identified the emotions with noticeably different accuracy, with Americans showing the highest average degree of accuracy (86%) and the Japanese the lowest (78%). Elfenbein and Ambady noted, however, that the task involved the recognition of emotions expressed by Americans. It turns out that there is a reliable in-group effect such that, although people are accurate in identifying emotional expressions in general, they tend to be better at identifying those emotions when expressed by people within their own culture. Furthermore, even though there is consistently high recognition of emotions in photographs, the accuracy rate is affected by how many generations a family of Chinese origin had lived in the United States and by whether the emotional expressions were displayed by people living in China or in the U.S.

Similarly, John Bowlby's (1988) conceptualization and Mary Ainsworth's research on attachment (Ainsworth, Blehar, Waters, & Wall, 1978) are predicated on the universality of the construct. Ainsworth's findings seem descriptively useful, but some (e.g., Keller, 2008) have argued that the conclusions regarding differences in attachment styles across cultures represent a bias toward Western culture. Keller stated that some conclusions include a heavy dose of judgment. For example, she suggested that inferences about maternal sensitivity associated with attachment reflect "a judgment on maternal adequacy, a way of distinguishing good from bad mothers" (p. 410).

An assessment of the research findings and subsequent interpretations suggests that attachment behaviors deemed undesirable or even pathological in one culture may be desirable and entirely acceptable in another (Rothbaum, Weisz, Pott, Kiyake, & Morelli, 2000). Thus, one could convincingly argue that attachment theory, often regarded as culture-free, is highly culture-bound.

Psychologists have regarded recognition of emotion and attachment styles as being universal. Thus, one might conclude that these topics should be easy to research: It would not matter where one conducted the research because people would not differ notably across different cultures. Unfortunately, current research on these topics belies the idea that cultural specifics are irrelevant. Consideration of attachment and of recognition of emotion reveals the difficulty that researchers face in trying to study constructs that may have some degree of universality.

A further indication of the complexity of these issues is that constructs that may be regarded as similar may require very different cultural assessment. For example, Smith, Spillane, and Annus (2006) have argued that anorexia nervosa is culturally invariant but that bulimia nervosa is highly Western in origin and prevalence.

## Issues in Culturally Relevant Research: Individualism and Collectivism

Psychologists have developed an awareness that they need to exercise caution in discussing supposedly universal traits or patterns of behavior. Even apparently simple cognitive acts like categorizing stimuli or remembering details of an experience involve important cultural components. For instance Ji, Zhang, and Nisbett (2004) reported that Chinese participants may group words according to how they relate whereas American participants group them according to taxonomy (e.g., in a *monkey–banana–panda* triad, Chinese participants group *monkey–banana*, but Americans pair *monkey–panda*).

Considerations of complex personality issues raise even more difficulties. For example, researchers have assumed that the need for self-esteem is a universal trait because the well-established body of literature has consistently shown such a need. However, that literature is based on North American culture; when psychologists have investigated self-esteem among the Japanese, the results diverge in critical ways from those involving North American participants (Heine, Lehman, Markus, & Kitayama, 1999). In fact, self-esteem as conceptualized in Western psychology may be fairly irrelevant in Eastern psychology.

Given that psychological theory is typically Western-based, the constructs that psychologists use and even the language may make it difficult to understand cultural differences and even to speak about them. Thus, researchers may be discussing what they think are etics that are really emics. In fact, there is still disagreement as to whether some psychological constructs are basically universal with different cultural manifestations or whether they are largely cultural (Smith et al., 2006).

One of the dimensions receiving considerable attention because of its cultural relevance involves the role of individualism and collectivism. According to Matsumoto and Yoo (2006), this is the most widely studied dimension in the field, and varied research projects have illustrated consistent behavioral differences associated with the individualistic-collectivist (IC) continuum. It will serve as a useful illustration of the nature of the problems associated with studying behaviors across cultures.

An initial caveat in discussing the effects of one's location on the IC continuum is that one must recognize that attributing differences in behavior to IC orientation is difficult because the investigator must be able to separate effects of culture (e.g., IC orientation) from other sources of variability. On an ecological level, there is a myriad of factors that affect behavior in different countries including affluence, population density, religious practice, and climate. As psychologists define *culture*, these ecological variables stand apart from cultural variables (Matsumoto & Yoo, 2006, p. 237).

Research on individualism and collectivism has revealed that people from collectivist cultures remember events differently than people from individualistic cultures. Individualist people tend to remember situations from the viewpoint of themselves as part of the situation. On the other hand, collectivist people tend to focus on the social situation with the perspective of an outsider looking in. A typical interpretation is that individualists focus on self and collectivists focus on other. If this difference in memory is true, then simple measurement of memories may be problematic across cultures because of the different ways that people conceptualize their world (Cohen & Gunz, 2002).

However, even if one were to resolve this dilemma, another problem arises in cultural research. Multiple cultures may exist and notable individual differences appear within a given country; unfortunately, researchers often equate country with culture, making the assumption that what is true generally within a country reflects differences in culture compared to another country. Thus, Iwata and Higuchi (2000) studied state and trait anxiety, finding that their Japanese participants had less positive views of themselves and higher levels of both state and trait anxiety than Americans. They attributed the variation across countries to differences in Japan and the United States on the IC continuum. But, as Matsumoto and Yoo (2006) pointed out, Iwata and Higuchi interpreted their data under the assumption that Japan is a collectivist society in which people are compliant in order to maintain social harmony and underestimate their own positive traits.

Matsumoto and Yoo identified seven assumptions that Iwata and Higuchi made regarding Japanese people. None of these assumptions was empirically tested. Matsumoto and Yoo did point out that Iwata and Higuchi's assumptions may be correct and that differences between Japanese and American students resulted from the relevant differences on the IC continuum. Their point was that psychologists should engage in research to verify such assumptions. The attribution of differences across groups to cultural factors when there is no empirical support for such an interpretation is known as the cultural attribution fallacy, a specific case of a larger problem that Campbell (1961) called the ecological fallacy.

Interestingly, Iwata and Higuchi (2000) couched their discussion of the Japanese-American differences using the American pattern as the norm. This type of inference poses behaviors of Americans as a standard against which others are compared, which Arnett (2008) has pointed out is common in discussing and interpreting research findings. This orientation to interpretation of research holds true for other types of comparisons as well, including gender differences (Hegarty & Buechel, 2006).

Another complicating factor here is that the IC dimension, as dominant as it is in cultural research, may not be the only construct with explanatory power. For example, as Matsumoto and Yoo (2006) pointed out, psychologists have listed 25 additional dimensions that distinguish cultures. As they noted, countries that differ on one dimension may also differ on others. For instance, on the IC continuum, the United States stands at first in individualism, whereas Japan is 27th out of 70 countries (which puts both Japan and the United States below the median in collectivist tendencies). At the same time, Japan is 8th in uncertainty avoidance, whereas the United States is 59th (Hofstede, 2001). Matsumoto and Yoo also noted that Japan ranks 4th in long- versus short-term orientation, with the United States at 26th out of 36 countries, which might explain differences in anxiety level differences among Japanese and Americans (Iwata & Higuchi, 2000) as well as or better than IC.

Finally, researchers must provide empirical assessment of characteristics of people in a particular culture in order to draw inferences about behaviors based on perceived differences across countries. Noting the great within-group variability in traits within a culture and, often, small across-group differences, McCrae and Terraccianno (2006) demonstrated that "there does not appear to be even a kernel of truth in the stereotypes of national character" (p. 160). There may be consensus about people in a given culture (e.g., the belief by Americans that the English have no sense of humor), but McCrae and Terraccianno note that consensus (i.e., reliability) does not equal validity. Hence, valid measurements of traits in a sample must accompany inferences of behaviors based on those traits.

## Culture and Its Relation to Thought and Language

The discussion above centers on the role of culture in attitudes, behaviors, and personality. But there is reason to believe that culture may affect the way people actually think about the world. The belief that Inuit people have a multitude of words for snow and that this linguistic abundance leads them to conceptualize their snow-filled world differently than people in moderate climates is just a myth. But the point behind that myth has a reality. One's cultural background, including one's language, seems to be causal in the development of a world view.

For example, as noted previously, Ji et al. (2004) presented their participants with word triads such as *monkey–panda–banana*. Participants selected two items that formed a group. A grouping like *monkey–panda* is categorical, whereas a grouping like *monkey–banana* is relational. The question that the researchers addressed was whether people of Chinese background and of American background responded similarly. The results confirmed that the Chinese participants were more likely to choose relational pairings (e.g., monkey–banana because monkeys eat bananas), whereas the American participants favored categorical pairings (e.g., monkey–panda because both are animals).

These results support the notion that people of East Asian backgrounds preferentially focus on overall context but that those with Western backgrounds make use of taxonomic concepts. Such findings are compatible with a collectivist, context-oriented perspective versus an individualistic perspective. Such sensitivity to context has appeared in numerous studies, including accuracy in identifying one's orientation in a rod-and-frame test (Ji, Peng, & Nisbett, 2000) and memory for focal versus background elements in visual display (Masuda & Nisbett, 2001).

However, explanations are always fraught with rival hypotheses. Simply because Ji et al.'s (2004) participants may have differed on the IC continuum, it does not necessarily follow that the differences in their patterns of responses in choosing a pair of words from the triad were due to collectivism versus individualism. Drawing such a conclusion may reflect an example of the cultural attribution fallacy.

For example, Matsumoto and Yoo (2006) have speculated that differences in memory for individual items in a visual display between Japanese and American participants may be due either to the greater emphasis on rote memorization in schools or on the visual computer game culture in Japan. Such memorial differences may be consistent across cultures, but those differences do not always signal cultural differences (as the term *culture* is used by psychologists). This difficulty with interpretations lies at the heart of the interpretation paradox (van de Vijver & Leung, 2000), which reflects the fact that large differences across groups are easy to spot, but hard to explain, whereas small differences are hard to spot, but easy to explain.

Similarly, differences in responses to stimuli may reflect a combination of culture and other factors. As noted above, Ji et al. (2004) reported that Chinese participants organized words relationally but Americans organized words categorically. At the same time, the language in which participants were tested affected their responses. Response patterns of some Chinese participants differed depending on whether the language of the experimental session was Chinese or English. This finding corresponds to differences that other investigators have noted. For instance, Marian and Neisser (2000) found that language itself provides a context for recall. When Russian–English bilinguals received a prompt in Russian, their memories for autobiographical details associated with living in Russia, whereas English prompts spurred better memory for events associated with speaking English. In addition, the researchers have noted differences in cognitive processes associated with language itself.

Similarly, cross-cultural research has revealed differences in recognition of emotions. Matsumoto, Anguas-Wong, and Martinez (2008) discovered that Spanish–English bilinguals recognized facial emotions more accurately when they were tested in English than in Spanish, and Matsumoto and Assar (1992) showed that Hindi–English bilinguals recognized facial emotions more accurately when tested in English than in Hindi.

These results based on language may extend beyond language itself. That is, it is possible that bilinguals who are bicultural engage in a kind of cultural frame switching, viewing their world in different ways depending on the context.

For example, Benet-Martínez, Leu, Lee, and Morris, (2002) assessed the degree to which participants saw their two cultures as being consistent with one another or contradictory to one another. They characterized the participants as either high in bicultural identity integration (BII, cultures were consistent) or low in BII (cultures were contradictory). In the experimental session, the researchers primed participants to think either of American culture (e.g., by presenting pictures of Mickey Mouse, the U.S. Capitol, etc.) or Chinese culture (e.g., by presenting pictures of a rice farmer, the Great Wall of China, etc.). Participants subsequently viewed an animation of a single fish swimming in front of a school of fish, and then the participants gave an explanation as to why the single fish was leading the pack. The researchers coded the responses as involving factors that were either internal (personal characteristics of the fish) or external (the fish being influenced by other fish).

The results revealed that people who saw their two cultures as consistent with one another (those high in BII) responded with internal attributes of the fish when primed with American symbols and with external attributes when primed with Chinese symbols. On the other hand, participants who saw their two cultures as contradictory (those low in BII) showed internal attributions when primed with Chinese symbols and external attributions when primed with American symbols.

The researchers concluded that those high in BII readily engaged in cultural frame switching because they were comfortable with both worldviews. In contrast, those low in BII reacted to cues in one culture by drawing to mind their affiliation with the other culture. This response resembles the behavior of tourists to foreign countries who have a heightened awareness of their affiliation with their culture but who rarely think of that affiliation in their home country. As Markus (2008) pointed out, ethnicity can affect the psychological experience even when people are not aware of it.

As these results show, culture plays a significant role in how people observe and respond to the world around them. But the issue is complex because behaviors change due to individual differences like the language that the person uses and the degree to which the person feels assimilated into the various cultures to which he or she is exposed. Depending on the sample used in a research project, results might show vastly different patterns. Furthermore, the nature of a prime could affect the outcome significantly. For example, Shih, Pittinsky, and Ambady (1999) primed women of Asian descent to their gender identities or to their cultural identities before asking them to solve math problems. When the women received the gender prime, they performed less well on the math task than when they received the culture prime.

Inzlicht and Ben-Zeev (2000) provided an example of what may be a very subtle prime that had a major effect on women's math performance. Simply being in the presence of men depressed women's math performance compared to being in a single-sex research session.

Priming is a useful technique for assessing the effect of group membership. Much of the work on performance after a prime as it systematically affects different groups has involved sex and gender (e.g., Inzlicht & Ben-Zeev, 2000); it is well known, but less studied, in the context of race (e.g., Aronson, Lustina, Good, Keough, Steele, & Brown, 1999; Steele & Aronson, 1995). There is a collection of additional research on other cultural groups whose members are affected by appropriate primes, including Canadian (Walsh, Hickey, & Duffy, 1999), Chinese (Lee & Ottati, 1995), French (Croizet & Claire, 1998), German (Keller, 2007), Italian (Muzzatti & Agnoli, 2007), and poor people (Croizet & Claire, 1998).

This complex pattern of factors that influence one's outlook and behavior reveals the caution one must exercise in attributing differences in performance simply to culture. As noted before, culture might be very important, but differences in behavior may reflect the moderating effect of other variables and of individual differences among participants. Thus, significant differences across groups might actually reflect a confounding variable that is correlated with cultural affiliation but the differences may not be due to that affiliation itself.

The Council of National Psychological Associations for the Advancement of Ethnic Minority Interests (2000) has developed guidelines for research in ethnic minority communities in the U.S. These guidelines were developed in the context of American culture, but they pertain to cross-cultural research of any kind. The principles involve (a) avoidance of treating all members of a group as being the same, (b) development of cultural competence by researchers, (c) use of multiple, valid, convergent measurements, (d) understanding of cultural context, (e) use of representative samples, and (f) avoidance of using race as a predictive construct.

## Methodological Issues

The cognitive and intellectual effects of culture on thought and behavior pose serious issues in interpretations of research results. But methodological questions that appear fairly simple in research with samples from a single culture turn out to be complicated in and of themselves. Failure to account for the effects of methodology across cultures can result in data that are, at best, uninterpretable or, at worst, entirely misleading. The present discussion of cross-cultural research will include a broad definition of cross-cultural, accepting that different cultures can exist across countries but also within countries.

In describing their research, authors should provide enough demographic information about participants to (a) allow valid interpretation of results, (b) generalize the results, and (c) provide useful information for further research in the area

(American Psychological Association, 2010, pp. 29–30). This information includes variables like age, race or ethnicity, sex, and socioeconomic status. As noted below, race and ethnicity are not useful explanatory constructs, but when demographic information appears in a published article, readers can use that information to put the results into context regarding to what groups the results might pertain.

A cursory examination of most research reports reveals a paucity of such information. Interestingly, the third edition of APA's publication manual (American Psychological Association, 1983) makes no mention of the importance of including culturally relevant information about participants. Not until the fourth edition does the manual provide detailed guidance about describing cultural characteristics of participants (American Psychological Association, 1994). This change across the publication manuals mirrors the increase in attention to the importance of culture in research.

The importance of these variables in behavior is obvious. But there are also potential surprises lurking where researchers are not likely to expect them. For example, Park and Gutchess (2006) have noted that the results of brain imaging studies show that culture is associated with differences in neural processing. Consequently, failure to recognize such cultural effects could blind researchers to confounding variables and problems in drawing inferences, and failure to indicate both age and ethnicity in a research report could hamper further research in the area.

Furthermore, some psychologists have questioned whether culturally relevant research involving race (as opposed to ethnicity) is well grounded. That is, does race actually represent a "naturally occurring" causal variable? Helms, Jernigan, and Mascher (2005) have argued that there are methodological problems associated with conceptualizing people from a given racial category as constituting an intact group. As a rule, researchers do not use empirical measures to verify that the members in a group actually share important characteristics other than race.

Even when investigators report demographics, one needs to be aware of potential problems with this information. When people self-report their race, they may alter their choices depending on type of question (e.g., forced choice vs. selecting all that apply) or perceived advantage of a given selection in a particular situation (Panter, Daye, Allen, Deo,& Wightman, 2009; Phinney, 1996). Thus, even if race is a viable conceptual variable, assignment to racial categories, whether by the researchers or by the participants, may be problematic. In fact, with respect to health-related research, Shields et al. (2005) have recommended that self-reported race may be useful for recruiting research participants, but that statistical analysis should not be based on self-reported race.

Another, related problem with categorizing by race or ethnicity is that such categories are often based on bureaucratic rather than on systematic and scientific denotations. Rodriguez (2000) pointed out that, if a researcher uses categories established by the United States government, the same individual may fall into different groups depending on what agency has collected the data. The Census Bureau does not include *Hispanic* as a racial category, but agencies responsible for civil rights issues do include such a racial category.

The Pew Research Center has illustrated the problem with categorization with a "quick primer" related to being Hispanic, at least in the eyes of the U.S. Census Bureau:

Q:   I immigrated to Phoenix from Mexico. Am I Hispanic?
A:   You are if you say so.
Q:   My parents moved to New York from Puerto Rico. Am I Hispanic?
A:   You are if you say so.
Q:   My grandparents were born in Spain but I grew up in California. Am I Hispanic?
A:   You are if you say so.
Q:   I was born in Maryland and married an immigrant from El Salvador. Am I Hispanic?
A:   You are if you say so.
Q:   I was born in Argentina but grew up in Texas. I don't consider myself Hispanic. Does the Census count me as an Hispanic?
A:   Not if you say you aren't. (Passel & Taylor, 2009)

With research involving comparisons across countries, the situation is equally or more murky. Researchers have often equated country and culture, so that all participants from a given country are seen as having the same cultural roots. Chang (2000) provided an example of the drawback in this approach, explaining that there is really no single cultural group that one can designate as Chinese. Considering historic, linguistic, and anthropological factors, one could identify over 50 different ethnic groups that are all labeled Chinese. In fact, some of these groups speak variants of Chinese that would be mutually incomprehensible. Some researchers have used strategies like labeling as Asian anybody who was born in Asia, which could include people from a vast array of countries that show notable cultural differences among themselves (Cohen & Gunz, 2002; Kim, Atkinson, & Yang, 1999).

Further difficulties arise in interpreting data based on cultural category. Kim et al. (1999) suggested that as people from Asian countries become familiar with the culture in the U.S., their behaviors may change quickly. However, their attitudes may change slowly, if at all. So in one sense, they become members of both cultures, with an outlook that may differ across individuals, depending on the degree to which they feel comfortable in both cultures (Benet-Martínez, Leu, Lee, & Morris, 2002).

## Stimulus Materials

A further, significant issue in cross-cultural research involves the materials (e.g., psychological tests, experimental stimuli) that investigators use. These materials might seem straightforward and noncontroversial within the context of single-culture research, but there are notable reasons to attend to them in cross-cultural research.

Researchers who measure a construct across different groups often assume that the measurement is invariant across groups (Chen, 2008). A second assumption is that the construct itself is the same across the groups (Arnett, 2008; Heine & Buchtel, 2009). Neither of these assumptions is guaranteed. For instance, Chen has pointed out regarding the question of measurement invariance that reliability (hence validity) is generally lower in educational measurement in underperforming groups. Furthermore, across groups, different factors may underlie a construct like self-esteem, so measuring the construct comparably in the different cultures is difficult or maybe not even possible (Smith et al., 2006).

When it is possible to assess personality across cultures that are related (e.g., American and European), language and stimulus issues can still be important. Studies of the Big Five model of personality lead to somewhat different results as a function of translating English words into other European languages (Peabody & De Raad, 2002). Similarly, the addition of contextual or situational information in self-reports of personal characteristics can affect the reliability of the measurements of the Big Five traits (De Raad, Sullot, & Barelds, 2008).

In addition to the problem of characterizing a construct, if a measurement instrument is to be used in groups with different languages, translation issues arise. The concept of *feeling blue* has been used to exemplify linguistic concerns. How does one translate it? A direct translation into Chinese produces an item with little meaning (Chen, 2008); trying to render it directly into Spanish leads to problems because the word for blue, *azul*, does not carry the same connotation as in English (Rogler, 1999). The use of back translation can help (Banville, Desrosiers, & Genet-Volet, 2000), although there are still reasons for concern when researchers attempt this. For example, Rogler reported that 36% of test items on the Spanish version of the Clinical Analysis Questionnaire had grammatical errors or direct translation of idioms that made no sense in Spanish.

There is a growing literature regarding the adequacy of assessment materials across cultures, but the issue is far from settled. The question of cultural competence on many levels in research remains an important concern.

## Ethics

A final set of issues in cross-cultural research revolves around ethics in research. In the present context, these issues are not associated with anonymity, confidentiality, informed consent, and other elements of planning and conducting research, although researchers must attend to them. Rather, the discussion here involves the implications of research with diverse populations.

Markus (2008) raised the question of whether research on race and ethnicity, in and of itself, leads to stereotyping or other ethically troublesome outcomes. The question is not moot. For example, Kirmayer and Young (1998) reported that somatization of psychiatric symptoms varies across cultures. In addition, some behaviors that are stereotypically associated with certain ethnic groups in the United States are also associated with personality disorders (Iwamasa, Larrabee, & Merritt, 2000). Researchers who are not sensitive to cultural variations could draw inferences that result in stigmatization and generally unwarranted conclusions. APA's ethical principles and standards are especially relevant here.

First, among the aspirational general principles cited by APA (2002), the issue of justice is quite relevant here. That is, psychologists need to recognize the limitations to their expertise and competence and to recognize their biases.

Second, psychologists must respect people's rights and dignity. This principle pertains to recognition of and respect for individual differences associated with "age, gender, gender identity, race, ethnicity, culture, national origin, religion, sexual orientation, disability, language, and socioeconomic status" (p. 1063). Furthermore, psychologists are enjoined to consider these factors when working with members of such groups.

Within the enforceable ethical standards set forth by APA, there are several specific elements related to culturally relevant research, including competence (boundaries and maintenance of competence, bases for scientific judgments) and assessments (use of assessments, interpreting assessment results, assessment by unqualified persons).

Researchers should not ignore the fact that research on populations with which they are unfamiliar is fraught with potential conceptual and methodological problems. The conclusions based on research with participants from diverse backgrounds have both theoretical and social implications that are connected to ethical issues.

## Conclusion

Cross-cultural research in American psychology has moved through several stages over the past century, from a relatively simple, descriptive depiction of people in varied cultures to a complex and nuanced recognition of the complex interplay between culture and behavior. The recent impetus among many psychologists to consider the relation of culture and behavior seems to mirror society's increased interest in cultural issues as American society has become more diverse; along the way ethnicity has become a more prominent facet of many people's lives.

Kim (2007; see also Chapter 1, this volume) has suggested that, just as societal ideas change, so do research ideas, positing that there are four "cultures" of cultural research. These so-called cultures include (a) the pre-encounter research culture: "I'm not interested"; (b) the initial encounter: "culture is a nuisance"; (c) the Captain Cook research culture: "let's explore and compare"; and (d) the paradigm shift research culture: "beyond ethnocentric paradigms." One might argue that psychology has entered the exploration/comparison phase. Development of ideas that may move psychological theory beyond ethnocentric paradigms would require a paradigm shift, according to Kim. So it is not immediately clear what the next phase would look like.

However, within the current paradigm, psychologists are only now successfully separating some culture-independent and -dependent processes. It has become apparent that some supposedly universal processes (e.g., recognition of facial emotions) are more intertwined with specifics of language than initially supposed, as shown in the recent research on the Big Five model of personality (Peabody & De Raad, 2002).

Furthermore, the use of an American-centered model of psychological processes still predominates. Models of attitude, personality, and behavior may undergo additional modification when what is considered standard (i.e., the American perspective) instead becomes simply one of many useful perspectives. And as researchers compare and explore psychological processes across cultures, it will be critical to define samples precisely and to document the validity of assumptions that participants show certain cultural characteristics, a practice that is largely honored in the breach.

Finally, because issues of race and ethnicity carry considerable emotional valence, researchers must show awareness of the implications of their findings. Obviously, all researchers need to show such awareness, but problems with stereotyping, prejudice, or simple misunderstanding are largely irrelevant in monocultural research with participants of the dominant culture.

Breaking new ground in any area of research poses distinct challenges. Cross-cultural research is no different than any other area. As noted here, psychologists have identified problems and posed solutions to a constellation of new issues with which researchers must contend when expanding the horizons of psychology to include the study and understanding of behavior across cultures.

# References

Ainsworth, M., Blehar, M., Waters, E., & Wall, S. (1978). *Patterns of attachment*. Hillsdale, NJ: Lawrence Erlbaum Associates.

American Psychological Association (1983). *Publication manual of the American Psychological Association* (3rd ed.). Washington, DC: Author.

American Psychological Association (1994). *Publication manual of the American Psychological Association* (4th ed.). Washington, DC: Author.

American Psychological Association (2002). Ethical principles of psychologists and code of conduct. *American Psychologist, 57*, 1060–1073.

American Psychological Association (2008). *A portrait of success and challenge: Progress report: 1997–2005*. Washington, DC: Author. Retrieved from http://www.apa.org/pi/oema/CEMRR_texecSUMM.pdf

American Psychological Association (2010). *Publication manual of the American Psychological Association* (6th ed.). Washington, DC: Author.

Arnett, J. J. (2008). The neglected 95%: Why American psychology needs to become less American. *American Psychologist, 63*, 602–614.

Aronson, J., Lustina, M. J., Good, C., Keough, K., Steele, C. M., & Brown, J. (1999). When white men can't do math: Necessary and sufficient factors in stereotype threat. *Journal of Experimental Social Psychology, 35*, 29–46.

Banville, D., Desrosiers, P., & Genet-Volet, G. (2000). Translating questionnaires and inventories using a cross-cultural translation technique. *Journal of Teaching in Physical Education, 19*, 374–387.

Benet-Martínez, V., Leu, J., Lee, F., & Morris, M. W. (2002). Negotiating biculturalism: Cultural frame switching in biculturals with oppositional versus compatible cultural identities. *Journal of Cross-Cultural Psychology, 33*, 492–516.

Bowlby, J. (1988). *A secure base: Parent–child attachment and healthy human development.* London: Routledge.

Campbell, D. T. (1961). The mutual methodological relevance of anthropology and psychology. In F. L. Hsu (Ed.), *Psychological anthropology* (pp. 333–352). Homewood, IL: Dorsey.

Chang, W. C. (2000). In search of the Chinese in all the wrong places! *Journal of Psychology in Chinese Societies, 1*, 125–142.

Chen, F. F. (2008). What happens if we compare chopsticks with forks? The impact of making inappropriate comparisons in cross-cultural research. *Journal of Personality and Social Psychology, 95*, 1005–1018.

Cheung, F. M., & Leung, K. (1998). Indigenous personality measures: Chinese examples. *Journal of Cross-Cultural Psychology, 29*, 233–248.

Cohen, D., & Gunz, A. (2002). As seen by the other …: Perspectives on the self in the memories and emotional perceptions of Easterners and Westerners. *Psychological Science, 13*, 55–59.

Council of National Psychological Associations for the Advancement of Ethnic Minority Interests (2000). *Guidelines for research in ethnic minority commun ities.* Washington, DC: American Psychological Association.

Croizet, J., & Claire, T. (1998). Extending the concept of stereotype threat to social class: The intellectual underperformance of students from low socioeconomic backgrounds. *Personality and Social Psychology Bulletin, 24*, 588–594.

De Raad, B., Sullot, E., & Barelds, D. P. H. (2008). Which of the Big Five Factors are in need of situational specification. *European Journal of Personality, 22*, 269–289.

Ekman, P. (1972). Universals and cultural differences in facial expressions of emotion. In J. Cole (Ed.), *Nebraska symposium on motivation, 1971* (pp. 207–283). Lincoln, NE: University of Nebraska Press.

Elfenbein, H. A., & Ambady, N. (2002). On the universality and cultural specificity of emotion recognition: A meta-analysis. *Psychological Bulletin, 128*, 203–235.

Elfenbein, H. A., & Ambady, N. (2003).When familiarity breeds accuracy: Cultural exposure and facial emotion recognition. *Journal of Personality and Social Psychology, 85*, 276–290.

Hegarty, P., & Buechel, C. (2006). Androcentric reporting of gender differences in APA journals: 1965–2004. *Review of General Psychology, 10*, 377–389.

Heine, S. J., Lehman, D. R., Markus, H. R., & Kitayama, S. (1999). Is there a universal need for positive self-regard? *Psychological Review, 106*, 766–794.

Heine, S. J., & Buchtel, E. E. (2009). Personality: The universal and the culturally specific. *Annual Review of Psychology, 60*, 369–394.

Helms, J. E., Jernigan, M., & Mascher, J. (2005). The meaning of race in psychology and how to change it: A methodological perspective. *American Psychologist, 60*, 27–36.

Herskovits, M. J. (1935). Social history of the Negro. In C. Murchison (Ed.), *Handbook of social psychology* (pp. 207–267). Worcester, MA: Clark University Press.

Hofstede, G. H. (2001). *Culture's consequences: Comparing values, behaviors, institutions and organizations across nations* (2nd ed.). Thousand Oaks, CA: Sage Publications.

Inzlicht, M., & Ben-Zeev, T. (2000). A threatening intellectual environment: Why females are susceptible to experiencing problem-solving deficits in the presence of males. *Psychological Science, 11*, 365–371.

Iwamasa, G. Y., Larrabee, A. L., & Merritt, R. D. (2000). Are personality disorder criteria ethnically biased? A card-sort analysis. *Cultural Diversity and Ethnic Minority Psychology, 6*, 284–296.

Iwata, N., & Higuchi, H. R. (2000). Responses of Japanese and American university students to the STAI items that assess the presence or absence of anxiety. *Journal of Personality Assessment, 74*, 48–62.

Ji, L.-J., Peng, K., & Nisbett, R. E. (2000). Culture, control, and perception of relationships in the environment. *Journal of Personality and Social Psychology, 78*, 943–955.

Ji, L.-J., Zhang, Z., & Nisbett, R. E. (2004). Is it culture or is it language? Examination of language effects in cross-cultural research on categorization. *Journal of Personality and Social Psychology, 87*, 57–65

Keller, H. (2008). Attachment—past and present. But what about the future? *Integrative Psychological and Behavioral Science, 42*, 406–415.

Keller, J. (2007). Stereotype threat in classroom settings: The interactive effect of domain identification, task difficulty and stereotype threat on female students' maths performance. *British Journal of Educational Psychology, 77*, 323–338.

Kim, B. S. K., Atkinson, D. R., & Yang, P. H. (1999). The Asian Values Scale: Development, factor analysis, validation, and reliability. *Journal of Counseling Psychology, 46*, 342–352.

Kim, M. S. (2007). The four cultures of cultural research. *Communication Monographs, 74*, 279–285.

Kirmayer, L. J., & Young, A. (1998). Culture and somatisation: Clinical, epidemiological, and ethnographic perspectives. *Psychosomatic Medicine, 60*, 420–430.

Lee, Y., & Ottati, V. (1995). Perceived in-group homogeneity as a function of group membership salience and stereotype threat. *Personality and Social Psychology Bulletin, 21*, 610–619.

Linton, R. (1945). *The cultural background of personality.* New York: Appleton-Century.

Marian, V., & Neisser, U. (2000). Language-dependent recall of autobiographical memories. *Journal of Experimental Psychology: General, 129*, 361–368.

Markus, H. R. (2008). Pride, prejudice, and ambivalence: toward a unified theory of race and ethnicity. *American Psychologist, 63*, 651–670.

Masuda, T., & Nisbett, R. E. (2001). Attending holistically versus analytically: Comparing the context sensitivity of Japanese and Americans. *Journal of Personality and Social Psychology, 81*, 922–934.

Matsumoto, D., Anguas-Wong, A. M., & Martinez, E. (2008). Priming effects of language on emotion judgments in Spanish–English bilinguals. *Journal of Cross-Cultural Psychology, 39*, 335–342.

Matsumoto, D., & Assar, M. (1992). The effects of language on judgments of universal facial expressions of emotion. *Journal of Nonverbal Behavior, 16*, 85–99.

Matsumoto, D., & Yoo, S. H. (2006). Toward a new generation of cross-cultural research. *Perspectives on Psychological Science, 1*, 234–250.

McCrae, R. R., & Terraccianno, A. (2006). National character and personality. *Current Directions in Psychological Science, 15*, 156–161.

Muzzatti, B., & Agnoli, F. (2007). Gender and mathematics: Attitudes and stereotype threat susceptibility in Italian children. *Developmental Psychology, 43*, 747–759.

Panter, A. T., Daye, C. E., Allen, W. R., Deo, M. E., & Wightman, L. F. (2009). It matters how and when you ask: Self-reported race/ethnicity of incoming law students. *Cultural Diversity and Ethnic Minority Psychology, 15*, 51–66.

Park, D., & Gutchess, A. (2006). The cognitive neuroscience of aging and culture. *Current Directions in Psychological Science, 15*, 105–108.

Passel, J., & Taylor, P. (2009, May 28). Is Sotomayor the court's first Hispanic? Retrieved from http://www.pewresearch.org/pubs/1238/sotomayor-supreme-court-first-hispanic

Peabody, D., & De Raad, B. (2002). The substantive nature of psycholexical personality factors: A comparison across languages. *Journal of Personality and Social Psychology, 83*, 983–997.

Phinney, J. S. (1996). When we talk about American ethnic groups, what do we mean? *American Psychologist, 51*, 918–927.

Riess, B. F., Schwartz, E. K., & Cottingham, A. (1950). An experimental critique of assumptions underlying the Negro version of the TAT. *Journal of Abnormal and Social Psychology, 45*, 700–709.

Rodriguez, C. E. (2000). *Changing race: Latinos, the census and the history of ethnicity in the United States*. New York: New York University Press.

Rogler, L. H. (1999). Methodological sources of cultural insensitivity in mental health research. *American Psychologist, 54*, 424–433.

Rothbaum, F., Weisz, J., Pott, M., Kiyake, K., & Morelli, G. (2000). Attachment and culture: Security in the United States and Japan. *American Psychologist, 55*, 1093–1104.

Samelson, F. (1978). From "race psychology" to "studies in prejudice": Some observations on the thematic reversal in social psychology. *Journal of the History of the Behavioral Sciences, 14*, 265–278.

Shields, A. E., Fortun, M., Hammonds, E. M., King, P. A., Lerman, C., Rapp, R., & Sullivan, P. F. (2005). The use of race variables in genetic studies of complex traits and the goal of reducing health disparities. *American Psychologist, 60*, 77–103.

Shih, M., Pittinsky, T., & Ambady, N. (1999). Stereotype susceptibility: Identity salience and shifts in quantitative performance. *Psychological Science, 10*, 80–83.

Smith, G. T., Spillane, N. S., & Annus, A. M. (2006). Implications of an emerging integration of universal and culturally specific psychologies. *Perspectives on Psychological Science, 1*, 211–233.

Steele, C. M., & Aronson, J. (1995). Stereotype threat and the intellectual test performance of African Americans. *Journal of Personality and Social Psychology, 69*, 797–811.

Thomas, W. I. (1937). *Primitive behavior: An introduction to the social sciences*. New York: McGraw-Hill.

Tylor, E. B. (1889). On a method of investigating the development of institutions; Applied to laws of marriage and descent. *Journal of the Anthropological Institute, 18,* 243–269.

Van de Vijver, F. J. R., & Leung, K. (2000). Methodological issues in psychological research on culture. *Journal of Cross-Cultural Psychology. Special Issue: Millennium, 31,* 33–51.

Walsh, M., Hickey, C., & Duffy, J. (1999). Influence of item content and stereotype situation on gender differences in mathematical problem solving. *Sex Roles, 41,* 219–240.

# 4

# Why Diversity Matters
## The Power of Inclusion in Research Methods

### Linda M. Woolf and Michael R. Hulsizer

As we look around the globe, one fact becomes immediately apparent—remarkable diversity, as well as similarity, characterizes humanity. The term *diversity* often refers to the varieties of human characteristics found within a culture, but also sometimes implies similar variety across cultures. Just within the United States, the population reflects a strikingly diverse tapestry composed of variations in gender, race, ethnicity, sexual orientation, language, ability, income, culture, and other elements of diversity. We live in a multicultural and international community with multi-layered, intersecting threads representing potential areas of study and understanding. Researchers may elect to study not only one element of diversity but also how this element may differ across cultures and/or interact with other elements of diversity. For example, one might choose to study gender differences within a culture, differences between two or more cultures related to gender, or the intersection of gender and sexual orientation either within or across cultures. Regardless, it is imperative that researchers conduct their investigations in a methodologically valid and culturally appropriate manner. It is not enough simply to include some element of diversity as a variable to study. Rather investigators must take care to insure that the methods chosen to research that variable are adequate, appropriate, and ethical. Failure to conduct cross-cultural or diversity research with an eye toward appropriate methodology may result in faulty results and erroneous conclusions.

Despite the spectrum of diversity as one looks around the globe, psychological research and study within the U.S. has failed to reflect that diversity. According to Louis Kincannon, Director of the United States Census Bureau (2007a),

> About one in three U.S. residents is a minority. To put this into perspective, there are more minorities in this country today than there were people in the United States in 1910. In fact, the minority population in the U.S. is larger than the total population of all but 11 countries. (para. 1)

The U.S. Census Bureau (2007b) also reported that the minority population is not localized in one region. Indeed, "nearly one in every 10 of the nation's 3,141 counties has a population that is more than 50 percent minority" (para. 1). Despite these figures, several researchers have noted a paucity of published research focusing on racial or ethnic minorities within psychology journals (e.g., Bernal, Trimble, Burlew, & Leong, 2003; Carter, Akinsulure-Smith, Smailes, & Clauss, 1998; Graham, 1992, Sue, 1999). According to a number of investigators, some researchers simply fail to report the racial and ethnic background of study participants (Buboltz, Miller, & Williams, 1999; Delgado-Romero, Galván, Maschino, & Rowland, 2005; Munley et al., 2002). Delgado-Romero and colleagues (2005) reported that only 57% of examined counseling articles published between 1990 and 1999 reported race and ethnicity. The results of their analysis revealed that White and Asian Americans were overrepresented, whereas African Americans, Hispanics, and Native American Indians tended to be underrepresented as compared to the U.S. population. Finally, it is also important to note that much of the traditional psychological curriculum has historically neglected issues of diversity (Guthrie, 1998). For example, despite the fact that approximately 45% of articles indexed in PsycINFO© included authors from outside the United States (Adair, Coelho, & Luna, 2002), introduction to psychology, life-span developmental psychology, and social psychology textbooks included little of this research (Woolf, Hulsizer, & McCarthy, 2002). Ultimately, it would seem that Betancourt and López's (1993) assertion that "the study of culture and related variables occupies at best a secondary place in American (mainstream) psychology" (p. 629) is as true today as it was almost two decades ago.

Fortunately, there has been a recent push to increase both an awareness of and research concerning diversity, cross-cultural issues, and international research within psychology. In January 2000, the Council of National Psychological Associations for the Advancement of Ethnic Minority Interests (CNPAAEMI) produced the *Guidelines for research in ethnic minority communities*. Five ethnic minority associations within the American Psychological Association (APA) collaboratively worked to create a document reflecting issues relevant to research with African American, Asian American, Hispanic, and American Indian populations. In 2003, the APA published the *Guidelines on multicultural education, training, research, practice, and organizational change for psychologists* and in 2005 and 2008 hosted Education Leadership Conferences devoted to diversity and international issues, respectively. Indeed, the APA (2009) vision statement now identifies the Association as

> A principal leader and global partner promoting psychological knowledge and methods to facilitate the resolution of personal, societal and global challenges in diverse, multicultural and international contexts. (para. 9)

In 2005, the APA Working Group on Internationalizing the Undergraduate Psychology Curriculum, in concert with the American Council on Education (ACE), published a set of recommended learning outcomes for psychology courses (Lutsky et al., 2005). The report noted that psychology has long been international both as a science and as a profession with early psychologists working in such diverse countries as Argentina, India, Japan, Mexico, New Zealand, and Russia. Goal 2 of the report focused on research methods and highlighted that "Students should be aware of research methods and skills necessary for international research competence" (p. 3). The report presented five learning outcomes in relation to research methods, specifically that students will develop: (1) the ability to access and read journals published outside the United States; (2) the ability to identify and appreciate the range of research methodologies used by psychologists around the globe (e.g., ethnographies, observations); (3) an awareness of ethical issues that may be of concern in other countries (e.g., protection from harm); (4) an understanding that many constructs may have different meanings in different cultures; and (5) an appreciation of the dangers associated with making broad generalizations based on small and potentially unrepresentative samples.

In this chapter, we focus on a number of issues related to the role of diversity in understanding research methods. It is important to note that we do not discuss all issues related to diversity concerns and research. Rather, we seek to introduce the topic by providing representative examples which highlight the complexity involved in conducting research responsibly—particularly research that involves diverse populations. Moreover, much of what we discuss in each section below describes research focusing on differences between groups (e.g., differences between two cultures). However, we would like to highlight that this does not negate the need for research to be more inclusive of diverse populations in non-diversity focused research. It is important that researchers endeavor to be more inclusive of diverse populations in all of their work.

## Validity

Marsella (2001) suggested that many psychologists are unwilling to "accept a very basic 'truth'—that western psychology is rooted in an ideology of individualism, rationality, and empiricism that has little resonance in many of the more than 5,000 cultures found in today's world" (p. 7). Indeed, as we saw in Chapter 1, psychology textbooks and journals are filled with psychological concepts, theories, and research findings that, at the surface, appear to be applicable to all humans. Yet, there is a great deal of cross-cultural as well as intra-cultural variability. Moreover, there is growing awareness that the use of homogeneous samples (e.g., introductory psychology students within the U.S.) has painted a somewhat distorted picture of psychological phenomena (Graham, 1992; Sears, 1986). Unfortunately, although homogeneous samples may increase the internal validity of a study, it is often at the expense of the ability to generalize to a range of diverse populations. All of the above highlights concerns related to the topic of research validity, specifically construct, internal, and external validity.

## Construct validity

Construct validity typically refers to the degree to which a variable has been operationally defined so that it captures the essence of a hypothetical construct under study. For example, does a particular depression scale adequately measure depression or is an IQ test a good measure of intelligence? If the answer is "yes," then the measure has good construct validity. If the answer is "no," then any research conclusions drawn from the use of the measure are, at best, limited. An examination of construct validity is necessary in any cross-cultural or diversity research.

When conducting cross-cultural research, experimenters must monitor the degree to which their methodology is equivalent across cultures and groups. In fact, Matsumoto (2003) suggested that researchers should strive to create the perfect cross-cultural study. To that end, Brislin (2000) asserted that investigators need to develop an awareness of three sources of nonequivalence—translation, conceptual, and metric. Translation equivalence is necessary when conducting research on one population using experimental measures developed and standardized with another population. For example, if a researcher plans to use a standardized questionnaire developed in the U.S., translation equivalence needs to be achieved prior to its use in another country. So, how should the researcher go about translating a scale or experimental measure? According to the *Guidelines for research in ethnic minority communities* (CNPAAEMI, 2000), the proper translation of experimental measures involves the use of the back-translation method. First, a bilingual translator converts the measure to the target language. Next, a second translator converts the translated measure back to the original language. Finally, a researcher compares the original version to the back-translated version to examine any existing differences. The process is repeated until translation equivalence is achieved.

Conceptual equivalence is the degree to which theoretical concepts or constructs are the same between two cultures. Unfortunately, researchers can introduce conceptual nonequivalence in a variety ways, even through something as seemingly innocuous as demographics. Although it is often useful to control for certain demographic variables, such as age, sex, and religious orientation, this may become problematic when conducting cross-cultural research. For example, a demographic question such as "age" would seem relatively innocuous. Yet, for the Ju/'hoansi, also known as the !Kung of the Kalahari, this would be not be a useful question, as the Ju/'hoansi use a culturally specific age categorization system as opposed to thinking of age in chronological years (Hames & Draper, 2004). The inclusion of an indigenous (local) investigator or collaborator may serve to increase the validity of cross-cultural research because this inclusion can better enable the research team to ask the right questions (CNPAAEMI, 2000).

Finally, researchers need to be concerned with metric equivalence—the ability to compare the specific scores on a scale of interest across cultures. For example, would a researcher interpret a score of 25 on the Beck Depression Inventory (Beck,

Ward, Mendelson, Mock, & Erbaugh, 1961) the same way across cultures? Would individuals living under repressive regimes, where government intrusion is a daily occurrence, score differently on the paranoia scale of the Minnesota Multiphasic Personality Inventory (MMPI-2; Butcher et al., 2001)? Additionally, metric equivalence may not exist within a culture when studying diverse populations. For example, researchers have rarely standardized measures of assessment used in research, particularly those related to personality assessment and psychopathology, for use with a disabled population (Elliott & Umlauf, 1995; Pullin, 2002). In addition, disabled individuals may score differently than others on the Hypochondriasis Scale of the MMPI-2 (Butcher et al., 2001), with seeming obsession over body functions. Varying cultural norms about time, differences in physical ability, and age may all impact completion of timed tests of intellectual ability.

Inadequately standardized measures that lack a representative normative group threaten construct validity by introducing the possibility that individuals are evaluated on performance as opposed to ability. Unfortunately, researchers rarely design studies to accommodate participants who are differently abled. Tasks designed to measure cognitive, personality, or other psychological abilities may instead be measuring primarily noncognitive or nonpsychological variables in research inclusive of participants with a range of abilities. For example, research on memory using computers to present stimuli may be more challenging for some older adults due to an increased incidence in susceptibility to glare from cataracts. Research participants of any age who are in ill health may fatigue more easily and perform poorly on outcome measures. Thus, differences found between participants may reflect visual or health differences as opposed to memory differences. Unless the researcher takes into account the impact of disability, age, or other factors, the resulting research conclusions may be biased and inaccurate.

## Internal validity

Internal validity reflects the confidence with which we can draw cause and effect conclusions from our research results. Of primary concern for researchers is the ability to eliminate, minimize, or hold constant all extraneous or confounding variables. Unfortunately, studies examining differences between various elements of diversity (e.g., gender, culture) are by their very nature quasi-experimental and hence limited in relation to cause and effect conclusions. Indeed, this issue may contribute to the paucity of diversity research within psychology. In a provocative article, Chang and Sue (2005) suggested that the current scientific paradigm, with its focus on experimental designs, has introduced a bias in psychology. Specifically, they asserted that mainstream journals systematically exclude multicultural research, thus devaluing existing multicultural research and impeding the growth of research in this area. Ideally, experimental research should be high in both internal validity and external validity. Unfortunately, it is very difficult to achieve both in experimental designs, and extremely problematic when using alternative designs (e.g., quasi-experimental, correlational, observational, ethnographic). Chang and Sue argued that the importance psychologists have placed on determining causality has led researchers to value internal validity over external validity.

Chang and Sue (2005) further asserted that the emphasis psychology places on causality (internal validity) has led to a host of additional research problems, which only serve to devalue external validity and the very nature of multicultural research. The problems they discussed included: (a) overuse of college students as research participants; (b) willingness to assume research conducted on one population (e.g., White, middle-class, U.S. citizens) can be generalized to other groups or contexts; (c) disregard for research seeking to explore cross-cultural differences as opposed to explaining such differences; (d) the tendency of journal reviewers to insist that researchers add a White control group when conducting research on ethnic minority groups; and (e) the formation of aggregate non-White populations to obtain a large enough sample size. The last issue is especially problematic due to the implied assumption of homogeneity among the non-White population, when in fact non-White groups may differ widely. Although the exclusion of diverse participants may enhance internal validity, the resultant homogeneous sample does not reflect the diversity of human experience.

## External validity

External validity is the degree to which research results can be generalized beyond one's sample. Often psychology focuses on the universality of human cognition and behavior. Researchers often refer to these universal concepts as etics. Concepts thought to be specific to a particular culture are called emics. Matsumoto (1994) suggested that, "most cross-cultural psychologists would agree that there are just as many, if not more, emics as there are etics" (p. 5). Many psychology textbook authors present traditional descriptions and recommended treatments for post-traumatic stress disorder (PTSD) as universal, or etics. Yet, PTSD symptoms and treatment are frequently culture-specific (Atlani & Rousseau, 2000; Bracken, 1998). The primary lesson of external validity is that researchers should exercise great care when extrapolating beyond their sample and this is particularly true when conducting cross-cultural or diversity research.

One of the primary issues at the core of external validity in relation to cross-cultural research is that variability exists within cultures. For example, the *Guidelines for research in ethnic minority communities* (CNPAAEMI, 2000), in relation to issues of using Hispanics or Asian/Pacific Islanders in research, stated that above all else, researchers need to be aware of the diversity of these populations. These broadly defined groups vary with respect to acculturation, language, race/ethnicity, beliefs, socioeconomic status, and educational background. Indeed, they do not represent homogenous cultures. Anyone critiquing research involving Asian/Pacific Islander or Hispanic participants must consider all these issues. These same issues are also fundamental to research guidelines associated with Native American Indians. In addition to research design concerns, investigators need to be prepared for small sample sizes. In fact, researchers may end up dealing with a single and consequently small population, given the fact that each tribe is a distinct cultural entity.

The issue of external validity also applies to diversity research within cultures. For example, Eichler (1991) cited the problem of overgeneralization in gender research—the propensity to extend concepts, theories, and research developed from studies involving participants of one gender to all individuals. Examples of overgeneralization ranged from the use of sexist language to the tendency of researchers to generalize the results of a study to all individuals when in fact the initial sample was composed only of men. Hyde (1996) also asserted that researchers often employ a "female deficit model" when drawing conclusions—the tendency to frame the results in such a fashion that women's behavior is seen as deficient or non-normative. Research conducted in highly patriarchal cultures may magnify this issue.

## Methodological Design Concerns

Many of the concerns we have discussed under validity intersect with methodological design concerns. However, several topics deserve further discussion and include methodological concerns related to demographics and sampling, experimenter bias, and the use of quasi-experimental design.

### Demographics and sampling

At first glance, the issue of demographics and sampling may appear to be simple. However, when one includes diverse populations or studies diversity both between and within cultures, these are highly complex and require careful thought and foresight. Some of the major issues impacting demographics and sampling involve: (1) self-identification; (2) hidden populations; (3) exclusion; and (4) faulty biologically based conclusions. Experimenter preconceptions about groups and cultures influence all of these issues.

When conducting research, it is important that investigators use culturally relevant and appropriate demographic categories regardless of whether the research involves participants within or between cultures. Particularly important is an appreciation for the role that culture may play in shaping a participant's self-identification. For example, if you are conducting cross-cultural research, is it more appropriate to use the word "Hispanic" or "Latino/a" in the United States? Can you include a broad category such as Asian or does one need to be more specific: "Japanese," "Chinese," "Hmong," or "Karen" (noting that this listing represents just a tiny fraction of the various ethnicities/cultures often lumped together under the term "Asian")? To better address questions such as these, researchers often collaborate with individuals who are native or knowledgeable about the cultures under study. Familiarity with the culture, including diversity within the culture under study (e.g., ethnic groups, language, religion), is essential to avoid bias and stereotypes on the part of the experimenter.

The issue of self-identification applies not just to cultural differences but also variations within culture, such as gender and sexual orientation. Gays and lesbians have often eschewed the term "homosexuality" because "homosexuality" has been historically associated with disease and mental illness. Today, some researchers elect to use "queer" as a more inclusive term replacing gay and lesbian and inclusive of bisexuals and transgendered individuals (Grace, Hill, Johnson, & Lewis, 2004). Moreover, it is not uncommon to see the abbreviation GLBTQI (gay, lesbian, bisexual, transgendered or transsexual, queer or questioning, intersex) used by sexual minorities within the U.S. Even more challenging, from a research perspective, is the fact that some individuals who have had same-sex sexual relationships may still self-identify as heterosexual (Savin-Williams, 2001) and transgendered or intersex (biological sex is ambiguous) individuals may identify as either male or female. This ambiguity and interplay among all these constructs makes simple, non-fluid gender and sexual orientation self-identification more ambiguous. Certainly, the juxtaposition of identity issues and the need for demographics creates the basis for problematic research hypotheses and sampling challenges. Nonetheless, researchers should avoid overly simplistic categorizations for the sake of expediency as this may introduce a source of bias into a research project.

Many groups around the globe are hidden from view due to cultural, religious, or legal strictures. For example, in some cultures, adultery may result in honor killings, homosexuality is punishable by death or banishment, and certain religious groups face imprisonment. Therefore, these populations often remain hidden as a matter of safety and to avoid oppression. Attempts to include and study such populations are thus difficult.

Even within the U.S., there remain hidden populations due to stigma and stereotype (see Chapter 12 in this volume). For example, attitudes concerning the subject of sexual orientation have changed significantly in the past 20 years. According to recent Gallup Polls (Saad, 2008), Americans have become increasingly more tolerant of homosexuality. In 1982, only 34% of participants agreed that homosexuality was an acceptable alternative lifestyle. This number had risen to 57% when participants responded to the same question in 2008. Despite these changing attitudes, research inclusive of or concerning sexual orientation remains a small fraction of the literature and appears largely in specialized journals or special issues of journals (Bowman, 2003). Many individuals may be reticent to self-identify as lesbian, gay, or bisexual due to fears concerning confidentiality or internalized homophobia. Thus, researchers are often limited to a very select group of the population who self-identify as lesbian, gay, or bisexual—typically White, formally educated, urban, and upper middle class. In response to the challenges associated with obtaining a representative sample, researchers are currently exploring new methodologies such as the use of the Internet for research purposes (Koch & Emrey, 2001) and the use of alternative and qualitative methodologies related to the study of sexual orientation (Morrow, 2003). It is important to note that this reflects just one instance of the difficulty of sampling hidden populations. Researchers studying any number of populations (e.g., the mentally ill or minority religions) that are not immediately identifiable based on some external character-istic, but belong to a class of individuals socially stigmatized because of group status, will experience difficulties, particularly with regard to sampling.

Unfortunately, researchers often exclude individuals, both intentionally and unin-tentionally, from research participation based on a variety of factors. Such factors include, but are not limited to, the ability to get to the site of the research, literacy, gender, language, political oppression, socioeconomic status, religious affiliation, and disability. Such exclusions limit the generalizability of the research. The pool of avail-able participants may be limited if participants are unable to read a questionnaire, lack the means to travel to the research site, or fear governmental reprisals for taking part in a research study. Consequently, those who become involved in the research may be different than those individuals who do not elect to or cannot participate.

Individuals with disabilities are often systematically excluded from research both in the U.S. and abroad. According to the World Programme of Action Concerning Disabled Persons (United Nations, 2009) at least 10% of the world's population is impaired by a physical, mental, or sensory disability. Within the U.S., researchers estimate that there are almost 44.1 million community dwelling peo-ple (5 years and older) with disabilities (U.S. Census Bureau, 2007c). Within the U.S. definitions of disability include sensory, physical, mental, self-care, homebound, and employment categories. Disabilities can be visible or hidden (e.g., heart defect), and individuals may or may not define themselves as disabled depending on the degree of limitation the disability has on their lives. Nonetheless, some investiga-tors fail to accommodate disabled participants, thereby systematically excluding them from research. Other researchers simply bar individuals with disabilities from research participation altogether, often as the result of experimenter bias—the assumption that disability has broad negative effects on cognition, personality, affect, or ability. Of course, this assumption is grounded largely in stereotype rather than reality (Dunn, 2000).

The five ethnic minority associations that compose the CNPAAEMI worked col-laboratively to create the *Guidelines for research in ethnic minority communities* (2000). The guidelines provided a wealth of information concerning research with ethni-cally diverse populations, with an important caveat. The CNPAAEMI warned that it is important for researchers to take care when using race as a demographic cat-egory, lest the variable become a proxy for biological explanations of behavior (Wang & Sue, 2005). Similar concerns surround the use of gender in psychological research. For example, McHugh and Cosgrove (2002) suggested that by attributing differences in men and women to gender differences "we risk essentializing gender, promoting a view of women as a homogenous group, and reinforcing the very mechanisms of oppression against which we are fighting" (p. 13) and note that the use of only "male/men" or "female/women" as categorical terms excludes those who identify as transsexual, transgender, or intersex.

Certainly, race and gender as variables are focal social and cultural constructs that, if used judiciously, can provide a wealth of information. The *Guidelines for research in ethnic minority communities* invited researchers to learn more about the rich diversity among individuals defined as belonging to a particular race and avoid treating racial categories as homogenous groups. They also recommended that researchers avoid non-representative but perhaps easy-to-reach samples. For example, it may be easy to conduct research on adolescents abroad, using as a sample those who attend a private English-speaking boarding school in another country, but this population may not be representative of the majority population in that country.

## Experimenter bias

In addition to the impact on participant demographics and samples, experimenter bias can also affect the nature of an investigator's worldview and subsequent research hypotheses. For any cross-cultural study, researchers must be familiar with all aspects of the society (e.g., language, religion, kinship patterns, etc.). Without such knowledge, any research questions, methods, and conclusions may be biased and untrustworthy. Moreover, it is imperative that researchers take into consideration the role of other diversity concerns within that culture as well. For example, research around the globe may be impacted by what Eichler (1991) termed androcentricity—the tendency for researchers to view the world from a male perspective. The research process perpetuates androcentrism in many ways. In an influential article, Denmark, Russo, Frieze, and Sechzer (1988) discussed several examples of sexism in research. For instance, the authors discussed the tendency for researchers to examine concepts such as leadership style in a fashion emphasizing male stereotypes (e.g., dominance, aggression) as opposed to a range of leadership styles, including those that are more egalitarian. Another example cited by Denmark and colleagues involved the propensity for some researchers to assume that topics relevant to White males are inherently more important than issues related to other groups. Binion (2006) argued that cultures have traditionally viewed women's human rights (e.g., marital rape and other forms of domestic abuse) as existing within the private sphere of the home outside of public view, and hence have often ignored them. The false dichotomy of public/private sphere has unfortunately negatively influenced the actions of communities and law enforcement, and has limited political asylum opportunities for women around the globe.

Experimenter bias has also impacted the conclusions reached by researchers studying disability both within and outside of the United States. According to Dunn (2000), "Insiders (people with disabilities) know what disability is like, whereas outsiders (people without disabilities) make assumptions, including erroneous ones, about it" (p. 574). Most notably, non-disabled individuals overestimate the effect of a disability on an individual's capacities and well-being. In addition, researchers explicitly studying participants with known disabilities may fail to consider all possible alternative explanations, such as cultural, situational, or interpersonal factors, and simply attribute the results to the disability. For example, researchers comparing math scores among disabled and non-disabled populations need to take into account the role of stereotype threat (Steele, Spencer, & Aronson, 2002) when discussing any performance differences between the groups.

## Research design

Typically, research examining cross-cultural differences or focusing on diversity-related variables such as gender, age, or sexual orientation, employs a quasi-experimental design. A researcher examining differences in age may compare younger and older adults or a cross-cultural psychologist may research differences between ethnic groups either within or across nations. Unfortunately, the use of distinct samples in a quasi-experimental design typically results in low internal validity. These samples may differ on any number of variables other than the one under investigation. In a cross-sectional study (in which two or more age groups are compared), age differences may be confounded with generational, non-shared cultural, or historical cohort experiences—making it difficult to determine causality. For example, early cross-sectional studies suggested progressive declines in intelligence following late adolescence and early young adulthood. However, research taking account of cohort effects (e.g., differences in educational levels) did not support this gloomy picture (Schaie, 1986; 2000).

Similarly, comparisons of ethnic groups or race within a culture may be confounded by differences in religion, language, socioeconomic status, or other factors not under study by the researchers. Unfortunately, researchers may assume differences in heredity or genetics to explain the results of cross-cultural studies or those involving race or ethnicity. This faulty assumption can lead to erroneous and potentially damaging conclusions. For example, throughout the twentieth century some researchers were still asserting that White Americans were intellectually superior to minority groups—specifically African Americans (e.g., Hernstein & Murray, 1994; Jensen, 1969). However, Sternberg, Grigorenko, and Kidd (2005) noted, "Race is a social construction, not a biological construct, and studies currently indicating alleged genetic bases of racial differences in intelligence fail to make their point even for these social defined groups" (p. 57).

Meta-analyses have become an increasingly popular tool for psychologists. For example, a search of PsycINFO© revealed dozens of meta-analyses examining gender as well as cultural differences across a variety of issues. Although meta-analyses have almost certainly added to psychologists' knowledge of humanity, researchers need to exercise caution when drawing conclusions from such studies. For example, in relation to gender, Halpern (1995) expressed concern that researchers ignore context when using benchmarks to determine whether a gender-related effect size is meaningful or important. The tendency to ignore context is further compounded by the fact that gender research often fails to use representative samples. Halpern cautioned that "as long as the research literature is based on a narrow selection of participants and assessment procedures, the results of any analysis will be biased" (p. 83).

## Research Ethics

The APA's *Ethical principles of psychologists and code of conduct* (2002) highlights a range of research ethics topics such as confidentiality, informed consent, the use of deception, and the obligation to be accurate in reporting results. Moreover, according to the *Ethical principles*, all psychologists must "strive to benefit those with whom they work and take care to do no harm" (p. 3). Although all of these concerns are fundamental to psychological research, issues of informed consent and confidentiality are especially important in cross-cultural research, particularly in relation to protection from harm.

In addition, according to the *Ethical principles*, researchers conducting any project must inform participants about a variety of features such as purpose, procedures, risks and benefits, the limits of confidentiality, and the right to withdraw from participation. As with all statements of informed consent, it is essential that the document be clear and unambiguous—this is particularly important in cross-cultural research. Researchers must develop consent forms with an understanding of the culture of participants in mind, inclusive of special needs related to language, reading ability, nation-specific legal standards, and cultural norms. Consequently, a "boiler-plate" statement simply translated into a different language often does not meet the standards of informed consent. Moreover, in some cultures, women may not be culturally free to give informed consent but must first receive the consent of a male guardian.

Individuals with developmental or cognitive disabilities represent a challenge to informed consent (Dresser, 2001). Informed consent rests on the premise that research participants can fully understand the procedures, risks, and benefits associated with a particular study and agree to participate. Unfortunately, individuals with significant cognitive impairment due to developmental disabilities, injury, or dementia may not fully understand the material provided to give informed consent. Researchers must take special care to protect participants who are unable to provide consent on their own, including situations where a guardian provides consent but the participants undergo experimental testing without their knowledge. Unfortunately, due to the potential risks involved, many researchers simply avoid research with cognitively disabled populations (Yan & Munir, 2004).

Researchers need to be particularly aware of issues of confidentiality when conducting cross-cultural research. Seltzer and Anderson (2001) noted that researchers should use care even with aggregate data, as some individuals or small groups may remain identifiable. Within this discussion, they highlighted the role that official statistics have played in historical incidents of forced migration, internment, and genocide. The United Nations Statistical Commission (1994) passed the *Fundamental principles of official statistics*, which stated, "Official statistics provide an indispensable element in the information system of a democratic society, serving the government, the economy and the public with data about the economic, demographic, social and environmental situation." Nonetheless, the UNSC asserted that researchers must protect individuals' privacy and guard against the misuse of statistics. It is clear that researchers must carefully protect the confidentiality of all participants (e.g., including no easily identifiable information about the participants on forms, questionnaires, etc.) in cultures where the researcher's data may be taken by family members, religious officials, or governmental agents for use against the well-being of the participant.

## Conclusion

Increasingly, we hear that we are living within a global community. If this is to be a true and inclusive statement, then research needs to reflect the tapestry of human existence, noting variations across a range of biological and social constructs (e.g., sex and race, respectively) and cultures. In this chapter, we have discussed a host of constructs such as gender and race but this does not represent the full spectrum of human expression. Other areas of diversity significantly impacting individuals' identities and their place in communities include, but are by no means limited to, socioeconomic status, linguistic variability, educational level, differing sects within religious groups, profession, marital status, physical and mental health, social class/caste, computer literacy, access to resources, political affiliation, and physical appearance. Ultimately, how we identify ourselves is incredibly variable and influenced by the currents of time, our communities, and our culture.

To become an effective and critical consumer and producer of research today requires cross-cultural and diversity-related understanding, knowledge, and skills. Individuals need to expand their horizons by reading research from around the globe, on a variety of topics and perhaps inclusive of research from related fields such as sociology, anthropology, history, and international studies. It is important to think of psychological research not so much as a template through which all topics can be studied (e.g., independent/dependent variables; experimental/control groups) but as a flexible tool that can be used creatively to explore topics of relevance across a range of populations and communities. With an awareness of alternative methodologies, input from collaborators with varying backgrounds, and an understanding of the unique ethical concerns involved in cross-cultural research, individuals can engage in exciting and important research that is both inclusive and reflective of human diversity across the global community.

# References

Adair, J. G., Coelho, A. E. L., & Luna, J. R. (2002). How international is psychology? *International Journal of Psychology, 37*, 160–170.

American Psychological Association (APA) (2002). Ethical principles of psychologists and code of conduct. Retrieved September 13, 2009, from http://apa.org/ethics/code2002.html

American Psychological Association (APA) (2003). Guidelines on multicultural education, training, research, practice, and organizational change for psychologists. *American Psychologist, 58*, 377–402.

American Psychological Association (APA) (2009). *Vision statement*. Retrieved September 1, 2009, from http://www.apa.org/about

Atlani, L., & Rousseau, C. (2000). The politics of culture in humanitarian aid to women refugees who have experienced sexual violence. *Transcultural Psychiatry, 37*, 435–449.

Beck, A. T., Ward, C. H., Mendelson, M., Mock, J., & Erbaugh, J. (1961). An inventory for measuring depression. *Archives of General Psychiatry, 4*, 561–571.

Bernal, G., Trimble, J. E., Burlew, A. K., & Leong, F. T. L. (2003). Introduction: The psychological study of racial and ethnic minority psychology. In G. Bernal, J. E. Trimble, A. K. Burlew, & F. T. L. Leong (Eds.), *Handbook of racial and ethnic minority psychology* (pp. 1–12). Thousand Oaks, CA: Sage.

Betancourt, H., & López, S. R. (1993). The study of culture, ethnicity, and race in American psychology. *American Psychologist, 48*, 629–637.

Binion, G. (2006). Human rights: A feminist perspective. In B. B. Lockwood (Ed.), *Women's rights: A Human Rights Quarterly reader* (pp. 70–86). Baltimore, MD: Johns Hopkins University Press.

Bowman, S. L. (2003). A call to action in lesbian, gay, and bisexual theory building and research. *The Counseling Psychologist, 31*, 63–69.

Bracken, P. J. (1998). Hidden agendas: Deconstructing post traumatic stress disorder. In P. J. Bracken & C. Petty (Eds.), *Rethinking the trauma of war* (pp. 38–59). New York: Free Association Books.

Brislin, R. (2000). *Understanding culture's influence on behavior* (2nd ed.). New York: Wadsworth.

Buboltz, W. C., Jr., Miller, M., & Williams, D. J. (1999). Content analysis of research in the *Journal of Counseling Psychology* (1973–1998). *Journal of Counseling Psychology, 46*, 496–503.

Butcher, J. N., Graham, J. R., Ben-Porath, Y. S., Tellegen, A., Dahlstrom, W. G., & Kaemmer, B. (2001). *Minnesota Multiphasic Personality Inventory-2 (MMPI-2): Manual for administration, scoring and interpretation* (rev. ed.). Minneapolis, MN: University of Minnesota Press.

Carter, R. T., Akinsulure-Smith, A. M., Smailes, E. M., & Clauss, C. S. (1998). The status of racial/ethnic research in counseling psychology: Committed or complacent? *Journal of Black Psychology, 24,* 322–334.

Chang, J., & Sue, S. (2005). Culturally sensitive research: Where have we gone wrong and what do we need to do now? In M. G. Constantine & D. W. Sue (Eds.), *Strategies for building multicultural competence in mental health and educational settings* (pp. 229–246). Hoboken, NJ: John Wiley & Sons.

Council of National Psychological Associations for the Advancement of Ethnic Minority Interests (CNPAAEMI) (2000). *Guidelines for research in ethnic minority communities.* Washington, DC: American Psychological Association.

Delgado-Romero, E. A., Galván, N., Maschino, P., & Rowland, M. (2005). Race and ethnicity in empirical counseling and counseling research: A 10-year review. *The Counseling Psychologist, 33,* 419–448.

Denmark, F., Russo, N. F., Frieze, I. H., & Sechzer, J. A. (1988). Guidelines for avoiding sexism in psychological research: A report of the ad hoc committee on nonsexist research. *American Psychologist, 43,* 582–585.

Dresser, R. (2001). Research participants with mental disabilities: The more things change. In L. E. Frost & R. J. Bonnie (Eds.), *Evolution of mental health law* (pp. 57–74). Washington, DC: American Psychological Association.

Dunn, D. S. (2000). Social psychological issues in disability. In R. G. Frank & T. R. Elliott (Eds.), *Handbook of rehabilitation psychology* (pp. 565–584). Washington, DC: American Psychological Association.

Eichler, M. (1991). *Nonsexist research methods: A practical guide.* New York: Routledge.

Elliott, T. R., & Umlauf, R. L. (1995). Measurement of personality and psychopathology following acquired physical disability. In L. A. Cushman & M. J. Scherer (Eds.), *Psychological assessment in medical rehabilitation* (pp. 301–324). Washington, DC: American Psychological Association.

Grace, P. A., Hill, R. J., Johnson, C. W., & Lewis, J. B. (2004). In other words: Queer voices/dissident subjectivities impelling social change. *International Journal of Qualitative Studies in Education, 17,* 301–324.

Graham, S. (1992). "Most of the subjects were White and middle class": Trends in published research on African Americans in selected APA journals, 1970–1989. *American Psychologist, 47,* 629–639.

Guthrie, R. V. (1998). *Even the rat was white: A historical view of psychology* (2nd ed.). Boston: Allyn and Bacon.

Halpern, D. F. (1995). Cognitive gender differences: Why diversity is a critical research issue. In H. Landrine (Ed.), *Bringing cultural diversity to feminist psychology: Theory, research, and practice* (pp. 77–92). Washington, DC: American Psychological Association.

Hames, R., & Draper, P. (2004). Women's work, child care, and helpers-at-the-nest in a hunter-gatherer society. *Human Nature, 15,* 319–341.

Hernstein, R. J., & Murray, C. (1994). *The bell curve: Intelligence and class structure in American life.* New York: Free Press.

Hyde, J. S. (1996). *Half the human experience: The psychology of women* (5th ed.). Lexington, MA: DC Heath and Company.

Jensen, A. R. (1969). How much can we boost IQ and scholastic achievement? *Harvard Educational Review, 33,* 1–123.

Koch, N. S., & Emrey, J. A. (2001). The Internet and opinion measurement: Surveying marginalized populations. *Social Science Quarterly, 82,* 131–138.

Lutsky, N., Torney-Purta, J., Veleyo, R., Whittlesy, V., Woolf, L., & McCarthy, M. (2005). *American Psychological Association Working Group on Internationalizing Undergraduate Psychology Curriculum: Report and recommended learning outcomes for internationalizing the undergraduate curriculum.* Retrieved September 14, 2009, from www.apa.org/ed/pcue/international.pdf

Marsella, A. J., (2001). Internationalizing the psychology curriculum. *Psychology International, 12*(2), 7–8.

Matsumoto, D. (1994). *Cultural influences on research methods and statistics.* Belmont, CA: Wadsworth.

Matsumoto, D. (2003). Cross-cultural research. In S. F. Davis (Ed.), *Handbook of research methods in experimental psychology* (pp. 189–208). Malden, MA: Blackwell.

McHugh, M. C., & Cosgrove, L. (2002). Gendered subjects in psychology: Satirical and dialectic perspectives. In L. H. Collins, M. R. Dunlap, & J. C. Chrisler (Eds.), *Charting a new course for feminist psychology* (pp. 3–19). Westport, CT: Praeger.

Morrow, S. L. (2003). Can the master's tools ever dismantle the master's house? Answering silences with alternative paradigms and methods. *The Counseling Psychologist, 31,* 70–77.

Munley, P. H., Anderson, M. Z., Baines, T. C., Borgman, A. L., Briggs, D., Dolan, J. P., Jr., et al. (2002). Personal dimensions of identity and empirical research in APA journals. *Cultural Diversity and Ethnic Minority Psychology, 8,* 357–365.

Pullin, D. (2002). Testing individuals with disabilities: Reconciling social science and social policy. In R. B. Ekstrom, & D. K. Smith (Eds.), *Assessing individuals with disabilities in educational, employment, and counseling settings* (pp. 11–31). Washington, DC: American Psychological Association.

Saad, L. (2008, June 18). *Americans evenly divided on morality of homosexuality: However, majority supports legality and acceptance of gay relations.* Princeton, NJ: The Gallup Organization.

Savin-Williams, R. C. (2001). *Mom, Dad. I'm gay. How families negotiate coming out.* Washington, DC: American Psychological Association.

Schaie, K. W. (1986). Beyond calendar definitions of age, time, and cohort: The general developmental model revisited. *Developmental Review, 6,* 252–277.

Schaie, K. W. (2000). The impact of longitudinal studies on understanding development from young adulthood to old age. *International Journal of Behavioral Development, 24,* 257–266.

Sears, D. O. (1986). College sophomores in the laboratory: Influences of a narrow data base on social psychology's view of human nature. *Journal of Personality and Social Psychology, 51,* 515–530.

Seltzer, W., & Anderson, M. (2001). The dark side of numbers: The role of population data systems in human rights abuses. *Social Research, 68,* 481–513.

Steele, C. M., Spencer, S. J., & Aronson, J. (2002). Contending with group image: The psychology of stereotype and social identity threat. In M. Zanna (Ed.), *Advances in experimental social psychology,* Vol. 34 (pp. 379–440). San Diego, CA: Academic Press.

Sternberg, R. J., Grigorenko, E. L., & Kidd, K. K. (2005). Intelligence, race, and genetics. *American Psychologist, 60,* 46–59.

Sue, S. (1999). Science, ethnicity, and bias: Where have we gone wrong? *American Psychologist, 54,* 1070–1077.

United Nations (2009). *World Programme of Action Concerning Disabled Persons.* Retrieved September 14, 2009, from http://www.un.org/disabilities/

United Nations Statistical Commission (1994). Fundamental principles of official statistics. Retrieved September 14, 2009, from http://unstats.un.org/unsd/methods/statorg/FP-English.htm

United States Census Bureau. (2007a). *Minority population tops 100 million.* Retrieved September 15, 2009, from http://www.census.gov/Press-Release/www/releases/archives/population/010048.html

United States Census Bureau. (2007b). *More than 300 counties now "Majority-Minority".* Retrieved September 15, 2009, from http://www.census.gov/Press-Release/www/releases/archives/population/010482.html

United States Census Bureau. (2007c). *2005–2007 American community survey.* Retrieved September 15, 2009, from http://www.census.gov/acs/www/index.html

Wang, V. O., & Sue, S. (2005). In the eye of the storm: Race and genomics in research and practice. *American Psychologist, 60,* 37–45.

Woolf, L. M., Hulsizer, M. R., & McCarthy, T. (2002). International psychology: A compendium of textbooks for selected courses evaluated for international content. *Office of Teaching Resources in Psychology.* Retrieved September 15, 2009, from http://teachpsych.org/otrp/resources/woolf02intcomp.pdf

Yan, E. G., & Munir, K. M. (2004). Regulatory and ethical principles in research involving children and individuals with developmental disabilities. *Ethics and Behavior, 14,* 31–49.

# Part III

# Development

In every culture, children are born, grow, develop to the extent their circumstances allow, and eventually die. Psychological researchers have studied development extensively, especially in the areas of cognition, psychosocial development, attachment, and temperament. And researchers interested in lifespan development have investigated various aspects of adulthood and aging. In Part III we will examine child development in some depth, and then go on to explore some of the fascinating cultural variations in perceptions of aging.

Nearly every psychology student studies development, including a common core of theoretical and empirical work in the areas noted above. However, in recent years investigators have begun to question to what extent these theoretical perspectives embody ethnocentric assumptions about their generality across cultures. Are traditional findings limited, for example, by the fact that many studies have been conducted on middle-class European American children? Fortunately, the field has advanced toward an appreciation of a much wider range of human settings, and the realization that there are significant developmental variations that must be understood in the cultural context.

In this section we will explore, then, the extent to which culture may shape cognitive development, psychosocial development, attachment, and temperament. We will also see that developmental aims or ideals may not be the same for all cultures. And of course we will raise the question: How universal is our understanding of human development?

We will also note coming changes in the population of elderly people in the world, with forecasters predicting large increases in the next few years. How will these people be perceived? How will they be treated? What role does culture play in determining the answers to these questions? And what are the effects of social, political, and economic variables on views of aging?

Culture, we will find, may shape the roles played by the elderly. They may be seen, for example, as grandparents, as advice-givers, or as sources of wisdom. Their relationship to younger generations may also vary across cultures, and their perceptions of death may be intertwined with religion, living arrangements, cultural values, and retirement policies.

In short, development is a fascinating, multi-faceted process. It is intimately related to, and strongly shaped by, culture; and it remains dynamic and malleable from birth to death.

# 5

# Child Development Across Cultures

## Adriana Molitor and Hui-Chin Hsu

During the latter half of the last century, developmental psychology earnestly began cross-cultural explorations. Although much remains unknown, great strides have been made in identifying similarities and variations in the development of children around the world. Despite the field's awareness of limitations in the universality of traditional theories and findings, the developmental phenomena and patterns discussed in undergraduate courses are often implicitly regarded as capturing unequivocal regularities in child development. However, the bulk of developmental knowledge has derived from research and theory focused on a small segment of the world's people—most often, middle-class European American children and families. This chapter considers the cross-cultural applicability of some of the most popular content addressed in undergraduate developmental psychology and reviews research that has revealed similarities and differences across cultures.

According to Super and Harkness (1986, 1994, 1997), three interconnected components of culture work together as a system (i.e., *a developmental niche*) to influence children's development. *Customs and practices* refer to normative and individual child-rearing practices within a culture that range from pragmatic strategies to symbolic or religious rituals. These culturally regulated behavioral practices incorporate sleeping and feeding routines, childcare arrangements, interpersonal interaction styles, and teaching approaches. *Settings* capture the physical, economic, and social contexts in which the child resides and include ecology, living space, family composition, and objects. Lastly, *caretaker psychology* encompasses not merely the psychological attributes of a parent but wider cultural belief systems, particularly shared understandings about the development and needs of children. These include implicit "ethnotheories" about how competencies unfold (e.g., nature vs nurture), timetables for expectations, desired competencies, and ultimate goals for development. Super and Harkness (1986, 1997) emphasized that the three components do not operate independently; rather, socialization practices are intimately tied to the cultural beliefs and ecology of a child's developmental niche.

Unfortunately, however, the interconnections are not consistently studied or uncovered in psychological research. As we review reports of cross-cultural differences in child development, it is nevertheless important to recognize that connections exist between cultural practices, beliefs, and settings even if they are not, as yet, fully understood.

## Cognitive Development

### Piaget's stages

The study of children's thinking traces its origins and inspiration to the pioneering research and prolific writings of Jean Piaget. Among the basic tenets of his integrative theoretical perspective (see Flavell, 1963, for a comprehensive review) is the renowned proposition that intellectual processes advance qualitatively in a series of four progressive stages. Although much of his research was conducted on his own children and children in Geneva, Switzerland, Piaget assumed he was uncovering universal patterns of thought and development (Crain, 2005; Dasen, 1994). Cross-cultural investigations indicate that in some respects, Piaget was correct in his depiction of cognitive growth; however, many aspects of his theory have not been supported even within Western samples. His perspective has been enormously influential, but the modern study of cognitive development now considers Piaget's stage portrayal inaccurate and insufficient in accounting for the full range of transformations in children's cognition.

*Sensorimotor intelligence*
Piaget described the period between birth and the second birthday as sensorimotor because infants rely on basic sensory and motor abilities to understand the world. He proposed that infants initially do not "think" about objects apart from acting on or perceiving them. Instead, thinking and behavior are fused as the dominant cognitive structures are simple action schemes. The ultimate achievement of this stage is the enduring and flexible capacity for symbolic schemes, enabling the toddler to internally represent objects, actions on those objects, and other complex experiences via mental imagery and symbols, including words (Piaget, 1964/1969). One means of displaying this cognitive advancement is the retrieval of hidden and invisibly displaced objects.

Although research by others has suggested that Piaget underestimated infants' capacity to represent and understand the object world (and social world) because of his reliance on infants' physical-motor execution, his description of sensorimotor task performance is considered universal. For example, in a well-known study of the rural Baoulé culture in Côte d'Ivoire, West Africa (see Berry, Poortinga, Segall, & Dasen, 1992), infants displayed the same sequence of sensorimotor substages proposed by Piaget. Minor variation occurred in the average month of onset with the Baoulé infants performing earlier on some tasks requiring object use—believed to be tied to these infants' extensive access to non-toy objects (Berry et al., 1992). Studies of infants in India (Kopp, Khoka, & Sigman, 1977), Guatemala (Kagan, 1977), and Zambia (Goldberg, 1972) also have reported similar unfolding of sensorimotor abilities in terms of sequencing, although with occasional delays in timing. Kopp et al. (1977) argued that cultural caregiving practices likely accounted for onset differences between Indian and American samples. For example, Indian mothers indirectly terminated hidden-object tasks by quickly comforting infants' frustration elicited by the give-and-take of these tasks.

Dasen and Heron (1981) pointed out that even at this first stage, performance is not driven entirely by maturational or equilibration factors (e.g., assimilation and accommodation). Rather, cultural experiences alter the rate of progression of particular substages, albeit minorly. Dasen and Heron otherwise emphasized the remarkable commonality among findings, not only in substage order but in the specific manipulative and exploratory behaviors described. Even chimpanzees exhibit the same sequence of sensorimotor performance described by Piaget (Cole, 2006).

## Preoperational thinking

The second cognitive stage is marked by the pervasive, enduring, and flexible use of symbolism to mentally represent objects and experiences. Thus, children in this stage (approximately 2 to 6 years) think in the conventional sense; they can reflect on absent objects and people, recall the past, and imagine future events. Symbolic capacity is evident in burgeoning language, imitation, and creative/imaginative play activities. Piaget, however, referred to this stage as preoperational because thought yet lacks operational structures enabling linked, reversible mental actions on objects (Piaget, 1964/1969). Overt limitations include unidimensional and end-state focusing, perception-bound reasoning, transductive causality, and egocentrism (see Trawick-Smith, 2010). Cognitive constraints lead to semi-logical thinking about objects and events, which is evident in basic scientific reasoning tasks.

The preoperational stage has been argued as universal (Dasen & Heron, 1981); however, this conclusion is chiefly supported by studies confirming that young children across cultures fail logical problem-solving tasks such as conservation of properties (i.e., that amount, number, etc. remain the same despite changes in appearance), multidimensional classification, and/or spatial reasoning. Nevertheless, available research supports the universality of some additional features of preoperational functioning. For example, in terms of the rapid development of language during this stage, psycholinguists confirm that by age 5 children around the world have mastered most of the basic rules of syntax of their native language (Trawick-Smith, 2010). In terms of emerging symbolism in play, Dasen and his colleagues (see Dasen & Heron, 1981) found that young children in the

Baoulé culture of West Africa displayed the same sequence of development (from conventional to symbolic play with objects) at about the same ages as French children even as the content differed.

Further preoperational depictions are equivocally supported within Western samples, although similarities in traditional conceptualizations have been found across cultures. For example, 3- to 5-year-olds across cultures display similar patterns of errors and age improvements in distinguishing appearance from reality (e.g., Flavell, Zhang, Zou, Dong, & Qi, 1983). Yet methodological probing of Western samples suggests that in some circumstances preschoolers can readily distinguish appearance from reality (see Deák, 2006). Cross-cultural studies also support the universality of traditional notions of egocentrism (i.e., viewing the world only through one's perspective). For example, Fahrmeier (1978) and Greenfield and Childs (1977) respectively found reversed linear age trends for egocentrism among children of the Hassau (Nigeria) and Zinacanteco Mayan (Mexico) cultures. Nonetheless, modern research suggests that young children are not as consistently egocentric as Piaget originally proposed, while it also confirms that perspective-taking and knowledge about the mind greatly increase with age (Flavell, 2000).

*Concrete operations*

In Piaget's third stage (beginning at approximately 5 to 7 years), the capacity for cognitive operations appears; that is, children can now perform linked, reversible mental actions on objects (Piaget, 1964/1969). Thus, thinking is no longer constrained by the limitations of the preoperational period and children can now understand the process of transformations, reversibility, etc. (see Trawick-Smith, 2010). This new operational capacity is evident in logical problem-solving and successful performance in basic scientific reasoning tasks. Nevertheless, Piaget referred to this stage as concrete because operations (and thus logical and systematic thinking) are limited to tangible objects and activities (i.e., real or readily imagined) and do not extend to ideas and hypothetical propositions (Crain, 2005; Piaget, 1964/1968).

Cross-cultural studies on concrete operational thinking are abundant and typically incorporate tasks assessing conservation, classification, and spatial skills. Considerable commonality has been found in children's performance, particularly among those who receive formal schooling. For example, Shayer, Demetriou, and Pervez (1988) uncovered strikingly similar patterns of emerging operations for British, Greek, Australian, and Pakistani school children (ages 6–12), regardless of socioeconomic background. Still, it is at this stage that remarkable cross-cultural heterogeneity appears particularly between Western and non-Western societies; however, disparate findings are not explained by this distinction alone.

Some studies of non-Western cultures have reported similar task performance for classification or conservation as in Western samples, including the same sequence of emergence (e.g., conservation of number, length, weight, area, then volume) and average age of onset. For example, comparable findings have been found for communities in Nigeria, Zambia (see Dasen, 1972), and Kenya (Kiminyo, 1977). Other studies of non-Western cultures have found concrete operations emerging at later ages than in Western samples. For example, in Papua New Guinea, conservation of number (which typically comes first) appears approximately three years later than in Western samples, while mastery of more complex tasks (e.g., conservation of area, volume) appears as much as six years later (Shea, 1985). Similarly later onsets, ranging from one to six years, also have been reported for other groups in non-Western cultures (e.g., Senegal, Algeria, Uganda) for various operational tasks (e.g., classification, conservation) (see Dasen, 1972). The eventual achievement of concrete operations (as well as the observation that tasks which are more difficult for Western children also are more difficult for many groups) suggests some degree of commonality across cultures (Shea, 1985).

The cross-cultural heterogeneity in operational mastery and onset rates is sometimes exacerbated by factors such as urban versus rural living, or years of schooling (e.g., Shea, 1985); however, these factors have not consistently led to differences (e.g., Kiminyo, 1977). On the other hand, immediate contextual factors seem to affect performance. For example, assessments using children's native language are associated with improved task execution (Gardiner & Kosmitzki, 2008). Even more so, children's performance seems to be greatly enhanced by familiarity of task materials (Rogoff, 2003). In terms of underlying developmental differences, Dasen and colleagues (Dasen 1977; Dasen & Heron, 1981; Segall, Dasen, Berry, & Poortinga, 1999) have argued that ecological demands, particularly those which are uniform within subsistence economies, may explain the diverse emergence of various domains of concrete operational reasoning. In their comparison of data from five cultures—the indigenous Aranda of Australia, the Inuit of Canada, the Ebrié and the Baoulé of Côte d'Ivoire, and the Kikuya of Kenya (Dasen, 1975; Segall et al., 1999)—Dasen and colleagues found that children's development of spatial and conservation reasoning varied according to the ecological pressures confronting the different subsistence groups (e.g., nomadic, hunting-gathering versus sedentary, agricultural farming). Overall, the strictly agricultural groups (Kikuyu and Baoulé) showed relatively rapid development of conservation reasoning (e.g., quantity), while the hunting and gathering groups (Aranda and Inuit) exhibited relatively later onsets. The researchers observed the opposite trend for spatial reasoning. The eco-cultural relevance of spatial reasoning appeared to be driving its rapid development among nomadic people, while the meaningfulness of conservation promoted its earlier onset among agriculturalists (Dasen & Heron, 1981). Thus, diverse cultural rates of development of operational domains may reflect the salience of what is, and is not, adaptive and valued within particular societies (Dasen, 1994).

### Formal operations

In Piaget's final stage (beginning around the time of puberty), cognitive operations are no longer limited to the physical realm. Thus, the adolescent can conduct mental actions not merely on objects, but on wholly abstract and hypothetical ideas; these ideas need no longer be attached to vivid representations that are supplied by external reality (Piaget, 1964/1968). Indeed, mental operations on operations become possible (Kuhn, 2008). "Concrete thinking is the representation of a possible action, and formal thinking is the representation of a representation of possible action" (Piaget, 1964/1968, p. 174). Formal operational structures include combinatorial and propositional logic (Piaget, 1972) and lead to various behavioral markers—hypothetical reasoning, isolation and control of variables, systematic combination (Kuhn, 2008), often collectively referred to as "scientific thinking."

Given the wide cross-cultural heterogeneity that began appearing in the concrete stage, it should be no surprise that researchers have not universally observed Piaget's final stage. Among unschooled subjects in traditional non-Western cultures, formal operational reasoning is typically not evidenced when assessed by standard tasks (Dasen, 1972; Dasen & Heron, 1981). Shea (1985) argued that such findings do not necessarily mean the absence of formal reasoning among entire cultures. In fact, formal-level thinking may be present in some remote non-Western communities when assessed via unconventional measures. For example, Tulkin and Konner (1973) suggested that preliterate tribal hunters of the Kalahari (Africa) displayed reasoning consistent with formal operations when working through issues dealing with the tracking of prey. Likewise, Saxe (1981) reported signs of a developmental trend in formal reasoning among Ponam islanders (ages 8–23) in Papua New Guinea. Specifically, combinatorial reasoning seemed evident by late adolescence during a task requiring construction of hypothetical families using an indigenous birth-order naming system for children. Although such findings are provocative in suggesting the development of formal operations even within remote settings, Segall et al. (1999) cautioned against assuming formal-level reasoning in the absence of standard criteria.

The achievement of Piaget's final stage seems to be strongly related to schooling. Among well-educated samples in non-Western cultures, evidence for formal operations does emerge. Orbell (1981) reported that 63% of high-achieving Zimbabwean male students in their fourth year of secondary education demonstrated formal operational thinking. Other researchers have reported similar evidence of formal operations among African students drawn from universities in Botswana, Kenya, and South Africa (e.g., Cherian, Kibria, Kiriuki, & Mwamwenda, 1988). However, secondary-level schooling alone is not sufficient to promote formal operational thinking, as it is not always evident even among educated non-Western samples (Dasen & Heron, 1981; Segall et al., 1999; Shea, 1985).

The cross-cultural trends mimic those within Western cultures. That is, most individuals do not achieve Piaget's final stage. Kuhn, Langer, Kohlberg, and Haan (1977) found that only about a third of adults in their U.S. sample showed consolidated formal operations. Though many appeared "transitional," a considerable percentage exhibited no signs of formal thinking. The general consensus is that, even among well-educated Americans, only a fraction display formal operations as assessed by traditional Piagetian tasks (Dasen & Heron, 1981; Neimark, 1979). When formal operations are employed, they tend to be exhibited in an area of specialty. For example, among college students, science majors outperformed non-science majors when tested on a traditional Piagetian balance task, and among non-science majors, seniors did not perform any better than freshmen (White & Ferstenberg, 1978). When assessments used formal-level tasks representing a range of specialty content, De Lisi and Staudt (1980) found that college students tended to exhibit formal reasoning only in tasks that corresponded to their major.

In response to emerging trends, Piaget (1972) acknowledged that his final cognitive stage may not be universally manifest, but believed it likely that all individuals eventually attain formal operations in an area of specialization. Thus, one's ultimate level of cognitive functioning would be reflected only under favorable circumstances (Berry et al., 1992; Dasen & Heron, 1981). The evidence available to date is insufficient to clarify this issue (Kuhn, 2008) and modern scholars have moved away from an assumption of generality in cognitive development and focused their scientific inquiry into domain- and context-specific processing (Rogoff, 2003).

## Modern approaches to cognitive development

A sociocultural perspective of cognitive development emphasizes that mental abilities do not develop in a vacuum. Rather, children learn, practice thinking, and develop their skills through participation in everyday activities organized by cultural conventions and routines (Gauvain, 1998; Rogoff, 2003). Cultural practices not only provide opportunities to support and maintain desired patterns of learning, but also impose constraints on cognitive growth (Gauvain, 2001). As a result, culture and cognition are inextricably interlinked. The development of two cognitive processes—attention and autobiographical memory—serve as illustrations of cultural influences.

### Attention
Mothers in different cultures employ different strategies to guide their infants' attention. For example, American mothers tend to encourage their infants to attend to the environment, whereas Japanese mothers tend to shift infants' attention away from the environment and toward the mother's face (Bornstein, Toda, Azuma, Tamis-Lemonda, & Ogino, 1990; Fernald & Morikawa, 1993). American and British mothers also show a preference for attention-following, where infants lead and mothers follow their infants' focus. By contrast, Chinese and Korean mothers prefer a style of attention-directing, where mothers scaffold their infants' attention to the object or event of their choice (Sung & Hsu, 2009; Vigil, 2002). These maternal attention regulation styles may reflect cultural values. Western mothers' style of following the child's lead encourages exploratory initiative and

reinforces individual interests and choices. By contrast, Asian mothers' style of using a directive tactic may strengthen mother–infant interpersonal connections and ensure the achievement of interpersonal harmony by considering the needs of others.

Childhood attention-deployment strategies also vary cross-culturally. For example, in response to several ongoing competing social events, Guatemalan Mayan toddlers and their mothers showed a pattern of simultaneous attention to multiple events, whereas middle-class European American dyads demonstrated a style of exclusive attention to one event at a time and alternating attention between events (Chavajay & Rogoff, 1999; Rogoff, Mistry, Göncü, & Mosier, 1993). American children with Mexican heritage also were more likely to display simultaneous attention than those with European heritage (Correa-Chávez, Rogoff, & Arauz, 2005). Furthermore, Mayan children spent more time in sustained attention to interactions not directed toward them, whereas middle-class European American children spent the majority of time either not attending to activity not involving them or only sporadically glancing at it (Correa-Chávez & Rogoff, 2009). These attentional patterns may reflect different cultural practices. In the traditional Mayan community, children are included in almost all activities. However, because learning situations are not specially designed, children are expected to learn by observing ongoing activity and keeping their attention broadly focused. In contrast, European American children tend to be the target of adults' exclusive attention. They are encouraged to focus on a particular age-appropriate task and sustain their attention.

Cultural differences in attentional socialization practices may contribute to contrasting adult cognitive styles (Cole & Cagigas, 2010). For example, East Asians exhibit a holistic or *field dependent* style that divides attention between contextual information and a focal object, whereas North Americans display an analytic or *field independent* style that emphasizes focal information about objects and is less sensitive to context (e.g., Kitayama, Duffy, Kawamura, & Larsen, 2003; Nisbett, Peng, Choi, & Norenzayan, 2001). Research indicates that American and Japanese children older than age 6 exhibit marked cultural differences in attention strategy that are similar to those of adults in their respective cultures, whereas those younger than 6 years do not (Duffy, Toriyama, Itakura, & Kitayama, 2009). This evidence supports the view that cultural socialization practices during very early childhood permanently shape how individuals allocate their attention and what information they process.

*Autobiographical memory*

An information-processing approach to memory focuses on encoding, recall, and recognition. People tend to remember things that are meaningful and relevant to their concerns. Culture can affect why and what people remember, and whether and how people use their past experiences to guide everyday decisions and actions. Studies regarding the effects of culture on children's memory have focused chiefly on autobiographical memory—recollections of personal events that occurred in one's past.

Our personal memories from early childhood are sparse. The inability of adults to recall events that occurred prior to age 3 is known as infantile amnesia, and seems to be a universal phenomenon (Fivush & Nelson, 2004; Wang, 2003). However, the onset and content of autobiographical memory varies cross-culturally. Adults from Western cultures with an emphasis on independence have an earlier age of first memory. On average, the earliest memory reported by American adults occurs at 3.5 years, six months earlier than those reported by Asians (Wang, 2003; Wang & Ross, 2007). Additionally, childhood memories reported by American adults tend to be more specific, detailed, and focused on self. By contrast, memories reported by individuals from Asian cultures tend to be more skeletal, generic, and centered on social relationships (Wang, 2003; Wang & Ross, 2007). Similar findings are observed in childhood. For example, American preschoolers reported more specific autobiographic memories than did Korean and Chinese preschoolers (Han, Leichtman, & Wang, 1998). Variations in belief systems, particularly "self-views," may account for cultural differences in memory onset and content. A social-cultural-developmental perspective (Fivush & Nelson, 2004; Wang, 2003) argues that cultural differences in how self is defined are reflected in how early and well people remember their past. Independent cultures place an emphasis on individuality. Thus, an autonomous sense of self guides cognitive resources into processing and remembering significant personal experiences. By contrast, in interdependent cultures such as China and Korea, because self is defined by people's social role and status in the family and community, a relational sense of self motivates individuals to prioritize information about significant others and social groups (Wang & Ross, 2007).

Early parent–child memory sharing is also critical to the development of autobiographical memory (Fivush & Nelson, 2004). Across cultures, memory conversations between parent and child differ in their style, content, and degree of maternal elaboration and support (e.g., Wang & Fivush, 2005). For example, European American mothers are likely to take a cognitive approach in memory sharing by engaging in elaborative talks with their children about positive and negative past events. These mothers tend to ask many questions and provide a great deal of nuanced information. They also frequently discuss children's desires, thinking, and feelings, highlighting them as separate and unique individuals. By contrast, Chinese mothers tend to use a behavioral approach during memory conversations. They are more likely to focus on moral lessons, discussing past wrong-doings and directing attention to behavioral conduct to avoid negative emotions in the future without giving causal explanations for the emotion itself. The style and content of children's memory reports mirror those observed in early parent–child reminiscing (e.g., Han et al., 1998; Wang, 2006; Wang & Leichtman, 2000). Compared to Asian children, American children provided elaborative and specific accounts of the past, more references to their own feelings, opinions, and preferences, and more mentions of themselves relative to others.

*Summary*

In summary, modern scholars argue that cognitive development cannot be fully or even meaningfully understood outside its cultural context. Researchers no longer question whether culture plays a role in the development of children's attention, thinking, and memory. Different cognitive tendencies and abilities develop in different social and cultural settings, depending on the demands placed on an individual's life. Through conversations and interactions with parents and others in their communities, children learn to pay attention, think, and remember in a culturally acceptable way. Continued research will increasingly clarify how culture-specific practices and cognitive processes are developmentally interlinked.

# Erikson's Stages of Psychosocial Development

In his classic reformulation and expansion of Freud's psychosexual stages, Erik Erikson (1963) proposed eight critical developmental tasks that individuals must sequentially resolve for healthy psychosocial adjustment. According to Erikson, each crisis is dominated by a subconscious struggle between opposing psychological attributes, and ultimately individuals must emerge from each stage possessing a favorable balance of the positive over the negative alternative (Crain, 2005). Erikson's field studies included the Sioux of South Dakota and Yurok of northern California and he believed his stages to be culturally universal. Erikson's efforts to explore the lives of healthy individuals into adulthood and in different cultural settings led his theory to be well-received beyond psychoanalytic circles. Nonetheless, authors have pointed out that Erikson takes an etic approach which imposes pre-formulated developmental themes, principally generated from observations of middle-class European and European American cultures, onto individuals of non-Western cultures (Gardiner & Kosmitzki, 2008). Such psychological issues may not be linearly addressed (e.g., Wang & Viney, 1997) and may not all be critical concerns within non-Western cultures that do not equally value free self-expression (Shiraev & Levy, 2007).

## Childhood crises

Four of Erikson's stages occur in childhood: *trust versus mistrust* in infancy, *autonomy versus shame/doubt* in toddlerhood, *initiative versus guilt* during preschool, and *industry versus inferiority* during school-age. The issue of forming trust by an infant toward his/her caregiver has been conceptualized and investigated more fully via the concept of secure attachment, now widely accepted as a basic and universal developmental task. Other developmental issues of childhood, prior to the onset of the proposed adolescent identity crisis, have generated less universal appeal and research scrutiny.

### Autonomy vs shame and doubt

According to Erikson, the issue of autonomy comes to a peak during the second and third year as biological maturation encourages the young child to act independently without parental control or assistance. This stage is characterized by a "sudden violent wish to have a choice" and becomes "decisive for the ratio of love and hate, cooperation and willfulness, freedom of self-expression and its suppression" (Erikson, 1963, pp. 252–254). Over-control by others during this period purportedly leads to a lasting propensity for doubt and shame. Although all societies, to some extent, manage to meet this basic human need for autonomous functioning or personal agency (Kagitcibasi, 2005), the idealization of autonomy comes from a Western perspective and is not universally valued or encouraged across cultures (Rogoff, 2003). For example, while European Americans typically advocate the importance of sleeping alone for a young child's developing self-reliance, co-sleeping is promoted within collectivist cultures. In fact, Guatemalan Mayan parents consider it cruel that American infants and young children are typically required to sleep in separate quarters (Morelli, Rogoff, Oppenheim, & Goldsmith, 1992; Rogoff, 2003).

Cultural differences in support for toddler autonomy also can be seen in subtle parental practices. During unstructured play times, Liu et al. (2005) reported that Chinese mothers exhibited greater overall involvement and encouraged more connectedness compared to Canadian mothers who encouraged more autonomy. Not surprisingly, the Chinese toddlers spent more time in connected joint play and less in autonomous activities. During meal-time interactions, Wang, Wiley, and Zhou (2007) found that European American viewers considered parental restraint of a toddler's autonomy as intrusive while Chinese Americans equated parental intervention as sensitivity. Thus, not only is the value of autonomy potentially contested across cultures, it has not been established even within Western samples that a lack of support for it during the toddler years, in particular, leads to heightened doubt and shame. Moreover, autonomy is often depicted as a developmental progression that continues through adolescence (e.g., Roer-Strier & Rivlis, 1998) rather than a critical task principally tackled in toddlerhood.

### Initiative vs guilt

In Erikson's third stage, children between 3 and 6 years experience a vigorous urge to contemplate goals and fantasize, and accordingly they take action via planning, constructing, and emulating with exuberance. "Initiative adds to autonomy the quality of undertaking, planning and 'attacking' a task for the sake of being active" (Erikson, 1963, p. 255). These pursuits naturally challenge what is permissible and, in resolution, children internalize social prohibitions; however, excessive external restriction risks engendering extreme guilt in the child (Crain, 2005; Erikson, 1963). To many developmentalists, preschoolers' need to express initiative is typically seen in their strong tendencies to solicit engagement and play with peers (Trawick-Smith, 2010) and those who fail to do so have been found to experience adjustment problems, including rejection by peers (Rubin et al., 2006). However, like autonomy, social initiative is not equally valued among cultures, particularly in East Asian and Latin American collectivistic societies (Chen & French, 2008). For example, in contrast to North American or Italian parents, Chinese parents consider restrained and cautious social behavior desirable (Rubin et al., 2006) and shy-inhibited Chinese children are likewise positively evaluated and accepted by peers and teachers (Chen, DeSouza, Chen, & Wang, 2006; Chen, Rubin, & Li, 1995).

In terms of creative initiative, Erikson's depiction of the young child's need to construct and plan is potentially supported by studies of children's play. For example, in her analyses of archived data from the classic anthropological six-culture study, Edwards (2000) reported that children in all six communities (located within Kenya, Mexico, Philippines, Okinawa, India, and the United States) showed strong tendencies for self-directed constructive play activities. Specifically, while role play subsided at whatever age children were required to make a significant contribution to the household and fantasy play was rarely observed in three of the samples, creative-constructive play was evident in all six communities. "Children seemed to have a developmental need to make and combine things, to make marks and draw, and to handle and reshape materials that could not be subdued" (Edwards, 2000, p. 336). Edwards further conjectured that in such creative-constructive pursuits, children's minds may have been "actively constructing stories or event scenarios for themselves and thus, either role play or fantasy play was taking place implicitly" (Edwards, 2000, p. 336).

Other studies affirm that pretend or fantasy play is not equally observed across cultures, even at preschool ages. In a study of Yucatec Mayan children, Gaskins (2000) reported that although play became the dominant activity during ages 3–5 and then receded, very little of it was pretend. Any pretend play was more likely initiated by older children, and still was relatively infrequent. Mayan children's play, in general, was not supported and was even discouraged, as it often conflicted with needed work and because Mayan parents did not view it as important for development (Gaskins, 2000). Similarly, Farver and colleagues (1995; 1997) consistently found that Korean American preschoolers engaged in more parallel play and less social and pretend play compared to European American counterparts. The dissimilarity is believed to reflect cultural differences in attitudes regarding play and thus corresponding differences in the ways that the preschool setting is physically and temporally structured (Farver et al., 1995; Farver & Shin, 1997).

Together, the findings suggest that although children across cultures spend time playing, often in the company of peers, cultural beliefs and conditions influence the frequency and type of peer engagement and play activities. It remains unclear how such attitudes or constraints influence children's long-term socioemotional functioning (Farver & Shin, 2000). As yet, there is no evidence to suggest that cultural restriction of children's social or creative initiative yields guilt or dysfunction.

*Industry vs inferiority*

According to Erikson (1963), the child around age 6 becomes ready to master skills, tools, and tasks, "which go far beyond the mere playful expression of his organ modes or limbs. His exuberant imagination is tamed and harnessed ... to the inorganic laws of the tool world" (pp. 258–259). It is in this striving for mastery and productivity that the preadolescent child unfortunately risks developing a sense of inadequacy due to executing an imbalance of achievements relative to disappointments. Modern psychologists recognize that self-evaluation is universal to the development of individuals across cultures, yet it is more complex and multi-faceted than Erikson depicted. Rather than merely possessing a global sense of self-worth, self-concept and its corresponding appraisal are believed to become increasingly differentiated and hierarchical in childhood with the individual developing self-esteem in various domains of competence (Harter, 1998, 2003, 2006; Marsh, Ellis, & Craven, 2002). Consistent with Erikson's discussion of differences between the tools of literate and preliterate societies, psychologists recognize that children across cultures do not base their self-evaluations on the same criteria. Moreover, just as ethnic minorities often do not equally value the same domains as the dominant culture (Trawick-Smith, 2010), children within cultures assign differential importance to various competency domains (Harter, 1998, 2003, 2006).

Empirical studies support Erikson's suggestion that self-evaluation becomes increasingly realistic during middle childhood as "the child must forget past hopes and wishes" (Erikson, 1963, p. 258). Preschoolers hold an inflated sense of what they can do compared to those in middle childhood and these elevated views are likely tied to an inability for extensive social and temporal comparison (Butler, 1998; Harter, 1998, 2006). Interestingly, researchers have found that East Asian children and adults (e.g., from Japan, China, and Korea) evaluate themselves less positively than counterparts in Western culture and that these self-critical effects are found even when there is no issue of self-presentation (Kitayama & Uchida, 2003). However, recent research that examines explicit versus implicit indicators of self-esteem suggests that implicit positive self-regard may be universally reported and needed (Kitayama & Uchida, 2003; Yamaguchi et al., 2007) despite cultural differences in explicit markers. Moreover, the issue of developing competence does not appear to be limited to grade school, particularly in other cultures. For example, in a study of Eriksonian tasks among Chinese children ages 6–18, Wang and Viney (1997) found that resolution of industry versus inferiority was the main focus of all the research participants, including those in late adolescence.

## Adolescent identity crisis

"With the advent of puberty, childhood proper comes to an end" and adolescents must define themselves as members of the society (Erikson, 1963, p. 261). Erikson (1968) argued that adolescents' critical task is to develop an integrated identity, with the ultimate goal being an individuated and separated self. Based on Erikson's emphasis on stable adherence to roles following a search, Marcia (1966) articulated four progressively mature identity statuses: *diffusion* (i.e., neither commitment nor search), *foreclosure* (i.e., commitment without exploration/questioning), *moratorium* (i.e., exploration), and finally *identity achievement* (i.e., commitment following crisis). Erikson's depiction of identity formation has received considerable scrutiny and is now viewed as inconsistent with experiences in diverse cultures and biased toward the upper social classes of Western societies (Schwartz & Hilda, 2006). In contrast to Erikson's conceptualization, the timing, degree, and psychological correlates of identity development differ markedly across cultures. For example, in a large-scale study of white and black men and women in South Africa, Ochse and Plug (1986) found that tasks described by Erikson as developing in childhood were strongly integrated only in white adolescents. On average, Black South African men resolved the identity crisis after age 40. Moreover, healthy psychosocial development as defined by Erikson related to well-being in White, but not Black, South Africans.

The modern version of Erikson's theory points to the central role of society and culture in identity formation (Côté, 1996). To achieve a coherent sense of self, adolescents actively select and modify their identities based on what would allow them to do best in the cultural context (Baumeister & Muraven, 1996). For example, in independent cultures where individualization and differentiation are valued, teenagers are encouraged to pursue personal choices. Consequently, following traditional goals and standards is viewed as insufficient in identity formation. By contrast, in interdependent cultures where familial values and cultural traditions still have a strong presence, adolescents are encouraged to conform to others' ideals. As a result, pursuit of personal goals and life plans is not encouraged when adolescents are in search for a meaningful self.

Research supports the idea that identity formation is an active cultural adaptation. For example, Hofter, Kärtner, Chasiotis, Busch, and Kiessling (2007) examined identity status among college students in Cameroon (Africa) and Germany. Cameroonian parents emphasize obedience and respect toward parents and elders, featuring socialization practices of an interdependent culture. By contrast, German parents emphasize individual distinctness and autonomy, representing the characteristics of an independent culture. As hypothesized, Cameroonian students reported more pronounced levels of foreclosure than German students, likely due to their greater acceptance of socially prescribed values and standards. Interestingly, more pronounced foreclosure was related to higher levels of negative affect among German students; yet, foreclosure was not related to well-being among Cameroonian students. Portes, Dunham, and Castillo (2000) likewise reported that American and Haitian adolescents scored significantly higher on commitment scores than did Colombians, even when age and socioeconomic status were controlled. Similarly, Taylor and Oskay (1995) found fewer Turkish, compared to American, college students attained the higher identity statuses of achievement and moratorium, with more classified as foreclosed. Thus, youth from interdependent cultures (e.g., Cameroon, Colombia, Turkey) tended to show patterns that were adaptive to their local cultural belief systems.

Even among independent cultures, domain-specific identity development varies. For example, both the U.S. and the Netherlands can be categorized as Western, democratic, and industrial/technological societies. Indeed, adolescents in both contexts showed decreased diffusion in the domains of relational and societal identity (Meeus, Iedema, Helsen, & Vollebergh, 1999). However, compared to Americans, Dutch adolescents displayed increased foreclosure in the domain of societal but not relational identity. Such cross-cultural differences appear due to the fact that Dutch youth experience greater imposed restrictions related to schooling and work. Because it is not always possible to contemplate commitments or make personal choices, Dutch adolescents are likely to remain in foreclosure in the domain of societal identity. Thus, both foreclosure and achievement served as the endpoint of identity development among Dutch adolescents. Similar patterns were observed when comparing American and South African college students' identity development (Low, Akande, & Hill, 2005). South Africans showed a greater tendency to be foreclosed in interpersonal domains of friendship and dating, yet achieved in ideological domains related to political issues and lifestyles. When making decisions about relationships, South African adolescents are more likely to rely on family and traditions. By contrast, social autonomy is highly valued in the U.S.; thus, dating and friendship are likely to be personal choices. On the other hand, because political responsibility is highly valued within the indigenous African populations in South Africa, these adolescents tended to achieve a higher status in this domain.

In summary, although the concept of identity formation is believed to apply to individuals across cultures, it is evident that universality does not exist in its development—whether in terms of timing, quality, progression, or psychological correlates. The findings clearly suggest that identity achievement is not necessarily the endpoint of development in all cultures, not even in all Western cultures. Healthy identity development during adolescence may be best viewed as a fit between personal needs and cultural demands. Positive adaptation to socially and culturally accepted guiding principles and constraints likely facilitates optimal development (Baumeister & Muraven, 1996; Schwartz & Hilda, 2006).

## Attachment

### Attachment theory

Attachment refers to the young child's emotional tie to his/her primary caregiver and was theorized by John Bowlby (1969/1982) to have a lasting impact on psychosocial development. He argued that an infant is biologically predisposed, as a result of natural selection, to form an attachment because it motivates proximity maintenance to the caregiver which facilitates protection during times of threat. Ultimately, the bond includes cognitive representations or "internal working models" (IWMs) of the attachment figure, self, and their relations. Constructed in the context of child–caregiver interactions, IWMs encompass relationship expectations, strategies, heuristics etc. and form the basis for how an individual maintains a close relationship with others (see Bretherton & Munholland, 2008). Bowlby's (1969/1982) theory underscores the role of the caregiver to serve as a "secure base" from which the infant can explore and learn about the environment.

Bowlby (1969/1982) distinguished four attachment phases: *undifferentiated reactivity* (0 to 2–3 months), *discriminating social responsiveness* (3 to 6–7 months), *clear-cut attachment* (7 months to 3 years), and finally a *goal-corrected partnership* (beginning around age 3). Attachment research has focused predominantly on phase three when infants demonstrate active maintenance of proximity and physical contact with a specific figure as well as evidence of using the figure as a base from which to explore. It is also when infants display separation and stranger anxieties. Attachment theory proposes important flexibility in the nature of the attachments that are formed in phase three as a result of caregiving (Ainsworth, 1967; Ainsworth, Blehar, Waters, & Wall, 1978; Bowlby, 1969/1982). The most widely used assessment of attachment variation is the Strange Situation, developed by Mary Ainsworth (1967; Ainsworth et al., 1978). In this procedure, an infant (12–24 months) is faced with an unfamiliar setting, a stranger, and brief separations from his/her caregiver. Three attachment patterns are traditionally classified (Ainsworth et al., 1978). Infants who express their distress, readily seek and achieve comfort from their caregivers upon reunion, and use the caregiver as a secure base for returning to exploration are classified as *secure*. Insecurely attached infants fail to use their attachment figure as a secure base for active exploration. Moreover, infants who convey little distress and avoid the caregiver upon reunion are classified as *insecure-avoidant*. Those who seek much proximity/contact with their caregivers yet resist interaction, exploration, and feeling comforted are classified as *insecure-resistant* (formerly *ambivalent*). They are often extremely distressed when separating from the caregiver; however, their reaction to reunion gives an impression that they find little security in the caregiver's return. According to a classic meta-analysis by

Van IJzendoorn and Kroonenberg (1988), the aggregate global distribution of patterns is approximately 65% secure, 21% insecure-avoidant, and 14% insecure-resistant.

## Limits to the universality of attachment theory?

Ainsworth's (1967) groundbreaking observations of Ugandan mothers and infants supported Bowlby's theory that infants develop attachment relationships in the phases described and that the majority develop a secure attachment with their mothers. A multitude of cross-cultural studies in Africa, East Asia, and Indonesia have since followed and indeed confirm that attachment is a universal phenomenon (i.e., the universality hypothesis) (Van IJzendoorn & Sagi-Schwartz, 2008). Nevertheless, important issues remain concerning the cross-cultural accuracy of other hypotheses of attachment theory. To date, researchers argue that a substantial core of attachment organization is exempt from cultural influence, including its nature (i.e., secure base hypothesis), optimality (i.e., secure-as-normative hypothesis), origins (i.e., sensitivity hypothesis), and consequences (i.e., competence hypothesis) (e.g., Van IJzendoorn & Sagi, 1999; Van IJzendoorn & Sagi-Schwartz, 2008). Even so, available evidence both supports and questions the universality of these core assumptions.

*Nature*
The nature of attachment is captured by the secure base hypothesis, which presumes infants use the caregiver as a secure base from which to safely explore the environment (Ainsworth et al., 1978; Bowlby, 1969/1982). Many studies confirm that the secure base phenomenon is observable in infant–mother dyads of industrialized nations, developing countries, and traditionally isolated societies (e.g., Kermoian & Leiderman, 1986; Posada et al., 1995; Valenzuela, 1997). Nevertheless, several cross-cultural researchers have contended that the focus on secure base relations to represent attachment quality places a biased emphasis on European American values of individuation and independence (e.g., Harwood, 1992; Rothbaum, Pott, Azuma, Miyake, & Weisz, 2000; Takahashi, 1990). In fact, cultures differ widely in the extent of exploration in everyday situations. For example, because of significant danger in immediate living situations (e.g., snakes), Dogon infants of Mali in West Africa are generally not permitted to explore freely (True, Pisani, & Oumar, 2001). The behavioral manifestation of secure base phenomenon in infant–mother dyads also varies across cultures. For example, whereas American infants increase maternal physical contact in an unfamiliar situation, infants in Germany increase visual reference to mothers (Zach & Keller, 1999). Finally, the link between attachment and dependence, rather than exploration, is more primary in non-Western cultures (e.g., Mizuta, Zahn-Waxler, Cole, & Hiruma, 1996). For example, Puerto Rican mothers prefer infants whose behaviors are inclined toward proximity maintenance rather than

exploration (Harwood, 1992). Thus, the conception and expression of secure base behavior appears to be largely influenced by cultural context.

*Optimality*

Strange Situation assessments gathered from more than 20 countries indicate that approximately two thirds of infants are classified as securely attached (Van IJzendoorn & Kroonenberg, 1988; Van IJzendoorn & Sagi, 1999). Attachment theorists view secure attachment as reflecting an appropriate balance between autonomy and relatedness in the infant–mother relationship, whereas insecure-avoidance represents high autonomy with low relatedness and insecure-resistant reflects the reverse (Lamb, Thompson, Gardner, & Charnov, 1985). Yet significant cross-cultural differences have been found in the distribution of attachment patterns, with more insecure-resistant infants in Japan and more insecure-avoidant infants in Germany and Israel (e.g., Grossmann, Grossmann, Spangler, Suess, & Unzner, 1985; Miyake, Chen, & Campos, 1985; Sagi et al., 1985; Sagi, Van IJzendoorn, Aviezer, Donnell, & Mayseless, 1994).

Several cross-cultural researchers have challenged the assumption that there is a single universal pattern of optimal functioning. They believe the labeling of a particular pattern as secure is merely a judgment regarding prevailing cultural ideals for child rearing and development (e.g., LeVine & Norman, 2008). For example, while self-reliance and obedience in infants are highly encouraged by German parents, interpersonal closeness and affective communication are discouraged. An insecure-avoidant attachment pattern exemplifying these ideal behaviors is likely to result (LeVine & Norman, 2008). By contrast, interpersonal harmony is emphasized in Japan (Rothbaum et al., 2000). Among Japanese infants, an insecure-resistant pattern may simply capture heightened emotional closeness and dependency in relating to their mothers. Finally, a social network of multiple caregivers who keep constant and close physical contact with infants is common among some traditional African communities (e.g., Keller, 2007; Tronick, Morelli, & Ivey, 1992; Tronick, Morelli, & Winn, 2008; True et al., 2001). As a result, Dogon infants do not approach their mothers during reunion as readily as do infants in other cultures (True et al., 2001). Thus, it appears that the optimal attachment organization may be constructed on the basis of cultural beliefs and socialization goals.

*Origins*

One of the central tenets of attachment theory is that variations in caregivers' sensitivity predict attachment quality (i.e., the sensitivity hypothesis) (Ainsworth et al., 1978). Indeed, a comprehensive meta-analysis confirmed that maternal sensitivity is modestly yet significantly associated with infant attachment security (De Wolff & Van IJzendoorn, 1997). Moreover, observations based on middle-class and very poor families in Colombia (Posada et al., 1999; Posada et al., 2002), chronically underweight Chilean infants living in urban poverty (Valenzuela, 1990, 1997), Dogon infants in Africa whose mothers have experienced multiple offspring losses (True et al., 2001), and well-educated Japanese mothers (Vereijken, Riksen-Walraven, & Kondo-Ikemura, 1997) all consistently reported that maternal sensitivity was associated with secure attachment.

Nevertheless, several cross-cultural researchers (e.g., Keller, 2007; Rothbaum & Morelli, 2005; Rothbaum et al., 2000) have questioned the Western conceptualization of sensitivity as a universal ideal for parenting. They argue that sensitivity as described by attachment theorists assumes that infants have both momentary and elemental needs that caregivers ought to fulfill and respect, and that these needs are readily agreed upon. However, because interpretations of sensitive caregiving incorporate varying cultural socialization goals, definitions may vary. For example, in the eyes of attachment theorists, mothers in both Japan and Puerto Rico may seem insensitive: Japanese mothers perhaps over-indulgent and Puerto Rican mothers over-controlling (Harwood, 1992; Rothbaum et al., 2000). Yet both styles may be appropriate for promoting socialization goals other than individuation and autonomy. In fact, greater maternal physical control was associated with secure attachment in middle-class Puerto Rican infants (Carlson & Harwood, 2003). From a sociocultural perspective, Puerto Rican mothers' persistent physical control is viewed as effective in raising a child well-accepted by the community (Harwood, 1992). Cameroonian rural Nso mothers also believe that a caretaker-centered concept of responsive control is the best parenting strategy for promoting optimal outcomes of obedience, respectfulness, and responsibility in children (Yovsi, Kärtner, Keller, & Lohaus, 2009). Taken together, an appreciation for culture-specific ideals of sensitive caregiving appears to be an important foundation for a better understanding of the sensitivity–security link.

### Consequences

Bowlby (1969/1982) and Ainsworth (Ainsworth et al., 1978) hypothesized that securely attached infants would become more socially and emotionally competent children and adults than those who were insecurely attached. Studies conducted in industrialized, independent cultures support the competence hypothesis. However, Rothbaum and colleagues (Rothbaum et al., 2000; Rothbaum & Morelli, 2005) have argued that the security–competence link needs to be considered within cultural contexts. For example, secure attachment has been theorized to be linked to direct communication and emotional openness (e.g., Bretherton, 1990). Yet, in cultures such as Puerto Rico, attachment security is associated with respect, obedience, and calmness, rather than self-expression (Harwood, 1992). And in Japan, coordinating one's needs with those of others is seen as essential to the goals of interpersonal unity and harmony. Thus, negative feelings are kept to oneself or expressed indirectly. Dependence on others is also more likely to be associated with attachment competence as prescribed in Japanese culture (Rothbaum, Kakinuma, Nagaoka, & Azuma, 2007). Thus, as with other propositions, the impact of attachment organization needs to be fully explored from a sociocultural as well as a universal perspective.

*Summary*
Focusing on the regularities of behaviors, attachment theorists tend to draw attention to the universality of attachment propositions. Nevertheless, the development of attachment may be best described as the interplay between biological and cultural input (Van IJzendoorn, Bakermans-Kranenburg, & Sagi-Schwartz, 2006). The recent call for reconsideration of cultural variations points to potentially divergent expressions and interpretations of secure attachment and sensitive caregiving. Moreover, the competence hypothesis is insufficiently tested cross-culturally and research is needed to examine the issue of sequelae more fully (Van IJzendoorn & Sagi-Schwartz, 2008).

# Temperament

## Thomas and Chess' Profiles

One of the most important contributions to the field of child development was the recognition that individual personality differences are evident at birth and do not simply emerge due to varying parental practices. Widespread appreciation of temperament can be traced to the pioneering work of child psychiatrists Alexander Thomas and Stella Chess in the New York Longitudinal Study. Since their introduction of the concept (Thomas & Chess, and colleagues, 1963, 1968, 1970, 1977), specific definitions of temperament have varied (see Goldsmith et al., 1987) but it is generally agreed that it refers to relatively consistent and stable behavioral differences among individuals that are genetically and biologically based.

From parental interviews, Thomas and Chess proposed nine dimensions on which infants appeared to differ (*sensory threshold, approach-withdrawal, reaction intensity, adaptability, predominant mood, rhythmicity, activity, distractibility,* and *persistence*). Based on clustering of these attributes, they clinically identified three temperament constellations. Infants with an *easy* temperament eagerly approach and adapt to novelty, exhibit low-to-moderate intensity reactions, are generally positive in mood, and readily establish routines. In contrast, *difficult* infants reject novel experiences, display intense and frequent negative reactions, and exhibit irregularity in their daily patterns. Finally, *slow-to-warm-up* infants have low activity levels, low-intensity reactions, respond to novelty with mild negativity, and adapt to it slowly. Thomas and Chess acknowledged that temperament was not immutable; environmental qualities could moderate or heighten characteristics. Nonetheless, they argued that a basic constancy of attributes was seen for most children. In terms of the distribution of profiles among the 141 infants in their sample, they found that approximately 40% qualified as easy, 15% as slow-to-warm-up, and 10% as difficult (Thomas et al., 1970).

In addition to formulating temperament profiles, Thomas and Chess proposed a connection to long-term adjustment. Of the nearly 30% of their sample who longitudinally showed clinical-level disturbances, those with a difficult constellation accounted for the largest proportion and those labeled slow-to-warm-up the next largest. An astounding 70% of difficult children, compared to 18% of easy participants, presented with problems requiring clinical intervention (Thomas et al., 1970). However, rather than suggesting that temperament alone predicted adjustment, Thomas and Chess proposed the concept of *goodness-of-fit*. That is, how well a child's environment accommodates his/her dispositional make-up greatly influences healthy psychosocial adjustment. A given set of circumstances will not have an identical impact on all children. It is the severity and duration of dissonance between environmental demand characteristics and a child's temperamental qualities that predict the likelihood of ensuing problems (Thomas et al., 1968, 1970).

Thomas and Chess based their work on a homogeneous sample of predominantly Jewish, educated, middle- and upper-class New York City families. Although Thomas and colleagues (Thomas et al., 1970) suggested that their dimensions and profiles could be used to characterize a range of populations, the ultimate utility of their approach has been challenged (Sanson, Hemphill, & Smart, 2002). The broad typologies have not been consistently useful in capturing temperament differences in other cultures. For example, in one study of Italian infants (Axia & Weisner, 2002), an overwhelming majority (90%) were easy. Other work suggested that many Chinese, Japanese, and Navajo neonates would be similarly characterized in this way (see Freedman & DeBoer, 1979), although much of this anthropological work preceded the popularity of Thomas and Chess' descriptions. Such findings not only suggest cultural differences in temperament, but also imply that within some cultures, the range of infant dispositional differences when using Thomas and Chess' broad typologies would be insufficient to study the role of temperament in developmental outcomes (Axia & Weisner, 2002).

The general consensus is that Thomas and Chess' dimensions and clusters are not universally applicable across cultures. One issue is that some traits may be interpreted, and thus measured, quite differently outside the U.S. For example, in a study of Malay infants (Bank, 1989), high sensory thresholds for responsiveness were not ascribed because infants and children were expected and presumed to be extremely aware of stimuli, especially anything uncomfortable. Malay parents also typically did not challenge infants' rejection of non-social experiences (e.g., new foods) because rejection was considered decisive; thus the concept of adaptability may not have been comparably measured. A further issue is that components of the difficult profile might not be considered elements of diagnostic difficulty within a different culture (Attili, 1989), and follow-up studies of U.S. samples have failed to support the constellations (Sanson et al., 2002). For example, rhythmicity and intensity—key components of the original conceptualization of difficultness—did not consistently relate to its other components (Daniels, Plomin, & Greenhalgh, 1984). Thus, developmentalists today concur that infants differ in temperament both within and across cultures, but do not advocate the framework established by Thomas and Chess. Recall that even a large percentage of the original sample (35%) could not be categorized into one of the three profiles (Thomas et al., 1970).

Further research on developmental outcomes soon suggested that the original clusters and their labels are inappropriately value-laden especially cross-culturally (Sanson et al., 2002). For example, in a study of working-class Puerto-Rican families in the U.S. (Korn & Gannon, 1983), characteristics of difficultness were not perceived as problematic and were not associated with later adjustment problems. Rather, because Puerto Rican parents made relatively few demands of their young children, the rearing environment did not conflict with the difficult constellation. Similarly, in his classic study of Masai infants in Kenya, DeVries (1984) also reported findings counter to Western expectations that infants with difficult temperaments are at greater risk for problems. On the contrary, mortality was greater for infants with an easy temperament because they received less attention and feeding compared to difficult counterparts. Such findings lent strong support for Thomas and Chess' proposition of goodness-of-fit; i.e., that different temperament characteristics are desirable depending on the context (Sanson et al., 2002) and that it is dissonance between environmental demands and temperament that leads to problems (Thomas et al., 1970). Despite the rejection of typologies (see Daniels et al., 1984), Thomas and Chess' conceptualization of the impact of temperament on a child's transactions with his/her environment is considered universally applicable both within and across cultures.

## Modern perspectives on temperament

In contrast to Thomas and Chess' clinical method, Mary Rothbart and her colleagues took a theoretical approach to identifying core constructs of temperament. Using a series of questionnaires developed to assess behavioral patterns in infants, toddlers, preschoolers, and school-aged children, a three-factor temperament structure emerged in data from infancy through childhood (Rothbart, 2007; Sanson et al., 2002). *Negative reactivity* reflects emotional mood and intensity and may be differentiated into anger and fearfulness. *Effortful control* refers to behavioral or physiological processes involving self-regulation that can modulate reactivity. *Inhibition/sociability* captures the tendency to approach or withdraw from novel situations and people, and includes positive affectivity. Rothbart (2007) has argued that although individual variations in components are genetic predispositions, environmental influences can further alter individual characteristics.

When using translated questionnaires, similar broad dimensions of temperament are often found in parental assessments across cultures. For example, the dimensions of emotionality and sociability were meaningfully derived from reports by American and Russian mothers of 3- to- 12-month-olds (Gartstein,

Knyazev, & Slobodskaya, 2005). A similar basic structure of temperament characteristics also emerged from Chinese, Japanese, and Australian parents' reports of their preschool- and school-aged children. Despite some minor variation, the three broad dimensions were extroversion/surgency, negative affectivity, and effortful control (Ahadi, Rothbart, & Ye, 1993; Rothbart, Ahadi, Hershey, & Fisher, 2001; Sanson, Smart, Prior, Oberklaid, & Pedlow, 1994). Thus, when taking an etic approach, where instruments devised in the U.S. were translated and applied directly to another culture, similar broad dimensions of temperament described infants and children within other cultures. However, these efforts have not resulted in identifying temperament characteristics or constellations that are unique to diverse cultures.

In taking an emic approach to potentially capture culture-specific aspects of temperament, Shwalb, Shwalb, and Shoji (1994) first asked Japanese mothers to freely describe their infants' behavioral styles; a standardized inventory followed. Many dimensions that emerged from analysis were similar to those found when using Western instruments. Yet, unique dimensions also appeared such as dependency/indulgence, which may be a reflection of the cultural emphasis on symbiotic harmony (Rothbaum et al., 2000) and on intense relatedness within Japanese mother–infant dyads. Even for dimensions that were conceptually similar to those found in Western research, the content differed. For example, "buries head in neck when embraced" is an item for assessing sociability. The findings suggest that the perceptual salience of infant behaviors varies depending on culture. The Japanese mothers tended to focus on tendencies related to the mother–child relationship.

Cultures vary in their temperament ideals and parents are indeed motivated to observe child characteristics that are culturally desirable (Kohnstamm, 1989). For example, in Russia, happiness is perceived as a transient, fleeting phenomenon that should be hidden and concealed from others. Thus, it is not surprising that compared to American parents, Russian parents reported lower positive emotionality and higher negative emotionality in their infants (Gartstein, Slobodskaya, & Kinsht, 2003). Anchored in Asian cultural ideals for compliant, obedient, and reserved behavior, Chinese mothers rated their infants as more sootheable, fearful, and prone to distress than did parents from the U.S. and Spain (Gartstein et al., 2006; Hsu, Soong, Stigler, Hong, & Liang, 1981). Chinese mothers and fathers also rated their preschoolers as less emotional than their American counterparts (Porter et al., 2005). Additionally, Japanese mothers rated their preschoolers as more withdrawal-oriented and as expressing less positive affect than did American mothers (Windle, Iwawaki, & Lerner, 1988).

Although the above differences in parental perception of child temperament may be tainted by cultural values, standardized laboratory observations have confirmed cultural differences. Most researchers agree that Chinese, Japanese, and Korean infants and toddlers are less behaviorally reactive, excitable, expressive, and irritable than their American and European counterparts (e.g., Camras et al. 1998; Kagan et al., 1994). Genetic differences may account for the distinction (see Kagan, 2009) although molecular genetic techniques have not been employed to substantiate this argument. Consistent with previous findings, when responding to inoculation, Japanese 4-month-olds showed less intense initial negative affect and took less time to quiet down than American infants. Surprisingly, their cortisol response was greater than that of American infants (Lewis, Ramsay, & Kawakami, 1993). This finding suggests that Japanese infants are not less reactive than their American counterparts; they are simply less behaviorally reactive. Differences in cultural values and socialization practices can contribute to variations in reactivity. For example, maternal encouragement of interdependence and thus closer infant–mother proximity (e.g., Rothbaum et al., 2000) may lead to Japanese infants' reduced signaling of distress compared to European American counterparts (Lewis et al., 1993). Indeed, mothers' interaction styles that are unique to their cultures can influence the development of self-regulation (e.g., Feldman, Masalha, & Alony, 2006).

The relation between temperament and developmental consequences has revealed both universal patterns and cultural differences. In terms of commonality, dispositional regulation and emotionality are consistently linked to social and emotional outcomes. Similar to European American children, low negative emotionality combined with high regulatory control predicted greater social competence and behavioral adjustment in Chinese (Zhou, Eisenberg, Wang, & Reiser, 2004; Zhou et al., 2008) and Indonesian children (Eisenberg, Liew, & Pidada, 2004; Eisenberg, Pidada, & Liew, 2001). The linkage of low positive emotionality to internalizing problems, and low regulation combined with high negative emotionality to externalizing problems, are also consistently found in both American and Chinese school-aged children (Zhou, Lengua, & Wang, 2009).

Nevertheless, the relation of temperament to adjustment also has demonstrated cross-cultural differences. For example, based on teachers' reports, Chinese children with externalizing problems displayed higher positive and negative emotionality than those with no adjustment problems, whereas the two groups did not differ among European American children (Zhou et al., 2009). In addition, the three core dimensions of temperament exhibited different association patterns among American and Chinese children. American children who were high in effortful control tended to exhibit lower negative affectivity, whereas Chinese children who were high in effortful control were more likely to show lower extraversion/surgency (Ahadi et al., 1993; Rothbart, 2007). Such patterns suggest that developmental outcomes are guided by cultural preferences: temperament characterized by low distress is favored in American culture, whereas low outgoing behavior and high inhibition are valued in Chinese culture.

### Summary

In sum, even though temperament reflects constitutionally based individual differences, culture may influence its expression and outcome by determining adaptive values. Cultural values have a significant impact on socialization goals and practices, which may alter the expression of temperamental traits. Additionally, the fit between children's biology and cultural ideals—or lack thereof—plays a role in the consequent adjustment of children. The same temperamental predisposition may contribute to adaptive or maladaptive outcomes in different cultures, depending on the attached positive or negative connotations and meanings that ultimately influence socialization experiences (Chen & French, 2008).

## Conclusions

Traditionally, the field of developmental psychology has been dominated by knowledge generated from Western European or European American theorists and researchers studying middle-class children of similar heritage. Fortunately, the last half-century has seen an exploding interest in moving beyond ethnocentric assumptions of generality and toward an appreciation of child development within a wide range of human settings. Although the state of our knowledge is far from ideal, the field has made great progress in identifying and understanding similarities and variations in the development of children worldwide.

A review of several topics popularly addressed in undergraduate courses leads to a conclusion often applied in reviews of specific developmental domains— that is, child development is neither entirely uniform around the world, nor totally culturally unique (Berry et al., 1992). Commonalities emerged within each content area. As Piaget observed, the development of cognition undergoes some remarkably similar transitions and tendencies particularly during early childhood. It also appears that Erikson identified some important human developmental tasks or trends such as developing trust in one's caregivers, creating and constructing through play, building and assessing one's competence compared to others, and identifying one's integrated beliefs and sense of purpose as a grown member of society. Likewise, as Bowlby and Ainsworth elaborated, all young humans face the essential task of forming an attachment and thus develop strategies and expectations for close relationships and for relating to the social world. Infants within all cultures also display biologically based dispositional differences. Moreover, as Thomas and Chess argued, these temperamental qualities have ramifications on children's later well-being because they greatly impact their rearing transactions.

A review of research across cultures also elucidates some of the inadequacies and errors associated with our most popular assumptions regarding regularities in children's development. As Super and Harkness (1994) astutely remarked, "In all societies, most children grow up to be competent adults; an important contribution of systematic cross-cultural comparisons has been to show how competence can be variously defined and how children come to achieve it" (p. 96). Indeed there are differences in developmental goals and outcomes across cultures. For example, it is evident that ideal reasoning and cognitive problem-solving skills may differ according to culture, as do emerging patterns of attending and remembering. Moreover, we see that issues surrounding autonomy or identity are often not viewed with the same ideals or timetables as observed in European American culture. Likewise, issues of personal initiative may not have the same indispensability to humans in all settings, and thus may not be imbued with the significance that Erikson supposed. Further, we can recognize the potential for societal conceptions of parental sensitivity to differ as well as the potential for diverging cross-cultural models regarding security and human relationships. Finally, it clear that temperament ideals vary across cultures and many European American preferences such as heightened positivity or sociability are not equally desired by all communities.

Beyond simply identifying global similarities and differences, the field has come to appreciate the cultural structuring of child development (Super & Harkness, 1997) and thus recognizes that significant variations must ultimately be understood within the cultural context in which they are observed. Different paths of development are not arbitrarily linked to different socialization experiences. Rather, rearing practices emerge from the settings and values of the larger cultural community. As Super and Harkness (1986, 1997) articulated in their conceptualization of the developmental niche, the subcomponents operate as an integrated system. Interconnections between cultural practices, beliefs and settings must be understood in order to appreciate the variations in developmental patterns and outcomes. Otherwise, a decontextualized approach offers little meaning (Super & Harkness, 1997).

# References

Ahadi, S., Rothbart, M. K., & Ye, R. (1993). Children's temperament in the U.S. and China: Similarities and differences. *European Journal of Personality, 7,* 359–377.

Ainsworth, M. D. S. (1967). *Infancy in Uganda: Infant care and the growth of love.* Baltimore, MD: Johns Hopkins University Press.

Ainsworth, M. D. S., Blehar, M. C, Waters, E., & Wall, S. (1978). *Patterns of attachment: A psychological study of the Strange Situation.* Hillsdale, NJ: Lawrence Erlbaum Associates.

Attili, G. (1989). The psychology of character and temperament in Italy: A historical review and recent trends. In G. Kohnstamm, J. Bates, & M. K. Rothbart (Eds.), *Temperament in childhood* (pp. 581–596). New York: Wiley.

Axia, V., & Weisner, T. (2002). Infant stress reactivity and home cultural ecology of Italian infants and families. *Infant Behavior and Development, 25,* 255–268.

Bank, E. (1989). Temperament and individuality: A study of Malay children. *American Journal of Orthopsychiatry, 59,* 390–397.

Baumeister, R., & Muraven, M. (1996). Identity as adaptation to social, cultural, and historical context. *Journal of Adolescence, 19,* 405–416.

Berry, J., Poortinga, Y., Segall, M., & Dasen, P. (1992). *Cross-cultural psychology: Research and applications.* New York: Cambridge University Press.

Bornstein, M. H., Toda, S., Azuma, H., Tamis-Lemonda, C., & Ogino, M. (1990). Mother and infant activity and interaction in Japan and in the United Sates: II. A comparative microanalysis of naturalistic exchanges focused on the organization of infant attention. *International Journal of Behavioral Development, 13*, 289–308.

Bowlby, J. (1969/1982). *Attachment and loss: Vol. 1. Attachment* (2nd rev. ed.). New York: Basic Books.

Bretherton, I. (1990). Open communication and internal working models: Their role in the development of attachment relationships. In R. A. Thompson (Ed.), *Nebraska Symposium on Motivation, 1988: Socioemotional development* (pp. 57–113). Lincoln, NE: University of Nebraska Press.

Bretherton, I., & Munholland, K. (2008). Internal working models in attachment relationships: Elaborating a central construct in attachment theory. In J. Cassidy & P. Shaver (Eds.), *Handbook of attachment: Theory, research, and clinical applications* (2nd ed., pp. 102–127). New York: Guilford.

Butler, R. (1998). Age trends in the use of social and temporal comparison for self-evaluation: Examination of a novel developmental hypothesis. *Child Development, 69*, 1054–1073.

Camras, L., Oster, H., Campos, J., Campos, R., Ujiie, T., Miyake, K., Wang, L., & Meng, Z. (1998). Production of emotional facial expressions in European American, Japanese, and Chinese infants. *Developmental Psychology, 34*, 616–628.

Carlson, V. J., & Harwood, R. L. (2003). Attachment, culture, and the caregiving system: The cultural patterning of everyday experiences among Anglo and Puerto Rican mother–infant pairs. *Infant Mental Health Journal, 24*, 53–73.

Chavajay, P., & Rogoff, B. (1999). Cultural variation in management of attention by children and their caregivers. *Developmental Psychology, 35*, 1079–1090.

Chen, X., DeSouza, A., Chen, H., & Wang, L. (2006). Reticent behavior and experiences in peer interactions in Chinese and Canadian children. *Developmental Psychology, 42*, 656–665.

Chen, X., & French, D. C. (2008). Children's social competence in cultural context. *Annual Review of Psychology, 59*, 591–616.

Chen, X., Rubin, K., & Li, B. (1995). Social and school adjustment of shy and aggressive children in China. *Development and Psychopathology, 7*, 337–349.

Cherian, V., Kibria, G., Kiriuki, P., & Mwamwenda, T. (1988). Formal operational reasoning in African university students. *Journal of Psychology, 122*, 487–498.

Cole, M. (2006). Culture and cognitive development in phylogenetic, historical, and ontogenetic perspective. In W. Damon & R. Lerner (Series Eds.) & D. Kuhn & R. Siegler (Vol. Eds.), *Handbook of child psychology: Vol. 2. Cognition, perception, and language* (6th ed., pp. 636–683). New York: Wiley.

Cole, M., & Cagigas, X. (2010). Cognition. In M. Bornstein (Ed.), *Handbook of cultural developmental science* (pp. 127–142). New York: Psychology Press.

Correa-Chávez, M., & Rogoff, B. (2009). Children's attention to interactions directed to others: Guatemalan Mayan and European-American patterns. *Developmental Psychology, 45*, 630–641.

Correa-Chávez, M., Rogoff, B., & Arauz, R. M. (2005). Cultural patterns in attending to two events at once. *Child Development, 76*, 664–678.

Côté, J. E. (1996). Sociological perspectives on identity formation: The culture–identity link and identity capital. *Journal of Adolescence, 19*, 417–428.

Crain, W. (2005). *Theories of development: Concepts and applications* (5th ed.). Upper Saddle River, NJ: Pearson/Prentice Hall.

Daniels, D., Plomin, R., & Greenhalgh, J. (1984). Correlates of difficult temperament in infancy. *Child Development, 55*, 1184–1194.

Dasen, P. (1972). Cross-cultural Piagetian research: A summary. *Journal of Cross-Cultural Psychology, 3*, 23–40.

Dasen, P. (1975). Concrete operational development in three cultures. *Journal of Cross-Cultural Psychology, 6*, 156–172.

Dasen, P. (1977). *Piagetian psychology: Cross-cultural contributions*. New York: Gardner Press.

Dasen, P. (1994). Culture and cognitive development from a Piagetian perspective. In W. Lonner & R. Malpass (Eds.), *Psychology and culture* (pp. 145–149). Boston, MA: Allyn and Bacon.

Dasen, P., & Heron, A. (1981). Cross-cultural tests of Piaget's theory. In H. Triandis & A. Heron (Eds.), *Handbook of cross-cultural psychology: Vol. 4. Developmental psychology* (pp. 295–341). Boston, MA: Allyn and Bacon.

Deák, G. (2006). Do children really confuse appearance and reality? *Trends in Cognitive Sciences, 10*, 546–550.

De Lisi, R. & Staudt, J. (1980). Individual differences in college students' performance on formal operations tasks. *Journal of Applied Developmental Psychology, 1*, 201–208.

DeVries, M. (1984). Temperament and infant mortality among the Masai of East Africa. *American Journal of Psychiatry, 141*, 1189–1194.

De Wolff, M. S., & Van IJzendoorn, M. H. (1997). Sensitivity and attachment: A meta-analysis on parental antecedents of infant attachment. *Child Development, 68*, 571–591.

Duffy, S., Toriyama, R., Itakura, S., & Kitayama, S. (2009). Development of cultural strategies of attention in North American and Japanese children. *Journal of Experimental Child Psychology, 102*, 351–359.

Edwards, C. P. (2000). Children's play in cross-cultural perspective: A new look at the six cultures study. *Cross-Cultural Research, 34*, 318–338.

Eisenberg, N., Liew, J., & Pidada, S. (2004). The longitudinal relations of regulation and emotionality to quality of Indonesian children's socioemotional functioning. *Developmental Psychology, 40*, 790–804.

Eisenberg, N., Pidada, S., & Liew, J. (2001). The relations of regulation and negative emotionality to Indonesian children's social functioning. *Child Development, 72*, 1747–1763.

Erikson, E. H. (1963). *Childhood and society* (2nd ed.). New York: W. W. Norton.

Erikson, E. H. (1968). *Identity: Youth and crisis*. New York: W. W. Norton.

Fahrmeier, E. (1978). The decline of egocentrism in Hausa children. *Journal of Cross-Cultural Psychology, 9*, 191–200.

Farver J. M., Kim, Y. K., & Lee, Y. (1995). Cultural differences in Korean- and Anglo-American preschoolers' social interaction and play behaviors. *Child Development, 66*, 1088–1099.

Farver J. M., & Shin, Y. L. (1997). Social pretend play in Korean- and Anglo-American preschoolers. *Child Development, 68*, 544–556.

Farver J. M., & Shin, Y. L. (2000). Acculturation and Korean-American children's social and play behavior. *Social Development, 9*, 316–336.

Feldman, R., Masalha, S., & Alony, D. (2006). Microregulatory patterns of family interactions: Cultural pathways to toddlers' self-regulation. *Journal of Family Psychology, 20*, 614–623.

Fernald, A., & Morikawa, H. (1993). Common themes and cultural variations in Japanese and American mothers' speech to infants. *Child Development, 64*, 637–656.

Fivush, R., & Nelson, K. (2004).Culture and language in the emergence of autobiographical memory. *Psychological Science, 15*, 573–577.

Flavell, J. H. (1963). *The developmental psychology of Jean Piaget.* Princeton, NJ: Van Nostrand.

Flavell, J. H. (2000). Development of children's knowledge about the mental world. *International Journal of Behavioral Development, 24*, 15–23.

Flavell, J. H., Zhang, X.-D., Zou, H., Dong, Q., & Qi, S. (1983). A comparison of the appearance–reality distinction in the People's Republic of China and the United States. *Cognitive Psychology, 15*, 459–466.

Freedman, D., & DeBoer, M. (1979). Biological and cultural differences in early child development. *Annual Review of Anthropology, 8*, 579–600.

Gardiner, H. W., & Kosmitzki, C. (2008). *Lives across cultures: Cross-cultural human development* (4th ed.). Boston, MA: Pearson/Allyn and Bacon.

Gartstein, M., Gonzalez, C., Carranza, J., Ahadi, S., Ye, R., Rothbart, M. K., & Yang, S. W. (2006). Studying cross-cultural differences in the development of infant temperament: People's Republic of China, the United States of America, and Spain. *Journal of Child Psychiatry and Human Development, 37*, 145–161.

Gartstein, M., Knyazev, G., & Slobodskaya, H. (2005). Cross-cultural differences in the structure of infant temperament: U.S. and Russia. *Infant Behavior & Development, 28*, 54–61.

Gartstein, M., Slobodskaya, H., & Kinsht, I. (2003). Cross-cultural differences in temperament in the first year of life: U.S. and Russia. *International Journal of Behavioral Development, 27*, 316–328.

Gaskins, S. (2000). Children's daily activities in a Mayan village: A culturally grounded description. *Cross-Cultural Research, 34*, 375–389.

Gauvain, M. (1998). Cognitive development in social and cultural context. *Current Directions in Psychological Science, 7*, 188–192.

Gauvain, M. (2001). Cultural tools, social interaction and the development of thinking. *Human Development, 44*, 126–143.

Goldberg, S. (1972). Infant care and growth in urban Zambia. *Human Development, 15*, 77–89.

Goldsmith, H. H., Buss, A., Plomin, R., Rothbart, M. K., Thomas, A., Chess, S., Hinde, R., & McCall, R. (1987). What is temperament? Four approaches. *Child Development, 58*, 505–529.

Greenfield, P., & Childs, C. (1977). Understanding sibling concepts: A developmental study of kin terms in Zinacantan. In P. Dasen (Ed.), *Piagetian psychology: Cross-cultural contributions* (pp. 335–358). New York: Gardner Press.

Grossmann, K., Grossmann, K. E., Spangler, G., Suess, G., & Unzner, L. (1985). Maternal sensitivity and newborns' orientation responses as related to quality of attachment in northern Germany. *Monographs of the Society for Research in Child Development, 50* (1–2, serial no. 209), 233–256.

Han, J., Leichtman, M., & Wang, Q. (1998). Autobiographical memory in Korean, Chinese, and American children. *Developmental Psychology, 34,* 701–713.

Harter, S. (1998). The development of self-representations. In W. Daman (Series Ed.) & N. Eisenberg (Vol. Ed.), *Handbook of child psychology* (5th ed., pp. 553–617). New York: Wiley.

Harter, S. (2003). The development of self-representations during childhood and adolescence. In M. Leary & J. Tangney (Eds.), *Handbook of self and identity* (pp. 610–642). New York: Guilford.

Harter, S. (2006). The self. In W. Damon, & R. Lerner (Series Eds.), & N. Eisenberg (Vol. Ed.), *Handbook of child psychology: Vol. 3. Social, emotional, and personality development* (6th ed., pp. 505–570). New York: Wiley.

Harwood, R. L. (1992). The influence of culturally derived values on Anglo and Puerto Rican mothers' perceptions of attachment behavior. *Child Development, 63,* 822–839.

Hofter, J., Kärtner, J., Chasiotis, A., Busch, H., & Kiessling, F. (2007). Socio-cultural aspects of identity formation: The relationship between commitment and well-being in student samples from Cameroon and Germany. *Identity: An International Journal of Theory and Research, 7,* 265–288.

Hsu, C., Soong, W., Stigler, J., Hong, C., & Liang, C. (1981). The temperamental characteristics of Chinese babies. *Child Development, 52,* 1337–1340.

Kagan, J. (1977). The uses of cross-cultural research in early development. In P. Leiderman, S. Tulkin, & A. Rosenfield (Eds.), *Culture and infancy: Variations in the human experience* (pp. 271–286). New York: Academic Press.

Kagan, J. (2009). Emotions and temperament. In M. Bornstein (Ed.), *Handbook of cultural developmental science* (pp. 189–208). New York: Psychology Press.

Kagan, J., Arcus, D., Snidman, N., Feng, W. Y., Hendler, J., & Greene, S. (1994). Reactivity in infants: A cross-national comparison. *Developmental Psychology, 30,* 342–345.

Kagitcibasi, C. (2005). Autonomy and relatedness in cultural context: Implications for self and family. *Journal of Cross-Cultural Psychology, 36,* 403–422.

Keller, H. (2007). *Cultures of infancy.* Mahwah, NJ: Lawrence Erlbaum Associates.

Kermoian, R., & Leiderman, P. (1986). Infant attachment to mother and child caretaker in an East African community. *International Journal of Behavioral Development, 9,* 455–469.

Kiminyo, D. (1977). A cross-cultural study of the development of conservation of mass, weight, and volume among Kamba children. In P. Dasen (Ed.), *Piagetian psychology: Cross-cultural contributions* (pp. 64–88). New York: Gardner Press.

Kitayama, S., Duffy, S., Kawamura, T., & Larsen, J. (2003). Perceiving an object and its context in different cultures: A cultural look at New Look. *Psychological Science, 14,* 201–206.

Kitayama, S., & Uchida, Y. (2003). Explicit self-criticism and implicit self-regard: Evaluating self and friend in two cultures. *Journal of Experimental Social Psychology, 39,* 476–482.

Kohnstamm, G. (1989). Temperament in childhood: Cross-cultural and sex differences. In G. Kohnstamm, J. Bates, & M. K. Rothbart (Eds.), *Temperament in childhood* (pp. 483–508). New York: Wiley.

Kopp, C., Khoka, E., & Sigman, M. (1977). A comparison of sensorimotor development among infants in India and the United States. *Journal of Cross-Cultural Psychology, 8,* 435–451.

Korn, S., & Gannon, S. (1983). Temperament, cultural variation, and behavior disorder in preschool children. *Child Psychiatry & Human Development, 13*, 203–212.

Kuhn, D. (2008). Formal operations from a twenty-first century perspective. *Human Development, 51*, 48–55.

Kuhn, D., Langer, J., Kohlberg, L., & Haan, N. (1977). The development of formal operations in logical and moral judgment. *Genetic Psychology Monographs, 95*, 97–188.

Lamb, M. E., Thompson, R. A., Gardner, W., & Charnov, E. L. (1985). *Infant–mother attachment: The origins and developmental significance of individual differences in Strange Situation behavior*. Hillsdale, NJ: Lawrence Erlbaum Associates.

LeVine, R. A., & Norman, K. (2008). Attachment in anthropological perspective. In R. A. LeVine & R. S. New (Eds.), *Anthropology and child development: A cross-cultural reader* (pp. 127–142). Malden, MA: Blackwell.

Lewis, M., Ramsay, D., & Kawakami, K. (1993). Differences between Japanese infants and Caucasian American infants in behavioral and cortisol response to inoculation. *Child Development, 64*, 1722–1731.

Liu, M., Chen, X., Rubin, K., Zheng, S., Cui, L., Li, D., Chen, H., & Wang, L. (2005). Autonomy- vs connectedness-oriented parenting behaviours in Chinese and Canadian mothers. *International Journal of Behavioral Development, 29*, 489–495.

Low, J., Akande, D., & Hill, C. (2005). A cross-cultural comparison of identity development: South Africa and the United States. *Identity: An International Journal of Theory and Research, 5*, 303–314.

Marcia, J. E. (1966). Development and validation of ego identity status. *Journal of Personality and Social Psychology, 3*, 551–558.

Marsh, H., Ellis, L., & Craven, R. (2002). How do preschool children feel about themselves? Unraveling measurement and multidimensional self-concept structure. *Developmental Psychology, 38*, 376–393.

Meeus, W., Iedema, J., Helsen, M., & Vollebergh, W. (1999). Patterns of adolescent identity development: Review of literature and longitudinal analysis. *Developmental Review, 19*, 419–461.

Miyake, K., Chen, S. J., & Campos, J. J. (1985). Infant temperament, mother's mode of interaction, and attachment in Japan: An interim report. *Monographs of the Society for Research in Child Development, 50* (1–2, serial no. 209), 276–297.

Mizuta, I., Zahn-Waxler, C., Cole, P. M., & Hiruma, N. (1996). A cross-cultural study of preschoolers' attachment: Security and sensitivity in Japanese and US dyads. *International Journal of Behavioral Development, 19*, 141–159.

Morelli, G., Rogoff, B., Oppenheim, D., & Goldsmith, D. (1992). Cultural variations in infants' sleeping arrangements: Questions of independence. *Developmental Psychology, 28*, 604–613.

Neimark, E. (1979). Current status of formal operations research. *Human Development, 22*, 60–67.

Nisbett, R., Peng, K., Choi, I., & Norenzayan, A. (2001). Culture and systems of thought: Holistic versus analytic cognition. *Psychological Review, 108*, 291–310.

Ochse, R., & Plug, C. (1986). Cross-cultural investigation of the validity of Erikson's theory of personality development. *Journal of Personality and Social Psychology, 50*, 1240–1252.

Orbell, S. (1981). Formal operational thinking among African adolescents. *Journal of Instructional Psychology, 8*, 10–14.

Piaget, J. (1964/1969). Development and learning. In R. Ripple & V. Rockcastle (Eds.), *Piaget rediscovered* (pp. 7–20). Ithaca, NY: Cornell University Press (1969).

Piaget, J. (1964/1968). *Six psychological studies* (A. Tenzer & D. Elkind, Trans.). New York: Vintage Books (1968).

Piaget, J. (1972). Intellectual evolution from adolescence to adulthood (J. Bliss & H. Furth, Trans.). *Human Development, 15*, 1–12.

Porter, C. L., Hart, C. H., Yang, C., Robinson, C. C., Olsen, S. F., Zeng, Q., Olsen, J. A., & Jin, S. (2005). A comparative study of child temperament and parenting in Beijing, China and the western United States. *International Journal of Behavioral Development, 29*, 541–551.

Portes, P. R., Dunham, R., & Castillo, K. D. (2000). Identity formation and status across cultures: Exploring the cultural validity of Eriksonian theory. In A. L. Comunian, & U. Gielen (Eds.), *International perspectives on human development* (pp. 448–459). Lengerich, Netherlands: Pabst Science Publishers.

Posada, G., Gao, Y., Fang, W., Posada, R., Tascon, M., Schoelmerich, A., … Synnevaag, B. (1995). The secure base phenomenon across cultures: Children's behavior, mothers' preferences, and experts' concepts. *Monographs of the Society for Research in Child Development, 60* (1–2, serial no. 244), 27–48.

Posada, G., Jacobs, A., Carbonell, O., Alzate, G., Bustamante, M., & Arenas, A. (1999). Maternal care and attachment security in ordinary and emergency contexts. *Developmental Psychology, 35*, 1379–1388.

Posada, G., Jacobs, A., Richmond, M., Carbonell, O., Alzate, G., Bustamante, M., & Quiceno, J. (2002). Maternal caregiving and infant security in two cultures. *Developmental Psychology, 38*, 67–78.

Roer-Strier, D., & Rivlis, M. (1998). Timetable of psychological and behavioural autonomy expectations among parents from Israel and the former Soviet Union. *International Journal of Psychology, 33*, 123–135.

Rogoff, B. (2003). *The cultural nature of human development.* New York: Oxford University Press.

Rogoff, B., Mistry, J. J., Göncü, A., & Mosier, C. (1993). *Guided participation in cultural activity by toddlers and caregivers.* Monographs of the Society for Research in Child Development, 58 (1, serial no. 236).

Rothbart, M. K. (2007). Temperament, development, and personality. *Current Directions in Psychological Science, 16*, 207–212.

Rothbart, M. K., Ahadi, S., Hershey, K., & Fisher, P. (2001). Investigation of temperament at three to seven years: The Children's Behavior Questionnaire. *Child Development, 72*, 1394–1408.

Rothbaum, F., Kakinuma, M., Nagaoka, R., & Azuma, H. (2007). Attachment and amae: Parent–child closeness in the United States and Japan. *Journal of Cross-Cultural Psychology, 38*, 465–486.

Rothbaum, F., & Morelli, G. (2005). Attachment and culture: Bridging relativism and universalism. In W. Friedlmeier, P. Chakkarath, & B. Schwarz (Eds.), *Culture and human development: The importance of cross-cultural research for the social sciences* (pp. 99–123). New York: Psychology Press.

Rothbaum, F., Pott, M., Azuma, H., Miyake, K., & Weisz, J. (2000). The development of close relationships in Japan and the U.S.: Paths of symbiotic harmony and generative tension. *Child Development, 71*, 1121–1142.

Rubin, K., Hemphill, S., Chen, X., Hastings, P., Sanson, A., LoCoco, A., ... Doh, H. S. (2006). Parenting beliefs and behaviors: Initial findings from the International Consortium for the Study of Emotional and Social Development (ICSSED). In K. Rubin & O. B. Chung, *Parenting beliefs, behaviors, and parent–child relations: A cross-cultural perspective* (pp. 81–103). New York: Psychology Press.

Sagi, A., Lamb, M., Lewkowicz, K. S., Shoham, R., Dvir, R., & Estes, D. (1985). Security of infant–mother, –father, and –metapelet attachment among kibbutz-reared Israeli children. In I. Bretherton & E. Waters (Eds.), Growing points of attachment theory and research. *Monographs of the Society for Research in Child Development, 50* (1–2, serial no. 209), 257–275.

Sagi, A., Van IJzendoorn, M., Aviezer, O., Donnell, F., & Mayseless, O. (1994). Sleeping out of home in a kibbutz communal arrangement: It makes a difference for infant–mother attachment. *Child Development, 65,* 992–1004.

Sanson, A., Hemphill, S., & Smart, D. (2002). Temperament and social development. In P. Smith & C. Hart (Eds.), *Blackwell handbook of childhood social development* (pp. 97–116). London: Blackwell.

Sanson, A., Smart, D., Prior, M., Oberklaid, F., & Pedlow, R. (1994). The structure of temperament from ages 3 to 7 years: Age, sex and sociodemographic influence. *Merrill-Palmer Quarterly, 40,* 233–252.

Saxe, G. (1981). When fourth can precede second: A developmental analysis of an indigenous numeration system among Ponam Islanders in Papua New Guinea. *Journal of Cross-Cultural Psychology, 12,* 37–50.

Schwartz, S. J., & Hilda, P. (2006). Identity development in adolescence and emerging adulthood: The interface of self, context, and culture. In A. M. Columbus (Ed.), *Advances in psychology research, Vol. 45* (pp. 1–40). New York: Nova Science Publishers.

Segall, Dasen, Berry, & Poortinga (1999). *Human behavior in global perspective: An introduction to cross-cultural psychology.* Boston, MA: Allyn & Bacon.

Shayer, M., Demetriou, A., & Pervez, M. (1988). The structure and scaling of concrete operational thought: Three studies in four countries. *Genetic, Social, and General Psychology Monographs, 114,* 307–376.

Shea, J. D. (1985). Studies of cognitive development in Papua New Guinea. *International Journal of Psychology, 20,* 33–61.

Shiraev, E., & Levy, D. (2007). *Cross-cultural psychology: Critical thinking and contemporary applications* (3rd ed.). Boston, MA: Pearson/Allyn and Bacon.

Shwalb, B. J., Shwalb, D. W., & Shoji, J. (1994). Structure and dimensions of maternal perceptions of Japanese infant temperament. *Developmental Psychology, 30,* 131–141.

Sung, J., & Hsu, H. (2009). Korean mothers' attention regulation and referential speech: Associations with language and play in one-year-olds. *International Journal of Behavioral Development, 33,* 430–439.

Super, C., & Harkness, S. (1986). The developmental niche: A conceptualization at the interface of child and culture. *International Journal of Behavioral Development, 9,* 545–570.

Super, C., & Harkness, S. (1994). The developmental niche and culture. In W. Lonner & R. Malpass (Eds.), *Psychology and culture* (pp. 95–99). Boston, MA: Allyn & Bacon.

Super, C., & Harkness, S. (1997). The cultural structuring of child development. In J. Berry, P. Dasen, & T. S. Saraswathi (Eds.), *Handbook of cross-cultural psychology: Vol. 2, Basic processes and human development* (2nd ed., pp. 1–39). Boston, MA: Allyn & Bacon.

Takahashi, K. (1990). Are the key assumptions of the "Strange Situation" procedure universal? A view from Japanese research. *Human Development, 33*, 23–30.

Taylor, R. D., & Oskay, G. (1995). Identity formation in Turkish and American late adolescents. *Journal of Cross-Cultural Psychology, 26*, 8–22.

Thomas, A., & Chess, S. (1977). *Temperament and development*. New York: Brunner/Mazel.

Thomas, A., Chess, S., & Birch, H. (1968). *Temperament and behavior disorders in children*. New York: New York University Press.

Thomas, A., Chess, S., & Birch, H. G. (1970). The origin of personality. *Scientific American, 223*, 102–109.

Thomas, A., Chess, S., Birch, H., Hertzig, M., & Korn, S. (1963). *Behavioral individuality in early childhood*. New York: New York University Press.

Trawick-Smith, J. (2010). *Early childhood development: A multicultural perspective* (5th ed.). Upper Saddle River, NJ: Merrill.

Tronick, E. Z., Morelli, G. A., & Ivey, P. K. (1992). The Efe forager infant and toddler's pattern of social relationships: Multiple and simultaneous. *Developmental Psychology, 28*, 568–577.

Tronick, E. Z., Morelli, G. A., & Winn, S. (2008). Multiple caregiving in the Ituri forest. In R. A. LeVine & R. S. New (Eds.), *Anthropology and child development: A cross-cultural reader* (pp. 73–83). Malden, MA: Blackwell.

True, M. M., Pisani, L., & Oumar, F. (2001). Infant–mother attachment among the Dogon of Mali. *Child Development, 72*, 1451–1466.

Tulkin, S., & Konner, M. (1973). Alternative conceptions of intellectual functioning. *Human Development, 16*, 33–52.

Valenzuela, M. (1990). Attachment in chronically underweight young children. *Child Development, 61*, 1984–1996.

Valenzuela, M. (1997). Maternal sensitivity in a developing society: The context of urban poverty and infant chronic undernutrition. *Developmental Psychology, 33*, 845–855.

Van IJzendoorn, M., Bakermans-Kranenburg, M., & Sagi-Schwartz, A. (2006). Attachment across diverse sociocultural contexts: The limits of universality. In K. H. Rubin & O. B. Chung (Eds.), *Parenting beliefs, behaviors, and parent–child relations: A cross-cultural perspective* (pp. 107–142). New York: Psychology Press.

Van IJzendoorn, M. & Kroonenberg, P. (1988). Cross-cultural patterns of attachment: A meta-analysis of the Strange Situation. *Child Development, 59*, 147–156.

Van IJzendoorn, M., & Sagi, A. (1999). Cross-cultural patterns of attachment: Universal and contextual dimensions. In J. Cassidy & P. R. Shaver (Eds.), *Handbook of attachment: Theory, research, and clinical applications* (pp. 713–734). New York: Guilford Press.

Van IJzendoorn, M. &, A. (2008). Cross-cultural patterns of attachment: Universal and contextual Sagi-Schwartz dimensions. In J. Cassidy & P. Shaver (Eds.), *Handbook of attachment: Theory, research, and clinical applications* (2nd ed., pp. 880–905). New York: Guilford.

Vereijken, C., Riksen-Walraven, J., & Kondo-Ikemura, K. (1997). Maternal sensitivity and infant attachment security in Japan: A longitudinal study. *International Journal of Behavioral Development, 21*, 35–49.

Vigil, DC (2002). Cultural variations in attention regulation: A comparative analysis of British and Chinese-immigrant populations. *International Journal of Language Disorders, 37*, 433–458.

Wang, Q. (2003). Infantile amnesia reconsidered: A cross-cultural analysis. *Memory, 11*, 65–80.

Wang, Q. (2006). Relations of maternal style and child self-concept to autobiographical memories in Chinese, Chinese immigrant, and European-American 3-year-olds. *Child Development, 77*, 1794–1809.

Wang, Q., & Fivush, R. (2005). Mother–child conversations of emotionally salient events: Exploring the functions of emotional reminiscing in European-American and Chinese families. *Social Development, 14*, 473–495.

Wang, Q., & Leichtman, M. (2000). Same beginnings, different stories: A comparison of American and Chinese children's narratives. *Child Development, 71*, 1329–1346.

Wang, Q., & Ross, M. (2007). Culture and memory. In S. Kitayama & D. Cohen (Eds.), *Handbook of Cultural Psychology* (pp. 645–667). New York: Guilford.

Wang, W., & Viney, L. (1997). The psychosocial development of children and adolescents in the People's Republic of China: An Eriksonian approach. *International Journal of Psychology, 32*, 139–153.

Wang, Y., Wiley, A., & Zhou, X. (2007). The effect of different cultural lens on reliability and validity of observational data: The example of Chinese immigrant parent–toddler dinner interactions. *Social Development, 16*, 777–799.

White, K., & Ferstenberg, A. (1978). Professional specialization and formal operations: The balance task. *Journal of Genetic Psychology, 133*, 97–104.

Windle, M., Iwawaki, S., & Lerner, R. M. (1988). Cross-cultural comparability of temperament among Japanese and American preschool children. *International Journal of Psychology. 23*, 547–567.

Yamaguchi, S., Greenwald, A., Banaji, M., Murakami, F., Chen, D., Shiomura, K., … Krendl, A. (2007). Apparent universality of positive explicit self-esteem. *Psychological Science, 18*, 498–500.

Yovsi, R. D., Kärtner, J., Keller, H., & Lohaus, A. (2009). Maternal interactional quality in two cultural environments: German middle class and Cameroonian rural mothers. *Journal of Cross-Cultural Psychology, 40*, 701–707.

Zach, U., & Keller, H. (1999). Patterns of attachment–exploration balance of 1-year-old infants from the United States and northern Germany. *Journal of Cross-Cultural Psychology, 30*, 381–388.

Zhou, Q., Eisenberg, N., Wang, Y., & Reiser, M. (2004). Chinese children's effortful control and dispositional anger/frustration: Relations to parenting styles and children's social functioning *Developmental Psychology, 40*, 352–366.

Zhou, Q., Lengua, L. J., & Wang, Y. (2009). The relations of temperament reactivity and effortful control to children's adjustment problems in China and the United States. *Developmental Psychology, 45*, 724–739.

Zhou, Q., Wang, Y., Deng, X., Eisenberg, N., Wolchik, S., & Tein, J.-Y. (2008). Relations of parenting and temperament to Chinese children's experience of negative life events, coping efficacy, and externalizing problems. *Child Development, 79*, 493–513.

# 6

# Cultural Variations
# in Perceptions of Aging

## James T. Gire

The past two decades have witnessed a tremendous increase in the population of the elderly, and estimates indicate that the rising elder population in the next two decades will be even more dramatic. Whereas the global population is expected to increase by 50% from 6 billion in 2000 to 9 billion in 2025, the population of the elderly, defined as those who are 60 years of age and older, is projected to grow by 300% within the same period. This increase in the absolute and relative number of the elderly will be much steeper in the developing world where it is expected to increase by 400% (United Nations Population Division, 2003). Thus, unlike the patterns observed in the middle of the twentieth century and earlier, when aging was a developed world phenomenon, the anticipated shift in demographic patterns will also encompass the developing world. According to the United Nations Population Division (2003) the year 2000 marked the first time when there were more people aged 60 years and older than children under 5 years of age in some developing countries. It is obvious that this rapid increase in the elderly population will impact all aspects of society. Therefore, it is imperative to gain a better understanding of the aging experience in order to ensure and enhance the well-being of the elderly and foster a greater understanding between demographic categories.

One area that has received research interest is the way in which the elderly are perceived. Therefore, this chapter will discuss the influence of cultural factors on perceptions of aging and their link to the physical and psychological well-being of the elderly. These perceptions—images, stereotypes, and attitudes about the old and about growing older—are important because they influence the way in which the elderly are treated, and often influence the way in which the elderly view themselves (e.g., Butler, 1980). Research has also indicated that both positive and negative perceptions of aging are associated with mental, affective, and cognitive well-being of individuals approaching the transition from middle adulthood into late adulthood. In some instances, there is a relationship between positive self perceptions of aging and longevity (e.g., Levy & Langer, 1994; Levy, Slade, Kunkel, & Kasl, 2002).

However, culture, rather than an individual's personal experiences of aging, appears to have a greater influence on perceptions of aging. A good deal of past research has found important differences across cultures in their beliefs about old age and attitudes toward the elderly (e.g., Brewer, Dull, & Lui, 1981; Levy, 1999; Levy & Langer, 1994; Schmidt & Boland, 1986). The fact that these perceptions are not usually biologically determined, means that they can vary, and indeed have varied, even within the same cultures over time. Thus, the source and flavor of our perceptions are determined by the prevailing beliefs and conditions in a given society over time. Because of intercultural communication, it is not surprising that there are also cultural similarities in perceptions of aging. The advent of globalization, greatly enhanced by advances in information and communication technology, is expected to result in even greater similarities, particularly among the educated class, across cultures. Regardless of the origins of perceptions of the elderly, they influence the views people across the age strata hold about their current and future selves with respect to physical declines, social roles, anxiety about aging, living arrangements and intergenerational relations. These issues will be examined in turn.

## Physical Declines

The most obvious image that comes to mind when most people talk about aging appears to be the physical declines that accompany longevity. However, it has become increasingly obvious to researchers that not everyone grows old in the same way. In fact, throughout history, societies have differed markedly in the meaning they have given to the same features of aging; these differences have also occurred in the same society across different times. A range of characterizations of aging includes positive, negative, ambivalent, and sometimes even contradictory images. These attitudes and perceptions have tended to mirror the successes, problems and challenges of aging arising from the social, political, cultural, and economic variables prevalent in a given society at the time.

Before we proceed, we need to make a distinction between primary and secondary aging. *Primary aging* refers to the irreversible (disease-free) changes in the biological, psychological, or sociocultural processes that arise as a normal course of development. *Secondary aging*, on the other hand, involves changes that are related to diseases (e.g., Alzheimer's and arthritis), lifestyle (e.g., smoking or diet), or environmental events (e.g., pollution or climate) that are not universally shared.

It had been presumed that negative views of aging were a recent phenomenon, a byproduct of major changes in economic development, aided by developments such as industrialization, which reshaped the balance of power between young adults and the elderly. However, the oldest reported work on depictions of the elderly by philosopher poet Ptah-hotep in Egypt in 2500 BC (cited in de Beauvoir, 1972) painted a rather bleak picture of aging:

How hard and painful are the last days of an aged man! He grows weaker every day; his eyes become dim, his ears deaf; his strength fades; his heart knows peace no longer; his mouth falls silent and he speaks no word. The power of his mind lessens and today he cannot remember what yesterday was like. All his bones hurt. Those things which not long ago were done with pleasure are painful now; and taste vanishes. Old age is the worst of misfortunes that can afflict a man. His nose is blocked, and he can smell nothing any more. (p. 92)

This very negative portrayal of the elderly was a largely Western conception, however. Ancient Asia had very positive images of aging, influenced by Confucian principles that extolled the virtues of old age. In describing moral development, Confucius suggested that great wisdom was to be found only in the latter stages of life (quoted in Achenbaum, 2005, p. 21):

At fifteen, I applied myself to wisdom; at thirty, I grew stronger at it; at forty I no longer had doubts; at sixty there was nothing on earth that could shake me; at seventy I could follow the dictates of my heart without disobeying the moral law.

The preeminence of age over other factors in Chinese society at the time ensured that older women had more authority than their sons and daughters (Thang, 2000).

Yet even in early Western civilization, images of the elderly were not always negative. In ancient Greece, Sparta was said to be ruled by a *gerousia*, which was a council of men who were at least 60 years of age, at the beginning of the seventh century BCE. This "council of elders" was selected on the basis of their wisdom, and they were expected to exercise their authority prudently. A similar view of aging was advanced by Cicero (106–43 BCE) who argued that what the elderly gained in wisdom based on years of experience, and characterized by reflection, force of character, and judgment, more than made up for the physical declines in muscle, speed, or physical dexterity (Achenbaum, 2005).

What is evident from these accounts is that perceptions of the elderly, and attitudes toward aging, derived from the physical characteristics of the aged, were usually correlated with chronological age, and have routinely associated old age with decline. The portrayed physical declines notwithstanding, perceptions of the aged have not been uniform across time, as indicated earlier. Negative views of aging and the elderly have been interspersed with positive images at other times in all societies. These changing perceptions may be due to several factors, but we will dwell on two such factors in this section: demographic patterns and economic transformation.

## Demographic patterns

Historically, old people have constituted a very small segment of society, seldom surpassing 2% of the population at any given time (Hauser, 1976). In fact, infant mortality rates were very high even at the beginning of the twentieth century.

In India, for example, Robinson (1989) reported that only one in three babies in Bombay survived to celebrate their first birthday. Considering that the definition of old age as beginning around the age of 65 years of age, plus or minus 15 years, has not changed, at least in Europe and North America, since 1700 (Harris, 1988), there were very few elderly in society. These small numbers made the elderly appear almost as strangers in the land of the young, a view that was unlikely to result in very positive images. If prejudice is presumed to derive, at least in part, from unfamiliarity with the targeted group, perceptions of the old as unfamiliar, unusual, and even worthy of suspicion and contempt, is not surprising. This dearth in numbers also meant that the aged had very limited support networks of their peers. Because most members of their generation had been lost to death, the elderly increasingly found themselves concerned with issues of very little interest to the young. Rather than living in the present or making plans for the future, they appeared to be preoccupied with the past. This, coupled with absence of social support of their age cohort, meant that the elderly were being cared for by the young. The end result was relatively negative perceptions of old age, by the elderly themselves, as lonely and dependent.

If the argument about demographic patterns holds, then it might explain the current upswing in attitudes toward the elderly in the West, and suggests that perceptions of the elderly should witness a more positive outlook with changes in the proportion of the elderly in the population. The example of Chile is suggestive of the changing demographic patterns of the future that could influence perceptions of the elderly. Of the cohort born in 1909, only 63% reached the age of 5 years, and only 13% were expected to live more than 85 years. In contrast, a mere 2% of the 1999 cohort had died before age 5 and at least 50% were projected to celebrate their eighty-fifth birthday (World Health Organization, 1999). With this expected dramatic change in demographic patterns, it is difficult to imagine that it will not impact the perceptions of aging. In democratic societies, this influence may be driven by political considerations as the elderly constitute a viable voting block that can influence election outcomes and policies. A glimpse of this effect can be inferred from the 2007–2008 primary and general election campaigns of candidates for the American presidency. It is no coincidence that health care (Medicare) and retirement (social security), two issues that are critical for elder well-being, received comparatively greater emphasis in states such as Arizona and Florida from the major candidates in the presidential election. These two states happen to have very large proportions of older voters.

## Economic transformation

Changes in the way in the elderly are perceived in different societies and within the same society over time, may have origins in the economic power that older people have held at different times. Achenbaum (2005) argued that during the times when agricultural activities were the predominant mode of economic attainment, the elderly were in a favorable position for a number of reasons. They had the know-how of agricultural production accrued from past experience, and even though they were diminished in physical strength, they had agricultural management skills and could supervise the work of others. Furthermore, because they had control over land, they had some measure of economic security. Children worked the land for their parents or grandparents, in the hope of getting title to these lands in the future. The elders ensured that they had made adequate provisions for themselves before they transferred ownership of the land. The belief, especially in more traditional societies, that elders were associated with magic powers thought to impact the viability of the land, further strengthened the position of the elderly.

The Industrial Revolution (late eighteenth century) suddenly changed the balance of power, and the economic status of the elderly declined significantly. Industrialization altered both the mode of production and patterns of consumption. Because machines could now perform the tasks hitherto performed manually, the elderly lost the expertise that was their strongest suit. In the new scheme of things, bureaucratic expertise, as opposed to preeminence in the family, became more valued, making it difficult for the elderly to cope with these changes and rendering older workers basically obsolete (Haber & Gratton, 1994). Particularly at the early stages of the Industrial Revolution, the elderly were treated as if they were disabled. Retirement programs were instituted mainly to get rid of workers whose skills were not valuable and were thus expendable (Achenbaum, 2005).

The preceding argument may provide a partial explanation for differences in elder perceptions across cultures, especially in the period following industrialization. The Industrial Revolution was principally in the West and only recently became a predominant influence in the developing world. To the extent that economic transformation was related to changing perceptions of the elderly, it would imply that countries in which industrialization took hold should display more unfavorable attitudes toward aging and the elderly. Indeed, some past research has found that Eastern societies adopt a more positive view of aging than Western cultures. Aging is associated with an increased reverence and a greater bearing in countries such as Japan, China, and South Korea, whereas North Americans appear to be more youth-oriented and hold more negative beliefs regarding the aging process (e.g., Chang, Chang, & Shen, 1984; Levy & Langer, 1994; Sung, 1994).

Considering the influence of industrialization and the more recent and powerful impact of information technology, views of aging would be more variegated even in non-Western cultures. That more recent studies would find mixed and inconsistent results, attests to this fact. For example, in an investigation of actual and ideal age-old concepts in China, India, and South Korea, Barak, Mathur, Lee, and Zhang (2001) reported trends similar to those found in Western societies. Arnhoff, Leon, and Lorge (1964) suggested that negative social attitudes toward the elderly are presumed to result in lower status and consequently, diminished roles for older people in the U.S. To the extent that this holds true, societies with more positive views of the elderly should be characterized by enhanced, or at least non-diminished, status and more positive roles for the elderly.

## Social Roles

An obvious way in which attitudes about and perceptions of aging can impact the elderly is manifested in the roles assigned to older adults in society, or roles older adults are presumed or expected to play. Researchers have used a variety of ways of inferring roles for the elderly, involving the portrayal of older adults in advertising, in examining images of older adults in children's drawings, and asking different segments of the population their views of elder roles. Some researchers (e.g., Frith, Shaw, & Cheng, 2005; Srikandath, 1991) have suggested that advertisements can provide a broad revelation of what cultures value, who is deemed to be important in a culture, and how certain groups and roles are represented in differing status positions. Using this premise that advertisements represent the prevailing ethos in a particular society, Raman, Harwood, Weis, Anderson, and Miller (2008) examined portrayals of older adults, as well as other groups, across a number of magazine advertisements in the U.S. and India to see how the elderly are valued and represented in the two cultures.

The results revealed very interesting cross-cultural similarities and differences. One of the similarities was the underrepresentation of the elderly (and the young) in advertisements in general, consistent with other studies suggesting an underrepresentation of the "tails" of the lifespan in media images (Harwood & Anderson, 2002). Cultural differences appeared in the kind of products with which the elderly were associated. In the U.S., the elderly were more often featured with health products, an indication of the negative stereotypes about old age and health. In India, on the other hand, older models were more extensively associated with advertisements for financial services, a finding that, in the opinion of Raman et al. (2008), was a reflection of the increasing financial uncertainty that may be related to the rapidly changing family structure in India. Another difference was in the portrayal of older adults in the U.S. with age peers while their Indian counterparts were associated with large extended families. This may be a reflection of differences in culturally appropriate roles for the elderly in the two cultures. This has implications for intergenerational relationships and living arrangements that will be discussed in the next section. Older peers may play a significant role in the U.S. because of age-segregated living arrangements in planned retirement communities. In India, however, the family is the focus for older adults, and they tend to live with or near their oldest child (usually the son).

Cultural differences in social roles for the elderly can also be inferred from the manner in which children view their grandparents. Hummel, Rey, and d'Epinay

(1995) examined drawings of grandmothers and grandfathers of 9,606 children, ages 6–14 years, in six countries: Bulgaria, the then Czechoslovakia, Guatemala, India, The Netherlands, and Switzerland. From an analysis of the drawings, the authors were able to identify three typologies. The first reflected a depiction of grandparents living alone, and spending time in leisure and self-care, an indication that they no longer had a viable social role in society. This was reflective of Switzerland and deemed to represent most of what obtained in industrialized European countries. The second typology also described grandparents as being isolated; however, they appeared to have the same roles as other adults that fit in the traditional gender-role division of labor, with grandmothers functioning mainly in the kitchen and grandfathers involved with outside work. This was represented mainly in Bulgarian drawings and associated with countries in which agriculture still plays an important role. The third typology was suggestive of grandparents as strongly integrated into society but primarily in a caregiving role. This was portrayed in drawings from India and converges somewhat with the Raman et al. (2008) findings in portrayals of the elderly in advertisements mentioned earlier in this section.

Societal expectations about roles for the elderly can also be obtained from asking people in different cultures to state the functions performed by or expected of older adults. Eyetsemitan and Gire (2003) conducted a seven-country study exploring several processes about aging in the developing world. The study included Bahrain, Bangladesh, Botswana, Brazil, Chile, Indonesia, and Nigeria. These nations are from different parts of the world and represented the low, medium, and high rankings of the United Nations Human Development Index (HDI). With respect to roles for the elderly, the authors found that older adults were expected to offer advice on both family and community disputes. They were also expected to preside over important social and spiritual functions, and were expected to be wise. These are very active roles for the elderly and would be considered a good way to age, from the standpoint of *activity theory* (Maddox, 1964).

However, this expected high level of activity seems to reflect Erikson's (1959) middle adulthood stage of *generativity versus stagnation* more than *ego integrity versus despair* that he theorized to characterize the late adulthood stage. In Erikson's late adulthood stage, ego integrity versus despair involves focusing on finding meaning to life through a review of what has transpired in one's life, rather than feeling despair or bitterness. This implies a shift in attention from other to self. The findings from Eyetsemitan and Gire's (2003) study suggest that Erikson's theory may apply to individualistic societies that may be related to the developed world dimension (Eyetsemitan, 2002) but that the shift from other to self may not be applicable to collectivist cultures that typically reflect the developing world dimension. This interpretation is consistent with the discussion of Erikson's stages in Chapter 5 of this volume. Even though they limit their discussion to the four of Erikson's eight stages that are presumed to occur in childhood, Molitor and Hsu point out that Erikson believed his stages to be culturally universal. However, they also cite numerous sources that question the presumptions of cultural universality in Erikson's theory. Thus, cultural variations in roles played by the elderly may impact the nature of intergenerational relationships and living arrangements in different cultures.

# Intergenerational Relationships and Living Arrangements

Cultural differences in intergenerational relationships and living arrangements may derive initially from different conceptions of what constitutes a family. In Western societies, the family most commonly refers to the nuclear family, consisting only of parents and their children, whereas for much of the non-Western world, families are viewed from an extended family model that tends to include grandparents and other relatives who usually reside with parents and their children. It should be noted, however, that there is a caveat to the generalities implied in this statement. Western and non-Western (usually developing) societies are not homogeneous entities—there are at times great disparities in cultural, social, demographic and family functions and forms within these categorizations.

## Intergenerational relationships

Differences in the conception of the family have been deemed to underlie the variations in family relationships of older people, especially in the area of elder support, in Western and non-Western societies. The prevailing situation seems to be that the extended family takes care of the needs of older people in developing countries, whereas very limited support is given to the elderly by family members in the Western (developed) world. One of the theories commonly used to explain this developed world–developing world disparity has been modernization theory. The basic tenets of modernization theory (e.g., Burgess, 1960; Cogwill, 1972, 1974) suggest that family support for the elderly is high in traditional, pre-industrial developing societies due to traditional values of familism and filial obligation, according to which people subordinate their individual interests to the demands and values of the family. Societies where these values predominate are referred to as collectivist cultures (Hofstede, 1980, 1983). In contrast, modernization loosens the grip that the family has on the individual; due to industrialization, urbanization, and other aspects of technological development, the family ceases to be the main unit of production and the process through which to attain social mobility. This is what is presumed to underlie the emergence of the nuclear family. The emphasis is shifted from devotion to the extended family to an emotional bond forged between spouses and their children. In Hofstede's categorization, countries in which these values predominate are termed individualistic societies.

These underlying differences in conceptions of the family have a direct impact on family support for the elderly because the erosion of the extended family brings with it a loss of the traditionally powerful status that older people wield in society. They no longer possess the powers to enforce the customary obligation of children to provide normative support for the older members of the extended family; they also lack the resources to give their children in return for support. Consequently, support for the elderly in modern societies derives not from binding customary obligations that were enforced by very stringent social, economic, and religious sanctions that were usually controlled by the elderly themselves; rather, it depends on the willingness of the children to undertake these tasks based on the level of sympathy or affection that they may have for their older relatives (Aboderin, 2005). Inherent in this viewpoint is the implication that family support for the elderly is a reciprocal interaction in which aged parents and relatives provide services such as advice in exchange for support from their children.

There have been many criticisms of modernization theory postulations, one of which is its implied linear, sequential mode of development with its presumed, fairly uniform characteristics in pre-industrial societies, to a pathway or transition to modernization and "development" via industrialization. It also implies that regardless of how one conceives of the terms "modern" and "developed," the pathway to modernization or development has to follow the historical processes of industrialization as attained in the West. Additionally, it seems to equate economic progress with development. However, even if one were to accept this premise with regard to disparities in intergenerational relationships, empirical support for this viewpoint in the developing world is inconclusive, at best. Some of the research suggests that despite technological change, family ties and support of the elderly have persisted; that many older people still live with their younger relatives in households of two or more generations, and that they tend to maintain close relations with their families and depend on them as their primary means of support. There have also been findings that do indicate some erosion of family relationships for support of older kin following technological change. This has prompted some governments, especially in East Asia, to initiate some public policies and avenues for providing elder support to replace some of the traditional roles hitherto played by the family (e.g., Aboderin, 2004; Hashimoto, 1993; Hermalin, 2003; Malhotra & Kabeer, 2002).

Notwithstanding the criticisms of modernization theory postulations, changes do occur in intergenerational relationships following technological change. Some of these relate to changes in demographic transition that we already touched upon, although in a different context, earlier in the chapter. To the extent that demographic shifts will significantly influence family relationships, especially with respect to care for the elderly, there is an emerging trend that requires urgent attention if the potentially far-reaching negative consequences for the elderly are to be forestalled. The urgency of the demographic changes in the developing world arises from the unparalleled pace at which the transition is occurring. For example, even though it took a country such as France 115 years to increase its older population from 7% to 14%, it may take most nations in the developing world just 20 years, perhaps even less, to accomplish that same feat (Randel, German, & Ewing, 1999).

Some have already identified the demographic changes in the developing world as the most significant contributor to changes in the structure and composition of families. Major advances in medical technology have increased longevity and contributed to the steadily declining fertility rates, treatment and prevention of infectious diseases, and reduction in infant mortality rates. These developments are poised to dramatically increase the numbers and proportion of the elderly in the next few decades (Sen, 1994). The projected increase in the proportion of the elderly in the population is expected to apply to Africa as well, despite high mortality and fertility rates, although the trajectory may be slightly different. The increase in Africa may also result from what is termed premature aging that is the result of the HIV/AIDS epidemic. These demographic shifts are expected to change family relationships in significant ways. For example, they will contribute to the decline in the number of younger family members available to provide support to older kin. The one-child policy in China easily comes to mind as a factor that probably contributes to this problem, and may be responsible for recent debates about possibly changing this policy.

Another factor that is credited with changes in family relationships is rural–urban migration. Presumably, high rates of urbanization in the West contributed to the reduction of family support for elderly kin. If the same process holds, the same might be expected of developing nations in the coming decades. According to the United Nations Population Division (2003), most countries in the developing world are experiencing very rapid rates of rural–urban migration and urbanization. These twin trends are expected to affect family structure and support in at least two ways. In the first instance, the out-migration is age-selective, with the younger kin more likely to leave rural areas to urban centers, leaving older people behind without younger family members to provide needed support. Second, even in cases where older people move to centers, they may encounter the loss of their traditional family support network. The loss in traditional support for elder kin is said to result primarily from the participation of women in the workplace. Because females in most societies tend to be saddled with the responsibility of providing care to older relatives, the increasingly competing demands on their time makes them less available for performing these traditional caregiving functions (Malhotra & Kabeer, 2002).

## Living arrangements

The conception of the family as consisting of a couple and their children has resulted in the elderly in the developed world living by themselves as couples, or if separated by death or divorce, for the older individual to live by himself or herself. With a high need for individualism, living alone is quite common, even among those elderly with declining health. But even within the developed world, wide disparities exist, depending on the socioeconomic status and ethnic compositions of the societies in question. For example, poor elderly in individualistic (usually developed) countries who experience serious declines in health or are unable to take care of themselves are often forced to live with their children (Worobey & Angel, 1990). In the U.S., a three-generation family living arrangement is much more likely among African Americans, Hispanics, or Asians than among White Americans (Choi, 1991). Because minority groups also happen to be more represented among the poor, it is difficult to determine whether or not multigenerational living arrangements are based on cultural values or necessitated by the economic need to share scarce resources.

Be it by desire for independence or other factors, the elderly in the developed world increasingly tend to live with their older peers. This has resulted in distinct housing arrangements in the form of age-segregated housing (e.g., Silverman, 1987), apartment complexes for the elderly (e.g., Hochschild, 1973), retirement communities (e.g., Heintz, 1976), and continuing care retirement communities (e.g., Sherwood, Ruchlin, & Sherwood, 1990; Thompson, 1994). There are a number of advantages to these age-segregated living arrangements in the sense that they are designed specifically to allow for care for the needs of the elderly, development of an elderly subculture, information sharing, and higher levels of social contact and morale (Lawton, Moss, & Moles, 1984). However, other studies have found a number of occupants in these settlements to be lonely and unhappy (e.g., Jacobs, 1974; 1975). Unfortunately, few studies, if any, have examined the effect that living in these communities designed specifically for the elderly have on elder perceptions by younger members of society and the elderly themselves.

Perhaps owing to the cultural conception of the elderly as part of the extended family in the developing world, it is uncommon for the elderly to live by themselves; even in situations where they do, it is usually not by their own volition. Independent living in the developing world connotes a co-residency arrangement (e.g., Ghana), with the elderly person as the head of the household (Apt, 1996). Just as in the developed world, the developing world is not monolithic. There are co-residency arrangements in which the elderly are not the head of household. In Taiwan, living with a married son is the ideal living arrangement for elderly parents, but here the strongest motive is poor health (Lee, Lin, & Chang, 1995). Even then, there are still very strong expectations that adult children should care for and support their aged parents, and that at least one child co-resides or lives in close proximity to them. Similarly, in the Philippines, most elderly people prefer co-residency with their children (Domingo & Asis, 1995).

Given this desire for co-residency with their children, it is not surprising that very few age-segregated housing arrangements exist for the elderly in the developing world (Choi, 1992). The family has traditionally taken care of housing needs of the elderly. However, as discussed earlier in this section, the projected changes in the proportion of elder population in the developing world, and the growing rural–urban migration could present serious challenges to the status quo. Proposals to change current patterns, such as having different housing arrangements, threaten to undermine customs and traditions that individuals expect to be in place when they age. Baihua (1987) reported that in China, the emphasis on family and community resources has hindered the development of long-term facilities that are intended for elderly people without family or sufficient income. Consequently, it is not uncommon to find up to three generations of families residing within the same household.

Besides the strong family ties and tradition, a majority of the elderly in the developing world live in rural areas. Therefore, it is not very practicable to develop elaborate age-segregated housing arrangements. Some of these are occurring by default as the young continue to migrate from the rural to urban areas in search of wage employment, leaving rural areas to be disproportionately populated by the elderly. In addition, considering the cost of occupancy in most age-segregated housing schemes, most elderly in the developing world could not afford these housing options due to less established old-age income programs. If changes in demographic patterns and migration bring age-segregated housing by fiat in the developing world, it will be interesting to see how this might impact elder percep-tions in these societies. Intergenerational relationships and living arrangements have some bearing on how the elderly view their last days and may play a key role in different conceptions and preparations for death across cultures.

## Death Anxiety: The Fear of Death

Most humans do not willingly welcome the idea of their own or their loved ones' death. In fact, the most common reaction to the thought of dying is fear. Some theorists (e.g., Becker, 1973) have suggested that fear of death is a major motivator of all behavior, with both positive and negative aspects. One way in which death anxiety can be a positive force is that people who are afraid of dying tend to do whatever it takes to ensure that they stay alive. Staying alive, in turn, contributes to the continuity and socialization of the species because people so driven are more likely to want to have children and to raise them according to their society's accept-able standards. However, the same death anxiety, if not properly handled, can become a destructive force and even result in both physical and mental problems. According to Fortner and Niemeyer (1999), high levels of death anxiety in older adults are associated with lower ego integrity and more physical and psychological problems relative to individuals with low death anxiety.

Death anxiety is a multifaceted construct that is difficult to define but has been conceptualized to include: fear of death of oneself; fear of death of others; fear of the dying of self; and fear of the dying of others. Fear of death of oneself has to do with the fear of the event of death and comprises such things as what happens to the individual after the experience of death. To some individuals, it could be fear about judgment—whether one would go to heaven or hell—or fear of cremation, earth burial, the donation of one's body to science, and what might happen to people and possessions that one may leave behind, including one's spouse, children, and businesses.

Fear of death of others encompasses the apprehension by an individual of death occurring to significant others in one's life, especially family members and friends. Fear of dying of one's self differs from fear of death of one's self in the sense that the former refers to the process of dying while the latter involves the event of death. A good number of people are not afraid of death itself, but are extremely anxious about how they will die. Anxieties here revolve around the notions of wasting away, the possible deterioration of one's physical appearance, and the pain that may be associated with dying. It is not uncommon for some also to worry about the possibility of being a burden to others, both in terms of time and financial costs. Fear of dying of others is similar to the fear of dying of self, the only difference being that the person in question may have anxieties about the process of dying of significant others in his or her life.

Each of these components can be examined at the public, private, and nonconscious levels. Thus, the fears about death that we may relay publicly may differ from what we may believe and express privately, which may be different from the fears that we may not, ourselves, be consciously aware that we are exhibiting. The complexity of this construct suggests that death anxiety is likely to manifest itself in various ways. One of the most obvious ways in which we display death anxiety is through avoidance (e.g., Kastenbaum, 1999). Avoidance may involve a public as well as a conscious manifestation of death anxiety. Some people consciously refuse to go to funerals or to visit friends and loved ones who are dying because it makes them uneasy or uncomfortable. Others may be unaware that their avoidance stems from their own fear of death. However, they have to find plausible explanations for not visiting loved ones who are dying. Being busy with other important issues is an excuse to mask the real (unconscious) motive – their own fear of death and dying. Other people may display death anxiety by engaging in activities that seem to confront or defy death (Kalish, 1984). These people may repeatedly engage in risky activities such as skydiving, rock climbing or becoming soldiers of fortune. Death anxiety can also manifest itself through changes in lifestyles, use of humor, or getting involved in jobs that deal with death such as funeral parlors or retirement facilities for the very old.

Death anxiety is not prevalent to the same degree across cultures. Roth (1978) suggested that death anxiety is related to how old age and the aged are perceived in a given society. According to Roth, unlike some Asian societies such as Japan where the elderly are respected and their advice valued, the elderly in the U.S. are not held in high regard and are constantly confronted with evidence that they are of very little value. For example, older adults are often forced into compulsory retirement at specified ages with little regard to the functional capacities and needs of the individual. Moreover, many older adults end up in retirement villages and other age-segregated living arrangements that deprive them of much needed beneficent stimulation from younger people, resulting in diminished self-esteem. Because their worth to the community is diminished, the elderly perceive a rather relentless push toward extinction. "Death is the compact expression of all anxieties of aging and of the troubles that older persons endure" (Roth, 1978, p. 557). Thus, one would expect higher levels of death anxiety in societies where the elderly are valued and held in high esteem than in those where older adults are devalued (Gire, 2002).

As stated earlier, death anxiety is a multifaceted concept; therefore, differences may exist between cultural groups or ethnicities on different aspects of death anxiety. In a study using a multifaceted measure called the Multidimensional Fear of Death Scale (MFODS; Hoelter, 1979; Niemeyer & Moore, 1994), DePaola, Griffin, Young, and Niemeyer (2003) found significant differences between elderly African Americans and Caucasian Americans on different dimensions rather than on more global death concerns. Specifically, Caucasians showed higher death anxiety on the MFODS Fear of the Dying Process subscale than their older African American counterparts. Some possible interpretations of this result by the authors are consistent with the varying effects that living arrangements can have on perceptions of old age and elder well-being. According to DePaola et al. (2003) death anxiety about the process of dying may be higher in Caucasian American elderly because the majority of Whites are likely to die in hospitals, nursing homes, hospices, or other institutions (Aiken, 1995). Thus, older Caucasians may fear dying in hospitals or nursing homes where they are very likely to be isolated from family members. Another reason for this difference may be related to the finding by Hummert and Nussbaum (2001) that dying patients who are able to communicate report that they often suffer moderate to severe pain during the last weeks of their lives that did not seem to be alleviated by medication. Therefore, the fear of a prolonged and painful dying process, particularly for older adults who are institutionalized, may be a rational response to their experiences. It also could explain why Caucasian families are more receptive of palliative care interventions at the terminal stages of their lives.

In contrast, African American participants in DePaola et al.'s (2003) study were more anxious than their Caucasian counterparts on the Fear of the Unknown, Fear of Consciousness When Dead, and Fear of the Body After Death subscales of MFODS. According to the authors, these are fears that might dispose African American elderly toward extending life by any means possible. This interpretation appears to be supported by the research finding that African Americans are more likely than Caucasians to want aggressive treatment at the end of life (Mouton, 2000). It might also explain the reluctance of Black elderly to utilize hospice care, as they are likely to perceive palliative care as somewhat synonymous with a denial of care. However, African Americans show very little anxiety on comfort care at the end of life, probably due to the traditional involvement of the family in providing care and support during terminal stages of their illness (Brown, 1990). Thus, differences in death anxiety and related aspects of elder well-being among ethnicities (cultures) are associated with intergenerational relationships, living arrangements, and other variables.

One of the cultural variables that has received extensive examination with respect to death anxiety is religiosity. Duff and Hong (1995) conducted a survey of 674 older adults and found that death anxiety was significantly associated with the frequency of attending religious services. This factor was particularly related to the belief in life after death. For example, Alvarado, Templer, Bresler, and Thomson-Dobson (1995) found a strong negative correlation between death anxiety and belief in after-life. That is, as the degree of certainty in afterlife increased, levels of death anxiety decreased. This was more explicitly confirmed in a recent study by Wink (2006) using mainly Caucasian Christian elderly in the U.S. He found that the relationship between religiousness and death anxiety was not as straightforward as may have been implied by these previous studies. Rather, religiousness interacted with a strong belief in a rewarding afterlife in predicting death anxiety. In other words, it was the consistency between a person's religious beliefs and their belief in afterlife, rather than religiousness in itself that predisposed the individual to either fear or not fear death. Neither variable by itself was a good predictor of death anxiety.

In a cross-cultural and cross-religious exploration of this belief in afterlife vari-able, Parsuram and Sharma (1992) compared people of three different religions in India: Hindus, Muslims, and Christians. They found that Hindus (who had the greatest belief in life after death) also tested lowest in death anxiety, followed by the Muslims, while the Christians showed the highest death anxiety. A few years later, Roshdieh, Templer, Cannon, and Canfield (1999) studied death anxiety and death depression among 1,176 Iranian Muslims who had war-related exposure dur-ing the Iran–Iraq war. They found that those who scored higher on death anxiety were those who also had weaker religious beliefs, did not believe in life after death, and did not assert that the most important aspect of religion is life after death.

Although few studies have empirically compared cultural groups on variables other than religion, we can extrapolate from these findings that death anxiety will be relatively lower among death-affirming societies than among death-denying or death-defying cultures. The United States, and probably most of the societies in the West, are death-denying/defying societies where even the idiom of expression is that of resistance. People conjure images of battling illness, or fighting the enemy (death) (Kalish & Reynolds, 1981). On the other hand, other societies appear to be more accepting of death. The Truskese of Micronesia would be an example of a death-affirming society, where people start preparing for death at age 40. Such acceptance ought to manifest itself in lower death anxiety levels—a notion that appeared to be validated by Benton, Christopher and Walter (2007), who found a relationship between the aging anxiety dimensions of physical appearance concern, the fear of losses, and death anxiety. Aging and impending death need not result in death anxiety, and even if or when they do, the impact could be positive or negative, depending on the individual and the cultural environment in which they find themselves. Thus, just like the other variables in aging, death anxiety is influenced by culture and may have an impact on elder well-being.

## Conclusion

Aging is an inevitable aspect of the developmental process. However, people do not age the same way; whereas some maintain considerable physical agility and robust health into the late stages of adulthood, others show obvious physical declines quite early and struggle with numerous health problems. Both physical and psychological variables combine to influence the experience of aging. The manner in which the elderly are perceived in society varies widely across cultures. These perceptions appear to be shaped by such factors as demographic patterns and transitions, economic transformation, the roles that a given society assigns to the elderly and intergenerational relations and living arrangements. These perceptions, in turn, affect attitudes that other members of society have about the elderly and how the elderly feel about themselves, thus affecting overall well-being of older adults, including longevity. One way of improving the quality of life of the elderly might involve inducing positive attitudes toward older adults by maintaining cultural practices (e.g., advice-giving, family connections) that promote positive perceptions while changing those (e.g., segregation, isolation) that tend to yield negative perceptions and unfavorable attitudes toward older citizens.

## References

Aboderin, I. (2004). Decline in material family support for older people in urban Ghana, Africa: Understanding processes and causes of change. *Journal of Gerontology: Psychological Sciences, Social Sciences, 59*, S128–S137.

Aboderin, I. (2005). Changing family relationships in developing nations. In M. L. Johnson (Ed.), *The Cambridge handbook of age and ageing* (pp. 469–475). New York: Cambridge University Press.

Achenbaum, W. A. (2005). Ageing and changing: International historical perspectives on ageing. In M. L. Johnson (Ed.), *The Cambridge handbook of age and ageing* (pp. 21–29). New York: Cambridge University Press.

Aiken, L. R. (1995). *Dying, death, and bereavement*. Boston, MA: Allyn & Bacon.

Alvarado, K. A., Templer, D. I., Bresler, C., & Thomson-Dobson, S. (1995). The relationship of religious variables to death depression and death anxiety. *Journal of Clinical Psychology, 51*, 202–204.

Arnhoff, F. N., Leon, H. V., & Lorge, I. (1964). Cross-cultural acceptance of stereotypes towards aging. *Journal of Social Psychology, 63*, 41–58.

Apt, N. A. (1996). *Coping with old age in a changing Africa: Social change and the elderly in Ghana*. Aldershot, UK: Avebury.

Baihua, J. (1987). An urban old people's home. *China Reconstructs, 36*, 32–33.

Barak, B., Mathur, A., Lee, K., & Zhang, Y. (2001). Perceptions of age identity: A cross-cultural inner-age exploration. *Psychology and Marketing, 18*(10), 1003–1029.

Becker, E. (1973). *The denial of death*. New York: Free Press.

Benton, J. P., Christopher, A. N., & Walter, M. I. (2007). Death anxiety as a function of aging anxiety. *Death Studies, 31*, 337–350.

Brewer, M. B., Dull, V., & Lui, L. (1981). Perception of the elderly: Stereotypes and prototypes. *Journal of Personality and Social Psychology, 41*, 656–670.

Brown, J. A. (1990). Social work practice with the terminally ill in the Black community. In J. K. Parry (Ed.), *Social work practice with the terminally ill* (pp. 67–82). Springfield, IL: Charles Thomas.

Burgess, E. D. (1960) (Ed.). *Ageism in Western societies*. Chicago: University of Chicago Press.

Butler, R. N. (1980). Ageism: A foreword. *Journal of Social Issues, 36*(2), 8–11.

Chang, B. L., Chang, A. F., & Shen, Y. (1984). Attitudes toward aging in the United States and Taiwan. *Journal of Comparative Family Studies, 15*(1), 109–130.

Choi, N. G. (1991). Racial differences in the determination of living arrangements of widowed and divorced elderly women. *The Gerontologist, 31*, 496–504.

Choi, S. J. (1992). Ageing and social welfare in South Korea. In D. R. Phillips (Ed.), *Ageing in east and south-east Asia* (pp. 148–166). London: Edward Arnold.

Cogwill, D. O. (1972). A theory of aging in cross-cultural perspective. In D. O. Cogwill & L. D. Holmes (Eds.), *Aging and modernization* (pp. 3–19). New York: Appleton-Century-Crofts.

Cogwill, D. O. (1974). Aging and modernization: A revision of the theory. In J. F. Gubrium (Ed.), *Late life* (pp. 123–145). Springfield, IL: Charles Thomas.

de Beauvoir, S. (1972). *The coming of age*. (Patrick O'Brian Trans.). New York: G. P. Putnam.

DePaola, S. J., Griffin, M, Young, J. R., & Niemeyer, R. A. (2003). Death anxiety and attitudes toward the elderly among older adults: The role of gender and ethnicity. *Death Studies, 27*, 335–354.

Domingo, J. L., & Asis, M. M. B. (1995). Living arrangements and the flow of support between generations in the Philippines. *Journal of Cross-Cultural Gerontology, 10*, 21–51.

Duff, R. W., & Hong, L. K. (1995). Age density, religiosity and death anxiety in retirement communities. *Review of Religious Research, 37*, 19–32.

Erikson, E. (1959). *Identity and the life cycle*. New York: Norton.

Eyetsemitan, F. E. (2002). Perceived elderly traits and young people's perception of helping tendencies in the U.S., Ireland, Nigeria and Brazil. *Journal of Cross-Cultural Gerontology, 17*, 57–69.

Eyetsemitan, F. E., & Gire, J. T. (2003). *Aging and adult development in the developing world: Applying Western theories and concepts*. Westport, CT: Praeger.

Fortner, B. V., & Niemeyer, R. A. (1999). Death anxiety in older adults: A quantitative review. *Death Studies, 23*, 387–411.

Frith, K., Shaw, P., & Cheng, H. (2005). The construction of beauty: A cross-cultural analysis of women's magazine advertising. *Journal of Communication, 55*(1), 56–70.

Gire, J. T. (2002). How death imitates life: Cultural influences on conceptions of death and dying. In W. J. Lonner, D. L. Dinnel, S. A. Hayes, & D. N. Sattler (Eds.), *Online readings in psychology and culture* (Unit 14, Chapter 2), Bellingham, WA: Center for Cross-Cultural Research, Western Washington University. Available from http://www.wwu.edu/~culture

Haber, C., & Gratton, B. (1994). *Old age and the search for security.* Bloomington, IN: Indiana University Press.

Harris, D. K. (1988). *Dictionary of gerontology.* New York: Greenwood Press.

Harwood, J., & Anderson, K. (2002). The presence and portrayal of social groups on prime-time television. *Communication Reports, 15*, 81–98.

Hashimoto, A. (1993). Family relations in later life: A cross-cultural perspective. *Generations, 17*, 24–26.

Hauser, P. (1976). Ageing and worldwide population change. In R. Binstock, & E. Shanas (Eds.), *Handbook of aging and the social sciences* (pp. 58–85). New York: Van Nostrand Reinhold.

Heintz, K. M. (1976). *Retirement communities.* New Brunswick, NJ: Rutgers University Center for Urban Policy Research.

Hermalin, A. I. (2003) (Ed.). *The well-being of the elderly in Asia: A four country comparative study.* Ann Arbor, MI: University of Michigan Press.

Hochschild, A. R. (1973). *The unexpected community.* Englewood Cliffs, NJ: Prentice-Hall.

Hoelter, J. W. (1979). Multidimensional treatment of fear of death. *Journal f Consulting and Clinical Psychology, 47*, 996–999.

Hofstede, G. (1980). *Culture's consequences: International differences in work-related values.* Beverly Hills, CA: Sage.

Hofstede, G. (1983). Dimensions of national cultures in fifty countries and three regions. In B. Deregowski, S. Dziurawiec, & R. C. Annis (Eds.), *Expiscations in cross-cultural psychology* (pp. 335–355). Lisse, The Netherlands: Swets and Zeitlinger.

Hummel, C., Rey, J. C., & D'Epinay, C. J. L. (1995). Children's drawings of grandparents: A quantitative analysis of images. In M. Featherstone & A. Wernick (Eds.), *Images of aging: Cultural representations of later life* (pp. 149–170). New York: Routledge.

Hummert, M. L., & Nussbaum, J. F. (Eds.) (2001). *Aging, communication and health.* Mahwah, NJ: Lawrence Erlbaum Associates.

Jacobs, J. (1974). *Fun city: An ethnographic study of a retirement community.* New York: Holt, Rinehart, & Winston.

Jacobs, J. (1975). *Older persons and retirement communities.* Springfield, IL: Charles Thomas.

Kalish, R. A. (1984). *Death, grief, and caring relationships* (2nd ed.). Pacific Grove, CA: Brooks/Cole

Kalish, R. A., & Reynolds, D. K. (1981). *Death and ethnicity: A psychocultural study.* Farmingdake, NY: Baywood.

Kastenbaum, R. (1999). Dying and bereavement. In J. C. Cavanaugh & S. K. Whitbourne (Eds.), *Gerontology: An interdisciplinary perspective* (pp. 155–185). New York: Oxford University Press.

Lawton, M. P., Moss, M., & Moles, E. (1984). The supra-personal neighborhood context of older people: Age heterogeneity and well-being. *Environment and Behavior, 16*, 89–109.

Lee, M., Lin, H., & Chang, M. (1995). Living arrangements of the elderly in Taiwan: Qualitative evidence. *Journal of Cross-Cultural Gerontology, 10*, 53–78.

Levy, B. R. (1999). The inner self of the Japanese elderly: A defense against negative stereotypes of aging. *International Journal of Aging and Human Development, 48*(2), 131–144.

Levy, B., & Langer, E. (1994). Aging free from negative stereotypes: Successful memory in China and among the American deaf. *Journal of Personality and Social Psychology, 66,* 989–997.

Levy, B. R., Slade, M. D., Kunkel, S. R., & Kasl, S. V. (2002). Longevity increased by positive self-perceptions of aging. *Journal of Personality and Social Psychology, 83*(2), 261–270.

Maddox, G. L. (1964). Disengagement theory: A critical evaluation. *Gerontologist, 6,* 80–82.

Malhotra, R., & Kabeer, N. (2002). *Demographic transition, inter-generational contracts and old age security: an emerging challenge for social policy in developing countries,* Working Paper No. 157. Brighton, UK: Institute for Development Studies.

Mouton, C. P. (2000). Cultural and religious issues for African Americans. In K. L. Braun, J. H. Pietsch, & P. L. Blanchette (Eds.), *Cultural issues in end of life decision making.* Thousand Oaks, CA: Sage.

Niemeyer, R. A., & Moore, M. K. (1994). Validity and reliability of the Multidimensional Fear of Death Scale. In R. A. Niemeyer (Ed.), *Death anxiety handbook: Research, instrumentation, and application* (pp. 103–117). Washington, DC: Taylor & Francis.

Parsuram, A., & Sharma, M. (1992). Functional relevance in belief in life-after-death. *Journal of Personality and Clinical Studies, 8,* 97–100.

Raman, P., Harwood, J., Weis, D., Anderson, J. L., & Miller, G. (2008). Portrayals of older adults in U.S. and Indian magazine advertisements: A cross-cultural comparison. *The Howard Journal of Communications, 19,* 221–240.

Randel, J., German, T., & Ewing, D. (1999) (Eds.). *The ageing and development report: Poverty, independence and the world's older people.* London: HelpAge International, Earthscan.

Robinson, F. (1989) (Ed.). *The Cambridge encyclopedia of India, Pakistan, Bangladesh, Sri Lanka, Nepal, Bhutan, and the Maldives.* Cambridge, UK: Cambridge University Press.

Roshdieh, S., Templer, D. I., Cannon, W. G., & Canfield, M. (1999). The relationship of death anxiety and death depression to religion and civilian war-related experiences in Iranians. *Omega: Journal of Death and Dying, 38,* 201–210.

Roth, N. (1978). Fear of death in the aging. *American Journal of Psychotherapy, 32,* 552–560.

Schmidt, D. F., & Boland, S. M. (1986). Structure of perceptions of older adults: Evidence for multiple stereotypes. *Psychology and Aging, 1,* 255–260.

Sen, K. (1994). *Ageing: Debates on demographic transition and social policy.* London: Zed Books.

Sherwood, S., Ruchlin, H. S., & Sherwood, C. C. (1990). CCRCs: An option for aging in place. In D. Tilson (Ed.), *Supporting the frail elderly in residential environments* (pp. 125–164). Glenview, IL: Scott, Foresman & Company.

Silverman, P. (1987). Community settings. In P. Silverman (Ed.), *The elderly as modern prisoners* (pp. 185–210). Bloomington, IN: Indiana University Press.

Srikandath, S. (1991). Cultural values depicted in Indian television advertising. *Gazette, 48,* 166–172.

Sung, K. T. (1994). A cross-cultural comparison of motivations for parent care: The case of Americans and Koreans. *Journal of Aging Studies, 8*(2), 195–209.

Thang, L. L. (2000). Aging in the East: Comparative and historical reflections. In T. R. Cole, R. Kastenbaum, and R. E. Ray (Eds.), *Handbook of aging and the humanities* (2nd ed. pp. 183–213). New York: Springer.

Thompson, I. (1994). Woldenburg Village: An illustration of supporting design for older adults. *Experimental Aging Research, 20,* 239–244.

United Nations Population Division (2003). *World population prospects—the 2002 revision.* New York: United Nations.

Wink, P. (2006). Who is afraid of death? Religiousness, spirituality, and death anxiety in late adulthood. *Journal of Religion, Spirituality and Aging, 18,* 93–110.

World Health Organization (1999). *World health report 1999.* Geneva.

Worobey, J. L., & Angel, R. J. (1990). Functional capacity and living arrangements of unmarried elderly persons. *Journal of Gerontology: Social Sciences, 45,* S95–S101.

# Part IV

# Cognition

Despite the fact that cultures vary widely, culture and cognition are intimately interconnected. That sentence is perhaps the central message of Part IV, "Cognition." Culture and the human brain have co-evolved, with cultural experience exerting an influence on the organization of the brain and, reciprocally, the brain's organization influencing culture. As a result, cultural practices produce variations in cognition, and culture provides the tools for human thought and action.

The relationship between culture and cognition can be seen at basic levels, including perception. As we will see in this section of the book, researchers have long been interested in cultural variations in perception, as evidenced in work conducted more than a century ago. Could culture play a role in the ability of individuals to judge the length of lines, or to perceive colors, or to recognize photographs or drawings of common objects? The research on these questions and others like them is sometimes surprising and always intriguing.

Many of us might have assumed that success in education might aid the success of cultures in the world—perhaps by fostering economic growth, cultural stability, and other group characteristics that enhance how countries fare in relation to others. But do teachers in different cultures really teach in significantly different ways? Could fundamentally different teaching styles result in very different student outcomes across a culture? Why might it matter?

Or, we might ask, how do we know whether there are important differences in the educational achievement of students from different cultures around the world? And why would psychologists be interested in this question? As we will learn in this section, educational assessment is an important contributor to strong educational systems, which in turn are instrumental to the ability of cultures to successfully compete in the world.

All of these issues and phenomena are of interest to researchers working within the broad scope of the field of cognitive psychology. These topics all have in common a connection to learning and to information processing—and they all bear strong relationships to culture.

# 7

# Culture and Cognition*

## Michael Cole and Martin Packer

## Introduction

From the earliest recorded accounts of people from one society meeting those from another, it is clear that such encounters engender the strong intuition that "those people" are fundamentally different than "we are." Often the word used to designate "us" is akin to "the human beings" while "they" are barbarians (Herodotus, 440 BCE / 2003). "They" make funny noises when they speak, they eat peculiar foods, and they live in ways that seem exotic and often inferior (see Chapter 2, this volume).

In the modern world, the academic study of this apparently universal tendency to evaluate others as somehow fundamentally different than we are is the province of psychologists who study the role of culture in human life (Cole, 1996; Kitayama & Cohen, 2007; Valsiner & Rosa, 2007). While in the past apparently deep and pervasive differences in modes of life and behavior were attributed to some deep, genetic variation associated with the concept of race, today it is recognized that whatever variations in skin color, hair, height, and other physical differences may distinguish members of different social groups, the variations that give rise to the intuition of fundamental difference in the accumulated knowledge of a social group are the exosomatic—external to the body—inheritance of the accumulated experience of earlier generations of that group. They are, that is to say, culturally organized, learned patterns of behavior, embodied in the group's everyday practices, its norms and values.

In this chapter we examine the relation between culture and cognition, conceiving it along two axes. The first is a synchronic axis, ignoring changes over time, of three distinguishable levels of social grouping: human beings as a mammalian species, societies (thought of as the population of a particular geographical and political region which shares cultural features), and cultural practices (thought of as recurrent ways of accomplishing valued social activities in concert with one's proximally circumscribed social unit). These levels are not independent. It is helpful to think of each "smaller" unit of cultural analysis as connected to, often embedded within, more inclusive levels. The second is diachronic, for it is essential to look upon culture as a process occurring over time. Just as geopolitically defined populations can be thought of as branches of a tree of human life extending back to *australopithecus*, the first bipedal ancestor to modern humans around four million years ago, so the cultural practices characteristic of a society represent various "ways of doing and thinking" that people have inherited from prior generations of "their kind" to organize everyday life. Hence, the study of culture and cognition requires a *developmental* analysis that extends across the domains of phylogeny (evolution), cultural history, ontogeny (the development of an individual), and micro-genesis (the moment-to-moment organization of daily human life) (Vygotsky, 1930/1997). Specifying the linkages among specific cultural practices within more inclusive sociocultural formations, and the linkages of those sociocultural formations within historically formed modes of life, is a major ongoing challenge to the study of culture and cognitive development.

Our presentation is organized as follows. We begin by providing working definitions of the core concepts of culture, cognition, and development. We then consider cognition at each of the synchronic levels of sociotemporal grouping associated with culture: cultural universals as they relate to human beings as a biological species, the cultural styles of large populations and social groups considered as historical configurations arising in particular ecological conditions, and cultural practices within social groups which, we will argue, are the proximal locus for the formation of both culture and cognition. Within each level, we introduce developmental considerations as they become relevant. We end by considering crucial issues that must be resolved in order to arrive at a more systematic understanding of the generality of cultural patterns across populations, their sources, and their consequences for cognition.

## Culture, Cognition, and Development: Some Definitional Considerations

In its most general sense the term *culture* as applied to human beings refers to the socially inherited body of past human behavioral patterns and accomplishments that serves as the resources for the current life of a social group (D'Andrade, 1986a). Although scholars usually agree that culture constitutes the social inheritance of a population, anthropologists have been divided in whether they focus on culture as "something out there" (the "man made part of the environment"; Herskovitz, 1948, p. 17) or as "something inside the head" ("what one needs to know to participate acceptably as a member in a society's affairs"; Goodenough, 1994, p. 265).

At present, many anthropologists and psychologists seek to transcend thinking about culture as either exclusively "ideal" or exclusively "material." For example, in linking culture and cognition, Geertz (1973) emphasized that

> human thought is basically both social and public—that its natural habitat is the house yard, the market place, and the town square. Thinking consists not of "happenings in the head" (though happenings there and elsewhere are necessary for it to occur) but of trafficking in ... significant symbols—words for the most part but also gestures, drawings, musical sounds, mechanical devices like clocks. (p. 45)

Our own proposal for transcending the ideal–material dichotomy with respect to culture is to think of culture as a dynamically changing environment that is transformed by the artifacts created by prior generations, extending back to the beginning of the species. As we employ the term, an artifact is an aspect of the material world that has been modified over the history of its incorporation into goal-directed human thought and action (Cole, 1996). By virtue of the changes wrought in the process of its creation and the way in which it has been appropriated as a tool of human thought, an artifact is *simultaneously ideal (conceptual) and material*. It is material in that it is embodied in physical form, whether in the morphology of a spoken, written or signed word, a ritual, or an artistic creation, or as a solid object such as a pencil. It is ideal in that this material form has been shaped by historical participation in the (successful, adaptive) human activities of which the artifact was previously a part and which it mediates in the present. D'Andrade (1986b) made this point when he wrote that "Material culture—tables and chairs, buildings and cities—is the reification of human ideas in a solid medium" (p. 22). The basic function of these artifacts and their deployment in various cultural practices is to coordinate human beings with the physical world and each other; in the aggregate, culture can be seen as the species-specific *medium* of human development, a medium which organizes and configures the human nervous system for interaction with the world.

This conception of artifacts extends to what Wartofsky (1973) referred to as secondary artifacts, representations of primary artifacts and their modes of use. Secondary artifacts play a central role in preserving and transmitting the kinds of social inheritance referred to as recipes, beliefs, norms, conventions, and the like. This extension brings the mental entities psychologists refer to as schemas or scripts into contact with their material instantiation in practical life. The term schema is ordinarily used by psychologists to refer to a mental structure that represents some aspect of the world. We find it more useful to adopt Bartlett's (1932) notion of schemas as *conventions*, because this usage emphasizes that schemas are simultaneously aspects of collective material practices and of mental structures/functions. Scripts are an especially important kind of schema for purposes of thinking about the role of culture in cognitive development because they represent the everyday, culturally organized events in which people participate. A script is an event schema that specifies the appropriate people who participate in that event, the social roles they play, the objects they use, and the sequence of actions and causal relations they perform (Nelson, 1986).

Both Bruner (1990) and Nelson (1981, 1986) accorded an important role to such event representations in cognitive development. Nelson (1981) referred to scripts as a "generalized event representation" (p. 101). In her view, which we share, scripts provide "a basic level of knowledge representation in a hierarchy of representations that reaches upward through plans to goals and themes" (p. 101). In her work on children's acquisition of event representations, Nelson highlighted other important properties of scripts as fundamentally important cultural artifacts. First, event schemas serve as guides to action. When someone participates in a novel event, they must seek an answer to the question, "What's going on here?" For example, once children acquire even a crude idea of the appropriate actions associated with going to a restaurant, they can enter the flow of this particular event with partial knowledge, "playing their role," which gets enriched in the course of the event itself, facilitating later coordination in new, unfamiliar events of a similar kind. As Nelson (1981) pointed out, "Without shared scripts, every social act would need to be negotiated afresh" (p. 109). Nelson also made the important observation that children grow up within contexts controlled by adults and hence they *participate in* and are *coordinated by* adult scripts. By and large, adults arrange the conditions for children's experiences, including culturally appropriate goals, rather than engage in direct teaching (Whiting, 1980). In effect, they use their notion of the appropriate script to provide constraints on the child's actions and allow the child to fill in the expected role activity in the process. In this sense, "the acquisition of scripts is central to the acquisition of culture" (Nelson, 1981, p. 110).

According to Bruner (2002), scripts are best considered constituents of a narrative. In his view narrative, the linking of events over time, lies at the heart of human thought. The re-presentation of experience in narratives provides a frame ("folk psychology") enabling humans to interpret their experiences and each other. If it were not for such narrativized framing, "we would be lost in a murk of chaotic experience and probably would not have survived as a species in any case" (Bruner, 1990, p. 56). Narrative has its correlates at the neurophysical level, as Luria (1974) has pointed out: he argued that all action involves a "kinetic melody," a smoothly patterned sequence of movements which, like narrative, organizes the purposive aspect of action into an integral embodiment. A kinetic melody represents not only the coordination of various afferent and efferent neural systems (those carrying messages to and from the brain respectively), but also their amalgamation with meaningful, skilled movements learned over time, enabling one to interact with, and act on, the world. A kinetic melody, therefore, illustrates the interpenetration of the cultural and the neural and provides an interwoven, dynamic unit of analysis that avoids reducing behavior to biology and opens the way to analysis of the ecological complexity of human experience.

We have devoted most of this section to a discussion of the definition of culture because this is central to our purpose in this chapter, but similar complexities apply to the definition of cognition and development. Generally speaking, the term *cognition* applies to the process of acquiring and deploying knowledge in a variety of manners, such as perceiving, attending, remembering, reasoning, linguistic ability, and so on. Equally generally, *development* as psychologists use that term refers to changes over time: both quantitative "growth" and qualitative change in the individual and how the person interacts with the physical environment and other people. Each of these concepts, no less than the concept of culture, is thoroughly saturated with theoretical commitments. For present purposes, we background such considerations to foreground the role of culture in the process of cognition, treating them in as neutral a fashion as possible.

## Culture and Cognitive Development: Universal Processes

Because of evidence for the presence of culture among the hominid precursors of modern humans for many hundreds of thousands, if not millions of years prior to the emergence of *Homo sapiens*, it is inappropriate to juxtapose human biology and human culture. The human brain and body have co-evolved over a long period of time with our species' increasingly complex cultural environment (Richerson & Boyd, 2005). The implications of this co-evolution of human culture and human biology were aptly summarized by Geertz (1973), who argued that as a result of their tangled relations in the course of human phylogeny, culture and biology are equally tangled in the course of human ontogeny:

> Rather than culture acting only to supplement, develop, and extend organically based capacities logically and genetically prior to it, it would seem to be ingredient to those capacities themselves. A cultureless human being would probably turn out to be not an intrinsically talented though unfulfilled ape, but a wholly mindless and consequently unworkable monstrosity. (p. 68)

At the time, Geertz was arguing from scanty data, but contemporary studies of hominization, the process of becoming human, have made clear the general principle that the contemporary human brain co-evolved with the accumulation of culture. Based on contemporary neuroscientific evidence, Quartz and Sejnowski (2002) declared that culture "contains part of the developmental program that works with genes to build the brain that underlies who you are" (p. 58). Donald (2001) made the same point in slightly different terms: "Culture actually configures the complex symbolic systems needed to support it by engineering the functional capture of the brain for epigenesis" (p. 23). (Epigenesis is the unfolding development of an organism from its earliest form.)

According to this logic, culture does not act independently of biological processes during ontogeny. Rather, to use a currently fashionable phrase, one needs to speak of "bio-cultural co-constructivism" (Li, 2006): the theoretical position that *both* culture, the historically accumulated artifacts that constitute the human-made part of the environment which greets a newborn at birth, *and* biological processes with a long phylogenetic history, operate simultaneously and interactively during ontogeny to provide the conditions for all of development, including its cognitive aspects.

## Universal Processes of Culture vis-à-vis Cognition and Development

With these considerations in mind, it should be clear from its place in the common history of *Homo sapiens* that culture plays a central role in cognitive development, regardless of which particular culture a child is born into. First, and most obviously, culture provides a vast storehouse of partial solutions to problems that human beings have previously encountered and solved (Hutchins, 1995). Put differently, culture provides a vast storehouse of tools to think and act with. While such tools/solutions routinely need modification because humans must constantly deal with changing circumstances, human infants do not encounter a world created *de novo* just for them. Rather, theirs is a world culturally prepared to provide them with cognitive resources, just as phylogeny has pre-adapted them to require and acquire such resources.

Second, the world that greets the newborn is a social world, populated by persons who have already acquired a great deal of the cultural knowledge that the child is going to have to acquire, and whose behavior is already shaped by this knowledge. The entire pattern of the child's early experiences takes place in an intricately choreographed set of scripted events, mediated by its caretakers using artifacts embodying the society's cultural heritage. These cultural resources include recipes for organizing babies' experiences so they will, in time, come to play the same role in the social group that their parents and older kin are currently playing, and that they will take their turn at organizing the experience of the next generation of children who will make possible the social group's continuation.

Our emphasis on culture as preceding the child and as a set of resources/ experiences arranged by adults who are heavily invested in the child's development should not distract attention from a third way in which culture plays an essential role in cognition. It requires active efforts by children to acquire the necessary cultural knowledge to become competent members of the social group, and thus to reduce their dependence on the ministrations of others and maximize their own potential to conduct their lives on their own terms. In short, children must learn to control their own behavior and their environments using the same cultural resources that their elders use if they are to thrive as members of the social group. From this perspective, cognitive development is a process of children learning to control the world and themselves by appropriating the cultural resources made available to them since birth by their families and community. If the process is successful they will eventually add to, and perchance transform, this set of cultural resources during the unforeseeable events of their own lives.

In summary, when considering the universal features of culture in human cognition what one sees is a three-sided process in which the social inheritance of the past is made available to children at birth in an ongoing process of enculturation which requires that both the social world and the child actively engage with their ideal/material social inheritance so that the child will become a competent adult member of the social group.

## Designs for Living and Cognitive Style

At present the most common way of studying the relations between culture and cognition is to make comparisons among populations in terms of cultural modes of being that are assumed to operate pervasively across particular cognitive domains. Often the populations selected are assumed to represent an entire society or nation, and sometimes even an entire civilization. For example, Nisbett and Masuda (2003) set out to compare the cognitive properties of societies descended from the Greek tradition with those of East Asian origin. Psychologists who conduct research at this level of cultural generality make a key assumption—that a society provides people with a shared, coherent, pervasive way of knowing and acting in the world around them. The anthropologist Ruth Benedict (1934) stated this assumption clearly, in her well-known statement concerning patterns of culture:

> A human society must make for itself some design for living. It approves certain ways of meeting situations and certain ways of sizing them up. People in that society regard these solutions as foundations of the universe. They integrate them no matter what the difficulties. Men who have accepted a system of values by which to live cannot without courting inefficiency and chaos keep for long a fenced-off portion of their lives where they think and behave according to a contrary set of values. They try to bring about more conformity. They provide themselves with some common rationale and some common motivations. *Some degree of consistency is necessary or the whole scheme falls to pieces.* (p. 53, emphasis ours)

Benedict's belief that the coherent shared patterning of psychological life is made possible by the cultural environment, and that each society's "design for living" provides its members with a system of values that ensures consistency, motivation, and rationale in their actions (ways of meeting situations) and conceptions (ways of sizing them up), was the basis during the last half of the twentieth century for a large program of cross-cultural work that has been termed an "eco-cultural" psychology (Berry, 1976; Greenfield, Keller, Fuligni, & Maynard, 2003; Whiting &

Whiting, 1975). The basic logic of this approach was to relate psychological patterns on the one hand to the sociocultural-ecological circumstances of the group on the other. These ecological circumstances were then assumed to establish the conditions within which configurations of economic activity/technology and social organization (kinship and the division of labor of adults) arise. These circumstances influence child-rearing practices which in turn shape the psychological characteristics of the children. Children were assumed to internalize the characteristics of their elders, owing to the patterned process of socialization they had undergone, and in this way given cultural designs for living are reproduced over generations (of course there will be at times changes in ecological circumstances, and these can be expected to instigate cultural changes, at a greater or lesser rate, that will in turn lead to patterned cognitive changes).

These cultural designs for living were assumed to be apparent in the individual in the form of what were referred to as *cognitive styles*. Generally these styles were conceived of as the preferred way in which a person processes information. Unlike cognitive *abilities*, such as IQ, which are typically considered in terms of degree along a single dimension, cognitive styles have typically been considered in terms of a bipolar scale, having two poles or extremes, each of which is a distinct cognitive style, a distinct tendency to behave in a certain manner.

A variety of terms has been used to characterize the cognitive styles associated with different cultural designs. Borrowing from Witkin (1967), Berry et al. (1986) coined the contrasting terms "field dependent" and "field independent." More recent research in this tradition has used such contrasts as "analytic/holistic," and "independent/interdependent" (Kitayama & Cohen, 2007). Although the specifics of the different approaches vary, as do the various tasks they use to assess the core cognitive styles, there is general agreement that cognitive styles apply across a wide spectrum of traditional psychological functions or processes, including perception, attention, reasoning, categorizing, self-construal, social inferences about others, and so on.

The early work of Berry, Witkin, and their colleagues set out to demonstrate that people in some cultures are more "field dependent" while those in other cultures are more "field independent," and to discover the relation between culture and cognition which leads to this difference. To say that a person is field dependent means they are more heavily influenced by the context in which stimuli are presented, or in which specific events of interest occur (Berry, 1976). "Field independence" means that perception of or cognition about a stimulus is not influenced by the context or setting. Field dependence in the perceptual and cognitive realms was operationally defined and experimentally tested using the Rod and Frame Test (RFT) and the Embedded Figures Test (EFT). The RFT consists of a rod inside a frame, both of which are moveable, and the participant must adjust the rod to what they consider a true vertical position as the position of the frame is changed. A field dependent person will judge whether or not the rod is vertical with reference to the frame that surrounds it, rather than relative to the floor or to their bodily position. The degree of error (the number of degrees away from 90) provides the measure of field dependence. The higher the score, the more field dependent the participant is considered to be. The EFT requires finding simple forms which are embedded in larger figures. Here, the field dependent person will have more difficulty separating the forms from the enclosing figures. The score is the average time in seconds to detect the simple forms, as well as the total number of correctly disembedded forms found within a fixed amount of time. Greater time and more incomplete tasks reflect greater difficulty in analyzing a part separately from a larger pattern, or viewing an object distinct from its context. Alternatively, they reflect a greater tendency to perceive complete patterns rather than their separate components. Both are more the case for the field-dependent cognitive style.

In the social realm, it was predicted that field-independent people would experience themselves as separate and distinct from others, that they would depend largely on internal referents, and that they would be more autonomous in their social relationships than field-dependent people. Or, to put the point in more contemporary terminology, a field-independent person's reasoning about themselves and others would be more focused on an autonomous agent, while a field-dependent person's reasoning would be more focused on an agent whose actions are importantly contingent on the social group.

Berry (1976) tested these ideas by gathering data from 18 subsistence societies ranging from West Africa to northern Canada and Australia, and from three industrialized groups. He used data from the Human Relations Area Files (HRAF) to code information about the ecological circumstances and culture of origin, as well as indications of acculturation to the larger national group of which the smaller group was a part, in order to obtain evidence concerning key elements of the ecocultural model. Berry and his colleagues purported to assess cognitive style in both the cognitive and social domains by administering the tests we have described. He interpreted the results as strongly supporting the ecocultural model relating environment, social structure, cultural practices, and cognitive style.

Some were skeptical about this research and raised questions about the methodology. In particular, it was pointed out that the distinction between perceptual and problem-solving tasks was suspect because the tasks used (such as the EFT and RFT) probably did not really sample different cognitive domains, so that demonstrating correlations between them was of doubtful significance, and that correlations between experimental tasks and actual social behavior were not adequately tested. Subsequently, a large-scale project to test the model, designed to overcome these objections, failed (Berry et al., 1986). For some years the general idea that cognitive styles are related to cultural configurations languished.

In recent years, however, as intercultural contact has accelerated in connection with the historical process referred to as globalization, psychologists have become increasingly aware of the importance of culture and an interest in cognitive styles has reappeared. It has done so in connection with the proposal that there is a basic distinction among the many societies on this planet between those that are "collectivist" and those that are "individualist" (Kitayama & Cohen, 2007).

## Collectivism and individualism

The description of cultures as either collectivist or individualist has a long history, not only in psychology but in sociology, anthropology, philosophy, and history. Individualistic cultures are generally considered to be ones in which the single human being is the fundamental building block of society, in which self-reliance and competitiveness are valued, and people are encouraged to cultivate their independence, self-reliance, and autonomy. Collectivist cultures, in contrast, are ones in which emphasis is placed on the group or community, commitment and group protection are emphasized, social norms and duties are valued, and people are encouraged to foster conformity and responsibility. Triandis (1988) suggested that this distinction is "perhaps the most important dimension of cultural differences in social behavior across the diverse cultures of the world" (p. 60). Hofstede (1980) identified four fundamental dimensions of cultural difference—*power distance, masculinity, uncertainty avoidance,* and *individualism* (later a fifth was added: *long-term orientation*). Of these, individualism has attracted by far the most attention.

An important contribution to this line of work was made by Markus and Kitayama (1991). They explored the psychological implications of individualist and collectivist cultures and suggested that they foster two distinct kinds of self: *independent* and *interdependent* selves respectively. Markus and Kitayama hypothesized that these two kinds of self would show differences in cognition, emotion, and motivation. They also pointed out the likely connection with cognitive style, noting that

> Witkin and his colleagues described a field dependent person as one who includes others within the boundaries of the self and who does not make a sharp distinction between the self and others. Many of the empirical findings ... about the interpersonal expertise and sensitivities of field dependent people are similar to those described herein for people with interdependent selves. (p. 247)

Since the 1980s the interest in individualism and collectivism has grown enormously. The basic idea of Witkin and Berry (1975), that culture produces a specific manner or style of thinking that spans all psychological domains, has been revived and elaborated upon well beyond the confines of their earlier theory and the data used to substantiate it.

## Systems of thought

Nisbett and colleagues (Nisbett, Peng, Choi, & Norenzayan, 2001; Nisbett & Masuda, 2003; Peng & Nisbett, 1999) have argued that sociocultural differences among societies have effects not only on their members' beliefs about the world but more profoundly on their "tacit epistemologies" and "even the nature of their cognitive processes" (Nisbett et al., 2001, p. 291). For example, they found that it is relatively more difficult for European Americans to detect changes in the background of scenes, suggesting that they are less field dependent, whereas it is more difficult for Asians to detect changes within objects in the foreground of a scene, suggesting that they are more field dependent. Nisbett has suggested that Eastern and Western cultures provide their members with distinct systems of thought. In the East, the system of thinking is holistic, with attention to objects, events, and people in the field in which they are seen or known. Eastern thinking relies more on a dialectical style of reasoning. In the West, the system of thinking is analytic, with perceptual attention focused on the object or event and its categories, and understanding focused on properties and behavior, conceived of in terms of formal rules. Nisbett and his colleagues speculate that these different ways of thinking originated in markedly different social systems. The Western style can be traced, they suggest, to ancient Greece, whose geography placed it at the center of routes of trade, and which had a coastline facilitating transportation and a mountainous terrain that supported herding more than agriculture. In such a society, agency and power were located in the individual. The Greeks passed down to Western cultures their emphasis on personal freedom and debate.

The ancient Chinese, in contrast, emphasized social obligation, collective agency, and harmony. Their civilization was based on agriculture, which required cooperation, and their society was complex and hierarchical. Their impressive technological innovations (including ink, porcelain, the compass, cartography, and seismographs) reflected, Nisbett proposed, practical ingenuity rather than scientific curiosity. Their worldview was one of overlapping or interpenetrating substances, in contrast to the Platonic worldview of essential forms underlying the apparent world.

Nisbett et al. (2001) proposed that not only is it possible to explain the intellectual differences between Chinese and Greek cultures through a reconstruction of their history, it is also possible to "build a psychological theory from the historical evidence" (p. 294). They suggest that what underlies habits of both attention (primarily to the field, on one hand, and primarily to the object, on the other) and cognition (explaining in terms of context, or explaining in terms of essential properties) are forms of social organization. Dialectical and logical thinking may have developed to deal with conflict in different kinds of society. From this perspective, culture not only provides the contents of individuals' beliefs, it also offers the general-purpose cognitive tools which individuals employ.

Experimental evidence for this kind of general cultural effect on cognition includes the finding that when an object is taken out of its original context, European Americans have relatively little difficulty identifying it as familiar, whether it is presented in isolation or with a new background, whereas Asians have greater difficulty identifying the object as the same when it is presented with a novel background than when it is presented in isolation (Ji, Peng, & Nisbett, 2000;

Masuda & Nisbett, 2001). Other researchers (making no mention of the demographic make-up of their sample) have suggested there is a universal bias toward processing objects in the foreground in human perception and categorization, but that semantic congruency between objects in the foreground and background increases accuracy (Davenport & Potter, 2004). Nisbett and colleagues, nevertheless, contend that Asians do not simply fail to process the object in the foreground, they incorporate the spatial context and somehow bind it into their representation of the object.

Similarly, Simons, and Levin (1997) explored the "change blindness" phenomenon, in which people fail to notice large changes in a visual scene that are made while it is briefly hidden or during an eye movement, and demonstrated that Asians more accurately detect changes to the background or environment, while European Americans more accurately detect changes to objects in the foreground. These findings may reflect the way cultures foster different patterns of attention by encouraging their members to incorporate more or less contextual information in decision-making processes (Ji et al., 2000; Masuda & Nisbett, 2001). More specifically, it is proposed that Asians focus attention on the interrelations between objects and the contexts in which these are embedded in visual space, whereas European Americans attend primarily to the object in the foreground and its salient characteristics.

Another recent study found that patterns in eye movements correlate with observed differences in cognitive style (Chua, Boland, & Nisbett, 2005). The eye movements of American (the ethnic make-up of this sample was not specified) and Chinese participants were measured using eye-tracking equipment while participants viewed photographs of a focal object superimposed on a complex background. The American participants fixated more often on focal objects and tended to fixate more rapidly after initial presentation of the photograph. In comparison, the Chinese participants made more eye movements to the background and took longer to direct their gaze specifically toward the focal object.

Linking these findings to their biological substrate, an investigation using functional magnetic resonance imaging (fMRI) of the brain (which measures changes in blood flow related to neural activity) during a visual learning task that required repetitive memorization and active recall of abstract geometric patterns (Grön et al., 2003) found that although behavioral performance (i.e., total recall and slope of learning) was identical for Europeans (Germans) and Chinese, the two groups demonstrated different patterns of neuronal activation. Initial learning for the Chinese participants activated bilateral frontal and parietal areas. The frontal lobes and the parietal area above and behind them form what is known as the "dorsal stream," the "where" system, which is apparently involved in guiding actions and recognizing where objects are in space. For the European American participants, in contrast, learning recruited what is known as the "ventral stream," posterior ventral regions such as the fusiform gyrus and the hippocampal complex. These areas are believed to be associated with object identification and to form the "what" system. The authors interpreted these results as demonstrating that differences in cultural upbringing influenced the initial attentional style with which the participants approached the geometrical patterns.

Such findings echo the earlier studies on differential levels of perceptual field dependence. It would seem that cultural differences in cognition *can* be observed in both behavioral performance and cerebral physiological activity. But, surprisingly and importantly, in the fMRI study mentioned above a crossover effect was observed in which Europeans for a time exhibited dorsal activation (upper brain areas) and Chinese participants for a time exhibited ventral activation (lower brain areas), before both returned to their initial baseline pattern. This shift in processing strategy midway through the learning process may be an attempt to more fully consolidate the percept to be learned by engaging the complementary analyzer. Once the representation of the figure had been stabilized in long-term memory, participants returned to their default attentional style. The fact that both European and Chinese groups were able to recruit both the ventral and dorsal streams suggests a significant degree of flexibility in the impact that their culture has had on their processing of visual information. That is to say, it is not the case that members of the more individualist culture *always* engage the ventral stream while members of the more collectivist culture *always* engage the dorsal stream.

## Priming cognitive style

This finding of flexibility is important because it raises some questions about theories that assume a direct connection from social organization to cognitive processes via generalized, culturally organized systems of thought. Moreover, a series of studies using an experimental technique known as "priming" has clearly shown that cultural style alone cannot fully explain the dynamic nature of differences between or within cultural groups.

Priming is the process of making something ready. For example, in past times one primed a pump by pouring a little water into it to seal the moving parts and make it ready to operate. In the same way, one paints a layer of "primer" first, to seal the surface before applying the final coat of paint. In psychological research priming is "preparing the mind" of the research subject for the task they are to undertake. For example, when a subject is asked for a word that begins with "tab," if they are first given a list of words that includes the word "table" they are more likely to respond with that word. Priming may be perceptual (showing an image) or conceptual (showing a meaningful stimulus).

The precise way that priming works is the topic of much debate, but that issue need not concern us here. What is important to the present discussion is that priming studies reveal variation *within* cultural groups in the degree to which people manifest the cognitive style assumed to be generally characteristic of the group. Priming studies offer researchers the opportunity to manipulate experimentally the factors that cross-cultural researchers typically employ only quasi-experimentally. That is to say, the researcher can systematically introduce, in the form of a prime, a factor assumed to play a role in producing cross-cultural differences in cognition. Cross-cultural comparison of people who grew up in different places with different cultural practices cannot separate the various aspects of these practices to see which is responsible for a measured difference in cognitive style. In priming studies, however, factors that seem likely to be important can be operationalized, assessed, and manipulated. Participants are typically primed by being presented a series of apparently unrelated tasks. Unknown to them, the first task is intended to prime them for subsequent tasks. By studying the "spillover" effect of the priming task on the focal task, manipulating it systematically, and comparing it with cross-national differences, researchers can test models of cultural influence on cognition (Oyserman & Lee, 2007).

With respect to the issue of pervasive cognitive styles, culture-priming tasks are designed to activate the elements of individualism or collectivism. Diverse primes have been used. They include asking people to think about how they are different from (individualism) or similar to (collectivism) family and friends; circling singular (*I, me, myself* …) or collective (*we, us, ourselves* …) pronouns in a passage; unscrambling sentences; subliminal presentation of words or pictures; reading a short story; and using a language assumed to be individualistic (English) or a language assumed to be collectivist (Russian, Chinese, Nepalese).

In a series of experiments, Oyserman, Sorensen, Reber and Chen (2009) demonstrated priming effects on visual memory, visual search, the Stroop color recognition task (reading aloud color names printed in different colors, such as the word 'green' printed in blue ink), a dichotic listening task (different auditory stimuli presented to each ear), and a test of academic preparedness. The participants for these experiments were from Eastern (Hong Kong and Korea) and Western (Norway and the United States) countries, as well as from a variety of American racial and ethnic groups (African Americans, Asian Americans and European Americans). Participants received instructions in their native language and were primed with a pronoun circling task. The results demonstrated that priming effects were similar in Eastern and Western societies (rather than it being the case that, for example, Westerners can be primed but not Easterners). They showed that the prime had an effect no matter what language was used. They also showed effects on a variety of kinds of cognitive tasks, including a real-world academic test. This included finding that once a cognitive style has been primed it "will be used even when it is ill suited to the task at hand" (Oyserman et al., 2009, p. 223). This last finding has important implications for performance on academic tests and tasks by different racial and ethnic groups. A meta-analysis of 67 studies (Oyserman & Lee, 2007) also found that priming had a significant, though only moderate-sized, overall effect on various measures of cognition.

Oyserman et al. (2009) interpret their findings as evidence for "the basic insight that how people think depends on the pragmatic imperatives of the context"

(p. 230). They suggest that culture does not produce "fixed and largely immutable patterned ways of thinking and of organizing the social world" (p. 230), but rather presents its members with specific "pragmatic imperatives" (p. 230) which cue relevant mind-sets. The results of cross-national investigations probably reflect the fact that societies differ in the frequency with which they cue or prime their members. As Oyserman et al. put it,

> Chronic between-society differences are likely importantly due to which mind-set is chronically accessible, suggesting that what appear to be fixed between-society differences are better understood as malleable differences in whether an individual or a collective mind-set is cued. (p. 230)

This work indicates that observable cross-cultural differences in cognition are not inherent in the people studied, but are results of the cues that are generally provided to people by their culture. It takes us beyond static models which presume that culture provides its members with enduring systems of thought by shaping persisting perceptual and cognitive habits, toward models in which culture presents moment to moment situations.

## Is the United States an individualistic culture?

An additional question about the research using cross-cultural comparisons to explore cultural influence on cognitive style concerns the legitimacy of its underlying claim that Eastern and Western cultures differ broadly and deeply on the collectivism–individualism dimension. It is generally assumed the United States is a highly individualistic culture, indeed, some have gone so far as to question the cross-cultural validity of psychological research as a whole because so much of it has been conducted with Americans. Oyserman, Coon and Kemmelmeier (2002) explored the question of whether Americans are more individualistic and less collectivistic than people in other cultures with a meta-analysis of 83 studies. They found that generally the data support the claim that Americans—or at least European Americans—differ on measures of individualism and collectivism when compared with people from other countries, and that individualism and collectivism do in fact influence basic psychological processes. However, they cautioned that "the empirical basis for this conclusion is not as firm as might be desired or as casual reading of textbooks in psychology would have the reader believe" (p. 43). The differences are not large, and they are not systematically patterned. In addition, researchers differ widely in the ways they define these characteristics. They have used different instruments to measure them, have studied small and selective samples and generalized to whole nations, and have frequently worked only with university students, who are unlikely to be representative of their society as a whole. Sometimes they have not measured these characteristics at all and simply compared people from two groups that they have *assumed* differ in collectivism or individualism or both (so they have ignored the other dimensions of cultural difference that Hofstede [1980] and others have pointed to). The consequence is "an emerging cultural tower of Babel in which cultural psychologists are quick to declare any cross-national differences to be 'cultural' and any cultural differences to be within the purview of IND–COL theory" (Oyserman et al., 2002, p. 44).

Oyserman (2006) also points out that cultures may vary independently on individualism and collectivism, so these are apparently not opposite poles on a bipolar continuum. Latin Americans, for example, are high on collectivism but also high on individualism. Although Americans are individualistic in their responses to standard measures they also show collectivist characteristics, such as valuing group membership and seeking advice from others. Furthermore, the evidence suggests that European Americans are less individualistic than African Americans. This highlights the likelihood that people in different subgroups and social strata differ in their socialization processes and their psychological characteristics. In short, the research comparing countries paints only a moderately convincing picture of national differences along an axis of individualism–collectivism, and only a moderately high degree of individualism among Americans.

## Cultural Practices as the Source of Variations in Cognition

Cultural practices can be thought of as the proximal units of culturally organized experience. Shweder and his colleagues (1998) expressed this idea when they wrote that whatever universal cognitive characteristics humans share as a species, these features "only gain character, substance, definition and motivational force … when they are translated and transformed into, and through, the concrete actualities of some particular practice, activity setting, or way of life" (p. 871). Culturally organized practices vary greatly within and between social groups, and so provide rich opportunities to study the relation of culture and cognition.

Authors who emphasize the idea of cognitive styles associated with the cultural patterns characteristic of large populations also assert the importance of cultural practice. So, for example, Nisbett and Masuda (2003) argued that "the differences in attention, perception, and cognition that we have shown are driven by differences in social structure and social practices" (p. 11169). Elsewhere, Nisbett and Norenzayan (2002) noted that "Societies differ in the cultural practices that they promote, affording differential expertise in the use of a cognitive strategy, or differential knowledge about a domain" (p. 28). However, these authors did not directly study cultural practices; instead their experimental studies investigated the presumed generalized cognitive outcomes of cultural practices which others had described.

By contrast, those who do directly study cultural practices as the proximal locus of culture–cognition relations are likely to combine direct ethnographic descriptions with experimental methods that model the practice they observe (Cole, 1996; Greenfield, 2004; Mejia-Arauz, Rogoff, & Paradise, 2005). The existing literature on culture and cognition provides many instructive examples. An early and compelling example can be found in the work of Serpell (1979). Having studied in Scotland but working at the time in Zambia in southern Africa, Serpell had become suspicious of a body of literature purporting to show that non-literate peoples were deficient in their ability to represent objects, due to a failure to develop appropriate habits of perceptual analysis. He conducted a study designed to distinguish between a generalized deficit in perceptual ability and culture-specific practices that promoted particular forms of representation. Four perceptual tasks were involved. The first required children to copy the positions of the experimenter's hands; the second to copy two-dimensional figures with pen and paper (drawing); the third to construct copies of two-dimensional wire objects with strips of wire; and the fourth to make copies of three-dimensional objects in clay.

Serpell's observations had led him to believe that that there were cultural differences in the frequency with which the children engaged in the practices required for these tasks. He predicted that Scottish and Zambian children would perform equally well in mimicking hand positions, because such actions were observed in both cultural groups. Children in both groups had experience modeling in clay, so no differences were expected for that task. But differences were expected in the use of pen and paper to represent a two-dimensional object, which was a frequent practice for the Scottish children, but not the Zambian children. Precisely the opposite expectation held for modeling using wire, which was a common practice among the Zambian children but not the Scottish children.

As one would predict if one believed that cultural practices are intimately related to cognitive processes, there were no differences among the two groups for mimicking hand positions or modeling with clay. But the Scottish children outperformed the Zambian children when asked to draw a picture of a two-dimensional object, while the Zambian children outperformed the Scottish children in modeling using wire.

Studies of the relation between cognitive processes and culture can also be carried out within a single culture, using the differential experience of adults in local practices as a means for making the relevant contrasts. For example, Saxe and Gearhart (1990) studied the development of topological concepts in 5- to 15-year-old unschooled child weavers (who made mats, hats, and other objects from straw) in rural communities in northeastern Brazil. Topology is the branch of mathematics that deals with spatial properties that are unchanged by transformations such as stretching, twisting, and bending. Saxe and Gearhart observed and videotaped everyday teaching interactions and analyzed the child weavers' topological understandings, contrasting weavers of different age levels and comparing weavers with age-matched non-weavers. The children who had become expert weavers presented more topological information (what goes on top of what, how straws are interlaced, etc.). Weavers showed greater skill with increasing age and were more able to construct relevant patterns for inexperienced weavers than could age-matched non-weavers. They were also more likely to provide novice weavers with effective demonstrations of weaving actions.

Another research strategy that adds to our understanding of culture-cognition relations takes advantage of historical change. For example, Greenfield and Childs (1977) went to a Mayan community in the state of Chiapas, Mexico, where they studied the cognitive and social consequences of learning to weave. Their work included careful descriptions of the weaving process engaged in by women and young girls who were being apprenticed into weaving. They analyzed the patterns of the weaving products and conducted experimental tests of the children's ability to reproduce weaving patterns using sticks of varying width and color and a model of the traditional loom. In the 1990s they returned to the same village and conducted parallel observations of parents (former child subjects) inducting their children into weaving to study the consequences of the changed weaving practices and products that had taken place over the years (Greenfield, 2004). In contrast to the late 1960s, by the mid-1990s this Mayan community had shifted from an economy based primarily on subsistence agriculture, relatively secluded from the modern state, to one based heavily on involvement in the money economy, and with much more frequent interaction with people from outside the village and the local region, including trade in woven cloth in a profusion of new patterns. The instructional mode that characterized the mother–child weaving sessions in the 1960s and 1970s consisted of mothers hovering close by and guiding the children with their own hands and bodies, using little verbal instruction. The entire system appeared to focus on maintenance of the "one right way" of the weaving tradition, a limited, relatively simple set of weaving patterns. In the 1990s, mothers who were more involved in the modern economy (for example, women who wove products for sale) instructed their children verbally from a distance, sometimes relying on older siblings to take over instruction, and their children learned by a process with a good deal more trial-and-error and self-correction of errors. There was no longer a small set of simple, "correct" patterns but many, varied patterns, indicating the increased respect paid to individual innovation which comes with a trial-and-error approach to learning. This proliferation in turn depended on, and contributed to, changes in weaving practices.

Accompanying these historical changes in economic practices and the complexity of woven products were changes in the way children represented weaving patterns in the experimental task. For example, instead of using three white sticks to represent a broad band of white cloth, a single broad, white stick was now more likely to be used, and those who attended school were more likely to be able to create novel patterns. These historical changes were accompanied by an unchanging pattern of representational development related to age: older children in both historical periods were more able than younger children to represent more complex visual patterns, a fact that Greenfield (2004) interprets as an indication of universal developmental processes accompanying culturally contingent ones.

Under some conditions, research focused directly on adults can be a strategy for those who are interested in the psychological consequences of cultural practices.

Scribner and Cole (1981) adopted this approach in their study of the cognition and literacy among the Vai, a tribal group residing along the northwest coast of Liberia. Although standard ethnographies of the Vai made them appear to be similar in most respects to their neighbors, they were in fact remarkable because they had been using a writing system of their own invention, acquired entirely outside of schools, for more than 100 years.

The key part of Cole and Scriber's work involved study of a variety of everyday tasks where literate people used written Vai to carry out culturally valued activities. From analysis of a large corpus of letters, for example, they discovered that although the contents were likely to be relatively routine, and hence easy to interpret, the letters nonetheless contained various "context setting" devices to take account of the fact that the reader was not in face-to-face contact with the writer. They reasoned that extended practice in letter writing to people in other locales ought to promote a tendency to provide fuller descriptions of local events. This notion was tested by creating a simple board game, similar to games common in the area but different enough to require rather explicit instructions. Literate and non-literate Vai people learned the game and then described it, either to another person, face to face, or by dictating a letter to someone in another village in enough detail for that person to be able to play the game on the basis of the instructions alone. Vai literates were far better at this task than non-literates, and among Vai literates their degree of experience in reading and writing was positively associated with performance.

Vai literates also excelled at analyzing spoken words into syllables and at synthesizing syllables into meaningful words and phrases (for example, the words for chicken [*tiye*] and paddle [*laa*], when combined, yield the word waterside), so by combining pictures it was possible to make entire "sentences." The same kind of result was found when tasks were modeled on Qur'anic literacy practices, wherein children learned to recite the Qur'an, the Islamic sacred book, by adding one word at a time to the first word of a passage. In an "incremental recall" task in which lists of words are built up by starting with a list length of one item and adding one item per trial, Qur'anic literates excelled. By contrast, when the order of the items changed from trial to trial (free recall) school literates performed better than Qur'anic literates.

Another example of cross-cultural research that focuses on the level of cultural practice is illustrated in research carried out by Rogoff, Paradise, Mejia-Arauz, Correa-Chávez, and Angelillo (2003), who have examined the proclivity of children from many low-technology cultures to learn by carefully observing what their peers and elders are doing. In a typical study, the researchers arranged for 6- to 8-year-old children to observe a 10-year-old child being instructed by a bilingual experimenter in how to accomplish an origami paper folding task (Mejia-Arauz et al., 2005). The children were either from Mexican heritage or European American heritage homes, living in a coastal town in California. Only half of the Mexican-heritage children had mothers with more than a high school education, while all of the European American heritage children had mothers with more than this level of education. On the basis of evidence from many non-industrial and indigenous societies, Mexican-heritage children were expected to observe more intently and ask for fewer explanations than their European-heritage counterparts. And this is what they found—for the Mexican-heritage children whose mothers had attained lower levels of education. However, those Mexican-heritage children whose mothers had gone beyond high school behaved more like their European American counterparts than their peers. They did not engage in as much intent observation, and they asked for a good deal more verbal explanation. These results led Mejia-Arauz and her colleagues (2005) to conclude that:

> Participation in school may socialize specific practices that then gradually become part of indigenous and indigenous-heritage people's own ways of doing things when former schoolchildren become parents, supplanting a traditional emphasis on learning by observation. (p. 290)

A final example of how cognitive skills develop when a society creates artifacts and cultural practices to support more complex cognitive achievements comes from studies of involvement in the use of an abacus in Japan (Hatano, 1997). An abacus, which consists of an oblong frame with rows of wires along which beads are slid to perform calculations, is an external memory and computational device. It registers a number as a configuration of beads, and operations of addition, subtraction, multiplication, and division are carried out by moving them. People can learn how to operate an abacus in an elementary but serviceable manner in a few hours when they participate in deliberate instruction. Advanced training is geared almost entirely to accelerating the speed of the operations involved. Values respecting the speed of calculation are shared among abacus operators.

As a result of extensive training, abacus operation tends to be gradually interiorized to such a degree that most abacus masters can calculate accurately and even faster without a physical abacus present than with the instrument itself. During mental calculation, it appears that they can represent an intermediate, resultant number on their "mental abacus," in the form of a mental image of the configuration of beads, onto which (mentally) they enter, or from which they remove, the next input number. In other words, abacus experts can solve calculation problems by mentally manipulating the mental representation of abacus beads. The interiorization of the operation is an important mechanism for accelerating the speed of calculation, because the mental operation is not constrained by the speed of muscle movement. Thus, expert abacus operators use the real abacus only when they calculate very large numbers that cannot be represented on their mental abacus. Abacus operators calculate extraordinarily rapidly (Hatano, 1997); when mixed addition and subtraction problems are presented in print, experts manipulate 5–10 digits per second. Remarkable speed is also observed for multiplication and division.

The case of gaining expertise in abacus operation (both material and mental) exemplifies the sociocultural nature of expertise (Hatano, 1997). Pupils who attend abacus classes are usually sent by their parents while they attend elementary school. The parents often believe that the exercise will foster children's diligence and punctiliousness as well as enhance their calculation and estimation ability. Young pupils are motivated to learn abacus skills to get parental praise, especially by passing an exam for qualification.

The students' motivation changes when they join an abacus club at school or become a representative of the abacus school—in other words, when the operation is embedded in a different kind of practice. Abacus enthusiasts compete in matches and tournaments, as tennis or chess players do. Also like these players, abacus club members not only engage in exercise at least a few hours every day but also seek knowledge of how to improve their skills. Their learning is strongly supported by the immediate social context of the club and the larger community of abacus operators.

Abacus operators are also socialized in terms of their values, for example, regarding the importance of abacus skills and their status in general education, as well as their respect for the speed of calculation mentioned above. In fact, the community of abacus educators and players constitutes a strong pressure group in the world of education in Japan. In this sense, gaining expertise is far from purely cognitive. It is a social process (Lave & Wenger, 1991), and it involves changes in values and identities (Goodnow, 1990). The experts' values and identities are undoubtedly forms of "culture in mind," acquired through internalization. They serve as the source of motivation for experts to excel in the target domain.

Expertise in mental abacus operation also induces changes at neural levels. For example, using event-related fMRI (high-speed mapping which makes it possible to study cerebral reactions to individual stimulus events), Tanaka, Michimata, Kaminaga, Honda, and Sadato (2002) showed that whereas ordinary people retain series of digits in verbal working memory (showing increased activation in the corresponding cortical areas including Broca's area, long associated with language), mental abacus experts hold them in visuospatial working memory, and show activations in bilateral superior frontal sulcus and superior parietal lobule, areas involved with spatial working memory and somatic perception respectively. Hanakawa, Honda, Okada, Fukuyama and Shibasaki (2003) demonstrated, also using fMRI, that when mental abacus experts and non-learners of abacus performed mental addition, the posterior superior parietal cortex was significantly more activated in the experts, suggesting again that they were using brain regions specialized for spatial and motor skills.

## Conclusions

These are only bare outlines of contemporary approaches to culture and cognitive development. It now is well established that culture is more than an "add on" to a phylogenetically determined process of human cognition. Culture matters. In Geertz's (1973) terms, it is "ingredient to the process" of cognitive development because the biological and cultural heritages of human beings have been part of the same process of hominization over millions of years. Claims for this interdependence are bolstered by modern brain imaging techniques that amply demonstrate that culturally organized experience, whether organized at the level of societies as a whole or at the level of cultural practices, have clear influences on brain organization and functioning and vice versa.

An issue that requires a good deal more thought concerns the connections among cultural patterns, cognitive styles, and cultural practices. On this point, there is as yet no firm agreement among scholars. Many adhere to the notion that broad cognitive styles, although acquired in specific cultural practices, are based on society-wide, historically accumulated, designs for living so that it makes good sense to speak of East Asian versus European or American cognitive styles that shape human cognition in virtually all domains of human experience from conceptions of the self to forms of perception, attention, problem solving, and social interaction. Even some who focus on cultural practices as the proximal locus of cultural influences on cognition believe that such practices are significantly shaped by overall cultural patterns that can be contrasted in terms of overarching binary oppositions such as interdependent versus independent cultural/cognitive styles.

Others place more emphasis on cultural practices as the primary locus of cultural variations in cognitive development, and take the view that the degree to which patterns of behavior learned in specific cultural practices become general in a cultural group is the result of the culturally organized linkages between practices which are never totalizing in their effects. Thus, for example, the range of literacy practices among the Vai is restricted relative to the range of practices associated with literacy in technologically advanced societies. The reasons for this restricted range among the Vai are many: absence of a technology of mass production, legal restrictions placed by the central government on the use of Vai script in civil affairs, adherence to a religion that uses a completely different writing system and a foreign language, and so on. Scribner and Cole's activity-based, cultural practice approach emphasized that, if the uses of writing are few, the skill development they induce will also be limited to accomplishing a narrow range of tasks in a correspondingly narrow range of activities and content domains.

However, when technological, social, and economic conditions create many activities where reading and writing are instrumental, the range of literacy skills can be expected to broaden and increase in complexity. In any society where literacy practices are ubiquitous and complexly interrelated, the associated cognitive skills will also become more widespread and complexly related, giving the (false) impression that literacy (usually attributed to engagement in schooling) induces generalized changes in cognitive development.

The literature on priming carried out within the research tradition that gave rise to the idea of cultural styles appears to be moving toward a similar conclusion from the opposite direction (e.g., Hong & Mallorie, 2004; Hong, Morris, Chiu & Benet-Martínez, 2000). Oyserman and her colleagues (2009) examined the proposal that there are cross-national differences in cognitive "mind-sets" (styles) and came to the conclusion that culture is situated cognition. In their view, such general processes as perceiving meaningful wholes or analyzing wholes in terms of their constituents are universal cognitive abilities, but whether people focus first on the whole or on its constituents depends upon the range of cultural practices which evoke one or the other cognitive strategy. As a result, particular cognitive strategies (mind-sets) "may appear stable within a particular context," but are "malleable and sensitive" to subtle changes in the setting (p. 230). What Oyserman and her colleagues refer to as "small interventions" (p. 233) that can evoke such changes include all of the experimental procedures that psychologists use to ground their inferences concerning culture cognition relations.

This line of thinking is strikingly similar to the conclusion of Cole, Gay, Glick, and Sharp (1971) almost 40 years ago that *"cultural differences in cognition reside more in the situations in which particular cognitive processes are applied than in the existence of a process in one cultural group and its absence in another"* (p. 233, original emphasis).

The difference between Mexican-heritage and European American-heritage children's proclivity to learn through intent observation is further evidence for this general line of thinking, for it implies that formal, literacy-based schooling is usefully considered as a complex set of cultural practices. Involvement in those practices induces practice-specific learning, but it may also seep into practices of the home and community. Hence, children's proclivities to engage in learning through intent observation change not because of a society-wide difference in cognitive style that shapes their involvement in specific practices (folding paper to make objects) but because of the interconnection of home and school practices in the lives of their parents, whose own lives were changed by the practices they engaged in as youngsters. As Rogoff and Angelillo (2002) described their approach, their aim

> is to examine a pattern of approaches to learning that relates to a constellation of cultural practices. This approach to culture, focusing on multifaceted and coherent cultural practices rather than on variables "independent" of each other, allows examination of cultural patterns that would be obscured if all but a few differences between communities were "controlled." (p. 290)

Running through most of the psychological research on culture and cognition is the assumption that the former has a causal and unidirectional influence on the latter. We have suggested that instead the relationship should be seen as one of *constitution*. Culture and cognition are not two separate phenomena: culture makes cognitive phenomena possible; humans cannot think except through culture. At the same time, culture is impossible without human thought and action. Neither would exist without the other. Of course biology cannot be left out; humans are an evolved species, and without brains and bodies we would not be capable of thinking, feeling, and acting. But biology alone is not sufficient, for humans have evolved to live cooperatively together and we raise our children in complex environments filled with the cultural artifacts we use to work and play. As children use these artifacts in interaction with significant other people their psychological functioning is transformed. In this sense, culture is the medium in which children grow.

The task that faces psychologists is that of untangling and articulating the character of this mutual constitution. Cross-cultural research plays an important part in this task, but the typical cross-cultural research design, in which the comparison of two or more cultures is treated as a quasi-experimental design, cannot avoid treating culture as a variable. Even experimental studies, such as the priming research, treat cultural factors as distinct from cognition, having an influence *on* it but not being inherent *to* it.

The relationship between cognition and culture is that of parts in an interrelated whole. Psychology still lacks the methodology adequate to the investigation of complex, holistic systems, but the way humans live, perceive, and think in cultural settings is surely one such system. Earlier we introduced Luria's concept of a kinetic melody as an illustration of the interpenetration of the cultural and the neural, and as a unit of analysis that captures something of the dynamic, interwoven character of human life and suggests how we might transcend the reductionism of much experimental design. The studies we described briefly in the final section of this chapter illustrate how cultural psychologists have begun to develop ways to investigate and understand the ecological complexity of human experience, and the part in this that is played by cognitive functioning. But there is still a long way to go before we can claim a firm understanding of the intricate ways in which culture and cognitive development relate to each other.

## Note

* The current paper draws upon an earlier paper by Cole and Cagigas (2009) but has been modified and updated to be appropriate to the present volume. Preparation of this manuscript was supported in part by funds provided to Cole by the University of California in his capacity as a University Professor.

## References

Bartlett, F. C. (1932). *Remembering*. Cambridge, UK: Cambridge University Press.
Benedict, R. (1934). *Patterns of culture*. New York: Houghton Mifflin.
Berry, J. W. (1976). *Human ecology and cultural style*. New York: Sage-Halstead.
Berry, J. W., Van de Koppel, J. M., Senechal, C., Annis, R. C., Bahuchet, S., Cavalli-Sforza, L. L., & Witkin, H. (1986). *On the edge of the forest: Cultural adaptation and cognitive development in Central Africa*. Lisse, The Netherlands: Swets and Zeitlinger.

Bruner, J. S. (1990). *Acts of meaning*. Cambridge, MA: Harvard University Press.

Bruner, J. S. (2002). *Making stories*. New York: Farrar, Strauss, & Giroux.

Chua, H. F., Boland, J. E., & Nisbett, R. E. (2005). Cultural variation in eye movements during scene perception. *Proceedings of the National Academy of Sciences, 102*(35), 12629–12633.

Cole, M. (1996). *Cultural psychology*. Cambridge, MA: Harvard University Press.

Cole, M., & Cagigas, X. (2009). Cognition. In M. H. Bornstein (Ed.). *Handbook of cultural developmental science* (pp. 127–142). New York: Psychology Press.

Cole, M., Gay, J., Glick, J. A., & Sharp, D. W. (1971). *The cultural context of learning and thinking*. New York: Basic Books.

D'Andrade, R. (1986a). Culture. In A. Kuper & J. Kuper (Eds.), *The Social Science Encyclopedia* (pp. 161–163). London: Routledge.

D'Andrade, R. (1986b). Three scientific world views and the covering law model. In D. Fiske & R. Shweder (Eds.), *Metatheory in social science* (pp. 19–41). Chicago: University of Chicago Press.

Davenport, J. L., & Potter, M. C. (2004). Scene consistency in object and background perception. *Psychological Science, 15*, 559–564.

Donald, M. (2001). *A mind so rare: The evolution of human consciousness*. New York: Norton and Co.

Geertz, C. (1973). *The interpretation of cultures*. New York: Harper & Row.

Goodenough, W. (1994). Toward a working theory of culture. In R. Borowsky (Ed.). *Assessing cultural anthropology* (pp. 262–273). New York: McGraw Hill.

Goodnow, J. J. (1990). Using sociology to extend psychological accounts of cognitive development. *Human Development, 33*, 81–107.

Greenfield, P. M. (2004). *Weaving generations together: Evolving creativity in the Maya of Chiapas*. Santa Fe, NM: School of American Research.

Greenfield, P. M., & Childs, C. P. (1977). Weaving, color terms and pattern representation: Cultural influences and cognitive development among the Zinacantecos of Southern Mexico. *Inter-American Journal of Psychology, 11*, 23–28.

Greenfield, P. M., Keller, H., Fuligni, A., & Maynard, A. (2003). Cultural pathways through universal development. *Annual Review of Psychology. 54*, 461–490.

Grön, G., Schul, D., Bretschneider, V., Wunderlich, A. P., & Riepe, M. W. (2003). Alike performance during nonverbal episodic learning from diversely imprinted neural networks. *European Journal of Neuroscience, 18*, 3112–3120.

Hanakawa, T., Honda, M., Okada, T., Fukuyama, H.. & Shibasaki, H. (2003). Neural correlates underlying mental calculation in abacus experts: A functional magnetic resonance imaging study. *NeuroImage,19*, 296–307.

Hatano, G. (1997). Commentary: Core domains of thought, innate constraints, and sociocultural contexts. In H. M. Wellman & K. Inagaki (Eds.), *The emergence of core domains of thought: Children's reasoning about physical, psychological, and biological phenomena.* (pp. 71–78). San Francisco: Jossey-Bass.

Herskovitz, M. (1948). *Man and his works: The sciences of cultural anthropology*. New York: Knopf.

Herodotus (440 BCE/2003). *Herodotus: The histories* (Aubrey de Sélincourt, Trans.). London: Penguin Books.

Hofstede, G. (1980). *Culture's consequences*. Newbury Park, CA: Sage.

Hong, Y.-y., & Mallorie, L. A. M. (2004). A dynamic constructivist approach to culture: Lessons learned from personality psychology. *Journal of Research in Personality, 38,* 59–67.

Hong, Y.-y., Morris, M. W; Chiu, C.-y., & Benet-Martínez, V. (2000). Multicultural minds: A dynamic constructivist approach to culture and cognition. *American Psychologist, 55,* 709–720.

Hutchins, E. (1995). *Cognition in the wild.* Cambridge, MA: MIT Press.

Ji, L., Peng, K., & Nisbett, R. E. (2000). Culture, control, and perception of relationships in the environment. *Journal of Personality and Social Psychology, 78,* 943–955.

Kitayama, S., & Cohen, D. (2007). *The handbook of cultural psychology.* New York: Guilford Press.

Lave, J., & Wenger, E. (1991). *Situated learning. Legitimate peripheral participation.* Cambridge, UK: Cambridge University Press.

Li, S.-C. (2006). Biocultural co-construction of lifespan development. In P. B. Baltes, P. A. Reuter-Lorenz, and F. Rösler, (Eds.). (2006). *Lifespan development and the brain: The perspective of biocultural co-constructivism* (pp. 40–57). New York: Cambridge University Press.

Luria, A. R. (1974). *Cognitive development: Its cultural and social foundations.* Cambridge, MA: Harvard University Press.

Markus, H., & Kitayama, S. (1991). Culture and the self: Implications for cognition, emotion, and motivation. *Psychological Review, 98,* 224–253.

Masuda, T., & Nisbett, R. E. (2001). Attending holistically vs analytically: Comparing the context sensitivity of Japanese and Americans. *Journal of Personality and Social Psychology, 81,* 922–934.

Mejia-Arauz, R., Rogoff, B., & Paradise, R. (2005). Cultural variation in children's observation during a demonstration. *International Journal of Behavioural Development, 29,* 283–291.

Nelson, K. (1981). Social cognition in a script framework. In J. H. Flavell & L. Ross (Eds.), *Social cognitive development: Frontiers and possible futures.* (pp. 97–118). Cambridge, UK: Cambridge University Press.

Nelson, K. (1986). *Event knowledge: Structure and function in development.* Hillsdale, NJ: Lawrence Erlbaum Associates.

Nisbett, R. E., & Masuda, T. (2003). Culture and point of view. *Proceedings of the National Academy of Sciences, 100*(19), 11163–11170.

Nisbett, R. E., & Norenzayan, A. (2002). Culture and cognition. In H. Pashler & D. Medin (Eds). *Steven's handbook of experimental psychology* (3rd ed.), *Vol. 2: Memory and cognitive processes* (pp. 561–597). Hoboken, NJ: John Wiley & Sons.

Nisbett, R. E., Peng, K., Choi, I., & Norenzayan, A. (2001). Culture and systems of thought: Holistic versus analytic cognition. *Psychological Review, 108,* 291–310.

Oyserman, D. (2006). High power, low power, and equality: Culture beyond individualism and collectivism. *Journal of Consumer Psychology, 16,* 352–356.

Oyserman, D., Coon, H. M., & Kemmelmeier, M. (2002). Rethinking individualism and collectivism: Evaluation of theoretical assumptions and meta-analyses. *Psychological Bulletin, 128,* 3–72.

Oyserman, D., & Lee, S. W.-S. (2007). Priming "culture": Culture as situated cognition. In S. Kitayama & D. Cohen (Eds.), *Handbook of Cultural Psychology* (pp. 255–282). New York: The Guilford Press.

Oyserman, D., Sorensen, N., Reber, R., & Chen, S. X. (2009). Connecting and separating mind-sets: Culture as situated cognition. *Journal of Personality and Social Psychology, 97*(2), 217–235.

Peng, K., & Nisbett, R. E. (1999). Culture, dialectics, and reasoning about contradiction. *American Psychologist, 54*, 741–754.

Quartz, S. R., & Sejnowski, T. J. (2002). *Liars, lovers, and heroes: What the new brain science reveals about how we become who we are.* New York: William Morrow.

Richerson, P. J., & Boyd, R. (2005). *Not by genes alone: How culture transformed human evolution.* Chicago: University of Chicago Press.

Rogoff, B., & Angelillo, C. (2002). Investigating the coordinated functioning of multifaceted cultural practices in human development. *Human Development, 45*, 211–225.

Rogoff, B., Paradise, R., Mejia-Arauz, R., Correa-Chávez, M., & Angelillo, C. (2003). Firsthand learning through intent participation. *Annual Review of Psychology, 54*, 175–203.

Saxe, G. B., & Gearhart, M. (1990). A developmental analysis of everyday topology in unschooled straw weavers. *British Journal of Developmental Psychology, 8*, 251–258.

Scribner, S., & Cole., M. (1981). *The psychology of literacy.* Cambridge, MA: Harvard University Press.

Serpell, R. (1979). How specific are perceptual skills? A cross-cultural study of pattern reproduction. *British Journal of Psychology, 70*, 365–380.

Shweder, R. A., Goodnow, J., Hatano, G., Levin, R. A., Markus, H., & Miller, P. (1998). The cultural psychology of development: One mind, many mentalities. In R. M. Lerner (Ed.), *Handbook of child psychology. Vol 1: Theoretical models of human development* (pp. 865–938). New York: Wiley.

Simons, D. J., & Levin, D. T. (1997). Change blindness. *Trends in Cognitive Sciences, 1*, 261–267.

Tanaka, S., Michimata, C., Kaminaga, T., Honda, M., & Sadato, N. (2002). Superior digit memory of abacus experts: an event-related functional MRI study. *NeuroReport, 13*, 2187–2191.

Triandis, H. C. (1988). Collectivism and individualism: A reconceptualization of a basic concept in cross-cultural psychology. In G. K. Verma & C. Bagley (Eds.), *Personality, attitudes, and cognitions* (pp. 60–95). London: Macmillan.

Valsiner, J., & Rosa, A. (Eds.). (2007). *The Cambridge Handbook of Sociocultural Psychology.* Cambridge, UK: Cambridge University Press.

Vygotsky, L. S. (1930/1997). *The collected works of L. S. Vygotsky, Vol. 4: The history of the development of higher mental functions* (R. W. Rieber, Ed.). New York: Plenum Press.

Wartofsky, M. (1973). *Models.* Dordrecht, The Netherlands: D. Reidel.

Whiting, B. B. (1980). Culture and social behavior: A model for the development of social behavior. *Ethos, 8*, 95–116.

Whiting, B. B., & Whiting, J. W. M. (1975). *Children of six cultures: A psycho-cultural analysis.* Cambridge, MA: Harvard University Press.

Witkin, H. A. (1967). A cognitive-style approach to cross-cultural research. *International Journal of Psychology, 2*, 233–250.

Witkin, H. A., & Berry, J. W. (1975). Psychological differentiation in cross-cultural perspective. *Journal of Cross-Cultural Psychology, 6*(1), 4–87.

# 8

# Cross-Cultural Differences in Visual Perception of Color, Illusions, Depth, and Pictures

## William L. Phillips

*I found myself ... on a high hill ... With me was a Pygmy youth, named Kenge ... Kenge was then about 22 yr. old, and had never before seen a view such as this ... Kenge looked over the plains and down to where a herd of about a hundred buffalo were grazing some miles away. He asked me what kind of insects they were, and I told him they were buffalo, twice as big as the forest buffalo known to him. He laughed loudly and told me not to tell such stupid stories.* (Turnbull, 1961, pp. 304–305)

Anecdotes like the one above from missionaries and anthropologists dating to the nineteenth century sparked curiosity as to whether visual perception is *innate* (we are biologically predisposed to see the world as it is, with no need for cues) or *learned* (we construct our perceptions from experience). You should recognize this as the *nature–nurture* debate espoused by the early philosophers Plato and Aristotle, and later by Descartes and Locke. When looking at this issue from a cross-cultural perspective, the question becomes, "Do group differences in perception result from *heritability* (genetic variation) or from differences in *culture* (how these groups live)?" The goal of this chapter is to illustrate some examples of differences in visual perception that exist among different cultural groups, so that we may develop a deeper understanding of people from other cultures. The main focus will be on *empirical research* performed on the perception of pictorial illusions and pictures, as researchers have consistently used these stimuli to examine cultural differences for over 100 years, exemplifying the importance of *replication* in science.

The origins of methodological cross-cultural perception can be traced to the work of W. H. R. Rivers (1864–1922), a neurologist and anthropologist who was the first scientist to systematically study cross-cultural perception while on an expedition to Torres Straits, between northeastern Australia and New Guinea, thus becoming the first cross-cultural experimental psychologist (Deregowski, 1998). In recognition of Rivers' pioneering work, the first section of this chapter will focus on color perception and pictorial illusions.

# Color Perception

Early work on the perception of color among different cultures typically reported that language is related to how different cultures sort color tiles. Rivers found that peoples from the Torres Straits area (Murray Island, Seven Rivers, Kuwai, and Mabuag) would sort color tiles into groups based on language (Slobodin, 1978). For example, inhabitants of Murray Island (whose language only has words for the colors black, white, and red) typically grouped green and blue tiles together. These findings were typical for other cultures (and languages) being studied at the time, and prompted the Whorf Hypothesis, which explicitly states that language determines our experience.

However, research has not fully supported this hypothesis. Rosch (1973) examined the color discrimination of the Dani tribe of Papua, New Guinea, and determined that although the language only has two terms (one for all dark colors and one for all light colors), the Dani were able to discriminate several colors from one another. This occurred even though, when given a sorting task, members of the Dani tribe typically sorted the color tiles into two groups. Davies and Corbett (1997) examined color sortings from native speakers of English, Russian, and Setswana. Though Russian has two words for blue (one for light blue and one for dark blue), the sortings from English and Russian speakers were very similar. The Setswana speakers, however, tended to sort the blues and greens together, and they used only one word for these colors. It seems, then, that language does not drive perception, but perhaps the importance of having particular words for different colors in a language is dependent upon the need for communicating those colors among individuals.

# The Müller-Lyer Illusion

When you first look at Figure 8.1, which of the lines appears longer? German psychiatrist Franz Müller-Lyer created this illusion in 1889 (Bermond & Van Heerden, 1996). Many people tend to judge the line segment on the left as shorter than the line segment on the right (the two lines are actually the same length—you can measure them with a ruler to confirm this).

Rivers sought to determine the effect of the Müller-Lyer illusion on three groups of Murray Islanders: men, boys, and girls. At the time it was believed that the Murray Islanders (being less "civilized") would be more susceptible to the illusion (that is, make greater errors). Participants were given a brass slide with convergent arrowheads (set at a standard length of 75 mm, and depicted as segment 'A') that contained an inner slide with a divergent arrowhead at one end (see Figure 8.2).

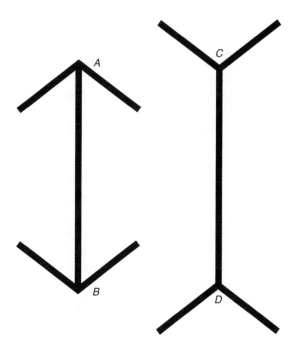

**Figure 8.1** Line segment *AB* is typically perceived to be shorter than line segment *CD*, though they are the same length.

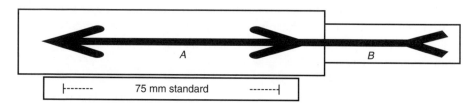

**Figure 8.2** Diagram of apparatus used by Rivers. The segment with divergent arrows (*B*) was to be extended to match the segment formed by the convergent arrows (*A*).

Rivers tested the three groups of Murray Islanders (men, boys, and girls) and compared their performance to three groups of English participants (students, adults, and schoolchildren). Interestingly, the Murray Islanders performed *better* than their English counterparts (they more accurately slid the guide so that the line segments had equal length).

Are these results reliable? Rivers believed that the differences were due to differences in culture between these groups (Slobodin, 1978). However, to be sure that culture is indeed the responsible factor, the result would have to be *replicated*—it must be shown that the result is consistent. Segall, Campbell, and Herskovits (1966) sought to determine whether culture was responsible for differences in performance on the Müller-Lyer stimulus, using 15 pictorial depictions of the illusion. Participants judged whether line *AB* was longer, line *CD* was longer, or if the two lines were equal. They tested more than 1,300 people in 17 different groups, including children (aged 6–11) from 12 of the groups. Most of the participants (more than 1,000) were from 10 different African countries, one small sample comprised Europeans in South Africa, another small sample included Hanunóo people in the Philippines, and 264 individuals were included in two American samples. Segall et al. found substantial differences among the groups. Data were collected in terms of the "percent error > standard"—referring to the percentage greater line *AB* had to be before it was judged equal to line *CD* (see Figure 8.1). Kalahari Bushmen and adult workers in South African gold mines showed virtually no effect of the illusion at all (their percent standard error (PSE) score was 1, meaning that they correctly judged when the two line segments were of equal length). The groups most susceptible to the illusion were the two American samples: a group of university students and children and adults from Illinois.

This pattern of results clearly demonstrated differences between groups. Moreover, the results also showed that children (regardless of group) were more susceptible to the illusion than adults, with the proportional difference between children and adults for any cultural group being fairly systematic (the correlation between children's and adults' ratings for all groups was 0.81). Segall et al. (1966) proposed the "carpentered-world hypothesis," which states that children who grow up and live in squared, city-block environments and rectangular buildings are more susceptible to the illusion (Figure 8.3). A second hypothesis that has been suggested is that differences in experience with pictures and drawings can explain group differences, although Segall et al. argued that this hypothesis did not fit their data as well.

How could one determine whether the differences reported by Segall et al. (1966) are due to culture (specifically, a carpentered world) or due to genetics? (It is apparent that the groups studied by Segall differed genetically.) One way to attempt to answer this question would be to select a pair of identical twins, then raise one in a "carpentered" environment and the other in a "non-carpentered" environment. Of course, there are probably ethical reasons why this should not be done (a good thing, too!). Pedersen and Wheeler (1983) did the next best thing: they tested 20 members of the Navajo Indian tribe, 10 of whom lived until at least age 6 in a *hogan* (the typical Navajo rounded house), and 10 of whom lived in a rectangular house. The results were consistent with predictions from the carpentered-world hypothesis—those Navajo students reared in rectangular houses were more susceptible to the Müller-Lyer illusion than those raised in the *hogan*. Other studies incorporating Chinese participants have also shown support for the carpentered-world hypothesis (Dawson, Young, & Choi, 1973).

Interestingly, most studies have used pictures (e.g., Segall et al., 1966) rather than the original hand-held apparatus incorporated by Rivers (illustrated in Figure 8.2). Bonte (1962) tested both methods of presenting the Müller-Lyer illusion on three groups of participants. The first group consisted of 150 Mbuti Pygmies from the Ituri rainforest located in the east of what is now named Democratic Republic of the Congo (formerly known as Zaire). The Mbuti are hunter-gatherers, living in

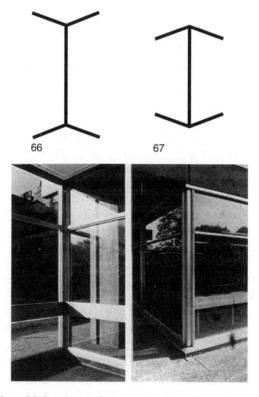

66                        67

**Figure 8.3** A real-world depiction of the Müller-Lyer illusion in a 'carpentered world setting'. Retrieved from http://www.cycleback.com/Müller_lyer_gregory.gif. Reprinted by permission of Richard L. Gregory.

small grass huts low to the ground, spending their lives almost exclusively in the forest. The second group was made up of 450 Bashi, who lived in the central Democratic Republic of the Congo. The participating Bashi lived near a large lake giving them a view of the horizon. They are largely agricultural, living in small, round huts. The third group consisted of 92 adult Europeans.

The Mbuti were unable to perform the task using the picture stimuli, so they were excluded from that analysis. Results revealed that, when using Rivers' apparatus, there was no difference in responses to the Müller-Lyer task. However, when using the pictures, Europeans were more susceptible to the illusion. You may recall that the differences obtained by Rivers were much smaller than those obtained by Segall. The discrepancies in Bonte's results (as compared to Segall) have been explained by methodological differences. For example, the Rivers apparatus (Figure 8.2) creates an artificial vertical line intersecting the line segments to be compared, which does not represent the original illusion (Rivers also saw this problem [Slobodin, 1978] and later created an apparatus that hid the line formed by the meeting point of the two movable pieces). Furthermore, Bonte presented the picture version using several stimuli per page, rather than one stimulus per page. She also used ink that faded with use, and failed to randomize the sequence of stimuli presentation (presenting length differences in ascending order—0%, 5%, 10%, etc.). Finally, Bonte did not explain how instructions were given to the non-English speaking groups, and she combined children and adults (however, she did explain that presenting stimuli one per page, in different orders, would be an improvement in the data collection process). These were exactly the kinds of changes employed by Segall et al. (1966). In addition, Segall et al. reported a strict procedure for administering the task, incorporated experimenters who were prepared for fieldwork, and gave test trials for each illusion used, to ensure comprehension. Though Bonte's results did partially support the results of Rivers, the work of Segall et al. (1966) demonstrated the importance of strict control in implementing a research design, incorporating repeated replication, and conducting thorough data analysis to support the hypothesis that ecological cues, especially experienced during the first 10 years, are largely responsible for the perception of the Müller-Lyer illusion.

## The Ponzo Illusion

A second size–depth illusion is shown in Figures 8.4–8.6. Created by (and named for) the Italian psychologist Mario Ponzo in 1913, the illusion depicts two converging lines (typically in the vertical plane) with two parallel horizontal lines intersecting the converging lines at different points. Though the two horizontal lines are of equal length, respondents typically judge the line closer to the convergent point as longer. A real-world example of this is shown in Figure 8.5 (also known as the "railway illusion").

Cultural differences have also been reported with respect to the susceptibility of different groups to this illusion (Brislin, 1974; Brislin & Keating, 1976; Segall et al., 1966). Though the data collected by Segall et al. were inconclusive, Smith found differences among three groups (N = 30) of Xhosa tribesmen (a group of undergraduates at a local South African university, a group of urban dwellers, and a group of rural dwellers). The rural dwellers would have lived in villages consisting of small rounded huts in an area described as an open vista. Smith hypothesized that the most "acculturated" group (the undergraduates) would be most susceptible to the Ponzo illusion. Results supported this hypothesis; the undergraduates were most susceptible and the rural dwellers the least susceptible. Unfortunately, there is no report whether the three groups of Xhosa men differed with respect to their surroundings while growing up, making it difficult to suggest that these results support the carpentered-world hypothesis. However, to the extent that these differences may be assumed, the data would support this hypothesis.

The situation became clearer in a study performed by Brislin (1974). He compared a group of individuals from Guam to a group from the mainland United States. At the time, Guam had very few long, straight roads, and no railroads.

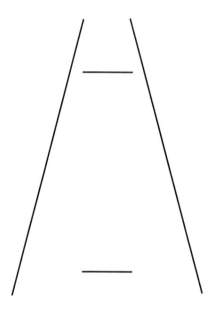

**Figure 8.4** The Ponzo illusion, in which the top line is perceived as longer than the bottom line.

**Figure 8.5** Railway version of the Ponzo illusion. Retrieved from http://www.richardgregory.org/papers/brainmodels/brain_model_fig7.jpg. Reprinted by permission of Richard L. Gregory.

**Figure 8.6** Popular variation on the Ponzo illusion. This drawing depicts several picture cues for depth: (1) relative height, (2) overlap, and (3) linear perspective. "Monster" image from *Mind sights: Original visual illusions, ambiguities, and other anomalies*, by Roger Shepard. New York: Freeman, 1990. Copyright © 1990 by Roger Shepard. Reprinted by arrangement with Henry Holt and Company, LLC.

Furthermore, the vistas were short due to either hills or trees. Brislin tested participants using standard two-dimensional representations of the Ponzo illusion drawn on cards (see Figure 8.4). The results were consistent with the ecological cue (or carpentered-world) hypothesis; participants from Guam were less susceptible to two-dimensional depictions of the Ponzo illusion than were the mainland Americans. Brislin and Keating (1976) sought to replicate these results in an environmental context. They reasoned that if exposure to open vistas and man-made environments were responsible for the susceptibility to the Ponzo illusion, then the illusion should be just as effective in a more natural setting. They compared a sample of 21 mainland U.S. students (all from urbanized areas) with 21 Pacific Islanders (all participants were between 22 and 40 years of age). The Pacific Islanders each had lived a minimum of their first 18 years on their home island. The islands represented had environments similar to that of Guam (described earlier) and included American Samoa, Fiji, Kauai, Marshals, Maui, Palau, Ponape, Solomons, Tonga, Truk, and Western Samoa. In addition, 10 participants (aged

22–40 years) from urbanized areas of the Philippines were tested as a third comparison group. Brislin and Keating created the "natural" setting by using boards that were each 3.2 m long, set up as the converging lines of the Ponzo illusion. A board 80 cm long (the standard) was placed near the apex, with comparison boards ranging in length from 77.6 cm to 92.8 cm in length. A wooden house served as the background to the scene, and participants stood 13.2 m away from the display at a point equidistant from the ends of one of the 3.2 m boards (resulting in the horizontal version of the Ponzo illusion).

The results replicated the earlier study performed by Brislin (1974). The participants from the United States were more susceptible to the illusion (as were participants from urban areas of the Philippines). Both these groups were significantly different from the Pacific Islanders. Furthermore, Brislin assessed the reliability of judgments using this procedure, testing 12 participants two months later. The correlation between test and retest judgments was $r = 0.75$, suggesting a consistent finding.

In another study investigating effects of age, schooling, and environment on perception of the Ponzo illusion in Moroccan males aged 6–22, Wagner (1977) analyzed the interaction among these three variables. When seen in pictures depicting it in relatively "natural" settings (a railroad track or a field), the Ponzo illusion produced increased susceptibility in older participants, and schooling and urban environments produced increased susceptibility for these same conditions.

The results of these studies (Brislin, 1974; Brislin & Keating, 1976; Wagner, 1977) once again support an ecological cue hypothesis. The major difference between groups was the environments in which they were reared, and not educational differences (all participants were attending post-baccalaureate courses in Hawaii), except for Wagner's participants, whose educational experience seemed to increase vulnerability to the illusion. These results also indicate that the Ponzo illusion persists under either two-dimensional or three-dimensional conditions. Moreover, these cues appear to be artifacts of constructed environments: straight paved roads, railroad tracks, and city-block matrices that give rise to the size–distance inference that objects farther away are larger than they appear. This inference would develop to a lesser degree in persons not exposed to great distances in their home environments. Interestingly, research has shown that differential exposure to environmental cues for the Ponzo illusion can also produce differing responses in nonhuman animals (e.g., Nakagawa, 2002). Curiously, however, Segall et al. (1966) reported that differences with respect to a similar perspective illusion were inconclusive.

## Picture Perception: Perceiving Depth in Pictures

Beyond the fact that the previously discussed illusions are depicted in line drawings, it will prove interesting to consider differences in the perception of whole pictures. There has been a considerable number of reports by missionaries, explorers, and anthropologists describing how different cultures interpret images in pictures and photographs (e.g., Kidd, 1904; Livingstone, 1857), and a long history of interest in pictures, spanning millennia (Halverson, 1992). These writers have reported how pictures or photographs were not well perceived, or perceived with some initial difficulty, by people who were not experienced with two-dimensional depictions of three-dimensional scenes. Thus, Kidd, writing about the Kafir of South Africa, related "The natives are frequently quite incapable of seeing pictures at first, and wonder what the smudge on the paper is there for" (1904, p. 282). According to these reports, children often perceived the image before adults, who after some instruction also could recognize objects such as a dog or ox. Other groups have reacted quite strongly to the sight of pictures, especially of slides projected on a large screen. Livingstone (1857) gave a rather interesting account of one such episode:

> Shinte was most anxious to see the pictures of the magic lantern ... he had his principal men and the same crowd of court beauties around him as at the reception. The first picture exhibited was of Abraham about to slaughter his son, Isaac; it was shown as large as life, and the uplifted knife was in the act of striking the lad; the Balonda men remarked that the picture was much more like a god than the things of wood or clay they worshipped ... The ladies listened with silent awe; but when I moved the slide, the uplifted dagger moving towards them, they thought it was to be sheathed in their bodies instead of Isaac's. "Mother, Mother!" all shouted at once, and off they rushed helter-skelter, tumbling pell-mell over each other, and over the little idol-huts and tobacco-bushes; we could not get one of them back again. (Ch. 16, Jan. 19)

Thus, it seems apparent that pictures are at one extreme (at least initially) not seen at all, to the extreme of believing they are real. However, it should also be noted that in one instance, the background was a small and glossy rectangle (the photographs) while in the other projections were made on a life-size wall or screen (Deregowski, 1999). More recent work has included scientific efforts to understand how people of differing cultures and backgrounds perceive pictorial stimuli.

Some of the pioneering cross-cultural experimental work on the perception of pictures was performed by Hudson (1960). Hudson was interested in how depth in pictures would be interpreted—specifically, the pictorial cues of relative size, overlap (or interposition) and linear perspective (see Figure 8.6 for an explanation of these cues). Hudson showed a series of pictures (like those in Figure 8.7) to 273 children and 289 adults in the Union of South Africa. The adults consisted of skilled and unskilled male mine workers with varying amounts of schooling. All the children attended school, and were in grades 1–12. One group of adults were teachers from area schools. The adults varied also in their territorial origin, which included South Africa, South West Africa, the High Commission Territories, Federation of Rhodesias and Nyasaland, East Africa, Mozambique, and Angola. Data were not reported by region, but whether the sample was of African or European descent and whether participants had experienced formal schooling.

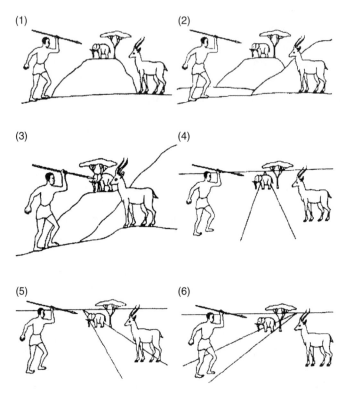

**Figure 8.7**    Six of the pictures used by Hudson. F7.1 depicts familiar size, F7.2 and F7.3 add the overlap cue, and F7.4—F7.6 depict linear perspective. From W. Hudson (1960), Pictorial depth perception in sub-cultural groups in Africa. *Journal of Social Psychology, 52*, 183–208. Reprinted by permission of the publisher (Taylor & Francis http://informaworld.com).

Hudson (1960) showed his participants the line drawings of various hunting scenes (Figure 8.7), first asking them to name all the elements depicted (to ensure they understood what the pictures represented). He then asked several questions about relations that were depicted, such as "What is the man doing?" and "What is nearer the man, elephant or antelope?" If participants answered "antelope" to the latter question, for example, they were classified as three-dimensional (3D) perceivers. Hudson found that educated people, both black and white (including schoolchildren and teachers), made significantly more 3D responses than unskilled laborers (whether schooled or not), and that within the unskilled laborers group those with schooling made more 3D responses. Hudson concluded from these data that formal schooling was an important factor in determining whether a person would be a 3D perceiver of pictures. Hudson's picture test was used on many different tribal groups within Africa (presumably without formal school-ing), with the majority of these investigations revealing that children and adults from these cultures tended not to perceive depth within these types of pictures (Deregowski, 1972).

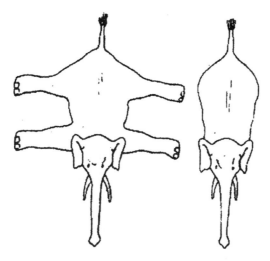

**Figure 8.8a** Example of the stimuli used by Hudson (1962). From J. B. Deregowski (1972). Pictorial perception and culture. *Scientific American, 227,* 82–88. Copyright © 1972 by Scientific American, Inc. All rights reserved.

**Figure 8.8b** Artistic "split" drawing of a bear by the Tsimshian Indians of the Pacific Northwest. From J. B. Deregowski, Pictorial perception and culture. Copyright © 1972 by Scientific American, Inc. All rights reserved.

In a second study, Hudson (1962; as cited by Deregowski, 1999) displayed images like those depicted in Figure 8.8a to 40 mine laborers from South Africa. Hudson asked the miners which of the two versions of the elephant they preferred. All but one of the miners preferred the "spread-eagle" version of the elephant. This split style is not wholly unique to these tribesmen, as this means of drawing is also depicted in the artwork of West Canadian Indians (Figure 8.8b), artwork depicted on an urn excavated near the Polish–Baltic coast and dating to the first century BCE, and in artwork from other cultures (Deregowski, 1999).

Kilbride and Robbins (1969) set out to replicate the findings of Hudson (1960) and to determine acculturation effects other than schooling that may be responsible for perceiving 3D representations in pictures. They presented the Hudson picture test to 104 rural-dwelling Baganda and 118 urban-dwelling Baganda. The rural Baganda lived on the northern and western shores of Lake Victoria in Uganda. This group were mostly farmers, having little or no access to television, movies, or magazines, and had an average of 3.36 years of schooling. In contrast, the urban group (living in Kampala, a city of over 200,000) reported having television sets in their homes (10%), owning cameras (14%), regularly reading magazines (89%), and averaging 7.47 years of schooling. The occupations of this group included teachers, administrators, nurses, engineers, clerks, and secretaries. Results indicated that even when controlling for educational differences, the urban group showed a greater tendency to be 3D perceivers. Thus, both formal education and urbanization (similar to that of Western culture) appear to influence the tendency for an individual to be a 3D perceiver.

Not all the picture research has involved samples from Africa. Jahoda and McGurk (1974b) tested the linear perspective cue by comparing 60 schoolchildren from Glasgow, Scotland, 60 urban schoolchildren from Hong Kong, 48 "boat" children from Hong Kong (these children spend most of their lives on junks, resulting in delayed or very limited schooling), and 59 schoolchildren from rural villages near Salisbury, Rhodesia. All participants viewed one of the four pictures shown in Figure 8.9 (Jahoda & McGurk, 1974a). One picture depicted only elevation as a depth cue, one employed elevation plus texture, one used elevation plus linear perspective, and one employed elevation, linear perspective, and texture as depth cues. Two female drawings were added to each picture along the diagonal depicting depth—girl and girl, girl and woman, woman and girl, and woman and woman (these two figures were identical except for size, with the larger representing the woman). Up to five different age groups (and thus levels of schooling) were tested from each sample. Each participant's task was to place two dolls on a green board (a physical model representing a 3D depiction of the picture) so as to represent the accurate size and spatial relationships depicted in the picture (see Jahoda & McGurk, 1974a, for a complete description of this task).

Replicating the results discussed earlier (Hudson, 1960; Kilbride & Robbins, 1969), the Scottish sample and the Rhodesian sample improved with age for both size and spatial relationships. However, this effect did not occur in either of the Hong Kong groups with respect to size. With respect to spatial relationships, the urban Hong Kong children did show an age effect, but the boat children did not. Of more interest to the present chapter is the difference in results between groups (not analyzed by Jahoda and McGurk). The urban groups (from Scotland and urban Hong Kong) had the advantage when making size judgments, while the two groups from Hong Kong were better at spatial relationships. This is a surprising

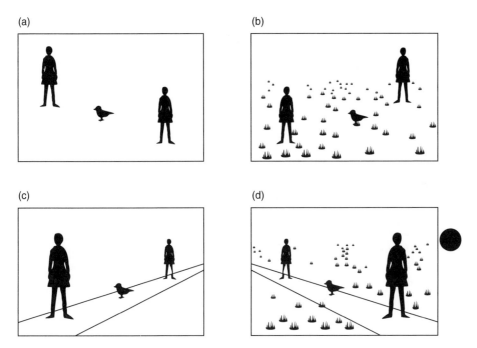

**Figure 8.9** Pictures used by Jahoda and McGurk (1974a). Participants represented the size and spatial relationships in a 3D model (see text for details). From H. McGurk & G. Jahoda, (1975). Pictorial depth perception by children in Scotland and Ghana. *Journal of Cross-Culural Psychology, 6*(3), p. 284. Copyright © 1975 by SAGE publications. Reprinted by permission of SAGE publications.

finding in light of the work of Hudson, who hypothesized that schooling was the major factor in perception of pictures. However, the Hong Kong groups showed little and no age–school effect for the urban and boat children, respectively. In other words, the ability to make size and spatial judgments for the Hong Kong children seemed to occur before schooling began; there is something else in their culture—which we will discuss in the following section—that seems to be responsible.

Bovet and Vauclair (2000) conducted a wide-ranging survey of research on picture recognition, not only in humans, but also in nonhuman animals. They concluded that picture recognition is present in humans from an early age, but that it is facilitated by previous exposure to pictures. Numerous researchers have concluded that, although naïve subjects can quickly learn to recognize objects in pictures, they may find the process effortful or stressful (e.g., Deregowski, Muldrow, & Muldrow, 1972). In addition to experience with pictorial stimuli, Bovet and Vauclair reported that familiarity with objects portrayed in pictures, as well as other characteristics of the stimuli (e.g., the presence of motion) contribute to individual responses.

## Picture Perception: Context and Wholeness

More recent research on cultural differences with respect to pictures has focused less on cues for depth and more on context and "wholeness." For example, Norenzayan, Smith, Kim and Nisbett (2002) investigated categorization differences among European Americans, Asian Americans, and East Asians. They hypothesized that Asians (who are more socialized to focus on interdependence within their culture) would attend more to family type characteristics than to single-rule based characteristics. Participants viewed two groups of objects like those presented in Figure 8.10a and 8.10b and attempted to determine the group to which each target was most similar. One hundred fifty-seven male and female students (52 European Americans, 52 Asian Americans, and 53 East Asians of both Chinese and Korean descent) rated the similarity of 20 stimuli. The results suggested that Asian Americans and East Asians were much more likely to judge similarity based on family resemblance (the whole stimulus) rather than one defining feature shared in common (the strategy employed by the European Americans).

Further evidence supporting the hypothesis that East Asians attend more to the "whole" rather than specific features of a stimulus comes from the work of Kitayama, Duffy, Kawamura and Larsen (2003). They presented 20 undergraduate university students from Japan and 20 from the United States the line drawing task described in Figure 8.11. Results revealed that Japanese students made fewer errors in the relative task, while Americans made fewer errors in the absolute task. This occurred even when the researchers instructed the participants to draw the absolute length of the line or the proportional length of the line! Participants could not overcome their pre-existing bias for drawing the line—with the Japanese students emphasizing the relational nature of the task, and the Americans the absolute.

The results of these two studies suggest that East Asians attend more to the entire or "whole" of a stimulus more than Americans. If this hypothesis is true, then it should occur in other, real-world contexts as well. Replications to test such hypotheses are performed to establish the *ecological validity* of a finding—obtaining a similar result under more naturalistic conditions. Masuda and Nisbett (2001) showed Japanese and American participants video clips of displays like that in Figure 8.12, and asked them to write a description of what they saw. Japanese participants were much more likely to begin their descriptions with a summary of the context (e.g., stationary objects in the display), whereas American participants tended to describe salient objects in the display (i.e., objects that were moving). Overall, Japanese participants reported nearly 60% more contextual information. Furthermore, in a follow-up recognition task that incorporated either the same, a novel, or no background, Japanese participants were influenced by the background while American participants were not (providing a novel background impaired Japanese participants' recognition of salient objects more than it did American participants' recognition).

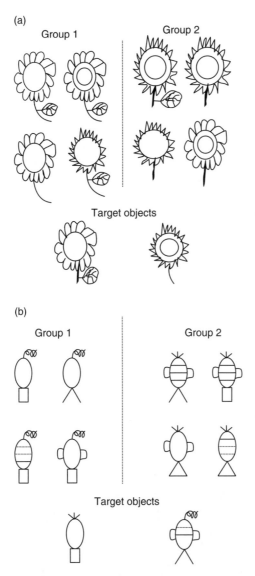

**Figure 8.10** Two stimuli used by Norenzayan et al. Given one of the two targets, participants were asked "Which group the target object is most similar to?" Participants could base their response on either a unidimensional rule shared by all members of the group (stem type or hair type) or choose based on overall family resemblance. From A. Norenzayan, E. E. Smith, B. J. Kim, & R. E. Nisbett (2002). Cultural preferences for formal versus intuitive reasoning. *Cognitive Science: A Multidisciplinary Journal, 26*(5), 653–684. Copyright © 2002 by Cognitive Science Society. All rights reserved.

Masuda, Gonzalez, Kwan and Nisbett (2008) also explored the perception of "wholes" and context in photography. Participants (37 Caucasians, 6 African Americans, 22 Taiwanese, 7 Koreans, 5 Japanese and 12 Chinese) were instructed to take four portrait photographs of a model (sitting or standing in either a lab or

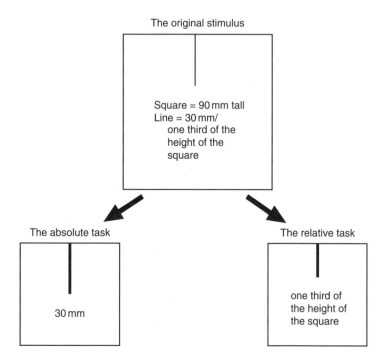

**Figure 8.11**   The task employed by Kitayama et al. They asked participants to either draw the test line the same size (in smaller box that was presented—the absolute task) or proportional to the size of the smaller box (the relative task). From S. Kitayama, S. Duffy, T. Kawamura, & J. T. Larsen (2003). Perceiving an object and its context in different cultures: A cultural look at new look. *Psychological Science, 14*(3), 201–206. Copyright © (2003) by Psychological Science. All rights reserved.

**Figure 8.12**   Example of the type of scene from video clips shown to participants by Masuda and Nisbett. Clips lasted approximately 20 seconds and were shown twice before data were collected. Photograph by author.

(a)

(b)

**Figure 8.13a** An example of the type of photograph taken by Americans. Photograph by author.

**Figure 8.13b** An example of the type of photograph taken by East Asians. Photograph by author.

an atrium setting). All participants were shown how to use the zoom lens and change focus on a digital camera, and all pictures were taken 9 ft from the subject. The findings were fascinating. Americans took portraits that depicted the face on average 35% larger than photographs taken by East Asians (Figure 8.13a and 8.13b, respectively)—a finding consistent with artists' paintings in each culture. American artists tend to emphasize the individual in portraits, and to be generally more object-oriented, whereas East Asian artists tend to portray individuals as part of a larger context, and to be generally more context-inclusive (Masuda et al., 2008).

## Summary

The preceding pages summarize more than 100 years of psychological research pertaining to differences in perception among cultures regarding color vision, visual illusions, pictorial depictions of depth, and the perception of "wholeness" in pictures and photographs. Where appropriate, I have provided non-scientific historical anecdotes as a comparison to emphasize the importance of the scientific method when drawing conclusions. Time and again, the data support the hypothesis that variables associated with cultural differences (both physical and social) contribute to perceptual differences found between groups. Thus, color sorting differences among cultures can be attributed to differences in language and vocabulary. Language does not influence the physiology of our perceptual systems *per se*, but it does drive the relationships we form among objects, leading to differences in attention, organization, and other cognitive processes. The relevance of this finding does not suggest that one language is more "primitive" than another, but rather illustrates that language meets the adaptive needs of those who employ it in a particular cultural context.

The carpentered-world hypothesis that physical environments (or ecological cues that relate to culture) affect our perception has been postulated to explain cultural differences in the Müller-Lyer and Ponzo illusions. Again, these conclusions do not imply that one culture is superior to another, but that our cognitive systems are adaptable to a variety of environments, and that our perceptual responses will vary accordingly. Moreover, this plasticity of cognitive functioning seems to be related to exposure at a young age more so than education, as indicated by the research of Pederson and Wheeler (1983), and that of Brislin (1974) (both of which controlled for education). The case is similar for the perception of depth in pictures. Interpretation of pictures is related to how pictures are used within a culture (whether pictures and paintings are purely ornamental and decorative or used as a means of communication), paired with ecological cues available from the environment.

Finally, socialization may be responsible for differences in perception and cognitive organization among cultures. East Asians consistently attend more to the context and wholeness of a scene, whereas Americans attend more to the salient features or objects. This may be related to the interdependence of East Asians versus the independence stressed by Western culture. Another example of socialization as a mechanism is found in the way Chinese mothers speak to their infants, in contrast to American mothers (Tardif, Shatz & Naigles, 1997). Chinese mothers tend to emphasize verbs, whereas American mothers emphasize nouns. This could lead Chinese children to attend more to relationships among objects in an entire scene (holistically), rather than to salient objects in a scene (analytically). Again, the socialization leads to differences in cognitive structure, highlighting that these structures are largely shaped by culture (Nisbett & Miyamoto, 2005).

In this chapter we have examined only a few of the fascinating perceptual phenomena that researchers have studied over many years. And, as we have seen, it is not sufficient to simply describe perceptual differences between cultures. Particular aspects of experience within cultures—education, specific forms of experience, the cultural emphasis on the context (or the individual), the role of relationships, and many more—are important influences on perceptual processes. We thus need continued research aimed toward unraveling these influences, studies that "unpackage" (Matsumoto, 2006; Whiting, 1976) these variables and expand our understanding.

# References

Bermond, B., & Van Heerden, J. (1996). The Müller-Lyer illusion explained and its theoretical importance reconsidered. *Biology and Philosophy, 11*, 321–338.

Bovet, D., & Vauclair, J. (2000). Picture recognition in animals and humans. *Behavioural Brain Research, 109*, 143–165.

Brislin, R. W. (1974). The Ponzo illusion: Additional cues, age orientation and culture. *Journal of Cross-Cultural Psychology, 5*(2), 139–161.

Brislin, R. W., & Keating, C. F. (1976). Cultural differences in the perception of a three-dimensional Ponzo illusion. *Journal of Cross-Cultural Psychology, 7,* 397–412.

Davies, I. R. L., & Corbett, G. G. (1997). A cross-cultural study of colour-grouping: Evidence for weak linguistic relativity. *British Journal of Psychology, 88,* 493–517.

Dawson, J. L., Young, B. M., & Choi, P. P. (1973). Developmental influences on geometric illusion susceptibility among Hong Kong Chinese children. *Journal of Cross-Cultural Psychology, 4*(1), 49–74.

Deregowski, J. B. (1972). Pictorial perception and culture. *Scientific American, 227*(5), 82–88.

Deregowski, J. B. (1998). W. H. R. Rivers (1864–1922): The founder of research in cross-cultural perception. *Perception, 27*(12), 1393–1406.

Deregowski, J. B. (1999). Pictorial perception: Individual and group differences within the human species. *Cahiers de Psychologie Cognitive/Current Psychology of Cognition, 18*(5), 1031–1063.

Deregowski, J. B., Muldrow, E. S., & Muldrow, W. F. (1972). Pictorial recognition in a remote Ethiopian population. *Perception, 1,* 417–425.

Hudson, W. (1960). Pictorial depth perception in sub-cultural groups in Africa. *Journal of Social Psychology, 52,* 183–208.

Jahoda, G., & McGurk, H. (1974a). Pictorial depth perception: A developmental study. *British Journal of Psychology, 65*(1), 141–149.

Jahoda, G., & McGurk, H. (1974b). Development of pictorial depth perception: Cross-cultural replications. *Child Development, 45,* 1042–1047.

Kidd, D. (1904). *The essential Kafir.* London: Adam and Charles Black.

Kilbride, P. L., & Robbins, M. C. (1969). Pictorial depth perception and acculturation among the Baganda. *American Anthropologist, 71*(2), 293–301.

Kitayama, S., Duffy, S., Kawamura, T., & Larsen, J. T. (2003). Perceiving an object and its context in different cultures: A cultural look at new look. *Psychological Science, 14*(3), 201–206.

Livingstone, D. (1857). *Missionary travels and researches in South Africa.* London: Royal Geographic Society. Retrieved from http://www.gutenberg.org/files/1039/1039-h/1039-h.htm

Masuda, T., Gonzalez, R., Kwan, L., & Nisbett, R. E. (2008). Culture and aesthetic preference: Comparing the attention to context of East Asians and Americans. *Personality and Social Psychology Bulletin, 34*(9), 1260–1275.

Masuda, T., & Nisbett, R. E. (2001). Attending holistically versus analytically: Comparing the context sensitivity of Japanese and Americans. *Journal of Personality and Social Psychology, 81*(5), 922–934.

Matsumoto, D. (2006). Are cultural differences in emotion regulation mediated by personality traits? *Journal of Cross-Cultural Psychology, 37,* 421–437.

McGurk, H., & Jahoda, G. (1975). Pictorial depth perception by children in Scotland and Ghana. *Journal of Cross-Cultural Psychology, 6,* 279–296.

Nakagawa, E. (2002). Rats respond to configurations of stimuli. *The Psychological Record, 52,* 531–558.

Nisbett, R. E., & Miyamoto, Y. (2005). The influence of culture: Holistic versus analytic perception. *Trends in Cognitive Sciences, 9*(10), 467–473.

Norenzayan, A., Smith, E. E., Kim, B. J., & Nisbett, R. E. (2002). Cultural preferences for formal versus intuitive reasoning. *Cognitive Science: A Multidisciplinary Journal, 26*(5), 653–684.

Pedersen, D. M., & Wheeler, J. (1983). The Müller-Lyer illusion among Navajos. *The Journal of Social Psychology, 121*(1), 3–6.

Rosch, E. H. (1973). Natural categories. *Cognitive Psychology, 4,* 328–350.

Segall, M., Campbell, D., & Herskovits, M. J., (1966). *The Influence of Culture on Visual Perception.* New York: The Bobbs-Merrill Company.

Shepard, R. N. (1990). *Mind sights: Original visual illusions, ambiguities, and other anomalies, with a commentary on the play of mind in perception and art.* New York: Freeman.

Slobodin, R. (1978). *W. H. R. Rivers.* New York: Columbia University Press.

Tardif, T., Shatz, M., & Naigles, L. (1997). Caregiver speech and children's use of nouns versus verbs: A comparison of English, Italian, and Mandarin. *Journal of Child Language, 24*(3), 535–565.

Turnbull, C. M. (1961). Some observations regarding the experiences and behavior of the BaMbuti Pygmies. *American Journal of Psychology, 74,* 304–308.

Wagner, D. A. (1977). Ontogeny of the Ponzo illusion: Effects of age, schooling, and environment. *International Journal of Psychology, 12,* 161–176.

Whiting, B. B. (1976). The problem of the packaged variable. In K. Riegel & J. Meacham (Eds.), *The developing individual in a changing world: Vol. 1* (pp. 303–309). Chicago: Aldine.

# 9

# Cross-Cultural Approaches and Issues in Educational Assessment

## Howard T. Everson

### Introduction

What is it that the Central Bank of Iceland, General Motors, the New York Yankees, and your local grocery store all have in common? Answer: their financial health and well-being are tied to the dramatic and unpredictable ups and downs of global financial markets. Financial giants and small investors alike are interconnected in a global economy. One may ask, reasonably, what have global economic growth and prosperity got to do with psychology and large-scale, international efforts to improve educational assessment? Answer: everything!

Recent research by two economists, Eric Hanushek of Stanford University and Ludger Woesssmann from the Ifo Institute for Economic Research and the University of Munich, relates growth in cognitive skills—knowledge and reasoning in mathematics and science, as well as basic literacy skills—to gains in gross domestic product (GDP) (Hanushek & Woessmann, 2010). Their research, sponsored by the Organization for Economic Cooperation and Development (OECD) used contemporary economic modeling methods to relate changes in cognitive skills, as measured by a number of large-scale international assessments such the Programme for International Student Assessment (PISA), to growth in per capita GDP, suggesting that "a modest goal of having all OECD countries boost their average PISA scores by 25 points over the next 20 years ... implies an aggregate gain of OECD GDP of USD 115 trillion over the lifetime of the generation born in 2010" (p. 6).

To survive and thrive, the educational policy argument goes, people, organizations and countries have to become smarter, not only about economics but about threats from climate change, political conflict, the environment, and disease, as well as about a host of other wide-ranging social and technological issues affecting our lives. Many progressive, forward-thinking policymakers and social critics believe, for example, that countries with strong educational systems, with schools that provide educational opportunities for all their citizens, will continue to prosper and grow more stable and democratic in the future. Those that fail to make these investments in education, the conventional wisdom suggests, will remain underdeveloped and relatively poor nations.

Writing recently in the *New York Times* (October 21, 2009) about the "New Untouchables"—those with education, imagination, and the ability to think in new and innovative ways—Thomas Friedman, the Pulitzer Prize-winning author and journalist, repeated the message heard more and more often in economic and policy circles that sustainable economic growth lies in understanding the importance of education for creating new knowledge, and advancing a country's economic growth through innovation and technological advances. A similar argument, detailing new forms of economic growth in a knowledge-based economy, is outlined by David Warsh (2006) in his recent book *Knowledge and the wealth of nations: A story of economic discovery.* Warsh tells about how in India, nearly five years earlier, the prime minister created a "Knowledge Commission to propound ideas for radical reform" (p. 401) in education. Warsh went on to discuss how most developed countries and their governments "get it"; they understand it is in their best interest to underwrite the production and dissemination of knowledge, to support the arts, promote literacy, and dramatically expand educational opportunity. He reported, for example, that in 2004 the German government began making massive investments in higher education. In Singapore, he reported, the pursuit of higher education has taken deep root in the society; China and India are training more PhDs in computer science, engineering, and mathematics than nearly the entire rest of the world. An investment in education is seen, increasingly, as the key to future growth and sustained economic development.

Increased interdependence and globalization, along with the recognition that economic growth in the twenty-first century will come from the development, diffusion, and application of new knowledge—new technologies and new insights and discoveries in the physical, biological, and social sciences—challenge us to improve education not only in the United States, but around the world. These forces, both directly and indirectly, have led to the development of large-scale, cross-cultural educational and psychological assessments, measures designed to provide government officials and public policymakers with the tools and information to gauge, accurately and comparatively, the literacy levels and quantitative skills of their citizens—assessments that provide benchmarks for comparing students' levels of attainment in critical areas of literacy, mathematics, and science.

The thesis of this chapter is not only that these large-scale assessments are necessary to promote strong education systems and contribute to economic growth and stability, but the development and use of these cross-cultural educational assessments can be substantially informed and improved upon by the application of contemporary thinking in psychology, particularly from advances in the learning sciences—the disciplines that focus on how people learn, and how to measure accurately and reliably the changes in learning that take place over many years of schooling. The remainder of this chapter is organized along the following lines.

The next section presents an overview of the movement to develop international, cross-cultural comparative educational assessments. This includes brief descriptions of the major international assessments currently in use, highlighting the long-standing efforts and successes of non-governmental organizations like the United Nations Educational, Scientific and Cultural Organization (UNESCO), the OECD, and the International Association for the Evaluation of Educational Achievement (the IEA). I also describe the increasing importance of the U.S. government sponsored large-scale assessment program, the National Assessment of Educational Progress (NAEP). This is followed by a review of some of the methodological challenges that have to be addressed when designing and implementing rigorous and systematic educational surveys, and reporting accurately and clearly their sometimes controversial results and findings. With this as background, a discussion of the role and influence of two contemporary interdisciplinary areas of research in psychology, cognitive and educational psychology, and psychometrics (i.e., educational and psychological measurement) is presented. The chapter concludes with a look at what lies ahead, with a focus on the potential role of computer-based technology and the Internet for developing new forms of assessment and promoting stronger cross-cultural collaborations.

## Overview of International Educational Assessments

The beginning of serious efforts to design and conduct cross-cultural, comparative educational assessments, at a relatively large and international scale, can be traced to the seminal efforts of the International Association for the Evaluation of Educational Achievement (the IEA). The IEA was founded in 1959 expressly for the purpose of designing and conducting comparative assessments so as to shed light on educational policies and practices in countries throughout the world. The first of these IEA sponsored studies, the Pilot Twelve-Country Study, was mounted nearly 50 years ago. From 1959 to 1962 the IEA conducted testing in mathematics, reading comprehension, geography, science, and non-verbal ability. Nearly 10,000 13-year-old students participated in this ground-breaking pilot study. The countries that took part in the IEA study included Belgium, England, Finland, France, the Federal Republic of Germany, Israel, Poland, Scotland, Sweden, Switzerland, the United States, and Yugoslavia (for more detail, see Foshay, Thorndike, Hotyat, Pidgeon, & Walker, 1962).

Over the past half-century, the IEA membership has grown to include more than 50 countries As Arthur Foshay noted in his *Brief history of IEA* (www.iea.nl/ brief_history_of_iea.html):

The very first IEA study was intended to investigate the feasibility of undertaking more extensive investigations of educational achievement … The study produced findings of academic and practical value, but more importantly it demonstrated the feasibility of conducting large-scale, cross-national surveys ... Furthermore, the study revealed that the effects of language differences can be minimized through the careful translation of instruments. (p. 1)

This early IEA initiative clearly showed that it was not only possible, but important for educational development reasons as well, to conduct meaningful cross-cultural assessments (Postlethwaite, 1985). Reports of this work were published in 1962, and motivated the IEA, in collaboration with the Educational Testing Service (ETS) and the survey and sampling organization, Westat, in the United States, and the Canadian Data Analysis Group to design and implement more and larger cross-cultural assessments. The IEA efforts were also strengthened with the help of the National Academy of Sciences in the United States. Over the past 50 years the IEA has conducted more than 20 large-scale assessment surveys. These included international comparative studies conducted between 1966 and 1975 examining the role of home and school factors on achievement in mathematics, science, reading comprehension, literacy, and civic education (Phillips, 2010; Phillips & Schweisfurth, 2007). Indeed, the IEA has expanded its reach over the years and now includes assessments of the Progress in International Reading Literacy Study (PIRLS) and the Trends in International Mathematics and Science Study (TIMSS). (For additional historical details about the long-term efforts of the IEA, see Foshay et al. [1962], Phillips [2010], and Postlethwaite [1985].)

The purpose of the more contemporary IEA assessments, PIRLS and TIMSS, is to collect and report data on what students know and can do in the areas of reading literacy, mathematics and science. Sketches of both of these assessments follow.


## Progress in International Reading Literacy Study (PIRLS)

The ability to read with comprehension and understanding is central to learning and to active participation in society and in economic life. The progressive views of the IEA, for example, clearly state that a literate citizenry is fundamental for a country's social and economic development. The PIRLS assessment program was designed to assess reading literacy and to monitor the progress of young students' reading achievement over time in the participating countries. Thirty-five countries from around the world participated in PIRLS 2001, and 41 countries participated in PIRLS 2006. Fifty-three countries plan to participate in PIRLS 2011 (For a complete listing of these countries see http://nces.ed.gov/Surveys/PIRLS/index.asp.)

PIRLS assessments are offered on a five-year cycle, and they measure trends in students' reading literacy, as well the participating countries' policies and practices with respect to promoting literacy. Through this complex survey and questionnaire design the participating countries can collect local and comparative information about changes and growth in levels of reading literacy and relate those trends to changes in reading instruction. The PIRLS literacy assessment framework reflects an attempt to measure students' understanding of a variety of text types with an emphasis on the purposes for reading—i.e., acquiring and using information and for literary experience. PIRLS asks students, for example, to demonstrate readings skills and strategies that include (1) retrieving information from text; (2) making inferences based on what they have read; (3) interpreting and synthesizing ideas and concepts; and (4) evaluating the features of the text they have been asked to read.

Interestingly, to provide policymakers and educators with a context for interpreting students' reading achievements, PIRLS also collects systematically, through the use of well-developed questionnaires, a range of data from the students themselves as well as from their parents, teachers, and school principals. By combining this background information with the student achievement data, it then becomes possible, using sophisticated psychometric methods and statistical techniques, to identify factors or combinations of factors—e.g., conditions in the home, school characteristics, instructional methods—that may be systematically associated with the observed trends in reading achievement. Through a collaborative process including researchers from IEA, the International Study Center at Boston College, the National Foundation for Educational Research in England and Wales (NFER), Statistics Canada, and an international panel of recognized experts in reading assessment, the results of the PIRLS surveys are described in well-documented reports that are then made available to the participating countries. In 2006, for example, 45 jurisdictions took part in PIRLS, which included 38 countries, five Canadian provinces, and both the Flemish-speaking and French-speaking schools systems in Belgium. U.S. fourth grade students had an average score of 540 (slightly above the worldwide average of 500), and a larger proportion of students scoring above the international benchmarks when compared with the international median of those benchmarks.

## Trends in International Mathematics and Science Study (TIMSS)

This large-scale international assessment program conducts comparisons of student achievement in mathematics and science trends over a four-year assessment cycle. Like PIRLS, in addition to collecting data on student achievement in mathematics and science, TIMSS also collects a rich set of information about the students' school and home contexts for learning in these two academic domains. The initial testing cycle for TIMSS occurred in 1995, and 41 countries took part in the assessment. The second cycle was in 1999 and 38 countries participated, with 26 of them included for the second time so as to begin a study of trends in student achievement. TIMSS in 2003 saw more growth, with more than 50 countries participating in the full assessment, and in 2007 58 countries took part in both the mathematics and science assessments.

Specific assessment frameworks were developed for assessing mathematics (number and operations, geometric shapes and measures, and data displays) and science (including life science, physical science, and earth science) for students in grade 4, elementary school. Students in grade 8 completed assessments in mathematics content areas of number properties, algebra, geometry, and data and probability; in science they were assessed in biology, chemistry, physics, and earth science. (For more complete details on the frameworks guiding the TIMSS assessments and the results of those assessments, see http://timss.bc.edu/TIMSS2007/release.htm.) In 2007, for example, the average mathematics scores of both U.S. fourth- and eighth-grade students were higher than the TIMSS scale averages (for the 4th graders the average was 529 versus the TIMSS scale average of 500; the U.S. 8th graders scored 508, on average, versus the TIMSS average of 500). The American fourth graders outpaced their peers in roughly two thirds of the other countries, yet scored lower, on average, in mathematics than students in eight countries; and had average math scores that were not statistically different from the average scores of students in four other countries. The score patterns for the U.S. eighth graders were similar, outpacing their peers in 37 of the 47 other countries participating in TIMSS 2007.

## Programme for International Student Assessment (PISA)

Another of the large-scale international assessments has been sponsored and developed recently by the member countries of the OECD. At last count, there were 60 countries (covering about 90% of the world economy) taking part in the OECD sponsored PISA.

Although similar to the earlier IEA assessments, PISA was designed to measure how much progress international cohorts of 15-year-old students are making in acquiring the knowledge and skills needed to be successful in the rapidly developing global knowledge society. The PISA surveys assess students' performance in a number of key subject areas, including reading (assessed in 2000), mathematics (2003), and science (2006). According to the OECD, the goals of PISA are: (1) to develop better methods for tracking students' progress as they move from elementary to secondary school; (2) to permit comparisons between student performance and forms of instruction by testing within and across particular grade levels, where appropriate; and (3) to make better use of computer-based assessments, so as to measure a broader range of knowledge and skills in reading, mathematics, and science using innovative, dynamic, and interactive tasks.

PISA has tested more than one million students thus far, using paper-and-pencil tests of reading, mathematics, and scientific literacy. In addition, the participating students also complete background questionnaires, and their school principals provide detailed information about their schools. This mixture of measures of cognitive abilities, demographic, and other student background information, as well as school-level characteristics allows researchers to examine outcomes over time and provide analyses using advanced statistical and psychometric methods that provide educators and policymakers with rich information for improving their countries' school systems. The OECD recently announced plans to implement additional rounds of surveys in 2012 and 2015. (For those interested in reading more about PISA and examining the results of the comparative, cross-national findings, detailed information can be found at http://www.pisa.gc.ca/what_pisa.shtml.)

There has been a good deal of discussion in education policy circles about comparing students' performance on international assessments, such as TIMSS and PISA, with samples of students drawn from NAEP, the large-scale assessment in the United States. NAEP is an ongoing, congressionally mandated project established to conduct national surveys of the educational attainments of students in the United States. In the U.S. NAEP is known as *the nation's report card*. Its primary goal is to determine and report the status of and trends over time in educational achievement. NAEP began in 1969 to obtain comprehensive and dependable national educational achievement data in a uniform, scientific manner, and is the nation's continuing assessment of what America's students know and can do in various subject areas. Assessments occur periodically in mathematics, reading, science, writing, the arts, civics, economics, geography, and U.S. history. NAEP provides results on subject-matter achievement, instructional experiences, and school environment for populations of students (e.g., all fourth-graders) and groups within those populations (e.g., female students, ethnic minority students). NAEP does not provide scores for individual students or schools, although state NAEP can report results by selected large urban districts. NAEP results are based on representative samples of students at grades 4, 8, and 12 for the main assessments, or samples of students at ages 9, 13, or 17 years for the long-term trend assessments. These grades and ages were chosen because they represent critical junctures in academic achievement. NAEP results serve as a common metric for all states and selected urban districts. Jones and Olkin (2004) have chronicled an interesting and informative history of NAEP in *The nation's report card: Evolution and perspectives*. (More detailed information about NAEP, including descriptions of its assessments and the results of those assessments is at the United States National Center for Education website at http://nces.ed.gov/nationsreportcard/about/.)

## Methodological Issues in Large-Scale International Assessments

Though brief, these sketches of PIRLS, PISA, TIMSS and NAEP provide a flavor for the global reach and scope of these assessment efforts, and underscore the increasing demand for these measures. Apparently, cross-cultural research in education and the psychology of learning is rapidly becoming a growth industry.

The intent of these cross-cultural assessments is to help reduce heretofore ethnocentric views of how students learn, and to reinforce the importance and efficacy of schooling for public policy and economic development. To make this all work in practice, and provide educators and policymakers with valid and reliable information on student learning and the effects of schooling, these large-scale, cross-cultural assessments must address a myriad of technical and measurement issues. The challenges include selecting the academic domains to be assessed, ensuring that the psychological constructs underpinning those domains (e.g., reasoning, problem solving, verbal comprehension) are validly represented by the test items and tasks, maintaining the psychometric infrastructure of the item banks and test forms that are used operationally, and the accurate translation of the test items and supplemental survey questionnaires. Other thorny measurement issues concern ensuring the reliability of the various measurement instruments and scaling them appropriately to ensure accurate score reporting across countries and cultures.

Countries, cultures, and peoples differ, obviously, not only in their languages and customs but also in their views on intelligence, aptitude, and achievement, and on the role of schooling (Sternberg, Lautrey, & Lubart, 2003). Psychologists and researchers working in this field also differ from time to time in their views of the cognitive processes (which ones and to what degree) at the root of measures of educational attainment (Samuda, Feuerstein, Kaufman, Lewis, & Sternberg, 1998). As Church (2010) noted recently in his insightful description of measurement issues in cross-cultural research, "from a cultural psychology perspective, cross-cultural comparison can only be made, if at all, after the investigation of each culture on its own terms" (p. 153). These cultural differences are handled, typically, in the early stages of the test design process by bringing together educators, psychologists, and measurement experts from the participating countries and having them reach consensus on many of these issues. For the most part, groups like the IEA, the OECD and, in the U.S., the NAEP design and analysis committees, are quite successful in achieving consensus and moving efforts forward toward large-scale, cross-cultural implementation.

An important point is that many of the measurement challenges stem from differing views of the psychological and educational constructs to be studied (i.e., literacy, reasoning, problem solving, and/or intelligence). Attention to this issue of construct equivalence (i.e., that the target of inference of the measurement instrument remains constant from one country and culture to another) is key to valid and accurate measurement. This is critical for ensuring reliable and valid comparisons of student achievement across international borders because it provides scientific evidence that the number of latent constructs or factors defining the overall structure of the assessment instruments stays the same from country to country, and across student samples within a country, particularly in those countries where regional distances and differences contribute to marked cultural and linguistic variation.

Similarly, concerns about measurement or method bias are often related to students having varying familiarity with item formats or methods of test administration that may appear strange or inappropriate in one country or cultural setting, while being seemingly typical in another cultural context. As I noted earlier, the need to maintain linguistic equivalence to ensure comparability and validity of measurement instrument translations from one language to another is an ever-present concern during the translation process. The methodological issues surrounding large-scale assessment in education, it should be noted, also pertain to many other applications of cross-cultural assessments in psychology, including measures of personality, psychopathology, and other clinically relevant psychological constructs and profiles. In this chapter I provide only a sampler of the issues that have to be addressed in cross-cultural educational research, highlighting those that directly impinge on the design of large-scale international assessments. More detailed treatments of the cross-cultural issues impinging on the definition and, therefore, the measurement, of central psychological constructs such as intelligence, aptitude, and personality, can be found in works edited by Sternberg, Lautrey, and Lubart (2003) and by Samuda et al. (1998). Church (2001; 2010) and Hambleton, Merenda, and Spielberger (2005) have reviewed methodological issues that must be addressed in large-scale, cross-cultural assessment, both generally, and with particular reference to other areas of psychology.

## How the Learning Sciences Inform Assessment Design

In the past quarter century a number of scientific disciplines have converged on the question of how people learn. This interdisciplinary effort is aimed at furthering our scientific understanding of human learning and thereby influencing the design and implementation of innovative approaches to curriculum, instruction, and assessment. Research in the learning sciences has traditionally focused on cognitive-psychological and social-psychological foundations of human learning, as well as on the design of learning environments and educational and psychological assessments. The primary contributing fields include cognitive science, computer science, cognitive psychology, educational psychology, and anthropology. The information processing view of the human mind embodied in modern cognitive science became dominant in psychology and education in the latter half of the twentieth century. Through the interdisciplinary lenses of the learning sciences, the field has begun to approach the study of intelligence, thinking and reasoning, problem solving, aptitude, and achievement in terms of the mental (i.e., cognitive) representations and processes that presumed to underlie observable behavior (National Research Council, 2001; Sternberg, 1984; Sternberg, Lautrey, & Lubart, 2003).

More than two decades ago, Samuel Messick (1984), a cognitive psychologist and educational measurement expert who worked for many years at the ETS, referred to the theoretical import of the learning sciences for the design of large-scale educational assessment when he wrote:

> Educational achievement refers to what an individual *knows* and *can do* in a specified subject area. At issue is not merely the amount of knowledge accumulated but its organization or structure as a functional system for productive thinking, problem solving, and creative invention in the subject area as well as for further learning. The individual's structure of knowledge is a critical aspect of educational achievement because it facilitates or hinders what he or she can do in the subject area. What a person can do in an area includes a variety of area-specific skills, such as extracting a square root or parsing a sentence or balancing a chemical equation, but also broader cognitive abilities that cut across subject areas, such as comprehension, memory retention and retrieval, reasoning, analysis and restructuring, evaluation or judgment, and fluency … Because cognitive abilities play a central role in both the acquisition and organization functions of educational achievement, their influence can hardly be suppressed or ignored in educational achievement testing that assesses knowledge structures. (p. 155)

Like others whose work borders on cognitive psychology and educational measurement, Messick's view of educational achievement and its measurement stresses knowledge structures as both a product of earlier learning and a vehicle for subsequent learning. It follows, then, that if our assessments can be designed to reveal precise weaknesses in an examinee's knowledge base, specific instructional prescriptions can be made. This capability would increase the utility and relevance of large-scale, cross-cultural assessments to educational reform (Leighton & Gierl, 2007).

With the emergence of the cognitive perspective in the learning sciences, the emphasis shifts from measures of how much a student has learned, or where he or she ranks on a continuum of achievement, to a focus on the importance of how knowledge is organized, and how students reorganize that knowledge to represent and solve problems. Thus, these educational assessments could begin to tell us more about *what* students know and what they can do—i.e., frame problems, develop multiple solution strategies, and evaluate the feasibility of those solutions. This theoretical shift further underscores the need for measurement models that distinguish learners in terms of their knowledge states, cognitive process abilities, and strategies for solving problems (Hunt, 1986; National Research Council, 2001; Reif, 2008).

New test items and tasks will be needed to capture the complexity of reasoning, problem solving, and strategic thinking that is emerging from the learning sciences. Test items and tasks that go beyond the four- or five-option multiple-choice format will be required, and are being developed. Nevertheless, it is certainly the case that even more painstaking work, work informed by theory, will be needed to perform the task analyses that must foreshadow the cognitive model development in various academic domains like mathematical problem solving or language learning and literacy. As the learning sciences, measurement techniques and statistical methods, and computer technologies advance, so, too, will our ability to gather rich, systematic cross-cultural evidence of student learning. Students' developed abilities in, for example, verbal reasoning, reading comprehension, writing, and mathematical problem solving may be assessed in the future with test items and tasks based on more firmly established theoretical foundations.

Achievement tests reflect what students know and can do in specific subject areas. Assessments of cognitive abilities, on the other hand, are not the same as subject-matter achievements. They are often more general, and when combined with measures of achievement they may provide more comprehensive diagnoses of academic potential. This view of educational achievement stresses not only knowledge as the product of learning but also knowledge as a means to more advanced levels of learning. Indeed, the potential exists for the design of cross-cultural educational assessments that provide educators with cognitive profiles of developed abilities not only in the traditional verbal and mathematical domains but also in the subject-specific domains such as mathematics, the sciences, writing, and reading comprehension, which, in turn, will provide direct connections to classroom learning and the effects of schooling. (The interested reader will find more elaborated descriptions of new constructs and discussions of the implications of developments in cognitive psychology for education assessment in Everson [1999, 2004].) By incorporating this view of learning in their frameworks, the international educational assessment programs discussed earlier can provide individual and group level data that may prove more direct and actionable for policy-makers focused on educational reform.

To recap, recent developments in cognitive and educational psychology suggest that test design in the future, including test specifications and frameworks, ought to be informed by this growing, interdisciplinary knowledge base of research that is contributing to our understanding of human thinking and reasoning. As cognitive analyses reveal the structure of competence in broad domains such as verbal comprehension and quantitative and scientific reasoning, as well as narrower, specialized achievement domains, these theory-based descriptions can provide a sound basis for principled, evidence-centered test design (Mislevy, Almond, & Lukas, 2003). Moreover, the application of cognitive theory, in turn, will allow us to draw interpretations and inferences from test performance that have sound theoretical underpinnings and more direct implications for teaching and learning.

## Advances in Psychometrics

Science instructs us that measurement is central to our understanding of the world. The better we measure, the more our knowledge of the world develops and, in turn, our ways of knowing and measuring improve. Early psychometric approaches, those developed in the early twentieth century, were based largely on classical test theory, what others have referred to as the *educational psychometric measurement* approach (Snow & Lohman, 1989). The dominant goal of this view of educational and psychological measurement was to estimate an examinee's position on a scale that measured a latent trait (e.g., intelligence, aptitude, or personality). This classical model developed largely to permit inferences about how much knowledge, aptitude, or ability an individual possessed. This came to be known more widely in psychology as the *standard test theory model*, and it proved useful for inferences related to selection, placement, and classification. With the advent of new knowledge about how people learn from instruction, the classical test theory approach has proven to be much less helpful for making instructional decisions or for diagnosing learning or achievement deficiencies—an often-stated measurement goal of many new assessments.

In response to the challenges articulated by the National Research Council's Committee on the Foundations of Assessment (National Research Council, 2001), which I discussed earlier, a number of new and promising psychometric approaches with a decidedly cognitive flavor are being developed. A number of these contemporary psychometric models are extensions of item response theoretic (IRT) models (Embretson & Reise, 2000). Others extend IRT work further and build on multidimensional latent trait IRT models introduced by Samejima (1988), Reckase (1985) and Embretson (1985). Still others, like those growing out of the work on Bayesian inference networks (Mislevy, 1995), represent attempts to capitalize on pattern recognition methods and conditional probability estimation techniques for gathering evidence and supporting inferences about examinee performance (Leighton & Gierl, 2007).

Although these measurement models may still rank students along a proficiency scale, their intent is to build on detailed task analyses and cognitively rich representations of how knowledge is structured from and by learning in school to produce assessments that inform instruction in ways that are diagnostic as well as prescriptive (Leighton & Gierl, 2007). Many of these newer psychometric models attempt to provide descriptions of the students' knowledge or ability structures, as well as bringing to the surface the cognitive processes presumed to underlie performance on single test items or tasks, or sets of tasks. Thus, if successfully developed and adapted—and much work is currently under way—these new developments in psychometrics hold promise not only for the design of large-scale, cross-cultural educational assessments, but also for dynamically linking assessment and instruction (Everson, 1995, 2004; Leighton & Gierl, 2007; Nichols, 1994; Nichols, Chipman, & Brennan, 1995).

Together, these relatively new psychometric models all take the important step of attempting to integrate cognitive psychology and educational measurement. It is important to restate, however, that to succeed a different breed of assessment is needed—test designs that will allow us to better understand what students know and can do after exposure to instruction, and identify the steps to take if we wish to improve their learning from instruction. If policymakers and educators wish to make claims about student knowledge, skills, or abilities—what students know and can do—test framework and design ought to specify:

1  the complex of knowledge, skills, and abilities to be tested—the achievement construct;
2  the level of fine-grained details about the students' knowledge and performances on a series of tasks that reflect the achievement construct, that allow inferences about what students know and can do in relation to the targeted achievement construct; and
3  the qualities of the test items and tasks that ensure students' performances provide evidence that is well aligned with the targeted achievement construct.

The Board on Testing and Assessment of the National Research Council (National Research Council, 2001) elaborated these three key aspects of assessment design in the influential work, *Knowing what students know: The science and design of educational assessment*. In this scheme, *curriculum* refers to the knowledge and skills in the subject or academic domain that students are expected to learn and teachers intend to teach. *Instruction* refers to the teaching methods and activities selected by the instructional designers to assist students as they attempt to master the course content. *Assessment* refers to how we measure what it is we want students to know and be able to do as a consequence of engaging in instruction. The framework outlined by the National Research Council will prove helpful as we plan the next generation of international educational assessments.

## Networks of Cross-Cultural Assessments

Personal computers are everywhere, and more and more they exist as addresses or nodes on a network of computers, on intranets and the Internet. In some sense the future is already here. Distance learning opportunities are becoming more widely available. Computer-based adaptive tests—assessments in which the examinee is presented with different test questions or tasks matched to his or her ability or skill levels—are becoming more widely used in large-scale assessment programs (e.g., in the U.S., the College Board's Computerized Placement Tests and the ETS Graduate Record Examination). And, as we have seen, a number of the cross-cultural assessment programs, such as PISA, are planning for computer-based assessments in the future. Bennett (1998, 2001, 2002) has framed the potential of computer-based testing for improving large-scale assessments. Bennett suggested the convergence of computer-based testing with advanced networks makes possible new forms of large-scale assessment—more complex items and tasks, seamless branching across content areas and domains, and modular testing components.

This merging of cognitive theory and new developments in psychometric modeling with computer technology also makes likely the introduction of new test delivery systems, remote scoring of constructed responses, and more powerful means for summarizing and communicating performance. These advances in information technologies, no doubt, will provide platforms for the next generation of the college admission tests. If Bennett (1998) is right, these new technologies will be the prime mover of innovation in educational testing. Indeed, Bennett makes a strong argument for future-oriented assessment design frameworks, ones that accommodate technological advances, foster improved measurement, and incorporate breakthroughs in the learning sciences. This convergence of technologies, moreover, will likely influence other forms of social measurement—including political polling methods and other large-scale international social science survey methodologies.

## Conclusion

There is little doubt that global educational reform movements will play out in important ways for advancing economic development. The central thesis of this chapter is that by employing theory-based assessment frameworks, we have the opportunity to introduce a new generation of large-scale, cross-cultural educational assessments—tests that measure a broader array of developed abilities (including both reasoning and achievement measures). Coupled with the emerging model-based measurement approaches and computing technologies described earlier, a theory-based focus ensures that, in the future, large-scale international assessments ought to be more aligned with emerging policy reforms in schooling. As Lane (1991) and others (Glaser, 1989; Mitchell, 1989) have noted, researchers working on the border between cognitive psychology and educational measurement have developed methods for assessing students' knowledge structures in a number of domains, including science, mathematics, reading comprehension, critical thinking, and analytical reasoning. Collectively, many working in these interdisciplinary fields see the possibility of leveraging this new knowledge to enrich our understanding of student learning. These efforts, in turn, will translate into new constructs, new item types, and, ultimately, new forms of assessment.

An ambitious program of research will be required, if we are to transform cross-cultural educational assessments in ways that make them useful not only for ranking and accountability, but also for placement and diagnosis. Such a research and development agenda, undoubtedly, would have to touch on four key areas:

1   developing new measurement constructs that go beyond what is currently assessed and include, for instance, reasoning within and across specific academic domains—the sciences, history, geography, and economics, for example;

2  designing new item types and response formats, and translating them across languages and cultures;

3  developing psychometric models for multidimensional scales and cognitive diagnosis; and

4  communicating examinee performances in ways that inform teaching and learning in the various participating countries and provinces.

The learning sciences and psychology, in particular, have great potential for contributing to the advancement of large-scale international test design.

This is an exciting time for large-scale cross-cultural educational assessment design and implementation. Change and innovation are in the air. Reform and innovation appear to be everywhere in education—particularly when it comes to large-scale assessment. Portfolios, standards-based assessment design, performance assessments, and computer adaptive test methods are just some of what we see in the future as we look across the landscape. Technological innovation, as noted earlier, will transform not only how we test but what we test. We can easily imagine, for example, networks of closely aligned tests, and ideas in this direction are already on the planning boards of a number of assessment design groups. It is clear, too, that rapidly advancing scientific areas like the brain sciences, artificial intelligence, and the psychology of learning will influence testing by reshaping the conceptual basis of teaching and learning in the future. As large-scale national and international surveys and assessments grow more influential, the psychologists, measurement scientists, and other social scientists responsible for developing them may find their work informed more and more by these interdisciplinary developments.

# References

Bennett, R. E. (1998). *Reinventing assessment: Speculation on the future of large-scale educational testing*. Princeton, NJ: Policy Information Center, Educational Testing Service. Available from: http://www.edt.org./research/pic/bennett.html

Bennett, R. E. (2001). How the Internet will help large-scale assessment reinvent itself. *Education Policy Analysis Archives*, 9(5). Available from http://epaa.asu./epaa/v9n5.html

Bennett, R. E. (2002). Inexorable and inevitable: The continuing story of technology and assessment. *Journal of Technology, Learning, and Assessment*, 1(1). Available from http://www.jtla.org.

Church, A. T. (2001). Personality measurement in cross-cultural perspective. *Journal of Personality, 69*, 979–1006.

Church, A. T. (2010). Measurement issues in cross-cultural research. In G. Walford, M. Viswanathan, & E. Tucker (Eds.), *The SAGE Handbook of Measurement* (pp. 151–176). London: SAGE Publications Ltd.

Embretson, S. E. (1985). Multicomponent latent trait models for test design. In S. E. Embretson (Ed.), *Test design: Developments in psychology and psychometrics* (pp. 195–218). Orlando, FL: Academic Press.

Embretson, S. E., & Reise, S. P. (2000). *Item response theory for psychologists*. London: Lawrence Erlbaum Associates.

Everson, H. T. (1995). Modeling the student in intelligent tutoring systems: The promise of a new psychometrics. *Instructional Science, 23*, 433–452.

Everson, H. T. (1999). A theory-based framework for future college admissions tests. In S. Messick (Ed.) *Assessment in higher education: Issues of access, quality, student development, and public policy,* (pp. 113–140). Mahwah, NJ: Lawrence Erlbaum Associates.

Everson, H. T. (2004). Innovation and change in the SAT: A design framework for future college admissions tests. In R. Zwick (Ed.), *Rethinking the SAT: The future of standardize testing in university admissions,* (pp. 75–92). New York: Routledge Falmer.

Foshay, A. W., Thorndike, R. L., Hotyat, F., Pidgeon, D. A., & Walker, D. A. (1962). *Educational achievements of thirteen-year-olds in twelve countries.* Hamburg, Germany: UNESCO Institute for Education.

Glaser, R. (1989). Expertise and learning: How do we think about instructional processes now that we have discovered knowledge structures? In D. Klahr & K. Kotovsky (Eds.), *Complex information processing: The impact of Herbert A. Simon* (pp. 269–282). Hillsdale, NJ: Lawrence Erlbaum Associates.

Hambleton, R. K., Merenda, P. F., & Spielberger, C. D. (Eds.) (2005). *Adapting educational and psychological tests for cross-cultural assessment.* Mahwah, NJ: Lawrence Erlbaum Associates.

Hanushek, E. A., & Woessmann, L. (2010). *The high cost of low educational performance: The long-run economic impact of improving PISA outcomes.* Paris: Organization for Economic Cooperation and Development.

Hunt, E. (1986). Cognitive research and future test design. *ETS Invitational Conference Proceedings.* Princeton, NJ: Educational Testing Service.

Jones, L. V., & Olkin, I. (Eds.) (2004). *The nation's report card: Evolution and perspectives.* Bloomington, IN: Phi Delta Kappan Foundation.

Lane, S. (1991). Implications of cognitive psychology for measurement and testing: Assessing students' knowledge structures. *Educational Measurement: Issues and Practice, 10*(1), 31–33.

Leighton, J. P. & Gierl, M. J. (2007). Cognitive diagnostic assessment for education. New York: Cambridge University Press.

Messick, S. (1984). Abilities and knowledge in educational achievement testing: The assessment of dynamic cognitive structures. In B. S. Plake, S. N. Elliott, & J. V. Mitchell, Jr. (Eds.), *Buros-Nebraska symposium on measurement and testing. Social and technical issues in testing: Implications for test construction and usage* (pp. 155–169). Hillsdale, NJ: Lawrence Erlbaum Associates.

Mislevy, R. J. (1995). Probability-based inference in cognitive diagnosis. In P. Nichols, S. Chipman, & R. Brennan (Eds.), *Cognitively diagnostic assessment* (pp. 43–71). Hillsdale, NJ: Lawrence Erlbaum Associates.

Mislevy, R. J., Almond, R. G. & Lukas, J. F. (2003). *A brief introduction to evidence-centered design.* ETS RR-03–16. Princeton, NJ: Educational Testing Service.

Mitchell, K. J. (1989). New concepts in large-scale achievement testing: Implications for construct and incremental validity. In R. F. Dillon & J. W. Pellegrino (Eds.), *Testing: Theoretical and applied perspectives* (pp. 132–145). New York: Praeger.

National Research Council (2001). *Knowing what students know: The science and design of educational assessment* (J. Pellegrino, N. Chudowsky, and R. Glaser, Eds.). National Research Council Committee on the Foundations of Assessment, Division of Behavioral and Social Sciences and Education. Washington, DC: National Academy Press.

Nichols, P. D. (1994). A framework for developing cognitively diagnostic assessments. *Review of Educational Research, 64*(4), 576–603.

Nichols, P. D., Chipman, S., & Brennan, R. (Eds.) (1995). *Cognitively diagnostic assessment.* Hillsdale, NJ: Lawrence Erlbaum Associates.

Phillips, D. (2010). International comparisons of educational attainment: Purposes, processes, and problems. In G. Walford, M. Viswanathan, & E. Tucker (Eds.), *The SAGE Handbook of Measurement* (pp. 203–220). London, SAGE Publications, Ltd.

Phillips, D., & Schweisfurth, M. (2007). *Comparative and international education. An introduction to theory, methods, and practice.* London: Continuum.

Postlethwaite, T. N. (1985). International Association for Evaluation of Educational Achievement (IEA). In T. Husen and T. N. Postlethwaite (Eds.), *The international encyclopedia of education. Research and studies* (pp. 2645–2646). Oxford: Pergamon Press.

Reckase, M. D. (1985). The difficulty of test items that measure more than one ability. *Applied Psychological Measurement, 9*, 401–412.

Reif, F. (2008). *Applying cognitive science to education.* Cambridge, MA: MIT Press.

Samejima, F. (1988). *Advancement of latent trait theory.* Office of Naval Research Report No. N00014–81-C-0569. Knoxville: University of Tennessee, Department of Psychology.

Samuda, R. J., Feuerstein, R., Kaufman, A. S., Lewis, J. E., & Sternberg, R. J. (Eds.) (1998). *Advances in cross-cultural assessment.* Thousand Oaks, CA: SAGE Publications.

Snow, R. E. & Lohman, D. F. (1989). Implications of cognitive psychology for educational measurement. In R. L. Linn (Ed.), *Educational measurement* (3rd ed., pp. 263–332). New York: Macmillan.

Sternberg, R. (1984). What cognitive psychology can (and cannot) do for test development. In B. S. Plake, S. N. Elliott, & J. V. Mitchell, Jr. (Eds.), *Buros-Nebraska symposium on measurement and testing. Social and technical issues in testing: Implications for test construction and usage* (pp. 39–60). Hillsdale, NJ: Lawrence Erlbaum Associates.

Sternberg, R. J., Lautrey, J., & Lubart, T. I. (Eds.) (2003). *Models of intelligence: International perspectives.* Washington, DC: American Psychological Association.

Warsh, D. (2006). *Knowledge and the wealth of nations: A story of economic discovery.* New York: W. W. Norton & Co.

# 10

# A Cross-Cultural Approach to Deconstructing Cognitive Processes in the Mathematics Classroom: Japan and the United States

## Noriyuki Inoue

### Introduction

A number of researchers have actively studied and discussed the sociocultural dependence of human cognition and learning (Luria, 1979; Cole, 1998; Lave, 1982). In recent decades, mathematical cognition has been one of the most widely studied domains among these researchers. For instance, it has been reported that mathematical concepts and skills develop as children dynamically interact with a wide variety of sociocultural activities such as the exchange of goods (Carraher, Carraher, & Schliemann, 1985; Saxe, 1988), schooling (Nunes, Schliemann, & Carraher, 1993), and play activities in daycare settings (Ginsburg, Inoue, & Seo, 1999). In this chapter I discuss, with a cross-cultural lens, the cultural foundation of students' learning and cognitive processes that takes place in mathematics classrooms. I also discuss key cross-cultural factors that shape cognition and learning in mathematics classrooms, with an emphasis on the studies of U.S.–Japan comparisons of mathematical learning.

In the past decade, a series of international comparison studies of mathematical achievement has stimulated interest in cross-cultural investigations of mathematical learning. Particularly, the finding that the U.S. largely lagged behind many of the industrialized nations in the Trends in International Mathematics and Science Study (TIMSS) and the Programme for International Student Assessment (PISA) motivated active discussions among researchers on the nature of learning in mathematics classrooms. These international comparison studies also motivated researchers to conduct closer investigations of how students in the countries that excelled in the international comparison studies learn mathematics in their classrooms. Among them, one of the most widely studied contexts is Japanese classrooms.

In these cross-cultural investigations, researchers looked for the answers to several questions, such as how mathematics is taught in Japanese classrooms, whether and how the students learn mathematics differently in Japan, and what the U.S. educators, school administrators, and policymakers could learn from the Japanese experience. In these investigations, the researchers conceptualized classroom learning activities as unique cultural practices situated in the cultural context, and attempted to identify meaningful educational implications for both educators and policymakers. In the following section I illustrate some of the key issues that are helpful for us in understanding the nature of mathematical learning in Japanese classrooms based on the cross-cultural investigations.

## Emphasis on Consensus Building

First of all, researchers found that how teachers teach mathematics in Japan differs significantly from the U.S. In the TIMSS 1999 Video Study (see Stigler & Hiebert, 1999), the researchers studied more than 1,000 eighth-grade mathematics classrooms in seven participating countries, including the U.S., Germany, and Japan, and identified several key differences in the ways mathematics is taught. The study found that: (1) the variability of teaching within each country is much smaller than the variability across these countries, and (2) typical mathematical learning activities in these countries follow distinctively different models. In the U.S., a typical mathematics lesson goes through the following sequence:

1   Homework check
    The teacher checks and reviews the students' answers to homework problems from the previous class.
2   Demonstration of examples
    The teacher introduces a set of new mathematical problems from the textbook or worksheet and solves them, with explanations, in front of the students.
3   Assign problem solving tasks
    The teacher assigns similar problems to the students from the textbook or worksheet.
4   Group work
    The students work on the assigned problems individually or in groups.
5   Check answers
    The teacher checks the students' answers.
6   Assign new homework
    The teacher distributes new homework based on the new mathematical skill that was taught in class.

This method of teaching emphasizes nurturing students' problem solving skills as the teacher models the use of the skills in front of the students, gives the students opportunities to practice the skills, and checks the students' answers to see whether they can demonstrate the skills. The teacher's role is mainly to help students acquire the techniques to solve the problems and check their performance. In contrast, Japanese mathematics instructions typically go through the following sequence.

1   *Hatsumon*
    After briefly reviewing prior knowledge, the teacher gives the students a rich mathematical problem that requires an understanding of key mathematical concepts.
2   *Kikanshido*
    Students solve the problem individually or in groups as the teacher walks past their desks and guides their thinking.
3   *Neriage*
    Students present their problem solving in front of the class, and the teacher facilitates a class discussion to evaluate and compare different strategies and build consensus on the mathematical concepts that are needed to solve the problem.
4   *Matome*
    The teacher summarizes the lesson and introduces a new set of problems for the students to consider.

In this instructional model, mathematical learning is shaped around the concept of inquiry, emphasizing students' deep thinking and social exchanges of mathematical ideas in which the students share their thinking and build consensus on key mathematical concepts (Fernandez & Yoshida, 2004; Inoue, in press). Among these components, *neriage* is viewed as the most important component of the lesson (Shimizu, 1999). During the *neriage* phase of the lesson, the students present their strategies and rationale for solving the problem in front of the class. Then the teacher asks the whole class which is the best strategy and facilitates a whole class discussion on the issue. In this process, the teacher rarely indicates if the answer is right or wrong. Instead, the teacher asks the students to carefully listen to everyone's ideas, even if they might be wrong, and think why each of the strategies the students present could (or could not) effectively solve the problem. The teacher facilitates the class discussion in such a way as to help students develop a conceptual realization (*kizuki*) as they build consensus. According to Takahashi (2006),

> This discussion is often called *Neriage* in Japanese, which implies polishing ideas. In order to do this, teachers need a clear plan for the discussion as a part of their lesson plans, which will anticipate the variety of solution methods that their students might bring to the discussion. These anticipated solution methods will include not only the most efficient methods but also ones caused by students' misunderstandings. (p. 42)

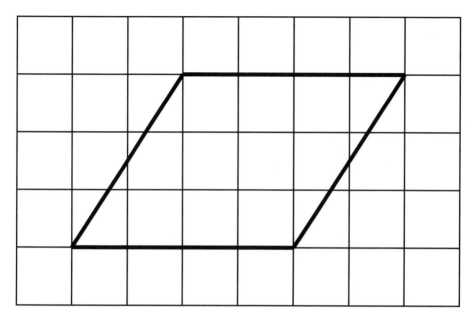

**Figure 10.1**   *Hastumon*: Find the area of the parallelogram.

Japanese teachers employ other methods for teaching, including direct instruction and drilling, but when they attempt to establish a firm conceptual understanding, they tend to follow this particular structure, especially in elementary schools (Fernandez & Yoshida, 2004).

As a further example of how the *neriage* method works, consider the situation in which a teacher could ask the students to think how to identify the area of the parallelogram in Figure 10.1 before learning the standard formula (area = base × height). In finding the area of the parallelogram, some students may count the number of unit squares within the parallelogram by ignoring the squares that are not fully included within the parallelogram, or estimating the areas of the squares that are not fully included (Figure 10.2). Other students may suggest cutting the triangular portion of the parallelogram on the left, moving it to the right side of the parallelogram, and creating a rectangle so that the area of the rectangle could be calculated instead (Figure 10.3).

At this point, the teacher would ask the students to think about the different strategies they have presented, and would build consensus on the best strategy. In the process, the teacher would ask the students to think about the strength and weakness of the presented ideas, discuss their rationales, and build consensus in the whole class discussion (e.g., "For the shapes that do not perfectly fit in the grids, moving the parts of the shape and making a rectangle can help us find the exact area of the original shape. Finding the number of unit squares is another way only if the area of the squares that do not fit in the grids can be accurately obtained."). Once the group has built consensus, the teacher would write the

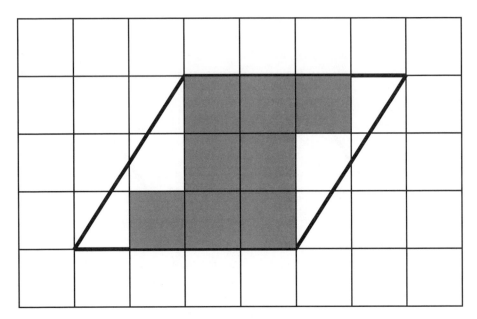

**Figure 10.2**   Counting the number of unit squares.

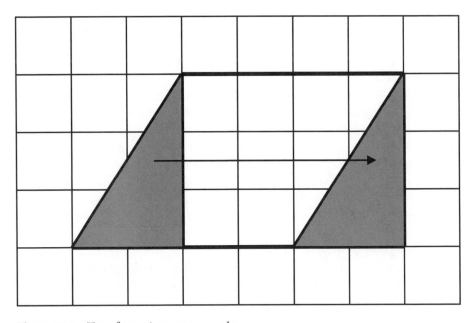

**Figure 10.3**   Transformation to a rectangle.

established understanding on the board, summarizing the discussion, and move on to the applications of the concept to different problems.

What characterizes this Japanese method of teaching is the pedagogical stance that learning mathematics is a group-based, collaborative activity, rather than an individually based, outcome-oriented activity. The emphasis is on listening to others' ideas and collaborating to think about different strategies together, compared to getting a right answer or competing against each other (Inoue, in press). This social-collaborative nature of mathematics instruction is in stark contrast with U.S. mathematics teaching. If the above situation took place in a U.S. classroom, the teacher might simply inform the first group of students their solution is wrong and tell the second group of students that their solution is right. The teacher may explain the rationale for right and wrong, but the other students would simply ignore the wrong answer and memorize the technique that leads to the right answer. In this sense, social-cognitive learning activity in Japanese classrooms is a very different type of learning activity from that occurring in many U.S. classrooms.

This emphasis on the social and collaborative nature of mathematical learning goes beyond learning in the classroom. To effectively implement this model of instruction (or *neriage*), Japanese teachers regularly engage in lesson study with their colleagues, especially in elementary and junior high schools (Stigler & Hiebert, 1999). In the lesson study, teachers in the same grade level or instructional group meet and build consensus on the goal of the lesson, plan a lesson together in relation to the overall goal, discuss how it can be improved, observe the actual lesson taught by one of the teachers, meet afterward to discuss the observed lesson, build consensus on how the lesson could be improved, and share their findings with their colleagues.

This form of professional development is increasingly employed for professional development in the U.S., but it is often the case that U.S. teachers who are not used to collaborating with others serve as a major stumbling block for these attempts (see Fernandez, Cannon, & Chokshi, 2003). Similarly, U.S. students are unaccustomed to collaborating and improving each other's thinking through listening to others, thinking deeply about different perspectives, and building consensus on different approaches and the concepts that underlie the approaches (Inoue, in press).

Researchers are now divided about whether the Japanese mathematics teaching, as a cultural practice, could be implemented in the U.S. context, and if so, how it would be possible. Nevertheless, these investigations and discussions establish a new understanding of mathematical learning; that is, the cultural dimension of mathematical learning plays an important role in shaping the nature of cognitive processes in classrooms.

## Students' Attitudes toward Mathematical Learning

Another cultural dimension that characterizes the difference in mathematics learning between Japanese and U.S. classrooms is students' attitudes toward mathematical learning. A series of cross-cultural studies has indicated that Japanese and American students significantly differ in their attitude toward mathematical learning (Lee, Ichikawa, & Stevenson, 1987; Stevenson et al., 1990; Stevenson, Lee, & Stigler, 1986;

Uttal, 1995). According to these studies, Japanese students are significantly more likely to agree with the statement, "Everyone in your class has the same amount of ability in math," while American students are significantly more likely to disagree with the statement. Similarly, Japanese students are significantly more likely to agree with the statement, "The best students in the class always work harder than the other students," while American students are significantly more likely to disagree with the statement. This implies that Japanese students tend to attribute their success and failure to their effort, while U.S. students tend to attribute their success and failure to their innate ability. This finding is more striking if we consider the fact that parents also possess the same attitudes toward mathematics, and decide the level of expectation for their children accordingly (Stevenson & Stigler, 1992; Uttal, 1995). In psychological terms, Japanese students and parents possess the tendency called effort attribution, while U.S. students and parents possess the tendency called innate ability attribution. Japanese students' inclination to listen to other students' ideas and learn even from mistakes in mathematics classrooms could be seen to stem from this culturally unique attitude toward mathematical learning.

The question is where this difference in attitudes toward mathematical learning comes from. Using a sociohistoric lens helps us make sense of this difference. For many centuries, East Asian societies have embraced the Confucian philosophy. As a result, people tend to possess a belief that social improvement is possible mainly through self-improvement. This could be seen to play an important role in nurturing effort attribution among Japanese students and parents (Uttal, 1995). In addition, since the arrival of industrialization in Japan about 150 years ago, the Japanese government's effort to modernize the nation and counter the Western nations' power created a social value system and attitude to "catch up with the West" using technology and scientific innovation (Duke, 1986). As a result, industrializing the country through technological advances became an important concern for Japanese society and the families who had internalized the value system over generations. Even after Japan became the number two economic power in the world, this sociocultural norm has not been easily wiped out. For example, in Japan, it is still not socially acceptable to say that one is not good at math, compared to the U.S. where this is completely acceptable (Uttal, 1995). This sociocultural norm on mathematics education could be seen as another reason why Japanese students make much more effort to learn mathematics, as compared to U.S. students. Again, using a cross-cultural lens could benefit our understanding of cognitive processes that take place in the mathematics classrooms.

## Culturally Unique Educational Themes

In introductory psychology courses, one of the most commonly used explanations to distinguish the U.S.–East Asian cultural difference is the individualist vs. collectivist contrast. However, to understand the nature of mathematical learning in

Japanese classrooms, it is important to go beyond this contrast and understand the complexity of the cultural practices more deeply. One way to do this is by looking into socially shared and valued concepts and themes that have influenced schooling in the culture (Duke, 1986; Lewis, 1995). In fact, the Japanese culture has a wide variety of culturally unique educational themes that are shared and valued by Japanese educators and parents.

The following section lists a few of these educational themes commonly valued and shared in the Japanese society. These culturally unique themes guide students' thinking as their teachers repeatedly emphasize their importance and design educational activities around the themes. As a result, the students gradually internalize them as important themes for their self-growth and anchor their thinking in the cultural concepts. In fact, in many Japanese schools, one could observe some of these words exhibited in the classrooms so that the students are constantly reminded of these themes. Since these terms do not have direct translations in English, the original terms are used here with additional explanations.

### Hansei

The direct translation of *hansei* is "reflection." In the U.S. context, reflection is often used to imply thinking about one's reasoning and decision-making for the purpose of trouble-shooting past actions. However, *hansei* involves much more than that. *Hansei* involves not only analyzing one's actions and thinking in the past, but also considering why it was not possible to meet responsibility and moral obligations, often with a sincere sense of regret and a firm determination to be a more responsible and integrated person (Lewis, 1995, Rohlen & LeTendre, 1999).

In the Japanese society, *hansei* is often considered to be an important path for gaining maturity (De Mente, 2004; White, 1987). In Japanese schools, students are often asked to engage in *hansei* and to reflect on their moral and social commitment to their responsibility (as students whose job is to learn). The students are often asked to engage in *hansei* not only during in-class learning activities, but also during after-school events such as field trips, sports competitions, and other extracurricular activities. It could be said that Japanese students' emphasis on effort and self-improvement is largely owed to this cultural theme that permeates the Japanese culture.

### Kizuna

In Japanese schools, this concept is emphasized on many different occasions. *Kizuna* implies a tight psychological bond that is created among people when they engage in the same activity or go through the same challenges and situations. This concept is considered one of the key ingredients for human development in the Japanese society (Nakayama, 1993). Japanese teachers usually consider developing *kizuna* among the students as one of the most important goals of education, and often facilitate learning activities around the theme so that the students can develop strong *kizuna* with their peers (Sato, 2004; Wray, 1999). Throughout the school year, Japanese schools offer many opportunities for students to develop *kizuna* with their peers and emphasize growing together as members of the society as they learn in the same classrooms, prepare for schools events, and engage in extracurricular activities. As a result, social dialogues, listening to each other, and collaborating with others (as in *neriage*) have a special meaning in Japanese classrooms.

Because of this educational theme, mathematics classes are not only an opportunity for students to learn important mathematical concepts, but also an arena for developing *kizuna* and pursuing self-growth as the students go through intellectual challenges and dialogues together. In this sense, the social-cognitive aspect of mathematical learning that takes place in Japanese classrooms is largely due to this educational theme and its value in the society. Although not every student internalizes this value system today, it is still the case that this theme repeatedly emerges as one of the goals in Japanese schools, and the majority of students understand that working with others, and developing *kizuna* with others, play an important role in their intellectual and personal development.

This also applies to teachers. Teachers develop strong *kizuna* as educators, as they work together in the lesson study, school meetings, and other school events. For many teachers, *kizuna* with their colleagues serves as a motivation that drives them to improve their teaching and become better *sensei*. This educational theme that penetrates Japanese education is not easily visible to outsiders, but plays a very important role in shaping learning activities that take place in Japanese schools.

### Omoi

*Omoi* plays a very important role in every aspect of the educational and professional activities in Japanese culture (McVeigh, 1998). The direct translation of *omoi* is "thinking," but it implies much more than that. *Omoi* involves an integrated form of thinking, feeling, and passion that penetrates and often defines one's personal and professional identity (Uchiyama, 2007, 2003). In daily Japanese conversations, the term is often used to share goals, thinking, passion, and feelings toward a person, group, situation, or workplace. Schools are generally considered an arena for students to develop and nurture *omoi*, including *omoi* about their friends, extracurricular activities, and school life. Using these opportunities, students are expected to develop strong *omoi* about their future, the community, and the society, and become fully developed members of society. In fact, for many Japanese teachers, being in touch with their *omoi* as a teacher and building their educational practices around their *omoi* is an important aspect of their growth as teachers.

Teachers often share their *omoi* with their students, and ask their students to share their *omoi* with their peers in many different occasions (Cave, 2007). In this sense, social interactions in the classroom are not merely social interactions. They serve as opportunities for the students to learn about each other's *omoi* and build strong *kizuna* with their peers. On these occasions, the students are expected to pursue self-growth in the form of development of their *omoi*, which is often shared at graduation ceremonies and other school events. Again, though it is not easily visible, this educational theme creates a special sociocultural atmosphere for classroom learning activities, often taking the form of students' respectful attitudes toward the teacher and collaborative relationship with their peers who share the same *omoi*.

These are just a few of the culturally unique educational themes valued and shared in Japanese schools, and that may help us to account for the behaviors and attitudes of Japanese students. One could find many more culturally unique themes shared and valued in Japanese schools and society by being fully immersed in the society. These themes set the tone of the classroom activities and drive the students' cognitive processes in the classroom. This must also be true in other cultures: Because education is an important cultural practice in every culture, we must be able to find many rich and deep culturally unique educational themes that may not be easily visible from outside, but are firmly ingrained in the culture's educational practices. Without considering such an important dimension of education, it would be difficult for us to fully understand how students think and learn in classrooms in different cultural contexts.

## Conclusion

In conclusion, in-depth analyses of the cultural foundations of cognition and learning serve as important dimensions for deconstructing the cognitive processes that take place in schools. The illustrations I have described came from the Japanese culture, but there must be many such examples from other cultures.

Regardless of which culture we are studying, it must be the case that the cross-cultural analysis of learning serves as an invaluable opportunity for us to understand how deep learning can be facilitated in schools, and what human development really means in different cultural contexts. Such investigations could equip us with rich resources that we could use to explore a wide variety of potentials that we could each pursue in our own societies. This is an opportunity that we cannot miss in the increasingly globalized world. This paper concludes with an invitation to other scholars and students of psychology to explore such potential and engage, with a cross-cultural lens, in deep analysis of the cultural foundations of cognitive activities.

# References

Carraher, T. N., Carraher, D. W., & Schliemann, A. S. (1985). Mathematics in streets and schools. *British Journal of Developmental Psychology, 3*, 21–29.

Cave, P. (2007). *Primary school in Japan: Self, individuality and learning in elementary education.* New York: Routledge.

Cole, M. (1998). *Cultural psychology: A once and future discipline.* Cambridge, MA: The Belknap Press of Harvard University Press.

De Mente, B. L. (2004). *Japan's cultural code words: 233 key terms that explain the attitudes and behavior of the Japanese.* North Clarendon, VT: Tuttle Publishing.

Duke, B. (1986). *The Japanese school: Lessons for industrial America.* New York: Praeger.

Fernandez, C., Cannon, J. & Chokshi, S. (2003). A U.S.–Japan lesson study collaboration reveals critical lenses for examining practice. *Teaching and Teacher Education, 19*, 171–185.

Fernandez, C., & Yoshida, M. (2004). *Lesson study: A Japanese approach to improving mathematics teaching and learning.* Mahwah, NJ: Lawrence Erlbaum Associates.

Ginsburg, H. P., Inoue, N. & Seo, K. H. (1999). Young children doing mathematics: Observation of everyday activities. In J. V. Copley (Ed.), *Mathematics in the early years.* Reston, VA: National Council of Teachers of Mathematics.

Inoue, N. (in press). Zen and the art of *neriage*: Facilitating consensus building in mathematics inquiry lessons through lesson study. *Journal of Mathematics Teacher Education.*

Lave, J. (1982). A comparative approach to educational forms and learning process. *Anthropology and Education, 8*, 181–187.

Lee, S. Y., Ichikawa, V., & Stevenson, H. W. (1987). Beliefs and achievement in mathematics and reading: A cross-national study of Chinese, Japanese, and American children. In D. A. Kleiber & M. L. Maehr (Eds.), *Advances in motivation and achievement: Enhancing motivation, Vol. 5* (pp. 149–179). Greenwich, CT: JAI Press.

Lewis, C. C. (1995). *Educating hearts and minds: Reflections on Japanese preschool and elementary education.* New York: Cambridge University Press.

Luria, A. (1979). *The making of mind: A personal account of Soviet psychology.* Cambridge, MA: Harvard University Press.

McVeigh, B. J. (1998). *The nature of the Japanese state: rationality and rituality.* New York: Routledge.

Nakayama, O. (1993). *Kizuna no shinri [Psychology of bonding].* Tokyo, Japan: Takarajima sha.

Nunes, T., Schliemann, A., & Carraher, D. (1993). *Street mathematics and school mathematics.* Cambridge, UK: Cambridge University Press.

Rohlen, T. P. & LeTendre, G. K. (1999). *Teaching and learning in Japan.* New York: Cambridge University Press.

Sato, N. E. (2004). *Inside Japanese classrooms: The heart of education.* New York: Routledge Falmer.

Saxe, G. B. (1988). Candy selling and math learning. *Educational Researcher, 17*, 14–21.

Shimizu, Y. (1999). Aspects of mathematics teacher education in Japan: Focusing on teachers' roles. *Journal of Mathematics Teacher Education, 2*, 107–116.

Stevenson, H. W., Lee, S., Chen, C., Stigler, J. W., Hsu, C., & Kitamura, S. (1990). *Contexts of achievement: A study of American, Chinese, and Japanese children.* Monographs of the Society for Research in Child Development, 55 (1–2, serial no. 221).

Stevenson, H. W., Lee, S. Y., & Stigler, J. W. (1986). Mathematics achievement of Chinese, Japanese, and American children. *Science, 231*, 693–699.

Stevenson, H. W., & Stigler, J. W. (1992). *The learning gap: Why our schools are failing and what we can learn from Japanese and Chinese education*. New York: Summit Books.

Stigler, J., & Hiebert, J. (1999). *The teaching gap: Best ideas from the world's teachers for improving education in the classroom*. New York: The Free Press.

Takahashi, A. (2006). Characteristics of Japanese mathematics lessons. *Tsukuba Journal of Educational Study in Mathematics, 25*, 37–44.

Uchiyama, K. (2007). *Genbano gakutositeno action research [Action research as a study of work-in-action]*. Tokyo, Japan: Hakuto Shobo.

Uchiyama, K. (2003). *The theory and practice of actuality: Reinterpreting soft systems methodology (SSM) from the Japanese point of view and its applications for management and information systems studies*. Tokyo, Japan: Institute of Business Research, Daito Bunka University.

Uttal, D. H. (1995). Beliefs, motivation, and achievement in mathematics: A cross-national perspective. In M. Carr (Ed.), *Motivation in mathematics* (pp. 25–37). Cresskill, NJ: Hampton Press, Inc.

White, M. (1987). *The Japanese educational challenge: A commitment to children*. New York: The Free Press.

Wray, H. (1999). Japanese and American education: Attitudes and practices. Westport, CT: Bergin & Garvey.

# Part V
# Gender and Sex Roles

Around the world, women and men exert control over different levels of resources and power, with women virtually always less influential than men. Women experience pressures to conform to cultural standards for physical appearance, and are victims of sexual violence in many countries. Although educational opportunities for women have improved in some places, they remain limited in many cultures, and both men and media control messages influencing women's self images—sometimes producing depression and lowered self-esteem.

Women's pay is usually lower than that of men, and such roles as motherhood, although varying across cultures, nevertheless define the lives of many women. Women are also disproportionately victims of violence, sometimes at the hands of acquaintances and family members. Women's rights and their treatment are thus major issues in cultures across the planet.

Despite this rather pessimistic picture of women's status and well-being, there are some reasons for optimism. Women have made gains in rights, opportunities, and treatment in some locales, and have attained positions of leadership and power in some governmental and other organizational structures. What cultural factors promote female power and leadership? How have women's advocates achieved their gains? These are the kinds of questions we raise in this section of the book.

We will also examine how some aspects of women's experience find parallels in the lives of individuals who differ from the dominant (heterosexual) pattern of sexual practices in many of the world's cultures. Those who differ from the dominant culture—homosexual, bisexual, transgendered, and transsexual individuals—have often been the subject of prejudice and discrimination. Such sexual stigma is frequently institutionalized in such cultural structures as laws and religions, and only a tiny percentage of countries have constitutional provisions prohibiting discrimination against sexual minorities.

Similarly, few cultures allow equal marriage and parenting rights for sexual minorities, and there are wide variations in personal attitudes toward homosexuality and other minority patterns of sexual behavior. Prejudice against sexual minorities can lead to problems of self-esteem and mental health, and we will find that education, religion, and socioeconomic status are correlated with prejudicial attitudes. We might ask why (and how) these attitudes come about, and the different ways cultures deal with them when they occur.

11

# Women Across Cultures

Hilary Lips and Katie Lawson

Women's lives differ, sometimes drastically, across cultures. Yet there are themes in their difficulties and challenges, in their strengths and successes, that link women's experiences across cultural boundaries. In diverse cultures, women face, for example, an emphasis on molding their bodies to fit cultural standards of physical appearance and beauty, an expectation that they will carry the major burdens of childrearing, and ascribed status that is lower than men's. Yet women in different cultures deal differently with such issues. This chapter examines some of the important commonalities and differences across cultures in women's lives. Included in our narrative are issues linked to physical bodies, motherhood and family, work and pay, violence, power and leadership, and feminist activism. A theme that links all these issues is the gendering of power. Women and men control different amounts and types of the resources upon which power is based; such differences in access to resources help shape gender differences in behavior in each of these realms.

## Physical Bodies

Worldwide, women face enormous pressure to adhere to strict standards of physical beauty—in part because a beautiful body is one resource a woman can use to gain status, solidify relationships, and attract other resources. Due to the body dissatisfaction that often results from this pressure to be beautiful, women go to great lengths to mold their bodies to conform to cultural standards. In parts of Africa and Thailand, girls as young as age 3 begin to wear rings around their necks in an attempt to make them appear longer, in order to attract an affluent husband as an adult. Over the years, additional rings (weighing up to 12 pounds) are added to the neck. The rings push down the collarbone and ribs to create the illusion of a neck up to 10 to 12 inches longer (Mydans, 2001). In the United States, nearly 91% of the 11.7 million cosmetic surgeries were performed on women in 2007 (American Society for Aesthetic Plastic Surgery, 2008). These surgeries include breast and buttocks implants, collagen lip injections, and liposuction (Gangestad & Scheyd, 2005).

Although women worldwide are often dissatisfied with their bodies, the type of dissatisfaction depends on the culture. Women in Western cultures often strive for thinness (which is associated with control, wealth, and happiness), while individuals in non-Western, poorer cultures often associate thinness with poverty, disease, and malnutrition, and thus admire larger women. Although traditionally more affluent cultures prefer thin women while poorer cultures prefer larger women, the gap between these cultural preferences has been shrinking due to the "Westernization" of many cultures (Grogan, 2008). Cultures not only differ on weight preferences, but also on desirable size for particular areas of the body. Women between the ages of 18 and 24 in Canada report more dissatisfaction and concern for the weight of their lower torso (abdomen, hips, thighs, and legs) whereas women in India report more concern for the weight of their upper torso (face, neck, shoulders, and chest) (Gupta, Chaturvedi, Chandarana, & Johnson, 2001).

## Theories

Research focuses on two main theories for women's dissatisfaction with their bodies. Sociocultural theories suggest that cultures influence body dissatisfaction through the media, family, peers, and other sources (Becker, Burwell, Gilman, Herzog, & Hamburg, 2002). According to this approach, women compare themselves to ideals presented by these sources to make judgments about their own body size. Upward social comparisons (comparisons made with other individuals who have a body closer to the cultural ideal) lead to more body dissatisfaction in women. Therefore, in cultures where women are constantly exposed to images of very thin women (e.g., the United States), women make numerous upward social comparisons daily, thus increasing body dissatisfaction (Leahey, Crowther, & Mickelson, 2007). The sociocultural theory is supported by the observation that "Westernization" appears to be correlated with the increasing preference of non-Western cultures for thin women (Grogan, 2008).

Feminist theories, on the other hand, suggest that women's cultural roles play a large part in body dissatisfaction. According to these theories, male power is a key issue in body dissatisfaction; body standards are used as tools for oppressing women. Unachievable body ideals, along with drastic amounts of pressure from society to attain the perfect body, can lead women to focus on these superficial aspects, rather than more important issues such as their own competencies. Therefore, in cultures where there is rapidly increasing equality in women's roles, feminist theories predict more body dissatisfaction in women (because there is more pressure for the perfect body as a backlash against women's advances). This interpretation is supported by research showing that Korean women (who are

living in an area with increasingly equal gender roles) reported more body dissatisfaction than women in the United States and China (Jung & Forbes, 2007).

## Consequences of body dissatisfaction

Body dissatisfaction in women is often associated with depression and lower levels of self-esteem (e.g., Paxton, Eisenberg, & Neumark-Sztainer, 2006). It also leads to actions with sometimes dire consequences for women's physical health. After years of wearing rings to elongate their necks, women in rural areas of Africa and Thailand lose the ability to hold up their heads with their own neck muscles if the rings are taken off (e.g., to punish the women for adultery). Even in countries with very sophisticated medical technology, cosmetic surgery can lead to deformed bodies, infection, or even death. Researchers also worry about the mental consequences of cosmetic surgery due to the fact that some patients have shown adjustment problems, anger toward surgeons, and isolation after surgery (Dittmann, 2005).

Body dissatisfaction can also lead to eating disorders (e.g., anorexia, bulimia), which have profound health effects on women. The Renfrew Center Foundation (2002) estimated that 70 million individuals worldwide have eating disorders, with 24 million of those in the U.S. Eating disorders are associated with mental health problems (e.g., depression, anxiety, substance abuse) and a number of physical health problems, including low blood pressure, anemia, osteoporosis, hair and bone loss, kidney failure, heart attacks, and even death (National Institute of Mental Health, 2008).

## Motherhood and Family

One reason women have traditionally been defined so strongly by their physical bodies is that the biological processes of reproduction—menstruation, pregnancy, childbirth, lactation—are so obvious in women. Historically, many cultures have surrounded these processes with myths and elaborate rituals and taboos, underscoring the importance (and dangers) of childbearing. For example, some Native American cultures regarded menstruating women as so powerful that they must stay away from men preparing for battle, lest their power interfere with the warriors' power (Allen, 1986). Indeed, the onset of menstruation, with its implication that pregnancy is now a possibility, is the trigger for new behavioral restrictions on young women in many cultures—from veiling in countries such as Saudi Arabia (Sasson, 1992) to increased parental control and admonitions about sexuality in North America (Lee, 1994).

Although constructed from a biological link between mother and child, motherhood is a profoundly cultural role and process. As Sudarkasa (2004) notes,

Even the act of childbirth itself varies according to culturally prescribed rules and expectations ... we are all aware that the typical contemporary Western mode of childbirth, where a woman lies on her back, with her legs spread apart is by no means the "natural" or relatively comfortable position for delivery. In parts of Africa and elsewhere in the world, the more traditional women still give birth from a kneeling position. (Introduction section, para. 4)

Clearly, this physical process of labor and delivery is shaped to some extent by cultural norms.

Aligned with the focus on reproduction is the notion, common to most cultures, that motherhood, and the domestic responsibilities that go with it, is a primary role for women—and that women are better suited to such work than men. Around the world, women devote vast amounts of their time to the bearing and rearing of children. One 10-country study showed that mothers spent from 5.2 to 10.7 hours daily on childcare, whereas fathers spent from 0.1 to 0.9 hours (Owen, 1995), and a more recent overview of time use studies carried out in 20 countries between 1965 and 2003 shows that men spent an average of only 14 minutes per day on childcare, thus leaving most of that work to women (Hook, 2006). Furthermore, women's family caring activities are not limited to children; women all over the world do most of the caring work for family members who are ill, disabled, or elderly (Forssén, Carlstedt, & Mörtberg, 2005).

Motherhood is understood to be a major aspect of women's identity (Wilson, 2007). In many cultures, a woman without children is considered a failure—perhaps not even a real woman. However, just producing children is not enough to succeed at this role. Depending on the culture, mothers may be held to high standards in terms of the ways they are expected to feel and behave toward their children. In North America and other Western cultures, motherhood is supposed to involve trying to live up to an ideal of love and self-sacrifice (Wilson, 2007) and conforming to an ideology of "intensive mothering"—an approach to mothering that is highly child-centered, labor-intensive, expensive, emotionally absorbing, and reliably puts the child's needs before the mother's (Hays, 1996). This ideology of motherhood appears to fit into a broader ideology that women are supposed to care for others—that they must be sensitive and responsive to the needs of others, even when they themselves are exhausted, stressed, and ill (Forssén et al., 2005). Women who fail to live up to this ideology may suffer guilt, anxiety, and a loss of self-esteem.

The ideology that a good woman ought to be caring does not portray mothers as particularly powerful—indeed, they even seem to be subservient to their children in some respects. Expectations are somewhat different across cultures, however. For example, the mother role for Japanese women has traditionally involved independence and power, with mothers having almost complete control over family decisions related to their children and having respected status as an influence group when speaking about children's needs to government officials. Japanese women report gaining status, respect, and self-worth from their roles as mothers

(Bankart, 1989). In some Igbo communities in Africa, as in other matrilineal cultures, family lineage is determined through the mother, making mothers a central force in defining their families (Nzegwu, 2004). Indeed, it is the mother role that brings power and prestige in both family and community settings to many African women (Sudarkasa, 2004).

Although mothers' relationships with their children are expected, in most developed cultures, to be defined by caring and attachment, there are numerous examples of mothers abandoning or even killing their babies. In cultures plagued by extreme poverty, where infant mortality is especially high, mothers may deliberately refrain from developing attachment to infants until they have survived their first months of life, sometimes not even naming them. Among the mothers observed in one desperately poor Brazilian shantytown, mothers expressed pity toward, but selectively neglected, infants who they thought would not survive— saying that it was best to let weak children die because they would never be strong enough to defend themselves as adults. Yet, these mothers were generally very affectionate toward their children and, in the few cases when neglected children actually managed to live, they were accepted and loved by their mothers (Scheper-Hughes, 1985). Based on her observations, this researcher argued that the mother–child bond is not necessarily automatic, and should be understood in the context of the culture and level of surrounding resources into which a child is born. Mothers in this impoverished Brazilian community were important to the survival of their children, but did not have the power to provide resources for their survival. In some respects, their only choice was whether to emphasize grief or resignation when faced with the imminent loss of a sickly child.

Across cultures, mothering and caregiving are viewed as women's work, but women are not necessarily given the resources and support they need to do that work. Furthermore, the high importance placed on motherhood does not mean that most women can choose to stay at home and focus on rearing children; the typical woman in most countries combines motherhood with economic activity outside the home.

## Work and Pay

Cultural norms play a large role in whether women work outside the home. For example, in Saudi Arabia, only 18% of women are economically active, compared with 92% in Burundi. However, over half of the women in a majority of the countries polled by the United Nations are economically active, suggesting that the worldwide norm is for women to carry the double burden of work both outside and in the home (United Nations Statistics Division, 2008a). In the United States, half of all paid workers are women, and women are two thirds of primary or co-breadwinners for families (Shriver & Center for American Progress, 2009).

Despite the fact that both men and women are economically active, women are paid less than men worldwide. Culture plays a large role in the extent of this gap. In 2008, the Nordic countries Norway and Sweden had the smallest gender wage gap in the world, with women earning 77% and 81% of men's wages, respectively, according to a survey by the World Economic Forum (Hausman, Tyson, & Zahidi, 2008). The same data source puts U.S. women's earnings at 67% of men's. Middle Eastern and North African countries are characterized by less equality in regard to gender, and have much wider gender wage gaps (e.g., women earn 30% of men's earnings in Yemen) (Hausmann et al., 2008). Depending on the measures used, the gender wage gap may appear smaller or larger (for example, according to the 2009 figures of the U.S. Census Bureau, women earn just under 78% of men's wages); however, there always seems to be a gap in favor of men.

## The cost of motherhood

One aspect of the gender pay gap is often referred to as the "motherhood penalty"; motherhood appears to be the number one influence on women's lower wages. In Anglo-American, continental European, and Nordic countries, mothers may earn less money than childless women and men because they work fewer hours due to other family responsibilities (and therefore have less work experience and job tenure), choose jobs based on flexibility, location, etc., that work better with childcare responsibilities (which leads to occupational segregation), and less successful women in occupations may choose, more often than successful women, to have children (Sigle-Rushton & Waldfogel, 2007).

### Occupational segregation

On average, men tend to work in higher paying and more powerful occupations than women. Such jobs are often less flexible, and require more time commitments that can be especially difficult for women with childcare responsibilities. Thus, the childcare responsibilities placed on women in many cultures indirectly contribute to the gendering of power seen across the world. For example, in 2006, according to statistics collected by the United Nations, only five out of 117 countries had at least 50% of legislative and managerial positions filled by women. In other countries, very few women hold these powerful positions (e.g., only 3% of all legislators and managers in Pakistan were women in 2006) (United Nations Statistics Division, 2008b). In other words, without cultural norms involving a more equal distribution of childcare responsibility, women will continue to struggle to obtain powerful and high-paying positions in society.

Countries that have attempted to reform cultural norms so that childcare responsibility is shared more equally between women and men have the most equal balance of men and women in high-paying jobs, and thus a narrower gender wage gap. For example, in Norway both men and women are given an opportunity for paid parental leave (approximately 42 to 52 weeks) when a child is born, thus reducing the time off women must take after having a child. Often, parents are paid 80 to 100% of their wages, provided by a social insurance fund. Yemen, on the other hand, gives shorter time periods for paid maternity leave (approximately 60 days), which is paid for by employers. These very different leave benefits for new parents might reasonably be expected to have a profound impact on the gender wage gap; indeed Norway has a significantly narrower gap than Yemen (Hausmann et al., 2008).

*Pay/hiring discrimination*
Even if a mother wants to work in a more powerful, higher-paying occupation, she is likely to face discrimination along the way. In many societies, mothers (but not childless women) are perceived as lacking the characteristics necessary for jobs (e.g. competence and availability), and are thus chosen less often for hire, for management positions and promotions, and are offered lower starting salaries (Correll, Benard, & Paik, 2007; Cuddy, Fiske, & Glick, 2004; Cunningham & Macan, 2007; Fuegen, Biernat, Haines, & Deaux, 2004). However, because most cultures do not place childcare responsibilities on men, fathers do not face the same discrimination in the workplace. In fact, often fathers are preferred as employees over men without children (Cuddy et al., 2004).

## Education/training

In much of the world, men and women have the same access to educational routes that will allow for higher-paying, more powerful positions. However, there are still places in Africa, the southern and western areas of Asia, and Arab states where opportunities for education are not equal for women and men. In these areas, approximately 100 million children, a majority of them girls, do not have access to primary education. In rural Africa specifically, 70% of young girls are not given the chance to finish primary school. Worldwide, for every 100 literate adult men, only 88 adult women are literate (Bureau of Public Information, 2006). Without an education, as adults these girls will not be in a position to become economically independent individuals, thus reducing their power. This, in turn, has a dramatic effect on many aspects of life, including the ability to escape from harmful, violent situations.

## Violence Against Women

In most cultures, men, far more often than women, are the targets of male violence, perhaps because many cultures stress a competitive, aggressive ideal of masculinity (Archer, 1994; Gilmore, 1990). However, around the world, women are the most frequent targets of intimate partner violence and sexual violence perpetrated by men. Both intimate partner violence and sexual violence have a private face; they often take place behind closed doors and are not reported by shamed and frightened victims. Indeed, underreporting makes it difficult to obtain accurate estimates.

A World Health Organization study of more than 24,000 women at 15 sites in 10 countries found that, depending on the site, between 15% and 71% of women interviewed reported they had been physically or sexually abused by a male partner during their lifetime; between 4% and 54% said they had been physically or sexually abused by a partner during the past year (Garcia-Moreno et al., 2006).

As for the prevalence of rape, researchers estimate that in industrialized countries one of every five women is raped sometime during her life (Parrot & Cummings, 2006). Research in non-industrialized countries is harder to come by, but all indications are that sexual violence directed at women is common all over the world, and that the younger a woman is at first intercourse, the more likely it is that she was forced (Watts & Zimmerman, 2002).

Common threads in these forms of violence against women are that they are often long-term, repeated patterns of abusive activity rather than isolated incidents; they are frequently perpetrated by men (spouses, relatives, acquaintances) who are known to the victims; and the female victims are often blamed for causing the violence (Watts & Zimmerman, 2002). Cultural norms and practices that grant higher status, power, and resources to men provide underlying support for these patterns. For example, the notion that men should be the heads of their households implies that they should be able to control "their" women, and women's dependence on men for economic and social resources can mean they have few options for leaving an abusive situation. Cultures in which there is an emphasis on male dominance, separate spheres for the two sexes, and high levels of interpersonal violence have a higher incidence of rape (Sanday, 1981), and women who report intimate partner violence are more likely than other women to be surrounded by men who engage in controlling and limiting behavior toward them (Ellsberg et al., 2008).

## Violence against women as public performance of the gender system

Although the kinds of violence described here are often hidden, both intimate partner violence and sexual violence also have a public face, and the connections between the private and public forms of violence against women are stark. In certain situations, violence against women becomes a public performance of gender hierarchy and male status: an overt statement about men's ownership of and right to authority over "their" women. The most dramatic example is honor killing: the murder of a woman whose behavior is deemed to have brought dishonor to her husband, father, and/or other family members. The behavior that prompts this reaction usually involves women transgressing cultural boundaries of propriety in ways that may range from dressing in unapproved ways, going unchaperoned to particular places, or being in the company of unrelated men, to having intimate relationships outside of marriage, being raped, or even marrying a man without family approval. Such killings, which are most often carried out by a male relative such as a brother, claim the lives of more than 5,000 women every year worldwide (United Nations Population Fund, 2000). They occur with some frequency in countries as diverse as Turkey, Jordan, Egypt, Pakistan, India, Israel, and Brazil, and are often treated leniently by legal systems (Parrot & Cummings, 2006).

Underpinning the practice of honor killings are cultural norms that not only assume higher status for men than women, but also tie a man's honor and standing in the community to his ability to control his wife and daughters. In certain poor communities where such norms are strong, the only possession of value a man may feel he owns is his honor. An indiscreet woman is seen as bringing shame on her family and destroying that one important possession—a possession that is clearly viewed as much more important than the woman herself. The cultural assignment of higher value to men's honor and community standing than to women's lives is a grim indicator that women's welfare is considered inconsequential relative to men's.

Ironically, rape (for which women are often punished) is also used as a *tool* of punishment against women for violating rules of sexual propriety, or even just for intruding into spaces, occupations, or situations where they "do not belong." Rape is also used as a tool of male–male hostility: one man can dishonor another by raping his wife, daughter, sister, or mother. In one case that stirred international protests, Mukhtaran Bibi, a young woman in rural Pakistan, was gang-raped by four men on the orders of the tribal council, and then forced to walk home naked in front of jeering villagers—all because her brother had been seen with a woman from that village (Kristof, 2005). The rape of women during war by enemy soldiers is a common way of dishonoring and demoralizing a community, leaving a lasting legacy of humiliation and bitterness. For example, during the war in Bosnia in the early 1990s, some estimate that more than 20,000 women were raped (Parrot & Cummings, 2006); during the genocide in Rwanda in 1994, between one-quarter and one-half million women were raped (Human Rights Watch, 1996). These women were then viewed by others in their societies as "ruined" and the pregnancies that often resulted from the rapes provided a constant reminder of the trauma and of this "spoiled" status. Under these circumstances, many women have killed themselves and/or their infants (Drakulic, 1994).

## The business of violence against women

In many contexts, the abuse of women is a for-profit enterprise. Sexual exploitation of girls and women, trafficking of women for the purpose of prostitution or forced labor, pornography that exploits images of female humiliation—all are thriving businesses in many parts of the world. For example, it has been estimated that as many as 800,000 persons, 80% of them women, are trafficked across national borders each year to find themselves caught in situations of forced servitude (U.S. Department of

State, 2008). Like other forms of violence against women, these practices are grounded in cultural norms and practices that provide men with more access to resources and in attitudes that women can be considered property. Although there are ongoing attempts, often through the United Nations and other non-governmental organizations, to stem these practices, many governments have responded weakly to the problem. Turning a blind eye suggests tacit support for male control over women and the primacy of male needs and wants over women's welfare.

## Impact of violence on women's health

Violence has a multitude of consequences for women's physical and mental health. In almost every site covered by a large international study, women who had experienced partner violence in their lifetimes were more likely than other women to report poor health; frequently reported problems included difficulty walking, trouble carrying out daily activities, pain, memory loss, dizziness, and vaginal discharge (Ellsberg et al., 2008). In the same study, women who reported experiencing intimate partner violence at least once in their lives were significantly more likely than other women to report emotional distress, suicidal thoughts, and suicide attempts.

The psychological impact of violence has profound implications for women's ability to achieve success, status, and power relative to men. Women who are victimized by partners often experience long-lasting anxiety, depression, and low self-esteem, making it difficult for them to function effectively (Matud, 2005). Women who live in situations where violence against women is common learn to be alert, careful, and avoidant (Khalid, 1997). Such caution limits their mobility and interferes with their economic and social opportunities. Thus, an atmosphere of violence against women, whether in the private context of the home or the public context of the street, serves as an effective way of controlling women.

Given these diverse consequences, violence against women is now viewed by international policy analysts as both a public health problem and a human rights issue. The shift from viewing violence against women as a private, interpersonal matter to viewing it as a public policy concern may be a direct result of women's increasing access to resources such as education, employment, and a voice in the media, that promote their movement into positions of public power and leadership.

## Power and Leadership

Across cultures, public positions of leadership are most often held by men. Women are routinely stereotyped as less powerful, dominant, and influential and are ascribed lower status and importance than men. Indeed, the association of men with power is so normative that, in many situations, women who behave in overtly powerful ways are disparaged as unfeminine, unattractive, and unlikeable

(Parks-Stamm, Heilman, & Hearns, 2008). If they persist, they may even become targets of violence—as in the case of Dr. Mina Hassan Mohammed, who received death threats when, as newly appointed first female director of an African hospital, she tried to exert her authority (Richburg, 1993) or of Malalai Kakar, the first Afghan woman to graduate from the Kandahar Police Academy, murdered by the Taliban in October 2008 for daring to step into a role reserved for men (BBC News, 2008).

It has not always and everywhere been the case, however, that powerful women are disparaged. For example, in certain Native American cultures, women were ascribed high levels of spiritual and political power (Kehoe, 1995). Some cultures make exceptions for older women, whose perceived power may increase with age (Freidman, Tzukerman, Wienberg, & Todd, 1992) and who may even, among groups such as the Maori and the Lahu, achieve high status as elders and as wise, powerful matriarchs (Dashu, 1990).

## Interpersonal power

The exertion of interpersonal influence is based upon control of resources: the capacity to reward, punish, or convince another to take an action or position s/he did not originally intend to take (French & Raven, 1959). Such resources may be relatively concrete (money, objective information, physical strength) or personal (expressed disapproval, affection, or admiration) and may involve mainly individual relationships or cultural expectations and norms.

The exertion of interpersonal power is gendered precisely because access to such resources is gendered. In many situations, for example, men have more access than women do to money and education, giving them more scope than women to exert interpersonal power by rewarding or convincing others. In the many cultural situations where men are deemed to have legitimate authority over women, the full force of cultural norms helps men to wield power over women. Thus, for example, if culture dictates that the man is "head of the house," a woman opposing her husband on some decision must push against not just her husband's individual arguments, threats, or promises, but the weight of cultural expectations that a wife should give in to her husband's wishes.

When the exertion of influence is viewed as illegitimate, the would-be influencer is pressured to use strategies that are indirect and hidden, rather than direct. Researchers have confirmed that, across at least some cultures, direct influence strategies are preferred over and valued more highly than indirect ones (Steil & Hillman, 1993). Because cultural norms so often dictate that women trying to influence men are acting illegitimately (i.e., in defiance of accepted social norms), women may often find themselves pushed toward using less-preferred influence strategies.

In cultures where power and dominance are viewed as unfeminine, research has shown that both men and women penalize women who exhibit these characteristics. This reaction includes the penalization of female workers who are successful in masculine occupations. The counterintuitive finding that women themselves penalize powerful, dominant women may be due to social comparison. Research suggests that women who also see themselves as possessing these masculine qualities are less likely to penalize powerful women (Lawson, 2009). Due to the possibility of penalization, often women who want to exert influence learn to do so by "softening" their approach and/or their image. Indeed, researchers find that women can defuse potentially negative reactions to their power by emphasizing such qualities as cooperativeness and concern for others (Carli, 2001). One recent study showed, for example, that providing information about a female leader's communal qualities prevented observers from judging her as unfeminine and interpersonally hostile (Parks-Stamm et al., 2008).

## Public leadership

Women are still far less likely than men to hold positions of public leadership. As of this writing, for example, women headed only 13 of 189 national governments (International Women's Democracy Center, 2008). The Gender Empowerment Measure (GEM), an index conceived by the United Nations Development Program, provides one way to quantify women's public power and compare it across countries (United Nations Development Program, 2008). Using this index, which includes measures of women's political participation and decision-making power, their workforce participation as managers and professional and technical workers, and their level of earned income, it is possible to see some of the large differences among countries in women's access to power and leadership. Recent statistics show Norway and Sweden as the countries with the highest GEM scores, and thus as the countries in which women's and men's public power is closest to equal. Both countries have index scores higher than 0.9, where 1.0 would indicate equality on the selected measures. By contrast, Yemen and Saudi Arabia have extremely low GEM scores (less than 0.3), indicating a great deal of inequality in the distribution of public power between women and men. The United States ranks fifteenth on the list, with a GEM score of 0.762 (United Nations Development Program, 2007/2008).

What cultural factors promote female leadership? One dimension appears to be the degree to which a culture accepts hierarchies and an unequal distribution of power. One 25-country study revealed that countries with strong acceptance of hierarchies are also characterized by high gender inequality (Glick, 2006). Other contextual issues also appear to be important. One review of leadership research revealed that women are most likely to be evaluated harshly as leaders in situations where people are not used to female leaders, settings where most of the participants are male, and leadership positions that seem to call for a directive "masculine" leadership style (Eagly, Makhijani, & Klonsky, 1992). Women political leaders have sometimes adjusted to these requirements by styling themselves as "mothers" of their countries—thus adopting a "feminine" aspect to their leadership role (Anuradha, 2008).

The presence of women in visible leadership positions may increase the perceived normalcy of female leadership and thus reduce resistance. It may also increase young women's sense of possibility that they can be leaders—a sense sometimes found to be weaker than men's (Killeen, López-Zafra, & Eagly, 2006; Lips, 2000, 2001). Thus, cultures in which women leaders are less rare may be supportive of increased female leadership. Apfelbaum (1993) suggested such a conclusion in a cross-cultural study which revealed that the experiences of female leaders in Norway and France differed greatly. Norwegian women in leadership relished and felt entitled to their power; French women felt isolated, lonely, and continually under siege in their positions. Apfelbaum attributed the difference in these women's experiences to their cultural context: women in Norway were in a culture where female leadership was common, expected, and supported; French women, by contrast, were trying to lead in a culture where female leaders were still an anomaly.

The legitimization of female leadership through explicit cultural rules and laws or by strong and obvious cultural norms is also likely to have a positive effect. For example, a laboratory study by Yoder and her colleagues (1998) compared the influence over an all-male group of a woman leader who either had or had not received special training and was said by a male experimenter to be either randomly appointed or especially trained to lead the group. Only the women who were both trained *and* legitimated by the experimenter were effective in influencing their groups' performance. It appears that simply placing women in leadership positions, without legitimizing them through some cultural authority, is not sufficient to ensure their power.

## Empowerment for women

The realization that women so frequently hold less power than men has led to calls for women's empowerment. Empowerment, a term that has been interpreted as a process by which people gain control over their own lives (Rappaport, 1987) or the ability to choose and achieve their own goals (Kasturirangan, 2008), has figured widely in discussions about how women's lives could improve in many cultural contexts. For many analysts, empowerment is facilitated by increasing women's access to resources—an approach that fits well with the social psychological analysis of power discussed above. Thus, for example, advocates urge that women who face domestic violence be given access to safe spaces in which they can define their own goals and determine appropriate actions to reach them (Kasturirangan, 2008). Increasing girls' access to education is also cited as a source of empowerment—something that will enable young women to improve many outcomes from jobs to health (Grown, Gupta, & Pande, 2005; Olateju, 2007). It is clear, however, that empowerment is not something that can be *given to* or *done for* any group of women—it must be achieved by women themselves. Women activists in many cultures have been striving to do just that.

## Feminist Activism

Much of the feminist activism that has improved the lives of women around the world started with small groups of concerned women. For example, many women of St. Croix (an island of approximately 50,000 people) came together for a Women Writers' Symposium in 1981. After listening to riveting feminist readings of poetry and writings, the women began discussing stories of abuse. About 20 local women exchanged contact information and continued this conversation at later informal meetings, which eventually led to the Women's Coalition of St. Croix. Today, this very successful organization continues to help abused women and children in a variety of ways, including providing intervention services 24 hours per day, 365 days per year, counseling, food, support groups, and training programs for police and teachers to help sensitize these workers to the needs of abused women and children. The group also owns and operates a crisis center and a shelter for battered women (Morrow, 1994).

Small group efforts such as this one can both progress to and stem from large-scale events, such as the World Conferences on Women, which are organized for the purpose of promoting the advancement of women worldwide. The Fourth Conference, hosted in Beijing in 1995, included 189 countries (attracting nearly 50,000 women and men) and led to the implementation of the *Beijing Declaration and Platform for Action*, which has promoted changes around the world through women's advocacy groups and governments (United Nations, 1997). For example, after its delegates attended the conference, Rwanda adopted a quota system for electing parliamentary and cabinet seats in their government, requiring 30% of the seats to go to women. In 2008, 56.3% of the members of Rwanda's lower or single House of Parliament were women (nearly a 40% increase since 1997). These women have provided the driving force behind many important legislative changes, including the overturning of sexist laws (such as one denying women the right to inherit land) and the passing of legislation aimed at ending domestic violence. These women plan to continue weeding out the discriminatory laws of Rwanda, including one that requires a husband's signature for a bank loan (McCrummen, 2008). This is just one example of a dramatic improvement in women's lives stimulated by the World Conferences on Women.

## Strategies

Feminist activists use a number of strategies to improve the lives of women. They may contribute to research on women's issues, provide economically for women, or teach women the skills to provide economically for themselves, work to change legislation, network, and/or educate the public about women's issues.

*Legislation*

Feminist activism can be quite effective at promoting equality for women by influencing legislation. Due to the increase of women in powerful, influential, and decision-making positions, women are in a better position to promote, support, and engage in feminist activism than ever before. For example, in 1972, inspired and pushed by the leadership of Senator Patsy Mink, the United States passed Title IX, which prohibits sex discrimination in any educational institution funded by the federal government. This legislation prohibits schools from excluding female students from classes, sports, or other activities held within the institution (U.S. Department of Labor, n.d.). This legislation has led to a number of significant changes within academic institutions, perhaps most notably within athletics at both the high school and college level. For high school students, girls' athletic participation increased by 847% after the passage of Title IX. For college students, women's athletic participation increased from 32,000 women prior to Title IX to 150,000 women in 2007 (National Council for Research on Women, n.d.).

Feminists have also supported legislation promoting pay equality in the workplace. Prior to 2009, workers in the United States were allowed to sue for pay discrimination only within six months after they received their first discriminatory paycheck. Unfortunately, this law did not take into account that an individual may work for an employer for years without realizing she is the victim of pay discrimination, as was the case for Lily Ledbetter. Ledbetter, a worker at Goodyear Tire & Rubber Company for 19 years, discovered at the end of her career that she had been receiving significantly lower pay than her male colleagues. Ledbetter sued the company for this discriminatory act, but the courts ruled in the favor of Goodyear because Ledbetter had not sued within six months of her first paycheck. Due largely to the efforts of feminist activism, the U.S. Congress reviewed this unfair law and supported its modification. In January of 2009, President Barack Obama signed a law stating that workers have the ability to sue companies for pay discrimination within six months of the last paycheck received (Goldstein, 2009). Without feminists (both in and out of the government) pushing for this change, this step toward equality might never have been taken.

*Networking*

Today's technology has provided feminists with the opportunity to network with others worldwide in order to communicate and organize activities to support women. Feminist groups develop websites to create awareness of various problems women are facing and to give individuals the chance to contribute money or time. For example, Women for Women International helps women who live in either war or post-war environments by providing financial support for basic necessities (food, water, etc.) and by teaching these women leadership and vocational skills for future jobs (Women for Women International, 2009). College students and others use social networking tools on the Internet, such as Facebook, to promote feminist activism. These students design and encourage others to join Facebook groups which provide information on women's issues, achievements of the group, and future events. Feminist groups have taken advantage of all the possibilities provided by the Internet to help women in a variety of ways, including raising public awareness of human rights.

*Education/public awareness*

The Internet is only one of many tools used to educate the public about issues women are facing around the world. In Nigeria, where rape is a serious problem and victims (rather than perpetrators) are often punished either physically or through ostracism for speaking about the incident, many victims of rape remain silent. A number of activist groups work with community leaders to change the community norms that force women into silence. In order to promote awareness of the human rights issues present in Nigeria, these feminist activists set up media interviews and press briefings, distribute information to promote awareness, and also use popular theater (Onyejekwe, 2008). Indian culture also uses a unique approach to promote awareness about women's issues. Individuals actually perform what is called "street theater" to communicate these problems (Garlough, 2008). Increased public awareness is essential in changing conditions for women throughout the world. Without knowing the existence and scope of a problem such as domestic violence, people cannot be mobilized to try to solve it. Education on feminist issues such as pressure to conform to destructive cultural standards of beauty, the gender pay gap, discrimination against mothers, and domestic violence are essential because these practices are often so ingrained in a culture that they are taken for granted and essentially invisible.

## Benefits of feminist activism

Examples of feminist activism can be found in most cultures today. Is such activism actually promoting change? At least in some cases, positive change has been a clear outcome. For example, legislative changes in the United States have led to more equality among the sexes. In 1972 (when Title IX was passed) 9% of medical degrees were earned by women, whereas in 2007 women earned 49.1% of the degrees (National Council for Research on Women, n.d.). The Beijing Platform for Action not only indirectly influenced legislative changes in Rwanda, but also led to increased public awareness about human rights in countries such as Guyana, which now includes human rights as a subject in school curricula, and Vietnam, which has attempted to remove school textbooks with gender stereotypes and has radio and television shows focusing on gender equality (Women's Environment and Development Organization, 2005).

Feminist activism also has personal psychological and social benefits. For example, after going through the Functional Adult Literacy Program in Turkey, women reported a more positive self-concept, along with more social integration and family cohesion (Kagitcibasi, Goksen, & Gulgoz, 2005). For activists themselves, feminist activism has also been found to be associated with mental and physical health. Feminist activists worry less about their weight, take fewer diet aids, report less disordered eating after perceiving sexist events, and report more satisfaction with their appearance than their non-activist counterparts (Haas, 2005; Sabik & Tylka, 2006). For lesbian women, activism is also associated with self-acceptance (Rand, Graham, & Rawlings, 1982). Overall, feminist activism has been effective in moving societies in the direction of greater gender equality and also has a number of health benefits for both the women receiving and those giving the help.

## Conclusion

All over the world, women's (and men's) roles, rights, and responsibilities have been shaped by cultural norms that support the assignment of more power and importance to men. The strength of these norms and the magnitude of the differences they support vary by culture, but there seems to be no country in which women and men enjoy equal access to political power and economic resources (Social Watch, 2008). Cultures with the highest levels of equality are not necessarily those with the most resources, but rather those for which gender equity is explicitly enshrined in policies such as labor-market regulations banning discrimination and gender quotas for political participation. Activism by women has been the driving force behind the development of such policies.

Worldwide, the situation is fluid: as women gain more control over their own lives, their sense of entitlement rises and they seek even more advances. The increasing capacity, nurtured by electronic media, for women to connect across cultures seems destined to speed up this process. Continuing progress toward equality is not inevitable, however, as illustrated by the dispiriting histories of countries (e.g., former Soviet bloc nations, Afghanistan, Iran) in which a shift in government sharply eroded women's rights. However, both positive examples of women's progress and negative examples of the ease which such progress can be reversed illustrate that women's position is very much a function of cultural agreement rather than a function of essential feminine qualities or female–male differences.

## References

Allen, P. G. (1986). *The sacred hoop: Recovering the feminine in American Indian traditions.* Boston, MA: Beacon Press.

American Society for Aesthetic Plastic Surgery (2008, February 25). *Cosmetic procedures in 2007.* Retrieved from http:// www.surgery.org/press/news-release.php?iid=491

Anuradha, C. S. (2008). Women political leadership and perception: A case study of South Asia. *International Journal of South Asian Studies, 1,* 1–8. Retrieved January 15, 2009 from http://www.pondiuni.edu.in/journals/ssas/13_anuradha.pdf

Apfelbaum, E. (1993). Norwegian and French women in high leadership positions: The importance of cultural context upon gendered relations. *Psychology of Women Quarterly, 17,* 409–429.

Archer, J. (1994). Violence between men. In J. Archer (Ed.), *Male violence* (pp. 121–140). London: Routledge.

Bankart, B. (1989). Japanese perceptions of motherhood. *Psychology of Women Quarterly, 13,* 59–76.

BBC News (September 28). Top Afghan policewoman shot dead. Retrieved September 28, 2008 from http://news.bbc.co.uk/1/hi/world/europe/7640263.stm

Becker, A. E., Burwell, R. A., Gilman, S., Herzog, D. B., & Hamburg, P. (2002). Eating behaviours and attitudes following prolonged exposure to television among ethnic Fijian adolescent girls. *Journal of Psychiatry, 180*(6), 509–514.

Bureau of Public Information. (2006). *Education of girls and women.* Retrieved January 16, 2009 from http://www.unesco.org/bpi/pdf/memobpi26_girlseducation_en.pdf

Carli, L. L. (2001). Gender and social influence. *Journal of Social Issues, 57,* 725–742.

Correll, S. J., Benard, S., & Paik, I. (2007). Getting a job: Is there a motherhood penalty? *American Journal of Sociology, 112*(5), 1297–1338.

Cuddy, A. J. C., Fiske, S. T., & Glick, P. (2004). When professionals become mothers, warmth doesn't cut the ice. *Journal of Social Issues, 60*(4), 701–718.

Cunningham, J. & Macan, T. (2007). Effects of applicant pregnancy on hiring decisions and interview ratings. *Sex Roles, 57,* 497–508.

Dashu, M. (1990). Women's power. (DVD). Transcript retrieved January 27, 2009 from http://www.suppressedhistories.net/womenspowerscript3.html

Dittmann, M. (2005). Plastic surgery: Beauty or beast? *Monitor on Psychology, 36*(8), 30. Retrieved from http://www.apa.org/monitor/sep05/surgery.html

Drakulic, S. (1994). The rape of women in Bosnia. In M. Davies (Ed.), *Women and violence: Realities and responses worldwide* (pp. 176–181). London: Zed Books.

Eagly, A. H., Makhijani, M. G., & Klonsky, B. K. (1992). Gender and the evaluation of leaders: A meta-analysis. *Psychological Bulletin, 111,* 3–22.

Ellsberg, M., Jansen, H. A. F. M., Heise, L., Watts, C. H., & Garcia-Moreno, C., on behalf of the WHO Multi-country Study on Women's Health and Domestic Violence against Women Study Team (2008). Intimate partner violence and women's physical and mental health in the WHO Multi-Country Study on Women's Health and Domestic Violence. *Lancet, 371,* 1165–1172.

Forssén, A. S. K., Carlstedt, G., & Mörtberg,C. M. (2005). Compulsive sensitivity—A consequence of caring: A qualitatitive investigation into women carer's difficulties in limiting their labours. *Health Care for Women International, 26,* 652–671.

French, J. R. P. Jr., & Raven, B. H. (1959). The bases of social power. In D. Cartwright (Ed.), *Studies in social power* (pp. 150–167). Ann Arbor: University of Michigan Press.

Friedman, A., Tzukerman, Y., Wienberg, H., & Todd, J. (1992). The shift in power with age: Changes in perception of the power of women and men over the life cycle. *Psychology of Women Quarterly, 16,* 513–525.

Fuegen, K., Biernat, M., Haines, E., & Deaux, K. (2004). Mothers and fathers in the workplace: How gender and parental status influence judgments of job-related competence. *Journal of Social Issues, 60*(4), 737–754.

Garcia-Moreno, C., Jansen, H. A. F. M., Ellsberg, M., Heise, L., & Watts, C. H., on behalf of the WHO Multi-country Study on Women's Health and Domestic Violence against Women Study Team (2006). Prevalence of intimate partner violence: findings from the WHO Multi-Country Study on Women's Health and Domestic Violence. *Lancet, 368*, 1260–1269.

Garlough, C. L. (2008). On the political uses of folklore: Performance and grassroots feminist activism in India. *Journal of American Folklore, 121*(480), 167–191.

Gangestad, S. W., & Scheyd, G. J. (2005). The evolution of human physical attractiveness. *Annual Review of Anthropology, 34*, 523–548.

Gilmore, D. G. (1990). *Manhood in the making: Cultural concepts of masculinity.* New Haven, CT: Yale University Press.

Glick, P. (2006). Ambivalent sexism, power distance, and gender inequality across cultures. In S. Guimond (Ed.), *Social comparison and social psychology. Understanding cognition, intergroup relations, and culture* (pp. 283–302). New York: Cambridge University Press.

Goldstein, A. (2009, January 28). Democrats overturn barrier to unequal-pay suits. *The Washington Post.* Retrieved May 4, 2009 from http://www.washingtonpost.com/wp-dyn/content/article/2009/01/27/AR2009012702279.html

Grogan, S. (2008). *Body image: Understanding body dissatisfaction in men, women, and children* (2nd ed). New York: Psychology Press.

Grown, C., Gupta, G. R., & Pande, R. (2005). Taking action to improve women's health through gender equality and women's empowerment. *The Lancet, 365*, 541–543.

Gupta, M. A., Chaturvedi, S. K., Chandarana, P. C., & Johnson, A. M. Weight-related body image concerns among 18–24-year-old women in Canada and India: An empirical comparative study. *Journal of Psychosomatic Research, 50*, 193–198.

Haas, A. E. (2005). *Political process, activism, and health.* Unpublished PhD dissertation, Ohio State University. Retrieved January 15, 2009 from http://www.ohiolink.edu/etd/send-pdf.cgi/Haas%20Anne%20E.pdf?acc_num=osu1127220576

Hausmann, R., Tyson, L. D., & Zahidi, S. (2008). *The global gender gap report 2008.* Retrieved from World Economic Forum: http://www.weforum.org/en/Communities/Women%20Leaders%20and%20Gender%20Parity/G enderGapNetwork/index.htm

Hays, S. (1996). *The cultural contradictions of motherhood.* New Haven, CT: Yale University Press.

Hook, J. L. (2006). Care in context: Men's unpaid work in 20 countries, 1965–2003. *American Sociological Review, 71*, 639–660.

Human Rights Watch (1996). *Shattered lives: Sexual violence during the Rwandan genocide and its aftermath.* New York: Human Rights Watch, Women's Rights Project.

International Women's Democracy Center (2008). *Fact Sheet: Women's political participation.* Retrieved December 19, 2008 from http://www.iwdc.org/resources/fact_sheet.htm

Jung, J. & Forbes, G. B. (2007). Body dissatisfaction and disordered eating among college women in China, South Korea, and the United States: Contrasting predictions from sociocultural and feminist theories. *Psychology of Women Quarterly, 31*(4), 381–393.

Kagitcibasi, C., Goksen, F., & Gulgoz, S. (2005). Functional adult literacy and empowerment of women: Impact of a functional literacy program in Turkey. *Journal of*

*Adolescent and Adult Literacy, 48*(6), 472–489. Abstract retrieved January 15, 2009 from http://www.reading.org/publications/journals/jaal/v48/i6/abstracts/JAAL-48–6-Kagitcibasi.html

Kasturirangan, A. (2008). Empowerment and programs designed to address domestic violence. *Violence Against Women, 14,* 1465–1475.

Kehoe, A. B. (1995). Blackfoot persons. In L. F. Klein & L. A. Ackerman (Eds.), *Women and power in Native North America* (pp.113–125). Norman, OK: University of Oklahoma Press.

Khalid, R. (1997). Perceived threat of violence and coping strategies: A case of Pakistan women. *Journal of Behavioral Sciences,* 8(1–2): 43–54.

Killeen, L. A., López-Zafra E., & Eagly, A. H. (2006). Envisioning oneself as a leader: Comparisons of women and men in Spain and the United States. *Psychology of Women Quarterly, 30,* 312–322.

Kristof, N. D. (2005, June 14). Raped, kidnapped and silenced. *The New York Times.* Retrieved January 15, 2009 from http://www.nytimes.com/2005/06/14/opinion/14kristof.html

Lawson, K. (2009). *The relationship among job suitability and attainability, agency, and women's penalization of successful women in masculine occupations.* Unpublished master's thesis. Radford University, Radford, VA.

Leahey, T. M., Crowther, J. H., & Mickelson, K. D. (2007). The frequency, nature, and effects of naturally occurring appearance-focused social comparisons. *Behavior Therapy, 38,* 132–143.

Lee, J. L. (1994). Menarche and the (hetero) sexualization of the female body. *Gender and Society, 8,* 343–362.

Lips, H. M. (2000). College students' visions of power and possibility as mediated by gender. *Psychology of Women Quarterly, 24,* 37–41.

Lips, H. M. (2001). Envisioning positions of leadership: The expectations of university students in Virginia and Puerto Rico. *Journal of Social Issues, 57*(4), 799–813.

Matud, M. P. (2005). The psychological impact of domestic violence on Spanish women. *Journal of Applied Social Psychology, 35* (11), 2310–2322.

McCrummen, S. (2008, October 27). Women run the show in a recovering Rwanda. *Washington Post Foreign Service.* Retrieved from http://www.washingtonpost.com/wp-dyn/content/article/2008/10/26/AR2008102602197.html

Morrow, B. H. (1994). A grass-roots feminist response to intimate violence in the Caribbean. *Women Studies International Forum, 17*(6), 579–592.

Mydans, S. (2001, May 20). Nai Soi's long-necked women. *The New York Times.* Retrieved from http://query.nytimes.com/gst/fullpage.html?res=9E0DEFDC173AF933A15756C0A9679C8B63&sec=travel&spon=&pagewanted=1

National Council for Research on Women (n.d.) *NCRW big five: Keeping the doors of opportunity open: Women, minorities and affirmative action* [fact sheet]. Retrieved from http://www.ncrw.org/ncrwbigfive/wp-content/uploads/2008/10/affirmative-action2.pdf

National Institute of Mental Health (2008). *What are eating disorders?* Retrieved from http://www.nimh.nih.gov/health/publications/eating-disorders/what-are-eating-disorders.shtml

Nzegwu, N. (2004). The epistemological challenge of motherhood to patriliny. *JENdA: A Journal of Culture and African Women Studies, Issue 5.* Retrieved January 19, 2009 from http://www.jendajournal.com/issue5/nzegwu.htm

Olateju, M. A. (2007). Reading kiosks: Literacy empowerment for the girl-child. *Language, Culture and Curriculum, 20*, 155–164.

Onyejekwe, C. J. (2008). Nigeria: The dominance of rape. *Journal of International Women's Studies, 10*(1), 48–64.

Owen, K. (1995, February 20). U.S. dads lag in childcare duties, global study finds. *Los Angeles Times*, p. 5.

Parks-Stamm, E. J., Heilman, M. E., & Hearns, K. A. (2008). Motivated to penalize: Women's strategic rejection of successful women. *Personality and Social Psychology Bulletin, 34*, 237–247.

Parrot, A., & Cummings, N. (2006). *Forsaken females: The global brutalization of women*. Lanham, MD: Rowman & Littlefield.

Paxton, S. J., Eisenberg, M. E., & Neumark-Sztainer, D. (2006). Prospective predictors of body dissatisfaction in adolescent girls and boys: A five-year longitudinal study. *Developmental Psychology, 42*(5), 888–899.

Rand, C., Graham, D. L., & Rawlings, E. I. (1982). Psychological health and factors the court seeks to control in lesbian mother custody trials. *Journal of Homosexuality, 8*(1), 27–39.

Rappaport, J. (1987). Terms of empowerment/exemplars of prevention: Toward a theory for community psychology. *American Journal of Community Psychology, 15*, 121–148.

Renfrew Center Foundation (2002). *Eating disorders 101 guide: A summary of issues, statistics, and resources*. Retrieved from www.renfrew.org

Richburg, K. B. (1993, February 18). "I would like to be president—really": Somali women defy repressive customs to help repair their damaged country. *Washington Post*, p. A35.

Sabik, N. J. & Tylka, T. L. (2006). Do feminist identity styles moderate the relation between perceived sexist events and disordered eating? *Psychology of Women Quarterly, 30*(1), 77–84.

Sanday, P. R. (1981). The socio-cultural context of rape: A cross-cultural study. *Journal of Social Issues, 37*, 5–27.

Sasson, J. P. (1992). *Princess: A true story of life behind the veil in Saudi Arabia*. New York: Avon.

Scheper-Hughes, N. (1985). Culture, scarcity, and maternal thinking: Maternal detachment and infant survival in a Brazilian shantytown. *Ethos, 13*, 291–317.

Shriver, M., & Center for American Progress (2009). The Shriver Report: A woman's nation changes everything. Retrieved January 25, 2010 from http://www.awomansnation.com/index.php

Sigle-Rushton, W. & Waldfogel, J. (2007). Motherhood and women's earnings in Anglo-American, continental European, and Nordic countries. *Feminist Economics, 13*(2), 55–91.

Social Watch (2008). *Gender Equity Index 2008—Progress and setbacks*. Retrieved January 15, 2009 from http://www.socialwatch.org/en/avancesyRetrocesos/IEG_2008/tablas/SWGEI.htm

Steil, J. M., & Hillman, J. L. (1993). The perceived value of direct and indirect influence strategies: A cross-cultural comparison. *Psychology of Women Quarterly, 17*, 457–462.

Sudarkasa, N. (2004). Conceptions of motherhood in nuclear and extended families, with special reference to comparative studies involving African societies. *JENdA: A Journal of Culture and African Women Studies, 5*. Retrieved January 19, 2009 from http://www.jendajournal.com/issue5/sudarkasa.htm

United Nations (1997, May 23). _Fourth World Conference on Women (1995)_. Retrieved from http://www.un.org/geninfo/bp/women.html

United Nations Development Program (2007/2008). _Human Development Report 2007/2008._ (Table 29: Gender Empowerment Measure). Retrieved December 18, 2008 from http://hdr.undp.org/en/media/HDR_20072008_GEM.pdf

United Nations Development Program (2008). _Measuring inequality: Gender-related Development Index (GDI) and Gender Empowerment Measure (GEM)_. Retrieved December 18, 2008 from http://hdr.undp.org/en/statistics/indices/gdi_gem/

United Nations Population Fund (2000). _State of the world population 2000_. Retrieved January 27, 2009 from http://www.unfpa.org/swp/2000/english/ch03.html

United Nations Statistics Division (2008a). _Statistics and indicators on women and men_. Table 5a: Economic activity. Retrieved January 16, 2009 from http://unstats.un.org/unsd/demographic/products/indwm/statistics.htm#Work

United Nations Statistics Division (2008b). _Statistics and indicators on women and men_. Table 5d: Women legislators and managers. Retrieved on January 16 from http://unstats.un.org/unsd/demographic/products/indwm/tab5d.htm, 2009

U.S. Census Bureau (2008). _Historical income tables—people_, Table P-40:Woman's earnings as a percentage of men's earnings by race and Hispanic origin: 1960 to 2007, retrieved September 7, 2009 from http://www.census.gov/hhes/www/income/histinc/p40.html

U.S. Department of State (2008). _Trafficking in persons report 2008_. Retrieved from http://www.state.gov/g/tip/rls/tiprpt/2008/ on December 19, 2008.

United States Department of Labor (n.d.). _Title IX, Education amendments of 1972_. Retrieved from http://www.dol.gov/oasam/regs/statutes/titleIX.htm

Watts, C. & Zimmerman, C. (2002). Violence against women: global scope and magnitude. _The Lancet, 359_, 1232–1237.

Wilson, S. (2007). "When you have children, you're obliged to live": Motherhood, chronic illness and biographical disruption. _Sociology of Health and Illness, 29_, 610–625.

Women's Environment and Development Organization (2005). _Beijing betrayed: Women worldwide report that governments have failed to turn the platform into action_. Retrieved from http://www.wedo.org/files/gmr_pdfs/gmr2005.pdf

Women for Women International (2009). _Helping women survivors of war rebuild their lives_. Retrieved from http://www.womenforwomen.org/index.php

Yoder, J. D., Schleicher, T. L., & McDonald, T. W. (1998). Empowering token women leaders: The importance of organizationally legitimated credibility. _Psychology of Women Quarterly, 22_, 209–222.

# 12

# Experiences of Sexual Minorities in Diverse Cultures

## Linh Nguyen Littleford and Mary E. Kite

Within all countries around the world, there have always been people whose sexual practices, orientation, and identity differed from the dominant group. It was not until the nineteenth century, mostly in Europe and North America, that people began to use labels to differentiate sexual minorities from sexual majorities (Bristow, 1997; Herek & Garnets, 2007); we begin by defining the terms commonly used in Western societies. *Heterosexuals* are believed to experience emotional, romantic, and sexual attraction to members of the other biological sex; for *homosexual people*, this attraction is to members of their own biological sex (American Psychological Association, 1998). *Bisexuals* have emotional, romantic, and sexual attraction to members of both the same and the other sex. Some people believe that their gender identity differs from the traditional notions of maleness and femaleness and/or that this identity does not correspond with their biological sex (Lev, 2007). These individuals are referred to as *transgendered people*. *Transsexuals* are people who are transgendered and who feel so strongly that they are "trapped in the body of the other sex" that they take sex hormones or have surgery to become the other sex (Hill, 2008).

As you have seen throughout this book, a society's culture is generally defined by the dominant group; across cultures, this privileged group comprises heterosexuals and people whose sense of being male or female is consistent with their biological sex. As we will discuss, individuals who differ from the dominant culture often experience prejudice and discrimination (Matsumoto & Juang, 2008) and this is especially true for people who identify as lesbians, gays, bisexuals, or transgendered (LGBTs); sexual minorities in all nations experience sexual stigma because they violate the norms established and are marked as "devalued, spoiled, or flawed in the eyes of others" (Crocker, Major, & Steele, 1998, p. 504).

Both lay people and researchers tend to view sexual orientation as a dichotomous variable; that is, they categorize people as either homosexual or heterosexual. However, it is more accurate to view sexual orientation on a continuum, ranging from completely homosexual to completely heterosexual, and with some individuals having a bisexual orientation. In addition, sexual minorities vary in if, how, and when they self-identify their affective or sexual orientation. Some individuals may feel sexual attractions, have same-gender sexual fantasies, and/or engage in same-gender sexual relations but do not consider themselves gay, lesbian, or bisexual (Garnets, 2002; Greene, 1994). Others may use different sexual identity labels to reflect their masculine or feminine roles, their status in the same-gender relationship, and their roles within sexual activities. For example, in Senegal, men who have sex with men self-identify as either *yoos* or *ibbis* (Niang et al., 2003). *Yoos* are more dominant, masculine, and often the insertive partners in sexual acts. They do not see themselves as homosexuals. In contrast, *ibbis* are more feminine, more passive in sexual acts, and have less status and power in the relationship. Similarly, in Peru (Caceras & Rosasco, 1999) and Turkey (Bereket & Adam, 2008), men who have sex with men select different identities depending on whether their relationships are egalitarian or adhere to traditional gender roles. Some sexual minorities, particularly those in developing countries and/or who are poor, engage in same-gender sexual behaviors for financial gains (Niang et al., 2003). Still others self-identify as LGB without ever having engaged in sexual relations (Rothblum, 1994). Consequently, defining sexual orientation based on same-gender sexual behaviors or on Western-based LGBT categories without considering other sociocultural factors can be both culturally insensitive and inaccurate (Zhou, 2006).

Accordingly, in this chapter we will discuss the experiences of sexual minorities, including those who self-identify as LBGT and those who have same-gender sexual fantasies and attractions, engage in same-gender sexual behaviors, and have atypical gender characteristics, whether or not they self-identify as LGBT. We will use *LGBT*, *LB*, or *GB* when reviewing research that included those labels. We will use *sexual minorities* to refer to LGBT people in cultures and countries where LGBT categories are not commonly used. Because gay men and lesbians in North America and Europe are the focus of most of the research and theory we discuss, our chapter primarily examines their experiences. When possible, we will also discuss how sexual stigma affects the lives of sexual minorities in other regions of the world and explore the heterogeneity of sexual minorities between and within countries.

Conceptually, we use Herek and colleagues' (Herek, Chopp, & Strohl, 2007; Herek, Gillis, & Cogan, 2009) sexual stigma framework and Meyer's (2003b, 2007) LGB minority stress model to discuss sexual minorities' experiences with stigma and its influence on their mental health. Both models propose that LGBT people face many forms of stigma and that these experiences have negative consequences. Herek et al. (2007, 2009) focus on how sexual stigma is transmitted and perpetuated in the U.S. and the extent to which both heterosexual and LGB people internalize these beliefs. Meyer's LGB minority stress model emphasizes how LGB individuals' expectations of, subjective experiences with, and interpretations of objective events such as exclusion, marginalization, prejudice, and discrimination affect their mental health outcomes. Both models focus on sexual stigma and its consequences primarily on people within the U.S.

We will discuss three levels of stigma: institutional, interpersonal, and intrapersonal. These levels are similar to the cultural and individual forms of stigma discussed by Herek et al. (2007, 2009), and the distal and proximal minority stressors presented by Meyer (2003b, 2007). Our institutionalized stigma category corresponds to Herek et al.'s (2009) cultural form of stigma. At this level of analysis, we will report the current laws and civil rights relevant to members of sexual minority groups. We will then divide Herek et al.'s (2009) *individual stigma* category into two levels (interpersonal and intrapersonal) to emphasize the ways in which sexual stigma similarly and differently affects sexual majorities and sexual minorities. Specifically, within our category of interpersonal stigma, we will focus on how sexual majorities internalize and exhibit sexual stigma toward sexual minorities. These types of sexual stigma parallel Meyer's (2003b, 2007) distal minority stressors. In contrast, within our category of intrapersonal stigma, we will highlight how sexual minorities internalize and cope with institutional and interpersonal forms of sexual stigma. These topics correspond to Meyer's (2003b, 2007) proximal minority stressors. We will conclude by reviewing what is currently known about sexual minorities' mental health outcomes.

## Prevalence of Sexual Minorities

When considering sexual minorities' experiences cross-culturally, it is important to consider their representation in the world's population. It is difficult to pinpoint the proportion of people who are LGBT and/or sexual minorities because these estimates are based entirely on self-report and individuals may choose not to self-disclose this information even on anonymous surveys. In addition, the prevalence rates differ depending on whether the surveys define LGB as ever having sexual relations with a same-gender other, as viewing one's sexual identity as LGB, or as being involved in the LGB community (Fox, 1995; Rothblum, 1994). Regardless of the method used, LGBTs are a numerical minority group. One common estimate is that approximately 10% of the population is gay or lesbian, but a closer look at the research shows that estimates vary from one to 17% (see Hill, 2008, for a review).

The percentage of women who self-identify as lesbian is generally smaller than the percentage of men who self-identify as gay, but national surveys of a representative sample of U.S. residents estimate both to be lower than 3% (Laumann, Gagnon, Michael, & Michaels, 1994). Estimating the percentage of women who identify as lesbian is further complicated by findings that women's sexuality is fluid. For example, a significant proportion of lesbian women report periodic attraction to men (Diamond & Savin-Williams, 2000). More men than women identify as transgendered, but we know of no research on the actual incidence of transgenderism. Based on U.S. samples, estimates of the prevalence of transsexualism range from one in 2,900 to one in 100,000 (de Cuypere et al., 2007).

## Institutionalized Sexual Stigma

Sexual stigma, or a system of beliefs that considers same-gender sexual practices as immoral or unacceptable and that deems sexual minorities inferior compared to sexual majorities, has been integrated into many societies. This belief system is embedded into virtually all aspects of society such that all individuals, regardless of their sexual orientation, identity, or personal views, know that sexual minorities are denigrated and treated more negatively than sexual majorities (Herek et al., 2007). One level in which people are socialized to stigmatize sexual minorities is through institutional structures, such as laws, that make explicit that sexual minorities do not have the same worth as sexual majorities and thus do not deserve equal rights.

Currently, many countries have laws that condemn same-gender sexual practices, punish people who are sexual minorities, and limit these individuals' civil rights. As of May 2009, 59% (115) of countries have laws that legalize same-gender sexual behaviors while 41% (80) consider the behaviors illegal (Ottosson, 2009). Same-gender behaviors for both sexes are illegal in most countries in Africa and Asia but are legal in all recognized countries in Europe and in all but one country in South America (i.e., Guyana). In Oceania, 8 of 17 countries and territories consider same-gender acts legal. In North America, homosexual acts are legal in 15 out of 25 countries and territories; in the U.S., the 2003 Supreme Court decision to overturn sodomy laws (Lawrence v. Texas, 2003) made it the third most recent country to decriminalize same-gender acts (Ottosson, 2009). In countries where engaging in homosexual acts is illegal, the typical punishment is imprisonment; however, in five countries in Africa (Mauritania and Sudan) and Asia (Iran, Saudi Arabia, and Yemen) and some parts of Nigeria and Somalia those persons are sentenced to death (Ottosson, 2009). Interestingly, 13% of countries have different laws for men and women who engage in same-gender behaviors (Ottosson, 2009). When differences exist, the laws permit women to have sex with women but punish men if they have sex with men; this punishment can be as severe as life imprisonment. The reverse pattern does not occur. Thus, no countries have laws that punish women who engage same-gender sexual behaviors while permitting men to engage in similar acts.

Of the countries that have decriminalized homosexual acts, only a few have laws that protect their sexual minority citizens from experiencing discrimination based on sexual orientation. Only 5% of the worlds' countries specifically prohibit discrimination based on sexual orientation in their constitutions. Employment discrimination based on homosexual orientation is banned in 25% of countries; 10% ban such discrimination based on gender identity (Ottosson, 2009). In addition, 2% of countries extend their institutionalized sexual stigma laws to non-citizens, prohibiting LGB people from entering their countries (Lesotho, Swaziland, Belize, and Trinidad and Tobago; Ottosson, 2009).

Very few countries, even with decriminalization, monitor and/or punish those who assault members of sexual minority groups (Ottosson, 2009; Stahnke et al., 2008). Just 5% of countries have hate crime laws providing harsher punishments for those inflicting physical violence because of the victims' sexual orientation (or perceived sexual orientation). Currently, 9% of countries legally recognize transsexuals' gender after gender reassignment treatment (Australia, Belgium, parts of Canada, Finland, Germany, Italy, Japan, the Netherlands, New Zealand, Panama, Romania, South Africa, Spain, Sweden, Turkey, United Kingdom, and parts of the U.S.; Ottosson, 2009). Only Uruguay and some parts of the U.S. punish more severely people who commit hate crimes based on the victims' gender identity (Ottosson, 2009).

Although a minority, there are countries in which citizens who are LGB have marriage and parenting rights comparable to their heterosexual counterparts. According to Ottosson (2009), 10% have laws that allow people who are LGB to marry (Belgium, Canada, Netherlands, Norway, South Africa, Spain, and Sweden, and six U.S. states) or to have civil partnerships or unions with most or all rights of marriage (Colombia, Denmark, Finland, Germany, Iceland, New Zealand, some parts of Australia, Switzerland, the U.K., and some U.S. states). Same-sex couples can jointly adopt children in 5% of countries (Andorra, Capital Territory and Western Australia in Australia, Belgium, the Brazilian city of São Paulo, most of the Canadian provinces, Iceland, Israel, the Netherlands, Norway, South Africa, Spain, Sweden, the U.K., and some parts of the U.S.). In addition, the non-biological parent in same-gender relationships may adopt her or his partner's children in 2% of countries (Denmark, Germany, Tasmania, and Alberta, Canada; Ottosson, 2009).

In summary, laws in the majority of the countries in the world allow same-gender sexual behaviors but explicitly limit sexual minorities' civil rights in multiple domains, including in marriage, adoption, employment, and protection from hate crimes. These laws reinforce the notion that members of sexual minority groups are abnormal and inferior relative to sexual majorities. Sexual minority citizens in many countries in Europe have more civil rights than their counterparts in other parts of the world. However, even in these countries, it was necessary to pass laws to ensure that sexual minorities have the same civil rights as sexual majorities—who have always enjoyed these rights without such legal proceedings. It appears, then, that sexual stigma still exists on some levels in these countries. In the next section, as we discuss sexual stigma at the interpersonal level, it will be evident that sexual majorities continue to view and treat sexual minorities negatively in all countries, including those in Europe.

## Interpersonal Forms of Sexual Stigma

### Sexual prejudice

The negative emotions and feelings sexual majorities have, as a result of internalized sexual stigma, toward individuals who are LGBT, are referred to as *sexual prejudice* (Herek et al., 2007). As is true for all cross-cultural research, to answer the question of whether sexual prejudice is higher in some countries than in others, researchers should ask equivalent samples (preferably representative of the population) the same questions using the same procedure. The questionnaires used should have linguistic equivalence—that is, the items must have the same meaning across the different languages used in the different countries. As Matsumoto and Juang (2008) note, failing to do so "creates the proverbial situation of comparing apples and oranges" (p. 29).

We are aware of only five studies that meet these criteria. Widmer, Treas, and Newcombe (1998) compared responses to the question "Is homosexual sex wrong?" across large and nationally representative samples from 24 countries; data were from the 1994 International Social Survey Program. As is true for each of the first three studies we describe, respondents were primarily from Eastern and Western Europe and North America. Respondents from the Netherlands, Norway, the Czech Republic, Canada, and Spain were most accepting of homosexual sex; those in Hungary, Bulgaria, Italy, Japan, Northern Ireland, the Philippines, Poland, and Slovenia were least accepting. It should be noted, however, that the majority of respondents in most countries (excepting the five most tolerant countries) reported that homosexual sex was always or almost always wrong.

Kelly (2001) reported responses from 29 nations who participated in the International Social Science Survey (ISSS) in 1999/2000. Results replicated Widmer et al. (1998) in that the same group of countries generally emerged as most and least accepting. However, note that Canada and Poland were not included in the 1999/2000 ISSS and that this survey included Switzerland, Denmark (both found to be accepting), and Chile (found to be unaccepting). Further, Kelly (2001) found Sweden and Germany among the most accepting, whereas Widmer et al. (1998) found somewhat less acceptance in those two countries. Štulhofer and Rimac (2009) reported responses from 31 European countries, based on the European Values Survey (EVS) in 1999/2000. Respondents answered whether homosexuality can be justified and whether they would like to have a homosexual neighbor. Similar to the other studies we have discussed, Scandinavians were most accepting and Eastern Europeans least accepting.

The Pew Global Attitudes Project (2007) examined attitudes toward homosexuality across 47 countries and, unlike the other surveys we summarize, included several African, Asian, South American, and Middle Eastern countries. Similar to the previously discussed surveys, in response to the question of whether homosexuality should be accepted or rejected, Western Europeans and Canadians were among the most accepting and Russians and Ukrainians were generally negative. Residents of South American countries and Mexico were also accepting (but not respondents in Venezuela and Bolivia). The majority of U.S. respondents were accepting of homosexuality. Residents of African countries were by far the least accepting; in most of those countries over 90% of the population believed homosexuality should be rejected. In South Africa, 64% rejected homosexuality. Residents of Asian countries, with the exception of Japan, also held anti-LG sentiments, with 69% or higher rejecting homosexuality. Israeli and Turkish citizens rejected homosexuality (50% and 57%, respectively), as did residents of the Palestinian territories (58%), but less so than did residents of other countries in the Middle East where rejection rates were 79% or higher.

**Table 12.1** Average rank of country based on attitudes toward homosexuality

| | |
|---|---|
| Lithuania | 1 |
| Hungary | 2 |
| Ukraine | 3 |
| Latvia | 4 |
| Bulgaria | 5 |
| Russia | 6 |
| Croatia | 7 |
| Portugal | 8 |
| Malta | 9 |
| Chile | 10 |
| Cyprus | 11 |
| Poland | 12 |
| Northern Ireland | 13 |
| Belarus | 14 |
| Japan | 15 |
| U.S.A. | 16 |
| Republic of Ireland | 17 |
| Italy | 18 |
| Slovenia | 19 |
| Slovakia | 20 |
| Finland | 21 |
| Britain | 22 |
| Belgium | 23 |
| Austria | 24 |
| France | 25 |
| Czech Republic | 26 |
| Germany | 27 |
| Spain | 28 |
| Luxembourg | 29 |
| Denmark | 30 |
| Iceland | 31 |
| Sweden | 32 |
| The Netherlands | 33 |

*Note*: For countries included in at least two surveys of nations (Kelly, 2001, Pew Global Attitudes Project, 2007, or Štulhofer & Rimac, 2009), average rank for attitudes toward homosexuality were computed. Higher ranks indicate countries with more positive attitudes.

To provide a general index of where acceptance of homosexuality is more or less likely, we computed a country's rank order of attitudes toward homosexuality, based on data reported in Kelly (2001), the Pew Global Attitudes Project (2007) and Štulhofer & Rimac (2009). Table 12.1 reports the average rank for those countries that were included in at least two surveys; higher ranks indicate countries more accepting of homosexuality. Because these surveys asked somewhat different questions, interpretation should be done with caution. Another limitation of this research is that attitudes were assessed with single-item measures that represent people's acceptance of homosexual behavior but not necessarily their acceptance of homosexual persons. Because the surveys we summarized were part of a larger study of social attitudes across nations, the use of one or two items is understandable. However, research conducted in the U.S. shows that people are generally more accepting of homosexual people than homosexual behavior (Kite & Whitley, 1996) and that people are more reluctant to deny gay men and lesbians basic civil rights than they are to disparage homosexual people or homosexual behavior (Herek, 2002). Overall acceptance rates might be different if, for example, attitudes toward civil rights were assessed, although it seems unlikely that the pattern of differences across countries would substantially change.

It is also important to point out that attitudes toward homosexuality are changing toward greater acceptance. In both Canada and the U.S., there has been a remarkable degree of change over the last 20 years (Andersen & Fetner, 2008). Similar to the results reported by Andersen and Fetner (2008), Adamczyk and Pitt (2009) found that younger people were more accepting than were older cohorts across 33 countries. Similarly, Kelly (2001) reported that Australians' attitudes toward homosexuality were much more accepting in 1999 than in 1984. Likewise, results on the General Social Survey, based on a U.S. sample, showed greater acceptance of homosexuality across time (Hurley, 2005). However, given the extreme negativity, the criminalization of same-gender behaviors, and the laws limiting sexual minorities' civil rights currently present in some countries, such as many African and Asian nations, this change is unlikely to be universal.

Religion appears to be one factor that differentiates between countries that are more accepting of homosexuality from those that are not. Štulhofer and Rimac (2009) found higher levels of acceptance of homosexuality in European countries whose major religion was Catholic or Protestant rather than Eastern Orthodox. Adamczyk and Pitt (2009) analyzed responses to the question of whether homosexuality can be justified in a study of 45,824 people from 33 nations. They found that people who lived in Catholic majority countries (Canada, Puerto Rico, Mexico, Venezuela, Spain, Argentina, Peru, Chile, Uganda, and the Philippines) and Protestant majority countries (U.S., South Korea, South Africa, and Zimbabwe) were more accepting of homosexuality than those in Muslim majority countries (Nigeria, Egypt, Tanzania, Indonesia, Singapore, Bosnia, Bangladesh, Algeria, Albania, Kyrgyz Republic, Jordan, and Pakistan). However, people in these Muslim majority countries had similar attitudes toward homosexuality as those in Christian Orthodox (Moldova, Serbia, Montenegro, and Macedonia), Buddhist (Japan and Viet Nam), and Hindu (India) countries.

In addition to religion, countries' levels of urbanization and economic development are associated with their citizens' acceptance of homosexuality (Adamczyk & Pitt, 2009; Štulhofer & Rimac, 2009). Adamczyk and Pitt (2009) theorized that in countries where there are economic uncertainties and the majority of the people still worry about their physical and basic needs (survival orientation), people cope by holding onto familiar cultural norms and laws. In contrast, within countries where there are economic stability and modernization, people can focus more on their psychological well-being and quality of life (self-expressive orientation). Therefore, they can be more accepting of unfamiliar cultural values and diverse worldviews. Consistent with their hypothesis, Adamczyk and Pitt found that people in self-expressive countries are more supportive of homosexuality than those in survival countries.

Interestingly, preliminary evidence indicates that people's acceptance of homosexuality is not significantly related to their countries' laws about sexual minorities (Adamczyk & Pitt, 2009). It is important to note that the researchers had to omit data from two countries in which sexual minorities are sentenced to death (Saudi Arabia, Iran) and from two countries where homosexual acts were illegal (Morocco) or unclear (Iraq). Thus, more research is needed to determine whether, and under what circumstances, people's acceptance of homosexuality reflects and perhaps influences the legal status of gays and lesbians in different countries.

Of course, within most countries, there are individual differences in acceptance of homosexuality. In fact, attitudes among people from the same country differ more than those held by people from different countries (71% versus 29% of the variance; Adamczyk & Pitt, 2009). We can identify a set of predictors of individuals' attitudes toward sexual minorities that appear to hold cross-culturally. First, research conducted in the U.S. has consistently shown that individuals who reported knowing a gay or lesbian person are more accepting of homosexuality (e.g., Herek & Capitanio, 1996). This relationship was also found in a study of Puerto Ricans' attitudes toward homosexuality (Bauermeister, Morales, Seda, & González-Rivera, 2007) and in samples of U.S. residents of Mexican descent (Herek & González-Rivera, 2006), Germans (Steffens & Wagner, 2004), and Italians (Lingiardi, Falanga, & D'Augelli, 2005). The available data suggest that this relationship holds up cross-culturally but we cannot say whether this factor predicts attitudes toward homosexuality *better* in any particular culture. And, of course, research based on samples from many more countries must be conducted before we can conclude that this relationship is universal.

Second, within countries, individuals with stronger religious beliefs, especially those from fundamentalist religions, are more negative toward gays and lesbians. Whitley (2009) found this relationship in a meta-analysis of 64 studies based on U.S. and Canadian samples. Cross-national studies indicated that church-goers (Kelly, 2001) and those who perceived religion as personally important (Adamczyk & Pitt, 2009) were less tolerant of homosexuality. The relationship between religiosity and sexual prejudice also emerged in samples from Canada (Andersen & Fetner, 2008; Hunsberger, Owusu, & Duck, 1999), Ghana (Hunsberger et al., 1999), Puerto Rico (Bauermeister et al., 2007), and of U.S. residents of Mexican descent (Herek & González-Rivera, 2006). Although Protestants had more negative attitudes toward homosexuality than Catholics, Orthodox Christians, Jews, and people with no religious affiliation, people's personal religiosity influenced their negative attitudes toward homosexuality significantly more in self-expressive oriented countries such as the U.S. than in survival-oriented countries such as Zimbabwe (Adamczyk & Pitt, 2009).

Third, the preponderance of evidence shows that, across cultures, women are more accepting of homosexuality than are men. Adamczyk and Pitt (2009) found that, across 33 nations studied, men held more sexual prejudice than women. This finding is consistent with research reported by Kelly (2001), who analyzed 29 nations. However, Kelly noted that these differences were larger in Scandinavian countries, Australia, Austria, France, Germany, Great Britain, and the U.S., but were non-significant in Russia, Chile, and the Philippines. The Pew Global Attitudes (2007) survey found women to be more accepting of homosexuality than men in Canada, Britain, Germany, France, the U.S., Pakistan, Turkey, Bangladesh, Lebanon, and Nigeria, but found no sex difference in Italy, Jordan, Uzbekistan, or Indonesia. In these countries, men were more intolerant of homosexuality than were women: Canada (Andersen & Fetner, 2008), Germany (Steffens & Wagner, 2004), Italy (Lingiardi et al., 2005), and the U.S. (Kite & Whitley, 1996). Studies comparing heterosexual men's and women's attitudes toward lesbians and gay men have been limited to the U.S. and the results are mixed. Kite and Whitley (1996) reported that, in U.S. samples, heterosexual men are especially intolerant of gay men. Similarly, Herek and González-Rivera (2006) found Mexican American men held more negative attitudes toward gay men than did women. However, Kite and Whitley (1996) found that men and women evaluated lesbians similarly whereas Herek and González-Rivera (2006) found that women were relatively negative toward lesbians. Bauermeister et al. (2007) found no sex difference in attitudes toward either gay men or lesbians in their Puerto Rican sample.

Finally, people with higher levels of education have shown greater acceptance of homosexuality than have those who are less educated. This finding has been reported for samples in the U.S. (Herek, 2002; Herek & Gonzáles-Rivera, 2006), Germany (Steffens & Wagner, 2004), Canada (Andersen & Fetner, 2008), the 21 nations in Kelly's (2001) study, and across the 33 countries included in Adamczyk and Pitt's (2009) study.

### Discrimination against sexual minorities

Sexual prejudice conveys sexual majorities' evaluations of sexual minorities; sexual discrimination is the negative differential *behavior* directed at members of the latter group. Sexual discrimination includes verbal and physical assaults, often referred to as anti-gay hate crimes or anti-LGBT violence, inflicted on people who are, or are perceived to be, LGBT. As mentioned earlier, not many countries ban anti-gay hate crimes specifically and even fewer have governmental organizations that monitor and report data on sexual orientation hate crimes. Of all hate crimes reported to police in 2007, the prevalence of incidents perpetrated specifically because of the victims' sexual orientation were 10% in Canada, 20.4% in Sweden, 8.3% in England, 5.6% in Northern Ireland, and 15.5% in the U.S. (Stahnke et al., 2008).

In several countries, non-governmental agencies have conducted surveys to assess the prevalence of anti-LGBT violence. In France, of all the reported hate crimes,

11% were due to sexual orientation and/or gender identity. In Germany, 35% of 24,000 gay and bisexual survey respondents reported that they had been victims of anti-LGBT violence within one year. In the U.K., 13% of LGBT people surveyed reported experiencing an anti-LGBT hate crime within the last year, and 20% within the last three years (Stahnke et al., 2008). Summarizing annual reports on hate crimes from nine countries, Stahnke et al. (2008) concluded that the rate of violence against people who are LGBT is high and may be increasing. And yet, these statistics may be much lower than actual incidence because, for many reasons, victims may not be able or willing to report these types of crimes to officials. Survey results revealed that only a small number of sexual minorities reported anti-LGBT violence to officials: 10% in Germany and 14% in the U.K. (Stahnke et al., 2008).

Sexual minorities are particularly vulnerable to physical and verbal assaults during adolescence and, as we will discuss later, these experiences may explain why younger LGBT people are at higher risk of suicide than their older cohorts. In Germany, 63% of respondents younger than 18 reported experiencing anti-gay violence (Stahnke et al., 2008). In the U.K., the percentage of GBT men who reported experiencing physical violence (being kicked or hit) while in school was equally high (68%; Rivers, 2001). Although fewer LBT women (31%) than GBT men experienced anti-gay violence, the rates were still significantly higher than those reported by the general student population (24%; Rivers, 2001). More frequent than the physical assaults, the majority of the LGBT respondents recalled experiencing verbal abuse (name calling: 82%, teasing: 58%, being ridiculed: 71%) as youths. In the U.S., Espelage and Swearer (2008) reported that 33% of students reported that they had been victims of anti-gay verbal harassment or physical assaults.

In short, in many countries, including those where laws exist to protect LGBT people's civil rights, sexual majorities continue to hold strong sexual prejudice and exhibit violent forms of discrimination toward people whom they perceive are LGBT. We will next discuss how members of sexual minority groups experience, and the extent to which they internalize, the dominant group's sexual stigma.

## Intrapersonal Forms of Sexual Stigma

### Perceptions of sexual stigma

Sexual minorities are aware of their minority status and the negative attitudes that members of the dominant group have toward them. As outlined by Meyer's (2003b, 2007) LGBT minority stress model, to understand how sexual stigma influences sexual minorities' mental health outcomes, we need to examine how they interpret their experiences of marginalization. A survey of 12,347 gay and bisexual men in eight countries in Europe found varying levels of perceived acceptance of their sexual minority status (Bochow, Chiarotti, Davies, & Dubois-Arber, 1994).

Specifically, most GB men in Denmark (61%) and the Netherlands (68%) believed that all of their family members, friends, and colleagues accepted their sexual orientation. However, the level of perceived acceptance was low for those in the other six countries (i.e., U.K. 34%, Germany [West: 32%, East 30%], Switzerland 28%, France 24%, Austria 19%, and Italy 9%). Gay and bisexual Latino men in three urban cities in the U.S. reported that their most common experiences with sexual stigma were to be told: that gays are not normal (91%); that gay people will be lonely (71%); and that gay people's sexual orientation causes family members to be embarrassed (70%; Diaz, Ayala, Bein, Henne, & Marin, 2001). Analyzing a nationally representative sample of 3,032 U.S. Americans aged 25 to 74 years, Mays and Cochran (2001) found that 42% of LGB participants reported that they have experienced sexual orientation-based discrimination (e.g., school, work, receiving financial and other services, and social hostility), compared to 2% of their heterosexual counterparts.

## Sexual self-stigma

Living in a culture where they are exposed to laws, attitudes, and behaviors that discriminate against non-heterosexuals, some sexual minorities accept these negative sexual stigma cultural norms. This acceptance of sexual stigma by members of sexual minority groups is known as *internalized homophobia* (Herek et al., 2007) or *sexual self-stigma* (Herek et al., 2009). Unlike some stigmas, such as racial or ethnic group membership, sexual orientation is concealable—that is, sexual minorities can choose whether or when to reveal their group membership and many choose to "pass" as a member of the dominant group. Sexual minorities who pass as heterosexuals may be doing so because of their internalized homophobia. In the U.S., LGB adults who endorsed more negative feelings toward LGB people were less likely to disclose their sexual identity to non-family members (Herek et al., 2009). However, many sexual minorities feel compelled to hide their sexual orientation out of fears of familial and social rejection, loss of employment, loss of parental rights, and physical and verbal violence. As discussed in the sections on institutionalized and interpersonal forms of sexual stigma, these concerns have their basis in reality.

How and why people conceal their sexual minority status may also be influenced by the norms within their cultures and their countries. For instance, some Korean (Kim & Hahn, 2006) and Chinese (Zhou, 2006) gay men conceal their sexual orientation by marrying women and producing children for fear of social ostracism, lower social status, and family dishonor and shame if they should fail to live up to their cultural and family expectations to continue their family lineage. Similarly, in the U.K., two-thirds of South Asian LGB people surveyed reported that they actively hid their sexual orientation because of incongruity with their Asian cultural expectations (Bhugra, 1997). Some Turkish gay men hide their

sexual minority status to maintain their family's honor and reputation (Bereket & Adam, 2008). Likewise, 64% of gay Latino American male participants in the U.S. presented themselves as heterosexuals (Diaz, Ayala, & Bein, 2004; Diaz et al., 2001). Interestingly, the Latino/Latina American community shows more disapproval toward people who identify as LGBT than they do toward those engaging in same-gender sexual activities (Greene, 1994). Racial/ethnic minorities in the U.S. (e.g., Hispanic/Latino Americans, Asian Americans, African Americans, and Native Americans) who identify as LGBT may feel additional pressure to conceal their sexual orientation. For some of them, identifying as LGBT may cause family members and those within their ethnic communities to perceive them as rejecting their cultural heritage, resulting in ostracism, coercion to conceal their sexual orientation, and withdrawal of social support (Greene, 1994). The loss of support from their own racial/ethnic communities can be more detrimental to ethnic minorities than to European Americans because ethnic minorities may already feel marginalized and excluded by the racial/ethnic dominant European American community (Greene, 1994).

Denying one's group membership does not alleviate the guilt and shame associated with the stigma and can actually heighten these feelings and cause additional stress (Pachankis, 2007). Withholding that one is a sexual minority means hiding an important part of one's identity; even casual details about one's intimate relationships must be kept secret, creating stress and anxiety for minority group members (Day & Schoenrade, 2000). In addition, not revealing their sexual minority status precludes opportunities to be accepted by other sexual minorities, to be exposed to more positive messages about their sexual orientation, and to learn protective strategies to address sexual stigma. McLaren, Jude, and McLachlan (2008) found that for Australian self-identified gay men, belonging to either a gay community or the general community led to fewer depressive symptoms. In addition, those who felt valued in a non-gay community also experienced more support in the gay community. The findings suggest that for self-identified gay men, having opportunities to connect with others and to feel valued will reduce depressive symptoms regardless of whether the support comes from sexual minorities or majorities. However, unlike people with a non-concealable stigma, sexual minorities are not born into a community of similar others and thus must seek out other sexual minorities to disclose their own group membership. Even when they wish to disclose their sexual minority status, LGBT people may not always be able to identify each other and thus may remain isolated (Frable, Platt, & Hoey, 1998). Therefore, because it is a concealable stigma, sexual orientation can have more deleterious effects on the individuals' self-esteem and mood than a visible stigma (Frable et al., 1998; Herek & Garnets, 2007).

To summarize, although their reasons may differ, many LGBT people conceal their sexual minority status from others, including their families and friends. Pretending to be heterosexuals or actively hiding their sexual minority status may exacerbate LGBT people's internalized sexual stigma. In addition, concealment can prevent access to social support and other benefits associated with being a part of the sexual minority community (e.g., community connection, protection, and more positive self-perception). However, research conducted on the benefits associated with participating in LGB communities has been limited to countries in which these communities are visible and where laws and social norms are more accepting of LGBT people. Sexual minorities may be more reluctant to participate in social support groups if they live in countries where disclosure of sexual orientation can result in death, imprisonment, and other legal sanctions. Also, prior research included participants from individualistic countries where it is normative to consider one's individual needs and happiness before the wishes of the family or community. Future research should include cultures in which people consider others' welfare before their own and should explore the extent to which sexual minorities adhere to the cultural norm of not seeking support outside one's immediate family and community. Thus, more cross-cultural studies are needed to determine whether the costs and benefits associated with disclosure are similar in cultures, communities, or countries where people are more collectivistic and where social norms and laws are more punitive of sexual minorities.

## Consequence of Sexual Stigma: Mental Health Outcomes

Regardless of where they live, sexual minorities experience some level of institutionalized and interpersonal forms of sexual stigma, which can impact their physical and mental health outcomes. The effects of sexual stigma on sexual minorities' physical health, particularly in relation to prevention and treatment of HIV / AIDS, are beyond the scope of this chapter (see Padilla, Vasquez del Aguila, & Parker, 2007, for an excellent review on this topic). We will focus instead on sexual minorities' mental health outcomes and discuss how these stem from people's experience of sexual stigma.

### Between group differences in mental health outcomes

Researchers have attempted to understand sexual minorities' mental health outcomes in two ways. The first approach is to determine whether sexual minorities' mental health outcomes differ from those of sexual majorities (Meyer, 2003b). Summarizing the research on mental health outcomes and sexual orientation, Herek and Garnets (2007) concluded that based on epidemiological surveys, generally, the rates of suicide and psychological distress are low. In other words, the majority of people surveyed (sexual minorities and sexual majorities) are psychological healthy. When researchers used global psychological distress measures, history of psychiatric hospitalizations, and self-esteem as indicators of mental health outcomes, they found that sexual minorities and majorities do not differ significantly from each other (Balsam, Beauchaine, Mickey, & Rothblum, 2005). However, when researchers used psychiatric disorder classifications, standardized measures, and suicide attempts/ideations as indicators of mental health outcomes, significant group differences emerged. In the most comprehensive analysis of studies on sexual orientation and mental health outcomes to date, King et al. (2008) found that LGB people are at significantly higher risks for experiencing psychological disorders than their heterosexual counterparts. They analyzed data only from studies that included LGB people and a comparable heterosexual cohort and those that used standardized scales and official psychiatric disorder classification systems. Of the studies published between January 1966 and April 2005, 25 met their criteria. Based on data from 214,344 participants, King et al. concluded that compared to heterosexuals, LBG people are 2.47 times more likely to attempt suicide in their lifetime, 1.5 times more likely to have depressive and anxiety disorders within a 12-month period, and 1.5 times more likely to have alcohol and other substance dependence disorders within 12 months (King et al., 2008). Depending on their gender, LGB people have different levels of risks on various psychological disorders. Women who were LB were at greater risk than heterosexual women for alcohol (4 times), drug (3.5 times), and any substance dependence (3.42 times). Men who were GB were four times more likely to attempt suicide in their lifetime than heterosexual men (King et al., 2008). However, King et al. analyzed data collected mostly in the U.S. (except Mathy, 2002), and did not compare mental health outcomes of sexual minorities in different countries. Nevertheless, more recent studies of people in the Netherlands (Sandfort, Bakker, Schellevis, & Vanwesenbeeck, 2006) and New Zealand (Meyer, 2003a) have reached a similar conclusion: LGB people are at greater risk of psychiatric illnesses than heterosexual people.

Mathy (2002) conducted the only known cross-national study on suicide and sexual orientation, surveying 37,432 participants in five continents. Analyzing men and women together, Mathy found that LGB in Asia, North America, and South America were more likely to both think about and attempt suicide than their heterosexual cohorts. In Australia, LGB were more likely to attempt suicide than heterosexuals. Therefore, Europe was the only continent in which people's sexual orientations did not predict suicidal thoughts or behaviors. But, when gender was considered, a different pattern emerged. For women, sexual orientation predicted both suicidal ideations and suicide attempts in only one continent: North America. The lack of differences between heterosexual and LB women in other continents should be interpreted with caution because of their small sample sizes (2 to 8). In contrast, compared to heterosexual men, GB men in Asia and Australia were more likely to only attempt suicide while those in North and South America were more likely to both think about and attempt suicide. Thus, for men, sexual orientation did not predict suicide attempts or ideations in Europe or Australia nor suicide ideations in Asia. However, more recently, de Graaf, Sandfort, and ten Have (2006) reported that, in the Netherlands, the prevalence of gay men (49%) with suicidal thoughts is comparable to that of LGB people in other countries in Europe and North America. These findings highlight the need for researchers to consider the heterogeneity within continents.

More recent studies have consistently shown that LGB people are more likely to have suicidal thoughts and attempts than heterosexuals. These results have been found in a nationally represented sample of 14,322 people between 18 and 26 years of age in the U.S., even after controlling for participants' race, gender, and age (Silenzio, Pena, Duberstein, Cerel, & Knox, 2007). Similarly, a longitudinal study of a large representative sample of Norwegian LGB youths revealed that, even after controlling for 16 risk factors for suicide attempts (e.g., depressed mood, alcohol and drug use, conduct problems, eating problems, loneliness, and social support), those who had same-gender sexual contact were more likely to have attempted suicide; and lesbian girls were at higher risks for attempting suicide in the future (Wichstrøm & Hegna, 2003).

## Within group differences in mental health outcomes

In contrast to ascertaining *whether* sexual minorities' mental health outcomes differ from those of sexual majorities, some researchers have sought to explain *why* the differences exist. Thus, the second approach is to assess the specific factors that affect sexual minorities' mental health. Researchers proposed that being LGB does not place people at risk for more psychological distress. Rather, it is that their sexual minority membership causes them to have experiences with sexual stigma and sexual prejudice which contribute to more psychiatric disorders (King et al., 2008; Savin-Williams & Ream, 2003).

Several studies showed that LGB people's perceptions of sexual stigma negatively affect their mental health. For example, Persian and Iranian LGB immigrants who perceived their culture of origin as more negative toward LGBs reported more stress. Similarly, European American LGBs who felt more negative cultural stigma reported more stress, depressive symptoms, and lower global self-esteem (Mireshghi & Matsumoto, 2008). In addition, LB women who internalized sexual stigma had more psychological distress (Szymanski & Owens, 2008). Herek et al. (2009) also found that internalized sexual stigma precipitated lower self-esteem, which led to more negative affect and more psychological distress.

Similarly, personal experience with sexual stigma has been found to be associated with worse mental health outcomes. Surveys of a representative sample of LG adults in the Netherlands showed that gay men who experienced more anti-gay discrimination reported more suicidality, even after controlling for their psychiatric history (de Graaf et al., 2006). Likewise, in the U.S., LGB participants who experienced sexual discrimination were 1.6 times more likely to have at least one psychiatric disorder (major depression, generalized anxiety disorder, panic disorder, alcohol dependence, and drug dependence) compared to LGB participants who had no experience with sexual discrimination (Mays & Cochran, 2001). Additionally, Polders, Nel, Kruger, and Wells (2008) reported that self-identified gay men and lesbian women in South Africa who experienced verbal abuse and had lower self-esteem were at the most risk of having depressive symptoms. Finally, de Graaf et al. (2006) reported that because fewer Dutch lesbian women experienced discrimination (18.6% versus 24.4% of men), sexual orientation discrimination did not correlate with suicidality for this group.

Experiences with interpersonal stigma can heighten risks of suicide and depression particularly for sexual minority youths because they are more likely to be victims of anti-gay violence than their adult counterparts. In a review of eight studies, Cochran (2001) concluded that sexual minority adolescents are at greater risk of suicide attempts than sexual majority adolescents or sexual minority adults. In the U.K., 53% of LGBT participants who had been bullied when they were in school had thought about self-harm and suicide; 40% had attempted suicide at least once (Rivers, 2001). In addition, LGBT people who had been bullied were more likely to report depressive symptoms compared to LGBs who did not experience bullying and to heterosexuals (both those who did and those who did not experience bullying; Rivers, 2001). Overall, these findings suggest that sexual minorities' negative mental health outcomes are not due to their sexual orientation or identity, per se, but rather to the negative treatment they receive based on their sexual minority membership.

## Conclusion and Future Directions

Currently, regardless of the countries considered, those with a heterosexual orientation and those with typical gender identity are the dominant group and, as such, enjoy many advantages (Herek, 2003). Although levels of institutionalized and interpersonal sexual stigma vary between and within countries, sexual minorities in most parts of the world do not have the same rights as sexual majorities. In contrast to sexual minorities, heterosexuals enjoy privileges such as the freedom to openly express affection for their partners and the absence of concern that their freedom, physical and mental well-being, livelihood, or familial and others' acceptance depends on their sexual orientation.

The empirical evidence suggests that sexual minorities who have worse mental health outcomes than sexual majorities tend to have experienced sexual stigma such as anti-gay attitudes and discrimination. However, because these studies have included only adults from North America, Europe, or Oceania, it is not known whether these findings generalize to people from countries that have yet to be researched. Although it will be a challenge, future studies need to include representative samples from African and Asian countries and to identify factors (institutional, cultural, individual, and familial) that heighten and buffer the negative impact sexual stigma has on sexual minorities' mental health outcomes. In addition, because of their high rates of suicide and experiences with anti-gay violence, it is vitally important to include adolescent sexual minorities in countries outside the U.S. and Europe in future research.

Future studies should also address the dearth of information about sexual minorities with multiple identities. For example, in the U.S., LGBT people who are also racial/ethnic minorities may experience racial discrimination from the European American gay community in addition to sexual prejudice from heterosexuals (Diaz et al., 2004). Thus, some researchers have proposed that membership in multiple minority groups may result in cumulative, additive minority stressors, precipitating in higher psychological distress (Diaz et al., 2001). In contrast, others have argued that being a minority member in one stigmatized cultural group (e.g., race/ethnicity, disabilities) may help an individual learn skills to cope with victimization associated with membership in another stigmatized cultural minority group (e.g., sexual minority, age; David & Knight, 2008). Therefore, future research should explore whether sexual minorities who have other minority identities (e.g., race/ethnicity, age, socioeconomic status, religion) have different experiences, coping styles, and mental health outcomes than sexual minorities who are members of other dominant groups. Researchers have only begun to explore these issues: Jewish gay men in the U.K. (Coyle & Rafalin, 2000); LGBT college students with disabilities in the U.S. (Harley, Nowak, Gassaway, & Savage, 2002); Greek and Turkish Cypriot gay men in London (Phellas, 2005); acculturated Chinese, Korean, and Filipino American men in the U.S. (Matteson, 1997); and LGB Korean, Japanese, and Chinese in their respective countries in Asia and in the U.S. (Kimmel & Yi, 2004). However, more researchers need to expand on the knowledge derived from these qualitative analyses and theoretical discussions. In summary, in addition to the cultural diversity between countries, researchers should examine the heterogeneity among members of sexual minority groups within the same countries when trying to understand sexual stigma and its consequences on people in diverse cultures.

# References

Adamczyk, A., & Pitt, C. (2009). Shaping attitudes about homosexuality: The role of religion and cultural context. *Social Science Research, 39*, 338–351.

American Psychological Association (1998). *Answers to your questions about sexual orientation and homosexuality* [Brochure]. Washington, DC: Author.

Andersen, R., & Fetner, T. (2008). Cohort differences in tolerance of homosexuality: Attitudinal change in Canada and the United States, 1981–2000. *Public Opinion Quarterly, 72*, 311–330.

Balsam, K. F., Beauchaine, T. P., Mickey, R. M., & Rothblum, E. D. (2005). Mental health of lesbian, gay, and heterosexual siblings: Effects of gender, sexual orientation, and family. *Journal of Abnormal Psychology, 114*, 471–476.

Bauermeister, J. A., Morales, M., Seda, G., & González-Rivera, M. (2007). Sexual prejudice among Puerto Rican young adults. *Journal of Homosexuality, 53*, 135–161.

Bereket, T., & Adam, B. D. (2008). Navigating Islam and same-sex liaisons among men in Turkey. *Journal of Homosexuality, 55*, 204–222.

Bhugra, D. (1997). Coming out by South Asian gay men in the United Kingdom. *Archives of Sexual Behavior, 26*, 547–557.

Bochow, M., Chiarotti, F., Davies, P., & Dubois-Arber, F. (1994). Sexual behavior of gay and bisexual men in eight European countries. *AIDS Care, 6*, 533–549.

Bristow, J. (1997). *Sexuality*. New York: Routledge.

Caceras, C. F., & Rosasco, A. M. (1999). The margin has many sides: Diversity among gay and homosexually active men in Lima. *Culture, Health and Sexuality, 3*, 261–275.

Cochran, S. D. (2001). Emerging issues in research on lesbians' and gay men's mental health: Does sexual orientation really matter? *American Psychologist, 56*, 931–947.

Coyle, A., & Rafalin, D. (2000). Jewish gay men's accounts of negotiating cultural, religious, and sexual identity: A qualitative study. *Journal of Psychology and Human Sexuality, 12*, 21–48.

Crocker, J., Major, B., & Steele, C. (1998). Social stigma. In D. T. Gilbert, S. T. Fiske & G. Lindzey (Eds.), *Handbook of social psychology, Vol. 2* (4th ed., pp. 504–553). Boston: McGraw-Hill.

David, S., & Knight, B. G. (2008). Stress and coping among gay men: Age and ethnic differences. *Psychology and Aging, 23*, 62–69.

Day, N. E., & Schoenrade, P. (2000). The relationship among reported disclosure of sexual orientation, anti-discrimination policies, top management support and work attitudes of lesbian and gay employees. *Personnel Review, 29*, 346–363.

de Cuypere, G., van Hemelrijck, M., Michel, A., Carael, B., Heylens, G., Rubens. R. … Monstrey, S. (2007). Prevalence and demography of transsexualism in Belgium. *European Psychiatry, 22*, 137–141.

De Graaf, R., Sandfort, T. G. M., & ten Have, M. (2006). Suicidality and sexual orientation: Differences between men and women in a general population-based sample from the Netherlands. *Archives of Sexual Behavior, 35*, 253–262.

Diamond, L. M., & Savin-Williams, R. C. (2000). Explaining diversity in the development of same-sex sexuality among young women. *Journal of Social Issues, 52*(2), 297–313.

Diaz, R. M., Ayala, G., & Bein, E. (2004). Sexual risk as an outcome of social oppression: Data from a probability sample of Latino gay men in three U.S. cities. *Cultural Diversity and Ethnic Minority Psychology, 10*, 255–267.

Diaz, R. M., Ayala, G., Bein, E., Henne, J., & Marin, B. V. (2001). The impact of homophobia, poverty, and racism on the mental health of gay and bisexual Latino men: Findings from three US cities. *American Journal of Public Health, 91*, 927–932.

Espelage, D. L., & Swearer, S. M. (2008). Addressing research gaps in the intersection between homophobia and bullying. *School Psychology Review, 37*, 155–159.

Fox, R. C. (1995). Bisexual identities. In A. R. D'Augelli & C. J. Patterson (Eds.), *Lesbian, gay, and bisexual identities over the lifespan* (pp. 48–68). New York: Oxford University Press.

Frable, D. E. S., Platt, L., & Hoey, S. (1998). Concealable stigmas and positive self-perceptions: Feeling better around similar others. *Journal of Personality and Social Psychology, 74*, 909–922.

Garnets, L. D. (2002). Sexual orientations in perspective. *Cultural Diversity and Ethnic Minority Psychology, 8*, 115–129.

Greene, B. (1994). Ethnic-minority lesbians and gay men: Mental health and treatment issues. *Journal of Consulting and Clinical Psychology, 62,* 243–251.

Harley, D. A., Nowak, T. M., Gassaway, L. J., & Savage, T. A. (2002). Lesbian, gay, bisexual, and transgender college students with disabilities: A look at multiple cultural minorities. *Psychology in the Schools, 39,* 525–538.

Herek, G. M. (2002). Heterosexuals' attitudes toward bisexual men and women in the United States. *Journal of Sex Research, 39,* 264–274.

Herek, G. M. (2003). Why tell if you're not asked? In L. D. Garnets & D. C. Kimmel (Eds.), *Psychological perspectives on lesbian, gay, and bisexual experiences* (2nd ed., pp. 270–298). New York: Columbia University Press.

Herek, G. M., & Capitanio, J. P. (1996). "Some of my best friends": Intergroup contact, concealable stigma, and heterosexuals' attitudes toward gay men. *Personality and Social Psychology Bulletin, 22,* 412–424.

Herek, G. M., Chopp, R., & Strohl, D. (2007). Sexual stigma: Putting sexual minority health issues in context. In E. H. Meyer & M. E. Northridge (Eds.), *The health of sexual minorities: Public health perspectives on lesbian, gay, bisexual and transgender populations* (pp. 171–208). New York: Springer.

Herek, G. M., & Garnets, L. D. (2007). Sexual orientation and mental health. *Annual Review of Clinical Psychology, 3,* 353–375.

Herek, G. M., Gillis, J. R., & Cogan, J. C. (2009). Internalized stigma among sexual minority adults: Insights from a social psychological perspective. *Journal of Counseling Psychology, 56,* 32–43.

Herek, G. M., & González-Rivera, M. (2006). Attitudes toward homosexuality among U.S. residents of Mexican descent. *Journal of Sex Research, 43,* 122–135.

Hill, C. A. (2008). *Human sexuality: Personality and social psychological perspectives.* Los Angeles, CA: Sage.

Hunsberger, B., Owusu, V., & Duck, R. (1999). Religion and prejudice in Ghana and Canada: Religious fundamentalism, right-wing authoritarianism, and attitudes toward homosexuals and women. *International Journal for the Psychology of Religion, 9,* 181–194.

Hurley, B. (2005, August). *Analyzing attitudes toward homosexuality over time.* Paper presented at the meeting of the American Sociological Association, Philadelphia.

Kelly, J. (2001). Attitudes toward homosexuality in 29 nations. *Australian Social Monitor, 4,* 15–21.

Kim, Y., & Hahn, S. (2006). Homosexuality in ancient and modern Korea. *Culture, Health and Sexuality, 8,* 59–65.

Kimmel, D. C., & Yi, H. (2004). Characteristics of gay, lesbian, and bisexual Asians, Asian Americans, and immigrants from Asia to the USA. *Journal of Homosexuality, 47,* 143–170.

King, M., Semlyen, J., Tai, S. S., Killaspy, H., Osborn, D., Popelyuk, D., & Nazareth, I. (2008). A systematic review of mental disorder, suicide, and deliberate self harm in lesbian, gay and bisexual people. *BMC Psychiatry, 8,* 1–17. Retrieved June 29, 2009 from http://www.biomedcentral.com/1471–244X/8/70

Kite, M. E., & Whitley, B. E., Jr. (1996). Sex differences in attitudes toward homosexual persons, behaviors, and civil rights: A meta-analysis. *Personality and Social Psychology Bulletin, 22,* 336–353.

Laumann, E. O., Gagnon, J. H., Michael, R. T., & Michaels, S. (1994). *The social organization of sexuality: Sexual practices in the United States.* Chicago: University of Chicago Press.

Lawrence *v.* Texas, 539 U.S. 538 (2003).

Lev, A. I. (2007). Transgender communities: Developing identity through connection. In K. J. Bieschke, R. M. Perez, & K. A. DeBord (Eds.). *Handbook of counseling and psychotherapy with lesbian, gay, bisexual, and transgender clients* (pp. 147–175). Washington, DC: American Psychological Association.

Lingiardi, V., Falanga, S., & D'Augelli, R. (2005). The evaluation of homophobia in an Italian sample. *Archives of Sexual Behavior, 34*, 81–93.

Mathy, R. M. (2002). Suicidality and sexual orientation in five continents: Asia, Australia, Europe, North America, and South America. *International Journal of Sexuality and Gender Studies, 7*, 215–225.

Matsumoto, D. J., & Juang, L. (2008). *Culture and psychology* (4th ed.). Belmont, CA: Thomson Wadsworth.

Matteson, D. R. (1997). Bisexual and homosexual behavior and HIV risk among Chinese-, Filipino, and Korean-American men. *Journal of Sex Research, 34*, 93–104.

Mays, V. M., & Cochran, S. D. (2001). Mental health correlates of perceived discrimination among lesbian, gay and bisexual adults in the United States. *American Journal of Public Health, 91*, 1869–1876.

McLaren, S., Jude, B., & McLachlan, A. J. (2008). Sense of belonging to the general and gay communities as predictors of depression among Australian gay men. *International Journal of Men's Health, 7*, 90–99.

Meyer, I. H. (2003a). Minority stress and mental health in gay men. In L. D. Garnets & D. C. Kimmel (Eds.), *Psychological perspectives on lesbian, gay, and bisexual experiences* (2nd ed., pp. 699–731). New York: Columbia University Press.

Meyer, I. H. (2003b). Prejudice, social stress, and mental health in lesbian, gay, and bisexual populations: Conceptual issues and research evidence. *Psychological Bulletin, 129*, 674–697.

Meyer, I. H. (2007). Prejudice and discrimination as social stressors. In E. H. Meyer & M. E. Northridge (Eds.), *The health of sexual minorities: Public health perspectives on lesbian, gay, bisexual and transgender populations* (pp. 242–267). New York: Springer.

Mireshghi, S. I., & Matsumoto, D. (2008). Perceived cultural attitudes toward homosexuality and their effects on Iranian and American sexual minorities. *Cultural Diversity and Ethnic Minority Psychology, 14*, 372–376.

Niang, C. I., Tapsoba, P., Weiss, E., Diagne, M., Niang, Y., Moreau, A. M. ... Castle, C. (2003). "It's raining stones": Stigma, violence and HIV vulnerability among men who have sex with men in Dakar, Senegal. *Culture, Health, and Sexuality, 5*, 499–512.

Ottosson, D. (2009). *State-sponsored homophobia: A world survey of laws prohibiting same sex activity between consenting adults. International Lesbian, Gay, Bisexual, Trans and Intersex Association (ILGA)*. Retrieved June 2, 2009 from http://www.ilga.org/statehomophobia/ILGA_State_Sponsored_Homophobia_2009.pdf

Pachankis, J. E. (2007). The psychological implications of concealing a stigma: A cognitive-affective-behavioral model. *Psychological Bulletin, 133*, 328–345.

Padilla, M. B., Vasquez del Aguila, E., & Parker, R. G. (2007). Globalization, structural violence, and LGBT health: A cross-cultural perspective. In E. H. Meyer & M. E. Northridge (Eds.), *The health of sexual minorities: Public health perspectives on lesbian, gay, bisexual and transgender populations* (pp. 209–241). New York: Springer.

Pew Global Attitudes Project (2007). *World publics welcome global trade—but not immigration.* Retrieved June 11, 2009, from http://pewglobal.org/reports/pdf/258topline.pdf

Phellas, C. N. (2005). Cypriot gay men's accounts of negotiating cultural and sexual identity: A qualitative study. *Qualitative Sociology Review, 1,* 65–82.

Polders, L. A., Nel, J. A., Kruger, P., & Wells, H. L. (2008). Factors affecting vulnerability to depression among gay men and lesbian women in Gauteng, South Africa. *South African Journal of Psychology, 38,* 673–687.

Rivers, I. (2001). The bullying of sexual minorities at school: Its nature and long-term correlates. *Educational and Child Psychology, 18,* 32–46.

Rothblum, E. D. (1994). "I only read about myself on bathroom walls": The need for research on the mental health of lesbians and gay men. *Journal of Consulting and Clinical Psychology, 62,* 213–220.

Sandfort, T. G. M., Bakker, F., Schellevis, F. G., & Vanwesenbeeck, I. (2006). Sexual orientation and mental and physical health status: Findings from a Dutch population survey. *American Journal of Public Health, 96,* 1119–1125.

Savin-Williams, R. C., & Ream, G. L. (2003). Suicide attempts among sexual-minority male youth. *Journal of Clinical Child and Adolescent Psychology, 32,* 509–522.

Silenzio, V. M. B., Pena, J. B., Duberstein, P. R., Cerel, J., & Knox, K. L. (2007). Sexual orientation and risk factors for suicidal ideation and suicide attempts among adolescents and young adults. *American Journal of Public Health, 97,* 2017–2018.

Stahnke, T., LeGendre, P., Grekov, I., McClintock, M., Aronowitz, A. & Petti, V. (2008). *Human rights first: 2008 hate crime survey.* Retrieved April 2, 2009 from http://www.humanrightsfirst.org

Steffens, M. C., & Wagner, C. (2004). Attitudes toward lesbians, gay men, bisexual women, and bisexual men in Germany. *Journal of Sex Research, 41,* 137–149.

Štulhofer, A., & Rimac, I. (2009). Determinants of homonegativity in Europe. *Journal of Sex Research, 46,* 24–32.

Szymanski, D. M., & Owens, G. P. (2008). Do coping styles moderate or mediate the relationship between internalized heterosexism and sexual minority women's psychological distress? *Psychology of Women Quarterly, 32,* 95–104.

Whitley, B. E., Jr. (2009). Religiosity and attitudes toward lesbians and gay men: A meta-analysis. *International Journal for the Psychology of Religion, 19,* 21–38.

Wichstrøm, L., & Hegna, K. (2003). Sexual orientation and suicide attempt: A longitudinal study of the general Norwegian adolescent population. *Journal of Abnormal Psychology, 112,* 144–151.

Widmer, E. D., Treas, J., & Newcombe, R. (1998). Attitudes toward nonmarital sex in 24 countries. *Journal of Sex Research, 35,* 349–358.

Zhou, Y. R. (2006). Homosexuality, seropositivity, and family obligations: Perspectives of HIV-infected men who have sex with men in China. *Culture, Health and Sexuality, 8,* 487–500.

# Part VI

# Health, Disorders, and Treatment

There is surprising variation across cultures concerning the definition and conceptualization of health. Is health simply the absence of disease? Does health imply a broad, holistic notion of balance in a person's life? Researchers working in a number of scholarly fields have produced an interdisciplinary understanding of health, especially in non-Western cultures and their perceptions of well-being. Clearly, the Western biomedical understanding is not the only view of health and illness in the world.

Different kinds of healers play a role in evaluation, diagnosis, and treatment across cultures. Thus, differing philosophies, religious influences, uses of such natural substances as medicinal plants, and Western medicines all play a role in defining and maintaining health. Culture is also significant in the conceptualization of mental health—in both its diagnosis and treatment. In particular, researchers recognize the importance of integration of cultural sensitivity with the need for empirically verifiable treatments in the realm of mental health. We will see an example in this section of some ways that treatments might be modified to achieve the aim of cultural sensitivity and effectiveness.

Finally, cross-cultural psychology has not given the attention it perhaps should have to intellectual disabilities. However, as individuals with intellectual disabilities occupy an increasingly important role in the work of cross-cultural psychologists, it becomes important to understand the extent to which disabilities in general, and intellectual disabilities in particular, represent ecologically and socially constructed phenomena, as opposed to fixed characteristics of individual people. Although different cultures have used different labels and diagnostic categories to describe individuals with disabilities, an important development in the field is the move toward an international consensus in a culturally relative world.

# 13

# Cultural Influences on Health

## Regan A. R. Gurung

For those raised in the Western world, there is an easy way to determine health. If we do not experience pain, are disease free, are at the right weight, and are not partaking in any obviously unhealthy behaviors (e.g., smoking, binge drinking) we feel confident in claiming we are healthy. The World Health Organization (WHO) describes health as "a state of complete physical, mental and social well-being and not merely the absence of disease or infirmity" (WHO, 1946, p. 100). What is not clear from this definition, and completely missing from the idea of health as just "the absence of disease" is the fact that health can vary according to where you live, how old you are, what your parents and friends think constitutes health, what your religious or ethnic background is, and what a variety of other factors indicate about you. The one word that nicely captures all these different elements that influence health is *culture*.

It is important to understand the role of culture in physical and mental health in today's global climate. Mental and physical health varies dramatically across cultural groups (Eshun & Gurung, 2009; Gurung, 2010). Not only is the world diverse, but every state, city, and county is getting increasingly more diverse. Both the objective indicators of physical health and the subjective nature of defining abnormality vary with culture, making an understanding of how culture impacts perceptions, conceptualizations, and treatment of health crucial. There are critical cultural variations in the conceptualization, perception, health-seeking behaviors, assessment, diagnosis, and treatment of abnormal behaviors and physical sickness. This chapter focuses on how different cultural approaches to health shape healthy behaviors, prevent illness, and enhance our health and well-being.

## What Is Culture?

Culture is varied, multilayered, and complex. A given individual may be a part of many different cultural groups, and some of those groups may have a larger influence on her health than others. Many people use the words *culture, diversity, ethnicity,* and *race*, as if they mean the same thing. Beyond these specific examples, people also think culture represents a set of ideals or beliefs or sometimes a set of behaviors, both of which are accurate components of what culture is. Although we rarely acknowledge it, culture has many dimensions. Keith (Chapter 1 in this volume) has already nicely reviewed definitions of culture. It is important to remember that culture can also include similar physical characteristics (e.g., skin color), psychological characteristics (e.g., levels of hostility), and common superficial features (e.g., hair style and clothing). The most commonly described objective cultural groups consist of grouping by ethnicity, race, sex, and age.

Two of the most important health-related aspects that define cultural groups are *socioeconomic status* (SES) and *sex*. Although sex (and, relatedly, gender) has found a place in curricula for some time now (e.g., gender studies, human sexuality classes, women's studies), socioeconomic status has only recently begun to be better incorporated into curricula. The poor make up a large percentage of Americans without health insurance, and SES is related to a higher occurrence of most chronic and infectious disorders and to higher rates of nearly all major causes of mortality and morbidity (Macintyre, 1997). Research has shown that SES is associated with a wide array of health, cognitive, and socioemotional outcomes, with effects beginning before birth and continuing into adulthood (Gottfried, Gottfried, Bathurst, Guerin, & Parramore, 2003) and is correspondingly a critical aspect of culture to be aware of.

Given the wide array of definitions of culture, it should come as no surprise that culture and its influences on life and health are studied by a number of different disciplines. For example, medical anthropologists are individuals who are committed to improving public health in societies in economically poor nations. Based on the biological and sociocultural roots of anthropology, medical anthropologists have long considered health and medical care within the context of cultural systems, although not necessarily using the tools or theoretical approaches of psychologists. That said, medical anthropology has paid more explicit attention to non-Western approaches to health and healing than mainstream psychology (Winkelman, 2009). In a related fashion, medical sociologists work within the framework of the medical model, focusing on the role of culture and a person's environment in health and illness. No one discipline is enough. In fact the complex interaction of cultural influences and health necessitates an interdisciplinary approach to studying the relationship and working toward elimination of health disparities (Anderson, 2009).

## Cultural Variations in Health: Health Disparities

Health disparities are "differences in health that are not only unnecessary and avoidable, but in addition, are considered unfair and unjust" (Whitehead, 1992, p. 433). There are many examples of disparities: e.g., the infant death rate among African Americans is still more than double that of European Americans, and heart disease death rates are more than 40% higher for African Americans than for European Americans (U.S. Department of Health and Human Services, 2009). Truly staggering is the disparity in life expectancy—there is a 35-year gap between groups with the shortest and longest life expectancies at birth (Murray et al. 2006). In general, health care, mental health, and disease incidence (e.g., tuberculosis) rates also vary significantly across ethnic groups. Thus, the suicide rate among American Indians is 2.2 times higher than the national average (Center for Disease Control, 2008), and those living below the poverty level are significantly more depressed that those higher in SES (Pratt & Brody, 2008).

The fact that there are differences in health behaviors and health in general has not escaped the notice of the American government, funding agencies, or health psychology researchers (the latter can do research to better the support of the first two). In fact the Healthy People 2010 project (U.S. Department of Health and Human Services, 2009), identified elimination of health disparities as one of its two overarching goals (the other is increasing the number and quality of years of life). In parallel, the American Psychological Association (APA) has also worked hard toward

the elimination of racial and ethnic disparities in health access and outcomes through an increased commitment to behavioral and biomedical research, improved data systems, culturally competent health care delivery, and efforts to increase public awareness of the existence of health disparities and the resources that are available to improve minority health outcomes. (American Psychological Association, 2009, para. 1).

APA's Office of Ethnic Minority Affairs released a special issue of its journal *Communique* in March 2009, focusing on psychological and behavioral perspectives on health disparities. APA's Division 38 (Health Psychology) has developed a Health Disparities webpage which introduces the key issues in health disparities research and provides resources to further aid research into this topic. As described on the webpage, the "overarching goals are to advance the understanding of (1) the nature and scope of health disparities and (2) the scientific study of health disparities, from description to intervention" (http://www.health-psych.org/ResourcesHealthDisparities.cfm, para. 2). Research specifically aimed to reduce health disparities, including interventions to reach out to negatively influenced parties, is under way and holds promise for major improvements. The federal government has also created cultural competency standards (National Standards for Culturally and Linguistically Appropriate Services, CLAS, https://www.thinkculturalhealth.org/), with corresponding training resources designed to help healthcare practitioners better serve patients from diverse populations. Where do these disparities spring from? There are many answers and a good start is to look to varying approaches to health.

# Cultural Variations in Approaches to Health

In most of the countries around the globe, health is understood using either the Western evidence-based medical approach or traditional indigenous approaches (Prasadarao, 2009). In traditional systems, a wide range of practitioners provides help. For example, in sub-Saharan Africa, four types of traditional healers provide health care, namely: (a) traditional birth attendants, (b) faith healers, (c) diviners and spiritualists, and (d) herbalists.

On a global level, health beliefs and practices are closely tied to religion and the country the religion is predominant in—components of culture (i.e., religion and nationality) not given enough attention in Western medicine. In predominantly Hindu countries such as India for example, modern medical practitioners are complemented by three types of traditional healers—*vaids* (healers practicing indigenous systems of medicine), *mantarwadis* (healers using astrology and charms for cure), and *patris* (healers who act as mediums for spirits and demons)—who offer treatment to physical and mental illness in rural villages of India (Kapur, 1979). The *vaids* believe that illness is due to "an imbalance between the natural elements" brought forth by environmental factors, certain diets, uninhibited sexual indulgence, and the influence of demons (Prasadarao, 2009, p. 153). These factors cause "excess heat, cold, bile, wind or fluid secretions" leading to the development of physical and mental illness. In Muslim countries such as Pakistan, traditional healers include *khalifs*, *gadinashins*, *imams*, *hakims*, and others who practice magic and sorcery (Karim, Saeed, Rana, Mubbashar, & Jenkins, 2004).

Long before there were medical degrees, hospitals, clinics, and pharmaceuticals, people were getting sick and receiving treatment. Yes, many of those treated by early healers and healing practices did not survive the treatment, let alone recover from the illness itself. This notwithstanding, people around the world have worked from the beginning of recorded history (and before) to prolong life and alleviate suffering from illness. There are three or four major philosophical approaches to health and healing that illustrate cultural differences in health. The one we may be most familiar with (and consequently, one I touch on only briefly) is referred to as conventional medicine, or *allopathy*. Western biomedicine is probably the most dominant form of healthcare in the world today. Hallmarks of this approach are an increasing reliance on technology and the use of complex scientific procedures for the diagnosis and treatment of illness. Treatments using this approach are designed to produce an opposite effect to that created by the disease. If you have a fever, you are prescribed medication to reduce the temperature. Western biomedicine views the body as a biochemical machine with distinct parts. Often called reductionist, Western biomedicine searches for the single smallest unit responsible for the illness.

## Traditional Chinese medicine

Traditional Chinese medicine (TCM) is probably used to treat more people than any other form of medicine. Even in North America, there are a large number of TCM schools and practitioners. In fact, acupuncture, one form of TCM, is covered by most health insurance policies. Two main systems categorize the forces identified in TCM that influence health and well-being: yin and yang and the five phases. According to one Chinese philosophy, all life and the entire universe originated from a single unified source called Tao. The main ideas about the Tao are encompassed in a 5,000-word poem called the *Tao Te Ching* written about 2,500 years ago. In TCM, health is the balance of the yin and yang, the two complementary forces in the universe. Yin and yang are mutually interdependent, constantly interactive, and potentially interchangeable forces. In TCM, 10 vital organs are divided into five pairs, each consisting of one "solid" yin organ and one "hollow" yang organ. TCM practitioners believe that the yin organs—the heart, liver, pancreas, spleen, kidneys, and lungs—are more vital than the yang organs, and dysfunctions of yin organs cause the greatest health problems. The yang organs are the gallbladder, stomach, small intestine, large intestine, and bladder (though an organ translated as 'triple burner' is also said to exist). A healthy individual has a balanced amount of yin and yang. If a person is sick, his or her forces are out of balance (Kaptchuk, 2000).

The yin and yang are often translated into hot and cold (two clear opposites), referring to qualities and not temperatures. To be healthy, what you eat and drink and the way you live your life should have equal amounts of hot qualities and cold ones. Balancing hot and cold is a critical element of many different cultures (e.g., Chinese, Indian, and even Mexican), although the foods that constitute each may vary across cultures. Some 'hot' foods include beef, garlic, ginger, and alcohol. Some 'cold' foods include honey, most greens, potatoes, and some fruits (e.g., melons, pears).

The five phases or elemental activities refer to specific active forces and illustrate the intricate associations that the ancient Chinese saw between human beings and nature. Energy or *qi*, another critical aspect of TCM, moves within the body in the same pattern as it does in nature with each season and with different foods helping to optimize energy flow within the body. The five elements of wood, fire, earth, metal, and water each link to a season of the year, a specific organ, and a specific food. Each element has specific characteristics, is generated by one of the other forces, and is suppressed by another. For example, wood generates fire that turns things to earth that forms metals. The heart is ruled by fire, the liver by wood, and the kidneys by water. Fire provides *qi* to the heart and then passes *qi* onto the earth element and correspondingly the stomach, the spleen, and pancreas. What you eat correspondingly can influence your different organs and your well-being in general (Kaptchuk, 2000).

## Ayurveda: Indian health beliefs

Ayurveda, a traditional Indian holistic system of medicine was developed by Charaka about 2,600 years ago (Lyssenko, 2004; Singh, 2007). Charaka described four causative factors in mental illness: (a) diet (incompatible, vitiated, and unclean food); (b) disrespect to gods, elders, and teachers; (c) mental shock due to emotions such as excessive fear and joy; and (d) faulty bodily activity. Thus, Ayurveda considers a biopsychosocial approach in formulating causative factors in mental disorders. Charaka, while emphasizing the need for harmony between body, mind, and soul, focused on preventive, curative, and promotive aspects of mental health. Ancient Indian court physicians further developed Ayurvedic practices and were given vast resources because the health of the king was considered equivalent to the health of the state (Svoboda, 2004). The use of Ayurveda flourished until 900 CE when Muslim invaders came into India and created a new form of medicine called *Unani*, a combination of Greek and Ayurvedic medicine with Arabic medicine (Udwadia, 2000). The use of plants and herbal remedies plays a major part in Ayurvedic medicine. About 600 different medicinal plants are mentioned in the core Ayurvedic texts. Western drug companies have used a number of plants originally used in India to cure diseases. For example, psyllium seed is used for bowel problems, and other plants are used to reduce blood pressure, control diarrhea, and lessen the risk of liver or heart problems. A substance called forskolin, isolated from the *Coleus forskohlii* plant, has been used in Ayurveda for treating heart disease, and its use has now been empirically validated by Western biomedicine (Ding & Staudinger, 2005).

TCM and Ayurveda share many basic similarities. Ayurvedic science also uses the notion of basic elements: Five great elements form the basis of the universe. Earth represents the solid state, water the liquid state, air the gaseous state, fire the power to change the state of any substance, and ether, simultaneously the source of all matter and the space in which it exists. Each of these elements can nourish the body, balance the body (serving to heal), or imbalance the body (serving as a poison). Achieving the right balance of these elements in the body is critical to maintaining a healthy state. These elements also combine to form three major forces (*doshas*) that influence physiological functions critical to healthy living (Svoboda, 2004). Ether and air combine to form the *vata dosha*, fire and water combine to form the *pitta dosha*, and water and earth elements combine to form the *kapha dosha*. *Vata* directs nerve impulses, circulation, respiration, and elimination. *Pitta* is responsible for metabolism in the organ and tissue systems as well as cellular metabolism. *Kapha* is responsible for growth and protection. We are all made up of unique proportions of *vata*, *pitta*, and *kapha* that cause disease when they go out of balance. These three *doshas* are also referred to as humors or bodily fluids and correspond to the Greek humors of phlegm (*kapha*) and choler (*pitta*). There is no equivalent to the Greek humor blood, nor is *vata* or wind represented in the Greek system. Similar to the meridians in TCM, the existence of these forces is demonstrated more by inference and results of their hypothesized effects than by physical observation. *Vata, pitta,* and *kapha* are also associated with specific body-type characteristics (Svoboda, 2004).

## Mexican American/Latino health beliefs

*Curanderismo* is the Mexican American folk-healing system that often coexists side by side with Western biomedicine. Coming from the Spanish verb *curar* meaning "to heal," *curanderos* are full-time healers. The *curandero's* office is in the community, often in the healer's own home. There are no appointments, forms, or fees, and you pay whatever you believe the healer deserves. This form of healing relies heavily on the patient's faith and belief systems and uses everyday herbs, fruits, eggs, and oils. In studies beginning as early as 1959, researchers first focused on "Mexican American cultural illnesses," such as *mal de ojo* (sickness from admiring a baby too much). More recent work (e.g., Trotter & Chavira, 1997) focuses on the healers themselves, their beliefs, training processes, and processes for treatment. Surveys of Mexican Americans show that even among highly assimilated Mexican Americans, traditional and indigenous practices still persist.

The Mexican American cultural framework acknowledges the existence of two sources of illness, one natural and one supernatural. When the natural and supernatural worlds exist in harmony, optimal health is achieved. Disharmony between these realms breeds illness. Beyond this supernatural balance component, the *curandero's* concept of the cause of illness parallels that of Western biomedicine. Like biomedical practitioners, *curanderos* believe that germs and other natural factors can cause illness. However, *curanderos* believe that there are supernatural causes to illness in addition to natural factors. If an evil spirit, a witch, or a sorcerer causes an illness, then only a supernatural solution will be sufficient for a cure. Illness can also be caused if a person's energy field is weakened or disrupted. Whether diabetes, alcoholism, or cancer, if a spirit caused it, supernatural intervention is the only thing that can cure it.

Unlike Western biomedicine and TCM, the practices of *curanderismo* are based on Judeo-Christian beliefs and customs. The Bible has influenced *curanderismo* through references made to the specific healing properties of natural substances such as plants (see Luke 10:34). *Curanderos'* healing and cures are influenced by the Bible's proclamation that belief in God can and does heal directly and that people with a gift from God can heal in his name. The concept of the soul, central to Christianity, also provides support for the existence of saints (good souls) and devils (bad souls). The bad souls can cause illness and the good souls, harnessed by the shamanism and sorcery of the *curanderismo*, can cure.

*Curanderos* use three levels of treatment depending on the source of the illness: material, spiritual, and mental (Trotter & Chavira, 1997). Working on the material level, *curanderos* use things found in any house (eggs, lemons, garlic, and ribbons) and religious symbols (a crucifix, water, oils, and incense). These material things often are designed to either emit or absorb vibrating energy that repairs the energy field around a person. Ceremonies include prayers, ritual sweepings, or cleansings (Torres & Sawyer, 2005). The spiritual level of treatment often includes the *curandero* entering a trance, leaving his or her body, and playing the role of a medium. This spiritual treatment allows a spirit to commandeer the *curandero*'s body, facilitating a cure in the patient. On some occasions, the spirit will prescribe simple herbal remedies (via the *curandero*). On other occasions, the spirit will perform further rituals. The mental level of treatment relies on the power held by the individual *curandero*, rather than on spirits or materials. Some illnesses (e.g., physical) often are treated by herbs alone (DeStefano, 2001), and psychological problems may be treated by a combination of all these types of treatments.

In a manner akin to that of health psychologists, *curanderos* explicitly focus on social, psychological, and biological problems (Trotter & Chavira, 1997). The difference is that they add a focus on spiritual problems as well. From a social perspective, the community where the *curanderos* work recognizes and accepts what the *curandero* is trying to achieve. The social world is important to the *curanderos*, who evaluate the patient's direct and extended support system. The patient's moods and feelings are weighed together with any physical symptoms. Finally, there is always a ritual petition to God and other spiritual beings to help with the healing process.

*Curanderos* each have their own set of specializations. For example, midwives (*parteras*) help with births, *sobaderos* treat muscle sprains, and herbalists (*yerberos*) prescribe different plants (Avila & Parker, 2000). For most Mexican Americans, the choice between *curanderismo* and Western biomedicine is an either/or proposition. Some individuals use both systems, and some stay completely away from Western hospitals as much as they can or because they do not have enough money to use them. Acculturated and higher social class Mexican Americans tend to rely exclusively on Western biomedicine. The existence of this strong cultural and historical folk medicine and the large numbers of its adherents make this approach to illness an important alternative style for us to consider in our study of the psychology of health.

### American Indian health beliefs

Many elements of the American Indian belief system and the approach to health are somewhat consistent with elements of *curanderismo* and TCM and provide a strong contrast to Western biomedicine. Although different tribes have different variations on the basic beliefs, four practices are common to most (Cohen, 2003): the use of herbal remedies, the employment of ritual purification or purging, the use of symbolic rituals and ceremonies, and the involvement of healers, also referred to as medicine men, medicine women, or shamans (though the latter is primarily used for the healers of northern Europe; Eliade, 1964). Native Americans have utilized and benefited from these practices for at least 10,000 years and possibly much longer.

Similar to the ancient Chinese, American Indians believed that human beings and the natural world are closely intertwined. The fate of humankind and the fate of the trees, the mountains, the sky, and the oceans are all linked. The Navajos call this "walking in beauty," a worldview in which everything in life is connected and influences everything else. In this system, sickness is a result of things falling out of balance and of losing one's way in the path of beauty (Alvord & Van Pelt, 2000). Animals are sacred, the winds are sacred, and trees and plants, bugs, and rocks are sacred. Every human and every object corresponds to a presence in the spirit world, and these spirits promote health or cause illness. Spiritual rejuvenation and the achievement of a general sense of physical, emotional, and communal harmony are at the heart of Native American medicine. Shamans coordinate American Indian medicine and inherit the ability to communicate with spirits in much the same way that Mexican American *curanderos* do. Shamans spend much of their day listening to their patients, asking about their family and their behaviors and beliefs and making connections between the patient's life and their illness. Shamans do not treat spirits as metaphors or prayers as a way to trick a body into healing. Shamans treat spirits as real entities, respecting them as they would any other intelligent being or living person.

Ritual and ceremony play a major role in American Indian medicine. One of the most potent and frequent ceremonies is the sweat lodge (Mehl-Medrona, 1998). Medicine men hold lodges or "sweats" for different reasons. Sometimes a sweat purifies the people present; at other times a sweat is dedicated to someone with cancer or another terminal illness. The ceremony takes place in a sweat lodge, which looks like a half dome of rocks and sticks covered with blankets and furs to keep the air locked in and the light out. The lodge symbolizes the world and the womb of Mother Earth. Heated rocks are placed in a pit in the middle of the half dome. Participants in the sweat sing sacred songs in separate rounds during the ceremony. After each round, a firekeeper brings in another set of hot rocks, and more songs are sung or prayers said. The sequence of prayers, chants, and singing following the addition of hot rocks continues until all the rocks are brought in. The hot stones raise the temperature inside the lodge, leading to profuse perspiration, which is thought to detoxify the body. Because of the darkness and the heat, participants often experience hallucinations that connect to spirit guides or provide insight into personal conditions.

Other ceremonies are also used. For example, the Lakota and Navajo use the medicine wheel, the sacred hoop, and the *sing*, which is a community healing ceremony lasting from two to nine days and guided by a highly skilled specialist called a *singer*. Many healers also employ dancing, sand painting, chanting, drumming (which places a person's spirit into alignment with the heartbeat of Mother Earth), and feathers and rattles to remove blockages and stagnations of energy that may be contributing to ill health. Sometimes sacred stones are rubbed over the part of the person's body suspected to be diseased. Although many American Indians prefer to consult a conventional medical doctor for conditions that require antibiotics or surgery, herbal remedies continue to play a substantial role in treatment of various physical, emotional, and spiritual ailments. The herbs prescribed vary from tribe to tribe, depending upon the ailment and what herbs are available in a particular area. Some shamans suggest that the herbs be eaten directly. Others suggest taking them mixed with water (like an herbal tea) or even with food. Healers burn herbs such as sage, sweet grass, or cedar (called a *smudge*) in almost every ceremony, and let the restorative smoke drift over the patient.

### African American folk medicine

In addition to these four basic approaches to health, there is also a wealth of other belief systems. One group not discussed as often as those above is African Americans. For many members of this cultural group, health beliefs reflect cultural roots that include elements of African healing, medicine of the Civil War South, European medical and anatomical folklore, West Indies voodoo religion, fundamentalist Christianity, and other belief systems.

African American communities have become very diverse, especially with the recent arrival of people from Haiti and other Caribbean countries and Africa. Similar to the American Indians, many people of African descent also hold a strong connection to nature and rely on *inyangas* (traditional herbalists). Even today in Africa, hospitals and modern medicines are invariably the last resort in illness. Members of some traditional African tribes seek relief in the herbal lore of the ancestors and consult the *inyanga,*who is in charge of the physical health of the people (Branford, 2005). When bewitchment is suspected, which happens frequently among the traditional people of Africa, or there is a personal family crisis or love or financial problem, the patient is taken to a *sangoma* (spiritual diviner or spiritual/traditional healer) who is believed to have spiritual powers and is able to work with the ancestral spirits or spirit guides (Branford, 2005). The *sangoma* uses various methods such as "throwing the bones" (*amathambo*, also known by other names depending on the cultural group) or going into a spiritual trance to consult the ancestral spirits or spirit guides to find the diagnosis or cure for the problem, be it bewitchment, love, or other problems. Depending on the response from the higher source, a decision will be made on what herbs and mixes (*intelezis*) should be used and in what manner (e.g., orally, burning). If more powerful medicine is needed, numerous "magical rites" can or will be performed according to rituals handed down from *sangoma* to *sangoma* (Branford, 2005). In South Africa, there are more than

70,000 *sangomas* or spiritual healers who dispense herbal medicines and even issue medical certificates to employees for purposes of sick leave.

Many African Americans believe in a form of folk medicine that incorporates and mirrors aspects of voodoo (really spelled "vodou"), which is a type of religion derived from some of the world's oldest known religions that have been present in Africa since the beginning of human civilization (Heaven & Booth, 2003). When Africans were brought to the Americas (historians estimate that approximately 650,000 slaves were imported by the 1680s), religious persecution forced them to practice voodoo in secret. To allow voodoo to survive, its followers adopted many elements of Christianity.

Today, voodoo is a legitimate religion in a number of areas of the world, including Brazil, where it is called *Candomblé*, and the English-speaking Caribbean, where it is called *Obeah*. In most of the United States, however, White slavers were successful in stripping slaves of their voodoo traditions and beliefs (Heaven & Booth, 2003). In some parts of the United States the remnants are stronger than in others. Some African American communities in isolated areas such as the coast and islands of North and South Carolina, survived intact well into the twentieth century. Here, *Gullah* culture involving the belief in herbalism, spiritualism, and black magic, thrived (Pinckney, 2003). What was called voodoo in other parts of the country was called "the root" (meaning charm). A number of other cultures, such as the American Indians described earlier and Hmong Americans, still believe that shamans and medicine men can influence health. Although shamanistic rituals and voodoo rites may seem to be ineffectual ways to cure according to Western science, the rituals have meaning to those who believe in them and should not be ignored or ridiculed.

## But does it work?

Many of the approaches described above may sound like folk medicine without any scientific basis. If you have never heard of them, you may wonder if they actually work. To take a truly culturally relativistic perspective (versus a biased ethnocentric perspective where one's own culture is always better) the simple answer is "in many cases." Indeed there are many anecdotal reports of the efficacy of the different cultural approaches to health described above. There is even a growing body of scientific evidence for many of the different treatments and approaches described (for a full review see Gurung, 2010). For example, much of the research conducted on TCM in America analyzes the constituents of herbs used in treatment, and many such studies show that the active ingredients of the herbs facilitate cures (Hon et al., 2007). Similarly, the Ayurvedic use of forskolin for treating heart disease has now been empirically validated by Western biomedicine (Ding & Staudinger, 2005).

## Culture and Mental Health

Culture influences how individuals manifest symptoms, communicate their symptoms, and cope with psychological challenges, and their willingness to seek treatment (Eshun & Gurung, 2009). Understanding the role of culture in mental health is crucial to comprehensive and accurate diagnoses and treatment of illnesses. Even the U.S. Surgeon General has recognized the importance of both a patient's culture, and that of the healthcare provider in mental health treatment, service use, and diagnosis (U.S. Department of Health and Human Services, 1999). A number of frameworks have been used to understand cultural influences on mental health including the sociobiological, ecocultural, and biopsychosocial perspectives (Eshun & Gurung, 2009). Another perspective that has become increasingly important in our postmodern world, with much migration and resettlement, is multiculturalism. It literally means many cultural views. It is a view that emphasizes importance, equality, and acceptance for all cultural groups within a society, and supports a strong desire to increase awareness about all groups to the benefit of the society as a whole (see Mio, Barker-Hackett, & Tumambing, 2006, for a review).

Overall epidemiological, clinical, and other studies suggest a "moderate but not unlimited impact of cultural factors" on mental health (Draguns, 1997). This implies that accurate evaluation and diagnoses of psychological disorders within the bounds of culture are crucial for appropriate and effective treatment and intervention (Arrindell, 2003). However, in spite of efforts in the field of counseling/clinical psychology to include or emphasize cultural influences on psychopathology in our traditional training programs, we are still limited in the depth and breadth of material available.

It is beyond the scope of this chapter to offer an in-depth review of the literature on culture and mental health, but I will briefly review some of the key issues involved. For example, it is important to remember that culture influences the client as well as the therapist. One needs also to focus on a wide range of processes: conceptualization, perception, health-seeking behaviors, assessment, diagnosis, and treatment, in the context of cultural variations. We need to consider issues related to reliability, validity, and standardization of commonly used psychological assessment instruments among different cultural groups, and the role of factors such as religion and stress as they relate to culture. It is also important to look at a bigger picture, focusing on psychotherapy in a culturally diverse world (see chapter 14, this volume), and to international perspectives on mental health (Prasadarao, 2009). Even specific disorders, such as eating disorders, mood disorders, anxiety disorders, post-traumatic stress disorder, and psychotic disorders, vary by culture (Eshun & Gurung, 2009). There are cultural differences and/or similarities in the symptoms reported, as well as the possibility of misdiagnosing mental illness among people who focus on specific symptoms (e.g., somatic) and less on others for varying reasons.

# Conclusion

One of the most pressing needs for cross-cultural psychology is to spend more time and energy on examining how cultural differences influence health and behavior. There is a strong emphasis for academic curricula to be culturally diverse (Gurung & Prieto, 2009), so why has there not been enough cultural research? The limited focus on cultural differences arises from a number of different factors. Mainstream psychology has tended to be blind to culture, not so much because of some explicit prejudice (although it has been argued that the primarily European American male researchers were biased; Guthrie, 2003), but because of the belief that there are commonalities to human behavior that transcend culture. Conceivably a function of its own individualistic bias, mainstream psychology has only recently begun to consider the theoretical and practical implications of a focus on the collective context—the family, peers, community, and culture, of the individual.

# References

Alvord, L., & Van Pelt, E. C. (2000). *The scalpel and the silver bear*. New York: Bantam.

Anderson, N. B. (2009). Health disparities: A multidimensional approach. *Communique*, March, 7–9.

American Psychological Association. (2009). *Racial and ethnic health disparities*. Washington, DC: Public Policy Office, American Psychological Association. Retrieved from http://www.apa.org/ppo/issues/phealthdis.html

Arrindell, W. A. (2003). Cultural abnormal psychology. *Behavior Research and Therapy, 41*, 749–753.

Avila, E., & Parker, J. (2000). *Woman who glows in the dark: A curandera reveals traditional Aztec secrets of physical and spiritual health*. New York: Tarcher Penguin.

Branford, D. (2005). *African herbalism and spiritual divination*. London: New Press.

Center for Disease Control. (2008, Summer). *Suicide facts at a glance*. Retrieved from http://www.cdc.gov/ViolencePrevention/pdf/Suicide-DataSheet-a.pdf

Cohen, K. (2003). *Honoring the medicine: The essential guide to Native American healing*. New York: Random House Ballantine Publishing Group.

DeStefano, A. M. (2001). *Latino folk medicine: Healing herbal remedies from ancient traditions*. New York: Ballantine Books.

Draguns, J. G. (1997). Abnormal patterns across culture: Implications for counseling and psychotherapy. *International Journal of Intercultural Relations, 21*(2), 213–248.

Ding, X., & Staudinger, J. L. (2005). Induction of drug metabolism by Forskilin: The role of the pregnana X receptor and the protein kinase A signal transduction pathway. *Pharmacology, 312*, 849–856.

Eliade, M. (1964). *Shamanism: Archaic techniques of ecstasy*. Princeton, NJ: Princeton University Press.

Eshun, S., & Gurung, R. A. R. (Eds.) (2009). Culture and mental health: *Sociocultural influences, theory, and practice*. Malden, MA: Wiley-Blackwell.

Gottfried, A. W., Gottfried, A. E., Bathurst, K., Guerin, D. W., & Parramore, M. M. (2003). Socioeconomic status in children's development and family environment: Infancy through adolescence. In M. H. Bornstein & R. H. Bradley (Eds.), *Socioeconomic status, parenting, and child development* (pp. 189–207). Mahwah, NJ: Lawrence Erlbaum Associates.

Gurung, R. A. R. (2010). *Health psychology: A cultural approach* (2nd ed.). San Francisco: Cengage.

Gurung, R. A. R., & Prieto, L. (Eds.) (2009). *Getting culture: Incorporating diversity across the curriculum*. Sterling, VA: Stylus.

Guthrie, R. E. (2003). *Even the rat was white: A historical view of psychology*. Boston, MA: Allyn & Bacon.

Heaven, R., & Booth, T. (2003). *Vodou shaman: The Haitan way of healing and power*. New York: Destiny Press.

Hon, K. L. E., Leung, T. F., Ng, P. C., Lam, M. C. A., Kam, W. Y. C., Wong, K. Y. ... Leung, P. C. (2007). Efficacy and tolerability of a Chinese herbal medicine concoction for treatment of atopic dermatitis: A randomized, double-blind, placebo-controlled study. *British Journal of Dermatology, 157*, 357–363.

Kaptchuk, T. (2000). *The web that has no weaver: Understanding Chinese medicine*. New York: McGraw-Hill.

Kapur, R. L. (1979). The role of traditional healers in mental health care in rural India. *Social Science and Medicine, 13B*, 27–31.

Karim, S., Saeed, K., Rana, M. H., Mubbashar, M. H., & Jenkins, R. (2004). Pakistan mental health country profile. *International Review of Psychiatry, 16*, 83–92.

Lyssenko, V. (2004). The human body composition in statics and dynamics: Ayurveda and the philosophical schools of Vaisesika and Samkhya. *Journal of Indian Philosophy, 32*, 31–56.

Macintyre, S. (1997). The Black report and beyond: What are the issues? *Social Science and Medicine, 44*, 723–745.

Mehl-Medrona, L. (1998). *Coyote medicine: Lessons from Native American healing*. New York: Touchstone.

Mio, J. S., Barker-Hackett, L., & Tumambing, J. (2006). *Multicultural psychology: Understanding our diverse communities*. Boston, MA: McGraw-Hill.

Murray, C., Kulkarni, S., Michaud, C., Tomijima, N., Bulzacchelli, M., Iandiorio, T., & Ezzati, M. (2006). Eight Americas: Investigating mortality disparities across races, counties, and race-counties in the United States. *PLoS Medicine, 3*(9), e260.

Pinckney, R. (2003). *Blue roots: African American folk magic of the Gullah people*. Orangeburg, SC: Sandlapper Publishing Co.

Prasadarao, P. S. D. V. (2009). Culture and mental health: An international perspective. In S. Eshun & R. A. R. Gurung (Eds.) *Culture and mental health: Sociocultural influences, theory, and practice* (pp. 149–178). Malden, MA: Wiley-Blackwell.

Pratt, L. A., & Brody, D. J. (2008). *Depression in the United States household population, 2005–2006*. National Center for Health Services Data Brief, 7. Retrieved from http://www.cdc.gov/nchs/data/databriefs/db07.pdf

Singh, A. (2007). Action and reason in the theory of Ayurveda. *AI and Society, 21*, 27–46.

Svoboda, R. E. (2004). *Ayurveda: Life, longevity, and health*. Albuquerque, NM: The Ayurvedic Press.

Torres, E., & Sawyer, T. L. (2005). *Curandero: A life in Mexican folk healing*. Albuquerque: University of New Mexico Press.

Trotter, R. T., & Chavira, J. A. (1997). *Curanderismo: Mexican American folk healing*. Athens, GA: University of Georgia Press.

Udwadia, F. E. (2000). *Man and medicine: A history*. London: Oxford University Press.

U.S. Department of Health and Human Services (1999). *Mental health: A report of the Surgeon General—Executive summary*. Rockville, MD: U.S. Department of Health and Human Services, Substance Abuse and Mental Health Services Administration, Center for Mental Health Services, National Institutes of Health, National Institute of Mental Health.

U.S. Department of Health and Human Services (2009). *Healthy People 2010*. Retrieved from www.healthypeople.gov

Whitehead, M. (1992). The concepts and principles of equity and health. *International Journal of Health Services, 22*, 429–445.

Winkelman, M. (2009). *Culture and health: Applying medical anthropology*. San Francisco: John Wiley and Sons.

World Health Organization (1946). Preamble to the Constitution of the World Health Organization as adopted by the International Health Conference, New York, 19–22 June, 1946; signed on 22 July 1946 by the representatives of 61 States (Official Records of the World Health Organization, no. 2, p. 100) and entered into force on 7 April 1948.

# 14

# Culture and Psychotherapy
## Searching for an Empirically Supported Relationship

### Junko Tanaka-Matsumi

*Life is animated by fission and fusion—separation and connection, isolation and relation, independence and dependence are not opposites but merely manifestations* of one nature. We must encourage and promote diversity even as we pursue unity. (Marsella, 2009, p. 134)

*Developing cross-cultural competence is a lifelong journey, replete with many joys and challenges* (Heppner, 2006, p. 147).

## Participant Observation of Culture and Psychotherapy

The purpose of this chapter is to examine ways to incorporate culture into empirically supported psychotherapies (Griner & Smith, 2006; Sue & Sue, 2008a; Tanaka-Matsumi, 2008). Keith (Chapter 1, this volume) reviewed various definitions of culture (e.g., Matsumoto & Juang, 2008) and stated that "increased understanding of culture—our own as well as others'—is perhaps the most pressing need for psychological science." (p. 16) Further, Keith articulated that understanding will come only on the strength of sound methodology and accurate data" (p. 16). The same applies to understanding of psychotherapies across cultures.

Psychotherapy outcome research has made great strides since the publication of Eysenck's (1952) critical report on the lack of clear evidence that any form of psychotherapy was particularly effective. Today, Paul's (1967) widely cited universal question on the need for identifying specific effects of psychological treatments has been answered to some degree: "What treatment, by whom, is most effective for this individual with that specific problem, and which set of circumstances?" (p. 111) We have increasing knowledge of what works for whom (Roth & Fonagy, 2004) for certain problems such as anxiety, depression, and childhood problems. What we do not know is in what *specific* ways culture matters in empirically supported psychological interventions (Chambless & Ollendick, 2001) and what we can do to accommodate cultural factors within them. Reflecting the pressing need of the diverse world, studies on the cultural adaptation of empirically supported psychological interventions are clearly increasing in number (Bernal, Jiménez-Chafey, & Rodriguez, 2009; Griner & Smith, 2006; Hays & Iwamasa, 2006).

Diversity issues in assessment and therapy occupy an important and legitimate place in the training and practice of professional psychology (Sue & Sue, 2008b). My personal story of becoming a professional psychologist in two culturally different countries (the United States and Japan) underscores the importance of looking at culture as a dynamic context for all our professional activities. I was trained in the scientist-practitioner model of clinical psychologist in the United States. I then taught in an American Psychological Association (APA) approved, combined clinical-school psychology PhD program for 20 years. I subsequently moved back to Japan and currently teach and practice clinical psychology and cross-cultural psychology at a university. In the U.S., I supervised a large number of assessment cases of culturally diverse clients at the university psychological research and therapy center. I also helped Japanese children and their families cope with acculturation stress and developmental issues as they made contacts with American culture.

My colleagues and I have been interested in two major questions (Tanaka-Matsumi, Higginbotham, & Chang, 2002). First, how does a cognitive behavior therapist conduct an assessment interview with a client from a culture or subculture different from his or her own? Second, and much more specifically, how can a cognitive behavior therapist use functional assessment (Haynes & O'Brien, 1990) to develop culturally sensitive case formulation and interventions that are culturally acceptable? We developed the Culturally Informed Functional Assessment Interview (Tanaka-Matsumi, Seiden, & Lam, 1996) to generate culture-relevant data from the client. We studied the relationship between culture and psychopathology and ways to advance culturally informed psychological assessment (e.g., Draguns & Tanaka-Matsumi, 2003; Tanaka-Matsumi, 2001; Tanaka-Matsumi & Draguns, 1997).

## Historical Antecedents of Empirically Supported Psychotherapies: Discovery of Placebo Effects and Common Factors in Psychotherapy

Modern Western history of psychotherapy began with Mesmer's magnetic therapy in Vienna and Paris in 1775 (Ellenberger, 1970). Mesmer's patients responded to the non-specific placebo effect of the unusual intervention in those days. Mesmer induced the placebo effect by the combination of a dramatic setting for demonstration, colorful therapist attire, and the presence of an intensively curious audience. Historically, the term "placebo" has referred to inactive medications prescribed primarily for purposes of placating or soothing the patient rather than directly treating any real disorder (Parloff, 1986). Placebo has two elements. First, the intervention lacks the specific ingredients for change, and, second, individuals who are offered such inactive interventions must nonetheless be led to believe in their potency (Frank & Frank, 1991; Parloff, 1986).

A study by Paul (1966) provided an example of the scientific rigor required to develop appropriate controls in psychotherapy research. Paul conducted the first controlled psychotherapy outcome research to test the effectiveness of Wolpe's (1958) systematic desensitization therapy with university students who were manifesting "performance anxiety" of speaking in public. Paul (1966) assigned participants to one of four groups: (a) insight oriented psychotherapy, (b) systematic desensitization, (c) attention placebo, and (d) no-treatment control. The participants who were assigned to the attention placebo group were led to believe that a "fast-acting tranquilizer" would help ameliorate their stress reactions. In reality, this was a placebo pill without any chemically active ingredients. The results indicated that the desensitization group improved significantly more than the rest of the groups on behavioral, physiological, and self-report measures of speech anxiety. The attention placebo group also improved more than the no-treatment group. Attention placebo effects include client's expectation of relief, relationship, the attention, warmth, suggestion, and interest of the therapist (Ullmann & Krasner, 1975).

Prince (1980) defined psychotherapy as "the mobilization of endogenous mechanisms" (p. 292) aimed at relieving an individual's suffering, and called attention to the wide variations in psychotherapeutic procedures. These included sleep, rest, social isolation, dreams, meditation, dissociation states, shamanism, and Western psychotherapies. Prince (1980) warned about the danger of focusing categorically on any one particular therapeutic mode and applying it to other cultures. In other words, therapists may not be aware of their own cultural bias when working with culturally different clients (Ridley, 2005). Over the years, with increased multicultural awareness of practitioners and societal claims for accountability, textbooks on multicultural counseling and therapy have come to clarify the types of cultural biases in psychotherapy, giving guidelines for addressing cultural complexities in the practice of psychotherapy (e.g., Hays, 2008; Sue & Sue, 2008b).

## Universal Functions of Psychotherapy and Culture-Specific Contents

Psychotherapy "alleviates distress, facilitates adaptive coping, and promotes more effective problem solving and decision making" (Draguns, 2008, p. 21) and takes place within the interactive cultural context of the therapist and the client (Draguns, 1975). As Hall (2001) defined them, culturally sensitive treatments involve "the tailoring of psychotherapy to specific cultural contexts" (p. 252). Different cultures practice healing systems in diverse forms that reflect indigenous views of health and illness and ways to help the individual in distress (e.g., Gielen, Fish, & Draguns, 2004; Moodley & West, 2005; Prince, 1980). Frank and Frank (1991) described universal features of broadly defined psychotherapies. These include: (a) helping seeker's state of demoralization, (b) availability of a socially recognized healer, (c) sharing of a world view by healer and client, (d) endorsement of cultural belief systems; and (d) sharing of cultural explanations of suffering. Attempts to link these cultural features to psychotherapeutic practices have developed into a major field of study with profound implications for teaching, research, and practice (e.g., Gerstein, Heppner, Stockton, Leong, & Aegisdottir, 2009; Gielen, Draguns, & Fish, 2008; Hays & Iwamasa, 2006; La Roche, 2005; Pedersen, Draguns, Lonner, & Trimble, 2008; Sue & Sue, 2008b), and for understanding the importance of quality of life across diverse cultures (Keith, 2000).

Techniques are important for behavior change; however, context is also important. Some techniques are frequently used in different cultural contexts to achieve therapeutic aims. For example, clients of Japanese Naikan therapy (Tanaka-Matsumi, 2004a) and clients of Western-derived cognitive behavior therapy (CBT) may both learn to use the same technique of self-observation and self-monitoring as a first step in directing attention to one's relationships with specific others. However, therapy rationale and cultural context of each therapy are very different. Japanese Naikan therapy clients would engage in self-observation to recall benevolences received from their mothers in terms of specific things mothers did for them to mobilize a forgotten sense of gratitude. European American clients of CBT may engage in self-observation of their interpersonal behavior to increase a sense of independence and autonomy. With regard to interpersonal relationships, assertiveness training was originally developed in the United States with its emphasis on advocating one's own rights. In Japan, assertiveness training is more functional when it accommodates a positive cultural contingency of using indirect verbal expressions of one's needs rather than using direct verbal expressions (Mitamura & Tanaka-Matsumi, 2009).

To give another example, Latino adults in the United States chose to engage in allocentric (other-oriented) relaxation imagery exercise more frequently than idiocentric (self-oriented) imagery exercise in culturally competent relaxation training (La Roche, D'Angelo, Gualdron, & Leavell, 2006). Anybody can learn to relax with training. In this case, however, the selected content of the imagery exercise matched with the allocentric cultural self-orientation of the Latinos. These examples suggest that psychotherapy's effectiveness depends on the cultural context of its application. That is, we need to stipulate salient cultural factors and seek empirical support for the claim through appropriate research design.

Psychotherapy researchers have been actively investigating the empirically verifiable bases of psychotherapies delivered to clients with a variety of presenting problems (Castonguay & Beutler, 2006). In both the United States and the United

Kingdom, healthcare providers mandate the practice of empirically supported psychotherapies for socio-economic reasons. In fact, evidence-based practice in psychology has been officially promoted by an American Psychological Association task force:

> Evidence-based practice in psychology (EBPP) is the integration of the best available research with clinical expertise in the context of patient characteristics, culture, and preferences. (APA Presidential Task Force on Evidence-Based Practice, 2006, p. 273)

As of 2001, there were over 130 different manualized treatments listed as empirically supported (Chambless & Ollendick, 2001), with more added each year (Nathan & Gorman, 2006). Most of the validated treatments are cognitive behavioral in orientation. The universal functions of these empirically validated interventions are tested increasingly and, at times, critically, in the age of globalization (La Roche & Christopher, 2008).

## Globalization, Diversity, and Dissemination of Evidence-Based Practices

The development of global transportation and communication systems has increased people's mobility and altered ethnic and cultural compositions of many countries of the world. The U.S. population, for example, is expected to reach over 380 million in 2050 and the current minority population will constitute the majority group, replacing the non-Hispanic white majority group (U.S. Census Bureau, 2002). Even within the same country, people hold different values and act according to sociocultural value systems which are institutionalized over the years, influencing help-seeking behaviors according to ethnic groups (Akutsu, Castillo, & Snowden, 2007; Comaz-Diaz, 2006; Snowden & Yamada, 2005). In this age of globalization, there is an increased need for training of culturally competent counselors and therapists to provide culturally informed and empirically supported counseling and therapy both within and outside their home countries (Hall, 2006; Marsella, 2009; Sue, 1998).

Globalization and diversification facilitate dissemination of information to those who benefit from the knowledge (Marsella, 1998). Psychologists in Europe perform professional activities across borders (Hall & Lunt, 2005). As an example of the cross-cultural spread of empirically supported psychotherapy, we may trace the development of the World Congress of Behavioural and Cognitive Therapy (WCBCT). Seven major associations around the globe participate in this international congress. The groups include the Association for Behavioral and Cognitive Therapies (ABCT) of North America and the European Association for Cognitive and Behavioural Therapies (EABCT) and other such umbrella associations located in all continents of the world. Almost 4,000 people from more than 70 countries attended the 2007 WCBCT in Barcelona. As an indication of strong Asian involvement, three associations jointly sponsored the 2004 WCBCT, held for the first time in Asia, in Kobe, Japan. The three sponsor associations were the Japanese Association for Behavior Therapy, the Japanese Association for Cognitive Therapy, and the Japanese Association for Behavior Analysis. The congress theme was "Toward a Global Standard." Further, in 2006, the first Asian Cognitive Behavior Therapy Conference was inaugurated in Hong Kong. The second meeting was held in Thailand (Bangkok) in 2008, and the third meeting is anticipated in Korea (Seoul) in 2011. These Asia-based conferences are particularly noteworthy from the viewpoint of cultural accommodation of CBT practices. The programs have emphasized culturally sensitive examination of evidence-based assessment and treatment. The practice of CBTs has been extended to Asia well beyond the cultural boundaries of their developmental origins in North America and Europe (Oei, 1998; Qian & Wang, 2005).

With its emphasis on empiricism, CBT is used on a national scale in the U.K. The Improving Access to Psychological Therapies (IAPT) program in the U.K. began in 2006 to support primary care trusts in implementing National Institute for Health and Clinical Excellence (NICE) guidelines for particularly underserved adults of working age suffering from depression and anxiety disorders (see http://www.iapt.nhs.uk/about-us/iapt-pathfinder-program/). IAPT utilizes CBT on a community basis to train and increase the number of CBT therapists, eventually by 10,000, to meet the society's needs for help.

In the United States, in a survey conducted every 10 years using Delphi methodology, a panel of 67 psychotherapy experts predicted that CBT, culture-sensitive/multicultural therapy, cognitive therapy, interpersonal therapy (IPT), and technical eclecticism would be the top five most influential theoretical orientations in psychotherapy by 2010 (Norcross, Hedges, & Prochaska, 2002). The survey results also predicted a required use of evidence-based psychotherapies by healthcare systems and the use of practice guidelines as part of standard clinical practice. Looking at the situation now, we can say these predictions have proven to be largely valid. However, the need for empirically supported and culturally sensitive psychotherapy at the level of community practice is yet to be fulfilled (Miranda et al., 2005; Snowden & Yamada, 2005; Sue & Sue, 2008a).

## Practitioners' Knowledge of Empirically Supported Therapies

It is frequently reported that there is a wide gap between clinical research and practice. Research-identified psychology treatments have produced efficacy data within an experimental paradigm but their effectiveness in day-to-day clinical practice is another matter (Kazdin, 2006). Psychotherapy outcome research has established outcomes based on multiple types of research evidence. Currently, there are two criteria for evaluating effectiveness of empirically supported psychotherapy outcomes. Treatment *efficacy* refers to outcomes obtained in an experimental research study and treatment *effectiveness* refers to outcomes in the naturalistic settings of clinical practice (Nathan, Stuart, & Dolan, 2000). The question is the utility of research-based treatments in day-to-day clinical work with individual clients from diverse cultural backgrounds.

One important move emerging out of the dissemination research concerns an empirical assessment of the practitioner's knowledge of "practice elements" of evidence-based treatments (Stumpf, Higa-McMillan, & Chorpita, 2009). Practice elements are "discrete clinical techniques or strategies, such as relaxation or self-monitoring, that are typically used as part of a larger intervention plan (e.g., a manualized treatment program for depression)" (Stumpf et al., 2009, p. 51). The practice elements are common elements empirically derived by using the "distillation and matching model" applied to a large number of evidence-based treatments for children and adolescents as reported in the literature (Chorpita & Daleiden, 2009). The practice elements (e.g., modeling, praise, and social skills training) are much more specific than the package intervention programs composed of different techniques in evidence-based treatments.

Stumpf et al. (2009) developed a 40-item test called the Knowledge of Evidence-Based Services Questionnaire (KEBSQ) in the treatment of child and adolescent mental health problem areas: anxious/avoidant, depressed/withdrawn, disruptive behavior, and/or attention/hyperactivity. A total of 184 community behavioral health practitioners from the American state of Hawaii participated in the study. The group consisted of almost equal proportions of White (34.4%) and Asian (32.5%) practitioners, reflecting the two largest subgroups in Hawaii. The KEBSQ includes 30 practice elements that are actually used in empirically supported treatment protocols for child/adolescent problems (e.g., exposure, relaxation, time out, feedback) and 10 items that are not directly relevant (e.g., play therapy). The KEBSQ proved sensitive to changes in knowledge of empirically supported psychological intervention protocols after the training in evidence-based treatments for youth. As expected, graduate students in clinical psychology scored significantly higher on the test than the community practitioners. This study demonstrated the importance of ascertaining a solid knowledge base when disseminating evidence-based treatments to community practitioners in order to evaluate the clinical effectiveness of efficacious treatments for children and adolescents (Weisz, Doss, & Hawley, 2005).

## Cultural Competencies in Psychotherapy

What are the competencies necessary to perform empirically supported and culturally responsive therapies? Cultural competencies should be generic to all forms of counseling and therapy (Hays, 2008; Pedersen, 2002) and encompass awareness, knowledge, and skills contributing to the practice of psychotherapy and counseling (Pedersen, 1997). Organizationally, the APA Presidential Task Force (2006) identified eight "components of clinical practice that promote positive therapeutic outcomes" (p. 276), each of which is highly relevant to the practice of culturally responsive assessment and therapy. The eight clinical components cover the whole range of clinical activities: (a) assessment, diagnostic judgment, systematic case formulation, and treatment planning; (b) clinical decision making, treatment and monitoring of progress; (c) interpersonal expertise, (d) self-reflection and skills acquisition: (e) empirical evaluation and research; (f) understanding the influence of individual and cultural differences on treatment; (g) seeking available resources; and (h) having a cogent rationale for clinical strategies. The eight clinical competencies are linked by empiricism, attention to individual differences, and multicultural perspectives.

Heppner (2006) addressed the same issue for counseling psychologists. He gave an extremely positive direction for the practice of multicultural counseling. Developing cross-cultural competence increases the sophistication of clinical research, expands the utility and generalizability of the knowledge bases in counseling psychology, promotes a deeper realization that counseling occurs in a cultural context, and increases not only counseling effectiveness but also the profession's ability to address diverse mental health needs across different populations around the globe. Gerstein et al. (2009) stated that there is a growing recognition that counseling and psychotherapy are embedded in the worldwide system of "interconnectedness" of the helping professions across cultures.

If cultural competencies are important, are professional psychologists practicing cultural competence? Empirical assessment is lacking in this area. In a national survey, Hansen et al. (2006) developed a 52-item Multi-cultural Practices and Beliefs Questionnaire and investigated the extent to which professional psychotherapists (N = 149, 93% European American) in the United States believe and actually engage in culturally competent practice. The authors found an overall significant difference between mean ratings for practices and beliefs. Among the universally endorsed cultural competence items are: (a) show respect for client's worldview; (b) avoid idealizing racial/ethnic groups; (c) take responsibility for transcending one's own negative racial/ethnic cultural conditioning; and (d) evaluate one's assumptions, values, and biases. Hansen et al. reported that only 22% of the practitioners used the Cultural Case Formulation in DSM-IV-TR (American Psychiatric Association, 2000) with ethnic clients, and only about 33% have used culturally sensitive data-gathering techniques in their practice. These results indicate that culturally adaptive protocols are not yet an integral part of assessment, case conceptualization, and intervention by professional psychologists. Furthermore, these psychologists reported that direct practices and experiences were most influential in developing multicultural competence, rather than guidelines and codes. The survey results indicate the importance of practicum with culturally diverse clients in training to increase self-assessment opportunities (American Psychological Association, 2003).

# Cultural Adaptation of Empirically Supported Psychotherapy

Cultural adaptation is the systematic modification of an evidence-based treatment or intervention protocol to consider language, culture, and context in such a way that it is compatible with the client's cultural patterns, meanings, and values. Adaptations that are well documented, systematic, and tested can advance research and inform practice (Bernal et al., 2009, p. 361). Cultural adaptation involves incorporation of culture-relevant and culture-sensitive information into the practice of psychotherapy with diverse clients. The multicultural literature has generated a series of guiding questions in order to accomplish cultural adaptation of a particular therapy.

Culturally sensitive therapists ask the following questions when working with clients in a cross-cultural setting (Higginbotham, 1984; Tanaka-Matsumi et al., 2002):

1　What is the culture-relevant definition of maladaptive behavior that is considered abnormal in the client culture?
2　What is the accepted standard of role behavior?
3　Who is sanctioned to provide help for the individual in distress?
4　What expectations does the client culture have for psychotherapy and counseling?

These questions are designed to raise the clinician's awareness of the fundamental elements of culture in the practice of helping professions. Heinchs et al. (2006) investigated the relationship between culture, social anxiety, and fear of blushing. The student participants were from individualistic (U.S.A., Australia, Canada, Germany, and the Netherlands) and collectivistic (Japan, Korea, and Spain) countries. Country-level standings on the individualism and collectivism cultural dimensions were determined according to Hofstede's (2001) work on cultural values and dimensions. They found that students from collectivistic cultures were more accepting toward socially withdrawn behaviors than students from individualistic countries. The authors also found significantly positive relations between the extent to which attention-avoiding behaviors are accepted in a culture and the level of social anxiety or fear of blushing symptoms. The results indicate cultural variations in the tolerance of socially withdrawn and anxious behaviors and suggest differences in normative standards of self presentation. These differences in cultural norms for expected behaviors can be clarified through negotiation (Kleinman, 1980) to resolve any misperception between the client and the therapist.

To identify common factors seen in different cultural adaptation guidelines, Van de Vijver and Tanaka-Matsumi (2008) reviewed models of cross-cultural assessment for case formulation. They reported considerable similarities among the models (see Andréas-Hyman, Ortiz, Añez, Paris, & Davidson, 2006; Evans & Paewai,

1999; Hays, 2008; Hwang, 2006; Hwang & Wood, 2006; Ridley, Li, & Hill, 1998; Sue, 1998; Tanaka-Matsumi et al., 1996; Weiss et al., 1992). The common cultural accommodation includes assessment of the following: (a) client's cultural identity and acculturation; (b) conflict with values; (c) client's own idiom (expressions) of distress; (d) client's causal explanatory model of presenting problems; (e) metaphors of health and well-being in the client's cultural group; (f) client's motivation for change; and (g) client's social support network.

Our impending question is whether there is evidence that culturally adapted therapies are actually more effective than those without particular cultural consideration. To what extent are they effective? Griner and Smith (2006) conducted a comprehensive literature search on culturally adapted mental health treatments and then performed a series of meta-analyses to determine effectiveness. They found 76 studies, with a total of 25,225 participants. Typically, studies included the comparison of a culturally adapted psychological intervention to a "traditional" intervention. Across all 76 studies, the average effect size was d = .45, indicating a moderately strong effect. The results were especially promising when the intervention was targeted for a specific cultural group (e.g., Hispanics) rather than a mixed group. The authors reported that as high as 84% of the total studies explicitly included cultural values and content into culturally adapted treatment such as the use of folk heroes for children. Griner and Smith's criteria of cultural adaptation included: (a) reference to cultural values and stories; (b) racial/ethnic matching of client and therapist, (c) service in client's native language, (d) multicultural paradigm of agency, (e) consultation with a culturally familiar individual, (f) outreach efforts, (g) extra service to retain clients, (h) verbal administration of materials for illiterate clients, (i) cultural sensitivity training for professional staff, and (j) referral to external agencies for additional services. The meta-analytic results (2006) showed the benefit of cultural adaptation of psychotherapy regardless of the technical content of each therapy. These culture-relevant variables are expected to interact with the client's presenting problems and the treatment process. Assessment is an on-going process within the interactive cultural context of client and therapist (Okazaki & Tanaka-Matsumi, 2004).

## Culturally Responsive CBT: Asking the Right Questions to Expand the Application

Cognitive behavioral therapists are trained to ask important questions with regard to the functional relationship between the expression of distress and cultural values, or the impact of client ethnicity and religiosity on coping with distress (Hofmann, 2006). Studies of culturally responsive CBT are available on such topics as somatic symptoms of post-traumatic stress disorder (PTSD; Hinton, Safren, Pollack, & Tran, 2006; Otto & Hinton, 2006; Schulz, Huber, &

Resick, 2006), panic attacks (Friedman, Braunstein, & Halpern, 2006; Zoellner, Feeny, Fitzgibbons, & Foa, 1999), and depression (Nicolas, Arntz, Hirsch, & Schmiedigen, 2009), among others.

In their textbook, *Foundations of counseling and psychotherapy: Evidence-based practices for a diverse society*, Sue and Sue (2008a) included a section called "Cultural diversity considerations" in each chapter on different forms of counseling and psychotherapy. The title and the content both suggest that the authors are making active efforts to advance evidence-based practices for diverse societies. While recognizing the importance of empirically supported therapies, the authors pay close attention to the quality of the relationship between the therapist and the client. They summarized the conclusions of the APA Division 29 Task Force (Ackerman et al., 2001) on empirically supported therapeutic relationship. The main conclusions are that the therapeutic relationship makes a contribution to psychotherapy outcome, independent of the specific type of treatment, and adapting the therapy relationship to specific client needs and characteristics enhances the effectiveness of treatment. The therapeutic alliance factors are considered to complement the practice of empirically supported therapies. Demonstrably effective "empirically supported relationship variables" (Ackerman et al., 2001, p. 495) included therapeutic alliance, cohesion in group therapy, empathy, goal consensus and collaboration, customizing therapy to deal with resistance or functional impairment, and management of countertransference. Castonguay and Beutler (2006) embarked on a synthesis of the literature related to empirically supported treatments and relationship factors that are effective for clients with depression, anxiety, personality disorders, and substance abuse problems. They asked: What is known about the nature of the participants, relationships, and procedures within treatment that induce positive effects across theoretical models and methods? And, how do the factors or variables that are related to participants, relationships, and treatments work together to enhance change?

Sue and Sue (2008a) included both technique and relationship factors as relevant to enhancing therapeutic effectiveness with diverse clients. Under cognitive behavior therapies for depression, the authors questioned if social and cultural influences are the cause of dysfunctional beliefs, if there are cultural factors and norms that need to be taken into consideration, and if the goals being considered are culturally appropriate for the client and his or her cultural group. Asking these and other diversity questions strengthens the cultural basis of empirically supported treatments, and practitioners would benefit from training in cultural orientation to the currently available guidelines.

As part of the case formulation methods, the cognitive behavior therapist gathers appropriate idiographic data from the client and other informants. A major advantage of the case formulation approach is its process orientation and individualized approach. The therapist's knowledge of the client's cultural definitions of problem behavior and cultural norms regarding behavior, change strategies, and culturally approved change agents will enhance the degree of cultural accommodation.

The functional analysis identifies antecedent events and consequences of problem behaviors within the client's social network. Cultural factors are embedded in the client's larger social environment and reinforcement history (Biglan, 1995; Hayes & Toarmino, 1995; Tanaka-Matsumi, 2004b).

At multiple clinical decision points during assessment, the therapist develops hypotheses for individual clients and probes for the contribution of contextual variables. As part of the case formulation methods, the therapist gathers appropriate idiographic data from the client and other cultural informants (Bruch & Bond, 1998; Nezu, Nezu, Friedman, & Haynes, 1997). The step-by-step functional approach helps the therapist with clinical judgments in seven domains: (a) the problem list, (b) core beliefs, (c) precipitating and activating situations, (d) the working hypothesis, (e) origins or early history of the problem, (f) the treatment plan, and (g) predicted outcome of treatment (Persons & Tompkins, 1997). A major advantage of the case formulation approach is its process orientation and individualized approach. To gather culture-relevant information from the client, it is important to establish a working alliance with the client, so that the therapist and the client can collaborate with each other.

La Roche et al. (2006) evaluated the effectiveness of the culturally sensitive relaxation method with Latino adults in a group setting. They used the Culturally Competent Relaxation Intervention (CCRI) which was designed especially for Latinos who hold allocentric self-orientation. Allocentrism at the individual level is connected with the collectivism cultural dimension. Relaxation for individualistic/idiocentric individuals directs attention to self rather than interconnectedness with the surroundings. The CCRI used a group socializing format before teaching guided imagery with either an allocentric imagery exercise of being with someone who makes one happy, or with an idiocentric imagery exercise of being by oneself on a beautiful beach. The authors reported preliminary results concerning Latinos' preference for allocentric imagery. The state of relaxation is a universal state of mind, but the content of relaxation exercise can be culturally variable to benefit the person using it. Future study could employ non-Latinos to examine whether allocentric preference is culture-related or more universal.

A series of studies conducted in Boston with the Asian community gives excellent examples of cultural adaptation of empirically supported CBT protocols for the treatment of specific anxiety disorders (Hinton et al., 2005; Hinton, Safren, Pollack, & Tran, 2006; Iwamasa, Hsia, & Hinton, 2006). Cognitive behavioral treatment has been recognized as evidence-based and several detailed manuals are available (e.g., Barlow & Craske, 1994; Craske & Barlow, 1994). One important component of these treatment protocols is the use of repeated exposure to feared situations to reduce the intensity of the fear response. In the case of panic attacks, clients are exposed to feared bodily sensations and taught to modify their maladaptive self-statements during exposure. Hinton and Otto (2006) conducted a cultural analysis of somatic symptoms of a panic attack in traumatized Cambodian refugees who received CBT in Boston. The authors introduced the Cambodian cultural syndrome of "weak heart" based on the ethnographic account of *wind* as the causal agent of anxiety symptoms that produced somatization of trauma-related distress. They hypothesized that "weak heart" produces catastrophic cognitions and somatic symptoms. According to the authors' cultural assessment, Cambodians construe a panic attack as a *wind* attack and consequently engage in self-statements to remove *wind*. Functional assessment of these "coining" and "cupping" statements indicated that these statements serve as the safety behaviors that maintain and perpetuate catastrophic cognitions about *wind*.

To accommodate cultural context, Otto and Hinton (2006) conducted therapy sessions in a local Buddhist temple with interpreters to help Cambodian refugee clients. They assessed the clinical relevance of culture-specific beliefs about *wind* travelling through vessels in the body and creating a dangerous bodily condition. They also encouraged the use of cultural metaphors of somatic symptoms and Cambodian cultural concepts whenever possible.

## Beyond Specific Therapies: Therapy as Negotiation in Cross-Cultural Context

Culturally adapted psychotherapy has components of "therapy as negotiation" (Kleinman, 1980). The interactive procedure is helpful for understanding the cultural meaning of the client's presenting problem. First, the therapist encourages clients to give their own explanation of the presenting problem. Second, the therapist discloses the explanation, or explanatory model, that he or she uses to interpret the problem. Third, the two frameworks are compared for commonalities and discrepancies. Finally, the client and clinician translate each explanatory model into mutually acceptable language, so that they may jointly set the content of therapy, the target behavior, and outcome criteria. In fact, reflecting Frank and Frank's (1991) definition of psychotherapy, effective communication between the therapist and the client in psychotherapy is based on the shared cultural meanings of the concepts and idioms of distress.

## Conclusion

The recent literature demonstrates successful applications of empirically supported treatment to culturally diverse clients. The cumulative empirical research on psychotherapy outcome amounts to hundreds of studies since the publication of Eysenck's (1952) critical report calling for scientific studies of psychotherapy outcome. Today, it is clear that psychotherapy has proven effective in general. More specifically, it is also clear that both techniques and relationship factors contribute to therapeutic effectiveness. A large number of empirically supported therapies are currently available for the treatment of specific disorders (Nathan & Gorman, 2006; Roth & Fonagy, 2004). Similarly, the literature on empirically supported relationship factors has helped direct our attention to the dynamic nature of interaction between the therapist and the client within the cultural context.

As I have reviewed in this chapter, there is an increasing number of studies on the adaptation of empirically supported therapy for specific cultural groups. The need for culture-specific clinical services will continue to increase in the near future. Furthermore, practitioners will be increasingly challenged to demonstrate that their services are evidence based. It can be expected, therefore, that there will be an increased need for systematic studies of culturally informed assessment and intervention methods. Finally, the training of culturally competent psychotherapists is expected to increase in the age of globalization.

# References

Ackerman, S. J., Benjamin, L. S., Beutler, L. E., Gelso, C. J., Goldfried, M. R., Hill, C. ... Rainer, J. (2001). Empirically supported therapy relationships: Conclusions and recommendations of the Division 29 Task Force. *Psychotherapy, 38*, 495–497.

Akutsu, P. D., Castillo, E. D., & Snowden, L. R. (2007). Differential referral patterns to ethnic-specific and mainstream mental health programs for four Asian American groups. *American Journal of Orthopsychiatry, 77*, 95–103.

American Psychiatric Association (2000). *Diagnostic and statistical manual of mental disorders IV-TR* (4th ed., text rev.) Washington, DC: Author.

American Psychological Association (2003). Guidelines on multicultural education, training, research, practice, and organizational change for psychologists. *American Psychologist, 58*, 377–402.

Andréas-Hyman, R. C., Ortiz, J., Añez, L. M., Paris, M., & Davidson, L. (2006). Culture and clinical practice: Recommendations for working with Puerto Ricans and other Latinas(os) in the United States. *Professional Psychology: Research and Practice, 37*, 694–701.

APA Presidential Task Force on Evidence-Based Practice (2006). Evidence-based practice in psychology. *American Psychologist, 61*, 271–285.

Barlow, D. H., & Craske, M. G. (1994). *Mastery for your anxiety and panic–II.* San Antonio, TX: Harcourt Brace.

Bernal, G., Jiménez-Chafey, M. I., & Rodríguez, M. M. D. (2009). Cultural adaptation of treatments: A resource for considering culture in evidence-based practice. *Professional Psychology: Research and Practice, 40*, 361–368.

Biglan, A. (1995). *Changing cultural practices: A contextualist framework for intervention research.* Reno, NV: Context.

Bruch, M., & Bond, F. (1998). *Beyond diagnosis: Case formulation approaches in CBT.* Chichester, UK: John Wiley & Sons.

Castonguay, L. G., & Beutler, L. E. (2006). Common and unique principles of therapeutic change: What do we know and what do we need to know? In L. G. Castonguay, & L. E. Beutler (Eds.), *Principles of therapeutic change that work* (pp. 353–369). New York: Oxford University Press.

Chambless, D. L., & Ollendick, T. H. (2001). Empirically supported psychological interventions: Controversies and evidence. *Annual Review of Psychology, 52,* 685–716.

Chorpita, B. F., & Daleiden, E. L. (2009). Mapping evidence-based treatments for children and adolescents: Application of the distillation and matching model to 615 treatments from 322 randomized trials. *Journal of Consulting and Clinical Psychology, 77,* 566–579.

Comaz-Diaz, L. (2006). Cultural variation in the therapeutic relationship. In C. D. Goodheart A. E. Kazdin, & R. J. Sternberg (Eds.), *Evidence-based psychotherapy: Where practice and research meet* (pp. 81–106). Washington, DC: American Psychological Association.

Craske, M. G., & Barlow, D. H. (1994). *Agoraphobia supplement to the MAP II program.* San Antonio, TX: Harcourt Brace.

Draguns, J. G. (1975). Resocialization into culture. The complexities of taking a worldwide view of psychotherapy. In R. W. Brislin, S. Bochner, & W. J. Lonner (Eds.), *Cross-cultural perspectives on learning* (pp. 273–289). Beverly Hills, CA: Sage.

Draguns, J. G. (2007). Psychotherapeutic and related interventions for a global psychology. In M. J. Stevens & U. P. Gielen (Eds.), *Toward a global psychology: Theory, research, intervention, and pedagogy* (pp. 233–266). Mahwah, NJ: Lawrence Erlbaum Associates.

Draguns, J. G. (2008). Universal and cultural threads in counseling individuals. In P. B. Pedersen, J. G. Draguns, W. J. Lonner, & J. E. Trimble (Eds.), *Counseling across cultures* (6th ed., pp. 21–36). Thousand Oaks, CA, US: Sage Publications.

Draguns, J. G., & Tanaka-Matsumi, J. (2003). Assessment of psychopathology across and within cultures: Issues and findings. *Behaviour Research and Therapy, 41,* 755–794.

Ellenberger, H. E. (1970). *The discovery of the unconscious. The history and evolution of dynamic psychiatry.* New York: Basic Books.

Evans, I. M., & Paewai, K. (1999). Functional analysis in a bicultural context. *Behaviour Change, 16,* 20–36.

Eysenck, H. J. (1952). The effect of psychotherapy: An evaluation. *Journal of Consulting Psychology, 16,* 319–324.

Friedman, S., Braunstein, J. W., & Halpern, B. (2006). Cognitive behavioral treatment of panic disorder and agoraphobia in a multiethnic urban outpatient clinic: Initial presentation and treatment outcome. *Cognitive and Behavioral Practice, 13,* 282–292.

Frank, J. D., & Frank, J. B. (1991). *Persuasion and healing: A comparative study of psychotherapy* (3rd rev.ed.). Baltimore, MD: Johns Hopkins University Press.

Gerstein, L. H., Heppner, P. P., Stockton, R., Leong, F. T. L., & Aegisdottir, S. (2009). The counselling profession in- and outside the United States. In L. H. Gerstein, P. P. Heppner, A. Aegisdottir, & A. A. Leung (Eds.), *International handbook of cross-cultural counseling. Cultural assumptions and practices worldwide* (pp. 53–67). Thousand Oaks, CA: Sage.

Gielen, U. P., Draguns, J. D., & Fish, J. M. (Eds.) (2008). *Principles of multicultural counseling and therapy.* New York: Routledge.

Gielen, U. P., Fish, J. M., & Draguns, J. G. (Eds.) (2004). *Handbook of culture, therapy, and healing.* Mahwah, NJ: Lawrence Erlbaum Associates.

Griner, D., & Smith, T. B. (2006). Culturally adapted mental health interventions. A meta-analytic review. *Psychotherapy: Theory, Research, Practice, Training, 43*, 531–548.

Hall, G. C. N. (2001). Psychotherapy research with ethnic minorities: Empirical, ethical, and conceptual issues. *Journal of Consulting and Clinical Psychology, 69*, 502–510.

Hall, J. (2006). Working in cross-cultural and international settings. In J. Hall & S. Llewelyn (Eds.), *What is clinical psychology?* (4th ed., pp. 313–330). Oxford: Oxford University Press.

Hall, J. E., & Lunt, I. (2005). Global mobility for psychologists: The role of psychology organizations in the United States, Canada, Europe, and other regions. *American Psychologist, 60*, 712–726.

Hansen, N. D., Randazzo, K. V., Schwartz, A., Marshall, M., Kalis, D., Fraziet, R., ... Norvig, G. (2006). Do we practice what we preach? An exploratory survey of multicututral psychotherapy competencies. *Professional Psychology: Research and Practice, 37*, 66–77.

Hayes, S. C., & Toarmino, D. (1995). If behavioral principles are generally applicable, why is it necessary to understand cultural diversity? *The Behavior Therapist, 18*, 21–23.

Haynes, S. H., & O'Brien, W. H. (1990). Functional analysis in behavior therapy. *Clinical Psychology Review, 10*, 649–668.

Hays, P. A. (2008). *Addressing cultural complexities in practice: A framework for clinicians & counselors* (2nd ed.). Washington, DC: American Psychological Association.

Hays, P. A., & Iwamasa, G. Y. (Eds.). (2006). *Culturally responsive cognitive behavioral therapy: Assessment, practice, and supervision.* Washington, DC: American Psychological Association.

Heppner, P. P. (2006). The benefits and challenges of becoming cross-culturally competent counseling psychologists: Presidential address. *Counseling Psychologist, 34*, 147–172.

Higginbotham, H. N. (1984). *Third world challenge to psychiatry: Culture accommodation and mental health care.* Honolulu: University Press of Hawaii.

Hinton, D. E., Chhean, D., Pich, V., Safren, S. A., Hofmann, S. G., & Pollack, M. H. (2005). A randomized controlled trial for cognitive-behavior therapy for Cambodian refugees with treatment-resistant PTSD and panic attacks: A cross-over design. *Journal of Traumatic Stress, 18*, 617–629.

Hinton, D. E., & Otto, M. W. (2006). Symptom presentation and symptom meaning among traumatized Cambodian refugees: Relevance to a somatically focused cognitive-behavior therapy. *Cognitive and Behavioral Practice, 13*, 249–260.

Hinton, D., Safren, S. A., Pollack, M. H., & Tran, M. (2006). Cognitive-behavior therapy for Vietnamese refugees with PTSD and comorbid panic attacks. *Cognitive and Behavioral Practice, 13*, 271–281.

Hofmann, S. G. (2006). The importance of culture in cognitive and behavioral practice. *Cognitive and Behavioral Practice, 13*, 243–245.

Hofstede, G. (2001). *Culture's consequences: Comparing values, behaviors, institutions, and organizations across nations* (2nd ed.). Beverly Hills, CA: Sage.

Hwang, W. C. (2006). The psychotherapy adaptation and modification framework: Application to Asian Americans. *American Psychologist, 61*, 702–715.

Hwang, W. C., & Wood, J. J. (2006). Cognitive-behavioral therapy with Chinese Americans: Research, theory, and clinical practice. *Cognitive and Behavioral Practice, 13*, 293–303.

Iwamasa, G. Y., Hsia, C., & Hinton, D. (2006). Cognitive-behavioral therapy with Asian Americans. In P. A. Hays & G. Y. Iwamasa (Eds.), *Culturally responsive cognitive-behavioral therapy: Assessment, practice, and supervision* (pp. 117–140). Washington, DC: American Psychological Association.

Kazdin, A. E. (2006). Assessment and evaluation in clinical practice. In C. D. Goodheart, A. E. Kazdin, & R. J. Sternberg (Eds.), *Evidence-based psychotherapy: Where practice and research meet* (pp. 153–178). Washington, DC: American Psychological Association.

Keith, K. D. (2000). Cross-cultural perspectives on quality of life. In K. D. Keith & R. L. Schalock (Eds.), *Cross-cultural perspectives on quality of life* (pp. 363–380). Washington, DC: American Association on Mental Retardation.

Kleinman, A. M. (1980). *Patients and healers in the context of culture.* Berkeley: University of California Press.

La Roche, M. J. (2005). The cultural context and the psychotherapeutic process: Toward a culturally sensitive psychotherapy. *Journal of Psychotherapy Integration, 15,* 169–185.

La Roche, M., & Christopher, M. S. (2008). Culture and empirically supported treatments: On the road to a collision? *Culture and Psychology, 14,* 333–356.

La Roche, M. J., D'Angelo, E., Gualdron, L., & Leavell, J. (2006). Culturally sensitive guided imagery for allocentric Latinos: A pilot study. *Psychotherapy: Theory, Research, Training, 43,* 555–560.

Marsella, A. J. (1998). Toward a "global-community psychology": Meeting the needs of a changing world. *American Psychologist, 53,* 1282–1291.

Marsella, A. J. (2009). Diversity in a global era: The context and consequences of differences. *Counseling Psychology Quarterly, 22,* 119–135.

Matsumoto, D., & Juang, L. (2008). *Culture and psychology* (4th ed.). Belmont, CA: Thomson/ Wadsworth.

Miranda, J., Bernal, G., Lau, A., Kohn, L., Hwang, W. C., & LaFromboise, T. (2005). State of the science on psychosocial interventions for ethnic minorities. *Annual Review of Clinical Psychology, 1,* 113–142.

Mitamura, T., & Tanaka-Matsumi, J. (2009). School-negotiation training for parents of developmentally disabled children: A functional assertiveness training. *Japanese Journal of Behavior Therapy, 35,* 257–270.

Moodley, R., & West, W. (Eds.). (2005). *Integrating traditional healing practices into counseling and psychotherapy.* Thousand Oaks, CA: Sage.

Nathan, P. E., & Gorman, J. (2006). *A guide to treatments that work.* New York: Oxford University Press.

Nathan, P. E., Stuart, S. P., & Dolan, S. L. (2000). Research on psychotherapy efficacy and effectiveness: Between Scylla and Charybdis? *Psychological Bulletin, 126,* 964–981.

Nezu, A. M., Nezu, C. M., Friedman, S. H., & Haynes, S. N. (1997). Case formulation in behavior therapy: Problem solving and functional analytic strategies. In T. D. Eells (Ed.), *Handbook of psychotherapy case formulation* (pp. 368–401). New York: Guilford.

Nicolas, G., Arntz, D. L., Hirsch, B., & Schmiedigen, A. (2009). Cultural adaptation of a group treatment for Haitian Americans. *Professional Psychology: Research and Practice. 40,* 378–384.

Norcross, J. C., Hedges, M., & Prochaska, J. O. (2002). The face of 2010: A Delphi poll on the future of psychotherapy. *Professional Psychology: Research and Practice, 33,* 316–322.

Oei, T. P. S. (Ed.). (1998). *Behaviour therapy and cognitive behaviour therapy in Asia.* Glebe, Australia: Edumedia Pty Ltd.

Okazaki, S., & Tanaka-Matsumi, J. (2006). Cultural considerations in cognitive-behavioral assessment. In P. Hays & G. Y. Iwamasa (Eds.), *Culturally responsive cognitive-behavioral therapy: Assessment, practice, and supervision* (pp. 247–266). Washington, DC: American Psychological Association.

Otto, M. W., & Hinton, D. E. (2006). Modifying exposure-based CBT for Cambodian refugees with posttraumatic stress disorder. *Cognitive and Behavioral Practice, 13*, 261–270.

Parloff, M. B. (1986). Placebo controls in psychotherapy research: A sine qua non or a placebo for research problems? *Journal of Consulting and Clinical Psychology, 54*, 79–87.

Paul, G. L. (1966). *Insight vs. desensitization in psychotherapy*. Stanford, CA: Stanford University Press.

Paul, G. L. (1967). Strategy of outcome research in psychotherapy. *Journal of Consulting Psychology, 31*, 109–118.

Pedersen, P. B. (1997). *Culture-centered counseling interventions: Striving for accuracy*. Thousand Oaks, CA: Sage.

Pedersen, P. B. (2002). Ethics, competence, and other professional issues in culture-centered counseling. In P. B. Pedersen, J. G. Draguns, W. J. Lonner, & J. E. Trimble (Eds.), *Counseling across cultures* (5th ed., pp. 3–28). Thousand Oaks, CA: Sage.

Pedersen, P. B., Draguns, J. G., Lonner, W. J., & Trimble, J. E. (Eds.). (2008). *Counseling across cultures* (6th ed.). Thousand Oaks, CA: Sage.

Persons, J. B., & Tompkins, M. A. (1997). Cognitive behavioral case formulation. In T. D. Eells (Ed.), *Handbook of psychotherapy case formulation* (pp. 314–339). New York: Guilford Press.

Prince, R. (1980). Variations in psychotherapeutic procedures. In H. C. Triandis & J. G. Draguns (Eds.), *Handbook of cross-cultural psychology: Vol. 6. Psychopathology* (pp. 291–350). Boston, MA: Allyn & Bacon.

Qian, M., & Wang, A. (2005). The development of behavioral therapy and cognitive behavioral therapy in P. R. China. *Japanese Journal of Behavior Therapy, 31*, 111–126.

Ridley, C. R. (2005). *Overcoming unintentional racism in counseling and psychotherapy* (2nd ed.). Thousand Oaks, CA: Sage.

Ridley, C. R., Li, L. C., & Hill, C. L. (1998). Multicultural assessment: Reexamination, reconceptualization, and practical application. *Counseling Psychologist, 26*, 827–910.

Roth, A., & Fonagy, P. (2004). *What works for whom? A critical review of psychotherapy research* (2nd ed.). New York: Guilford.

Schulz, P. M., Huber, L. C., & Resick, P. A. (2006). Practical adaptations of cognitive processing therapy with Bosnian refugees: Implications for adapting practice to a multicultural clientele. *Cognitive and Behavioral Practice, 13*, 343–344.

Snowden, L. R., & Yamada, A. M. (2005). Cultural differences in access to care. *Annual Review of Clinical Psychology, 1*, 143–166.

Stumpf, R. E., Higa-McMillan, C. K., & Chorpita, B. F. (2009). Implementation of evidence-based services for youth. *Behavior Modification, 33*, 48–65.

Sue, S. (1998). In search of cultural competence in psychotherapy and counseling. *American Psychologist, 53*, 440–448.

Sue, D., & Sue, D. M. (2008a). *Foundations of counseling and psychotherapy: Evidence-based practices for a diverse society*. Hoboken, NJ: John Wiley & Sons.

Sue, D. W., & Sue, D. (2008b). *Counseling the culturally diverse: Theory and practice* (5th ed.). New York: John Wiley & Sons.

Tanaka-Matsumi, J. (2001). Abnormal psychology and culture. In D. Matsumoto (Ed.), *Handbook of culture and psychology* (pp. 256–286). New York: Oxford University Press.

Tanaka-Matsumi, J. (2004a). Japanese forms of psychotherapy: Naikan therapy and Morita therapy. In U. P. Gielen, J. M. Fish, & J. G. Draguns (Eds.), *Handbook of culture, therapy, and healing* (pp. 277–291). Mahwah, NJ: Lawrence Erlbaum Associates.

Tanaka-Matsumi, J. (2004b). Behavioral assessment and individual differences. In M. Hersen, S. Haynes, & E. M. Heiby (Eds.), *The comprehensive handbook of assessment. Vol. 3: Behavioral assessment* (pp. 359–393). New York: John Wiley.

Tanaka-Matsumi, J. (2008). Functional approaches to evidence-based practice in multicultural counseling and therapy. In U. P. Gielen, J. G. Draguns, & J. M. Fish (Eds.), *Principles of Multicultural Counseling and Therapy* (pp.169–198). Routledge.

Tanaka-Matsumi, J., & Draguns, J. G. (1997). Culture and psychopathology. In J. Berry, M. Segall, & Ç. Kağitçibaşi (Eds.), *Handbook of cross-cultural psychology, Vol. 3: Social psychology, personality and psychopathology* (2nd ed., pp. 449–491). Boston, MA: Allyn & Bacon.

Tanaka-Matsumi, J., Higginbotham, H. N., & Chang, R. (2002). Cognitive behavioral approaches to counseling across cultures: A functional analytic approach for clinical applications. In P. B. Pedersen, J. G. Draguns, W. J. Lonner, & J. E. Trimble (Eds.), *Counseling across cultures* (5th ed. pp. 337–354). Thousand Oaks, CA: Sage.

Tanaka-Matsumi, J., Seiden, D., & Lam, K. (1996). The Culturally Informed Functional Assessment (CIFA) interview: A strategy for cross-cultural behavioral practice. *Cognitive and Behavioral Practice, 3*, 215–233.

Ullmann, L. P., & Krasner, L. (1975). *A psychological approach to abnormal behavior* (2nd ed.) Englewood Cliffs, NJ: Prentice-Hall.

U.S. Census Bureau (2002, November). *Demographic trends in the 20th century: Census 2000 special reports*. Retrieved July 11, 2009, from http:// www.census.gov / prod/ 2002pubs / censr-4.pdf.

Van de Vijver, F. J. R., & Tanaka-Matsumi, J. (2008). Cross-cultural research methods. In D. McKay (Ed.), *Handbook of research methods in abnormal and clinical psychology* (463–481). Thousand Oaks, CA: Sage.

Weiss, M. G., Doongaji, D. R., Siddhartha, S., Wypij, D., Pathare, S., Bhatawdekar, M., ... Fernandes, R. (1992). The Explanatory Model Interview Catalogue (EMIC) contribution to cross-cultural research methods from a study of leprosy and mental health. *British Journal of Psychiatry, 160*, 819–830.

Weisz, J. R., Doss, A. J., & Hawley, K. M. (2005). Youth psychotherapy outcome research: A review and critique of the evidence base. *Annual Review of Psychology, 56*, 337–363.

Wolpe, J. (1958). *Psychotherapy by reciprocal inhibition*. Stanford, CA: Stanford University Press.

Zoellner, L. A., Feeny, N. C., Fitzgibbons, L. A., & Foa, E. B. (1999). Responses of African American and Caucasian women to cognitive behavioral therapy for PTSD. *Behavior Therapy, 30*, 581–595.

# 15

# Evidence-Based Interventions for Culturally Diverse Children and Adolescents*
## The Case of Mexican American Youth

### Kristen McCabe and Allison Christian

As noted in Chapter 24 of this volume, the United States is a diverse country comprising many subcultures. Of these, Latinos are the largest ethnic minority group, representing 15% of the total population (U.S. Census Bureau, 2007). Among Latinos, Mexican Americans constitute the largest subgroup, at 64% of U.S. Latinos (U.S. Census Bureau, 2009). Developing effective mental health services for the Mexican American population is an urgent public health priority (Bernal & Sáez-Santiago, 2006; Vega & Lopez, 2001). Mexican American children are a particularly large group, given that the median age of Mexican Americans is 25 years, a full 10 years younger than the non-Hispanic White (NHW) population (U.S. Census Bureau, 2007). Thus, Mexican American children are a large and growing segment of the U.S. population.

Furthermore, Mexican American children have particularly high rates of mental health needs. Mexican American youth have higher rates of conduct disorder (Vazsonyi & Flannery, 1997), delinquency (Farrington, 1987; Rutter & Giller, 1983), anxiety disorders (Glover, Pumariega, Holzer, Wise, & Rodriguez, 1999), depression (Hill, Bush & Roosa, 2003; Joiner, Perez, Wagner, Berenson & Marquina, 2001; Wight, Aneshensel, Botticello & Sepúlveda, 2005), school dropout (National Center for Educational Statistics, 2003), and drug use and suicide (Grunbaum et al., 2004; Swanson, Linskey, Quintero-Salinas, Pumariega, & Holzer, 1992) compared with NHWs. However, despite this elevated need for mental health services, Latino youth are less likely to receive such services, more likely to receive low-quality services, less likely to receive evidence-based treatments (EBTs), and more likely to drop out of treatment prematurely than NHWs (McCabe, 2002; McCabe et al., 1999; U.S. DHHS, 2001; Villalba, 2007). Mexican Americans as a subgroup are also underrepresented in care and are more likely to receive poor-quality care (Abreu & Sasaki, 2004; Bein, Torres, & Kurilla, 2000; Kataoka et al., 2002; Vega, Kolody, & Aguilar-Gaxiola, 2001). Given this combination of high need and low service utilization,

Mexican American youth are a population in great need of high-quality culturally sensitive mental health services.

Unfortunately, the evidence base regarding effective mental health services for Mexican American youth has lagged far behind the need for those services. Clinical trials of psychosocial interventions have historically not included sufficient numbers of Mexican Americans or other Latino subgroups to allow generalization of findings to those populations, leaving doubt as to whether existing EBTs are as effective with Mexican Americans as with NHWs. Some researchers have suggested that, because many EBTs have yet to demonstrate equivalent outcomes with ethnic minority families to those found in studies with Caucasians, the widespread use of standard EBTs with ethnic minorities may be premature (Piña, Silverman, Fuentes, Kurtines, & Weems, 2003; Polo & López, 2009; Wood, Chui, Hwang, Jacobs & Ifekwunigwe, 2008). These researchers point to the comparatively poorer outcomes from community-based effectiveness studies that include greater ethnic diversity than most clinical trials in support of this argument (e.g., Chambless & Ollendick, 2001), and conclude that EBTs are likely to require significant adaptations to be effective with ethnic minority families (Bernal, Bonilla, & Bellido, 1995; Hall, 2001).

## Why Might EBTs Need to Be Modified for Mexican Americans?

Arguments that EBTs may need to be modified to be effective with Mexican Americans have been based on research indicating that a range of factors important to the way Mexican American families engage with and respond to psychosocial interventions for children differ significantly from the norm found in NHW populations. For example, Latino culture has been described as family oriented (Rogler & Cooney, 1984; Zayas, 1993; Zinn, 1982), hierarchical (Fontes, 2002), collectivistic (John, Resendiz, & De Vargas, 1997), traditional in regard to gender roles (Shapiro & Simonsen, 1994), and as placing a high degree of value on warm interpersonal relationships, or *personalismo* (Santiago-Rivera, Arredondo, & Gallardo-Cooper, 2002). Although there is a great deal of variability in the degree to which individual Latino families fit this description, these cultural characteristics have important implications for psychotherapy. With the exception of *personalismo*, all these factors have been found to be associated with less help seeking (Acosta, Yamamoto, & Evans, 1982; Santiago-Rivera et al, 2002; Shapiro & Simonsen, 1994). For example, the value that many Latinos place on family may lead to a great deal of support from family members, but also may contribute to the fact that Latinos are more likely to turn to family members for help with their child's problems, as opposed to professionals outside the family (Forehand & Kotchick, 1996; Parra-Cardona, Córdova, Holtrop, Villarruel, & Wieling, 2008;

Rogler, Malgady, & Rodriguez, 1989). Turning to family members as a resource may mean Latinos are less open to ideas and suggestions that are not congruent with the current practice within their family. A qualitative study of Mexican American parents of children receiving mental health services supported this view. McCabe, Yeh, Garland, Lau, and Chavez (2005) found that over half of those parents were strongly discouraged from seeking mental health services for their child by a family member, often a grandparent or spouse, who believed that the child did not have a mental health problem, treatment would not work, or that seeking treatment reflected badly on the family.

Latinos may also differ from NHWs in how they define mental disorders, and which child problems they consider to be mental health problems as opposed to disciplinary or physical health problems. Yeh, Hough, McCabe, Lau, and Garland (2004) interviewed a large multiethnic sample of parents whose children had identified mental health problems about what they felt the causes of those problems were. Latino parents were less likely than NHW parents to endorse causes for their child's problems that were consistent with biopsychosocial beliefs about mental illness, the belief system that is most prevalent in Western mental health treatment. An extension of this study revealed that the relative lack of endorsement of biopsychosocial beliefs about the causes for mental health problems explained a significant portion of service underutilization by Latino families (Yeh et al., 2005). Research has found Latinos often endorse folk illness and physical illness as causes of problems, which is related to seeking fewer mental health services (Acosta, Yamamoto & Evans, 1982; Shapiro & Simonsen, 1994; Vazquez-Nuttal, Avila-Vivas & Morales-Barreto, 1984) and may favor spiritual/folk healers (Zea, Quezada & Belgrave, 1994) and medical doctors (Vega, Kolody, Aguilar-Gaxiola, & Catalano, 1999) over mental health professionals. Latino parents who do not consider their child's behavior problems to be a mental health issue may be less likely to seek psychological services to aid them with those problems, may be less open to referrals to mental health services, and may be less likely to engage with those services that they do receive. It is possible that the stigma associated with mental illness, which has been found to predict treatment dropout (Bein et al., 2000; Levine & Padilla, 1980; Rogler et al., 1989), could also be related to the ways in which parents define children's problems.

Latinos also face a number of other attitudinal barriers to accessing and benefiting from child mental health services. Lack of knowledge about services and what to expect from them may result in fears about seeking treatment; while mismatches between expectations and treatment received may lead to premature dropout (Bein et al. 2000; Keefe & Casas, 1980). Research suggests many Mexican American families are unaware of services (e.g., Rogler et al., 1989). In one study, when asked why many Latino families do not seek mental health services for their children, parents cited lack of knowledge about available services as an important factor, in addition to stigma and desire to deal with problems "within the family" (McCabe et al., 2005). In another study, McCabe (2002) found that parents who were less educated, who felt that emotional/behavioral problems should be handled within the family, and who felt that increased discipline was the appropriate response to children's emotional/behavior problems, were also more likely to terminate therapy after one session. In addition, parents who had more perceived barriers to treatment, and who expected their child to recover quickly, were more likely to drop out of treatment.

A larger, quantitative study of the barriers experienced by Latino families who had a child with significant mental health needs (Yeh, McCabe, Hough, Dupuis, & Hazen, 2003) further elucidated the practical and attitudinal barriers that Latino families face when seeking mental health services for their child. This study found that the most frequently cited barriers to treatment were concerns about what might happen in treatment (e.g., services would not be confidential), followed by the belief that services would not be helpful or effective, practical barriers such as lack of transportation, child care, or ability to pay, and stigma. A smaller, but significant proportion (18%) were discouraged from seeking services by language barriers. Thus, negative attitudes toward psychotherapy, and lack of knowledge about psychotherapy, may play a role in discouraging Latino families from seeking treatment, and distrust of services may lead to poorer engagement in treatment.

Parenting style is another important factor that has been found to differ across Mexican Americans and NHWs, and which has the potential to affect the way Mexican American families respond to many child and family psychosocial treatments, particularly those that are parent-mediated. Research on Latino parenting paints a somewhat contradictory picture. For example, Latino cultures have been described as placing a high value on family closeness and interconnectedness or *familismo*, respect, and obedience to authority (Fontes, 2002; Parra-Cardona et al., 2008; Wilkinson, 1987). This cultural value is consistent with research that has found the authoritarian parenting style to be more prevalent among Latino families, which emphasizes obedience and family loyalty, in contrast to Caucasian parents who tend to value independence and assertiveness in their children (Calzada & Eyberg, 2002; Domenech Rodríguez, Donovick, & Crowley, 2009; Darling & Steinberg, 1993; Hammer & Turner, 1990). Latino parents have been reported to be more likely than Caucasian parents to use direct demands, physical punishment such as spanking, and criticism (MacPhee, Fritz, & Miller-Heyl, 1996).

In contrast to findings which suggest greater authoritarianism among Latino families, other studies have described Latino and Mexican American parents as high in warmth and nurturance (Vega, 1990), permissiveness (Carlson, Uppal, & Prosser, 2000; Chilman, 1993; Radziszewka, Richardson, Dent, & Flay, 1996; Vega, 1995), or authoritative parenting style (Domenech Rodríguez et al., 2009). Some researchers suggest stricter parenting and hostile control are only more common among less acculturated Mexican Americans (Buriel, 1993; Chun & Akutsu, 2003; Hill, Bush & Roosa, 2003). This could be due to more individualistic and egalitarian views of parenting; more knowledge of alternative, less coercive forms of discipline (Parke et al., 2004); and to the relatively higher income and education levels of more acculturated Mexican Americans. For example, when controlling for factors such as education level, financial difficulties, and parenting stress, Rodriguez (2007) and Uno, Florsheim, and Uchino (1998) found Mexican American and European American parents were equally likely to engage in harsh parenting. Some suggest the commonly used parenting categories (Baumrind, 1967) are not appropriate for Latinos and Mexican Americans. Rather, they believe Latinos/Mexican Americans fall into their own category of supportive yet harsh parenting (Buriel, 1993; Chun & Akutsu, 2003; Manongdo & Ramírez García, 2007). Although these cultural differences in parenting style have the potential to either increase or reduce fit with existing EBTs, the fact that EBTs were largely developed based on experience with NHW families makes it more likely that parenting styles differing from the NHW average will be a poor fit for existing treatments.

Finally, the ways in which symptoms are expressed differ significantly across cultures. For instance, Mexican Americans experience more psychosomatic problems than other ethnicities (Laval, Gomez, & Ruiz, 1989; Piña & Silverman, 2004; Varela et al., 2004). Furthermore, Mexican Americans may also experience culture-bound syndromes, defined by the DSM-IV TR (American Psychiatric Association, 2000) as "recurrent, locality-specific patterns of aberrant behavior and troubling experiences that may or may not be linked to a particular DSM-IV diagnostic category" (p. 898). Many of these patterns are indigenously considered to be "illnesses," or at least afflictions, and most have local names. An example of a culture-bound syndrome that is found among Mexican Americans is *ataque de nervios*, a syndrome that does not correspond to any DSM-IV TR diagnosis, but which can include symptoms of depression, anxiety, dissociation, and seizures or fainting (American Psychiatric Association, 2000). Although this syndrome has been studied less in children than adults, recent studies confirm that it is quite common among children (Guarnaccia, Canino, Rubio-Stipec, & Bravo, 1993) and has been found to relate to impairment and psychiatric problems in a child population. It is quite possible that symptoms of other disorders may also be experienced and expressed differently among Mexican Americans.

## Can EBTs Work for Mexican Americans Without Modifications?

The range of cultural differences described in the previous section that may have an influence on engagement and benefit from psychotherapy would seem to suggest that EBTs are unlikely to be effective with Mexican American families without significant modification. However, The Surgeon General's report on *Mental Health, Culture, Race, and Ethnicity* (U.S. DHHS, 2001) concludes that in general, EBTs still represent the best treatments available to ethnic minorities, and what is needed is an understanding of when these EBTs should be used with minority groups in standard form, when they require significant cultural modifications to be effective, and when they may be contraindicated for specific cultural groups. Recently, some have begun to argue that there are reasons to believe that EBTs may well be effective with Mexican Americans and other ethnic minority groups. These theorists argue that it is not feasible to develop separate treatments for each subgroup and each disorder and that the behavioral principles (e.g., reinforcing child behavior with praise or consistently applying a time-out from reinforcement following child noncompliance) that underlie many EBTs are likely to be universal, or at least apply across a wide range of different cultures (e.g., Kazdin, 2008). They point out that therapists are trained to tailor EBTs to the individual client; working with a client from a cultural group for which the EBT was not originally designed, and adapting language, involvement of multiple family members, and ethnicity/culture of the client may simply represent a form of such tailoring (Kazdin, 2008).

Several recent reviews (Ho, McCabe, Yeh, & Lau, in press; Huey & Polo, 2008; Miranda et al., 2005) have concluded that when EBTs have been tested with ethnic minority families without cultural modifications, they have usually been found to be effective with those groups. However, the evidence base is far from complete, and many EBT/ethnic minority group combinations remain to be tested. Furthermore, evidence pertaining to ethnic subgroups, such as Mexican Americans, is particularly sparse. Below, we describe several psychosocial interventions that have been tested with Mexican Americans and other Latinos that exemplify different approaches to addressing cultural factors. The studies reviewed here are not an exhaustive list of interventions that have been tested with Mexican Americans; rather, they can be considered examples of interventions that have been evaluated with this ethnic group to date.

## Identifying EBTs for Mexican American/Latino Children and Families

We reviewed published controlled clinical trials to select examples of evidence-based psychosocial treatments for emotional and conduct problems that have been evaluated with Mexican American youth. To be consistent with recent reviews (e.g., Huey & Polo, 2008), we did not include interventions involving (a) medication only, (b) reading only, (c) teaching/tutoring focus only, and (d) relocation only (e.g., moving child to a foster placement). We described trials that included a substantial number of Mexican Americans or Latinos in their sample (i.e., more than 25 Mexican American participants). Finally, the treatments reviewed have been evaluated with "well-conducted" trials with clear inclusion/exclusion criteria, appropriate control or comparison conditions, random assignment, reliable measures to assess outcomes, and clearly described statistical procedures (Brestan & Eyberg, 1998).

These procedures led to the isolation of a group of studies that examined interventions with Latino/Mexican American children and families that varied along a continuum of cultural modification. It is important to note that all of the studies reviewed utilized some form of cultural modification. We have classified the studies according to the following criteria:

1   Minimal cultural modification: Studies included in this category involved relatively few formal modifications to the original intervention. For example, in these studies the treatment may have been provided by bilingual and bicultural providers, who presumably would have made adjustments to their language and interpersonal styles that may have been more congruent with those of their Latino clients. They may also have translated the intervention and related materials into Spanish, delivered the intervention in a space decorated to reflect Latino culture, or provided toys to children that would be culturally familiar. However, these studies did not systematically alter the treatment manual or intervention procedures in any way to address cultural needs of Latino children and families.

2   Culturally modified treatments (CMTs): CMTs have gone beyond treatment delivery by bilingual/bicultural providers and translation into Spanish, and have systematically adapted the treatment protocol to meet the cultural needs of Latino families. These modifications are reflected in the treatment manual and the culturally modified version is clearly distinguishable from the standard version of the intervention.

3   Culture-specific treatments (CSTs): CSTs are treatments that have been designed with a particular cultural group in mind from their inception. Although these treatments may rely on principles from therapeutic traditions that began with other cultural groups, the treatment offered has been constructed from the ground up with Latino/Mexican American families in mind. Cultural considerations pervade both the delivery of the treatment and the core concepts, goals, and techniques used in the treatment.

## Minimal cultural modification

### School-based child-centered play therapy (CCPT)

Garza and Bratton (2005) conducted one of the few studies to examine the efficacy of a psychosocial intervention for Mexican Americans with minimal cultural modifications. This study randomly assigned 30 Mexican American children in kindergarten through fifth grade who were referred to school counseling for behavior problems to receive 15 weeks of child-centered play therapy or curriculum-based small-group counseling. Both groups received their respective interventions in

Spanish and English, and toys for play therapy were specially chosen to be culturally familiar to Mexican American children. The CCPT protocol focused on principles that included creating an accepting environment, encouraging self-directed
play, decision making, problem solving, following the child's lead, reflecting
thoughts, feelings, and behaviors, enhancing child self-esteem, and setting therapeutic limits. At post-treatment, children assigned to CCPT had significantly
lower parent- and teacher-reported externalizing, but not internalizing problems
compared with controls.

### Schools and Homes in Partnership (SHIP) program

Already shown to be effective among Caucasian children, the comprehensive
intervention program SHIP was examined among a sample of 284 elementary-
aged schoolchildren exhibiting aggressive behaviors and reading difficulties
(Barrera et al., 2002). Of the 284 participants, 116 were Mexican American, 52
were non-Mexican Latinos, and 116 were Caucasian. Bilingual therapists and
Spanish-language assessments were used, because a majority of the families primarily spoke Spanish (85%). In comparison to a no-treatment control condition,
children who received cognitive behavioral therapy (CBT), extra reading instruction, and had parents who received training in behavior management exhibited
fewer aggressive social behaviors post-treatment. A year later, parents from the
intervention group reported less coercion and fewer anti-social behaviors among
their children. The Latino children benefited equally from the intervention compared to European Americans with one exception: teachers reported fewer internalizing difficulties among European American students post-treatment, but not
for Latino students.

## Culturally modified treatments

### Guiando a Ninos Activos (GANA)

McCabe and colleagues (2005) developed a culturally adapted version of parent–
child interaction therapy (PCIT; Eyberg & members of the Child Study Laboratory,
1999), an evidence-based psychosocial treatment for young children (ages 3–7
years) with externalizing behavior problems that has demonstrated efficacy across
a number of clinical trials. The adaptation process involved gathering information
regarding potential cultural adaptations to PCIT from the clinical literature, the
empirical literature, expert opinion, and qualitative data collected from Mexican
American parents and therapists. The proposed modifications were reviewed by a
group of researchers with expertise in the adaptation of mental health treatments,
a panel of Mexican American therapists who work clinically with Mexican
American families, and Sheila Eyberg, the creator of PCIT.

The resulting GANA program adopted a public health approach (Bruce, Smith,
Miranda, Hoagwood, & Wells, 2002; U.S. DHHS, 2001), in which the program

provider plays an active role in engaging families in the program, addressing barriers to participation, and preventing treatment dropout. In addition, the GANA program recognizes that Mexican Americans are heterogeneous, such that adaptations that might enhance the program for one family would actually decrease fit for another. To ensure that parenting experts are able to tailor the GANA program to the needs of individual families, a detailed assessment of a number of culturally influenced concepts that may have an important effect on how parents respond to the program is conducted in the first session. For example, parents are asked to provide information on their conceptualization of their child's problems, their beliefs about the causes of their child's problems, the role of extended family members in raising the child, beliefs about discipline, attitudes and expectations for the program, and use of alternative treatments (a complete list can be found in McCabe et al., 2005). These concepts are referenced throughout treatment so that the program can be presented in ways congruent with the parents' belief system about the causes of their children's problems and the types of intervention that they believe will be helpful. In addition, some constructs are assessed continuously throughout treatment because they may change, such as the degree to which an extended family member is supportive or unsupportive of the child's participation in the program, so that the therapist will be able to address changes as they occur and before a family drops out. Other adaptations to the program include: (a) framing the program as an educational/skill building intervention to reduce the stigma associated with seeking "mental health services"; (b) showing families two 15-minute videotape presentations that describe the phases of the program and show examples of families in PCIT sessions (Zebell & Urquiza, 2002a, 2002b) before treatment to reduce unrealistic expectations that have been found to predict treatment dropout for Mexican American families (McCabe, 2002); (c) increasing therapist training about Mexican American culture; (d) giving GANA therapists extra time during each session to focus on rapport building and training in establishing rapport with Mexican Americans; (e) eliciting complaints during each session to ensure that respect for authority does not prevent the parent from voicing complaints that, left unaddressed, might lead to treatment dropout; (f) translating and simplifying written handouts used in each session of PCIT, as well as including pictures of Mexican American families engaged in PCIT so that parents could more readily identify with the examples; and (g) implementing a comprehensive engagement protocol based on the approach of McKay, Stoewe, McCadam, and Gonzales (1998) that explicitly targets mothers, fathers, and grandparents.

Finally, a randomized controlled trial (RCT) was conducted in which 58 Mexican American families whose 3- to 7-year-old child suffered from clinically significant behavior problems were randomly assigned to receive either GANA, standard PCIT, or treatment as usual (TAU; McCabe & Yeh, 2009). Ninety-three percent (N = 54) of families completed a post-treatment assessment. All three treatment approaches produced significant pre–post improvement in conduct problems across a wide variety of parent-report measures. GANA produced results that were significantly superior to TAU across a wide variety of both parent-report and observational indices; however, GANA and PCIT did not differ significantly from one another. PCIT was superior to TAU on two of the parent-report indices and almost all of the observational indices. There were no significant differences among the three groups on treatment dropout, and families were more satisfied with both GANA and PCIT than with TAU. These data suggest that both PCIT and GANA are probably efficacious with Mexican American youth.

*Parent management training (PMT)*
Martinez and Eddy (2005) conducted a randomized controlled trial of PMT, culturally modified for Latino families, called *Nuestras Familias*. PMT, a highly effective intervention (Brestan & Eyberg, 1998), involves instruction, modeling, role playing, and home practice in order to increase encouragement, monitoring, discipline, and problem solving by parents. Researchers randomly assigned 73 Spanish-speaking Latino parents (90% Mexican American; 10% Central American) and their at-risk middle school-aged children to the intervention in a community setting or the control (no project-related services). PMT served as the core of the program, with aspects adapted to address specific needs of Latinos. Parents participated in 12 weekly, two and a half hour-long group sessions, and received notebooks, homework, and telephone calls for support and check-up. By the end of the study, 70% of families had completed a minimum of 10 sessions. The culturally modified version of PMT proved highly efficacious. Weekly parent satisfaction surveys indicated that 100% of participants found the intervention somewhat or very helpful, and intervention participation, attendance, and general satisfaction with the program were high. At termination of treatment, the intervention significantly improved general parenting, skill encouragement, and overall effective parenting as well as significantly decreased youth aggression, externalizing behaviors, and likelihood of smoking, and marginally decreasing drug use.

*Cognitive Behavioral Intervention for Trauma in Schools (CBITS)*
CBITS was developed by Jaycox (2000, as cited in Kataoka et al., 2003) for use with multicultural inner city youth with post-traumatic stress disorder, depression, and other anxiety symptoms related to community violence exposure. CBITS employs standard CBT techniques (i.e., education about reactions to trauma, relaxation training, cognitive therapy, real life exposure, stress or trauma exposure, and social problem solving) in an eight-session, school-based group format, with four two-hour optional multifamily group sessions offered to parents focused on immigration-related stressors and parenting. CBITS was offered to students as part of a package of school services designed to support immigrants. Participants were 199 students ages 10 to 15 years, 57% of whom were Mexican American, with the remainder from Central American countries. Sixty-seven youths were randomized to CBITS and 46 to the wait-list control; however, an

additional 85 students were assigned (non-randomly) to CBITs so they would have a chance to receive the intervention before the close of the school year. Significant improvements in depression and PTSD symptoms were observed among those who received the intervention at three-month follow-up relative to controls. However, Mexican Americans showed less improvement in symptoms than did other Latinos in the study, suggesting that modifications may need to be made to increase the fit of the intervention for Mexican Americans. In 2003 Stein et al. conducted a RCT of CBITS among 126 Mexican American sixth-grade students with a history of exposure to violence and clinically significant levels of PTSD. Compared with a wait-list control, children receiving group CBITS from school-based mental health providers had significantly lower levels of depression, PTSD symptoms, and psychosocial dysfunction, with results maintained at six months.

## Culture-specific treatments

*Cuento therapy*
Ramirez, Jain, Flores-Torres, Perez, and Carlson (2009) examined the effectiveness of *cuento* therapy on self-esteem, depression, anxiety, and reading test performance among 58 low-income Mexican American third-grade students between the ages of 8 and 10 referred for school failure. *Cuento* therapy, which uses cultural storytelling as a means of modeling pro-social behaviors, ideas, and thoughts in a culturally relevant manner, was originally developed by Constantino, Malgady, and Rogler (1986) for use with a Puerto Rican population. Following treatment, global, academic, and general self-esteem scores of the treatment group increased significantly and physiological anxiety decreased, while the control group had no change in the former, and an increase in the latter. There were no differences between treatment and control groups in terms of reading test performance—both increased post-study.

## Summary and Conclusions

Mexican Americans represent a large and growing segment of the child and adolescent population in the United States, with high rates of mental health needs and many barriers to receiving high-quality, culturally effective mental health services. Low rates of service utilization and high rates of treatment dropout as well as significant cultural differences in familial relationships, cultural values, parenting styles, and conceptualization of emotional and behavioral problems in children that exist between Mexican Americans and mainstream American culture suggest that interventionists must pay careful attention to the cultural fit of mainstream interventions with this cultural group. The field is just beginning to conduct studies that can provide guidance to practitioners on how to modify EBTs to maximize cultural fit for Mexican Americans. As this review demonstrates, some progress has been made in testing psychosocial interventions with Mexican Americans over the past decade.

Without exception, the studies described here made at least minimal modifications to the treatment being delivered to Mexican American or other Latino families; most often they used translation of intervention materials into Spanish, and bilingual and either bicultural or culturally knowledgeable therapists. Although in the absence of studies that compare culturally naïve, non-Spanish speaking therapists delivering the EBT to bilingual/bicultural therapists we cannot draw empirical conclusions regarding the importance of this feature, the field has assumed that employing therapists who can communicate effectively with their clients and have an understanding of the client's cultural background represents a minimal standard of culturally competent care. This is supported by findings of studies which indicate better client retention and outcomes for Mexican Americans when they are ethnically matched with their therapists (e.g., Flicker, Waldron, Turner, Brody, & Hops, 2008). In general, these studies have demonstrated that some interventions require only these minimal cultural modifications to be effective with Mexican American clients (e.g, Barrera et al., 2002; Garza & Bratton, 2005). However, it is important to keep in mind that, given the low number of bilingual/bicultural providers relative to the mental health needs of Mexican American and other Latino clients, this minimal standard is often unmet in usual clinical practice.

Other studies have gone beyond translation and the use of bilingual and bicultural therapists and have made more extensive cultural modifications that significantly alter the standard techniques and procedures of the EBT. These adaptations have generally retained the majority of the core features of the EBT, but have made notable modifications to the ways in which the treatments are presented to clients, techniques for engaging family members, treatment rationales, and/or orientation to treatment. Three such studies have specifically examined culturally modified EBTs with Mexican Americans. Two of these studies demonstrated positive outcomes comparable to those found in clinical trials for Caucasian families, Martinez & Eddy (2005) for PMT and McCabe & Yeh (in press) for PCIT. McCabe & Yeh (in press) additionally provided an important comparison between the culturally modified version of PCIT (GANA) and both standard PCIT and TAU. This design established that standard PCIT (which for the purposes of this review would be classified as using minimal cultural modification, because bilingual/bicultural therapists delivered the treatment) was highly effective for young children with behavior disorders, and although few differences were found between standard PCIT and TAU on parent report measures, standard PCIT was significantly superior to TAU on observational measures. GANA significantly outperformed TAU on both parent report and observational indices, but the differences between GANA and PCIT did not reach significance. This pilot study suggests modest advantages to cultural modification are possible, and future research should examine this issue with larger sample sizes. Furthermore, many of the modifications described in both of these studies are techniques or concepts that may generalize to other interventions and other ethnic groups, including Caucasian families. For example, the use of a general cultural assessment at the outset of treatment to inform the way in which the therapist presents particular concepts is one that could theoretically be applied to any ethnic group.

Finally, one study demonstrated positive outcomes for *cuento* therapy, a culture-specific psychotherapy for Mexican American youth (Ramirez, Jain, Flores-Torres, Perez, & Carlson, 2009). At first glance the approach of developing culture-specific treatments may seem like an arduous way of approaching the development of treatments that can be used in typical community clinics serving multicultural populations. However, much as EBTs that have been developed with largely Caucasian populations are beginning to demonstrate generalizability to other ethnic minority populations (sometimes with cultural modifications, and sometimes without), it may also be the case that interventions developed with a particular ethnic minority group in mind may one day generalize to Caucasian and other ethnic minority populations as well. Thus, the approach of developing an intervention within a specific cultural context may represent a way of bringing innovative ideas into the field that can then be tested with a wider array of ethnic groups.

This review demonstrates that important work is taking place to examine the efficacy of a range of psychosocial interventions for Mexican American families. Using a variety of different approaches, all of the studies described here make a contribution to our understanding of how to provide culturally effective psychotherapy to Mexican American youth. However, much work remains to be done. Clearly, the studies reviewed do not address the full range of EBTs that might be beneficial for Mexican Americans. Many clinical conditions have gone unstudied, and there are many gaps in the developmental stages of the children included in the trials. However, pursuing all three of these lines of research is likely to bear fruit in the future. Designs that compare these different approaches to one another are particularly important, because in the absence of such designs it is difficult to know whether cultural modifications have improved outcomes relative to standard treatments, or whether those outcomes may in fact be no better (or even worse; e.g., Kumpfer, Alvarado, Smith & Bellamy, 2002). Given the urgency of providing effective cultural mental health treatment to this large and growing segment of the population, this work is likely to have an important public health impact.

# Note

*   This research was supported by NIMH grant KO1MH1924 to Kristen McCabe.

# References

Abreu, J. M., & Sasaki, H. M. (2004). Physical and mental health concerns of Hispanics. In D. R. Atkinson (Ed.), *Counseling American minorities* (6th ed., pp. 300–316). New York: McGraw-Hill.

Acosta, F. X., Yamamoto, J., & Evans, L. A. (Eds.). (1982). *Effective psychotherapy for low-income minority patients*. New York, NY: Plenum.

American Psychiatric Association (2000). *Diagnostic and statistical manual of mental disorders* (4th ed., text revision). Washington, DC: Author.

Barrera, Jr., M., Biglan, A., Taylor, T. K., Gunn, B. K., Smolkowski, K., Black, C. … Fowler, R. C. (2002). Early elementary school intervention to reduce conduct problems: A randomized trial with Hispanic and non-Hispanic children. *Prevention Science, 3*, 83–94.

Baumrind, D. (1967). Childcare practices anteceding three patterns of preschool behavior. *Genetic Psychology Monographs, 75*, 43–88.

Bein, A., Torres, S., & Kurilla, V. (2000). Service delivery issues in early termination of Latino clients. *Journal of Human Behavior in the Social Environment, 3*, 43–59.

Bernal, G., Bonilla, J., & Bellido, C. (1995). Ecological validity and cultural sensitivity for outcome research: Issues for cultural adaptation and development of psychosocial treatments with Hispanics. *Journal of Abnormal Child Psychology, 23*, 67–82.

Bernal, G., & Sáez-Santiago, E. (2006). Culturally centered psychosocial interventions. *Journal of Community Psychology, 34*, 121–132.

Brestan, E. V., & Eyberg, S. M. (1998). Effective psychosocial treatments of conduct-disordered children and adolescents: 29 years, 82 studies, and 5,272 kids. *Journal of Clinical Child Psychology, 27*, 180–189.

Bruce, M. L., Smith, W., Miranda, J., Hoagwood, K., & Wells, K. (2002). Community-based interventions. *Mental Health Services Research, 4*, 205–214.

Buriel, R. (1993). Childrearing orientations in Mexican American families: The influence of generation and sociocultural factors. *Journal of Marriage and the Family, 55*, 987–1000.

Calzada, E. J., & Eyberg, S. M. (2002). Self-reported parenting practices in Dominican and Puerto Rican mothers of young children. *Journal of Clinical Child and Adolescent Psychology, 31*, 354–363.

Carlson, C., Uppal, S., & Prosser, E. (2000). Ethnic differences in processes contributing to the self-esteem of early adolescent girls. *Journal of Early Adolescence, 20*, 44–67.

Chambless, D. L., & Ollendick, T. H. (2001). Empirically supported psychological interventions: Controversies and evidence. *Annual Review of Psychology, 52*, 685–716.

Chilman, C. S. (1993). Mexican and Spanish-origin American families. In H. P. McAdoo (Ed.), *Family ethnicity: Strength in diversity* (pp. 141–163). Thousand Oaks, CA: Sage Publications.

Chun, K. M., & Akutsu, P. D. (2003). Acculturation among ethnic minority families. In K. M. Chun, P. B. Organista, & G. Marin (Eds.), *Acculturation: Advances in theory, measurement and applied research* (pp. 95–119). Washington, DC: American Psychological Association.

Constantino, G., Malgady, R. G., & Rogler, L. H. (1986). *Cuento* therapy: A culturally sensitive modality for Puerto Rican children. *Journal of Consulting and Clinical Psychology, 54*, 639–645.

Darling, N., & Steinberg, L. (1993). Parenting style as context: An integrative model. *Psychological Bulletin, 113,* 487–496.

Domenech Rodríguez, M., Donovick, M. R., & Crowley, S. L. (2009). Parenting styles in a cultural context: Observations of "protective parenting" in first-generation Latinos. *Family Process, 48,* 195–210.

Eyberg, S. M., & members of the Child Study Laboratory (1999). Integrity checklists and session materials. *Parent–child interaction therapy manual.* Available on-line at www.PCIT.org.

Farrington, D. P. (1987). Epidemiology. In H. C. Quay (Ed.), *Handbook of juvenile delinquency* (pp. 33–61). New York: John Wiley and Sons.

Flicker, S. M., Waldron, H. B., Turner, C. W., Brody, J. L., & Hops, H. (2008). Ethnic matching and treatment outcome with Hispanic and Anglo substance-abusing adolescents in family therapy. *Journal of Family Psychology, 22,* 439–447.

Fontes, L. A. (2002). Child discipline and physical abuse in immigrant Latino families: Reducing violence and misunderstandings. *Journal of Counseling and Development, 80,* 31–40.

Forehand, R., & Kotchick, B. A. (1996). Cultural diversity: A wake-up call for parent training. *Behavior Therapy, 27,* 187–206.

Garza, Y., & Bratton, S. (2005). School-based child-centered play therapy with Hispanic children: Outcomes and cultural considerations. *International Journal of Play Therapy, 14,* 51–79.

Glover, S. H., Pumariega, A. J., Holzer, C. E., Wise, B. K., & Rodriguez, M. (1999). Anxiety symptomatology in Mexican American adolescents. *Journal of Child and Family Studies, 8,* 47–57.

Grunbaum, J. A., Kann, L., Kinchen, S., Ross, J. G., Lowry, R., Harris, W. A. ... Collins, J. (2004). *Youth risk behavior surveillance—United States.* Washington, DC: Center for Disease Control.

Guarnaccia, P. J., Canino, G., Rubio-Stipec, M., & Bravo, M. (1993). The prevalence of *ataque de nervios* in the Puerto Rican disaster study: The role of culture in psychiatric epidemiology. *Journal of Nervous and Mental Disease, 181,* 157–165.

Hall, G. C. (2001). Psychotherapy research with ethnic minorities: Empirical, ethical, and conceptual issues. *Journal of Consulting and Clinical Psychology, 69,* 502–510.

Hammer, T. J., & Turner, P. H. Z. (Eds.). (1990). *Parenting in contemporary society.* Englewood Cliffs, NJ: Prentice Hall.

Hill, N. E., Bush, K. R., & Roosa, M. W. (2003). Parenting and family socialization strategies and children's mental health: Low-income Mexican-American and European-American mothers and children. *Child Development, 74,* 189–204.

Ho, J., McCabe, K. M., Yeh, M., & Lau, A. S. (in press). Evidence-based treatments for conduct disorder among ethnic minorities. In R. C. Murrihy, A. Kidman, & T. H. Ollendick (Eds.), *A clinician's handbook for the assessment and treatment of conduct problems in youth.*

Huey, S., & Polo, A. (2008). Evidence-based psychosocial treatments for ethnic minority youth: A review and meta-analysis. *Journal of Clinical Child and Adolescent Psychology, 37,* 262–301.

John, R., Resendiz, R., & De Vargas, L. (1997). Beyond familism? Familism as explicit motive for eldercare among Mexican American caregivers. *Journal of Cross-Cultural Gerontology, 12,* 145–162.

Joiner, T. E., Perez, M., Wagner, K. D., Berenson, A., & Marquina, G. S. (2001). On fatalism, pessimism, and depressive symptoms among Mexican-American and other adolescents attending an obstetrics-gynecology clinic. *Behaviour Research and Therapy, 39,* 887–896.

Kataoka, S., Stein, B. D., Jaycox, L. H., Wong, M., Escudero, P., Tu, W., Zaragosa, C. … Fink, A. (2003). A school-based mental health program for traumatized Latino immigrant children. *Journal of the American Academy of Child and Adolescent Psychiatry, 42,* 311–318.

Kataoka, S. H., Zhang, L., & Wells, K. B. (2002). Unmet need for mental health care among U.S. children: Variation by ethnicity and insurance status. *American Journal of Psychiatry, 159,* 1548–1555.

Kazdin, A. E. (2008). Evidence-based treatments and delivery of psychological services: Shifting our emphases to increase impact. *Psychological Services, 5,* 201–215.

Keefe, S. E., & Casas, M. J. (1980). Mexican Americans and mental health: A selected review and recommendations for mental health service delivery. *American Journal of Community Psychology, 303,* 319–320.

Kumpfer, K. L., Alvarado, R., Smith, P., & Bellamy, N. (2002). Cultural sensitivity and adaptation in family based prevention interventions. *Prevention Science, 3,* 241–246.

Laval, R. A., Gomez, E. A., & Ruiz, P. (1989). A language minority: Hispanic-Americans and mental health care. In D. R. Atkinson, G. M. Morten, & D. W. Sue (Eds.), *Counseling American minorities,* (3rd ed., pp. 242–255). Dubuque, IA: William C. Brown.

Levine, E. S., & Padilla, A. M. (Eds.). (1980). *Crossing cultures in therapy: Pluralistic counseling for the Hispanic.* Monterey, CA: Brooks/Cole Publishing Corporation.

MacPhee, E., Fritz, J., & Miller-Heyl, J. (1996). Ethnic variations in personal social networks and parenting. *Child Development, 67,* 3278–3295.

Manongdo, J. A., & Ramirez Garcia, J. I. (2007). Mothers' parenting dimensions and adolescent externalizing and internalizing behaviors in a low-income, urban Mexican American samples. *Journal of Clinical Child and Adolescent Psychology, 36,* 593–604.

Martinez, Jr., C. R., & Eddy, J. M. (2005). Effects of culturally adapted parent management training on Latino youth behavioral health outcomes. *Journal of Consulting and Clinical Psychology, 73,* 841–851.

McCabe, K. (2002). Factors that predict premature termination among Mexican-American children in outpatient psychotherapy. *Journal of Child and Family Studies, 11,* 347–359.

McCabe, K., & Yeh, M. (2009). Parent–child interaction therapy for Mexican Americans: A randomized clinical trial. *Journal of Clinical Child and Adolescent Psychology, 38,* 753–759.

McCabe, K. M., Yeh, M., Garland, A. F., Lau, A. S., & Chavez, G. (2005). The GANA program: A tailoring approach to adapting parent–child interaction therapy for Mexican Americans. *Education & Treatment of Children, 28,* 111–129.

McCabe, K., Yeh, M., Hough, R., Landsverk, J., Hurlburt, M., Culver, S., & Reynolds, B. (1999). Racial/ethnic representation across five public sectors of care for youth. *Journal of Emotional and Behavorial Disorders, 7,* 72–82.

McKay, M. M., Stoewe, J., McCadam, K., & Gonzales, J. (1998). Increasing access to child mental health services for urban children and their caregivers. *Health and Social Work, 23,* 9–15.

Miranda, J., Bernal, G., Lau, A., Kohn, L., Hwang, W. C., & LaFromboise, T. (2005). State of the science on psychosocial interventions for ethnic minorities. *Annual Review of Clinical Psychology, 1,* 113–142.

National Center for Educational Statistics (2003). *Dropout rates in the United States: 2002 and 2003*. Washington, DC: U.S. Department of Education: Institute of Education Sciences.

Parke, R. D., Coltraine, S., Duffy, S., Buriel, R., Dennis, J., Powers, J. ... Widaman, K. F. (2004). Economic stress, parenting, and child adjustment in Mexican American and European American families. *Child Development, 75*, 1632–1656.

Parra-Cardona, J. R., Córdova, D., Holtrop, K., Villarruel, F. A., & Wieling, E. (2008). Shared ancestry, evolving stories: Similar and contrasting life experiences described by foreign born and U.S. born Latino parents. *Family Process, 47*, 157–172.

Piña, A. A., & Silverman, W. K. (2004). Clinical phenomenology, somatic symptoms, and distress in Hispanic/Latino and Euro-American youths with anxiety disorders. *Journal of Clinical Child and Adolescent Psychology, 33*, 227–236.

Piña, A. A., Silverman, W. K., Fuentes, R. M., Kurtines, W. M., & Weems, C. F. (2003). Exposure-based cognitive behavioral therapy treatment for phobic and anxiety disorders: Treatment effects and maintenance for Hispanic/Latino relative to European-American youths. *Journal of the American Academy of Child and Adolescent Psychiatry, 42*, 1179–1187.

Polo, A. J., & López, S. R. (2009). Culture, context, and the internalizing distress of Mexican American youth. *Journal of Clinical Child and Adolescent Psychological, 38*, 273–285.

Radziszewka, B., Richardson, J. L., Dent, C. W., & Flay, B. R. (1996). Parenting style and adolescent depressive symptoms, smoking, and academic achievement: Ethnic, gender, and class differences. *Journal of Behavioral Medicine, 19*, 289–305.

Ramirez, S. Z., Jain, S., Flores-Torres, L. L., Perez, R., & Carlson, R. (2009). The effects of *cuento* therapy on reading achievement and psychological outcomes of Mexican-American students. *Professional School Counseling, 12*, 253–262.

Rodriguez, C. M. (2007). Ecological predictors of disciplinary style and child abuse potential in a Hispanic and Anglo-American sample. *Journal of Child and Family Studies, 17*, 336–352.

Rogler, L. H., & Cooney, R. S. (1984). *Puerto Rican families in New York City: Intergenerational processes* (Hispanic Research Center Monograph No. 11). Maplewood, NJ: Waterfront Press.

Rogler, L. H., Malgady, R. G., & Rodriguez, O. (Eds.). (1989). *Hispanics and mental health: A framework for research*. Malabar, FL: Krieger.

Rutter, M., & Giller, H. (1983). *Juvenile delinquency: Trends and perspectives*. Harmondsworth, England: Penguin.

Santiago-Rivera, A., Arredondo, P. M., & Gallardo-Cooper, M. (2002). *Counseling Latinos and* la familia: *A practical guide*. Thousand Oaks, CA: Sage.

Shapiro, J., & Simonsen, D. (1994). Educational/support group for Latino families of children with Down syndrome. *Mental Retardation, 32*, 403–415.

Stein, B. D., Jaycox, L. H., Kataoka, S. H., Wong, M., Tu, W., Elliott, M. N., & Fink, A. (2003). A mental health intervention for schoolchildren exposed to violence: A randomized controlled trial. *Journal of the American Medical Association, 290*, 603–611.

Swanson, J. W., Linskey, A. O., Quintero-Salina, R., Pumariega, A. J., & Holzer, C. E. (1992). A bi-national school survey of depressive symptoms, drug use, and suicidal ideation. *Journal of the American Academy of Child and Adolescent Psychiatry, 31*, 669–678.

United States Census Bureau (2007). *The American community—Hispanics: 2004*. Washington, DC: Author.

United States Census Bureau (2009). *Latino or Hispanic origin by race*. Washington, DC: Author.

United States Department of Health and Human Services (USDHHS) (2001). *Mental health: Culture, race, and ethnicity: A report of the Surgeon General*. Washington, DC: Author.

Uno, E., Florsheim, P., & Uchino, B. N. (1998). Psychosocial mechanisms underlying quality of parenting among Mexican-American and white adolescents mothers. *Journal of Youth and Adolescence, 27* 585–605.

Varela, R. E., Vernberg, E. M., Sanchez Sosa, J. J., Riveros, A., Mitchell, M., & Maskunkashey, J. (2004). Anxiety reporting and culturally associated interpretation biases and cognitive schemas: A comparison of Mexican, Mexican American, and European American families. *Journal of Clinical Child and Adolescent Psychology, 33,* 237–247.

Vazquez-Nuttal, E., Avila-Vivas, Z., & Morales-Barreto, G. (1984). Working with Latin-American families. *Family Therapy Collections, 9,* 74–90.

Vazsonyi, A. T., & Flannery, D. J. (1997). Early adolescent delinquent behaviors: Associations with family and school domains. *Journal of Early Adolescence, 17,* 271–293.

Vega, W. A., & Lopez, S. R. (2001). Priority issues in Latino mental health services research. *Mental Health Services Research, 3,* 189–200.

Vega, W. A. (1990). Hispanic families in the 1980s: A decade of research. *Journal of Marriage and the Family, 52,* 1015–1024.

Vega, W. A. (1995). The study of Latino families: A point of departure. In R. Zambrana (Ed.), *Understanding Latino families: Scholarship, policy, and practice* (pp. 3–17). Thousand Oaks, CA: Sage.

Vega, W., Kolody, B., & Aguilar-Gaxiola, S. (2001). Help seeking for mental health problems among Mexican Americans. *Journal of Immigrant Health, 3,* 133–140.

Vega, W., Kolody, B., Aguilar-Gaxiola, S., & Catalano, R. (1999). Gaps in service utilization by Mexican Americans with mental health problems. *American Journal of Psychiatry, 156,* 928–934.

Villalba, J. A. (2007). Health disparities among Latina/o adolescents in urban and rural schools: Educators' perspectives. *Journal of Cultural Diversity, 14,* 169–175.

Wight, R. G., Aneshensel, C. S., Botticello, A. L., & Sepúlveda, J. E. (2005). A multilevel analysis of ethnic variation in depressive symptoms among adolescents in the United States. *Social Science and Medicine, 60,* 2073–2084.

Wilkinson, D. (1987). Ethnicity. In S. Steinmetz & M. B. Sussman (Eds.), *Handbook of marriage and the family* (pp. 345–405). New York: Plenum.

Wood, J. J., Chui, A. W., Hwang, W., Jacobs, J., & Ifekwunigwe, M. (2008). Adapting cognitive-behavioral therapy for Mexican American students with anxiety disorders: Recommendations for school psychologists. *School Psychology Quarterly, 23,* 1045–3830.

Yeh, M., Hough, R. L., McCabe, K., Lau, A., & Garland, A. (2004). Parental beliefs about the causes of child problems: Exploring racial/ethnic patterns. *Journal of the American Academy of Child and Adolescent Psychiatry, 43,* 605–612.

Yeh, M., McCabe, K., Hough, R. L., Dupuis, D., & Hazen, A. (2003). Racial/ethnic differences in parental endorsement of barriers to mental health services for youth. *Mental Health Services Research, 5,* 65–77.

Yeh, M., McCabe, K., Hough, R. L., Lau, A., Fakhry, F. & Garland, A. (2005). Why bother with beliefs? Examining relationships between race/ethnicity, parental beliefs about causes of child's problems, and mental health service use. *Journal of Consulting and Clinical Psychology, 73*, 800–807.

Zayas, L. H. (1993). Childrearing, social stress, and child abuse: Clinical considerations with Hispanic families. *Journal of Social Distress and the Homeless, 1*, 291–309.

Zea, M. C., Quezeda, T., & Belgrave, F. Z. (1994). Cultural values and adjustment to disability among Latinos. *Journal of Social Behavior and Personality, 9*, 185–200.

Zebell, N. (producer), & Urquiza, A. J. (producer). (2002a). *Compliance Video / Dando ordenes efectivas—SER DIRECTO—*(Spanish language version) [Video]. (Available from UCDMC CAARE Center, PCIT Training Services, 3300 Stockton Blvd. Sacramento, CA 95812.)

Zebell, N. (producer), & Urquiza, A. J. (producer). (2002b). *Relationship enhancement "Fortaleciendo la relación familiar—A DIARIO"* (Spanish language version) [Video]. (Available from UCDMC CAARE Center, PCIT Training Services, 3300 Stockton Blvd. Sacramento, CA 95812.)

Zinn, M. B. (1982). Familism among Chicanos: A theoretical review. *Humboldt Journal of Social Relations, 10*, 224–238.

# 16

# International Perspectives on Intellectual Disability

Robert L. Schalock

## Introduction and Overview

In a recent editorial titled "Intellectual disability in a global context," Emerson, McConkey, Walsh, & Felce (2008) summarized three trends appearing in the international literature regarding persons with intellectual disability (ID): (a) a refocus from a concentration on individuals with disability to studying them within the social contexts in which they live; (b) the critical influence of the family and society on the lives of persons with ID; and (c) a shift away from an emphasis on specialists and disability services toward empowering and enabling mainstream provision to meet the needs of people with ID. This chapter expands on these three trends and discusses the broader context within which they are occurring from three perspectives: understanding the construct of ID; performing clinical functions in regard to diagnosis, classification and planning supports; and impacting public policy.

At the outset it is important to realize that detailed international information pertaining to persons with ID is available primarily for those countries within the upper middle and high World Bank income categories (Emerson, Fujiura, & Hatton, 2007; Emerson, Graham, & Hatton, 2006; Fujiura, Park, & Rutkowski-Kmitta, 2005; Mercier, Saxena, Lecomte, Cumbrera, & Harnois, 2008). In an article describing the *WHO ATLAS on Global Resources for Persons with Intellectual Disabilities* (World Health Organization, 2007), the authors pointed out that "The low and middle income countries are particularly at a disadvantage [in regard to data on persons with ID], with a high proportion of countries without any documentation of ID, or any management systems, epidemiological data, or national research capacities" (Mercier et al. 2008, p. 87). Furthermore, the most striking differences between the poorest and the richest countries of the world in relation to ID pertain to the areas of information, judicial protections, government benefits, financing, availability of services, and access to those services (Mercier et al., 2008).

It is also important to realize that I used a number of information gathering strategies in writing this chapter. In reference to the discussion of "naming and defining," major data came from an international survey Schalock and Verdugo (2008) conducted in early 2008. Information used in subsequent sections was synthesized from published literature in the field of ID and my involvement in cross-cultural research (Jenaro et al., 2005; Keith & Schalock, 2000; Schalock, Verdugo, Bonham, Fantova, & van Loon, 2008; Schalock et al., 2005). Finally, some of the material included in the chapter derives from my work with the Terminology and Classification Committee of the American Association on Intellectual and Developmental Disabilities (AAIDD, formerly AAMR) which has developed and published the 11th edition of the AAIDD Manual: *Intellectual disability: Definition, classification, and systems of supports* (Schalock et al., 2010).

Throughout the chapter, the term *intellectual disability (ID)* denotes persons who exhibit significant limitations in intellectual functioning and adaptive behavior, and whose "condition" originates during the developmental period or before cultural norms of adulthood are reached. As discussed more fully in Parmenter (2004), Schalock et al. (2007), and Schroeder, Gertz, and Velazquez (2002), the term ID is used increasingly internationally due to the fact that the term is preferable for a number of reasons. Chief among these are that the term ID: (a) reflects the changed construct of disability described by AAIDD (Wehmeyer et al., 2008) and the World Health Organization (WHO) (2001); (b) aligns better with current professional practices that focus on functional behaviors and contextual factors; (c) provides a logical basis for individualized supports provision due to its basis in a social-ecological framework; (d) is less offensive to persons with the disability; and (e) is more consistent with international terminology, including journal titles, published research, and organization names (Schalock et al., 2007).

## Understanding the Construct of Intellectual Disability

There have been significant conceptual and empirically based changes over the last few decades in the way the international community views the construct of disability, explains human functioning, and understands the etiology of ID. Although these changes are not equivocal, they do reflect the new "mental model" of ID that is emerging internationally (Schalock et al. 2008).

### The construct of disability

The construct of intellectual disability belongs within the general construct of disability, which focuses on the expression of limitations in individual functioning within a social context and represents a substantial disadvantage to the individual. Disability has its genesis in a health condition that gives rise to impairments in body functions and structures, activity limitations, and participation restrictions within the context of personal and environmental factors (Luckasson et al., 2002; WHO, 2001).

The current construct of disability has emerged over the last two decades due primarily to an increased understanding of the process of disablement and its amelioration. Major factors in this evolution include: (a) research on the social construction of illness and the extensive impact that societal attitudes, roles, and policies have on the ways that individuals experience health disorders (Aronowitz, 1998); (b) blurring of the historical distinction between biological and social causes of disability (Institute of Medicine, 1991); and (c) recognition of the multidimensionality of human functioning (Buntinx, 2006; Luckasson et al., 2002; Wehmeyer et al., 2008; WHO, 2001). Because of these factors, the concept of disability has evolved from a person-centered trait or characteristic (often referred to as a "deficit") to a human phenomenon with its genesis in organic and/or social factors. These organic and social factors give rise to functional limitations that reflect an inability or constraint in both personal functioning and performing roles and tasks expected of an individual within a social environment (Bach, 2007; DePloy & Gilson, 2004; Hahn & Hegamin, 2001; Nagi, 1991; Oliver, 1996; Rioux, 1997; Schalock, 2004).

This social-ecological conception of disability is reflected well in current publications of both AAIDD and the WHO. The importance of this evolutionary change in the construct of disability is that IDis no longer considered entirely an absolute, invariant trait of the person (DeKraai, 2002; Devlieger, Rusch, & Pfeiffer, 2003; Switzky & Greenspan, 2006). Rather, this social-ecological construct of ID: (a) exemplifies the interaction between the person and the environment; (b) focuses on the role that individualized supports can play in enhancing individual functioning; and (c) allows for the pursuit and understanding of "disability identity" whose principles include self-worth, subjective well-being, pride, common cause, policy alternatives, and engagement in political action (Powers, Dinerstein, & Holmes, 2005; Putnam, 2005; Schalock, 2004; Vehmas, 2004).

## Multidimensionality of human functioning

As proposed by the WHO (2001), human functioning is an umbrella term for all life activities and encompasses body structures and functions, personal activities, and participation. Limitations in functioning are labeled a "disability" that can result from problem(s) in body structures and functions and personal activities. For purposes of understanding what ID refers to, the WHO's ICF domains of "body functions" (impaired intellectual functioning) and "activities" (limitations in adaptive behavior) are important because they refer to the diagnostic criteria specified in the operational definition of ID. Because all dimensions of human functioning and impacting factors are important to fully understand a person with ID, the current conceptual framework of human functioning emphasizes its multidimensional nature as reflected in the following five domains (Wehmeyer et al., 2008):

- **Intellectual abilities**. Intelligence is a general mental capability. It includes reasoning, planning, solving problems, thinking abstractly, comprehending complex ideas, learning quickly, and learning from experience (Gottfredson, 1997; Neisser, Boodo, Bouchard, & Boykin, 1996).
- **Adaptive behavior**. Adaptive behavior is the collection of conceptual, social, and practical skills that have been learned and are performed by people in their everyday lives (Schalock et al., 2010).
- **Health**. Health is a state of complete physical, mental, and social well-being (WHO, 1993).
- **Participation**. Participation is the performance of people in actual activities in social life domains and is related to the functioning of the individual in society. It refers to roles and interactions in the areas of home living, work, education, leisure, spiritual, and cultural activities (Wehmeyer et al., 2008).
- **Context**. Context describes the interrelated conditions within which people live their everyday lives. It includes environmental and personal factors that represent the complete background of an individual's life (WHO, 2001). Environmental factors make up the physical, social, and attitudinal environment in which people live and conduct their lives. Personal factors are characteristics of the person such as gender, race, age, motivation, lifestyle, habits, upbringing, coping styles, social background, educational level, past and current experiences, character style, and individual psychological assets. All or any of these characteristics may play a role in the manifestation of a disability (Schalock et al., 2010).

## The etiology of ID

Increasingly, researchers conceptualize etiology of ID as a multifactorial construct composed of four categories of risk factors that interact across time, including across the life of the individual and across generations from parent to child. This multifactorial understanding of etiology is replacing the historical approach that divided etiology of ID (referred to then as mental retardation) into two broad types: those due to biological origin and those due to psychosocial disadvantage. The multifactorial approach to etiology expands the list of causal factors in two directions: types of factors and timing of factors (Schalock et al., 2010). In reference to types of factors, there are four categories of risk factors:

- **Biomedical**: factors related to biologic processes, such as genetic disorders or nutrition, maternal illness, or parental age.
- **Social**: factors that relate to social and family influences, such as poverty, maternal malnutrition, stimulation, and adult responsiveness.

**Table 16.1**   Exemplary prenatal, perinatal, and postnatal risk factors in intellectual disability

---

*Prenatal*
- Biomedical: chromosomal disorders, metabolic disorders, transplacental infections (e.g. rubella, herpes, HIV), exposure to toxins or teratogens (e.g. alcohol, lead, mercury), undernutrition (e.g. maternal iodine deficiency)
- Social: poverty, maternal malnutrition, domestic violence, lack of prenatal care
- Behavioral: parental drug use, parental immaturity
- Educational: parental disability without supports, lack of educational opportunites

*Perinatal*
- Biomedical: prematurity, birth injury, hypoxia, neonatal disorders, rhesus incompatibility
- Social: lack of access to birth care
- Behavioral: parental rejection of caretaking, parental abandonment of child
- Educational: lack of medical referral for intervention services at discharge

*Postnatal*
- Biomedical: traumatic brain injury, malnutrition, degenerative / seizure disorders, toxins
- Social: lack of adequate stimulation, family poverty, chronic illness, institutionalization
- Behavioral: child abuse / neglect, domestic violence, difficult child behaviors
- Educational: delayed diagnosis, inadequate early intervention, inadequate special education services, inadequate family support

---

- **Behavioral**: factors that relate to potentially causal behaviors, such as dangerous (injurious) activities or maternal substance abuse.
- **Educational**: factors that relate to the availability of educational supports promoting mental development and the development of adaptive skills.

In reference to timing, the occurrence of causal factors can take place prenatally, perinatally, or postnatally. Table 16.1, based on the work of Emerson et al. (2007), Schalock et al., (2010), and Walker et al. (2007), summarizes key risk factors from each of these three perspectives.

## Performing Clinical Functions

### Best practices

Best practices regarding the performance of clinical functions related to diagnosis, classification, and planning supports are based on current terminology, an operational definition of the ID construct, and an assessment framework that aligns the three clinical functions. These three factors provide a sound conceptual and meas-urement framework for the three clinical functions discussed later in this section.

*Current terminology*
Currently one finds internationally a number of terms that refer to what is most commonly known as intellectual disability. As Brown (2007) and Brown and Radford (2007) noted, these terms include mental deficiency, mental disability, mental handicap, mental subnormality, developmental disability (especially in Canada), and learning disabilities (especially in the United Kingdom).

To address this situation, Luckasson et al. (2002) and Luckasson and Reeve (2001) stressed the importance of differentiating between naming and defining. Specifically,

- In naming, a specific term is attached to something or someone. Naming is a powerful process that carries many messages about perceived value and human relationships.
- In defining, the name or term is explained as precisely as possible. The defini-tion should establish the boundaries of the term and separate who or what is included within the term from who or what is outside the term. The impor-tance of an operational definition is that it establishes meaning and helps meet the basic human drive for understanding.

To help clarify the naming phenomenon (i.e. terminology) in more detail, Schalock & Verdugo (2008) conducted an e-mail survey of 35 colleagues in 30 countries. These colleagues were either in adult rehabilitation or special education services to per-sons with ID, or were familiar with the field of ID and closely related developmen-tal disabilities. Schalock and Verdugo obtained responses from 30 respondents representing 27 countries (South America, 10 countries), Central America (2), Caribbean (2), North America (2), Europe (7) and the Pacific Rim (4). The general results were: (a) the term intellectual disability was the term reportedly used most frequently, with the exceptions of "learning disability" (Canada and the United Kingdom), "mental deficiency" (China), "mental handicap" (Taiwan and France), and "a person carrying a mental handicap" (Brazil); and (b) the term used most widely in the respective country is generally the term most frequently used by poli-cymakers, adult service providers, schools, diagnostic teams, and researchers.

*Operational definition*
Based on a review of the international literature (along with the above-referenced survey) the most commonly referenced operational definition of ID is that prom-ulgated by AAIDD. According to this operational definition:

> Intellectual disability is characterized by significant limitations both in intellectual functioning and in adaptive behavior as expressed in conceptual, social, and practical adaptive skills. This disability originates before age 18. (Schalock et al., 2010, p. 1)

**Table 16.2**   An assessment framework

| Function | Purposes | Exemplary measures and tools |
|---|---|---|
| Diagnosis | Establishing eligibility:<br>– services<br>– benefits<br>– legal protections | Intelligence tests<br>Adaptive behavior scales<br>Documented age of onset |
| Classification | Grouping for:<br><br>– reimbursement/funding<br>– services/supports<br>– communication<br>– education/rehabilitation<br>– services | Support needs intensity assessments<br>IQ ranges or levels<br>Environmental assessments<br>Etiology risk factors<br>Mental health measures<br>Benefit categories |
| Planning supports | Enhancing outcomes:<br>– personal<br>– family<br>– societal | Person/family centered planning<br>Self appraisal<br>Individual plan elements<br>Functional behavior assessments |

Assumptions are an explicit part of a definition because they clarify the context from which the definition arises, and indicate how the definition must be applied. Thus, the definition of ID cannot stand alone. The following five assumptions are essential to the application of the definition just stated: (a) limitations in present functioning must be considered within the context of community environments typical of the individual's age peers and culture; (b) valid assessment considers cultural and linguistic diversity as well as differences in communication, sensory, motor, and behavioral factors; (c) within an individual, limitations often coexist with strengths; (d) an important purpose of describing limitations is to develop a profile of needed supports; and (e) with appropriate personalized supports over a sustained period, the life functioning of the person with intellectual disability generally will improve (Schalock et al., 2010).

*Assessment framework*

Internationally, there is a growing consensus regarding the need for a holistic approach to the assessment of persons with ID. Such an approach involves three clinical functions: diagnosis, classification, and planning supports. Table 16.2 presents an assessment framework that shows this alignment. Material in the table is based on the work of Luckasson et al. (2002) and Schalock et al. (2010). The importance of this framework is that it shows clearly the primary purposes for diagnosis, classification, and supports planning, and lists a number of exemplary measures or tools that can be used to assess the person in reference to each purpose or clinical function. As countries integrate this assessment framework into their service delivery system, one can expect to see a better alignment among the clinical functions of assessment, diagnosis, and planning individualized supports (Schalock & Luckasson, 2005).

## Diagnosis

Based on the operational definition of ID presented earlier, the identification of ID is based on three criteria: significant limitations in intellectual functioning, adaptive behavior as expressed in cognitive, social, and practical adaptive skills, and age of onset prior to age 18. Each of the first two criteria (significant limitations in intellectual functioning and adaptive behavior) is *defined* in terms of cutoff scores and *interpreted* in reference to a confidence interval (Schalock et al., 2010).

- The "significant limitations in intellectual functioning" criterion for a diagnosis of ID is an IQ score that is approximately two standard deviations below the mean, considering the standard error of measurement for the specific instruments used and the instruments' strengths and limitations (within the cultural context).
- The "significant limitations in adaptive behavior" criterion for a diagnosis of ID is performance that is approximately two standard deviations below the mean of either (a) one of the following three types of adaptive behavior: conceptual, social, or practical, or (b) an overall score on a standardized measure of conceptual, social, and practical skills. As with the intellectual functioning criterion, the assessment instruments' standard error of measurement must be considered when interpreting the individual's obtained score.
- Confidence interval. The results of any psychometric assessment must be evaluated in terms of the accuracy of the instrument used. Any obtained score is subject to variability as a function of a number of potential sources of error including variations in test performance, examiner's behavior, cooperation of the test taker, and other personal and environmental factors. The term standard error of measurement (SEM), which varies by test, sub-group, and age group, is used to quantify this variability and provide a statistical confidence interval around the obtained score within which the person's true score falls. From the properties of the normal curve, a range of statistical confidence can be established with parameters of at least one SEM (66% probability) or parameters of two SEM (95% probability).

## Classification

All classification systems have as their fundamental purpose the provision of an organized scheme for the categorization of various kinds of observations. Classification systems are used typically for four purposes: funding, research, services/supports, and communication about selected characteristics of persons and their environments. Many different classification systems are currently used internationally in the field of ID. Chief among these are:

- ICD-9-CM (Medicode, 1998) and ICD-10 (WHO, 1993). Within these two classification systems, mental retardation (the term ID is not used) is coded primarily on the basis of full-scale IQ scores.
- ICF (WHO, 2001). As a classification instrument, the ICF is complementary to the ICD-10, but extends beyond the medical perspective and includes an ecological perspective that is oriented toward human functioning and health.
- DSM-IV (American Psychiatric Association, 2000). The DSM-IV is a multiaxial system that provides potential information about an individual in five domains. Mental retardation (the term ID is not used) is included in Axis II, with classification based on assessed IQ scores.

The IQ-based classification systems used historically are insufficient for at least two reasons: First, their conceptual basis and operational definition are limited to intellectual functioning; and second, they do not reflect either current terminology or the emerging conception of disability. In reference to their conceptual basis, in a recent article summarizing international trends in the field, Emerson et al. (2007) observed that,

> When classification practices and service supports based on constructions of intellectual disability are imposed on societies with different conceptions of competence, tension, conflict, and resistance are likely to arise....[and furthermore] classification systems and services that start from local conceptions of competence and the proper social role of a competent person may be more productive. (p. 607).

Second, a unidimensional, IQ-based classification system is not based on either a multidimensional model of human functioning or an ecological construct of disability. As the field of ID moves increasingly to an ecological focus and a supports paradigm, a number of current policies and practices that have emerged will require a broader, multidimensional approach to classification than the unidimensional (i.e., IQ-based) approach used previously. Chief among these are: (a) grouping for reimbursement/funding on the basis of some combination and weighting of levels of assessed support need, level of adaptive behavior, health status, and/or contextual factors such as residential platform and geographical location; (b) research methods that focus on ecologically based predictors of desired outcomes; and (c) individualized services and supports based on the pattern and intensity of assessed support needs across the five dimensions of human functioning (intellectual functioning, adaptive behavior, health, participation, and context). As a result of these changes in policies and practices, increasingly one finds multidimensional classification systems being used that reflect the multidimensionality of human functioning (Schalock et al., 2010).

## Planning individualized supports

Since the mid-1980s the supports paradigm has made at least two significant impacts internationally on education and (re)habilitation programs. First, the pattern and intensity of a person's support needs are used as the basis for individual support plan development, agency and systems planning, and resource allocation. Second, the supports orientation has brought together the related practices of person-centered planning, personal growth and development opportunities, community inclusion, and empowerment. Although the concept of supports is by no means new, what is new is the belief that the judicious application of individualized supports can improve human functioning and enhance personal outcomes.

Supports can be defined as resources and strategies that aim to promote the development, education, interests, and personal well-being of a person and that enhance human functioning (Thompson et al., 2009). Internationally, we have observed four key aspects of the provision of supports to persons with ID: supports enable people to access resources, information, and relationships within their local communities; individualized supports result in increased integration and enhanced personal growth and development; support needs can be assessed in psychometrically sound ways; and the impact of supports can be evaluated in reference to personal and family outcomes.

Internationally, the concept of supports is being applied to persons with ID in different ways. For some, the supports orientation has brought together (generally within an individual support plan) the related practices of person-centered planning, personal growth and development opportunities, community inclusion, self-determination, empowerment, and the application of a "system of supports" that includes policies and practices, incentives, cognitive supports (i.e., assistive technology), prosthetics, skills and knowledge, and environmental accommodation (Thompson et al., 2009). For others, we have seen the integration of a quality of life framework into an individualized planning process so as to align supports provision within the quality of life framework, and thus focus on the potentially effective role that individualized supports play in the enhancement of quality of life-related personal outcomes (van Loon, 2008). And for others, supports are provided through a community-based rehabilitation model, which consists of small programs implemented through the combined efforts of those with disabilities, their families, and the community using indigenous supports (McConkey & O'Toole, 1995). According to Emerson et al. (2007), this model remains the centerpiece of international development strategies.

## Impacting Public Policy

Changes in policies and practices regarding persons with ID can come from the microsystem (i.e., the person), the mesosystem (e.g., the agency or organization), or the macrosystem (e.g., governments). The significant changes across systems that have occurred over the last four decades reflect the power of advocacy groups and clearly focused efforts by multiple stakeholders. But, we are not there yet (Verdonschott, de Witte, Reichrath, Buntinx, & Curfs, 2009). Thus in thinking about impacting public policy I encourage the reader, in this final part of the chapter, to consider public policy principles, an array of services and supports, and measuring public policy outcomes.

### Public policy principles

International disability policy regarding persons with ID is currently premised on a number of principles that are: (a) person-referenced, such as inclusion, empowerment, individualized and relevant supports, productivity and contribution, and family integrity and unity; and (b) service-delivery referenced, such as antidiscrimination, coordination and collaboration, and accountability (Brown & Percy, 2007; Montreal Declaration, 2004; Salamanca Statement, 1994). These principles have resulted in significant changes in service delivery policies and practices, and a significant effort to conceptualize and measure important life domains. In reference to significant service delivery policies and practices, we have seen internationally policies and practices enacted that provide education, community living and employment opportunities, technological supports and assistive technology, person-centered planning, and a framework to assess person- and family-referenced value outcomes. In reference to life domains, the principles mentioned above have been operationalized in the following eight universally recognized life domains (United Nations, 2006): rights (access and privacy); participation; autonomy, independence, and choice: physical well-being; material well-being (work and employment); inclusion, accessibility, and participation; emotional well-being (freedom from exploitation, violence, and abuse); and personal development (education and rehabilitation). Although there is considerable variability across countries, the net effect of these principles and related changes has been the development of an array of services and supports for persons with ID and an increasing focus on measuring public policy outcomes.

### Array of services and supports

As discussed more fully by Emerson et al. (2007) and Mercier et al. (2008), persons with disabilities, including those with ID, are provided with an array of educational, residential, occupational, and support services. Although

the availability and composition vary across countries, the general parameters of this array are:

- educational opportunities which vary from highly segregated classrooms, to
  resource rooms, to schools providing full inclusion for students with ID;
- residential options which vary from large, congregate living facilities and nursing homes, to group homes, to supported community living private residences.
  It should be noted, however, that across the globe, only a small proportion of
  persons with ID live in residential settings; most reside with their family
  (Emerson et al., 2007);
- occupational (i.e., vocational, work) opportunities which vary from day activity centers, to sheltered workshops, to general work skills and vocational preparation, to integrated employment;
- support services including leisure activities, transportation, assistive technology, rights and advocacy support, and/or nutritional assistance.

## Measuring public policy outcomes

As additional resources are devoted to the development of this array of services
and supports, policymakers and funders are increasingly asking questions related
to the outcomes of the services and supports provided to persons with ID and
their families. Public policy outcomes can be used for multiple purposes, including
analyzing the impact of specific public policies, monitoring the effectiveness and
efficiency of services and supports, providing a basis for quality improvement
and performance enhancement, meeting the increasing need for accountability,
and helping establish the parameters of best practices (Schalock et al., 2010).

Although just appearing in the field of ID (even in the upper middle and high
country income categories) public/social policy outcomes are being assessed in
three broad areas: personal, family, and societal. The framework used to measure
these outcomes is based on the delineation of valued life domains and the assessment of core indicators associated with each life domain. Table 16.3 summarizes
exemplary outcome domains.

## Conclusion

The international trends and changes discussed in this chapter regarding the construct of ID, clinical functions, and public policy are occurring within the broader
context of: (a) an emerging disability paradigm that includes a multidimensional
model of human functioning and an ecological construct of disability; (b) a supports

**Table 16.3**  Public policy outcome measures: domains and referent group

| *Person-referenced outcome domains** | | | |
|---|---|---|---|
| Rights | Personal development | Self-determination | Physical well-being |
| Inclusion | Emotional well-being | Material well-being | Participation |
| *Family referenced outcome domains*** | | | |
| Family interaction | Emotional well-being | Personal development | |
| Parenting | Physical well-being | Financial well-being | |
| Community / civic involvement | Disability-related supports | | |
| *Societal-referenced outcomes**** | | | |
| Socioeconomic position | Health | Subjective well-being | |

\* Based on the work of Alverson, Bayliss, Naranjo, Yamamoto and Unruh (2006), Gardner and Caran (2005), Bradley and Moseley (2007), Schalock and Verdugo (2002).

\*\* Based on the work of Aznar and Castanon (2005), Isaacs et al. (2007), Summers et al. (2005).

\*\*\* Based on the work of Arthaud-Day, Rode, Mooney, and Near (2005), Emerson et al. (2006), Emerson and Hatton (2008).

paradigm that focuses on the assessment of a person's support needs and the mainstream provision of individualized strategies that enable people to receive a modicum of support irrespective of where they live, while also encouraging their social inclusion; and (c) a quality revolution with its focus on outcomes rather than inputs and processes, and the use of outcome-related information as a basis for quality management and quality improvement (Emerson et al., 2007; Schalock, Bonham, & Verdugo, 2008; Wehmeyer et al., 2008).

Even though our current understanding of ID is based primarily on data from higher-income countries, the issues surrounding the understanding, acceptance, and inclusion of persons with ID extends beyond national income categories. Thus, in addition to international efforts to improve services and supports to persons with ID, there will continue to be considerable and intense discussion internationally about the construct of disability, how intellectual disability fits within the general construct of disability, and the relation of ID to other developmental disabilities (Brown & Percy, 2007; Finlay & Lyons, 2005; Schalock & Luckasson, 2005; Switzky & Greenspan, 2006). Furthermore, there will continue to be serious discussion regarding the social construction of ID (Rapley, 2004), the ethical analysis of the concept of disability (Vehmas, 2004), and whether the elements of the ID construct and the construct itself are relevant internationally due to the cultural relativity of the constructs of intellectual functioning and adaptive behavior (Emerson et al., 2007). More specifically, in the future we can expect further discussions within the international community related to refining the construct of intellectual disability; improving the reliability of diagnosis; expanding classification systems to reflect the multidimensional nature of human functioning; understanding better the nature of intelligence, adaptive behavior, and disablement; and evaluating the impact of individualized supports on individual functioning and personal outcomes.

# References

Alverson, C. Y., Bayliss, C., Naranjo, J. M. Yamamoto, S. H., & Unruh, D. (2006). *Methods of conducting post-school outcomes follow-up studies: A review of the literature.* Eugene, OR: National Post-School Outcomes Center, University of Oregon.

American Psychiatric Association (2000). *Diagnostic and statistical manual of mental disorders* (4th ed. text rev.). Washington, DC: Author.

Aronowitz, R. A. (1998). *Making sense of illness. Science, society, and disease.* Cambridge, UK: Cambridge University Press.

Arthaud-Day, M. E., Rode, J. C., Mooney, C. H., & Near, J. P. (2005). The subjective well-being construct: A test of its convergent, discriminate, and factorial validity. *Social Indicators Research 74,* 445–476.

Aznar, A. S. & Castanon, D. G. (2005). Quality of life from the point of view of Latin American families: A participative research study. *Journal of Intellectual Disability Research, 49,* 784–788.

Bach, M. (2007). Changing perspectives on developmental disabilities. In I. Brown and M. Percy (Eds.), *A comprehensive guide to intellectual and developmental disabilities* (pp. 35–57). Baltimore, MD: Paul H. Brookes.

Bradley, V. J. & Moseley, C. (2007). National core indicators: Ten years of collaborative performance measurement. *Intellectual and Developmental Disabilities, 45,* 354–358.

Brown, I. (2007). What is meant by intellectual and developmental disabilities? In I. Brown & M. Percy (Eds.), *A comprehensive guide to intellectual and developmental disabilities* (pp. 3–15). Baltimore, MD: Paul H. Brookes.

Brown, I. & Percy, M. (Eds.) (2007). *A comprehensive guide to intellectual and developmental disabilities.* Baltimore, MD: Paul H. Brookes.

Brown, I. & Radford, J. P. (2007). Historical overview of intellectual and developmental disabilities. In I. Brown and M. Percy (Eds.), *A comprehensive guide to intellectual and developmental disabilities* (pp. 17–33). Baltimore, MD: Paul H. Brookes.

Buntinx, W. H. E. (2006). The relationship between WHO-ICF and the AAMR 2002 system. In H. Switzky and S. Greenspan (Eds.), *What is mental retardation? Ideas for an evolving disability in the 21st century* (pp. 303–323). Washington, DC: American Association on Mental Retardation.

DeKraai, M. (2002). In the beginning: The first hundred years (1850 to 1950). In R. L. Schalock (Ed.), *Out of darkness and into the light: Nebraska's experience with mental retardation* (pp. 103–122). Washington, DC: American Association on Mental Retardation.

DePloy, E. & Gilson, S. F. (2004). *Rethinking disability: Principles for professional and social change.* Belmont, CA: Thompson Books/Cole.

Devlieger, J. P., Rusch, F., & Pfeiffer, D. (Eds.) (2003). *Rethinking disability: The emergence of new definition, concepts, and communities.* Antwerp, Belgium: Garant Publishers.

Emerson, E., Fujiura, G. T., & Hatton, C. (2007). International perspectives. In S. L. Odom, R. H. Horner, M. E. Snell, and J. Blacher (Eds.), *Handbook of developmental disabilities* (pp. 593–613). New York: Guilford Press.

Emerson, E., Graham, H., & Hatton, C. (2006). The measurement of poverty and socio-economic position in research involving people with intellectual disability. In L. M. Glidden (Ed.), *International review of research in mental retardation* (pp. 77–108). New York: Academic Press.

Emerson, E. & Hatton, C. (2008). Self-reported well-being of women and men with intellectual disabilities in England. *American Journal on Mental Retardation, 113,* 143–155.

Emerson, E., McConkey, R., Walsh, P. N., & Felce, D. (2008). Editorial. Intellectual disability in a global context. *Journal of Policy and Practice in Intellectual Disabilities, 5,* 79–80.

Fujiura, G. T., Park, H. J., & Rutkowski-Kmitta, V. (2005). Disability statistics in the developing world: A reflection on the meanings of our numbers. *Journal of Applied Research in Intellectual Disability, 18,* 295–304.

Finlay, W. M. L. & Lyons, E. (2005). Rejecting the label: A social constructionist analysis. *Mental Retardation, 43,* 120–134.

Gardner, J. F. & Caran, D. (2005). Attainment of personal outcomes by people with developmental disabilities. *Mental Retardation, 43,* 157–174.

Gottfredson, L. S. (1997). Mainstream science on intelligence: An editorial with 52 signatories, history, and bibliography. *Intelligence, 24,* 13–23.

Hahn, H. & Hegamin, A. P. (2001). Assessing scientific meaning of disability. *Journal of Disability Policy Studies, 12,* 114–121.

Institute of Medicine (1991). *Disability in America: Towards a national agenda for prevention.* Washington, DC: National Academy Press.

Isaacs, B. J., Brown, I., Brown, R., Baum, N., Meyerscough, T., Neikerg, S. (2007). The international family quality of life project: Goals and description of a survey tool. *Journal of Policy and Practice in Intellectual Disabilities, 4,* 177–185.

Jenaro, C., Verdugo, M. A., Caballo, C., Balboni, G., Lachapelle, Y., Otrębski, W., & Schalock, R. L. (2005). Cross-cultural study of person-centered quality of life domains and indicators: A replication. *Journal of Intellectual Disability Research, 49* (Part 10), 734–739.

Keith, K. D. & Schalock, R. L. (Eds.) (2000). *Cross-cultural perspectives on quality of life.* Washington, DC: American Association on Mental Retardation.

Luckasson, R., Borthwick-Duffy, S., Buntinx, W. H. E., Coulter, D. L., Craig, E. M., Reeve, A. ... Tasse, M. J. (2002). *Mental retardation: Definition, classification, and systems of supports* (10th ed.). Washington, DC: American Association on Mental Retardation.

Luckasson, R. & Reeve, A. (2001). Naming, defining, and classifying in mental retardation. *Mental Retardation, 39,* 47–52.

McConkey, R., & O'Toole, B. (1995). Towards the new millennium. In B. O'Toole & R. McConkey (Eds.), *Innovations in developing countries for people with disabilities* (pp. 3–14). Chorley, UK: Lisieux Hall.

Medicode (1998). *International classification of diseases (9th rev.): Clinical modification* (6th ed.). Salt Lake City, UT: Medicode Publications.

Mercier, C., Saxena, S., Lecomte, J., Cumbrera, M. G., & Harnois, G. (2008). WHO ATLAS in global resources for persons with intellectual disabilities 2007: Key findings relevant to low- and middle-income countries. *Journal of Policy and Practices for Persons with Intellectual Disabilities, 5*, 81–88.

Montreal Declaration (2004). *Montreal Declaration on intellectual disability*. Montreal, Canada: PAHO/WHO Conference.

Nagi, S. Z. (1991). Disability concepts revisited: Implications for prevention. In A. M. Pope & A. R. Tarlov (Eds.), *Disability in America: Toward a National Agenda for Prevention* (pp. 309–327). Washington, DC: National Academy Press.

Neisser, U., Boodo, G., Bouchard, T. J. & Boykin, A. W. (1996). Intelligence: Knowns and unknowns. *American Psychologist, 51*, 77–101.

Oliver, M. (1996). *Understanding disability from theory to practice*. Basingstoke, UK: Palgrave Macmillan.

Parmenter, T. R. (2004). Contributions of IASSID to the scientific study of intellectual disability: The past, the present, and the future. *Journal of Policy and Practice in Intellectual Disabilities, 1*, 71–78.

Powers, L., Dinerstein, R., & Holmes, S. (2005). Self-advocacy, self-determination, social freedom, and opportunity. In K. C. Lakin and A. Turnbull (Eds.), *National goals and research for people with intellectual and developmental disabilities* (pp. 257–287). Washington, DC: American Association on Mental Retardation.

Putnam, M. (2005). Conceptualizing disability: Developing a framework for political disability identity. *Journal of Disability Policy Studies, 16*, 188–198.

Rapley, M. (2004). *The social construction of intellectual disability*. Cambridge, UK: Cambridge University Press.

Rioux, M. H. (1997). Disability: The place of judgment in a world of fact. *Journal of Intellectual Disability Research, 41*, 102–111.

Salamanca Statement. (1994). *Salamanca statement and framework for action in special needs education*. Salamanca, Spain: University of Salamanca, Department of Psychology.

Schalock, R. L. (2004). The emerging disability paradigm and its implications for policy and practice. *Journal of Disability Policy Studies, 14*, 204–215.

Schalock, R. L., Bonham, G. S., & Verdugo, M. A. (2008). The conceptualization and measurement of quality of life: Implications for program planning and evaluation in the field of intellectual disabilities. *Evaluation and Program Planning, 31*, 181–190.

Schalock, R. L., Borthwick-Duffy, S. A., Bradley, V. J., Buntinx, W. H. E., Coulter, D. L., Craig, E. M. ... Yeager, M. H. (2010). *Intellectual disability: Definition, classification, and systems of supports* (11th ed.). Washington, DC: American Association on Intellectual and Developmental Disabilities.

Schalock, R. L. & Luckasson, R. (2005). AAMR's definition, classification, and systems of supports and its relation to international trends and issues in the field of intellectual disabilities. *Journal of Policy and Practice in Intellectual Disability, 1*, 136–146.

Schalock, R. L., Luckasson, R., Shogren, K., Borthwick-Duffy, S., Bradley, V., Buntinx, W. H. E. ... Yeager, M. H. (2007). The renaming of mental retardation: Understanding the change to the term intellectual disability. *Intellectual and Developmental Disabilities, 45*, 116–124.

Schalock, R. L. & Verdugo, M. A. (2002). *Handbook on quality of life for human services practitioners*. Washington, DC: American Association on Mental Retardation.

Schalock, R. L. & Verdugo, M. A. (2008). *AAIDD international survey on terminology, definition, and classification.* Unpublished study.

Schalock, R. L., Verdugo, M. A., Bonham, G. S., Fantova, F., & van Loon, J. (2008). Enhancing personal outcomes: Organizational strategies, guidelines, and examples. *Journal of Policy and Practice in Intellectual Disabilities, 5*, 276–285.

Schalock, R. L., Verdugo, M. A., Jenaro, W., Wang, M., Wehmeyer, M., Xu, J., & Lachapelle, Y. (2005). A cross-cultural study of quality of life indicators. *American Journal on Mental Retardation, 110*, 298–311.

Schroeder, S. R., Gertz, G., & Velazquez, F. (2002). *Final project report: Usage of the term "mental retardation": Language, image and public education.* Lawrence, KS: Kansas University Center on Developmental Disabilities.

Summers, J. A., Poston, D. J., Turnbull, A. P., Marquis, J., Hoffman, L., Mannan. H. … Wang, M. (2005). Conceptualizing and measuring family quality of life. *Journal of Intellectual Disabilities Research, 49*, 777–783.

Switzky, H. N. & Greenspan, S. (2006). Summary and conclusion: Can so many diverse ideas be integrated? Multiparadigmatic models of understanding MR in the 21st century. In H. N. Switzky and S. Greenspan (Eds.), *What is mental retardation? Ideas for an evolving disability* (pp. 337–354). Washington, DC: American Association on Mental Retardation.

Thompson, J. R., Bradley, V., Buntinx, W. H. E., Schalock, R. L., Shogren, K. A., Snell, M. … Yeager, M. H. (2009). Conceptualizing supports and support needs. *Intellectual and Developmental Disabilities, 47*, 135–146.

United Nations (2006). *Convention on the rights of persons with disabilities.* Available at: http://www.un.org/disabilities/convention.

Van Loon, J. (2008). Aligning quality of life domains and indicators with SIS data. In R. Schalock, J. Thompson, & M. Tasse (eds.), *The support intensity scale companion guide: A resource for SIS users* (pp. 80–87). Washington, DC: American Association on Intellectual and Developmental Disabilities.

Vehmas, S. (2004). Ethical analysis of the concept of disability. *Mental Retardation, 42*, 209–222.

Verdonschott, M. M. L., de Witte, L. P., Reichrath, E., Buntinx, W. H. E., & Curfs, L. M. G. (2009). Community participation of people with intellectual disability: A review of empirical findings. *Journal of Intellectual Disability Research, 53*, 303–318.

Walker, S. P., Wachs, T. D., Gardner, J. M., Losoff, B., Wasserman, G. A., Pollitt, E. (2007). Child development: Risk factors for adverse outcomes in developing countries. *The Lancet, 369*, 145–157.

Wehmeyer, M. L., Buntinx, W. H. E., Coulter, D. L., Lachapelle, Y., Luckasson, R. A., Verdugo, M. A. … Yeager, M. H. (2008). The intellectual disability construct and its relation to human functioning. *Intellectual and Developmental Disabilities, 46*, 311–318.

World Health Organization (1993). *International statistical classification of diseases and related health problems* (10th ed.). Geneva: Author.

World Health Organization (2001). *International classification of functioning, disability, and health*: ICF. Geneva: Author.

World Health Organization (2007). *ATLAS on global resources for persons with intellectual disabilities.* Geneva: Author.

# Part VII

# Emotion and Well-Being

The study of basic emotions is one of the most compelling of research areas in cross-cultural psychology, and gave rise to early demonstrations of universality in facial expressions of emotion that are still considered standard in the field. Researchers, dating from the time of Charles Darwin, have long considered emotional expression innate and adaptive in its contribution to survival and well-being. In this section we will examine evidence that provides additional strong support for the innate biological nature of expressions of emotion.

Researchers have also studied human happiness across many cultures. Most people, according to these studies, are happy, and most people value happiness. However, people's happiness varies across cultures, and investigators continue to develop ways to study how culture may influence happiness and well-being. This research area demands a sensitive understanding of the role of language and measurement techniques, and respect for the ways people around the world define such constructs as happiness and well-being.

People may, for example, define well-being in terms of such measures as health or wealth, or they may attempt to measure personal satisfaction. Some of these measures are objective in nature, involving tangible or easily quantifiable entities like income. However, some of the most important facets of well-being are the subjective aspects of satisfaction. Thus, an individual could have large amounts of money, but remain unhappy or dissatisfied with life; or, conversely, a person with little money might be quite satisfied with his or her existence.

Contemporary investigators have begun to investigate the possibility that subjective well-being, like a number of other psychological constructs, may be influenced, at least in part, by an adaptive, homeostatic process. At the same time, sociocultural variables also serve to buffer or to moderate individual subjective well-being. And this area, like others in cross-cultural psychology, is fraught with the difficulties inherent in cross-cultural measurement.

# 17

# Culture, Emotion, and Expression

## David Matsumoto and Hyi Sung Hwang

### Basic Emotions

One of the most powerful concepts that has emerged in the last several decades in psychology is that known as *basic emotions*. These emotions—anger, disgust, fear, joy, sadness, surprise—are thought to be biologically wired in humans, and shared with nonhuman primates such as chimpanzees. Over the years research has indicated that a number of characteristics distinguish basic emotions from other emotions: (1) distinctive universal signals, (2) presence in other primates, (3) distinctive physiology (both in the autonomic nervous system—ANS—and the central nervous system—CNS), (4) distinctive universal antecedent events, (5) coherence among emotional responses, (6) quick onset and brief duration, (7) automatic appraisal, and (8) unbidden (Ekman, 1992).

One of these characteristics is especially central to the idea of basic emotions, that of the universality of facial expressions of emotion. In actuality, Darwin (1872/1998) was the first to argue that emotions are biologically innate and evolutionarily adaptive. According to Darwin, basic emotions involve universal signals that help people survive. Emotions are transient, biopsychosocial reactions programmed to help individuals to adapt to and cope with events related to survival and well-being. They are biological and innate because they involve physiological responses from the nervous systems, and prime skeletal muscle activities. They are psychological because they involve specific mental processes required for elicitation and regulation of response. And because they are reactions to events that have meaning to us, their expression is very important so that others in our surroundings immediately know what is going on.

The universal expression and recognition of emotion has been documented in numerous studies (Elfenbein & Ambady, 2002; Matsumoto, 2001; Matsumoto,

Keltner, Shiota, Frank, & O'Sullivan, 2008). These expressions have very rapid onsets, made possible by automatic appraisal with little awareness, and involuntary changes in expression and physiology in a coherent package. This assertion has been supported by studies of the ANS and CNS, supporting the fact that emotions are the products of evolution, with biological givens (Ekman, 1999).

Despite the overwhelming evidence concerning the universality of emotional expression and recognition, there have been controversies surrounding their source. Essentially, there are two potential sources of universal expressions: culture constant learning and biological innateness. Researchers supporting the learning perspective in emotion point out that the universality of facial expressions of emotion may actually be due to the ability of some people to learn how to spontaneously and automatically express emotions (Feldman Barrett & Russell, 1999; Fernandez-Dols & Ruiz-Belda, 1997; Russell, 1991). Thus, all people around the world learn to smile at happy events because they see others doing so, and are reinforced for doing it. An evolutionary viewpoint, however, would suggest that the universal facial expressions of emotion are biologically hardwired from birth, and present in all humans.

Clearly, merely documenting the universality of emotional expression in many cultures around the world does not resolve questions concerning the source of the universality; other methodologies are necessary, including studies of the developmental emergence of facial expressions (Oster, 2005), the similarities across nonhuman primates (Parr, Waller, Vick, & Bard, 2007; Vick, Waller, Parr, Pasqualini, & Bard, 2007), and the facial expressions of emotion in people with disabilities. One type of study that can help resolve this question involves the study of blind individuals, especially those born blind (congenital blindness). If people who are congenitally blind produce the same facial expressions of emotions as those with sight, that would be strong evidence for the biological innateness of facial expressions of emotion because there is no possible way they could have learned to produce those expressions by watching others. Moreover, if congenitally blind people all around the world from different cultures did so, that would be even stronger evidence for a biologically resident source for facial expressions of emotion. Thus, the study of the facial expressions of blind individuals is an interesting and important method by which to address this very basic question about emotions and culture.

In this chapter we describe two recent studies from our laboratory that address questions concerning the source of universal facial expressions of emotion by examining congenitally blind individuals in naturalistic settings. We believe these studies provide strong evidence for the biological innateness of the universality of facial expressions of emotion. We begin below with a brief review of previous studies of the expressions of blind individuals.

# Previous Studies Examining the Facial Expressions of Emotion in Blind Individuals

Over the years there have been a number of studies that have examined the expressive behavior of blind persons. Some of these examined voluntarily produced expressions, and indicated that blind individuals have difficulties posing emotional expressions (Dumas, 1932; Fulcher, 1942; Galati, Scherer, & Ricci-Bitti, 1997; Mistschenka, 1933; Ortega, Iglesias, Fernandez, & Corraliza, 1983; Rinn, 1991; Webb, 1977). But voluntarily produced expressions are not the same as involuntary, spontaneous expressions; they differ in many characteristics (Ekman, Hager, & Friesen, 1981; Hager & Ekman, 1985). And of course they cannot inform us as to whether blind individuals produce the same expressions spontaneously.

Other studies of blind individuals have examined spontaneous expressions, all reporting that blind individuals spontaneously produced the same types of emotional expressions as sighted individuals. But some of these studies relied on observation by the experimenter or assistants (Charlesworth & Kreutzer, 1973; Eibl-Eibesfeldt, 1973; Freedman, 1964; Goodenough, 1932; Thompson, 1941); thus it is not clear what expressions actually occurred in these studies because observation is not as precise as careful measurement of the actual behaviors that occurred. The others measured facial muscle movements (Cole, Jenkins, & Shott, 1989; Galati, Miceli, & Sini, 2001; Galati, Sini, Schmidt, & Tinti, 2003; Ortega et al., 1983; Peleg et al., 2006). But with the exception of Duchenne smiling (smiles involving the muscle around the eye and the muscle the pulls the lip corners up), no study examined the existence of specific facial *configurations* associated with emotions. Studying facial configurations is important because emotional expressions typically involve various combinations of facial muscle movements in specific configurations, and without examining the configurations, it is difficult if not impossible to draw any conclusions about emotional expressions.

# Recent Evidence Concerning the Source of Universal Facial Expressions of Emotion

Recently, we conducted two studies that examined the spontaneous facial expressions of emotion in a highly emotionally charged event—a medal round competition at the Olympic Games. The first study investigated the expressions of sighted athletes in the judo competition of the 2004 Athens Olympic Games (Matsumoto & Willingham, 2006). This study provided additional evidence for the universal production of facial expressions of emotion, and served as an important comparison base for the second study, which examined the spontaneous facial expressions of emotion of blind athletes competing at the 2004 Athens Paralympic Games just two weeks later (Matsumoto & Willingham, 2009). Our interest in this chapter is in the findings of the blind athletes, but let's first discuss what was found for the sighted athletes.

## Spontaneous expressions of sighted athletes

In the first study (Matsumoto & Willingham, 2006), we examined the expressions of the 84 gold, silver, bronze, and fifth place winners of the judo competition at the 2004 Athens Olympic Games, who came from 35 countries and six continents. They constituted a sample of the most culturally diverse individuals in whom spontaneous expressions that occurred in a highly charged, emotional event in three situations have been examined. We used high-speed photography to capture their facial reactions immediately at the end of the match and twice during the medal ceremonies. Their expressions were coded using the Facial Action Coding System (FACS) (Ekman & Friesen, 1978), and FACS codes were then compared to the Emotion FACS (EMFACS) dictionary to obtain emotion predictions (Ekman & Friesen, 1982; Matsumoto, Ekman, & Fridlund, 1991). EMFACS identifies facial muscle movements that are theoretically related to facial expressions of emotion posited by Darwin (1872/1998) and later Tomkins (1962, 1963), and empirically verified by studies of spontaneous expression and judgments of expressions by Ekman and colleagues over 20 years (Ekman, Davidson, & Friesen, 1990; Ekman & Friesen, 1971; Ekman, Friesen, & Ancoli, 1980; Ekman, Friesen, & Ellsworth, 1972; Ekman, Friesen, & O'Sullivan, 1988; Ekman, Sorenson, & Friesen, 1969).

The first set of analyses focused on the athletes' expressions produced immediately at match completion, when they knew they had either won a medal or not, and what medal. There were several theoretically important questions, the first of which was whether or not emotional expressions occurred at all. Until this study, no previous study had documented the existence of the universal facial expressions of emotion in a naturalistic field setting, so this very basic question was one of the primary foci of the study. In fact, of the 84 athletes photographed at match completion, there were no usable photos for six. Of the remaining 78, 67 (86%) provided at least one expression that was FACS codable. Of these, 33 (49%) provided two expressions, 13 (19%) provided three, and 5 (7%) provided four. Of the 118 expressions coded, only four did not produce an emotion prediction by the EMFACS dictionary. There was a considerable range of expressions, including different types of smiles, and expressions of contempt, disgust, fear, and sadness. Thus, the vast majority of the athletes produced expressions at match completion, and these corresponded to emotions predicted by EMFACS.

Another important theoretical question was whether or not the expressions differentiated between winners and the defeated. The results indicated that this was indeed the case; winners (gold and bronze medalists) were much more likely to smile than the defeated, while the latter (silver medalists and fifth placers) were much more likely to display sadness, contempt, disgust, or no expression.

We then examined whether the distribution of expressions differed according to culture. Because of small sample sizes for individual countries, we combined them into three categories: North America/Western Europe, East Asia, and all others. No analysis, however, produced a significant cultural difference, providing evidence for the universality of the expressions.

An additional merit to the focus on medal matches is the fact that the medalists participated in the medal ceremony. Medal ceremonies occurred in the middle of the competition area, and generally about 30 minutes after the completion of the last match of the day. Athletes marched in single file, stood behind the podium, stood up onto the podium when their names were called, and received their medal and wreath from a dignitary. After all athletes had received their medals, they stood for the playing of the national anthem of the gold medalist, and then gathered on the gold medal podium for a group photo. They then marched around all four sides of the field of play, stopping to greet fans and allow their photos to be taken. Although the medal matches are likely to lead to relatively uninhibited expressions because of the nature of the situation and competition, the medal ceremonies are clearly a social event, produced for the purpose of a viewing audience both in the arena and on television. By focusing on the athletes in the medal matches, we had a chance to observe and measure their spontaneous behavior in two very different situations.

Despite the fact that none of the silver medalists had smiled when they lost their medal match, almost all (54 of 56) of the athletes who participated in the medal ceremonies smiled when they received their medal. This finding spoke to the power of the social situation to change the nature of the expressions produced. When the specific type of smile was differentiated, however, differences emerged according to place finish. Gold and bronze medalists (i.e., those who had won their last match to take a medal) were much more likely to display Duchenne smiles, and especially uncontrolled Duchenne smiles,[1] than were the silver medalists (who lost their medal match). The silver medalists indeed did not display felt, enjoyable emotions as much as either the gold or bronze medalists.

We tested for cultural differences in these expressions using the country classification described above. No analysis, however, produced a significant result. Thus there were no cultural differences in smiling behavior when athletes received their medals. Essentially the same results were found when athletes' expressions were examined at the point in the medal ceremonies when they posed on the podium after the playing of the national anthem of the gold medalist.

This study produced strong evidence that the facial expressions of emotion previously reported in laboratory studies to be universal also occur in emotionally charged, naturalistic situations. That there were no cultural differences in the first expressions at match completion is supportive of the universality of these expressions when emotion is aroused. The expressions clearly differentiated between victors and the defeated. The facial signs of victory were Duchenne smiles; the expressions of the defeated athletes were strikingly different. Of the 42 athletes who lost their medal match, only one smiled; the others showed a variety of negative emotions, including sadness, contempt, disgust, and fear. Moreover, a not insubstantial number of them also displayed no emotion. That they did not simply show less smiling strongly suggests that their emotional experiences were substantially different than the gold and bronze medalists; thus there is not a linear decrease in smiling from gold, silver, and bronze medalists. Finally, nearly all athletes spontaneously smiled during both periods of the medal ceremonies, probably due to the highly staged and public nature of the ceremonies, demonstrating the powerful influence of social context on expressive behavior. But the smiles of the silver medalists were differentiated from the smiles of the gold and bronze medalists. Gold and bronze medalists displayed Duchenne smiles, while silver medalists were more likely to display controlled Duchenne smiles, non-Duchenne smiles, or smiles blended with sadness. On the podium, after receiving the medal and the national anthem of the gold medalist was played, some silver medalists did not smile at all, instead displaying contempt, sadness, or uninterpretable expressions.

## Spontaneous expressions of blind individuals

Our second study (Matsumoto & Willingham, 2009)—and the one we highlight in this chapter—compared the spontaneous facial expressions of congenitally blind and non-congenitally blind judo athletes at the 2004 Athens Paralympic Games with the sighted athletes reported above. The athletes in this study came from 23 cultures. If congenitally blind individuals from vastly different countries and cultures produce exactly the same facial configurations of emotion in the same emotionally evocative situations, this is strong evidence for the biological basis of their source, because these individuals could not possibly have learned to produce these expressions through visual observation. Some may argue that these individuals may have learned to produce those expressions tactilely, but one would have to argue that they are able to feel different expressions that occur spontaneously—i.e., rapidly, automatically, and unconsciously—on themselves or others, and then be able to spontaneously produce them, and that this occurs across all cultures studied. This proposition is hardly defensible.

This study was conducted in exactly the same manner as the study of sighted athletes reported earlier. Basically we identified expressions that occurred immediately at the end of the medal matches, and during the medal ceremonies. The expressions were coded by FACS, and then classified into emotion categories using the EMFACS dictionary. We compared the expressions of the blind and sighted athletes on both the levels of individual facial muscle movements and emotion categories. We also examined the difference between congenitally and non-congenitally blind athletes, and found no significant differences between them; thus we refer to them as one group below.

We essentially found near-perfect concordance between the expressions of the blind and sighted athletes. For example, correlations between the frequencies of the blind and sighted athletes' individual facial muscle behaviors were $r(32) = .94$, $p < .01$; $r(32) = .98$, $p < .01$; and $r(32) = .96$, $p < .01$, for match completion, receiving medal, and on the podium, respectively. These data are especially impressive given the fact that FACS coding identifies over 40 individual facial muscle movements that can occur at any one time, allowing for thousands of combinations of expressions. Despite this potential for great variety, the expressions were amazingly similar between the blind and sighted athletes.

Moreover, the expressions of the blind athletes functioned in exactly the same ways as the sighted athletes. For example, winners displayed all types of smiles, especially Duchenne smiles, more frequently than the defeated athletes, who displayed more disgust, sadness, and combined negative emotions. When receiving the medal, winners (gold and bronze) displayed all types of smiles and Duchenne smiles more frequently than did the defeated (silver medalists), who displayed more non-Duchenne smiles. Thus, not only were the expressions comparable; similar types of expressions occurred at similar times and in reaction to similar events. These findings lead us to believe that the emotions and their expressions functioned the same way for the blind individuals. (See Figures 17.1–17.4 for examples and comparisons.)[2] These findings provided strong support for the notion that blind individuals produce exactly the same facial expressions of emotion as sighted individuals when emotions are spontaneously aroused. Thus, we believe that there is a biologically based emotion–expression linkage that is universal to all people of all cultures.

# Conclusion

Emotions, and especially basic emotions, have been incredibly adaptive in our evolutionary history. They prepare individuals to respond to events in their environment immediately, automatically, and unconsciously. They are rapid

(a) **Blind athlete**        (b) **Sighted athlete**

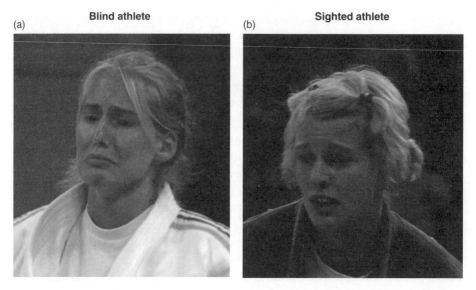

**Figure 17.1**   Comparison of blind and sighted athletes who just lost a match for a medal.

(a) **Blind athlete**        (b) **Sighted athlete**

**Figure 17.2**   Comparison of blind and sighted athletes who just won a match.

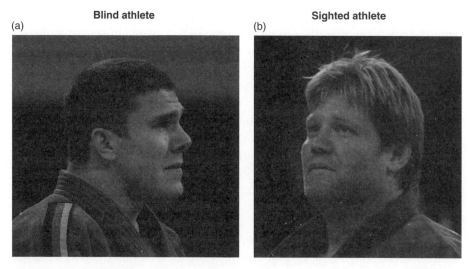

**Figure 17.3** Comparison of blind and sighted athletes who just won a match and were overcome with emotion.

**Figure 17.4** Comparison of blind and sighted athletes on the podium.

information-processing systems that help us deal with threats from predators, problems of nature, and problems based in the social complexity of human life. Thus, we would not be here today if it were not for our emotions and the way they have evolved and were naturally selected because emotions allow for complex social networks and relationships, and enhance the meaning of normal, daily activities. Emotions also drive us to pursue happiness, and to be creative in music, art, drama, and work. They motivate us to seek recreation and to engage in sports and organize competitions, whether in the local community Little League or the Olympic Games. They inspire us to search the sea and space, to create mathematics, an achievement no other species can claim, as well as an educational system. Furthermore, they allow us to go to the moon, to create a research laboratory on Antarctica, and send probes to Mars and Jupiter.

Cross-cultural research on emotion was particularly instrumental to the field of cross-cultural psychology in general, and contributed much to today's fervor with culture in psychology. The findings documenting the universality of facial expressions of emotion served as the backbone for much interest in culture, and spoke to something unique about humans and humanity that transcended culture. Moreover, facial expressions of emotion are the closest thing we have to a universal language.

However, doing behavioral research on emotion across cultures is incredibly difficult, even though now we have the tools and technologies to do so. Behavior coding is also labor intensive, and all of the caveats that are associated with cross-cultural research are magnified in the world of behavioral studies. Although there are challenges to this area of research in the future, these challenges bring with them opportunities and potential to make strong contributions to our knowledge of this very basic area of psychological science. Future studies promise to develop our societies and social relationships, not only for our survival but also for our common well-being.

# Notes

1   Controlled smiles were those that co-occurred with buccinator (AU 14), sometimes in combination with mentalis and/or orbicularis oris (AUs 17 and 24). These lower face actions give the appearance that the expressor is making a conscious effort to control their facial behaviors and/or words, as if they are "biting their lip." That they often occurred with both Duchenne and non-Duchenne smiles suggested that these facial actions qualified the meaning of the smile, adding information to the message of the smile beyond the signal of enjoyment.
2   All photographs courtesy of Bob Willingham.

# References

Charlesworth, W. R., & Kreutzer, M. A. (1973). Facial expressions of infants and children. In P. Ekman (Ed.), *Darwin and facial expression* (pp. 91–168). New York: Academic Press.

Cole, P. M., Jenkins, P. A., & Shott, C. T. (1989). Spontaneous expressive control in blind and sighted children. *Child Development, 60*(3), 683–688.

Darwin, C. (1872/1998). *The expression of emotion in man and animals.* New York: Oxford University Press.

Dumas, F. (1932). La mimique des aveugles [Facial expression of the blind]. *Bulletin de l'Academie de Medecine, 107,* 607–610.

Eibl-Eibesfeldt, I. (1973). The expressive behavior of the deaf-and-blind born. In M. von Cranach & I. Vine (Eds.), *Social communication and movement* (pp. 163–194). London: Academic Press.

Ekman, P. (1992). An argument for basic emotions. *Cognition & Emotion, 6*(3–4), 169–200.

Ekman, P. (1999). Basic emotions. In T. Dalgleish & T. Power (Eds.), *The handbook of cognition and emotion* (pp. 45–60). Chichester, UK: John Wiley and Sons, Ltd.

Ekman, P., Davidson, R. J., & Friesen, W. V. (1990). The Duchenne smile: Emotional expression and brain physiology: II. *Journal of Personality and Social Psychology, 58*(2), 342–353.

Ekman, P., & Friesen, W. V. (1971). Constants across culture in the face and emotion. *Journal of Personality and Social Psychology, 17,* 124–129.

Ekman, P., & Friesen, W. V. (1978). *FACS: Investigator's guide.* Palo Alto, CA: Consulting Psychologists Press.

Ekman, P., & Friesen, W. V. (1982). *EMFACS.* Unpublished manuscript.

Ekman, P., Friesen, W. V., & Ancoli, S. (1980). Facial signs of emotional experience. *Journal of Personality and Social Psychology, 39,* 1125–1134.

Ekman, P., Friesen, W. V., & Ellsworth, P. (1972). *Emotion in the human face: Guide-lines for research and an integration of findings.* New York: Pergamon Press.

Ekman, P., Friesen, W. V., & O'Sullivan, M. (1988). Smiles when lying. *Journal of Personality and Social Psychology, 54*(3), 414–420.

Ekman, P., Hager, J., & Friesen, W. V. (1981). The symmetry of emotional and deliberate facial actions. *Psychophysiology, 18,* 101–106.

Ekman, P., Sorenson, E. R., & Friesen, W. V. (1969). Pancultural elements in facial displays of emotion. *Science, 164*(3875), 86–88.

Elfenbein, H. A., & Ambady, N. (2002). On the universality and cultural specificity of emotion recognition: A meta-analysis. *Psychological Bulletin, 128*(2), 205–235.

Feldman Barrett, L., & Russell, J. A. (1999). The structure of current affect: Controversies and emerging consensus. *Current Directions in Psychological Science, 8,* 10–14.

Fernandez-Dols, J. M., & Ruiz-Belda, M. A. (1997). Spontaneous facial behavior during intense emotional episodes: Artistic truth and optical truth. In J. A. Russell & J. M. Fernandez-Dols (Eds.), *The psychology of facial expression* (pp. 255–274). New York: Cambridge University Press.

Freedman, D. G. (1964). Smiling in blind infants and the issue of innate versus acquired. *Journal of Child Psychology and Psychiatry, 5,* 171–184.

Fulcher, J. S. (1942). "Voluntary" facial expression in blind and seeing children. *Archives of Psychology, 272,* 5–49.

Galati, D., Miceli, R., & Sini, B. (2001). Judging and coding facial expression of emotions in congenitally blind children. *International Journal of Behavioral Development, 25*(3), 268–278.

Galati, D., Scherer, K. R., & Ricci-Bitti, P. E. (1997). Voluntary facial expression of emotion: Comparing congenitally blind with normally sighted encoders. *Journal of Personality and Social Psychology, 73*(6), 1363–1379.

Galati, D., Sini, B., Schmidt, S., & Tinti, C. (2003). Spontaneous facial expressions in congenitally blind and sighted children aged 8–11. *Journal of Visual Impairment and Blindness,* July, 418–428.

Goodenough, F. L. (1932). Expression of emotions in a blind-deaf child. *Journal of Abnormal and Social Psychology, 27,* 328–333.

Hager, J. C., & Ekman, P. (1985). The asymmetry of facial actions is inconsistent with models of hemispheric specialization. *Psychophysiology, 22*(3), 307–318.

Matsumoto, D. (2001). Culture and emotion. In D. Matsumoto (Ed.), *The handbook of culture and psychology* (pp. 171–194). New York: Oxford University Press.

Matsumoto, D., Ekman, P., & Fridlund, A. (1991). Analyzing nonverbal behavior. In P. W. Dowrick (Ed.), *Practical guide to using video in the behavioral sciences* (pp. 153–165). New York: John Wiley & Sons.

Matsumoto, D., Keltner, D., Shiota, M. N., Frank, M. G., & O'Sullivan, M. (2008). What's in a face? Facial expressions as signals of discrete emotions. In M. Lewis, J. M. Haviland, & L. Feldman Barrett (Eds.), *Handbook of emotions* (pp. 211–234). New York: Guilford Press.

Matsumoto, D., & Willingham, B. (2006). The thrill of victory and the agony of defeat: Spontaneous expressions of medal winners at the 2004 Athens Olympic Games. *Journal of Personality and Social Psychology, 91*(3), 568–581.

Matsumoto, D., & Willingham, B. (2009). Spontaneous facial expressions of emotion of congenitally and non-congenitally blind individuals. *Journal of Personality and Social Psychology, 96*(1), 1–10.

Mistschenka, M. N. (1933). Über die mimische Gesichtsmotorik der Blinden [Facial mimicking motor behavior in blind individuals]. *Folida Neuropathologica Estoniana, 13,* 24–43.

Ortega, J. E., Iglesias, J., Fernandez, J., M., & Corraliza, J. A. (1983). La expression facial en los ciegos congenitos [Facial expression in the congenitally blind]. *Infancia y Aprendizaje, 21,* 83–96.

Oster, H. (2005). The repertoire of infant facial expressions: An ontogenetic perspective. In J. Nadel & D. Muir (Eds.), *Emotional development* (pp. 261–292). New York: Oxford University Press.

Parr, L., Waller, B. M., Vick, S.-J., & Bard, K. A. (2007). Classifying chimpanzee facial expressions using muscle action. *Emotion, 7*(1), 172–181.

Peleg, G., Katzir, G., Peleg, O., Kamara, M., Brodsky, L., Hel-Or, H., … Nevo, E. (2006). Heriditary family signature of facial expression. *Proceedings of the National Academy of Sciences, 103*(43), 15921–15926.

Rinn, W. E. (1991). Neuropsychology of facial expression. In R. Feldman & B. Rime (Eds.), *Fundamentals of nonverbal behavior* (pp. 3–70). New York: Cambridge University Press.

Russell, J. A. (1991). Culture and the categorization of emotions. *Psychological Bulletin, 110,* 426–450.

Thompson, J. (1941). Development of facial expression of emotion in blind and seeing children. *Archives of Psychology, 37,* 1–47.

Tomkins, S. S. (1962). *Affect, imagery, and consciousness.* Vol. 1: *The positive affects.* New York: Springer.

Tomkins, S. S. (1963). *Affect, imagery, and consciousness*. Vol. 2: *The negative affects*. New York: Springer.

Vick, S.-J., Waller, B. M., Parr, L. A., Pasqualini, M. S., & Bard, K. A. (2007). A cross species comparison of facial morphology and movement in humans and chimpanzees using the Facial Action Coding System (FACS). *Journal of Nonverbal Behavior, 31*, 1–20.

Webb, C. (1977). The use of myoelectric feedback in teaching facial expression to the blind. *Biofeedback and Self-Regulation, 2*(2), 147–160.

# 18

# Happiness Around the World

## Jennifer Zwolinski

*We believe that a psychology of positive human functioning will arise that achieves a scientific understanding and effective interventions to build thriving in individuals, families, and communities.* (Seligman & Csikszentmihalyi, 2000)

Just six years after this prediction, the American Psychological Association honored Seligman with an Award for Scientific Contributions for his creation and development of the field of positive psychology—a field of study including well-being, engagement, meaning, and life satisfaction. One of the subfields of positive psychology receiving significant research attention has been the topic of happiness. Although this focus has remarkably increased with the growth of the positive psychology movement, scholars have been publishing scientific reports of happiness around the world for over 60 years. The earliest published empirical comparison of happiness across nations involved nine countries in 1948 (Buchanan & Cantril, 1953). This was followed by a comparative study in 1960 of 14 nations (Cantril, 1965), and a global survey in 1975 (Gallup, 1976) in which happiness in all parts of the world was assessed. Several ongoing international survey programs have also been developed, including the Eurobarometer (since 1973), the World Values Survey (since 1980) and the European Welfare study (Kalmijn & Veenhoven, 2005). Findings from these surveys as well as other large-scale cross-national comparisons of happiness and subjective appreciation of life as a whole have been gathered in Veenhoven's (2009a) World Database of Happiness, an ongoing register of scientific research on the world literature on happiness. To date, this collection includes more than 1,000 measures of happiness in more than 4,000 national surveys in 206 nations yielding over 10,000 correlational findings. The World Database of Happiness can be found at http://worlddatabaseof-happiness.eur.nl

The main goal of this chapter is to provide a general overview of some of this literature on happiness around the world. The first part of the chapter will focus on methodological issues when evaluating happiness across nations. The second section will review cross-national data on happiness, and the third part will include a discussion of how the empirical literature on happiness can facilitate well-being through government policy in the form of assessment and intervention.

## Happiness Applied to Culture: Methodological Considerations

### How is happiness generally defined?

To date, there is no universally accepted definition of happiness (for a review of the different definitions of happiness across cultures, see Harper, Guilbault, Tucker & Austin, 2007). According to the World Database of Happiness, happiness refers to "the subjective enjoyment of one's life as-a-whole" (Veenhoven, 2009b, para. 1). Individuals consider two components in evaluating their lives (Veenhoven, 2004a), specifically the hedonic level of affect (the degree to which pleasant affect dominates) and contentment (perceived realization of wants). These two components represent "affective" and "cognitive" appraisals of life, respectively. Together they create an overall evaluation of life, called "overall" happiness (Veenhoven, 2009c).

Veenhoven (2009d) has compiled numerous examples of both the affective and cognitive components in the World Database of Happiness. The Database evaluates and describes these assessments in terms of their substantive meaning (e.g., *focus* of assessment such as affect, and *timeframe* of happiness), method of assessment (e.g., *mode*, such as the technique by which happiness is assessed, *scale range*, and *scale type*) and subvariant of assessment (e.g., *wording* or variation of an otherwise similar phrase). These multiple methods of evaluating overall happiness have led to a better understanding of the ways in which happiness is experienced by diverse cultural groups.

The World Database of Happiness conception of happiness is similar, yet distinct, from other related terms used in the literature. For example, happiness and life satisfaction have been shown to be correlated yet there is evidence that they do not belong to the same latent variable ($\gamma = -.71$; happiness, but not life satisfaction, was reverse scored; Gundelach & Kreiner, 2004). It is not entirely correct to state that happiness refers solely to the affective component alone and life satisfaction refers entirely to the cognitive component, as some scholars have suggested, because these two components are related and therefore both should be considered in evaluating happiness (Haller & Hadler, 2006). It would not be accurate to suggest, for example, that a person is genuinely happy if that happiness is based entirely on faulty cognitive assumptions (Haller & Hadler, 2006) regarding life satisfaction. Therefore, a consideration of both the cognitive and affective components, as is included in the World Happiness Database, would be expected to yield a more comprehensive understanding of how people experience overall happiness.

## Is the experience of happiness universal?

The experience of happiness is likely to be universal (Ryan, Sheldon, & Deci, 1996), and people everywhere are likely to prefer the desirable to the undesirable, and the pleasant over the unpleasant (Diener & Diener, 1995; Michalos, 1991; Veenhoven, 1991). However, because the perception of what is desirable or pleasant varies substantially across cultures (Diener & Suh, 2000; Kitayama & Markus, 2000), it is reasonable to expect cross-cultural variations in what constitutes happiness and in the predictors of happiness.

For example, the definition and experience of well-being are different between North America and East Asia, likely because of divergent cultural models of the self (Uchida, Norasakkunkit, & Kitayama, 2004). Unlike Western cultures in which happiness is likely to be constructed as personal achievement, in East Asian cultures happiness is grounded in social harmony and connectedness (Uchida et al., 2004). Diener and Diener (1995) also provided support for diverse cultural models of the self in a 31-country investigation in which they found that self-esteem was more strongly correlated with subjective well-being in individualistic (e.g., European American) cultures than in collectivistic (e.g., East Asian) cultures.

Lu and Gilmour (2004) examined the lay conceptions of happiness between Chinese and American participants by examining free responses on a formal essay in response to the question "What is happiness?" They found distinct differences in the conception of happiness between the two groups. Whereas socially oriented subjective well-being emphasized role obligations as well as harmony and balance within the individual and one's surroundings among Chinese participants, individually oriented subjective well-being emphasized personal accountability and achievement for Euro American participants. The authors suggested that these different conceptions of happiness provide data to support the idea that culture molds the meaning of happiness.

One way to study how culture molds the meaning of happiness is to examine differences in emotional norms between collectivistic and individualistic cultures. Eid and Diener (2001) investigated intracultural variation in emotion norms in two individualistic groups (U.S. and Australia) and two collectivistic groups (China and Taiwan). They found that with respect to norms for positive emotions (pride, contentment, joy, and affection), the individualistic nations were very homogeneous, whereas the more collectivistic nations were rather heterogeneous. The nations did not have one set of norms that applied to all people. Instead, results suggested variability of emotional norms across society (Eid & Diener, 2001).

A lot of what is known about emotional norms in collectivistic cultures (especially in relation to individualistic cultures) has focused on Asian nations as representative of collectivistic cultures (Kim-Prieto & Eid, 2004). To examine the divergences in emotions and emotion norms that may be observed in other collectivistic cultures, Kim-Prieto and Eid (2004) studied the emotion norms of five African nations (Ghana, Nigeria, South Africa, Tanzania, and Zimbabwe). Results indicated emotion norms that replicated those of the collectivistic cultures of East Asia, but also found numerous exceptions. In terms of positive affect, African nations were less hedonic than Western nations but more hedonic than Eastern cultures, particularly China. Consistent with Eid and Diener's (2001) work, these results highlight the need to consider both within-nation and between-nation variability in emotional norms, especially as they relate to positive affect. More insight into cultural norms or biases that may influence these findings will lead to a better understanding of how emotions are experienced across different cultural groups.

## Could observed differences in happiness simply be due to cultural bias?

The focus of this section is on the methodological literature that is specific to happiness. A more thorough examination of the methodological issues associated with the related concept, subjective well-being, is described by Robert A. Cummins and Anna L. D. Lau in this volume. As in the subjective well-being literature, numerous scholars have examined whether cross-national differences in happiness were due to cultural bias or social inequality. In response to the issue of language and/or translation issues, many studies fail to show consistent differences due to subtle variations in the meaning of key terms used in the questions in different languages (Ouweneel & Veenhoven, 1991). Gundelach and Kreiner (2004) found that language alone did not account for differences in cross-cultural variation in happiness. For example, in Austria, where the language is German, Austrians reported higher levels of happiness than Germans reported in Germany. Veenhoven (1993) also maintains that there are no consistent language effects although some researchers still argue that happiness can be interpreted differently in different non-English languages (Mathews, 2006).

Even if the term "happy" in itself does not make a difference in how people respond to assessments in different languages, culture may play a role (Gundelach & Kreiner, 2004). To address this concern, Ouweneel and Veenhoven (1991) evaluated the possibility that cross-national differences in happiness were due to differences in social desirability (e.g., whether there was a greater difference in responses regarding "general happiness" compared to responses about "happiness in the past few weeks"). They assumed that the latter would be less vulnerable to desirability distortion because it is less of a failure to report being more recently let down than to admit one's life is unsatisfactory in general. They did not find support for this assumption.

Still, other researchers have observed cultural differences in how individuals respond to questions about happiness. Argyle (2001) compared countries and groups with a positive happiness bias to those with a negative happiness bias. For example, North Americans report more positive self-views and self-serving biases, and engage in more self-enhancement than East Asians (Suh, 2000). The high happiness scores reported in the U.S. may be partly due to social norms toward positive affect (Argyle,

2001). In individualistic cultures, there is more pressure to display positive emotions, whereas collectivistic cultures seem to be less restrictive toward positive emotions (Safdar et al., 2009). This might explain why Chinese participants display the lowest frequency and intensity for positive emotions (e.g., happiness or joy) compared to Australian and American participants (Eid & Diener, 2001). Similarly, when shown a disgusting film with an interviewer (as opposed to watching it alone), Japanese participants masked their negative emotions by smiling when in the presence of an interviewer, whereas the American participants looked disgusted in the presence of the interviewer (Friesen, 1972). In China, people focus more on negative events, are less optimistic than Americans, and tend to have a more modest demeanor (Lee & Seligman, 1997), all of which may influence their responses to these assessments.

Still, not all Eastern groups are drastically different from their Western counterparts. Diener, Suh, Smith, and Shao (1995) found that U.S. college students viewed life satisfaction, happiness, joy and contentment as more important than Chinese college students. However, there were no differences on these variables between U.S. and Korean college students. U.S. college students also reported feeling and expressing positive affect to be more desirable and appropriate than did the Chinese and Korean groups. Chinese students thought that experiencing and expressing negative affect were more desirable and appropriate than U.S. students (Diener et al., 1995). These results suggest that the local social context should be considered in order to fully understand happiness across cultures (Mathews, 2006).

Perhaps observed group differences in happiness are part of broader differences in well-being which result from "quality of society" or societies with better living conditions (Ouweneel & Veenhoven, 1991). After controlling for real national income, Ouweneel and Veenhoven (1991) found that happiness tended to be higher in countries that provided citizens with material comfort, social security, education, healthcare, and political rights—explaining 80% of the variance in average happiness in the 28-nation sample. Further, happiness was strongly related to life expectancy and less anxiety and/or psychological distress (Ouweneel & Veenhoven, 1991). Overall, these results showed that there are sizeable differences in happiness between countries and that there was little support for the notion that these differences are entirely due to cultural bias.

Some people or cultural groups may simply be unhappy, and this may not be attributable to methodological issues. Since the 1980s, Russians' reported happiness has been low in comparison to other nations and Russians have been less happy than during the Communist period. Doubts were raised about the validity of these self-reports, indicating that the data may not actually reflect their self-appraisals, due to distortions in translation and to a differential response bias. Veenhoven (2001) sought to examine unhappiness reports in Russia, including whether this tendency to report unhappiness may be due to unfavorable comparison to the West. Results indicated that Russians understood the questions well and that their responses about life were consistent. Their unhappiness was consistent with the problematic economy and their average satisfaction was lower than predicted given their life expectancy, mood, and suicide rates. Overall, these results suggest that Russians were as unhappy as they reported, and Veenhoven (2001) proposed that this was not due to the Russian character as much as to social transitions that were occurring during the time of the study.

The fact that there may be important methodological considerations that influence how researchers interpret cross-cultural differences or similarities in happiness does not minimize the value of what we know about happiness. There may be measurement errors or interview/assessment biases that influence the results; however, this is common to all social sciences (Schimmel, 2009). As with all scientific literature, these methodological issues emphasize the need to be sensitive to how assessment and/or cultural explanations may have impacted the results of these studies, as well as the extent to which the results can be generalized to other groups. Given these considerations, the next section will review some of the findings on people's happiness in relation to others around the world.

## Ratings of Happiness Around the World

### Are most people happy?

Diener and Diener (1996) examined cross-national data and reported that most people are happy (i.e., most report positive or above neutral levels of well-being). However, these data came almost entirely from people in industrialized societies and most participants were college students. As a result, it is unclear whether some factor related to life in industrialized culture contributed to these reports, such as individualistic definitions of the self (Triandis, 1995) and/or industrialized society meeting more human needs (e.g., better healthcare and more formalized social welfare systems).

To more thoroughly examine the influence of industrialization on perceived happiness, Biswas-Diener, Vittersø, and Diener (2005) extended Diener and Diener's original (1996) analyses to cultures that were substantially different than industrialized cultures, including collectivistic and materially simple cultures, namely the Kenyan Maasai, the U.S. Amish, and the Greenlandic Inughuit. These results for non-industrialized cultures indicated that 84% of the sample scored above neutral levels of well-being, providing further support for Diener and Diener's original findings and also providing evidence that wealth and the material comforts of industrialized cultures are not essential for happiness.

Still, this does not mean that all people are happy. Data are still limited from the poorest nations of the world (e.g., Rwanda, Mozambique, Afghanistan; Tov & Diener, 2007). Relative to what is known about happiness in modern societies, few quantitative studies have examined well-being in smaller cultures (for a review, see Tov & Diener, 2007).

## Do national happiness reports change over time?

In order to examine whether this tendency toward happiness is stable across time, Inglehart, Welzel, and Foa (n.d.) examined happiness trends in 24 countries, from 1946 to 2006. Using Veenhoven's World Database of Happiness, which included data from the first four waves of the Values Surveys, they found that among the countries for which there were long-term data, 19 of the 26 countries showed rising happiness levels and some of these were steeply rising trends (India, Ireland, Mexico, Puerto Rico, and South Korea). However, the publics of some societies did not report being any happier. For example, the U.S., which had the most extensive time series data, showed a flat trend from 1946 to 2006. The British dataset, which has the second fullest time series, showed a downward trend for this same time period, and an upward trend for the period of 1980 to the time of the study. Only four countries showed downward trends in happiness (Austria, Belgium, the U.K., and West Germany).

More representative data support the idea that happiness is increasing across time and for most people. Data from 1981 to 2007 including 88 countries containing 90% of the world's population showed that happiness rose in 45 of the 52 countries that had substantial time series data (Inglehart, Foa, Peterson, & Wetzel, 2008). This rise was particularly likely in countries that allowed people relatively free choice in how to live their lives. The perception of free choice has been shown to increase with factors such as economic development, democratization, and increasing social tolerance (Inglehart et al., 2008).

Some scholars have expanded the study of cross-national long-term happiness states to "happy life years," which refers to an estimate of how long and happy the average citizen will live in a nation in this era (Veenhoven, 2006). A formula for happy life years takes into account life expectancy:

Happy life years = Life expectancy at birth × 0–1 happiness.

Assume that life expectancy in a country is 50 years, and that the average score on a 0- to 10-point happiness scale is 5. Converted to a 0–1 scale, the happiness score is 0.5. The product of 50 and 0.5 is 25. So the number of happy life years is 25 in that country (Veenhoven, 2004b).

Using this formula for data from 95 nations between 1995 and 2005, Veenhoven (2006) provided results in terms of three happy life year groups: top (or > 60 years), middle (or +/− 40 years), and bottom (or < 25 years). The top five nations with the greatest number of happy life years were Switzerland (63.9 years), Denmark, Iceland, Austria, and Australia, whereas the nations with the fewest happy life years were Moldova (23.7 years), Uganda, Angola, Tanzania, and Zimbabwe (11.5 years). The difference between the highest and lowest nations in terms of happy life years was more than 50 years. Research has shown that people live longer, happier lives in nations characterized by economic affluence, freedom, and justice (Veenhoven, 2005); these three qualities explained 66% of the variance in happiness life years.

The relation between income and happiness is one area of cross-cultural research as it relates to well-being that has received significant research attention. Easterlin (1974) investigated the relation between happiness and income using a dataset involving 30 surveys in 19 countries from 1946 to 1970. His findings indicated a positive association between happiness and income for within-country comparisons. However, cross-country comparisons and time series data yielded a weaker relation between income and happiness.

In their more recent reassessment of the Easterlin paradox using multiple longitudinal datasets spanning decades, Stevenson and Wolfers (2008) found a clear relation between economic growth and happiness. Their results indicate a clearer relation between absolute income and rising happiness and a more limited role for relative income comparisons. They were also interested in studying whether the happiness–Gross Domestic Product (GDP) gradient systematically differed from the satisfaction–GDP gradient by examining datasets (1975 Gallup-Kettering survey, the First European Quality of Life Survey conducted in 2003, and the 2006 Eurobarometer) that asked respondents about both happiness and life satisfaction. Results indicated that the happiness–GDP relation was roughly similar to, although slightly weaker than, the life satisfaction–GDP relation.

Deaton's (2008) review of the data concerning happiness and income provide further evidence against the Easterlin paradox. First, richer countries have been shown to be happier. Second, the cross-country effect of income on happiness tended to be larger than the within-country effect of income and happiness. Finally, results indicated that among rich countries, there is no correlation between national income and national happiness. Most of these findings were based on the World Values Survey, which includes data from both rich and poor countries. (For an additional review of the relation between income and happiness within and between countries, see Arthaud-Day and Near (2005).)

In response to recent dissenting views of the income–happiness association, Easterlin and Angelescu (2009) argue that this may be due to the failure to distinguish between the short- and long-term temporal relationship between happiness and income. In the short term, when fluctuations in macroeconomic conditions dominate the association, happiness and income are positively related. However, in the long term, happiness and income are unrelated (Easterlin & Angelescu, 2009).

The assumption that economic growth is a sure route to well-being requires further investigation (Easterlin & Angelescu, 2009). Based on some of the findings presented earlier in this section, specifically, that happiness around the world has been shown to be related to social factors other than simply economic growth, such as personal freedom and justice, should increasing happiness around the world be a goal of public policy? The next section will attempt to answer this question.

# What Should Be Done with These Findings on Culture and Happiness?

Before answering this question, it is important to note that most people value happiness. In an unpublished study, Diener and Oishi (2006) asked over 10,000 respondents in 48 nations to rate the average importance of happiness in their lives (as cited in Oishi, Diener, & Lucas, 2007). Results indicated that happiness was the highest of 12 possible attributes, with a mean of 8.03 on a nine-point Likert-type scale (compared to 7.54 for success and 6.84 for material wealth).

Most people not only value happiness; they also benefit from happiness. Happiness is not just about feeling good for the individual; it also has a positive impact on society. Happy people fare much better on the domains of love, work, and health, compared to unhappy people, according to meta-analytic research evaluating 225 reports (Lyubomirsky, King & Diener, 2005). Happy people participate more in community organizations, are more liked by others, are less likely to get divorced, tend to live slightly longer, perform better at work, and earn higher incomes. Although the effect sizes observed by Lyubomirsky, King and Diener (2005) were modest at best ($r = .20–.30$), they were almost never negative, suggesting that harmful effects of subjective well-being were extremely unlikely.

## How can the literature on happiness inform social policy?

In light of the fact that happiness is valued by most people and that it is associated with better outcomes for society, national findings about happiness can help to inform social policy decisions in order to increase happiness. Veenhoven (2004a) argued that research on happiness can serve social policy in several ways. First, this research can assist in evaluating citizens' dissatisfaction that is not traditionally considered in the political process. Second, the findings provide information about the effectiveness of governmental interventions, including income supplementation, job creation, and housing programs. Third, the findings provide feedback on the relative effectiveness of the policy regime as a whole. These findings are discussed in more detail in Veenhoven's (1993, 1994, 2000) prior work.

## Should government strive to increase individuals' happiness?

Haybron (2008a) addressed this question by considering the kinds of environments that are conducive to human flourishing. Do individuals fare best when they have the greatest possible freedom to share their own lives based on their own priorities? Or do they fare best when given social or physical contexts that influence or constrain individuals' choices (e.g., by favoring certain ways of living or goods)?

Haybron (2008a) argued that individuals may fare best with the latter (i.e., *contextualism* as opposed to *individualism*), because individuals have human needs that are not best left to individual choice. Despite the controversy, this stance is worth considering. Happiness may be less influenced by individual choice and more influenced by social and physical support networks that shape the way individuals live (Haybron, 2008a), further suggesting that government does have a role in promoting individual happiness.

Similarly, Huppert (2009) supports the role of a broad population-based approach for enhancing well-being. Western psychology has traditionally emphasized the individual rather than the collective and so explanations of psychological dysfunction as well as treatments are usually conceptualized on the individual level. Given that individuals reflect the characteristics of the population in which they live, Huppert suggests a population-based approach for reducing disorder and improving well-being. The aim of interventions, therefore, should not be on reducing distressing symptoms or enhancing thriving in individuals (individual approach), but rather on reducing the number of people who have the distressing symptoms and increasing the number of thriving individuals (population approach). A small shift in the population mean of the underlying risk factors or symptoms can do more to improve well-being and decrease distress than that which would be observed at the individual treatment level (Huppert, 2009).

## Where to begin? Assessment and application

One way to begin making these changes on a more population-based (or government) level is to simply try to start making citizens or other cultural groups around the world as happy as possible. However, the effects of happiness on important life outcomes appear to be non-linear (Diener, Nickerson, Lucas, & Sandvik, 2002; Oishi & Koo, 2008). For example, although cheerfulness generally has a positive effect on current income, the association is curvilinear with current income increasing more rapidly at lower than at higher cheerfulness ratings (Diener et al., 2002). Large-scale cross-sectional survey data show that the optimal level of happiness varies across context (Oishi et al., 2007). Thus, individuals with the highest levels of happiness tended to fare best in terms of close relationships and volunteer work, whereas individuals with slightly lower levels of happiness tended to fare best on income and education. Optimal levels of happiness might differ in various domains because complete satisfaction with one's current circumstances might prevent pursuit of change in achievement domains like education and income (Oishi et al., 2007). More research is needed to examine how the optimal level of happiness might differ for diverse cultural groups and / or nations.

This is one reason why any attempt at increasing happiness should begin with assessment to determine where intervention can best be applied. To facilitate this role for government, psychologists have led the call for measures of subjective well-being to form the basis of government policy and the political assessment of a nation's success (Diener, 2000). Psychological researchers such as Ed Diener, Martin Seligman and Nobel laureate Daniel Kahneman have encouraged governments to create national well-being accounts to supplement existing economic data (Huppert et al., 2006). Some psychologists argue that public policy decisions at the organizational, corporate, and government levels should be more heavily influenced by issues relating to well-being, encouraging systematic assessment of well-being so that policy makers can have these findings for implementation into policy-making decisions (Diener & Seligman, 2004).

Psychologists and economists have recently created numerous large-scale studies that track well-being over time with the goal of enabling decision-makers to use information about well-being to guide public policy (for a review, see Oishi et al., 2007). According to the Cambridge Well-being Institute (WBI), a group of interdisciplinary scholars that aims to promote the highest quality research in the science of well-being, the measurement of well-being should incorporate multiple domains, including how people feel and function, emphasize social well-being, and incorporate two complementary methodologies (general evaluative questions and more specific questions about the person's recent events) (Huppert et al., 2006).

Annual national indicators of subjective well-being would provide valuable information that potentially could enlighten policy decisions and individual choices (Diener, 2000). According to Diener, there are a number of advantages to a national indicator of subjective well-being, especially one that that tracks the same individuals over time to see where changes are most needed:

- First, it would be valuable in determining the domains in which people are more and less satisfied, thus suggesting where interventions might be most needed.
- Second, a national index would provide an educational function, alerting people to the factors that influence their subjective well-being.
- Finally, the development of a national survey to track subjective well-being would increase the likelihood that it will become an outcome variable that is considered in policy decisions.

Schimmel (2009) provided a good example of why ongoing well-being or happiness assessment is needed to complement social policy decisions. He examined the extent to which happiness research was complementary to the United Nations Development Programme's (UNDP)[1] main indicator, the Human Development Index (HDI). Happiness in this context refers to the degree to which an individual judges the overall quality of his/her life favorably, whereas the HDI focuses on poverty, wealth, and development. The happiness data from Schimmel's investigation are from Veenhoven's 2006 World Database of Happiness, and the HDI ranking is based on the year 2005 (UNDP, 2005: 219–222). Happiness rankings ranged from 8.2 in Denmark to 3.9 in Tanzania (higher scores translate to increased happiness), and the HDI was ranked by high, medium, and low levels of human development for 177 countries. Results indicate that happiness tends to follow the human development ranking; for example, Denmark shows a high levels of development (14th position) and Tanzania shows a low level of development (164th position).

However, Schimmel (2009) also observed some important exceptions. First, some countries are in a better position on happiness than in the HDI ranking. Columbia and Switzerland are in second position for happiness (average of 8.1), yet they are in the medium (69th) and high (7th) positions, respectively, for human development. Second, other countries have a worse position in happiness than the HDI would suggest. Hungary and Slovakia are among the last 30 countries in the happiness ranking, while they are high on HDI. Clearly, individuals' subjective experience of happiness is different from the UNDP's vision of development, indicating that despite advances in human development, people are not necessarily any happier (Schimmel, 2009). These findings suggest that happiness studies should be complementary to the HDI in order to obtain a more comprehensive understanding of well-being especially as it relates to policy. The integration of a happiness indicator that incorporates additional dimensions of happiness detected by research is indispensable for UNDP to correct its analytical approach to development from "development as freedom" to "development as happiness" (Schimmel, 2009).

Once comprehensive assessments including measures of happiness or well-being are conducted to see where intervention is needed, then culturally appropriate, empirically validated treatments can be applied. Members of the WBI emphasize that interventions need to be evidence-based; accordingly, they are developing criteria for empirically based interventions including specific characteristics of the intervention (e.g., content, mode of delivery, duration, standardization), characteristics of the evidence for effectiveness (e.g., whether the trial was double-blind and placebo controlled), and characteristics of the individual (e.g., individual differences in temperament, affect, age, gender, education). They recognize that treatments will likely need to be tailored to the groups they are serving. Their website offers information about ongoing intervention programs that focus on children, patients, and the workplace (http://www.cambridgewellbeing.org/).

The WBI website also offers links to other ongoing policy programs such as the "Foresight Project on Mental Capital and Well-being." The goal of this project has been to advise the government on how to achieve the best possible mental development and mental well-being for citizens in the U.K. (http://www.foresight. gov.uk/OurWork/ActiveProjects/Mental%20Capital/Welcome.asp). Beddington et al. (2008) completed a report for this project, involving more than 450 experts from 16 countries evaluating 80 peer-reviewed papers, with numerous international workshops addressing the challenges and opportunities that lie ahead in the next 20 years for policy-makers in the U.K. and around the world. They emphasized that in order to prosper economically and socially, countries must learn how to capitalize on their citizens' cognitive resources. Governments have tremendous opportunities to create environments in which citizens' well-being can flourish through early intervention which can assist in reducing crime, improving work productivity, and decreasing pressure on health and care systems by preserving mental capital in older age. Inaction can lead to numerous challenges to well-being across the lifespan, including learning disabilities, depression, and dementia. These interventions will require significant changes in the nature of governance by placing mental capital and well-being at the heart of policy-making (Beddington et al., 2008).

Other scholars have also offered specific social policy suggestions that aim to increase happiness. For example, the New Economics Foundation (nef) is an independent "think-and-do tank" that aims to improve quality of life by challenging mainstream thinking on economic, environmental, and social issues (http://www. neweconomics.org/). As part of nef's "Well-being Manifesto," they challenged the assumption that government's primary role is to improve the economy. Instead, the nef maintains that a greater effect on well-being can be accomplished by changing work–life balance, one's living environment, and the vibrancy of local communities.

Shah and Marks (2004) of nef reported eight inter-related guideline areas where government in the U.K., and perhaps in other developed nations, could take more effective actions to promote well-being. First, they suggested the nations should create a set of national well-being accounts. Next, they can create a well-being economy with emphasis on employment, meaningful work, and environmental taxation. Third, government should help citizens reclaim time by improving the work–life balance, gradually reducing the maximum working week to a 35- or 30-hour week. Fourth, create an education system that promotes flourishing so people can reach performance goals. Fifth, refocus the National Health Service (NHS) to promote complete health making patients "co-creators" or partners in promoting health. Sixth, invest in the very early years and parenting, which may include paid parental leave to cover at least the whole of a child's first two years of life. Seventh, discourage materialism and promote authentic advertising, including a decline in commercial advertising aimed at young children. Eighth, strengthen active citizenship, social well-being and civil society. These guidelines offer a valuable effort to stimulate evidence-based policy-making by translating results of social research into a practical political program. Such efforts can improve the quality of democracy and political decisions (Ott, 2005). Ongoing standardized assessments are needed to determine whether these policy standards are culturally appropriate for certain countries and how best to evaluate these recommendations.

One country that has successfully tracked and integrated well-being standards into public policy is Bhutan. King Jigme Singye Wangchuk of Bhutan puts more emphasis on happiness than on economic development in his statement that "Gross National Happiness is more important that Gross Domestic Product" (Royal Government of Bhutan, 2002). The government of Bhutan is aware that certain approaches to development may lead to an increase in unhappiness, so it minimizes any initiatives that it believes will contribute to this dissatisfaction. The process of review is apparent in a series of five-year plans. The king recognizes that "if at the end of a plan period, our people are not happier than they were before, we should know that our plan has failed" (as cited in Shrotryia, 2006).

The plan has been effective. Conditions in the 1990s were better than they were in the 1960s (for a review, see Shrotryia, 2006). For example, over 90% of the population had access to primary healthcare, more than 90% of children were immunized, life expectancy at birth had gone up to 66 years, although adult literacy remained low at 54%. Data from the Royal Government of Bhutan (2006; as cited in Shrotryia, 2008) also indicated a very high percentage of people enjoying a happy status of life. In a study of 126,115 citizen of Bhutan, a total of 45.2% reported they were "very happy" while 51.6% reported being "happy" using a three-point scale (1 = very happy, 2 = happy, and 3 = not very happy). Bhutan is in the eighth position on the World Map of Happiness (White, 2007) based on life expectancy, access to education, GDP per capita, and life satisfaction (for more information and to see a map of the Happy Planet Index, see the nef's website at http://www.happyplanetindex.org/). Although Bhutan lags behind in GDP and the HDI, the country has a much higher status on happiness, especially compared to many developed nations (Shrotryia, 2008). Clearly, Bhutan's policy toward "Gross National Happiness" is working in terms of improving overall quality of life.

## Further considerations when implementing intervention

Even if an ideal policy is to increase happiness for citizens, it is not entirely clear, from an empirical point of view, how these policies should be implemented (Coyne & Boettke, 2006) for diverse groups of people around the world. Some questions to be addressed in this section are as follows: What are some considerations for governments in the application of the happiness literature to public policy? Can peoples' expectations about happiness be set too high? Is happiness the most desirable goal?

One way for government to help individuals realize what will genuinely lead to happiness comes from research on important life outcomes with the knowledge that what is beneficial for one cultural group may not apply to another group. For example, Oishi and Diener (2001) asked European American and Asian American participants to list five important goals they hoped to accomplish in the next month. The participants then judged the extent to which each goal was related to independence (i.e., an attainment of one's own fun or enjoyment). One month later, participants evaluated their prior month's life satisfaction as well as the extent to which their goals had been achieved. For the European American sample, happiness increased as more independent goals were achieved. On the other hand, for the Asian sample, happiness increased as a function of goal achievement rated to be less independent (and therefore probably more interdependent; e.g., bringing happiness to parents). This is consistent with prior studies cited in this chapter showing that in some European American cultures, happiness tends to be defined and experienced as personal achievement, whereas in some East Asian cultures it tends to be defined and experienced as a manifestation of social harmony.

Another way that governments can use the happiness literature is by implementing programs that educate individuals about cognitive errors when trying to anticipate what will increase their happiness. For example, people often make important life decisions (such as the decision to get married or change careers) based in part on the predicted level of happiness or life satisfaction that would result, and yet these predictions may be wrong (Wilson & Gilbert, 2005). Individuals are not very good at *affective forecasting*, or knowing what will make them happy (Gilbert, 2006) and they tend to adapt relatively quickly and return to their prior level of happiness (*hedonic adaptation*). Diener's (2000) review of the literature suggests that at the individual level, people must realize that lasting happiness may come, in part, from activities such as working for one's goals, being involved in "flow" activities, being a part of close social relationships, and experiencing renewable physical and mental pleasures.

If individuals are poor at affective forecasting, then they may also have a tendency toward *positive illusions*, which can lead to problems with inflated self-evaluations as well as personal overestimations of control over future outcomes (Haybron, 2008b), which may facilitate poor choices (Taylor & Brown, 1988). One of these poor choices may be explained by *lay rationalism* or the tendency to base decisions on rationalistic "hard" attributes (e.g., economic values) as opposed to "soft" attributes (e.g., happiness) (Hsee & Hastie, 2006). Some individuals may choose "hard" criteria even when they predict that those options will lead to the individual being worse off (e.g., when making a career choice between a higher and lower paying job).

An important question for all scholars and governments working to increase happiness was raised by Oishi et al. (2007): Can people's expectations for happiness sometimes be set too high, and can these expectations lead to negative outcomes for the individual? Certain problems can arise when focusing on attaining ultra-happiness such as adaptation (Diener, Lucas, & Scollon, 2006; Wilson & Gilbert, 2005), and that finding that people's happiness is influenced in part by their temperaments (Lykken & Tellegen, 1996). Trying to obtain continuously high levels of happiness and positive affect could require risky behaviors (e.g., thrill-seeking activities, drug use) as well as novelty-seeking (e.g., constantly seeking new relationships and activities so positive affect or arousal levels are maintained). These forms of intense happiness-seeking behaviors are likely to lead to instability in a person's life (Oishi et al., 2007).

Although it is not clear how much happiness is "enough", what is clear is that extremely high levels of happiness may not be the most desirable goal (Oishi et al.,

2007) for the individual or society. The type of happiness may also differ for different groups. Whereas Western cultures tend to focus on individual happiness or self-happiness, some Asian and African cultures focus on how individual happiness can be derived from group or family happiness (Harper, Guilbault, Tucker, & Austin, 2007). Cultural awareness can facilitate an understanding of the difference between individual (*one-directional*) happiness from within-group (*two-directional*) happiness when applying well-being interventions to diverse groups (Harper et al., 2007).

Happiness is not static, and subjective well-being may vary over time for different individuals, so a policy implemented at one period may not apply at a future period of time (Coyne & Boettke, 2006), hence the need for continual assessment. Although psychologists have an important role to play in educating lay people about optimal levels of happiness and the levels of happiness that are realistic, they have not yet been able to give much advice with confidence, because no data have existed on these issues until very recently (Oishi et al., 2007). An optimal level of happiness for an individual is likely influenced by that individual's personal resources, challenges, the behavioral domain being assessed (e.g., work or personal relationships), and the type of well-being being evaluated (Oishi et al., 2007). All of these factors may be influenced by specific cultural factors and these should be considered when applying any form of assessment or intervention with diverse groups of individuals.

## Conclusion

Numerous cross-national studies on happiness have provided valuable information on happiness around the world. We now know, for example, that most people around the world are happy (Biswas-Diener et al., 2005; Diener & Diener, 1996) and most people value happiness (Oishi et al., 2007). We also know that citizens' happiness tends to benefit society in numerous ways.

To increase happiness around the world, interdisciplinary researchers have led the call for national assessments of well-being (Huppert et al., 2006) and are offering suggestions on how to implement national well-being standards (Shah & Marks, 2004). For example, members of the WBI are working with government and social policy organizations to ensure that the measurement of well-being is considered an important indicator of the success of governmental policies and that associated interventions are scientifically grounded. Some countries (e.g., Bhutan) have already successfully applied well-being standards to public policy (Shrotryia, 2006).

Despite these promising advances in the areas of assessment and intervention, more empirical consideration is needed to further understand culture-dependent influences on happiness and well-being (Uchida et al., 2004). More work is also needed on designing and implementing culturally sensitive and effective interventions that can be applied individually or through public policy. When an individual or governmental intervention is applied, it is important to be culturally sensitive in interactions with all individuals who are being served, including the use of culturally sensitive measures, an understanding of the culture (especially their own values and beliefs), and the language. In this way, individuals with an interest in increasing the well-being of citizens can find effective ways to best apply empirical knowledge to help these citizens to lead better. It appears that scholars are well on their way to help individuals, families, and communities to live better lives, just as Seligman and Csikszentmihalyi (2000) predicted.

# Note

1 The 2005 UNDP Report is the "UN's global development network, advocating for change and connecting countries to knowledge, experience and resources to help people build a better life." (UNDP, 2005: E-5–2). The UNDP is composed of an independent worldwide advisory team of leaders in academia, government and civil society with the aim of contributing data, ideas, and best practices to support the analysis and proposals in the 2005 UNDP Report.

# References

Argyle, M. (2001). *The psychology of happiness* (2nd ed.). Hove, UK: Routledge.

Arthaud-Day, M., & Near, J. (2005). The wealth of nations and the happiness of nations: Why "accounting" matters. *Social Indicators Research, 74*(3), 511–548.

Beddington, J., Cooper, C. L., Field, J., Goswami, U., Huppert, F. A., Jenkins, R. ... Thomas, S. M. (2008). The mental wealth of nations. *Nature, 455*, 1050–1060.

Biswas-Diener, R., Vittersø, J., & Diener, E. (2005). Most people are pretty happy, but there is cultural variation: The Inughuit, the Amish, and the Maasai. *Journal of Happiness Studies, 6*(3), 205–226.

Buchanan, W., & Cantril, H. (1953). *How nations see each other: A study in public opinion.* Urbana, IL: University of Illinois Press.

Cantril, H. (1965). *The pattern of human concern.* New Brunswick, NJ: Rutgers University Press.

Coyne, C. J., & Boettke, P. J. (2006). Economics and happiness research: Insights from Austrian and public choice economics. In Y. K. Ng & L. S. Ho, (Eds), *Happiness and public policy: Theory, case studies, and implications* (pp. 89–105). New York: Palgrave Macmillan.

Deaton, A. (2008). Income, aging, health and well-being around the world: Evidence from the Gallup World Poll. *Journal of Economic Perspectives, 22*(2), 53–72.

Diener, E. (2000). Subjective well-being: The science of happiness, and a proposal for a national index. *American Psychologist, 55*, 34–43.

Diener, E., & Diener, M. (1995). Cross-cultural correlates of life satisfaction and self-esteem. *Journal of Personality and Social Psychology, 68,* 653–663.

Diener, E., & Diener, C. (1996). Most people are happy. *Psychological Science, 7,* 181–185.

Diener, E., Lucas, R. E., & Scollon, C. N. (2006). Beyond the hedonic treadmill: Revisions to the adaptation theory of well-being. *American Psychologist, 61,* 305–314.

Diener, E., Nickerson, C., Lucas, R. E., & Sandvik, E. (2002). Dispositional affect and job outcomes. *Social Indicators Research, 59*(3), 229–259.

Diener, E., & Seligman, M. E. P. (2004). Beyond money: Toward an economy of well-being. *Psychological Science in the Public Interest, 5,* 1–31.

Diener, E., & Suh, E. M. (Eds.) (2000). *Cultural and subjective well-being.* Cambridge, MA: MIT Press.

Diener, E., Suh, E. M., Smith, H., & Shao, L. (1995). National differences in reported subjective well-being: Why do they occur? *Social Indicators Research, 34,* 7–32.

Easterlin, R. (1974). Does economic growth improve the human lot? In P. A. David & M. W. Reder (Eds.), *Nations and households in economic growth: Essays in honor of Moses Abramovitz* (pp. 88–125). New York: Academic Press, Inc.

Easterlin, R., & Angelescu, L. (2009). Happiness and growth the world over: Time series evidence on the happiness–income paradox. *IZA Discussion Paper No. 4060.* Retrieved August 24, 2009, from http://ftp.iza.org/dp4060.pdf

Eid, M. & Diener, E. (2001). Norms for experiencing emotions in different cultures: Inter-and intranational differences. *Journal of Personality and Social Psychology, 81,* 869–885.

Friesen, W. F. (1972). *Cultural differences in facial expressions in a social situation: An experimental test of the concept of display rules.* Unpublished doctoral dissertation, University of California, San Francisco.

Gallup, G. H. (1976). Human needs and satisfaction: A global survey. *Public Opinion Quarterly, 40,* 459–467.

Gilbert, D. (2006). *Stumbling on happiness.* New York: Knopf.

Gundelach, P., & Kreiner, S. (2004). Happiness and life satisfaction in advanced European countries. *Cross-Cultural Research: The Journal of Comparative Social Science, 38*(4), 359–386.

Haller, M., & Hadler, M. (2006). How social relations and structures can produce happiness and unhappiness: An international comparative analysis. *Social Indicators Research, 75,* 169–216.

Harper, F., Guilbault, M., Tucker, T., & Austin, T. (2007). Happiness as a goal of counseling: Cross-cultural implications. *International Journal of Advanced Counseling, 29,* 123–136.

Haybron, D. (2008a). Happiness in context. In D. Haybron (Ed.), *The pursuit of unhappiness: The elusive psychology of well-being* (pp. 254–279). Oxford: Oxford University Press.

Haybron, D. (2008b). The pursuit of unhappiness. In D. Haybron (Ed.), *The pursuit of unhappiness: The elusive psychology of well-being* (pp. 225–252). Oxford: Oxford University Press.

Hsee, C. K., & Hastie, R. (2006). Decision and experience: Why don't we choose what makes us happy? *Trends in Cognitive Sciences, 10*(1), 31–37.

Huppert, F. (2009). A new approach to reducing disorder and improving well-being. *Perspectives on Psychological Science, 4*(1), 108–111.

Huppert, F., Marks, N., Clark, A., Siegrist, J., Stutzer, A., & Vittersø, J. (2006, June). *Personal and social well-being module for the European Social Survey, Round 3*. Retrieved August 20, 2009, from http://www.cambridgewellbeing.org/policy.html

Inglehart, R., Foa, R., Peterson, C., & Welzel, C. (2008). Development, freedom, and rising happiness: A global perspective (1981–2007). *Perspectives on Psychological Science, 3,* 264–285.

Inglehart, R., Welzel, C., & Foa, R. (n.d.). *Happiness trends in 24 countries, 1946–2006.* Retrieved August 20, 2009, from http://www.worldvaluessurvey.org/happiness trends/

Kalmijn, W. M., & Veenhoven, R. (2005). Measuring inequality of happiness in nations: In search for proper statistics. *Journal of Happiness Studies, 6,* 357–396.

Kim-Prieto, C., & Eid, M. (2004). Norms for experiencing emotions in sub-Saharan Africa. *Journal of Happiness Studies, 5*(3), 241–268.

Kitayama, S., & Markus, H. R. (2000). The pursuit of happiness and the realization of sympathy: Cultural patterns of self, social relations, and well-being. In E. Diener and E. M. Suh (Eds.), *Cultural and subjective well-being* (pp. 113–161). Cambridge, MA: MIT Press.

Lee, Y., & Seligman, M. (1997). Are Americans more optimistic than the Chinese? *Personality and Social Psychology Bulletin, 23,* 32–40.

Lu, L., & Gilmour, R. (2004). Culture and conceptions of happiness: Individual oriented and social oriented SWB. *Journal of Happiness Studies, 5*(3), 269–291.

Lykken, D., & Tellegen, A. (1996). Happiness is a stochastic phenomenon. *Psychological Science, 7,* 186–189.

Lyubomirsky, S., King, L. A., & Diener, E. (2005). The benefits of frequent positive affect. *Psychological Bulletin, 131,* 803–855.

Mathews, G. (2006). Happiness and the pursuit of a life worth living: An anthropological approach. In Y. K. Ng & L. S. Ho, (Eds.), *Happiness and public policy: Theory, case studies, and implications* (pp. 147–169). New York: Palgrave Macmillan.

Michalos, A. C. (1991). *Global report on student well-being, Vols. 1–4.* New York: Springer-Verlag.

Oishi, S., & Diener, E. (2001). Goals, culture, and subjective well-being. *Personality and Social Psychology Bulletin, 27,* 1674–1682.

Oishi, S., Diener, E., & Lucas, R. (2007). The optimum level of well-being: Can people be too happy? *Perspectives on Psychological Science, 2*(4), 346–360.

Oishi, S., & Koo, M. (2008). Two new questions about happiness: "Is happiness good?" and "Is happier better?" In M. Eid & R. J. Larsen. (Eds.), *The science of subjective well-being* (pp. 290–306). New York: Guilford Press.

Ott, J. (2005). Book reviews: Well-being manifesto for a flourishing society. Netherlands: New Economics Foundation, Erasmus University, Rotterdam. *Journal of Happiness Studies, 6*(2), 187–193.

Ouweneel, P., & Veenhoven, R. (1991). Cross-national differences in happiness: Cultural bias or societal quality? In N. Bleichrodt & P. J. D. Drenth (Eds.), *Contemporary issues in cross-cultural psychology* (pp. 168–184). Lisse, Netherlands: Swets & Zeitlinger Publishers.

Royal Government of Bhutan (2002). *9th five year plan (2002–2007).* Main Document, Planning Commission, April. Thimphu, Bhutan.

Ryan, R. M., Sheldon, T. K., & Deci, E. L. (1996). All goals are not created equal: An organismic perspective on the nature of goals and their regulation. In P. M. Gollwitzer and

J. A. Bargh (Eds.), *The psychology of action: Linking cognition and motivation to behavior* (pp. 7–26). New York: Guilford Press.

Safdar, S., Friedlmeier, W., Matsumoto, D., Yoo, S., Kwantes, C., Kakai, H. … Shigemasu, E. (2009). Variations of emotional display rules within and across cultures: A comparison between Canada, USA, and Japan. *Canadian Journal of Behavioural Science, 41,* 1–10.

Schimmel, J. (2009). Development as happiness: The subjective perception of happiness and the UNDP's analysis of poverty, wealth, and development. *Journal of Happiness Studies, 10,* 93–111.

Seligman, M. E. P., & Csikszentmihalyi, M. (2000). Positive psychology: An introduction. *American Psychologist, 55,* 5–14.

Shah, H., & Marks, N. (2004). *A well-being manifesto for a flourishing society.* London: New Economics Foundation.

Shrotryia, V. K. (2006). Happiness and development: Public policy initiatives in the Kingdom of Bhutan. In Y. K. Ng & L. S. Ho, (Eds.), *Happiness and public policy: Theory, case studies, and implications* (pp. 193–208). New York: Palgrave Macmillan.

Shrotryia, V. K. (2008, November). *Shift in the measures of quality of life vis-à-vis happiness—A study of Phongmey geog and Trashigang town in Eastern Bhutan.* Paper presented at the 4th International Gross National Happiness Conference, Centre for Bhutan Studies, Thimphu, Bhutan. Retrieved March 12, 2009, from http://www.bhutanstudies.org.bt/main/pub_detail.php?Pubid=106

Stevenson, B., & Wolfers, J. (2008, August). *Economic growth and subjective well-being: Reassessing the Easterlin paradox.* 3rd Annual Conference on Empirical Legal Studies Papers. Retrieved January 13, 2009, from http://ssrn.com/abstract=1121237

Suh, E. M. (2000). Self, the hyphen between culture and subjective well-being. In E. Diener and E. M. Suh (Eds.), *Subjective well-being across cultures* (pp. 63–86). Cambridge, MA: MIT Press.

Taylor, S. E., & Brown, J. D. (1988). Illusion and well-being: A social psychological perspective on mental health. *Psychological Bulletin, 103,* 193–210.

Tov, W., & Diener, E. (2007). Culture and subjective well-being. In S. Kitayama & D. Cohen (Eds.), *Handbook of cultural psychology* (pp. 691–713). New York: Guilford Press.

Triandis, H. (1995). *Individualism and collectivism.* Boulder, CO: Westview Press.

Uchida, Y., Norasakkunkit, V., & Kitayama, S. (2004). Cultural constructions of happiness: Theory and empirical evidence. *Journal of Happiness Studies, 5,* 223–239.

United Nations Development Programme (UNDP), *Human Development Report (2005).* Oxford: Oxford University Press.

Veenhoven, R. (1991). Is happiness relative? *Social Indicators Research, 24,* 1–34.

Veenhoven, R. (1993). *Happiness in nations: Subjective appreciation of life in 56 nations 1946–1992.* Rotterdam: Erasmus University.

Veenhoven, R. (1994). Is happiness a trait? *Social Indicators Research, 32,* 101–160.

Veenhoven, R. (2000). The four qualities of life: Ordering concepts and measures of the good life. *Journal of Happiness Studies, 1*(1), 1–39.

Veenhoven, R. (2001). Are the Russians as unhappy as they say they are? *Journal of Happiness Studies, 2*(2), 111–136.

Veenhoven, R. (2004a). World database of happiness: Continuous register of research on subjective appreciation of life. In W. Glatzer, S. VonBelow, & M. Stoffregen (Eds.),

*Challenges for quality of life in the contemporary world: Advances in quality-of-life studies, theory and research* (pp. 75–89). Dordrecht, Netherlands: Kluwer Academic Publishers.

Veenhoven, R. (2004b). Happy life years: A measure of Gross National Happiness. In U. Karma & G. Karma (Eds.). *Gross national happiness and development, Proceedings of the first international seminar on "Operationalization of Gross National Happiness"* (pp. 287–318). Center of Bhutan Studies, Thimphu, Bhutan.

Veenhoven, R. (2005). Apparent quality-of-life in nations: How long and happy people live. *Social Indicators Research, 71*(1), 61–86.

Veenhoven, R. (2006). *Happy Life Years in 95 nations 1995–2005, World Database of Happiness, Rank Report 2006–2b.* Retrieved August 20, 2009, from http://worlddatabaseofhappiness. eur.nl

Veenhoven, R. (2009a). *World Database of Happiness, Structure of the collections.* Erasmus University, Rotterdam. Retrieved August 20, 2009 from http://worlddatabaseofhappiness. eur.nl

Veenhoven, R. (2009b). *World Database of Happiness, Item Bank.* Erasmus University, Rotterdam. Retrieved August 20, 2009 from http://worlddatabaseofhappiness.eur.nl

Veenhoven, R. (2009c). *World Database of Happiness, Item Bank: Introductory Text.* Erasmus University, Rotterdam. Retrieved August 20, 2009, from http://worlddatabaseofhappiness. eur.nl

Veenhoven, R. (2009d). *World Database of Happiness, Item Bank: Classification.* Erasmus University, Rotterdam. Retrieved August 20, 2009, from http://worlddatabaseofhappiness. eur.nl

White, A. (2007). A global projection of subjective well-being: a challenge to positive psychology? *Psychtalk, 56*, 17–20.

Wilson, T. & Gilbert, D. (2005). Affective forecasting: Knowing what to want. *Current Directions in Psychological Science, 14*, 131–134.1.

# 19

# Well-Being Across Cultures
## *Issues of Measurement*
## *and the Interpretation of Data*

### Robert A. Cummins and Anna L. D. Lau

At the heart of human striving, there must be a common need for well-being. But discovering how this well-being should be measured and described is an intellectual challenge. Even the most basic notion of what "well-being" might be differs between disciplines and between cultures. Economics equates well-being with money and medicine equates it with health, while the social sciences regard well-being as an over-arching construct, incorporating issues of money and health but much broader in scope. Further differences are introduced by culture. Some of these are easy to understand, such as the societal value of family name. Others are more subtle, such as differences in cultural response style to questions of personal satisfaction. This chapter will document such disciplinary and cultural views and, in the process, attempt to discover aspects of well-being that are universal.

Traditional measures of well-being focus on the objective circumstances of living (e.g. Human Development Index, 2007/2008). For example, wealth, medical health, and living standards are commonly used to define well-being and life quality. The attraction of these objective variables is they are tangible and so can be measured in familiar ways through frequencies or quantities. Moreover, in the tradition of the physical sciences, the results can be verified by any number of people using the same techniques of measurement. Because of this, the objective measures travel well cross-culturally. Medical health is defined by universal criteria and all currencies can be standardized through conversion to American dollars.

All this is very comforting to people who define well-being by what they can see and touch. The measures are clearly reliable. Less comforting, however, is the knowledge that such measures are not, of themselves, valid measures of life quality. That is, well-being also contains a subjective dimension which involves how good people feel about their lives. Even less comforting is our understanding that the objective measures cannot reliably predict the subjective measures. People who are rich and medically healthy can also be depressed. People who are not rich and in poor health can also be happy.

An additional challenge to the traditional measures of life quality is that, of the two dimensions, the subjective is by far the most important. If people feel their lives are not worth living, then as Schalock (1997) asked, what is the use of life? So the first section of this chapter examines subjective well-being (SWB) in terms of its character and measurement. The second section then discusses the application of such measurement across different cultures.

## The Character of Subjective Well-Being

Subjective well-being has been a topic of scientific study for over 30 years. The publications of Andrews and Withey (1976) and Campbell, Converse, and Rodgers (1976) launched the area into scientific prominence. Both texts demonstrated that SWB data could be reliably measured and that the statistical analysis of such data, using ordinary linear statistics, produced interesting results. Of particular importance, they found their measures of SWB to be remarkably stable. It is this stability and reliability of measurement that has made SWB such an attractive new area for quantitative investigation. However, researchers in this area have also encountered many problems in their attempts to create a systematic body of knowledge. Two of the most difficult issues are the lack of a standardized terminology (see Diener, 2006 for a review) and the huge number of instruments that measure different aspects of SWB (ACQOL, 2009).

The problems with terminology have been very serious. Even as the early researchers used the term "happiness" to describe the area of their study, they recognized that the term was ambiguous. For example, Fordyce (1983) grappled with his use of the term, describing happiness as "an emotional sense of well-being—that goes by many names (contentment, fulfilment, self-satisfaction, joy, peace of mind, etc.)" (p. 484). The problem that Fordyce recognized is that, in common English usage, happiness generally refers to a state of mind caused by an acute emotional experience, such a enjoying a cup of tea on a hot day. But this is not what the well-being researchers generally intend to measure. They strive to measure a dispositional state of mood happiness that is much more stable. So, to make this distinction, "trait" or "mood" happiness has come to be known as SWB in order to reduce terminological confusion. (See Chapter 18 in this volume for a further review of current conceptions and study of happiness.)

Measuring SWB in a consistent manner has posed the other major challenge to research cohesion. This problem arises as a direct consequence of terminological confusion. The lack of an agreed terminology means that opinions vary as to what questions should be asked to measure the construct. Consequently, a surprisingly high proportion of researchers find it necessary to invent their own scale. The result is a huge legacy of instruments. The Australian Centre on Quality of Life (ACQOL, 2009) lists many hundreds of scales that purport to measure SWB in one form or another. This has greatly limited progress in understanding. These scales are of very mixed psychometric quality and many of them measure quite different constructs. The unfortunate result is a confused and massive literature that, despite three decades of research, still lacks simple conceptual cohesion.

Notwithstanding these difficulties, understanding of SWB has advanced to the point that coherent and testable theories have been developed. This is a fascinating intellectual challenge because such theories must attempt to account for the rather odd psychometric properties of SWB. These include its relationship with other variables, such as depression, and the nature of its relationship with the objective measures of life quality. One such theory proposes that SWB is being managed by a psychological system that we call SWB homeostasis (see Cummins, 2003; Cummins, Gullone, & Lau, 2002).

Homeostasis involves various mechanisms. Some of these are dispositional and include processes of adaptation, selective-attention, and social comparison. Other mechanisms are resources external to the person, such as money and close relationships, that can be used to shield the person from adversity. These various devices act in concert to maintain an average level of SWB that is stable and predictable within countries like Australia (Cummins, Eckersley, Pallant, Van Vugt, & Misajon, 2003). However, the average level of SWB is not constant across the world, as it is for the physiologically managed systems, such as body temperature. SWB differs quite markedly between nations, for reasons that we will discuss later.

## Subjective Well-Being Homeostasis

The theory of subjective well-being homeostasis proposes that, in a manner analogous to the homeostatic maintenance of body temperature, SWB is actively controlled and maintained as a positive mood (see Cummins & Nistico, 2002, for an extended description). This implies that almost everyone has the experience of their overall lives as positive, and this is empirically demonstrated in Figure 19.1. This figure is reproduced from Cummins et al. (2009) and represents the combined data from some 40,000 respondents in Australia derived from general population surveys. SWB is depicted on a standardized 0 to 100 scale.

SWB homeostasis is attempting to maintain a normal positive sense of well-being as a generalized and rather abstract view of the self. It is exemplified by a response to the classic question "How satisfied are you with your life as a whole?" Given the extraordinary generality of this question, the response that people give does not represent a cognitive evaluation of their life. Rather it reflects a deep and stable positive mood state that we used to call *core affect* (Davern, Cummins, & Stokes, 2007) but which we now call *homeostatically protected mood* (HPMood) (Cummins, 2010). This is a mood state, dominated by a sense of contentment, flavored with a touch of happiness and excitement. It is this general and abstract

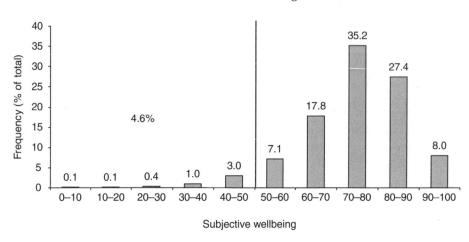

**Figure 19.1.**   Frequency distribution of Personal Wellbeing Index.

state of SWB which the homeostatic system seeks to defend. As one consequence, the level of SWB that people experience has the following characteristics:

1  It is normally very stable. Although unusually good or bad events will cause it to change in the short term, over a period of time homeostasis will normally return SWB to its previous level (Hanestad & Albrektsen, 1992; Headey & Wearing, 1989).

2  Each person has a level of HPMood that is set genetically. This "set-point" lies in the "satisfied" sector of the dissatisfied–satisfied continuum. That is, on a scale where zero represents complete dissatisfaction with life and 100 represents complete satisfaction, people's set-point normally lies within the range of about 60–90 points (Cummins et al., 2002).

3  At a population level within Western nations, the average set-point is 75. In other words, on average, people feel that their general satisfaction with life is about three-quarters of its maximum extent (Cummins, 1995, 1998).

While this generalized sense of well-being is held positive with remarkable tenacity, it is not immutable. A sufficiently adverse environment can defeat the homeostatic system and, when this occurs, negative affect dominates conscious awareness and people lose touch with HPMood. When this happens, their perceived level of SWB falls below its homeostatic range. For example, people who experience strong, chronic pain from arthritis or from the stress of caring for a severely disabled family member at home have low levels of subjective well-being (Cummins, 2001; Cummins, Hughes, et al., 2007). However, for people who are maintaining a normally functioning homeostatic system, their levels of SWB will show little relationship to normal variations in their chronic circumstances of living.

So, how does homeostasis manage to defend SWB against the unusually good and the unusually bad experiences of life? The answer we propose is that there are two levels of defense (internal and external) that we call "buffers."

## Homeostatic buffers

Interaction with the environment constantly threatens to move well-being up or down in sympathy with momentary positive and negative experience. And to some extent this does occur. However, most people are adept at avoiding strong challenges through the maintenance of established life routines that make their daily experiences predictable and manageable. Under such ordinary life conditions, the level of their mood-state varies by perhaps 10 percentage points or so from one moment to the next, and this variation represents their *set-point range* (Cummins et al., in press). Homeostasis works hardest at the edges of this range to prevent more drastic mood changes which, of course, do occur from time to time. Strong and unexpected positive or negative experience will shift the sense of personal well-being to abnormally higher or lower values, usually for a brief period, until adaptation occurs. However, if the negative experience is sufficiently strong and sustained, homeostasis will lack the power to restore equilibrium and SWB will remain below its set-point range. Such homeostatic defeat is marked by a sustained loss of positive mood and a high risk of depression (Cummins et al., in press).

So the first line of defense for homeostasis is to avoid, or at least rapidly attenuate, negative environmental interactions. This is the role of the external buffers.

## External buffers

The two most important sources for the defence of our SWB are close relationships and money. Of these two, the most powerful buffer is a relationship with another human being that involves mutual sharing of intimacies and support (Cummins, Walter, & Woerner, 2007, Report 16.1). Almost universally, the research literature attests to the power of such relationships to moderate the influence of potential stressors on SWB (for reviews see Henderson, 1977; Sarason, Sarason, & Pierce, 1990).

Money is also a very important external buffer, but there are misconceptions as to what money can and cannot do in relation to personal well-being. As far as we know, it cannot shift the set-point to create a perpetually happier person. Set-points for SWB are proposed to be under genetic control (Braungart, Plomin, DeFries, & Fulker, 1992; Lykken & Tellegen, 1996), so in this sense money cannot buy happiness. No matter how rich someone is, their average level of SWB cannot be sustained higher than one that approximates the top of their set-point range. People adapt readily to luxurious living standards, so genetics trumps wealth after a certain level of income has been achieved.

The presence of this upper limit to SWB is supported by the findings of a recent report. Cummins, Walter, et al. (2007) studied the cumulative data from the Australian Unity Well-being Index, which comprises SWB data from about 30,000

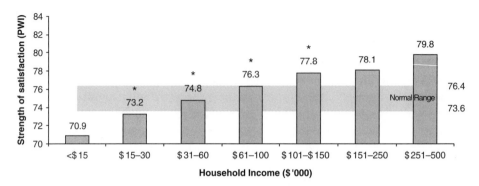

**Figure 19.2.**    Income and the Personal Wellbeing Index (combined surveys).

Australians. The purpose of the analysis was to determine the demographic groups with the highest and the lowest well-being. It is reported that the maximum average subgroup score considered to be reliable is about 81.0 points. Thus, this seems to be the maximum SWB that can be maintained as a group average even for people who have close relationships and plenty of money.

The reason for the ceiling of about 80 points is the normal distribution of set-points, approximately represented by Figure 19.1. It is approximate because the extremes of this distribution are likely caused by extraneous factors. Values below 60 are likely the result of homeostatic defeat caused by either momentary emotion or depression. Values above 90 probably reflect the influence of recent positive emotional events. So, omitting these extreme values, the distribution of individual set-points extends from about 60 to 90, and the top of these set-point-ranges extends from about 65 to 95. Thus, assuming a normal distribution of set-points, the average of any optimally functioning sample cannot exceed the average of the range 65–95, which is about 80 points. This theoretically derived estimate fits quite well the empirically determined maximum value of about 80 points shown in Figure 19.2.

The true power of wealth is not to buy short-term emotional happiness, but rather its capacity to protect HPMood through its use as a highly flexible resource (Cummins, 2000) that allows people to defend themselves against potentially negative experiences. Wealthy people pay others to perform tasks they do not wish to do themselves. Poor people, who lack such resources, must fend for themselves to a much greater extent. Poor people, therefore, have a level of SWB that is far more at the mercy of their environment.

## Internal buffers

When we fail to control our external environment and SWB is threatened, our internal buffers come into play. These comprise protective cognitive devices that are designed to minimize the impact of personal failure on positive feelings about our self. There are many such devices, collectively called *secondary control techniques* (Rothbaum, Weisz, & Snyder, 1982) and a detailed discussion of these systems in relation to SWB appears in Cummins and Nistico (2002) and Cummins et al. (2002). They have the role of protecting our SWB against the conscious reality of life. They do this by altering the way we see ourselves in relation to some challenging agent. As a consequence of such cognitive restructuring, the negative potential of a challenging experience to damage well-being is deflected away from the core view of self. So the role of these buffers is mainly to mini-mize the impact of personal failure. The ways of thinking that can achieve this are highly varied. For example, one can find meaning in the event ("God is test-ing me"), fail to take responsibility for the failure ("It was not my fault") or regard the failure (e.g., dropping a vase) as unimportant ("I did not need that old vase anyway.")

In summary, the combined external and internal buffers ensure that our well-being is robustly defended. There is, therefore, considerable stability in the SWB of populations and, as has been stated, the mean SWB for Western societies like Australia are consistently at about 75 points on a 0 to 100 scale. However, comparisons of SWB between countries are complicated by two forces. One is living standards that are severe enough to cause widespread homeostatic defeat. The other is a cultural response bias in the way that people project their SWB onto measurement scales.

## Cross-Cultural Differences in SWB

Within the Western media it is common to find reports that compare the levels of SWB or happiness between countries. The assumption in such reports is that the data being compared are valid between cultures, such that the differences repre-sent meaningful international comparisons of life quality. This assumption is incorrect and simplistic (for a critique of the Economist Intelligence Unit's 'Quality of Life Index' see Cummins et al., 2005). There are two reasons.

The first is the simple problem of translation—that there is often no simple equivalence between the terms used to describe affective states in different languages. The second reason is more important and concerns cultural response bias (for an interesting review of such biases due to Confucian cul-ture, see Kim, Peng, & Chiu, 2008). The consequences of response bias have been well documented (e.g. Lee, Jones, Mineyama, & Zhang, 2002; Stening & Everett, 1984). Essentially, when data are compared between equivalent demo-graphic groups, people from East and Southeast Asian cultures score lower on measures of well-being because they are more reticent to rate themselves at the ends of the response scale when compared to people from Western cul-tures. The reasons for this bias, as documented by Lau, Cummins and

McPherson (2005) in Hong Kong, are a combination of modesty, concern at tempting the fates by rating oneself too high, and having a different view of what the maximum scale score represents.

As a consequence of response bias, Asian cultures tend to report lower average levels of SWB. This is because the Asian response distribution has a lower proportion of high values than is normal for samples which exhibit the Western bias. That is, people in Asia tend to respond 7 or 8 (on a 0–10 scale) whereas they would, in the context of Western culture, respond 9 or 10. The operation of this bias then gives the appearance that, on average, the people from these cultures have lower levels of SWB than do people from the West.

Not all reports of cultural response bias are reliable. For example, Kim et al (2008) have claimed that Chinese respondents have a greater tendency to agree with negatively worded self-esteem items (thereby giving rise to the differences in self-esteem commonly reported between East Asians and North Americans). However, the authors have misreported their own data. Their results actually show that when the items in the Rosenberg Scale (five positive and five negatively worded items) were rephrased to be consistently either all positive or all negative, the cultural difference between the means was almost identical for both formats. Nevertheless, the differential response bias for SWB as reported above appears to be a robust finding.

## Response bias and living standards

The first report showing that population mean scores could be combined to produce a "gold standard" for SWB (Cummins, 1995), used data only from Western countries. When non-Western countries were included (Cummins, 1998) it became evident that this combination produced far higher variation in SWB. This is hardly surprising. Countries differ in both wealth and culture, and SWB is sensitive to both types of influence. Figure 19.3 shows the relationship between national wealth and SWB.

The difficulties of dealing with the combination of cultural response bias and lower living standards are demonstrated in a study by Lau et al. (2005), who compared the SWB of Hong Kong Chinese and Australians. Apart from the differential cultural response bias between these two countries, the lowest incomes in Hong Kong are relatively much lower that they are in Australia. This can be seen from the respective Gini coefficients as Hong Kong 52.5 and Australia 35.2 (United Nations, 2006). Gini coefficients represent the distribution of wealth in a country and values range from 0 (everyone has the same level of wealth) to 1 (one person owns all the wealth). So the comparative SWB data will reflect both of these two influences as follows:

1  Because people in Hong Kong will be avoiding the ends of the response scale, the cultural response bias will tend to truncate the distribution, making it more

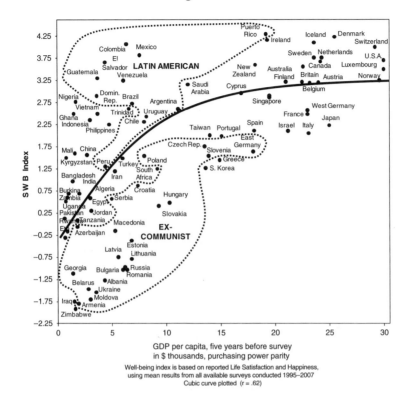

**Figure 19.3.** Subjective well-being (SWB), per capita gross domestic product (GDP), and different types of societies. Wellbeing Index is based on reported life satisfaction and happiness, using mean results from all available surveys conducted 1995–2007 (cubic curve plotted; r = .62). PPP = purchasing power parity estimates.

    leptokurtic or peaked. The result will be a smaller standard distribution and a reduced mean score because the effect of the bias will be most evident at the top of the distribution.

2   Because more people in Hong Kong will be in economic distress, this will tend to extend the SWB distribution downwards, making the distribution more negatively skewed and platykurtic or flat. This will tend to decrease the mean and raise the standard deviation.

In summary, the mean score should be less in Hong Kong due to the combined influences of the response bias and income inequality. The standard deviation, on the other hand, should remain much the same due to the opposing forces. And this is what we found. The mean SWB was higher for the Australian sample and there was no difference in the standard deviations of the two samples. We conclude that this is evidence of a cultural response bias because the effects of the income inequality alone would act to both reduce the mean and extend the standard deviation.

## Culture as a moderator variable

Many papers question the nature of the relationship between SWB and other variables. For example, is the relationship between SWB and life aspects (e.g., family life, work) the same the world over or does the relationship vary according to the cultural group? It is very common for researchers to report their monocultural results as though they are pancultural, but it takes only a moment of thought to realize this is almost certainly naïve. Cultures differ hugely in the emphasis they put on different life aspects. It is therefore both logically intuitive and empirically supported from the literature, that different cultures impart different value systems. These, in turn, moderate the relationship between the experience of life aspects and SWB. Thus, the nature and strength of the connection between almost any life aspect and SWB will be somewhat dependent on culture.

Two examples will serve to make this point. The first involves religion, and there are very stark differences in the kinds of values espoused by the different religious teachings. The impact of Confucian teachings on response bias has already been mentioned. But such cultural differences also moderate the relationship between religious beliefs and SWB. Indeed, Lavric and Flere (2008) found that not only the strength but also the direction of the correlation between positive affect and religious beliefs depends to a great extent on religious culture.

As the second example, it is well known that cultures differ markedly in the level of social capital that they support and that this is an effective moderator of common mental disorders (for a review see de Silva, Huttly, Harpham, & Kenward, 2007; de Silva, McKenzie, Huttly, & Harpham, 2005). It might therefore be expected that the negative impact of caring for a disabled child is likely to vary between cultures according to the level of support that the mother receives. Social capital at the level of families is called *familism*, described by strong feelings of loyalty, reciprocity, and solidarity among family members (Marin & Marin, 1991). It concerns support provided by the family collective to one another, one's obligations to the family, and the involvement of relatives with the family (Sabogal, Marin, Otero-Sabogal, Marin, & Perez-Stable, 1987). So it should be no surprise that the level of familism is an important factor with respect to caring for a disabled child (Aranda & Knight, 1997; Magilvy, Congdon, Martinez, Davis, & Averill, 2000; Shurgot & Knight, 2004). For example, it is generally found that familism is higher in Latino compared with White families in the USA. Thus, probably due to the level of support that they receive within the family, Latina mothers are less likely to report negative aspects of such caregiving than non-Latina White mothers (Magana & Smith, 2006). Thus, culture is moderating the link between caring for a disabled child and the mothers' psychological well-being.

What is clear from this account is that the interpretation of international SWB comparisons must be done very cautiously. But a simpler form of comparison involves the within-country change in SWB over time. Because such comparisons will necessarily hold cultural response bias constant, changes over time will reflect the relative ability of the population to manage their well-being and, in particular, the proportion of the population who are suffering homeostatic failure. So let us now consider the process of measuring SWB in an international context.

## Measuring Subjective Well-Being

The *Directory of instruments* available through the Australian Centre on Quality of Life (ACQOL, 2009) lists over 1,000 scales that purport to measure well-being in some form. So how can a researcher make a choice from such a daunting list? From the perspective of SWB we have given in this paper there are three scales that we recommend.

The first is one of the oldest. It is the single question "How satisfied are you with your life as a whole?" (Andrews & Withey, 1976). This question perfectly fulfills the criteria for an item measuring SWB to be both personal and abstract. No one can compute the answer to the question in terms of cognition. So it is answered in reference to the ongoing mood state, which normally approximates the set-point of HPMood (Davern et al., 2007). The drawback to using this question, however, is that it is a single item. As such it is not as reliable as a multi-item scale, so two alternative scales are recommended.

The first is the most widely used instrument to measure SWB, the Satisfaction with Life Scale (SWLS; Diener, Emmons, Larsen, & Griffin, 1985). This scale is designed to measure global life satisfaction through five items, each of which involves an overall judgment of life in general. The scores from these items are then summed as a measure of SWB. For a copy of the scale go to http://s.psych.uiuc.edu/~ediener/hottopic/hottopic.html.

The importance of the SWLS is that it represents an expanded version of "life as a whole." The items are not designed to give individual insights into the structure of SWB. This differs from the second scale to be recommended. The Personal Wellbeing Index (PWI; International Wellbeing Group, 2006) has a quite different design as the "first-level deconstruction" of life as a whole. It contains eight items, referred to as "domains," where each item represents a broad, semi-abstract area of life. The theoretical basis for the PWI is that the domains together describe the experience of overall life satisfaction. Empirically they tend to explain about 50–60% of the variance in "life as a whole." The manual is available from http://www.deakin.edu.au/research/acqol/instruments/wellbeing_index.htm.

The PWI is designed to be a work in progress, with the scale evolving as new data show ways for it to be successfully modified. The International Wellbeing Group oversees this evolution and the eighth domain, spiritual/religious satisfaction, was added to the scale in 2006.

The disadvantage of the PWI, compared to the SWLS, is that, because the domains are slightly more specific in their focus than "life as a whole," they have rather more cognitive content. This adds variance related to the cognitive target of the domain, making the PWI somewhat less reliable in reflecting HPMood than the SWLS. On the other hand, this additional variance can also be used to advantage. Because of this additional information, the scale can be analyzed at either the level of individual domains or at the level of a single combined score. Finally, the PWI has parallel versions for adults who have a cognitive or intellectual disability, schoolchildren, and pre-school children (International Wellbeing Group, 2006).

## Summary

In order to make a comprehensive assessment of life quality within a nation, it is necessary to employ both objective and subjective indicators. Both kinds of measure provide different and useful information for policy planners. Making comparisons between countries, however, is hazardous. While such comparisons based on objective measures appear valid and reliable, those based on subjective measures are not. Making SWB comparisons between nations is a fraught process because the ways culture and living standards interact to influence reported SWB are poorly understood. At this time, the direct comparison of inter-nation SWB levels is invalid as an indicator of true differences in subjective life quality.

The major usefulness of SWB measurement is as an indication of homeostatic failure and risk of depression. It is, thus, a useful measure by which to identify areas of relative need and also as a way of tracking the effectiveness of government interventions that involve the allocation of resources. Giving attention to the resources necessary to maintain normative SWB for disadvantaged population sub-groups may be one of the most effective initiatives to enhance population well-being and national productivity around the world.

## References

ACQOL. (2009). *Australian Centre on Quality of Life—Directory of Instruments*. Retrieved 27 December, 2006, from http://www.deakin.edu.au/research/acqol/instruments/index.htm

Andrews, F. M., & Withey, S. B. (1976). *Social indicators of well-being: American's perceptions of life quality*. New York: Plenum Press.

Aranda, M., & Knight, B. (1997). The influence of ethnicity on the caregiver stress and coping process: A sociocultural review and analysis. *The Gerontologist, 37*, 342–354.

Braungart, J. M., Plomin, R., DeFries, J. C., & Fulker, D. W. (1992). Genetic influence on tester-rated infant temperament as assessed by Bayley's infant behavior record: Nonadoptive and adoptive siblings and twins. *Developmental Psychology, 28*, 40–47.

Campbell, A., Converse, P. E., & Rodgers, W. L. (1976). *The quality of American life: Perceptions, evaluations, and satisfactions.* New York: Russell Sage Foundation.

Cummins, R. A. (1995). On the trail of the gold standard for life satisfaction. *Social Indicators Research, 35*, 179–200.

Cummins, R. A. (1998). The second approximation to an international standard of life satisfaction. *Social Indicators Research, 43*, 307–334.

Cummins, R. A. (2000). Personal income and subjective well-being: A review. *Journal of Happiness Studies, 1*, 133–158.

Cummins, R. A. (2001). The subjective well-being of people caring for a severely disabled family member at home: A review. *Journal of Intellectual and Developmental Disability, 26*, 83–100.

Cummins, R. A. (2003). Normative life satisfaction: Measurement issues and a homeostatic model. *Social Indicators Research, 64*, 225–256.

Cummins, R. A. (2010). Subjective wellbeing, homeostatically protected mood and depression: A synthesis. *Journal of Happiness Studies, 11*, 1–17. DOI: 10.1007/s10902–009–9167–0.

Cummins, R. A., Eckersley, R., Pallant, J., Van Vugt, J., & Misajon, R. (2003). Developing a national index of subjective wellbeing: The Australian Unity Wellbeing Index. *Social Indicators Research, 64*, 159–190.

Cummins, R. A., Gullone, E., & Lau, A. L. D. (2002). A model of subjective well being homeostasis: The role of personality. In E. Gullone & R. A. Cummins (Eds.), *The universality of subjective wellbeing indicators: Social Indicators Research Series* (pp. 7–46). Dordrecht, The Netherlands: Kluwer.

Cummins, R. A., Hughes, J., Tomyn, A., Gibson, A., Woerner, J., & Lai, L. (2007). *Australian Unity Wellbeing Index: Report 17.1 The wellbeing of Australians—carer health and wellbeing.* Melbourne: Australian Centre on Quality of Life, School of Psychology, Deakin University. Retrieved June 30, 2009, from http://www.deakin.edu.au/research/acqol/index_wellbeing/index.htm

Cummins, R. A., & Nistico, H. (2002). Maintaining life satisfaction: The role of positive cognitive bias. *Journal of Happiness Studies, 3*, 37–69.

Cummins, R. A., Stokes, M., Michalos, A., Vitterso, J., Steel, P., Okerstrom, E., & Clay, N. (2005). The world's best country. *Social Indicators Network News, 81*, 1–4,11. http://www.isqols.org/.

Cummins, R. A., Walter, J., & Woerner, J. (2007). *Australian Unity Wellbeing Index: Report 16.1—The wellbeing of Australians—groups with the highest and lowest wellbeing in Australia.* Melbourne: Australian Centre on Quality of Life, School of Psychology, Deakin University. Retrieved June 30, 2009, from http://www.deakin.edu.au/research/acqol/index_wellbeing/index.htm

Cummins, R. A., Woerner, J., Gibson, A., Lai, L., Weinberg, M., & Collard, J. (2009). *Australian Unity Wellbeing Index:—Report 20.0. The wellbeing of Australians—money, debt and loneliness.* Melbourne: Australian Centre on Quality of Life, School of Psychology, Deakin University. Retrieved May 5, 2010, from http://www.deakin.edu.au/research/acqol/index_wellbeing/index.htm

Davern, M., Cummins, R. A., & Stokes, M. (2007). Subjective wellbeing as an affective/cognitive construct. *Journal of Happiness Studies, 8*(4), 429–449.

de Silva, M. J., Huttly, S. R., Harpham, T., & Kenward, M. G. (2007). Social capital and mental health: A comparative analysis of four low income countries. *Social Science & Medicine, 64*(1), 5–20.

de Silva, M. J., McKenzie, K., Huttly, S. R., & Harpham, T. (2005). Social capital and mental illness: A systematic review. *Journal of Epidemiology and Community Health, 59*(8), 619–627.

Diener, E. (2006). Guidelines for national indicators of subjective well-being and ill-being. *Journal of Happiness Studies, 7,* 397–404.

Diener, E. D., Emmons, R. A., Larsen, R. J., & Griffin, S. (1985). The satisfaction with life scale. *Journal of Personality Assessment, 49,* 71–75.

Fordyce, M. W. (1983). A program to increase happiness: Further studies. *Journal of Counseling Psychology, 30,* 483–498.

Hanestad, B. R., & Albrektsen, G. (1992). The stability of quality of life experience in people with Type 1 diabetes over a period of a year. *Journal of Advanced Nursing, 17,* 777–784.

Headey, B., & Wearing, A. (1989). Personality, life events, and subjective well-being: Toward a dynamic equilibrium model. *Journal of Personality and Social Psychology, 57,* 731–739.

Henderson, S. (1977). The social network, support and neurosis. The function of attachment in adult life. *British Journal of Psychiatry, 131,* 185–191.

Human Development Index. (2007/2008). *Fighting climate change: Human solidarity in a divided word.* New York: United Nations Development Programme and Palgrave Macmillan.

International Wellbeing Group. (2006). *Personal Wellbeing Index Manual.* Melbourne, Australia: Deakin University. Retrieved June 30, 2009, from http://www.deakin.edu.au/research/acqol/instruments/wellbeing_index.htm

Kim, Y. H., Peng, S. Q., & Chiu, C. Y. (2008). Explaining self-esteem differences between Chinese and North Americans: Dialectical self (vs. self-consistency) or lack of positive self-regard. *Self and Identity, 7*(2), 113–128.

Lau, A. L. D., Cummins, R. A., & McPherson, W. (2005). An investigation into the cross-cultural equivalence of the Personal Wellbeing Index. *Social Indicators Research, 72,* 403–430.

Lavric, M., & Flere, S. (2008). The role of culture in the relationship between religiosity and psychological well-being. *Journal of Religion and Health, 47*(2), 164–175.

Lee, J. W., Jones, P. S., Mineyama, Y., & Zhang, X. E. (2002). Cultural differences in responses to a Likert scale. *Research in Nursing and Health, 25,* 295–306.

Lykken, D., & Tellegen, A. (1996). Happiness is a stochastic phenomenon. *Psychological Science, 7,* 186–189.

Magana, S., & Smith, M. J. (2006). Psychological distress and well-being of Latina and non-Latina White mothers of youth and adults with an autism spectrum disorder: Cultural attitudes towards coresidence status. *American Journal of Orthopsychiatry, 76*(3), 346–357.

Magilvy, J., Congdon, J., Martinez, R., Davis, R., & Averill, J. (2000). Caring for our own: Health care experiences of rural Hispanic elders. *Journal of Aging Studies, 14,* 171–191.

Marin, G., & Marin, B. (1991). *Research with Hispanic populations.* Newbury Park, CA: Sage.

Rothbaum, F., Weisz, J. R., & Snyder, S. S. (1982). Changing the world and changing the self: A two-process model of perceived control. *Journal of Personality and Social Psychology, 42,* 5–37.

Sabogal, F., Marin, G., Otero-Sabogal, R., Marin, B. V., & Perez-Stable, E. J. (1987). Hispanic familism and acculturation: What changes and what doesn't. *Hispanic Journal of Behavioral Science, 9*, 397–412.

Sarason, I. G., Sarason, B. R., & Pierce, G. R. (1990). Social support: The search for theory. *Journal of Social and Clinical Psychology, 9*, 137–147.

Schalock, R. L. (1997). The conceptualization and measurement of quality of life: Current status and future considerations. *Journal of Developmental Disabilities, 5*, 1–21.

Shurgot, G., & Knight, B. (2004). Preliminary study investigating acculturation, cultural values, and psychological distress in Latino caregivers of dementia patients. *Journal of Mental Health and Aging, 10*, 183–194.

Stening, B. W., & Everett, J. E. (1984). Response styles in a cross-cultural managerial study. *Journal of Social Psychology, 122*(2), 151–156.

United Nations. (2006). *Table 15: Inequality in income or expenditure (PDF). Human Development Report 2006 335. United Nations Development Programme.* Retrieved 21 May 2007, from http://hdr.undp.org/hdr2006/pdfs/report/HDR06- complete.pdf#page=335

World Bank. (1997). *World Values Surveys; GNP/capita purchasing power estimates from World Bank, World Development Report, 1997.* Retrieved June 30, 2009, from http://margaux.grandvinum.se/SebTest/wvs/articles/folder_published/article_base_5

# Part VIII

# Language
# and Communication

People of all cultures communicate and use language—a major similarity across people around the globe. And language also stands out as one of the most obvious differences observed across cultures. Language contributes to both understanding and misunderstanding between peoples. No matter how different they may seem, however, all languages have in common certain key characteristics, while continuing to possess their obvious discrepancies.

Researchers have studied common communicative gestures in babies born across cultures and the development of language in children as they mature and become enculturated. Although they certainly learn through the efforts of parents and others, children also seem to learn language without formal training.

The study of language can tell us something about how people think and about how they perceive their world. And, of course, differences in thinking and perception can provide the basis for cross-cultural misunderstanding. Further, overcoming such misunderstanding may require much more than the literal translation of words from one language to another, and such subtleties as humor and metaphor may prove particularly difficult to communicate across cultures.

Cross-cultural communication is particularly important as the world becomes a smaller place—in terms of ease of travel and electronic exchange of information. Therefore, research on how we encode and decode messages becomes increasingly significant, especially when we attempt to communicate with strangers and members of other groups. To aid cross-cultural communication, researchers have examined the role of various dimensions of culture, as well as such cultural features as the role of context as a contributor to communication.

Some researchers have argued that nonverbal aspects of communication, in the form of gestures, intonation, and body language, may carry a larger portion of an intended message than the words embodied in language. Recognition of the role of nonverbal communication is yet another fascinating facet of our understanding of language and communication across cultures.

# 20

# Language and Culture
## *Commonality, Variation, and Mistaken Assumptions*

### David S. Kreiner

There may be nothing more obvious about cultural differences than the variability in our languages. At the same time, perhaps there is nothing more striking about humans than our remarkable similarity in the use of this complex communication system. Language can be revealing about culture, culture can help us better understand language, and their interplay can give us insight into what it means to be human.

This chapter will examine both commonalities and differences in language across cultures. We will first explore the idea that language is universal across cultures. We will then see how similarities and differences in language across cultures may be revealing about the relationship between language and thought. Finally, we will examine how both mistaken assumptions and cultural differences in language can lead to misunderstandings.

## Is Language Universal Across Cultures?

Although there are obvious differences between languages, it is often claimed that we all communicate in essentially the same way: human language. A group of extraterrestrials observing our planet might assume that all human beings rely on the same communication system, but from our perspective as humans, we tend to notice the differences among human languages. As a result, we overlook the remarkable consistency across human languages. Hockett (1966) noted a number of characteristics that languages share; these are often described as linguistic universals. Human language is distinguished by these features from other systems of communication. Examples of linguistic universals include the following.

1   Language is discrete. Any two different sentences that we choose to compare will differ in one or more specific features. *I ate a handful of beans* differs from *I ate a mouthful of beans* in that one morpheme has changed. A morpheme refers to the smallest unit of language that carries meaning by itself. In this example, the two sentences are similar in every respect except for the difference between the morphemes *hand* and *mouth*. Similarly, *I ate a handful of beans* differs from *I ate a handful of beets* in only one sound. Individual speech sounds are called phonemes. Hockett compares the discreteness of language to another communication system, the dances of honeybees, which can be "indefinitely similar to one another" (Hockett, 1966, p. 10).

2   Language is hierarchical, meaning that small units are combined into larger ones. Phonemes are combined into morphemes, which are combined into phrases, which are combined into sentences.

3   All human languages contain words that fall into different grammatical categories, such as nouns and verbs.

4   All languages provide a way to create new sentences, making the number of possible sentences in any language infinite. This creative property of language is a consequence of its discrete and hierarchical nature. Languages contain rules about how to combine discrete units. A new sentence can always be created by adding a phrase to an existing sentence.

5   Languages have to be acquired. In other words, they are transmitted culturally. As humans, we are not born knowing a particular language; instead, we are born with the ability to learn language based on input from the environment. Our genetic make-up provides us with the ability to learn language. For example, a honeybee cannot learn to speak French no matter how much education it receives.

The above are just a few examples of commonalities across human languages. The degree of similarity across human languages, combined with the relative ease with which humans acquire language, has led to the claim that human language is instinctual (Pinker, 1994). The language instinct provides us with a set of abilities that drive us to acquire and use language. The assumption is that our brains come prepared to learn a communication system that is discrete and hierarchical, contains grammatical categories, and so on. Languages differ, in this view, only in the details.

The universality of language may extend to nonverbal gestures that babies use to communicate. Blake, Vitale, Osborne, and Olshansky (2005) studied the development of gestures in infants from different cultures. Changes in the use of different types of gestures were similar across groups. For example, Italian Canadian infants were as similar to other cultures (e.g., Japanese) in their gestures as they were to English Canadian infants, despite the similarity in cultural environments for the two groups of Canadian infants. These findings suggest a common human facility for the development of communication.

Any neurologically normal child acquires language without the need for formal training (Pinker, 1994). If there is a language in the environment, children will learn it. If individuals find themselves in an environment lacking a common language, they will invent one. Some of the clearest examples of this tendency arise from the need for deaf individuals to communicate with each other when they find themselves in an environment that lacks sign language.

The development of Nicaraguan Sign Language (NSL), as described by Senghas, Kita, and Özyürek (2004), illustrates the typical pattern by which a new language comes into existence. First, a pidgin system develops; individuals agree on signs or words that are contributed and combined from their own home languages. The same process has occurred many times historically when individuals from different language backgrounds have been brought together. For example, slaves in the Americas developed pidgin systems by contributing words from their many native languages as well as combining them with words from the dominant language in the environment (e.g., English). In the case of NSL, Senghas et al. (2004) have described how children came from different areas in Nicaragua to attend a central school for the deaf. Many of the children had developed systems of home signs that they used to communicate with their families, but these systems were idiosyncratic. The beginnings of NSL constituted a pidgin system in which the children implicitly came to agree on what particular signs represented. Pidgin systems tend to lack regular grammatical rules for combining units. As new cohorts of children came to the school, they not only learned the pidgin signs, but they also regularized the grammatical system. Similarly, children of first-generation slaves regularized the pidgin of their parents. At this stage, the communication system is typically described as a creole. The result is a full-fledged language characterized by the linguistic universals described above.

A fascinating example is Al-Sayyid Bedouin Sign Language (ABSL), a relatively new language that is still in the early stages of its development. Sandler, Meir, Padden, and Aronoff (2005) have described the development of ABSL. Many of the residents of the village of Al-Sayyid (located in Israel) are deaf due to a hereditary condition. Interestingly, the deaf individuals in the village are not treated differently from hearing individuals. Most of the hearing individuals are able to communicate with their relatives and friends using ABSL. Sandler et al.'s investigation has revealed that ABSL is developing on its own, not as a derivative of an existing language. Part of the reason for this is that Al-Sayyid is isolated from other linguistic communities. ABSL is currently in its third generation, meaning that the grandchildren of the individuals who originated the first pidgin system are now learning the language, their parents having added grammatical rules to the signs originated by their grandparents. In studying the second generation users of ABSL, Sandler et al. have demonstrated that the language contains linguistic universals, such as a preferred word order. ABSL prefers the SOV (subject–object–verb) word order, as in *I the food ate*. The SOV word order occurs in a number of other languages, such as Japanese, but does not occur in languages spoken in the areas surrounding Al-Sayyid. ABSL continues to evolve, as do other languages. For example, the hierarchical property of words being composed of smaller units is developing with the third generation of ABSL users. The story of ABSL is interesting in and of itself (see Fox's 2007 account), and it supports the claim of commonality across human languages.

Hockett (1966) acknowledged that linguistic universals could not be proven to be true, as all human languages could not be studied. We do not know, for instance, whether all human languages have a preferred word order, only those that have been studied. Hockett pointed out that it would be impossible to study every language that exists in addition to every language that ever existed. The best we can do is to continue to collect information about human languages. Ultimately, we need to make inferences about the general nature of human language based on the languages that have been studied.

The usefulness of continuing to collect information is illustrated by the Pirahã language, spoken by an Amazonian culture in Brazil. Pirahã appears to lack some of the so-called universal features present in other languages that have been studied, notably words for numbers and counting. Everett (2005) proposed that the Pirahã culture constrains the language in the sense that the Pirahã only think and communicate about immediate experience. At the request of the Pirahã, Everett and his family attempted to teach them to count in Portuguese, but they were unable to master it. Everett reports that the Pirahã are often cheated by Brazilians with whom they trade because they are unable to determine whether they are getting a good deal or not. Everett also points out that the Pirahã have remained monolingual despite having contact with other languages for over 200 years, suggesting that they do not pick up languages which display ways of thinking that are inconsistent with their culture.

Human languages have remarkable similarity. Languages tend to have the same basic properties, they tend to be acquired by individuals in the same way, and they tend to develop within cultures in the same way. As Hockett (1966) acknowledged, however, properties of human languages may not be universal in an absolute sense. The extent to which characteristics of human language vary across cultures can be revealing about both how we communicate with each other and how we think.

## Language, Culture, and Thought

Although human languages have much in common with each other, they obviously are different enough that a speaker of one language may have difficulty understanding a speaker of another language. Do differences between languages reflect cultural differences in the way that we think about the world, and do similarities indicate the shared conceptions that we have of the world? Does knowing a particular language shape the way that we think? In this section, we will explore how the relationship between language and thought may be revealed by comparing speakers of different languages.

The most widely discussed idea about the relationship between thought and language was proposed by Whorf (Carroll, 1956). Whorf proposed that the way we think about the world could be affected by the language that we know. Knowledge of a particular language could limit the sorts of concepts and ideas about which we can think. In his position as an insurance inspector, Whorf considered the possibility that the way an individual thinks about a situation could be limited by language. Whorf found that an employee in a warehouse had dropped a match into a gasoline drum. The gasoline drum had been located in an area of the warehouse that displayed a sign indicating *empty*. Whorf proposed that the word *empty* was understood as meaning that nothing at all was inside the drum. Based on this assumption about the meaning of the word, the employee was not able to think about the possibility of flammable vapors in the drum.

Similarly, it is often stated that the Inuit language (spoken by Aleut peoples) contains many words for snow. The assumption is that speaking a language with many words for snow provides a way to think about distinctions that speakers of other languages (with fewer words for snow) cannot. This analysis of Inuit turns out to be erroneous, as it fails to distinguish different root words from a single root word that is modified by suffixes (Martin, 1986). Nevertheless, Whorf's proposal that language limits the way we think about the world has been influential and has stimulated a great deal of research.

There is now a considerable research literature comparing speakers of languages that vary in their terms for describing colors. Languages differ widely in their use of color terms. Basic color terms refer to names of colors that are understood by all speakers of the language and are not combinations of other color terms or contained in the meaning of other terms. English has 11 basic color terms, while Russian has 12, with separate terms for light blues and dark blues. Berinmo is a language spoken in Papua New Guinea, a nation located in the South Pacific near Australia and Indonesia. Berinmo has five basic color terms, with, for example, the term for red also covering pink and orange (Roberson, Davies, Corbett, & Vandervyver, 2005).

The Dani language of New Guinea contains only two basic color terms. The word *mola* refers to bright colors, while *mili* refers to dark colors. Rosch (1973) compared speakers of Dani and English on their ability to remember seeing particular colors. Of course, Dani speakers are able to perceive differences between other colors; their language just does not contain different words for them. Within a particular color category, an individual can select a shade of that color that represents the best example; this is called a focal color. The best example of blue is the focal blue; the best example of red is the focal red; and so on. Rosch reported that English speakers and Dani speakers both displayed better memory for focal colors than for non-focal colors. Despite the fact that Dani speakers do not have separate color terms, they still demonstrated better memory for focal colors. Rosch's results were taken to contradict Whorf's hypothesis; cognition was similar across different groups despite differences in their languages.

More recent research has suggested that there may in fact be language-related differences in how we think about color. Recall that the Berinmo language has five basic color terms, and that these do not correspond directly to color terms in English. Roberson, Davies, and Davidoff (2000) measured how well speakers of both Berinmo and English could learn and remember color categories. The results, for both Berinmo and English speakers, indicated that we can more easily perceive differences between colors when our language uses different color terms to label them. For example, the Berinmo word *nol* includes both blue and green. Roberson et al. (2000) found that English speakers were better at discriminating shades of blue from shades of green than they were at discriminating within blue or within green. Berinmo speakers did not show this pattern. The boundary between the Berinmo words *nol* and *wor* is within the green category for speakers of English. Roberson et al. found that Berinmo speakers were better able to distinguish shades of *nol* from shades of *wor* than shades within these two colors. English speakers did not show this pattern. The important thing about these findings is that individuals are better able to discriminate among different colors if their language contains different words for those colors. This research is consistent with Whorf's idea that the way we think can be influenced by the structure of the language that we speak.

It appears to be the case that language can influence how we categorize colors. Whether language can actually *limit* what we are able to think is a different question. Roberson et al. (2005) asked speakers of several different languages to sort a set of 65 color chips so that more similar colors were grouped together. The researchers found both differences and similarities in how the colors were sorted. Speakers of languages that had separate color words for green, blue, and purple were more consistent in how they grouped those color chips than were speakers of languages that did not contain the separate color terms. However, speakers of different languages were similar in placing more importance on hue than on lightness. This similarity occurred even when the color terms in the speaker's own language emphasized lightness more than hue. A particularly interesting finding was that speakers of the same language varied on how they grouped the color chips. It is also interesting that individuals generally grouped the color chips into more categories than they had color terms in their language. These latter two points suggest that we are able to make distinctions even without having specific words to do so. Thus, results from studies on color perception present a mixed picture about the relationship between a language's color terms and how speakers of the language think about color.

Differences in color terms have received a great deal of attention in language research, but languages can differ in other ways. Recall that the Pirahã language appears to lack words for numbers and counting. Frank, Everett, Fedorenko, and Gibson (2008) explored whether speakers of Pirahã might be limited in how they are able to think about numbers. Frank et al. used an exact matching task in which a particular number of spools of thread were displayed by the experimenter. The task was to match the number of spools by counting out balloons. Pirahã speakers were able to complete this exact matching task. However, when they were asked to match the number of spools from memory, they had difficulty completing the task accurately. The results indicate that the Pirahã participants were capable of exact counting, but had more difficulty with it when the task required memory. Everett (2005) suggested that the Pirahã have cultural constraints against thinking outside immediate experience. Everett argued that there is not a useful distinction between culture and language; thus the constraints of one's language are really cultural constraints. Everett's suggestion is that the Pirahã have constraints against thinking about numbers in certain ways, not that they are incapable of different ways of thinking.

Are such differences in how people think about the world a result of the language that they know, or is the language a byproduct of cultural differences in how people think about the world? Ji, Zhang, and Nisbett (2004) pointed out that studies comparing individuals from different cultures often confound culture with language, as individuals are usually responding to questions that have been translated into their own language. This problem makes it impossible to tell whether any differences that emerge from such studies are the result of cultural differences, language differences, or both. To address this concern, Ji et al. tested bilingual individuals in both languages. Eastern cultures tend to emphasize relationships more than objects, whereas Western cultures tend to show the opposite pattern. For example, when given the words *seagull, tree, squirrel* and asked which two words go with each other, a Chinese speaker is likely to choose *tree* and *squirrel* because of the relationship between them. An English speaker is more likely to choose *seagull* and *squirrel"* because they are members of the same category, *animal*. Ji et al. suggest that different languages may be associated with different ways of thinking. For example, a Chinese–English bilingual may be more likely to think of the world in terms of categories when tested in English because the English language provides cues about categories. When Chinese speakers (Mandarin or Cantonese) were tested in English, they made more categorical choices than Chinese speakers who were tested in Chinese. However, this effect did not hold for Chinese speakers from Hong Kong and Singapore, suggesting that the findings were due to differences in cultural experience rather than differences in the language in which they were tested.

Grammatical gender is another way that language might affect the way that individuals in different cultures think. In some languages, such as Spanish, nouns are categorized as belonging to the masculine or feminine gender, whereas languages such as English do not include a grammatical gender system. Does grammatical gender affect our perception of objects as being more masculine or feminine? Flaherty (2001) compared Spanish speakers and English speakers on their conception of various objects. Participants rated drawings of objects on whether they were male or female and gave them either male or female names. Grammatical gender was related to how participants classified the gender of the object for Spanish-speaking adults and older children, but not for younger Spanish-speaking children (5 to 7 years old). English speakers assigned gender of the objects consistently with the animate–inanimate distinction, which is the tendency in English to associate inanimate objects with the pronoun "she" and animate nouns with "he."

Similarly, Sera et al. (2002) found that speakers of French and Spanish were influenced by grammatical gender in how they assigned male or female voices to inanimate objects, but German speakers were not. German nouns are not consistently marked for grammatical gender, whereas Spanish and French nouns are consistently marked for gender. Further, Sera et al. reported that French and Spanish speakers tended to agree on gender assignment of inanimate nouns when their languages assigned them the same gender but disagreed when their languages assigned different genders to the nouns.

In another experiment, Flaherty (2001) found that Spanish speakers were more likely to classify objects according to grammatical gender than according to gender-related attributes of the objects, such as associating "big" with males and "small" with females. Perceived attributes had a stronger relation to assigned gender of the objects for younger Spanish speakers, similar to the results for English speakers. These findings suggest that, as we acquire a language, the distinctions that the language makes gradually come to influence the way that we think.

Research on the development of cognition also supports the idea that the distinctions we learn can change our perceptions. Scott and Monesson (2009) investigated the effect of learning a category on infants' ability to discriminate among individuals within a category. They asked parents to read picture books to their 6-month-old infants for three months. In one condition, the picture books contained individual names for six monkeys (e.g. Dario, Boris). In another condition, all six monkey faces were simply labeled categorically as *monkey*. Infants who learned the category had more difficulty discriminating among the six individual monkeys. These results suggest that the learning of categories can change the way that we perceive the world.

Özyürek et al. (2008) studied how expression of motion develops in both verbal language and gestures. They compared how Turkish-speaking and English-speaking children described motion in animated movies. Manner refers to the way in which something or someone moves (e.g., walking) while path refers to the direction of the movement (e.g., up). In Turkish, manner and path are typically communicated in different verbs; thus Turkish speakers usually express manner and path in different clauses (e.g., *She ascended the hill while walking*). In English, manner and path are often expressed in a single clause (e.g., *She walked down the hill*). Özyürek et al. found that 3-year-olds used language consistent with adult speakers of their language. English-speaking children tended to use single clauses to represent manner and path while Turkish-speaking children used multiple clauses. However, the use of gestures was similar in younger children (ages 3 to 5).

Whether they spoke English or Turkish, the children used separate gestures for manner and path. At age 9 and older, English-speaking children tended to combine manner and path into one gesture, while Turkish-speaking children continued to use separate gestures, consistent with their language. Özyürek et al. interpreted the results as evidence that gestural expression is shaped by language, reflecting language-influenced representations of motion.

We have seen that learning a language can influence the way we perceive reality. Yet, this does not capture the entirety of the relationship between language and thinking. Pinker (2007) examined the relationship between language and thought from another direction. He suggested that there is much to learn about the way the human mind works by examining how humans use language. Pinker argued that there are some basic but uniquely human ways of understanding the world that are reflected in language. One illustration is that the world presents a continual flow of sensory information, but the human mind breaks this flow of information into discrete units of meaning that can then be expressed in language. Pinker proposed that human thought is based on units such as objects, events, and goals. This view implies that, even though individuals and cultures can vary in their languages and the ways that they view the world, the essential machinery underneath is something we have in common.

Whorf's hypothesis is sometimes expressed as having a strong form and a weak form (Hunt & Agnoli, 1991). The strong form claims that we are not able to think about a distinction that is not made in our language. This hypothesis is untenable in the sense that we can think about a concept even if we do not have a specific word for it. We can tell the difference between two different shades of green, for example, even if our language does not include separate words for them like *wor* and *nol*. Similarly, Pirahã speakers can perform an exact matching task even though they lack words for exact numbers (Frank et al., 2008). Even in the presence of differences in cognition depending on language, we have seen similarities, such as the tendency to place more importance on hue than on lightness in grouping colors.

The evidence that we have reviewed here indicates that language can affect thinking even if it does not limit what we can think about. This is consistent with the weak form of Whorf's hypothesis. We perceive the world differently depending on the categories in our language and the preferences of our cultures.

## Assumptions and Misunderstandings

Ironically, our ability to communicate with each other depends on a communication system that itself shapes our perceptions of reality. Differences in ways of perceiving, thinking, and communicating can result in misunderstandings. In this final section, we will start by examining causes of misunderstanding between individuals. We will end with a few examples of misunderstandings about language in general. A better understanding of what language is and how it varies across cultures can prevent both types of problems.

A failure to communicate can be much more than an inconvenience. For example, what happens when a patient and a doctor fail to communicate accurately? Roberts, Moss, Wass, Sarangi, and Jones (2005) analyzed communication between patients and doctors in London, an environment in which many languages are spoken. Their analysis revealed misunderstandings between patients and doctors in 31% of the consultations they recorded. Two thirds of the misunderstandings occurred with patients who had limited English language skills. The vast majority of these misunderstandings had to do directly with language issues rather than with differing cultural beliefs about health. Consider the following example: A patient from Nigeria was talking with his physician in London. The patient had been bitten by a dog, and the physician was trying to determine whether a rabies vaccination was needed for the patient. When the physician asked the patient if the dog was a stray, the patient indicated that he knew the dog's owner. Further, the patient explained that the dog's owner stated that the dog received regular veterinary care. The physician appeared satisfied with this, apparently assuming that it would not be necessary to vaccinate the patient. However, the physician failed to appreciate the culture-specific meaning of the patient's intonation. In reference to the claim that the dog received veterinary care, the patient stated, "that's *what* they said" (the italicized word indicating stress). In Nigerian English, this intonation pattern signals skepticism. In contrast, a British or American English speaker would be likely to stress the verb (*said*) rather than the content (*what*) to indicate skepticism. As a result, the physician failed to understand that the patient was expressing skepticism. The patient continued to express discomfort with this interaction until the physician understood that the dog might not have been vaccinated. Had the patient not been persistent in correcting the miscommunication, the interaction with the physician could have resulted in a serious health problem.

Another consequence of miscommunication is that immigrants may fail to obtain services to which they are entitled because of a language barrier. Kretsedemas (2005) pointed out that these difficulties in communication vary depending on both the particular immigrant group and the linguistic, ethnic, and racial backgrounds of caseworkers. In a study conducted in Florida, Kretsedemas found that Haitian clients had significantly more difficulty communicating with their caseworkers than did Hispanic clients. This resulted in delays in receiving services and the need for multiple visits in order to have an application accepted. The Haitian clients also perceived their caseworkers as more biased than did the Hispanic clients. Kretsedemas suggested that these differences might be explained by the fact that Hispanic clients had no difficulty finding Hispanic caseworkers, but Haitian clients often had caseworkers who did not speak their language.

Grice (1975) provided a useful framework for understanding how language users successfully (or unsuccessfully) communicate their intended messages.

Language is not just about the sounds (or signs), morphemes, phrases, and rules of grammar. Grice outlined four rules, or maxims, for successful communication of intent. The maxim of quality means that the speaker makes every effort to communicate only accurate information. A speaker who provides enough information to make his or her meaning clear, but not more information than necessary, is adhering to the maxim of quantity. By providing information that is germane to the topic being discussed, the speaker follows the maxim of relevance. Finally, by avoiding ambiguity in language, the speaker is adhering to the maxim of manner. Accurate communication depends on the listener being able to assume that the speaker is following conversational rules. For example, if a speaker is attempting to be sarcastic but the listener assumes that the speaker is following the maxim of quality, the intended meaning will be misunderstood. The meaning of "Yes, that is so true" reverses depending on whether the speaker is being indirect (violating quality) or direct (adhering to quality).

Failure to understand a conversational partner's level of directness can result in misunderstandings. Holtgraves (1997) defines conversational indirectness as a difference between sentence meaning (as determined by the words and syntax, without use of context) and the speaker's intended meaning. This may occur, for example, when a speaker phrases something so as not to hurt the listener's feelings, but intends for the listener to understand a different message. A host may say, "Please stay for tea," but the intended meaning is "It is time for you to leave." An individual who tends to speak more directly may perceive someone who speaks indirectly as being evasive, while an individual with a more indirect style may perceive a direct speaker as being rude. Holtgraves found that Koreans scored higher on a measure of indirectness than did Americans. Although Holtgraves related this difference to the collectivistic-individualistic difference in cultures, indirectness also depends on the social context within cultures.

One way that conversational directness can vary is in terms of work and non-work contexts. Directness may be the norm for informal communication between family members ("Did you bathe recently?"), while indirectness may be expected in more formal settings such as at work ("There's a great sale on body wash.") Sanchez-Burks et al. (2003) investigated the hypothesis that reliance on relational cues involved in indirect communication varies between work and non-work settings more for individuals in cultures that rely on Protestant relational ideology (PRI). In the PRI belief system, a focus on maintaining harmonious relationships is not appropriate in a work setting; thus, indirect communication to spare a co-worker's feelings is not emphasized. Sanchez-Burks et al. provided several types of evidence suggesting that Americans tend to show less reliance on indirect communication in work settings than social settings, but this difference does not occur for East Asians (who do not have PRI as part of their culture). The researchers concluded that this cultural difference in communication styles has important consequences for multicultural or multinational work settings. The possibility of a serious misunderstanding or social gaffe could be reduced by increasing our awareness that other individuals may not share our assumptions about the appropriate level of directness in conversation.

We should also be aware that figurative language, such as idioms and metaphors, may not translate well across languages and cultures. Sakuragi and Fuller (2003) asked college students in the U.S. and Japan to rate how easily metaphors could be translated to other languages. Both Japanese-speaking and English-speaking (U.S.) college students rated metaphors as less easy to translate the more they perceived a target language as different from their own. For both Japanese and English speakers, across several target languages, there was a similar pattern indicating the types of metaphors that were considered easier to translate. Generally, when the literal meaning of a metaphor is more similar to its intended figurative meaning, it is considered more likely to translate accurately into a different language. Sakuragi and Fuller found that similarity in appearance was more important than similarity in function in predicting ease of translation. For example, one item the students rated was *hurricane eye*. Students who rated this metaphorical eye as similar in appearance to the eye as a literal body part were likely to indicate it would translate to a different language. If the *foot of a bridge* was rated as similar in function to the foot as a body part, that was less important in predicting how well the metaphorical phrase would translate. Although a metaphor in one language may not always translate well to another language, these results suggest that the processes used to understand metaphors may be quite similar across languages.

Bell (2007) examined the use of humor in conversations between native and non-native speakers of English. Both native and non-native speakers made adjustments in their use of language. For example, both parties tended to avoid controversial topics. Native speakers tried to avoid idioms and other usages that they thought might be difficult for their non-native conversational partners to understand. Similarly, non-native speakers avoided using jokes that they thought would not translate well into English. These findings again support the idea that an increased awareness of cultural variability can prevent misunderstandings.

We have seen several ways that individuals can get mistaken ideas about what their conversational partners mean. On a broader level, mistaken ideas about language and its relationship to culture can have serious social implications. One example of this is mistaken assumptions about differences among dialects. Pinker (1994) addressed the belief that the version of English spoken by some African Americans in the U.S. is a degraded, inferior version of standard English. Sometimes referred to as Ebonics, Black English Vernacular (BEV) is just as rule-governed as Standard American English (SAE). Dialects of any language differ from each other in features such as vocabulary and patterns of syntax. When one dialect, such as SAE, is spoken by a dominant majority, it is often assumed that the dialect is the "correct" one. Any deviations from SAE are then perceived in terms of lack of effort or lack of ability.

One misconception that Pinker (1994) addressed is the belief that BEV speakers tend to be lazy in their speech, leaving out words and word endings. In fact, BEV simply uses different rules than SAE. As a normal part of the development of a language over time, patterns of syntax change. On the surface, these changes may be perceived as a decrease in rigor, as when individuals complain about the lax speaking patterns of a younger generation. In modern SAE, for instance, it is acceptable in speech to contract "I have not" into "I haven't" or "I am going to" to "I'm gonna." In SAE, a speaker might say, "She's swimming." This utterance could mean either, "She is swimming right at the moment," or "She generally swims." The meaning is ambiguous in SAE. In contrast, a BEV speaker might say "She swimming" to mean specifically that she is swimming right at the moment. It appears that a word (*is* or at least the contraction *'s*) has been omitted when compared to SAE, but this is misleading. If the BEV speaker wants to indicate that the person swims regularly, the utterance "She be swimming" indicates that meaning unambiguously. The BEV pattern in this example is more informative than the SAE pattern. Of course, this example does not demonstrate that BEV is superior to SAE, only that dialects can differ in their patterns. A better understanding of how dialects may vary across cultures can prevent us from reaching erroneous conclusions about the speakers of those dialects.

Another assumption we may make is that language systems that differ significantly must be learned in very different ways. One obvious difference is in the writing systems used in different languages. Some languages, such as English, rely on writing systems that are largely phonetic; written characters represent sounds. Chinese is written using characters that are largely ideographic; symbols represent words or morphemes. Given the dramatic differences in what must be learned in order to read using these different systems, we might expect substantial differences in learning how to read. McBride-Chang and Kail (2002) compared reading acquisition by students learning to read Cantonese or English. The children learning Cantonese (in Hong Kong) were in a very different cultural setting than the children learning English (in the U.S.). One important difference is that children in Hong Kong begin learning to read several years before children in the U.S. typically begin. Another important difference is in methods of reading instruction. Children in Hong Kong are taught to read by sight, associating characters with the words they represent. Most children in the U.S. are taught to read primarily with phonics instruction, learning which letters represent which sounds. Further, children in Hong Kong schools learn English and Mandarin in addition to Cantonese, while children in U.S. schools rarely receive foreign language instruction in the early grades. Surprisingly, McBride-Chang and Kail found that predictors of early reading were quite similar between children learning English and children learning Cantonese. For example, phonological awareness (knowledge of the sound structure of the language) was highly predictive of the ability to recognize words or characters in both groups. Visual processing ability was not very predictive of reading ability in either group. Thus, we should not assume that learning processes must be different just because language systems differ on the surface.

To conclude the final section of this chapter, we will consider how cultural differences are important in language research. Knowledge that we gain on both the individual and scientific levels is not culture-free. Often it is necessary for researchers to translate a questionnaire from its original language into one or more other languages. How does the researcher know that the instrument will maintain reliability and validity after being translated? Cha, Kim, and Erlen (2007) described different solutions to this dilemma. The most common solution is the use of back-translation. In this method, an individual who speaks both languages translates the items on a questionnaire to the target language. Then, another bilingual individual translates the items back to the original language. The original and back-translated versions are then compared. If any of the back-translated items do not match with the original items in concept, then another bilingual individual translates the items. Cha et al. pointed out that it is difficult to predict how many translators will be needed in order to complete this process. Further, it may be difficult to locate enough translators who are sufficiently knowledgeable about both the research and the cultures involved. Cha et al. used a combined approach to translate instruments from English to Korean. Their method included having the instruments translated to Korean and back-translated to English. The process also included a review of the back-translated instruments by monolingual individuals who were knowledgeable about the content of the instruments. They noted a number of translation difficulties that can occur. One example is that a word may exist in one language but not another. An item on the English version of an instrument contained the word *party*, but there is no corresponding word in Korean. The translators resolved this by using a combination of words in Korean. Cha et al. also pointed out that it can be very difficult to translate an idiom. They recommended that scale developers avoid the use of idiomatic expressions. Note that the researcher who develops the scale must anticipate possible cross-cultural use in order for this advice to be useful.

The failure to take into account different experiences can produce misleading assumptions about group differences. Bartoshuk, Fast, and Snyder (2005) highlighted the problem of making sensory or hedonic comparisons across groups. When asked to rate the intensity of a stimulus, or their liking for something, individuals' ratings depend on the anchors used on the rating scale. Because the meaning of these anchors can vary based on one's experiences, comparison of the ratings across groups can be misleading. For example, suppose respondents rate an experience of pain from 0 (none at all) to 100 (strongest imaginable pain). If two groups (say, men and women) differ on their numerical responses, it may be interpreted as meaning that one group experiences the same stimulus as being more painful than does the other group. But, as Bartoshuk et al. explain, this misses the fact that the groups are likely to differ on how they interpret the anchors of the scale. If the two groups differ in their experiences, then the strongest imaginable pain could be quite different for one group than for the other. Thus, a research finding indicating a group difference in sensory judgments may be misleading. The same issue can occur outside the context of research whenever two individuals are communicating. When we anchor our judgments in different experiences, we may think we are talking about the same thing even though we are not.

## Concluding Comments

We began this chapter with an examination of the idea that human language is universal. Although it is not possible to prove that all human languages share a particular feature, the evidence for commonality is quite strong. Despite variability across human languages, they have much in common. One of the central lessons about language is that the important similarities are not always obvious on the surface.

We have learned that language can affect the way we perceive each other and the world around us. The way we carve up the world in different categories is, to some extent, related to the language that we know. We saw this pattern with color terms, grammatical gender, and ideas about motion. It is important that we distinguish between differences in the *ability* to think about certain distinctions and differences in our *habits* of thinking. For example, we have the ability to think about color categories even when we do not habitually make those distinctions in our language.

In the same way, an awareness of how our assumptions can differ from those of others can help us avoid misunderstandings. We have discussed examples of cultural differences in directness, figurative language, and humor. We have seen how mistaken assumptions can affect our ability to obtain services, our views of people who speak differently, and the meaning of research results. The good news is that we also have the flexibility to make adjustments in our language use and in our assumptions about the language use of others. Our shared capacity for flexible thinking opens the door to understanding other cultures. But an open door is only useful when we realize that it is there.

## References

Bartoshuk, L. M., Fast, K., & Snyder, D. J. (2005). Differences in our sensory worlds: Invalid comparisons with labeled scales. *Current Directions in Psychological Science, 14,* 122–125.

Bell, N. D. (2007). How native and non-native English speakers adapt to humor in intercultural interaction. *Humor, 20,* 27–48.

Blake, J., Vitale, G., Osborne, P., & Olshansky, E. (2005). A cross-cultural comparison of communicative gestures in human infants during the transition to language. *Gesture, 5,* 201–217.

Carroll, J. B. (Ed.). (1956). *Language, thought, and reality: Selected writings of Benjamin Lee Whorf.* New York: Technology Press of Massachusetts Institute of Technology; London: John Wiley & Sons, and Chapman & Hall, Limited.

Cha, E., Kim, K. H., & Erlen, J. A. (2007). Translation of scales in cross-cultural research: Issues and techniques. *Journal of Advanced Nursing, 58,* 386–395.

Everett, D. L. (2005). Cultural constraints on language and cognition in Pirahã. *Current Anthropology, 46,* 621–646.

Flaherty, M. (2001). How a language gender system creeps into perception. *Journal of Cross-Cultural Psychology, 32,* 18–31.

Fox, M. (2007). *Talking hands.* New York: Simon & Schuster.

Frank, M. C., Everett, D. L., Fedorenko, E., & Gibson, E. (2008). Number as a cognitive technology: Evidence from Pirahã language and cognition. *Cognition, 108,* 819–824.

Grice, H. P. (1975). Speech acts. In P. Cole & J. Morgan (Eds.), *Syntax and semantics 3* (pp. 26–40). New York: Academic Press.

Hockett, C. F. (1966). The problem of universals in language. In J. H. Greenberg (Ed.), *Universals of language* (2nd ed., pp. 1–29). Cambridge, MA: MIT Press.

Holtgraves, T. (1997). Styles of language use: Individual and cultural variability in conversational indirectness. *Journal of Personality and Social Psychology, 73,* 624–637.

Hunt, E., & Agnoli, F. (1991). The Whorfian hypothesis: A cognitive psychology perspective. *Psychological Review, 98,* 377–389.

Ji, L., Zhang, Z., & Nisbett, R. E. (2004). Is it culture or is it language? Examination of language effects in cross-cultural research on categorization. *Journal of Personality and Social Psychology, 87,* 57–65.

Kretsedemas, P. (2005). Language barriers and perceptions of bias: Ethnic differences in immigrant encounters with the welfare system. *Journal of Sociology and Social Welfare, 32,* 109–123.

Martin, L. (1986). "Eskimo words for snow": A case study in the genesis and decay of an anthropological example. *American Anthropologist, 88,* 418–423.

McBride-Chang, C., & Kail, R. V. (2002). Cross-cultural similarities in the predictors of reading acquisition. *Child Development, 73,* 1392–1407.

Özyürek, A., Kita, S., Allen, S., Brown, A., Furman, R., & Ishizuka, T. (2008). Development of cross-linguistic variation in speech and gesture: Motion events in English and Turkish. *Developmental Psychology, 44,* 1040–1054.

Pinker, S. (1994). *The language instinct: How the mind creates language.* New York: William Morrow and Company.

Pinker, S. (2007). *The stuff of thought: Language as a window into human nature.* New York: Viking Penguin.

Roberson, D., Davies, I. R. L., Corbett, G. G., & Vandervyver, M. (2005). Free-sorting of colors across cultures: Are there universal grounds for grouping? *Journal of Cognition and Culture, 5,* 349–386.

Roberson, D., Davies, I. R. L., & Davidoff, J. (2000). Color categories are not universal: Replications and new evidence in favor of linguistic relativity. *Journal of Experimental Psychology: General, 129,* 369–398.

Roberts, C., Moss, M., Wass, V., Sarangi, S., & Jones, R. (2005). Misunderstandings: A qualitative survey of primary care consultations in multilingual settings, and educational implications. *Medical Education, 35,* 465–475.

Rosch, E. (1973). On the internal structure of perceptual and semantic categories. In T. E. Moore (Ed.), *Cognitive development and the acquisition of language* (pp. 111–144). New York: Academic Press.

Sakuragi, T., & Fuller, J. W. (2003). Body-part metaphors: A cross-cultural survey of the perception of translatability among Americans and Japanese. *Journal of Psycholinguistic Research, 32,* 381–395.

Sanchez-Burks, J., Lee, F., Choi, I., Nisbett, R., Zhao, S., & Koo, J. (2003). Conversing across cultures: East–west communication styles in work and nonwork contexts. *Journal of Personality and Social Psychology, 85,* 363–372.

Sandler, W., Meir, I., Padden, C., & Aronoff, M. (2005). The emergence of grammar: Systematic structure in a new language. *Proceedings of the National Academy of Sciences, 102,* 2661–2665.

Scott, L. S., & Monesson, A. (2009). The origin of biases in face perception. *Psychological Science, 20,* 676–680.

Senghas, A., Kita, S., & Özyürek, A. (2004). Children creating core properties of language: Evidence from an emerging sign language in Nicaragua. *Science, 305,* 1779–1782.

Sera, M. D., Elieff, C., Forbes, J., Burch, M. C., Rodriguez, W., & Dubois, D. P. (2002). When language affects cognition and when it does not: An analysis of grammatical gender and classification. *Journal of Experimental Psychology: General, 131,* 377–397.

# 21

# Crossing Boundaries
## *Cross-Cultural Communication*

### Leeva C. Chung

In our quest to stabilize the global economy amid fast and furious advances in technology, the world is becoming a village of intersecting webs. We find ourselves having increased face-to-face contact with people who appear to be different from ourselves. Transiting across borders or moving from one space to another, we may find more diversity and cultural values in flux. Now more than ever, we face the daily challenge to communicate effectively with individuals who may have little, if anything, in common with us.

The study of cross-cultural communication is about the study of communication that involves, to varying degrees, cultural group membership differences. It is about acquiring the necessary tools and skills to manage such differences appropriately and effectively in ways that make sense to us. It is also about developing an alternative frame without rigid biases. On a practical level, there are many reasons to understand the role of culture in our basic communication encounters, even if we decide not to travel beyond national borders. Within the U.S., cultural diversity is a part of our everyday experience, and is especially critical for several reasons. For example, in school and in the workplace, it is inevitable that students and employees from dissimilar cultures are in constant contact with one another— whether face to face, or via phone or social networking. Our ability to value different approaches to problem solving and mindfully move away from traditional "either/or" binary thinking about groups can create and expand diverse options in managing intercultural problems. According to creativity research (Sternberg, 1999), we learn more from people who are different from us than from those who are similar to us.

The picture of a simple life with "like-minded" similar people is no longer accurate, wherever you call home. In what was once a homogeneous community, we may now find more diversity and cultural values in flux. In the U.S., for example, census projections suggest that racial and ethnic minorities between the ages of 18 and 34 will become the majority by the year 2039. Another current phenomenon is online dating, both domestically and globally. No longer private issues, online dating services, chat rooms, and services allow us to meet on the basis of various criteria. Some people may disclose their ethnicities, and some people may not. Brooks (2003) reported that 40 million U.S. individuals date online. The success of various dating services clearly suggests that this service is in demand in this hook-up age. With the dramatic rise of cross-cultural marriages and children, intimate relationships are a fertile ground for bumps and clashes. Taking this all into account, the boundaries that shape how we perceive others and how we value culturally intact groups will change. These boundaries that mark whom we include and exclude become pivotal as we try to understand how to get along in a diverse world. With such rich layers of domestic and global cultural issues, we need an alternative perspective to understand our complex interactions. This chapter will explore the necessity to study cross-cultural communication in our twenty-first century global world. As we move across physical and emotional borders, how do we learn to negotiate our communication, culture, and identity in a cross-cultural context, and how can we understand the logic that motivates our actions or behaviors?

## Communication, Culture, and Cross-Cultural Communication

I am often asked: What do cross-cultural/intercultural communication scholars do? And how is this similar to cross-cultural psychology? To attempt to answer this question, I will begin by defining communication, culture, and cross-cultural communication. Then I will highlight shared research concepts and summarize cross-cultural communication theories.

### Communication and culture

To think about communicating effectively with those who are culturally different, we must understand the major characteristics that make up the process of communication. Both culture and communication reciprocally influence one another. Culture is created, passed down, and adapted from one generation to the next. To distinguish between the characteristics of culture and communication, we will discuss the complex relation between them.

The concept *communication* is dynamic and subject to multifaceted interpretations. Although there are many working definitions of communication, Griffin (2009) perhaps best described it, as the relational process of creating and interpreting messages that elicit some form of response. Thus, messages are the core of communication. In any communication encounter, we use verbal and nonverbal messages to get our ideas across to each other. We can exchange messages, but we cannot exchange meanings. No two people will interpret a message in the same way because of our unique lived experience (Gudykunst, 1994). Communication is a symbolic exchange process, between two individuals who attempt to accomplish shared meanings.

With many existing definitions of culture (see, for example, Chapter 1 in this volume), it is safe to say that *culture* is an elastic concept that takes on multiple layers of meaning. Culture is basically a learned system of meanings that helps us to make sense, or explain, what is going on around us. Individuals within a cultural group share complex patterns of traditions, beliefs, values, norms, meanings, and symbols that are passed on from one generation to the next and are shared to varying degrees by interacting members of a community (Ting-Toomey, 1999). Culture can be compared to an iceberg: the deep invisible layers (e.g., traditions, beliefs, values) are hidden but have a direct influence on our behavior. It is the uppermost layers of cultural artifacts (e.g., fashion, language, pop music) that we typically learn about another culture.

To understand what culture does for us, Ting-Toomey (1999) summarized three functions of culture that appear to be critical: (a) culture gives us a frame of reference to understand who we are, which is an identity meaning function; (b) culture satisfies our need for membership affiliation and belonging, which is the need for group inclusion; and (c) culture shapes our attitudes toward in- and out-group members. These three functions serve as an invisible cultural boundary—a particular sense of shared identity and solidarity among group members, reinforcing the boundary of "we" as an in-group, and "dissimilar others" as belonging to distant out-groups. At the same time, culture can also foster exclusive boundaries within the group; individual group members may feel ostracized by the cultural in-group and be cast as out-group members. Communication serves as an intricate piece of the cultural puzzle, linking these various needs and processes together.

### Cross-cultural communication

Cross-cultural communication involves comparisons of communication across cultural groups rather than between individuals within particular cultural groups (Gudykunst, 2002). Our communication interactions affect and influence our behavior with strangers. While considering cross-cultural communication, it is important to include both global and domestic/local comparisons. More importantly, it is critical that we conceptualize the use of culture as a frame to understand our behavior and our messages, and their impact and influence in shaping our interactions. For example, cultural groups may approach decision-making or nonverbal gestures differently. They may develop friendships and romantic relationships with different, mismatched expectations and speed, or have different communication desires, goals, and motivation. Although a successful cross-cultural encounter encourages a competent approach and a healthy outlook, difficulties emerge from the residue of behaviors, ideas, and beliefs that are comfortable and considered to be proper or "the right way" (Brislin, 1981). For example, even with people who want to have intercultural interactions (have positive attitudes), there are intercultural communication difficulties to overcome (e.g., in a high-context situation, where I am supposed to be very sensitive to subtle situational cues, but I may not have been socialized this way in my low-context culture).

Putting this all together, cross-cultural communication scholars and researchers are fundamentally trying to determine how we can be flexible, competent communicators when we interact with cultural strangers. This is no easy task, a bit like learning how to dance. During our cross-cultural encounters, we may step on people's toes, feel out of sync, or have mismatched ideas about our own ethnocentric viewpoint. With time and struggle, we learn to observe how to act appropriately, flow in our encounters, and adjust our perspective. Thankfully, culture is not a static web. It is a dynamic, evolutionary process. Similarly, human beings are not static individuals—we change. In learning about another culture, or about dissimilar groups, we can expand our ways of thinking and find new insights to strengthen our own identity.

Anthropologist Edward T. Hall (1959) stated it best: communication *is* culture and culture *is* communication. Communication is central to the definition of our cultural experience. Investigating the comparative nature of the communicative process is at the core of cross-cultural communication. But what makes cross-cultural communication and cross-cultural psychology similar and different? Are these two mutually exclusive fields of study? Let's examine how we share our research sandbox and draw boundaries in this field of study.

## Sharing the sandbox

Cross-cultural psychology and communication researchers share very similar contemporary elements, despite inhabiting two different fields of study. While communication scholars focus on behavior and interaction among cultural strangers, psychologists acknowledge the influence of culture on the behavior of an individual. Contemporary research examines cultural similarities and differences using cultural-level and/or individual-level dimensions. There are two central aspect of cultures frequently discussed in cross-cultural communication and psychology research: general and specific cultural value comparisons.

Many cross-cultural researchers have identified Hofstede's (1980) cultural value dimensions of individualism-collectivism (IC), power distance (OD), uncertainty avoidance (UA), and masculinity-feminism (MA) as useful general comparative cultural constructs. IC appears to be the major dimension of cultural variability used to explain similarities and differences across cultural groups (Triandis, 1988). The strength of this dimension lies in the fact that it possesses the "clearest individual-level equivalents in cultural level tendencies" (Gudykunst & Kim, 1997, p. 56).

While individualistic cultures, such as the United Kingdom, emphasize individual goals, collectivistic cultures, such as Guatemala, stress the primacy of group goals over individual preferences. As a result of this value dimension, important relationships and connections have emerged:

- the importance of measuring in-group versus out-group boundary comparisons (Tajfel, 1978)
- identifying high- versus low-context communication patterns (Hall, 1976)
- expanding individual personality variables such as idiocentrism and allocentrism to advance individualism versus collectivism (Triandis, Leung, Villareal & Clack,1985)
- incorporating interdependent versus independent self construals (Markus & Kitayama, 1991) to explain a wide variety of communication phenomena.

As you can see, the IC dimension provides a potentially rich explanatory framework for understanding similarities and differences in cross-cultural studies by extending the frame of a simple continuum. Hofstede's (1980) other dimensions (i.e., PD, UA, and MA) also provide similar continua by which to analyze cultural phenomena. Thus, researchers have treated culture as a central construct to explain how communication varies across and between cultural groups. Despite problems and criticisms associated with Hofstede's conceptualization, these dimensions can be useful when monitored carefully as an individual assessment rather than generalized large group comparisons.

## Drawing lines in the sand

Currently, there is a plethora of cross-cultural communication research attempting to explain cultural-level and/or individual-level differences in language, relational attraction, emotions, perceptions, identity, nonverbal communication, conflict, and intergroup behavior (to name a few), that have contributed to the growth of the field of communication. Gudykunst and Lee (2002) have summarized some of the contemporary theories as follows:

1  Gudykunst's (1995) Anxiety/uncertainty management theory (AUM) explains the importance of information-seeking behavior to reduce our anxiety and uncertainty when we interact with cultural strangers. Effective communication only occurs when we can mindfully manage our anxiety and uncertainty.
2  Ting-Toomey's (1998; 2004) face negotiation theory (FNT) provides us with a general framework to understand how we manage face and conflict situations as a result of our cultural differences in norms and values. *Face* is the respect for identity issues during an interaction or the emotional significance we attach to our own worth and the self-worth of others (Ting-Toomey, 2004). *Facework* is

the verbal and nonverbal strategies we use to maintain, defend, or upgrade our self-image and attack or defend (or "save") the images of others.

3   Burgoon's (1995) expectancy violations theory (EVT) refers to expectations we have of ourself and others when we cross cultural boundaries. Violations occur when our expectations become discrepant from our initial anticipations and give us pause (e.g., personal space violations) and arousal. In addition, communicator valence refers to whether we perceive interaction with a particular communicator as rewarding or costly. Burgoon (1995) suggested that the concept of communication expectancy is a universal one, including the meanings, tolerable range, and evaluations (positive–negative valence) of our expectancy violations.

4   Gallois, Giles, Jones, Cargile, and Ota (1995) proposed communication accommodation theory (CAT), a theory of what happens during interactions with different groups by focusing on the language, nonverbal behavior, and paralanguage we use in conversation. When two people from different ethnic or cultural groups interact, they tend to accommodate each other in the way they speak in order to gain the other's approval. Gallois et al. contrasted two strategies—convergence and divergence—that we use when interacting with in- and out-group members. Convergence occurs when the individual adapts his or her communication behavior in such a way as to become more similar to the other person. Divergence accentuates the differences between onerself and another.

This is a brief summary of what we know about explaining cross-cultural similarities and differences in communication across cultural groups. Research in cross-cultural communication is exciting, flourishing, and popular. But as we move forward, there are some obstacles and challenges cross-cultural researchers must face. Let's discuss this is in more detail.

## Challenges in cross-cultural communication research

According to Levine, Park, & Kirschbaum (2007), three areas will be challenging for future cross-cultural research: theory, definition, and situational contexts. Although investigators use the cross-cultural theories sampled above in current research, Levine and colleagues believe there are persisting problems in using the IC (and other related constructs) dimension in research. The reliance on this one dimension to characterize distinct cultural groups limits the scope of inquiry. The IC dimension can explain some, but not all communication attitudes and behaviors. Kim (2001) argued that this conceptualization can lead to dangerous categorizations. Presenting cultures in either/or terms can lead to grave misunderstandings in research and analysis. As a result, we can safely say this area is ready for new perspectives and new theory.

Secondly, Levine et al. (2007) argued that as we compare and contrast communication patterns between different cultural groups, the findings don't always predict what happens when interaction takes place between individuals. Culture is typically viewed as a collective framework. In research, the individual may or may not be the most meaningful unit in cross-cultural comparisons. Culture gives us commonality and belonging within the group, but not necessarily with other individuals. But shared cultural knowledge is impossible to determine, given that culture is shared to varying degrees by individual group members. As mentioned above, a culture gives us a shared sense of identity and belonging. Looking at *individual* accounts of in-group membership and identity may provide the added explanatory strength to determine what happens during interaction.

Finally, communication does not take place in a vacuum, but in a context. Cross-cultural researchers need to investigate specific situational and/or relational contexts rather than being uniform in agreement that culture is the main influence. Thus, questions like "In what situation is preference for direct communication favored over indirect styles?" are more careful (and precise) than implying "Culture X prefers direct communication over indirect styles."

These points raise some very intriguing issues for researchers, and the implication is simple. As changing demographics are widespread and accelerated, we are all crossing boundaries and shifting identities. Whether through marriage, immigration, adoption, or work, individuals can no longer claim a monocultural communication or cultural behavior pattern. Sharing space and language results in shared identity space. Collectivistic individuals may find compatible behavioral patterns among fellow individualistic workers; or individualistic low-context communicators may adopt more high-context frames with relational partners. Thus, our measurements are in need of updating and framing at the level of the individual.

Cross-cultural research in communication presents some special challenges as we share and negotiate our boundaries. Specifically, crossing boundaries of culture, communication, and identity presents a new frame or lens to understand our cross-cultural encounters. In the final section, fleshing out the intersection of these three components raises two important questions: (1) How does the relationship among culture, communication, and identity play out? and (2) What are the research implications?

## The intersection of communication, culture, and ethnic identity

Viewing cultural variation based on group membership is an important concern because individuals born into cultural groups are generally characterized as in-group members. Previous research has shown that individuals tend to see themselves in light of their respective cultural group membership (Brewer, 1997; Miller & Brewer, 1984). But what are we doing with out-group members? How do we address intact cultural individuals who have been cast aside and *perceived* as out-group members?

*Who are you?*

Much social science research has studied how our identities affect us during the lifespan. We all have a complete image of our *self* that is an outcome of the interactions we have within our social environment. Significant people within their social world influence how individuals come to view who they are. Personal identity is a theory of self that is formed and maintained through actual or imagined agreement (Schlenker, 1985). How we see ourselves is shaped and molded by the feedback we receive from others (Mead, 1934).

Although culture plays the larger role in shaping our view of ourselves, it is through multiple channels that we acquire and develop our own values, norms, and baseline for behavior in our lives. For example, our families pass on values and norms from one generation to the next. Parents teach their children the difference between right and wrong, and acceptable and unacceptable ways of behaving, through the language they use and through role modeling these actions. During their early years, children internalize what to value and devalue, what to appreciate and reject, and what goals are important in their culture, through the influence of their family system and via pervasive messages from popular culture and contemporary media. It is through the pervasive cultural value patterns—as filtered through the family and media systems—that meanings and values of identity are differentiated and defined (Moran & Chung, 2008). We all have identity goals, which refer to our need for respect/disrespect or approval/disapproval when interacting with others. Self-identification provides the motivational key to communicative actions. How we conceive our sense of self and how we want to be perceived by others are fundamental communicative questions. It is through communication that we can reframe and modify our self views, in a continuous cycle of negotiation.

*One day you're IN, the next, OUT*

We all have primary personal identities that include any unique attributes that we associate with our self in comparison with those of others. Groups play a significant role in the development of self, and as individuals support their social identities by acquiring group memberships, the salience and formation of cultural identity are integral. Development of identity does not occur in the same manner across societal boundaries. Thus, how an individual expresses his/her identity may be vastly different in India than in Cuba. One may emphasize the integration of an individualized identity or more collectivistic/familial connection. The cultural and ethnic identities acquired during the childhood and adolescent years influence with whom we associate, the food we eat, the language or dialect we speak, and the nonverbal styles we are at ease with in communicating with others. In being aware of our multifaceted self-concept, it is important that we gain a deeper awareness of the complex, multifaceted identities of culturally different others. Ethnic identity is one such fact that intersects with culture and communication.

Multicultural individuals are increasing in numerical proportion and live on the border between two or more cultural groups (Martin & Nakayama, 2009). Across social science disciplines, researchers are determined to understand the persistence of ethnic identities in countries with a variety of ethnic groups with strong, dominant identities. Throughout much of the history of the U.S., the country been compared to a melting pot (Zangwill, 1909) where immigrants were assumed to blend and melt into the society, encouraging a process of Americanization (Glazer, 1997; Gordon, 1964). However, ethnic individuals have consistently embraced, adopted, and formed ethnic identities despite integration pressures within the society. The melting pot metaphor suggests a type of conformity and a reminder of the difficulty many groups have had assimilating into the society; many individuals have continued to embrace an ethnic identity despite the pressure to assimilate.

Defining ethnic identity is no doubt problematic across several disciplines. Although there are hundreds of definitions of ethnic identity, Alba (1990) provided a strong definition, proposing that ethnic identity is "inherently a matter of ancestry, of beliefs about the origins of one's forebears" (p. 37). The dominant society is a major force influencing the components of ethnic identity (Sue, Mak & Sue, 1998). How does one develop a sense of ethnic identity? A developing sense of personal and social identity can be combined into development of an ethnic identity. According to Phinney (1992), there are three areas of identity construction: affect, cognition, and behaviors. *Affect* describes the labels we use to self-identify, our sense of belonging, being in the in-group, and feeling content as a member of the group. *Cognition* comprises the history and knowledge of the group. Finally, *behaviors* include group involvement and the practice of celebrating group membership, although an individual associated with a particular ethnic group may not actually behave in accordance with her or his ethnic norms or behaviors. In other words, skin color or other ethnic traits do not automatically guarantee ethnic in-group membership. In the U.S., although ethnic minorities strive hard to be "Americans," they are constantly reminded by the media or in actual interactions that they may not belong to the larger U.S. society.

Ethnic identity can be sustained by shared characteristics, such as language or religion. It is also a subjective sense of "in-groupness," as individuals perceive themselves and each other as members of the same in-group through shared historical and emotional ties. However, for many ethnic minority group members living in the larger U.S. society, a constant struggle exists between perception of their own ethnic identity and the perception of others' questioning of their ethnic heritage or role. Often, this results in a sense of both ethnic and cultural identity crisis. By understanding how we define ourselves and how others define themselves ethnically and culturally, we can communicate with more cultural sensitivity and understanding.

Realizing that ethnic group membership does not necessarily correspond to cultural group membership and identification with the dominant group can help explain what makes the group "common" and what separates one ethnic group from others. We cannot assume that all individuals in an ethnic group will share a single, common identification when group culture is rich in linguistic and religious diversity. Ethnic identity appears to have subjective and objective layers. Just how cross-cultural psychologists and communication scholars approach ethnic identity will be summed up briefly.

First, ethnic identity can be viewed as a sense of group membership based on shared political and economic conditions. A popular theme in this literature holds that positive group interaction is an essential component of ethnic identity. This idea incorporates both sociological and psychological perspectives, including theories of assimilation (Gordon, 1964), acculturation (Berry, 1980), and social identity (Tajfel, 1974). Second, ethnic identity has been addressed in a developmental model. In this perspective, identity transformation occurs throughout the lifespan of an individual and is based on experiences of ethnic discovery (see Cross, 1991; Parham & Helms, 1985). Third, the process of identity formation is concerned with how individuals understand the implications of their ethnic identity (Erikson, 1968; Phinney, 1989). Finally, communication has been linked with ethnic identity as an outcome of adaptation (Kim, 1988) and negotiation within the individual and among ethnic group members (Ting-Toomey, 1993). These two communication theories (adaptation and negotiation) are important to explore further because how we view ourselves inversely affects how we communicate with others.

*Adaptation and identity*

As more minorities cross boundaries, one outcome of successful adaptation is an intercultural identity (Kim, 1995). By combining psychological (affective, behavioral, and cognitive), social (interpersonal and mass communication), and environmental explanations, we can explain the stress–adaptation–growth process of an individual. The social and psychological dimensions of adaptation are different but interrelated facets of cross-cultural adaptation. Identity is dynamic and evolving. Kim (1988, 1995) argued that during the process of adaptation, stress is an underlying factor motivating an individual to make the necessary adjustments to find some form of balance. The degree of intercultural development influences an individual's capacity to function in a multicultural society by undergoing the struggle to manage the stress, the need to successfully adapt, and the maintenance of ethnic identity distinctiveness. The result is an intercultural identity, defined as an increase in the individual's capacity to integrate conflicting cultural demands into a cohesive new whole (Kim, 1995).

Identity has universalized and individualized orientations: universalized to transcend the ascribed cultural parameters, and individualized as the self–other orientation becomes more particularized and personalized (Kim, 2001). Although most social scientists have devoted time to drawing boundaries between ethnic group memberships, emphasis should be placed on merging boundaries without the need to lock oneself in a single identity (Kim, 1995). In essence, an individual who expands his/her identity by incorporating new cultural elements should not be perceived as a disloyal ethnic group member. Rather, the merging of ethnic boundaries is perceived as a matter of personal necessity and value for the ethnic individual.

*Identity negotiation*

Ting-Toomey (1993) developed a theory of identity negotiation, drawing on social identity theory (Tajfel & Turner, 1979), acculturation theory (Berry, Kim, Power, Young, & Bujaki, 1989), and racial identity development scales (Cross, 1991; Helms, 1990). Ting-Toomey viewed ethnic identity as a multidimensional construct including aspects of personal and collective self-concept, affiliation with in-group and out-group members, attitudes, and feelings. According to Ting-Toomey, humans have universal needs for security and inclusion. Ethnic identity represents a contradictory state between a sense of group belonging and a sense of wanting to become separate from the group, which accounts for group inclusion or differentiation.

The contradictory state takes the form of a dialectical tension, which is "the simultaneous presence of two relational forces that are interdependent and mutually negating. Their interdependence is evident in that the forces define each other" (Montgomery, 1992, p. 207). Thus, the ultimate challenge for an individual is to find the balance between both states. This tension, between in-group membership and individuality, is anchored in the daily life and social practices of ethnic individuals.

What the adaptation and negotiation theories have in common is that membership in an in-group is a matter of degree and variation. If norms, values, and social relationships within an in-group influence the communication patterns of group members, the influence should depend on the extent to which one shares the group's norms (Kim, 1988). Admission to the in-group and acceptance by the in-group, on the basis of shared norms and values, are interrelated: The more an individual associates with the in-group, the greater the conformity that is expected and reinforced. At the same time, if the in-group does not approve of an individual's behavior, it can reject the in-group member. Because of this variation in conformity among in-group members, the boundary lines of in-group and out-group are sometimes blurred. Although our in-groups offer us a sense of belonging and security, they also have the power to reject us.

The process of identity formation is concerned with how individuals understand the implications of their ethnic identity. We communicate who we are on a daily basis. Our identities have a profound influence on when we feel secure, when we are at our most vulnerable, and when we feel obligated to mask our authentic self. We struggle with and against our identity. But how can we connect identity with a cross-cultural frame? Making a distinction between cultural variability and ethnic identity salience is clear. The social construction of the self may be the determining factor in understanding the context of cultural differences. By using the identity pulls of security–vulnerability and inclusion–differentiation, we can understand that it is not easy to neatly fit into an in- or out-status.

# Implications in Cross-Cultural Communication

The intersection and boundaries of identity, communication and culture are dynamic and constantly transformed to fit the needs of individuals in complex settings. The situational nature of identity challenges cross-cultural communication scholars to understand the impact of prescribing a general "group membership" ethnic identity which is not the ascribed self-identity. The other challenge is to find the behavioral cues associated with in-group or out-group status during an interaction with a member of the same ethnic group, and how the individual perceives these cues.

The importance of the behavioral cues associated with out-group perception during interaction may help address our differences in getting together, and explain why we have different goals, values, proxemics, and needs during conversations. More importantly, fleshing out our behavioral cues can be a major contributor to a successful or failed cross-cultural encounter.

## Language rules

Language plays a key role in cross-cultural communication. Language is closely tied to our claimed identity. We use language to agree or disagree with people, to offer or decline requests, enforce goals, and defuse tension. Language frames our perceptions and interpretations of everyday events happening around us; it is a taken-for-granted aspect of our life. We acquire meanings for words (e.g., collaboration, peace) or phrases (e.g., deal with it) via the value systems of our culture. Though language can easily create misunderstandings, it can also clarify misunderstandings and minimize tense moments.

Across the globe, languages are constructed with words or symbols that are arranged in patterned ways and governed by a set of rules. The semantic rules of language are based on the meaning we attach to words. Words do not have self-evident meanings. Humans consensually establish shared meanings for specific words and phrases. For example, *hot* has a feature of temperature, and *mess* has a feature of organization. If we combine hot with mess as *hot mess* the concept takes on a whole range of different meanings. Beyond using vocabulary, we need to apply the appropriate cultural meaning features that are indicated by different word pairings. Without such cultural knowledge, we may have the right vocabulary but an inappropriate meaning association system.

Another important component of language is pragmatics. Pragmatics of a language refers to the contextual rules that govern language usage in a particular culture. Pragmatics concerns the rules of how to say what, to whom, and under what situational conditions, in a speech community (Hymes, 1972). These two rules of language give rise to the diverse functions of languages across cultures and answer the question of why language plays such a critical role within each culture. Language is an integral part of both a sense of identity and the mindset that goes with it.

For example, think about how you want to persuade your boss to allow you to take a week off. Cross-culturally, there are two modes you can choose from. The first is called the self-enhancement mode. This mode focuses on boasting about one's credentials, accomplishments, and special achievements and abilities. In Switzerland and the U.S., encouraging individuals to sell themselves and highlight their achievements during a job interview is an example of self-enhancement. On the other hand, the self-effacing verbal mode emphasizes the importance of modest talk, hesitant speech, and the use of self-deprecation concerning one's effort or performance. The self-humbling mode is a fundamental part of the Puerto Rican verbal style. In your request for a week off, which do you choose? Who could understand what a self-effacing individual wanted? Research indicates that in many Latin, Native American, and Asian cultures, individuals believe that if their performance is good, or if time off is needed, others will notice. However, from the Western cultural standpoint, if their performance is good, or time off is needed, individuals should document or be direct so that those in charge will be sure to take notice.

Thus, language rules during an interaction are about much more than what words are spoken: it is the *way* words are spoken that plays an enormous role in how a cross-cultural encounter unfolds, possibly resulting in mismatched expectations, assumptions, and/or stereotypes. How language interacts with our nonverbal behavior adds an additional factor to our discussion of the intersection of culture, identity, and communication.

## Nonverbal communication

Nonverbal communication is a powerful form of human expression. It is all around us. Nonverbal messages are often the primary means of signaling our emotions, attitudes, and the status of our relationships with others. Although our communication with others consists of verbal messages, nonverbal communication is equally important as verbal communication (Andersen, 2008). Many nonverbal experts estimate that in every encounter, nonverbal channels convey about 60–65% of the message. Nonverbal messages signify who we are, based on what we wear, how we speak, and how we present ourselves. Nonverbal communication is both a conscious and an unconscious aspect of our everyday life. We can communicate with people without speaking a word, intentionally or not. Because nonverbal communication occurs with or without verbal messages, nonverbal messages provide the context for how an accompanying verbal message should be interpreted and understood. They can either create confusion or clarify communication. Often, nonverbal messages can create cross-cultural friction and miscommunication because (1) the same nonverbal signal can mean different things to different people in different cultures, (2) we often send multiple nonverbal cues, and (3) there are many display rule variations to consider, such as personality, gender, relational distance, socioeconomic status, and situation.

Our culture shapes the display rules for when, where, with whom, and how different emotions should be expressed or suppressed. Nonverbal cues are the markers of our identities. The way we dress, the way we talk, and our nonverbal gestures, all tell something about who we are and how we want to be viewed. We rely on nonverbal cues as our "name badge" to identify what group we belong to and what groups we are *not* members of. Our accent, posture, and hand gestures further reveal our group membership. Many misunderstandings occur when we try to infer the meaning behind nonverbal codes, especially with someone who is from a different culture. Decoding nonverbal messages with 100% accuracy is like making predictions about who will win the Super Bowl— before the season starts.

Nonverbal communication includes a wide variety of behaviors, including the study of *kinesics* (facial expressions, posture, and body movement), *proxemics* (space), *vocalics* (silence and the meaning behind how we say our words), *haptics* (contact, touch behavior), *artifacts* (objects and appearance), *oculesics* (eye behavior), and *chronemics* (time) (Andersen, 2008). Each of these behaviors has generated numerous research studies, as investigators try to understand these nonverbal cues cross-culturally.

## Regulating our boundaries

Space and time are boundary regulation issues. When we feel threatened by an intrusion into our space or territory, we are sensitive and vulnerable. Marking our territory has more to do with psychological ownership than physical ownership. This is the feeling we have of owning the particular spot. If our territory is taken over, we react without taking a moment to think about our behavior and our actions, because we perceive a violation. Students in classes will often complain when someone "is sitting in my seat." Although classroom seats are open game, it is a personal affront, creating a sense of violation if one's "psychologically owned" spot is invaded.

Humans communicate personal closeness and space through a series of actions, especially nonverbal actions, called *immediacy* behaviors by interpersonal communication scholars. This dimension is reflected in actions that communicate warmth, closeness, approach, and accessibility, or, at the other extreme, by behaviors expressing avoidance and distance (Andersen, 1985, 2008). Our immediate behaviors may include smiling, touching, eye contact, open body positions, closer distances, and more vocal animation. High-contact cultures are those in which people stand closer, touch more, and prefer more sensory stimulation than do people in low-contact cultures (Hall 1976). High-contact cultures include South American, southern European, and Arab nations. Moderate-contact cultures include Australia, Canada, and the U.S. Low-contact cultures include Asia and Eastern Europe. According to Andersen (2008), high-contact cultures are located in warmer climates and lower contact cultures reside in cooler climates and high altitudes. What is the reason for this phenomenon? "Cultures in cooler climates tend to be more task oriented and interpersonally 'cool,' whereas cultures in warmer climates tend to be more interpersonally oriented and interpersonally 'warm'" (Andersen, 1999, p. 91).

In a study comparing seating arrangements between Taiwan and the U.S., Cline and Puhl (1984) found that Taiwanese prefer side-by-side seating among same-sex partners. Participants in the U.S. generally preferred corner seating for intimate matters and use seating to connect opposite-sex partners and separate same-sex partners. In terms of rules about touch, same-sex touch and handholding in Malaysia, China, Sudan, Japan, Nepal, and Saudi Arabia are acceptable and part of daily life. However, such contact with the opposite sex may be considered taboo. In the U.S., same-sex handholding may occur between gay/lesbian/bisexual individuals, whereas opposite-sex handholding is an appropriate public display of heterosexual affection.

It is tempting to draw conclusions about people without understanding their culture. When someone from a different culture does not look at you directly, it is easy to assume that he or she may disrespect you, is shy, or is not interested. However, some cultural groups believe that looking someone in the eyes is disrespectful (e.g., Thailand, Navajo Indians). Before judging an action, it is best to engage in conversation and find the meaning behind the gestures. Nonverbal cues communicate status, power, in-group and out-group differences, and unique identities. In attempting to understand within culture and across culture nonverbal variations, flexibility, respect, and patience serve as good first steps in gaining nonverbal entrance to a culture.

## The Intersection and Boundaries of Identity: What This All Means

Behavioral cues are related to our nonverbal messages. Nonverbal cues communicate status, power, in-group and out-group differences, and unique identities. If we believe that our self-concept influences how we feel, think, and act toward others, we can see how this may explain the need we have to draw boundaries in our constant negotiation of identity. Individuals may be grouped together under one categorical ethnic label, but a global label may utterly fail to explain the variety of associations each of those individuals has made in the process of forming an ethnic identity.

As our global cities merge, the need to look "global," and even culturally ambiguous, has interesting implications. Marketing cosmetic and plastic surgery around the globe is a lucrative enterprise. For example, according to Schuman (2001), some Korean women have increasingly widened their eyes in a relentless drive to attain a Western image of beauty. For similar reasons, some young Korean women undergo nose reconstruction, breast implants, construction of false buttocks, face lifts, and Botox® injections. In China, some people have surgery to elongate their legs in an effort to compete globally and stand as tall as their Western counterparts. According to Sciolino (2000), Iran ranks high among countries in which individuals are not content with their noses, making plastic surgery popular. Body and face alterations definitely serve the nonverbal function of intentional identity negotiation. If used successfully, surgery can enhance an individual's self-esteem and appearance. However, if an operation fails, the results may damage an individual's remaining self confidence or distinctive personality.

The tension between seeking in-group membership and avoiding out-group rejection may be anchored in the daily life and social practices in which cross-cultural communication encounters occur. The contradictory nature of an identity may be accounted for in two ways: (1) ethnicity and ethnic identity are contextual and situational; and (2) ethnic identity is less a static group phenomenon than a social process of becoming. These two issues have clear implications for communication research and for advancing theoretical applications.

## Contextual frame

Social identity theory indicates that the more strongly one identifies with the group, the more bias one shows in favor of his or her group against salient out-groups (Brewer, 1997). But what if one perceives the internal ethnic group as the out-group? Thus, being, for example, "German" or "Tanzanian" may be highly contextual, and membership in such a collective group may not imply or allow for either ethnicity or cultural variability, resulting in individual conflict. Attempts to expand the framework of social identity theory to understand the structural features of the social environment, perceptions, and motivations at the individual level will be important for cross-cultural studies. In this way we can perhaps identify the contextual and situational parameters that trigger affective responses to in-group and out-group membership, and further explicate the determinants of social category salience. Examining group salience will help develop a broader understanding of the nature of internal group differences. Research in this area may also shed further light on the role of interpersonal attraction within and across cultural groups.

According to interethnic attraction research, the strength of individuals' ethnic identities is related to intergroup attraction and dating (Chung & Ting-Toomey,

1999). Individuals with assimilated, bicultural, or marginal identities have a greater tendency to date and/or marry out of their own groups than those who view their ethnic identities and traditions as very important aspects of their self-concept. There are also times during which individuals are attracted to culturally dissimilar others because they perceive these partners as typical or atypical of their own culture. This means that people activate stereotyping processes in initial intercultural attraction stages—be they positive or negative stereotypes. Chung and Ting-Toomey (1999) studied Asian and Asian American groups concerning the influence of identity on relational expectations of potential dating partners. They found that Asian Americans who rated themselves high in ethnic identity tended to hold unfavorable attitudes toward out-group dating. Conversely, Asian Americans who had weaker ethnic identities held favorable attitudes toward out-group dating.

## Ethnic identity—living with tension

Ethnic identity is less a static group phenomenon than a social process of becoming. For people in the U.S., this dialectical tension, between the need to be recognized as a member of the ethnic group in America, and as a member of an ethic community, supports Ting-Toomey's (1993) identity negotiation perspective. This view holds that the contradictory state existing between a sense of group belonging and a sense of wanting to become separate from the group is associated with ethnic identity. To achieve balance between both states, the individual must constantly and consciously negotiate and renegotiate identities. This state of needing to belong to both groups equally is, in one sense, a form of self-actualization, to the extent this implies having a universal identity/intercultural identification (Kim, 1995).

Inevitably, as we become an international community, there are further implications of the balance between inclusion and differentiation. The drive to appear "global" (or perhaps more specifically, Hollywood Western) has some interesting influences on identity management.

For example, an "e.net identity" (Ting-Toomey & Chung, 2005) is a composite identity shaped by technology, popular culture, and mass consumption. An e.net self can have both internal and external facets. Internally, one can hold both components of ethnic-cultural values (e.g., collectivism and individualism) and contemporary value orientations. An individual with an e.net identity has a sense of belonging on a global level and is connected with diverse yet like-minded individuals who actively carve out a distinctive "adopted community" (e.g., by hobbies or game types) and communicate fervently via chat rooms or e-discussion groups.

This new global, ambiguous identity creates a tension: the pull between becoming global and remaining local. The global identity may be a person who adopts and embraces the practices of Western culture, is open to receiving non-traditional information, and may select the foreign product because it is different from his or her local culture. The global child may be eager to embrace a new custom and challenge the tradition of the local group. A global child is likely to eagerly watch *Dora the Explorer* and *Pucca* and be ready to move to programming on MTV as he or she grows older. Preference for, and acceptance of, foreign programming may increase the influence of the values presented (Elasmar, 2003), and increase the tension between global and local cultures.

## Wrapping Up

The intersection of culture, communication, and identity holds hope for improving and carving out our understanding of crossing boundaries. A cross-cultural lifestyle demands both negotiation and flexibility to navigate through life's misunderstandings. The process of discovery may be filled with trials and tribulations, some bumps in our journey. However, an understanding of how we can support, embrace, and understand those who are different from us can open our minds and eyes to the diverse richness of human expresssion.

With an increase in groups transcending boundaries and moving around the globe, the question of identification and group membership is an important concern. The range of issues is enormous, but a common thread is the individual effort to achieve identity in the context of a large, stereotypical group. Thus, social identity theorists continue to address questions of group homogeneity, and understanding the complexity of ethnic identity as it is shaped and molded by group- and society-level influences constitutes a major challenge for future communication researchers.

The situational nature of identity challenges communication scholars to understand the impact of prescribing a general "group membership" ethnic identity which is not the ascribed self-identity. A second challenge is to find the behavioral cues associated with in-group or out-group status during interactions with members of the same ethnic group, and to determine how individuals perceive these cues.

To understand the person with whom you are communicating, you need to understand the identity domains which this individual deems important. For example, if the person strongly values broad cultural membership identity you need to find ways to validate and be responsive to that identity. Conversely, if the person strongly values her personal identity above and beyond a certain cultural membership, you need to uncover ways to positively affirm her desired personal identity. The capacity to do this will depend upon our ability to validate the individual and group differences we encounter in our everyday interactions with people across cultural boundaries.

# References

Alba, R. (1990). *Ethnic identity*. New Haven, CT: Yale University Press.

Andersen, P. A. (1985). Nonverbal immediacy in interpersonal communication. In A. W. Siegman & S. Feldstein (Eds.), *Multichannel integrations of nonverbal behavior* (pp. 1–36). Hillsdale, NJ: Lawrence Erlbaum Associates.

Andersen, P. (1999). *Nonverbal communication: Forms and functions*. Mountain View, CA: Mayfield.

Andersen, P. (2008). *Nonverbal communication: Forms and functions* (2nd ed.). Long Grove, IL: Waveland Press.

Andersen, P., Hecht, M., Hoobler, G., & Haywood, M. (2002). Nonverbal communication across cultures. In W. B. Gudykunst & B. Moody (Eds.), *Handbook of International and in intercultural communication* (pp. 89–106). Newbury Park, CA: Sage.

Berry, J. (1980). Acculturation as adaptation. In A. Padilla (Ed.), *Acculturation: Theory, models, and some new findings* (pp. 9–26). Boulder, CO: Westview Press.

Berry, J., Kim, U., Power, S., Young, M., & Bujaki, M. (1989). Acculturation attitudes in plural societies. *Applied Psychology, 38*, 185–206.

Brewer, M. (1991). The social self: On being same and different at the same time. *Personality and Social Psychology Bulletin, 17*, 475–482.

Brewer, M. (1997). On the social origins of human nature. In C. McGarty & S. A. Haslam (Eds.), *The message of social psychology* (pp. 54–62). Cambridge, MA: Blackwell Publishers Ltd.

Brewer, M., & Miller, N. (1996). *Intergroup relations*. Pacific Grove, CA: Brooks/Cole.

Brislin, R. (1981). *Cross-cultural encounters*. New York: Pergamon Press.

Brooks, D. (2003, November 8). Love, Internet syle. *New York Times*. http://www.nytimes.com/2003/11/8/opinion/08BROO.html?th

Burgoon, J. (1995). Cross-cultural and intercultural applications of expectancy violations theory. In R. Wiseman (Ed.), *Intercultural communication theory* (pp. 194–214). Thousand Oaks, CA: Sage.

Chung, L. C., & Ting-Toomey, S. (1999). Ethnic identity and relational expectations among Asian Americans. *Communication Research Reports, 16*, 157–166.

Cline, R. J. & Puhl, C. A. (1984). Genger, culture, and geography: A comparison of seating arrangements in the United States and Taiwan. *International Journal of Intercultural Relations, 8*, 199–219.

Cross, W., Jr. (1991). *Shades of Black: Diversity in African-American identity*. Philadelphia, PA: Temple University Press.

Elasmar, M. (2003). *The impact of international television: A paradigm shift*. Hillsdale, NJ: Lawrence Erlbaum Associates.

Erikson, E. (1968). *Identity, youth and crisis*. New York: Norton.

Gallois, C., Giles, H., Jones, E., Cargile, A., & Ota, H. (1995). Accommodating intercultural encounters. In R. Wiseman (Ed.), *Intercultural communication theory* (pp. 115–147). Thousand Oaks, CA: Sage.

Glazer, N. (1997). *We are all multiculturalists now*. Cambridge, MA: Harvard University Press.

Gordon, M. (1964). *Assimilation in American life*. New York: Oxford University Press.

Griffin, E. (2009). *A first look at communication theory* (9th ed.). New York: McGraw Hill.

Gudykunst, W. B. (1994). *Bridging differences: Effective intergroup communication* (2nd ed.). Thousand Oaks, CA: Sage Publications.

Gudykunst, W. B. (1995). Anxiety/uncertainty management (AUM) theory: Current status. In R. L. Wiseman (Ed.), *Intercultural communication theory* (pp. 8–58). Thousand Oaks, CA: Sage.

Gudykunst, W. B. (2002). Cross cultural communication. In W. B. Gudykunst & B. Moody (Eds.), *Handbook of international and intercultural communication* (pp. 19–23). Newbury Park, CA: Sage.

Gudykunst, W., & Kim, Y. (1997). *Communication with strangers* (3rd ed.). New York: McGraw Hill.

Gudykunst, W. B., & Lee, C. (2002). Cross cultural communication theories. In W. B. Gudykunst & B. Moody (Eds.), *Handbook of international and intercultural communication* (pp. 213–235). Newbury Park, CA: Sage.

Hall, E. T. (1959). *The silent language.* New York: Doubleday.

Hall, E. T. (1976). *Beyond culture.* New York: Doubleday.

Helms, J. (1990). *Toward a theory of black and white racial identity: Research and practice.* New York: Greenwood Press.

Hofstede, G. (1980). *Culture's consequences: Comparing values, behaviors, institutions, and organizations across nations.* Beverly Hills, CA: Sage.

Hymes, D. (1972). Models of the interaction of language and social life. In J. Gumperz & D. Hymes (Eds.), *Directions in sociolinguistics: The ethnography of communication.* (pp. 35–71). New York: Holt, Rinehart & Winston.

Kim, Y. Y. (1988). *Communication and cross-cultural adaptation: An integrative theory.* Clevedon, UK: Multilingual Matters.

Kim, Y. Y. (1995). Identity development: From cultural to intercultural. In H. Mokros (Ed.), *Information and behavior: Interaction and identity* (pp. 347–369). New Brunswick, NJ: Transactions Publishers.

Kim, Y. Y. (2001). *Becoming intercultural: An integrative theory of communication and cross-cultural adaptation.* Thousand Oaks, CA: Sage.

Levine, T., Park, H. S., & Kirschbaum, K. (2007). Some conceptual challenges for cross-cultural communication research in the 21st century. *Journal of Intercultural Communication, 36,* 205–221.

Markus, H., & Kitayama, S. (1991). Culture and the self: Implications for cognition, emotion, and motivation. *Psychological Review, 2,* 224–253.

Martin, J., & Nakayama, T. (2009). *Intercultural communication in contexts* (5th ed.). New York: McGraw Hill.

Mead. G. H. (1934). Mind, self and society from the standpoint of a social behaviorist. Chicago: University of Chicago Press.

Miller, N., & Brewer, M. B. (1984) (Eds.). *Groups in contact: The psychology of desegregation.* New York: Academic Press.

Montgomery, B. (1992). Communication as the interface between couples and culture. In *Communication Yearbook 15* (pp. 476–508). Newbury Park, CA: Sage.

Moran, K., & Chung, L. (2008, April). Global or local identity? A theoretical analysis of the role of Viacom on identity formation among children in an international context. *Global Media Journal, 7*(12), article no. 4. Retrieved from http://lass.calumet.purdue.edu/cca/gmj/sp08/gmj-sp08-moran-chung.htm

Parham, T., & Helms, J. (1985). Relation of racial identity attitudes to self-actualization and affective states of Black students. *Journal of Counseling Psychology, 32*, 431–440.

Phinney, J. (1989). Stages of ethnic identity development in minority group adolescents. *Journal of Counseling Psychology, 9*, 34–49.

Phinney, J. (1992). The multigroup ethnic identity measure. A new scale for use with diverse groups. *Journal of Adolescent Research, 7*, 156–177.

Schlenker, B. R. (Ed.). (1985). *The self and social life*. New York: McGraw Hill.

Schuman, M. (2001, February 21). Out on a limb: Some Korean women are taking great strides to show a little leg. *Wall Street Journal*, A1.

Sciolino, E. (2000, September 22). Iran's well-covered women remodel a part that shows. *New York Times*, A1.

Sternberg, R. J. (Ed.). (1999). *Handbook of creativity*. New York: Cambridge University Press.

Sue, D., Mak, W., & Sue, D. (1998). Ethnic identity. In L. Lee & N. Zane (Eds.), *Handbook of Asian American psychology* (pp. 289–323). Thousand Oaks, CA: Sage Publications.

Tajfel, H. (1974). Social identity and intergroup behaviour. *Social Science Information, 13*, 65–93.

Tajfel, H. (Ed.). (1978). *Differentiation between social groups: Studies in the social psychology of intergroup relations*. New York: Academic Press.

Tajfel, H., & Turner, J. (1979). An integrative theory of intergroup conflict. In W. G. Austin & S. Worchel (Eds.), *The social psychology of intergroup relations* (pp. 94–109). Monterey, CA: Brooks-Cole.

Ting-Toomey, S. (1988). Intercultural conflict styles: A face-negotiation theory. In Y. Y. Kim & W. Gudykunst (Eds.), *Theories in intercultural communication* (pp. 213–235). Newbury Park, CA: Sage.

Ting-Toomey, S. (1988). A face negotiation theory. In Y. Kim & W. Gudykunst (Eds.), *Theories in intercultural communication* (pp. 213–235). Newbury Park, CA: Sage Publications.

Ting-Toomey, S. (1993). Communication resourcefulness: An identity-negotiation perspective. In R. Wiseman & J. Koester (Eds.), *Intercultural communication competence* (pp. 72–111). Newbury Park, CA: Sage.

Ting-Toomey, S. (1999). *Communicating across cultures*. New York: Guilford Press.

Ting-Toomey, S. (2004). The matrix of face: An updated face-negotiation theory. In W. Gudykunst (Ed.), *Theorizing about intercultural communication* (pp. 71–92). Thousand Oaks, CA: Sage.

Ting-Toomey, S. & Chung, L. (2005). *Understanding intercultural communication*. New York: Oxford University Press.

Triandis, H. C. (1988). Collectivism vs. individualism: A reconceptualization of a basic concept in cross-cultural psychology. In G. Verma & C. Bagley (Eds.), *Cross-cultural studies of personality, attitudes, and cognition* (pp. 60–95). London: Macmillan.

Triandis, H. C., Leung, K., Villareal, M., & Clack, F. (1985). Allocentric versus idiocentric tendencies. *Journal of Research in Personality, 19*, 395–415.

Zangwill, I. (1909). *The melting pot*. New York: Macmillan Co.

# Part IX

# Personality

People have long wondered why humans are the way they are—how individuals arrive at their conceptions of self, and the traits that define them. The theories that attempt to describe and explain personality have arisen within both Eastern and Western traditions.

Although Western courses in psychology and in personality theory have typically described European American approaches to the field, they have less frequently presented an understanding of personality deriving from the cultures of the East. So, just as the student of personality should be aware of the psychoanalytic, behavioral, humanistic, cognitive, and trait theories of the West, so too should the student understand such Eastern perspectives as those originating with Confucius and the Buddha.

These Eastern viewpoints describe a different relationship between individuals, families, and communities. They see well-being as an aspect of social relations and the extent to which the individual fulfills them. Further, in the Buddhist view, we will inevitably experience suffering, and we are defined by how we respond to it.

Eastern and Western perspectives produce very different views of the self, at least in part because they present fundamentally different views of reality. In particular, in this section we will see how the Western idea of self as a "thing" within the person differs from the Eastern view that self can exist only in the connections among its constituent parts.

# 22

# Culture and Theories of Personality*

## Western, Confucian, and Buddhist Perspectives

### Peter J. Giordano

Some of the most compelling questions that humans ask are "What makes people tick?" "What factors coalesce to form our personalities?" or "How do we change?" These perennial questions have been asked for centuries, millennia even, by philosophers, theologians, epic storytellers, novelists and, most recently, by psychologists. These queries continue to animate discussions in one form or another in local pubs and in college classrooms around the globe. These questions will not let us rest because they are central to our identities and because they defy easy answers.

Psychology as an academic discipline started systematically to probe these questions when Sigmund Freud began to sculpt his theory beginning in the late nineteenth century. His was the first comprehensive theory of personality offered in the West. His thinking has not only shaped a good deal of how we imagine ourselves and others, but also has led to intellectual debates that in turn generated competing understandings of human personality. The richness of these perspectives continues to drive thinking and research in this domain.

All of us, whether trained as psychologists or not, are implicit personality theorists (Anderson, Rosenfeld, & Cruikshank, 1994), drawing on our personal experiences to mold our views of self and others. At the level of formal theory construction, personal experiences have shaped how theorists have constructed the ideas in their theories. For example, the context of Freud's life clearly influenced how he thought about the dynamics and motivations of human personality (Gay, 1988). The same holds true for the difficult interpersonal relations in Maslow's home of origin or for the religious overtones in Carl Rogers' childhood and adolescence. We easily accept that the personal experiences of these theorists structured their approach to understanding the development of persons. And we readily allow that the wider sociocultural conditions surrounding their lives shaped their thinking about human behavior and motivations. For example, Freud's witness of the tragedy of World War I and the events leading up to the explosion of World War II molded his understanding of the motivations of the human psyche.

In our contemporary world, advances in genetics and brain biochemistry are influencing discourse about personality development and change.

Locked within our own cultural context, however, we may be less perceptive of how the *wider* circumstances of our cultural heritage shape our thoughts on these matters. By "wider" circumstances I am not referring to specific world events, such as those I cite with regard to the development of Freud's thinking. Rather, by "wider" circumstances I denote those cultural beliefs or expectations that are so much a part of how we think about ourselves that we accept them without critical examination.

Consider this recent example to illustrate my point. My youngest son just graduated from high school and, during his senior year, had the good fortune of taking a course titled *The History of Ideas* from a very gifted teacher. The course was essentially a "great books" course, and Michael read and discussed some of the celebrated works of literature and philosophy by writers such as Plato, Homer, Plutarch, Descartes, Shakespeare, Sartre, Tolstoy, and many others. What a course for a young student to experience. Missing from this list, however, were great works of literature and philosophy from half a world away—works by Confucius, Laozi, Zhuangzi, Xunzi, or the Buddha. The course was wonderful, but would have been enriched had Michael had the opportunity to explore the work of these persons as well. I do not fault the teacher. I think it merely reflects a cultural bias that most of us hold.

We have a corresponding situation in our understanding of theories of personality. We study powerful theoreticians from Western culture, but we may omit important material from Eastern traditions. As a specific example in this domain, one that I introduce now and work with in more depth later in this chapter, reflect on how in the West we construe the notion of personal identity. Typically, we think of a person as an autonomous actor who, despite external forces, is largely in charge of his or her own destiny. Consider the personal story of Barack Obama, someone who rose above difficult personal beginnings and, by the sheer power of his intellect and personality, overcame many obstacles to become President of the United States. How did this happen? we might ask. A typical answer we offer is that he "pulled himself up by his own bootstraps" and worked diligently to achieve what he has. His is a great American story because it embodies ideas that Americans hold dear.

Other cultures, particularly those in the East, however, might take a different approach to understanding the developmental trajectory of Mr. Obama's life. Rather than focusing on his *individual* abilities, dispositions, and accomplishments, those from an Eastern culture might instead concentrate on how his *relationships with others* contributed to the narrative of his life, how he fulfilled the various obligations to those relationships, and how those relational activities shaped his identity, his understanding of the complexities of working with others, and his ultimate rise to the presidency. The differences in these explanations, the autonomous actor versus the relationally constructed person, are important and reflect significant cultural differences in how we think about human personality.

The aim of this chapter is to explore how some Eastern traditions might understand human personality. Because of increasing global interconnectedness (e.g., economic, social, and political intersections), it is more and more imperative to do so. It is intellectually short-sighted to believe that Western approaches to personality theory have the final say in approaching the question of what makes us tick. My emphasis in this chapter, I should note, will be on theoretical thinking, rather than on cross-cultural investigations of individual differences derived from empirical research in personality psychology. My assumption is that if we seek to understand Eastern perspectives on personality *in their own right*, rather than compare them to Western approaches, we will be better equipped to generate more ecologically valid studies of the utility and validity of these approaches. In so doing, we will also avoid the tendency to judge other cultures and their ideas as inferior to our own (Keith, 2008). The scientific challenges are great, of course, as investigators empirically examine Eastern approaches to personality. Issues of translation of important texts, as one case in point, are significant, although I do not address this topic in this chapter. As we shall see, some of this empirical work is already well under way (e.g., Hwang, 2006; Wallace & Shapiro, 2006), although even some of our best efforts (e.g., Wallace & Shapiro, 2006) encounter significant challenges to how language is used and concepts are understood (Sugamura, Haruki, and Koshikawa, 2007).

In the remainder of this chapter, I will first give a brief overview of the primary personality theories that have dominated Western discourse on this topic. Later in the chapter, I present two Eastern systems for approaching questions of personality, the Confucian and the Buddhist traditions, both having their origins in Asia, the former in China and the latter in India then migrating to China, Korea, Japan, and ultimately to the West.

A legitimate question at this juncture is why deal with the Confucian and Buddhist traditions? Isn't it true that these two approaches are philosophical systems for understanding the human condition and for offering suggestions on how to live? Why are they presented in this chapter? I work with these two traditions because I believe they can be viewed as case examples from the East of potent systems for understanding human personality. We can understand them as theories of personality because they deal with the same issues and questions that formal Western theories do. For example, each of these approaches, using different constructs and technical vocabulary than ones Westerners may be accustomed to, posits basic elements of personality, presents ideas for how personality develops, offers explanations for why people suffer, and suggests activities for alleviating suffering. They also each present a model for the mature and mentally healthy personality, something that has been a focus of all the great Western personality theories and that reflects the contemporary Western emphasis now known as positive psychology (Seligman & Csikszentmihalyi, 2000).

I should note that approaching Eastern traditions in this way is not new, although it is something that has not been a focus of attention in the past several decades, particularly as the empirical foundations of personality psychology have been more firmly established. For example, with a Tibetan mandala on the front cover, the third edition of Hall and Lindzey's classic *Theories of personality* (1978) text contained an extensive discussion of Eastern psychology, whereas the fourth and last edition of this book (Hall, Lindzey, & Campbell, 1997) did not retain the chapter on this topic. Moreover, the edited volume *Asian psychology* (Murphy & Murphy, 1968) presented a wide ranging discussion of some ideas within the "psychologies" (their term) of India, China, and Japan. The material in this book is largely of historical interest at this point in time, however, because the editors did not have the benefit of recent scholarship (e.g., recent translations and empirical work) in this domain. It is also well known that Carl Jung made contact with Eastern thought (e.g., Jung, 1963a, Wilhelm & Jung, 1962) in his theoretical formulations. His interest, however, leaned toward a mystical approach, something this chapter does not emphasize. To be fair, I should note that in the psychotherapeutic domain (one dimension of most personality theories) there has been a relatively stable interest in Eastern therapy techniques (Corsini & Wedding, 2008) and some, though not many, personality theory texts have maintained an interest in Eastern ideas (Frager & Fadiman, 2005).

Decades ago, Allport (1938) observed that psychologists are sometimes deficient in their attempts to describe personality with any degree of richness or detail, particularly when compared to the skill of novelists. Novelists, Allport argued, are able to capture a complexity of description that can leave contemporary theories appearing to be insipid. I believe Allport's observation is still relevant today, despite remarkable advances in the field. We have made great strides in empirically investigating the claims of personality theories with the aim of refining their precision and accuracy. Indeed, one measure of the validity of these perspectives is the degree to which they may be empirically verified. Clearly, Western psychology has made important progress in this domain, enhancing our ability to retain that which appears to be valid and reliable. Many chapters in the present volume highlight important advances in this domain.

However, in a line of thinking similar to Allport's, Monte (1999) asserted that the individual found in a scientifically verifiable theory may not resemble too closely the individual sitting across from you in a restaurant or beside you in a movie theater. Both Allport's and Monte's opinions point to the continuing need to refine our *theoretical* thinking so as to best capture the nuances of human personality. Looking East to other perspectives may help us create a more comprehensive and culturally sensitive understanding of personality function, something that is one goal of this chapter.

But one might also ask if we are not diluting the science of psychology by adopting what sounds like a non-empirical approach. This concern is legitimate. However, there are a number of reasons for looking to Eastern systems of personality to help inform our thinking. First, it is not unique that these systems, at this point in time, are difficult to investigate empirically. The same is true of many

Western approaches, including a number of ideas in Freud's thinking and the work of many neo-psychoanalytic theorists. Though empirically difficult to investigate (Popper, 1959), these theories still make important contributions because they are comprehensive, useful, and internally consistent, and provide important heuristic functions, all qualities of solid theoretical systems.

Second, working with Eastern perspectives brings into clearer focus how Western ideas may seem alien in other cultures, and may not apply very well to persons living in those cultures. The converse of course is that Eastern ideas may seem foreign to Westerners, a problem for Western personality teachers and researchers. If our aim, however, is to understand personality in a more three-dimensional or holistic way, then we do well to consider conceptualizations that may run in new directions from our ordinary way of thinking. Again, in a world in which we increasingly interact with others from cultures different than our own, we do well to understand a variety of cultural perspectives.

## Western Theories of Personality

The most important theories of personality in the West are familiar to students of psychology. These personality systems include the psychoanalytic, humanistic-existential, behavioral, cognitive, and trait approaches. In this section of the chapter, I briefly summarize these approaches with an eye toward understanding the primary emphases of these perspectives. In so doing, I pay scant attention to important considerations such as the application of these theoretical ideas to helping people, the primary research methods used by the various theorists, or the status of empirical support for these perspectives. A more extensive treatment of these theories can be found in any text on theories of personality or elsewhere in condensed form (Giordano, 2008; Lewis, 2008).

### The psychoanalytic perspective

The psychoanalytic perspective, originating with the thinking of Viennese physician Sigmund Freud, who worked tirelessly on the construction of his theory from the late nineteenth century (Breuer & Freud, 1895) until his death in 1939, is one of the most dominant and controversial theories of personality in the West. So powerful are his ideas that we tend to think as Freudians without even knowing it. If you believe your personality was formed largely because of how you were parented early in life, you can write Freud a thank-you note (Cohen, 1999; Hamer & Copeland, 1998; Harris, 1998). Despite the influence of his ideas, however, some have argued that his thoughts are so flawed that we should no longer teach them in psychology (Macmillan, 1991), although others believe we should tread more lightly on those kinds of assertions and recognize the value in his perspective (Westen, 1998).

Psychoanalytic theory adopts four assumptions about human personality: (1) that much of our basic inclinations are driven by primitive biologically based instincts of sex (Eros) and aggression (Thanatos), (2) that all behavior is unconsciously determined, (3) that early childhood experiences are primary in shaping who we are, and (4) that intrapsychic conflict characterizes the human psyche. This intrapsychic conflict is generated by the constant interaction among the id, ego, and superego, three so-called structures or agencies of personality that evolve over time during the stages of psychosexual development. The ego, the mediator among the demands of the id, superego, and reality, demonstrates psychological maturity to the extent that it can adequately manage and balance all these often conflicting demands.

The scope of Freud's vision and the power of his personality spawned theoretical offshoots including Jung's analytical psychology and Adler's individual psychology, as well as a number of neo-psychoanalytic and objects relations theorists such as Erik Erikson (1963), Erich Fromm (1973), Melanie Klein (1964), D. W. Winnicott (1965) and others. All these theorists retained some core elements of Freud's thinking, but modified other ideas to extend the original psychoanalytic formulation.

## The behavioral perspective

The chief architect of the behavioral approach was B. F. Skinner (1938), who developed his ideas beginning in the 1930s in America to counter what he regarded as the mentalism and non-scientific nature of Freud's perspective. Elegant in its parsimony, Skinner's operant conditioning approach rejected non-observable explanations for behavior. As a radical behaviorist, Skinner suggested that a person is a complex organism behaving in lawful ways. Although any psychologist worth her or his salt would agree with this tenet, Skinner was one of the strongest proponents of this viewpoint. The task of the psychologist therefore is to utilize the methods of experimental analysis to determine the general laws of behavior, which take the form of contingencies of reinforcement and punishment. Whereas Freud embraced a determinism rooted in the unobservable dynamics of the unconscious, Skinner adopted an environmental determinism—behavior is lawful (i.e., not random) and the causes of behavior are directly observable and located in the external environment of the behaving person. Internal explanations for behavior, Skinner believed, were explanatory or redundant fictions and only served to impair our ability to predict future behavior (Skinner, 1953, 1974). Skinner did not reject the existence of subjective experience or internal states, as is sometimes believed (Debell & Harless, 1992). Instead, he discarded the use of these as causal explanations of behavior.

Like Freud, Skinner's theoretical viewpoint produced a number of derivative perspectives. In general, these perspectives adhered to Skinner's scientific approach, although these new developments began once again to look inside the person for causal explanations. These newer perspectives therefore initiated a scientific study of the role of cognition in shaping personality, a movement that Skinner thought was wrong headed until the time of his death in 1990 (Skinner, 1990). I will return to this discussion after we consider the humanistic-existential point of view.

## The humanistic-existential perspective

The personality theorists in this tradition rejected both the unconscious determinism of psychoanalysts and the environmental determinism of behaviorists. Instead, theorists like Carl Rogers (1942, 1951, 1957) and Abraham Maslow (1968/1999, 1971) emphasized the freedom of persons to construct their own personalities and in so doing to be responsible for the life they pursue. Emphasizing psychological health and well-being, Rogers and Maslow helped lay the foundation for the contemporary positive psychology movement (Seligman & Csikszentmihalyi, 2000). In his relatively complex theory, Rogers asserted that conditions of worth in the family of origin could deform authentic personality development. Overcoming these limitations would allow the person to become more fully functioning and healthy (Rogers, 1951). Less complex in his theoretical formulations, Maslow nevertheless made important contributions to our understanding of healthy personality development in the form of self-actualization and the experience of a fulfilling, vibrant life. Rollo May (1953) and Viktor Frankl (1959) were theorists who shared a somewhat similar approach to Rogers and Maslow, although their body of work is not as comprehensive.

## The cognitive perspective

The family of cognitive theories shares the conviction that inner states such as beliefs, expectations, emotional arousal, and any number of mental events are viable avenues for investigation, as long as these constructs are studied with the methods of science. Thus, these approaches share with the Skinner an empirical methodology, although they widen the range of appropriate subject matter. Inner states, for these theorists, are important dimensions of personality, in terms of personality structure, development, and change. The personal construct theory of George Kelly (1955) was foundational to work in this area, although Albert Bandura's social cognitive theory (1965, 1977, 1986) and its variations (1997, 2006) are better known and more influential. From the cognitive perspective, personality is seen as a complex, organized, and predictable system of cognitive structures.

These structures, which develop over time, drive behavior; they are also recipro-cally determined *by* behavior as well as by environmental forces.

## Types, traits, and the biological underpinnings of personality

This approach to understanding personality is one of the oldest traditions in the West and at the same time is enjoying extreme popularity in the present. A diverse set of perspectives, these approaches all tend to value the biological underpinnings of personality, made more possible today by methods of modern neuroscience, and tend to see the essential components of personality as either traits (individual characteristics or dispositions) or types (broad categories of persons). Traits and types help account for individual differences in personality. The type A personality pattern (Friedman and Rosenman, 1974) is a well known example of the latter. Many of the theorists in this domain have used a powerful statistical approach known as factor analysis to aid in their understanding of the structure of personal-ity. Researchers and theorists such as Raymond Cattell (1952, 1965), Hans Eysenck (1967), and more recently McCrae and Costa (1987), have all made important con-tributions in this domain.

McCrae and Costa's Big Five, five robust factors, or supertrait theory (neuroti-cism, extraversion, openness, agreeableness, and conscientiousness) enjoys partic-ular popularity in contemporary psychology. From the vantage point of this perspective, personality consists of a pattern of traits of varying strengths, with a healthy dose of biological determinism.

Big Five theorists assert that these supertraits are independent of one another and describe personality structure across cultures. However, evidence suggests there may be differences in relative strength across cultures and sex differences within cultures (Paunonen, 2003), or that the five-factor solution may not be a perfect match for all cultures (Xinyue, Saucier, Gao, & Liu, 2009).

## Some summary comments

There are several important themes in the preceding discussion that I would like to highlight and that will provide a contrast for the discussion to follow. First, all the Western perspectives, with the exception of a behavioral viewpoint, assume an inde-pendent actor who initiates action, an autonomous identity so to speak, whether the actor consists of an agency such as an ego or a constellation of independent traits. Second, with the exception of trait and type approaches, the dominant Western theories typically find families as a primary source of psychopathology in individu-als. Families are seen to disrupt and distort personality development, leading to any number of personal ills. Whether through unresolved intrapsychic conflicts origi-nating in parent–child interactions, conditions of worth, narcissistic parents, or maladaptive contingencies of reinforcement, families are often construed as places from which one needs to escape in order to become fully functioning.

## Two Eastern Approaches to Understanding Personality

Having reviewed some of the major ideas in the dominant Western theories of personality, I now consider two important traditions for understanding personality that have evolved over the past 2,500 years in Asia. As mentioned previously, these two approaches are the Confucian and the Buddhist traditions. Obviously, it is difficult to do justice to these two traditions in only a few pages, just as doing so is problematic when discussing the Western perspectives. However, the danger is probably even more acute when discussing Confucianism or Buddhism because, as Westerners, we carry stereotypes and inaccuracies about what these approaches represent. Regarding Confucianism, for example, our exposure to these ideas may run as deep as having opened a fortune cookie to read the phrase, "Confucius say …. [fill in the aphorism]." Compounding the problem, Confucianism is often seen as antiquated, feudalistic, coercive, and paternalistic (Littlejohn, 2009; Rosemont & Ames, 2009), although the so-called new Confucianism (Bell, 2008; Makeham, 2003) is reviving Confucian ideas in a way that is more relevant to contemporary thinking. Similar problems arise when we discuss Buddhism. Unfortunately, our notions of Buddhism (and other Eastern philosophies) have often been shaped by an emphasis on rather arcane and exotic notions of altered states of consciousness (Tart, 1990; White, 1972), rather than on how Buddhist ideas might inform a more familiar understanding of the shaping of human character and personality (Brazier, 2002), the enhancement of personal relationships (Beck, 1989), or a healthier experience of everyday life (Kabat-Zinn, 1994).

When reading this section of the chapter, please keep in mind too that these Eastern traditions have evolved over a span of time centuries longer than Western approaches. In addition, these perspectives have undergone significant development as they have encountered other cultures. As Buddhism migrated, for example, from India to China it took on new forms in the structure of Chan Buddhism (Hershock, 2004) and then further evolved as Zen developed in Japan (Kasulis, 1981). And of course Zen evolved again much later as it immigrated to the United States via writers such as Alan Watts (1957) or Shunryu Suzuki (1970). The modification of ideas in this way is not uncommon. In a similar fashion, psychoanalytic ideas have developed significantly over the last century, as they crossed the Atlantic to the U.S.

### Confucianism as personality theory

The primary architect of Confucian thought is obviously Confucius (551–479 BCE), whose *Analects* (Ames & Rosemont, 1998) express much of the ideals of

Confucianism. By way of background and for the reader interested in exploring the Confucian tradition in greater depth, the *Analects of Confucius* is considered one of the "four books" (i.e., canonical material) of Confucianism, with the other three being the *Zhongyong*, the *Da Xue*, and the *Mencius*. Although Confucianism is typically described as a system of philosophy or political thought (Bell, 2008), I believe this tradition can also be understood as a theory of personality, a point I made earlier in this chapter. To review, I make this assertion because the Confucian tradition shares five important characteristics with Western theories of personality—it posits basic elements or agencies of personality, presents ideas for how personality develops, offers explanations for why people suffer, suggests activities for alleviating suffering, and presents a model for the mature and mentally healthy personality.

As with any Western theory, Confucianism works with these five elements to a greater or lesser degree; some are fully developed and others less so. One cannot dismiss the idea that Confucianism is a personality theory because, for example, it does not do a very adequate job of describing activities to alleviate mental suffering. We could level this same criticism at trait or factor analytic approaches to personality, and yet we would not question its status as a viable Western model. My contention is that *in addition to* understanding Confucianism as a philosophical, religious, or political system of thought, we may also view it as an explanation of how personalities develop, change, and reach optimal functioning.

Henry Rosemont and Roger Ames, two leading Asian scholars and philosophers by training, make assertions that sound remarkably like personality theorists. For example, in their important new translation and interpretation of the Xiaojing, *The Chinese classic of family reverence* (Rosemont & Ames, 2009), they contend that "The family is where much of our personality develops and continues to develop even after we mature and become parents ourselves" (p. 4). In a similar vein, they aver that reading the Xiaojing "can thus serve as a mirror of our own family past, helping us to reflect on how and why we have become who we are, on whom we are becoming, and on how we might become better" (p. 4). Such discourse clearly fits within the tradition of personality theorizing. If you did not know these statements pertained to Confucianism, it would be difficult to distinguish them from any number of Western personality theories.

To consider Confucianism in more depth, let's start at the end point of personality development. A central and perennial question asked in the Confucian tradition is how a person becomes consummately human (Ames, in press). This question takes us to the heart of the Confucian understanding of persons; the answer presents a clear contrast to typical Western approaches and a nice connection to positive psychology concerns. One becomes a consummate human or an exemplary person by dedication to a path of *fulfilling one's interpersonal roles and responsibilities*. In other words, one becomes consummately human only in relationship with others, and in particular in one's immediate and extended families (Ames, in press; Rosemont & Ames, 2009).

On the face of it, this idea seems simple and straightforward, and yet it is a markedly different perspective than that adopted by most Western personality theorists. As I discussed previously, in Western perspectives the family is often portrayed as a primary source of emotional suffering and psychopathology. We must break free of our families, these traditions assert, to demonstrate our maturity and to develop our individual identities. In the Freudian tradition, we have blamed parents, particularly mothers, for significant individual suffering. The schizophrenogenic mother (Fromm-Reichmann, 1948) and the refrigerator mother (Bettelheim, 1967; Kanner, 1949) are two sad and noteworthy examples of how parents have been causally linked to significant psychopathology, schizophrenia in the former and autism in the latter. And more contemporary object relations theorists such as Alice Miller (1981) blame the family crucible for the deformed psychological lives of their children. Equally damning to the family is Rogers' (1951) perspective that families of origin create conditions of worth, which stunt the psychological growth of their members, particularly children.

This view of family as toxic is a bedfellow with the person as autonomous and independent, and may in part be a result of the industrial revolution and the rise of consumerism and individualism so prevalent in the West in general and in America in particular (Cushman, 1995). One of the primary tasks of budding adulthood, we tend to believe as Westerners, is that we must separate from our families in order to "grow up" and become our own independent selves. This idea permeates our culture to such a degree that we hardly see things in any other way. But this notion of family and individual independence is alien to a Confucian point of view and therefore would be seen as foreign to an understanding of how a person develops and changes over time, especially if that person is to evolve into an exemplar of psychological health and well-being (Ames, in press; Rosemont & Ames, 2009).

The essential idea when understanding personality within the Confucian tradition is that human beings or, better put, human becomings (Ames, in press) are fundamentally relationally defined—we develop our identities to the extent that we fulfill our role expectations in our immediate and extended families and in the broader social community. Personalities mature as they fulfill these roles in wider and wider concentric circles of relationship (Tu, 1994). Personality development, therefore, is always a communal affair. Personality is a dynamic system, ever fluid and flexible (cf. Carl Rogers), as the relational contexts of our lives change. The person I am today evolves as a function of how my relationships change, as I get married, divorced or widowed, as I become a parent or grandparent, or as I move into and out of employment positions (Rosemont, 1997).

A number of important implications of this theoretical perspective are evident. First, from this viewpoint, it makes little sense to construe the person as an independent, autonomous self. These are not roles one plays; negotiating and fulfilling these roles is *who one is* (Rosemont, 1997). When lived with maturity, these roles are something one fulfills not out of duty merely to please others (e.g., parents, employers), but out of an intrinsic motivation to attend to and fulfill communal needs. Nor does it make sense to speak in terms of psychological well-being as an independent project, a venture one undertakes alone, even with the help of a therapist. Psychological well-being is inextricably bound to social relationships.

Consider too the idea of self-description. I might describe myself in the following manner: I am a middle-aged man, who has a wife and two boys, and who teaches students in a university setting. Such a description locates my identity as separate from ("I *have* a wife and two boys") the important persons in my life. An alternative description, and one that would be more true to a Confucian appreciation of personality, would be as follows: I am a middle-aged man, the son of two elderly parents, the husband of my wife, the father of two boys, the teacher of my students, and so on. This latter description underscores the centrality of the relationships in my life. Indeed, "I" do not exist as an autonomous self; rather "I" exist in between all these relationships. I am these relationships and I change (my personality changes) as the configuration of these relationships evolves in developmental time. To say that I *have* a son who is going off to college thus creating an "empty nest" misses the important nuance that my personality will reconfigure as the relationship with my son changes, as will the relationship with my wife, as will the relationship with my other son. In terms of mature personality development, I become an exemplary person and exhibit consummate behavior to the extent that I adequately fulfill the responsibilities of *all* these relationships, starting at home and working outward, in what Tu Wei-ming (1994) has called the "ceaseless process of human flourishing" (p. 183).

But how does one fulfill these relational expectations to the highest degree so as to become an exemplary person, which is after all a central concern of Confucian thought? Confucians acknowledge that we do come into the world with a certain set of inclinations and proclivities, certain dispositions if you will, but we must change and develop through years of self-conscious effort (Tu, 1994). Invoking both nature and nurture, Rosemont and Ames (2009) suggested,

> In a Confucian world, because persons are born into family relations that are considered constitutive of their persons, their "natures," or perhaps better, "natural tendencies," are a combination of native instinct and the cultivated cognitive, moral, aesthetic, religious sensibilities provided by their family locus and initial conditions. (p. 41)

Thus, the Confucian approach to personality change is action and results oriented. Self-conscious effort is the key. In Confucianism, one must "walk the walk" (i.e., talk is cheap), not just read, write, or speculate about these inspiring ideals (Bell, 2008). Persons become exemplary through ongoing efforts first within the family context and then expanding outward to fulfill adequately the roles that constitute personal identity. In this discussion, I have emphasized relationships among family members, something that is consistent with the "five relationships" highlighted in the Confucian tradition: father–son, husband–wife, elder brother–younger brother, ruler–subject, and friend–friend (Rosemont & Ames, 2009). The latter two relationships, of course, point us outside the immediate family and also suggest that, although these five relationships are central in traditional Confucianism, the communal context of living *in all its variations* is the foundational idea.

Moreover, because families are no more separate and independent than individuals (i.e., families themselves are embedded in a social context), families are responsible to other families in the ever-widening relational concentric circles that I mention above. Personality dysfunction results to the extent that one does not fulfill these roles and responsibilities. If such dysfunction occurs, it is the responsibility of the social network to bring the person back into harmonious relationships. Persons do not flourish or suffer in isolation. If one person suffers, so do others. Thus, psychological health and well-being are the responsibility of all persons in the social network, in this case the family.

In my discussion thus far, I have avoided a principal criticism of traditional Confucianism—that it advocates a strict hierarchy in the structure of relationships. The hierarchy exists to insure that roles are adequately understood and carried out. Indeed, the Chinese terms used to describe these relationships indicate there are those who are above (superior) and those who are below (inferior), as in the father is "above" the son or the man is "above" the woman (Rosemont & Ames, 2009). Given the space constraints of this chapter, I will not discuss this important issue at length. I refer the interested reader to the excellent discussion by Rosemont and Ames, who are careful to point out that the terms typically translated as "above" and "below" may also be read to indicate "benefactor" and "beneficiary," that the structure of these relationships has never implied blind obedience on the part of the beneficiary, that elitism is not a necessary byproduct of hierarchy, and that benefactor–beneficiary hierarchies are ever-shifting, as when I help a friend and a week later he helps me. Nor does it follow, as Rosemont and Ames reveal, that coercion and oppression are necessary components of hierarchy. A young person may derive wonderful fulfillment by learning to defer to and care for his or her grandparent, for example. Finally, despite stereotypes to the contrary, many of the great Confucian thinkers, including Confucius himself, have been vociferous critics of the status quo (Bell, 2008). Why not continue this tradition as our understanding of Confucianism continues to evolve?

To sum up, the Confucian approach to personal development, change, and mental well-being can be understood as a theory of personality in the same way that the ideas of Freud, Rogers, and others are viewed in this way. The notion of the relational self and Confucian role ethics (Ames, in press), however, run against the typical Western idea of the autonomous actor, the one who must break free of the restrictions of family (or other social structures), so as to "stand on one's own two feet" and develop into maturity.

Despite the divergence from a typically Western approach, I hope you can sense also that there are points at which Confucian ideas interact with some Western ways of thinking. For example, there are recent developments in the West in the psychotherapeutic literature and in recent treatments of male and female psychology in which the relational self is highlighted, although the Confucian tradition is not part of the discussion (Jordan, 2002; Levant & Pollack, 1995; Miller & Stiver, 1997). It is also true that the concept of the relationally defined self in Confucianism intersects with some of Triandis's (1989) notions of the private self and the collective self. Another noteworthy connection is Bronfenbrenner's bioecological model of human development (Bronfenbrenner, 1979; Bronfenbrenner & Morris, 1998). While building some of these bridges, however, it is important to understand Confucian ideas in their own right and in their own context, rather than filtering them through a Western interpretive lens. The same will hold true as we examine a Buddhist understanding of personality.

## Buddhism as personality theory

In contrast to Confucianism, which has not had much dialogue with Western psychology, Buddhism has a longer and more extensive history of interaction with the West, dating at least to William James in the early twentieth century (Michalon, 2001). However, it was Carl Jung and his far-ranging explorations into Eastern thought, including Buddhism, who created more interest by publishing a number of essays utilizing Eastern ideas to illustrate some of the principles of analytical psychology (Jung, 1963a, 1963b). Unfortunately, despite the interest that Jung's thought engendered in Eastern ideas, his speculations have been perceived by many as mired in mysticism, an issue that created distance between Jung and other, more scientifically oriented, personality psychologists. In recent decades, however, partly in response to the positive psychology movement, there has been a renewed interest in creating a rapprochement between Buddhism and Western scientific psychology. Some of this interest is observed in empirical studies of Buddhist (and other) meditative strategies (Walsh & Shapiro, 2006) and in applications of Buddhist psychology to remedy dysfunctional behavioral patterns such as anxiety disorders (Toneatto, 2002), substance abuse problems and other addictive behaviors (Marlatt, 2002), HIV risk behaviors in drug-using populations (Avants & Margolin, 2004), and as an approach to alleviating grief reactions (Michalon, 2001).

Note in the previous paragraph that I used the term Buddhist *psychology*. Although Buddhism is typically thought of as a philosophical system, recent psychological explorations into Buddhist thought have underscored the connections between Buddhist beliefs and ideas in the discourse of contemporary Western psychology (Dahlsgaard, Peterson, & Seligman, 2005; Wallace & Shapiro, 2006; Walsh & Shapiro, 2006). The reader interested in exploring these intersections in greater depth should consult the references cited in this section of the chapter.

For this chapter, whose purpose is to appreciate Buddhism as a theory of personality, I will emphasize the degree to which Buddhism shares characteristics with Western approaches. I should note that some aspects of Buddhism emphasize meditation induced higher states of consciousness, similar to ideas presented by

James (1902/1958), Jung (1963b), or Maslow (1968/1999, 1970, 1971). Although these states of consciousness are important in Buddhist thought and practice, my emphasis will be on Buddhist formulations of what human cognition and personality are like, how suffering arises, and the steps we can take to alter our personalities to lead to more fulfilling, mentally healthy lives.

The Buddhist tradition is remarkably complex, as it has evolved over time and in geographic expansion and assimilation into a variety of cultures. It is sometimes described as the *Middle Way* because it eschews the extremes of either self-indulgence or self-mortification. Buddhism derives its name from its founder, the Buddha or enlightened one, who lived and taught in northern India at roughly the same time as Confucius (probably 563–483 BCE). Siddhartha Gautama, the Buddha's given name, left his wife and son and a life of relative luxury at the age of 29 to pursue an understanding of the nature of suffering and its cure (Edwards, 1972). Today Buddhism is commonly classified into three main schools—Theraveda Buddhism in Southeast Asia, Mahayana Buddhism in East Asia, and Vajrayana Buddhism in the Indo-Tibetan region (Edwards, 1972; Wallace & Shapiro, 2006).

Buddhism is often regarded as the most psychological of the Eastern systems of thought (Wallace & Shapiro, 2006) or as offering the world's first psychology textbooks (Brazier, 2002). As we discuss a Buddhist conception of personality, the ideas I present are necessarily general and leave out the sometimes great differences across the various schools of Buddhism. It is fair to say, however, that the principles I outline capture the essence of Buddhist psychology. As I indicate above, I will emphasize the practical, everyday challenge of personality and character development in Buddhist theory, rather than the more esoteric notions of metaphysics or states of consciousness. These latter two aspects of Buddhism are important to greater or lesser degrees in the various Buddhist traditions, but they are less germane to the topic of this chapter. In adopting this strategy, I clearly short-change, if not short-circuit, important elements of Buddhism, a problem that has been clearly articulated by Sugamura, Haruki, and Koshikawa (2007).

The essence of Buddhist teachings is said to reside in a talk the Buddha gave a short time after his enlightenment or his awakening to a more authentic way of life. The talk, known as the *Setting in motion of the wheel of the Dharma*, outlined the Four Noble Truths, which are the foundational ideas in Buddhism. In the description that follows, I rely heavily, though not exclusively, on Brazier (2002), who acknowledged that some Buddhists might strongly disagree with his rendering of these ideas. The usefulness of Brazier's analysis for our purposes, however, is that it highlights the psychological dimensions of Buddhist thinking.

The Four Noble Truths are as follows:

*Dukkha* (from the Sanskrit): Affliction—is a fact of life. It is real. Suffering is often a term used instead of affliction.

*Samudaya*: Arising—in this world of affliction, something arises within us. Feelings arise in response to the affliction. These feelings are real and they often take the form of desiring things to be other than the way they are. For example, we may believe that some pleasurable activity or object can relieve our suffering and bring satisfaction. In fact, the activity or object does not bring satisfaction; it is the temporary lack of desire that constitutes the satisfaction (Levine, 1979).

*Nirodha*: Containment—what arises in us can be contained. We can harness or control these feelings. They can then become the fuel for personal transformation.

*Marga:* Path or track—characteristics of a constructive, enlightened life. This Fourth Noble Truth consists of the Eightfold Path (the Middle Way), which leads to a fulfilled life.

The Eightfold Path consists of:

Right View (understanding)—listening and seeing deeply.

Right Thought—keeping in mind the thought of a higher purpose, leading to greater compassion.

Right Speech—speak in ways that inspire.

Right Action—begins with self-restraint. Do good for others.

Right Livelihood—not just a question of doing the right job, but always keeping in mind what the job is and doing it for the good of others.

Right Effort—becoming aware of the feelings that arise in us in response to affliction.

Right Mindfulness—living in the present moment, recollecting always the true purpose of life.

Right *Samadhi* (concentration or rapture)—the highest understanding of the purpose of life. A *cultivated* state of mind that "naturally finds the bliss in all the eventualities of everyday life and so enables us to fulfill our purpose in being alive" (Brazier, 2002, pp. 182–183).

In a sense, the first two aspects of the Eightfold Path reflect early efforts in the life of the developing person who is working toward psychological maturity, the next three are ethical requirements for mature behavior, and the latter three pertain to meditative techniques designed to enhance personal development (Edwards, 1972). Properly understood, the Eightfold Path should not be seen as a linear eight-step process to enlightenment. In a sense, there are many paths to maturity, and what works well for one person may not be the path for another. A Buddhist teacher cannot directly enlighten the student, but merely points the way toward an authentic life. This notion is reflected in the Buddhist aphorism that your path in life is to find your path in life.

Considered as a whole, the Four Noble Truths (the Eightfold Path constitutes the Fourth Noble Truth) describe the central problem of existence and the strategies for leading a noble life of mature character. We all will experience affliction and suffering. How we respond to it defines who we are. The task of the developing person is, through sustained effort and practice, to transcend one's own circumstances so as to live a life of doing good for others.

The Buddhist framework, however, presents a very real problem for Western thought. Who is the developing person? What constitutes this individual identity? As with Confucianism, our task as Westerners is to grasp the idea that this person is not a separate self. In fact, the sense of self as separate, autonomous, or independent is a central form of psychopathology in this tradition. Brazier (2002) de-emphasized this aspect of Buddhist thought, although because many interpreters of Buddhism see it as important, we should work with the idea here.

The idea of an independent ego is one that creates mental suffering because it leads to self-focused pleasure-seeking, fear, greed, loneliness, pride, conceit and a host of other negative feelings or experiences. Buddhism teaches that the idea of a separate self is merely an illusion created by our ongoing experience. What we experience as our "self" is really an impermanent and ever-changing series of thoughts, emotions, sensations, impulses, and so on (Mosig, 2006). Also of relevance and to further complicate our understanding of personal identity is the Buddhist concept of independent co-origination or the idea that all things can be understood only in relation to all other things (Sugamura, Haruki, & Koshikawa, 2007). Things do not exist in and of themselves. It makes little sense, therefore, to consider personal identities as separate or independent. Persons can only be defined in relation to other persons, an idea akin to the Confucian relational self. Construing the person in this way brings us full circle to Brazier's (2002) emphasis on living a life in service to others—by caring for others, I care for myself, because I exist only in terms of my relationships and the quality of my life derives from the quality of these relations. The Buddhist construal of self is elaborated in more detail in Chapter 23 of this volume.

Where then does this discussion leave us in terms of a Buddhist understanding of personality? Clearly, this conceptualization differs from dominant Western approaches when considering personal identity and personality development. The Buddhist tradition underscores the inevitability of suffering (both physical and mental) and how we might construct our lives and, through disciplined practice (typically strategies of mental training in meditation), arrive at a more fulfilling, noble, and other-centered existence. As with our discussion of Confucianism, you will likely see connections with Western theories that are more familiar to you. However, I encourage you as much as possible to understand Buddhism on its own terms, without interpreting it through the lens of Western theory.

## Conclusion

In this chapter, I have briefly reviewed the dominant Western theories of personality and have proposed that Confucianism and Buddhism, although traditionally viewed as philosophical systems, may also be understood as theories of personality. I make this assertion because they share important dimensions of Western theories, including describing basic elements of personality, presenting ideas for how personality develops, offering explanations for why people suffer, suggesting activities for alleviating suffering, and proposing a model of the mature and mentally healthy person. As a Westerner, it may be difficult to assimilate these approaches into existing schemas because they are in some ways alien to our usual way of conceptualizing persons and their lives.

We might therefore ask if we can authentically adopt these ways of thinking. Bell (2008), who is not Chinese, worked with this question in his playful yet serious discussion of his own grappling with this issue. How much of a Confucian can he be? Can any of us who were not born into the Confucian tradition really think and behave and construct our lives in these ways? From a different perspective, Michalon (2001) concluded that, although he does not consider himself a Buddhist, he benefitted greatly from the practice of Buddhist meditation. He poignantly shared the story of the accidental death of his only child and how Buddhist meditation helped him cope with the profound grief of this experience.

Michalon (2001) and Bell (2008) may have something to teach us. Although we may not be Buddhists or Confucians perhaps we can profit from these powerful ideas as we construct our own lives and become intentional in how we develop our personalities. After all, both Confucianism and Buddhism address the same "big potato" questions (Monte, 1999) of human existence and identity construction as do the grand Western theories. I leave it to you, the reader, to explore these perspectives more fully and to decide their utility in understanding both others and yourself.

## Note

*   I thank my Belmont friends and colleagues Seraphine Shen-Miller, Assistant Professor of Psychology, and Ronnie Littlejohn, Chair of Philosophy and Director of Asian Studies, who offered insightful comments on a draft of this chapter. I also thank Roger Ames for sharing his recent scholarly work on the lovely notion of virtuosic relationality.

## References

Allport, G. W. (1938). Personality: A problem for science or a problem for art? *Revista de Psihologie, 1*, 1–15.

Ames, R. T., & Rosemont Jr., H. (1998). *The Analects of Confucius: A philosophical translation.* New York: Ballantine Books.

Ames, R. T. (in press). *Confucian role ethics: A vocabulary.* Hong Kong: Chinese University Press.

Anderson, D. D., Rosenfeld, P., & Cruikshank, L. (1994). An exercise for explicating and critiquing students' implicit personality theories. *Teaching of Psychology, 21*, 174–177.

Avants, S. K., & Margolin, A. (2004). Development of spiritual self-schema (3-S) therapy for the treatment of addictive and HIV risk behavior: A convergence of cognitive and Buddhist psychology. *Journal of Psychotherapy Integration, 14*, 253–289.

Bandura, A. (1965). Influence of models' reinforcement contingencies on the acquisition of imitative responses. *Journal of Personality and Social Psychology, 1*, 589–595.

Bandura, A. (1977). *Social learning theory.* Englewood Cliffs, NJ: Prentice-Hall.

Bandura, A. (1986). *Social foundations of thought and action: A social cognitive theory.* Englewood Cliffs, NJ: Prentice-Hall.

Bandura, A. (1997). *Self efficacy: The exercise of control.* New York: Freeman.

Bandura, A. (2006). Toward a psychology of human agency. *Perspectives on Psychological Science, 1*, 164–180.

Beck, C. J. (1989). *Everyday Zen.* New York: Harper Collins.

Bell, D. A. (2008). *China's new Confucianism: Politics and everyday life in a changing society.* Princeton, NJ: Princeton University Press.

Bettelheim, B. (1967). *The empty fortress: Infantile autism and the birth of self.* New York: Free Press.

Brazier, D. (2002). *The feeling Buddha: A Buddhist psychology of character, adversity, and passion.* New York: Palgrave Macmillan.

Breuer, J., & Freud, S. (1895). *Studies on hysteria.* New York: Basic Books.

Bronfenbrenner, U. (1979). *The ecology of human development: Experiments by nature and design.* Cambridge, MA: Harvard University Press.

Bronfenbrenner, U., & Morris, P. A. (1998). The ecology of developmental processes. In R. M. Lerner (Ed.), *Handbook of child psychology, vol. 1, Theoretical models of human development* (5th ed., pp. 535–584). New York: Wiley.

Cattell, R. B. (1952). *Factor analysis.* New York: Harper.

Cattell, R. B. (1965). *The scientific analysis of personality.* Baltimore, MD: Penguin.

Cohen, D. B. (1999). *Stranger in the nest: Do parents really shape their child's personality, intelligence, or character?* New York: Wiley.

Debell, C. S., & Harless, D. K. (1992). B. F. Skinner: Myth and misperception. *Teaching of Psychology, 19*, 68–73.

Corsini, R. J., & Wedding, D. (2008). *Current psychotherapies* (8th ed.). Belmont, CA: Thomson Brooks/Cole.

Cushman, P. (1995). *Constructing the self, constructing America: A cultural history of psychotherapy.* Reading, MA: Addison-Wesley.

Dahlsgaard, K., Peterson, C., & Seligman, M. E. P. (2005). Shared virtue: The convergence of valued human strengths across culture and history. *Review of General Psychology, 9*, 203–213.

Edwards, P. (Ed.) (1972). *The encyclopedia of philosophy* (vol. 1). New York: Macmillan.

Erikson, E. H. (1963). *Childhood and society* (2nd ed.). New York: Norton.

Eysenck, H. J. (1967). *The biological basis of personality.* Springfield, OH: Charles C. Thomas.

Frager, R., & Fadiman, J. (2005). *Personality and personal growth* (6th ed.). Upper Saddle River, NJ: Prentice-Hall.

Frankl, V. E. (1959). *Man's search for meaning.* New York: Simon & Schuster.

Friedman, H. S., & Rosenman, R. H. (1974). *Type A behaviour and your heart*. London: Wildwood House.

Fromm, E. (1973). *The anatomy of human destructiveness*. New York: Holt, Rinehart, and Winston.

Fromm-Reichmann, F. (1948). Notes on the development of treatment in schizophrenics by psychoanalytic psychotherapy. *Psychiatry, 11*, 263–273.

Gay, P. (1988). *Freud: A life for our time*. New York: Norton.

Giordano, P. J. (2008). Personality psychology. In S. F. Davis & W. Buskist (Eds.) *21st century psychology: A reference handbook* (Vol. 1, pp. 402–412). Thousand Oaks, CA: Sage.

Hall, C. S., & Lindzey, G. (1978). *Theories of personality* (3rd ed.). New York: Wiley.

Hall, C. S., Lindzey, G., & Campbell, J. B. (1997). *Theories of personality* (4th ed.). New York: Wiley.

Hamer, D., & Copeland, P. (1998). *Living with our genes*. New York: Anchor.

Harris, J. R. (1998). *The nurture assumption: Why children turn out the way they do*. New York: The Free Press.

Hershock, P. (2004). *Chan Buddhism*. Honolulu: University of Hawai'i Press.

Hwang, W. (2006). The psychotherapy adaptation and modification framework: Application to Asian Americans. *American Psychologist, 61*, 702–715.

James, W. (1902/1958). *The varieties of religious experience*. New York: Mentor.

Jordan, J. V. (2002). A relational-cultural perspective in therapy. In R. F. Massey & S. D. Massey (Eds.) *Comprehensive Handbook of Psychotherapy* (Vol. 3, pp. 233–254). New York: Wiley.

Jung, C. G. (1963a). *Psychology and religion: West and East*. In *Collected Works*, Vol. 11. Princeton, NJ: Bollingen Series/Princeton University Press.

Jung, C. G. (1963b). *Mysterium Coniunctionis*. In *Collected Works*, Vol. 14. Princeton, NJ: Bollingen Series/Princeton University Press.

Kabat-Zinn, J. (1994). *Wherever you go, there you are*. New York: Hyperion.

Kanner, L. (1949). Problems of nosology and psychodynamics of early infantile autism. *American Journal of Orthopsychiatry, 19*, 416–426.

Kasulis, T. P. (1981). *Zen action Zen person*. Honolulu: University of Hawaii Press.

Keith, K. D. (2008). Cross-cultural psychology and research. In S. F. Davis & W. Buskist (Eds.) *21st century psychology: A reference handbook* (Vol. 2, pp. 483–490). Thousand Oaks, CA: Sage.

Kelly, G. A. (1955). *The psychology of personal constructs* (Vols. 1 and 2). New York: Norton.

Klein, M. (1964). *Contributions to psychoanalysis, 1921–1945*. New York: McGraw Hill.

Levant, R., & Pollack, W. (1995). *A new psychology of men*. New York: Basic Books.

Levine, S. (1979). *A gradual awakening*. Garden City, NY: Anchor Books.

Lewis, P. (2008). Personality development. In S. F. Davis & W. Buskist (Eds.) *21st century psychology: A reference handbook* (Vol. 1, pp. 392–401). Thousand Oaks, CA: Sage.

Littlejohn, R. (2009, March 5–8). *Hidden commensurabilities? Tu Weiming's new Confucian political theory and the Lockean civil libertarian tradition*. Paper presented at the National Conference of Asian Studies Development Program, Philadelphia, PA.

Macmillan, M. (1991). *Freud evaluated: The completed arc*. Amsterdam: North Holland.

Makeham, J. (2003). (Ed.). *New Confucianism: A critical examination*. New York: Palgrave Macmillan.

Marlatt, G. A. (2002). Buddhist philosophy and the treatment of addictive behavior. *Cognitive and Behavioral Practice, 9*, 44–49.

Maslow, A. (1968/1999). *Toward a psychology of being* (3rd ed.). New York: Wiley.

Maslow, A. (1970). *Religions, values, and peak experiences.* New York: Penguin Books.

Maslow, A. (1971). *The farther reaches of human nature.* New York: The Viking Press.

May, R. (1953). *Man's search for himself.* New York: Norton.

McCrae, R. R., & Costa, P. T. (1987). Validation of the Five Factor Model across instruments and observers. *Journal of Personality and Social Psychology, 52*, 81–90.

Michalon, M. (2001). "Selflessness" in the service of the ego: Contributions, limitations and dangers of Buddhist psychology for Western psychotherapy. *American Journal of Psychotherapy, 55*, 202–218.

Miller, A. (1981). *The drama of the gifted child.* New York: Basic Books.

Miller, J. B., & Stiver, I. P. (1997). *The healing connection: How women form relationships in therapy and in life.* Boston, MA: Beacon Press.

Monte, C. F. (1999). *Beneath the mask: An introduction to theories of personality* (6th ed.). Fort Worth, TX: Harcourt Brace.

Mosig, Y. D. (2006). Conceptions of the self in Western and Eastern psychology. *Journal of Theoretical and Philosophical Psychology, 26*, 39–50.

Murphy, G., & Murphy, L. B. (1968). *Asian psychology.* New York: Basic Books.

Paunonen, S. V. (2003). Big Five factors of personality and replicated predictions of behavior. *Journal of Personality and Social Psychology, 84*, 411–422.

Popper, K. R. (1959). *The logic of scientific discovery.* London: Hutchinson.

Rogers, C. R. (1942). *Counseling and psychotherapy: New concepts in practice.* Boston, MA: Houghton Mifflin.

Rogers, C. R. (1951). *Client-centered therapy.* Boston, MA: Houghton Mifflin.

Rogers, C. R. (1957). The necessary and sufficient conditions of therapeutic personality change. *Journal of Consulting Psychology, 21*, 95–103.

Rosemont, Jr., H. (1997). Classical Confucian and comtemporary feminist perspectives on the self: Some parallels and their implications. In D. Allen (Ed.), *Culture and self: Philosophical and religious perspectives, East and West* (pp. 63–82). Boulder, CO: Westview Press.

Rosemont, Jr., H., & Ames, R. T. (2009). *The Chinese classic of family reverence: A philosophical translation of the Xiaojing.* Honolulu: University of Hawai'i Press.

Seligman, M. E. P., & Csikszentmihalyi, M. (2000). Positive psychology: An introduction. *American Psychologist, 55*, 5–14.

Skinner, B. F. (1938). *The behavior of organisms: An experimental analysis.* New York: Appleton-Century-Crofts.

Skinner, B. F. (1953). *Science and human behavior.* New York: The Free Press.

Skinner, B. F. (1974). *About behaviorism.* New York: Knopf.

Skinner, B. F. (1990). Can psychology be a science of mind? *American Psychologist, 45*, 1206–1210.

Sugamura, G., Haruki, Y., & Koshikawa, F. (2007). Building more solid bridges between Buddhism and Western psychology. *American Psychologist, 62*, 1080–1081.

Suzuki, S. (1970). *Zen mind, beginner's mind.* New York: Weatherhill.

Tart, C. T. (Ed.) (1990). *Altered states of consciousness.* New York: Harper Collins.

Toneatto, T. (2002). A metacognitive therapy for anxiety disorders: Buddhist psychology applied. *Cognitive and Behavioral Practice, 9,* 72–78.

Triandis, H. C. (1989). The self and social behavior in differing cultural contexts. *Psychological Review, 96,* 506–520.

Tu, W. (1994). Embodying the universe: A note on Confucian self-realization. In R. T. Ames, W. Dissanayake, & T. P. Kasulis (Eds.), *Self as person in Asian theory and practice.* Albany, NY: State University of New York Press.

Wallace, B. A., & Shapiro, S. L. (2006). Mental balance and well-being: Building bridges between Buddhism and Western psychology. *American Psychologist, 61,* 690–701.

Walsh, R., & Shapiro, S. L. (2006). The meeting of meditative disciplines and Western psychology: A mutually enriching dialogue. *American Psychologist, 61,* 227–239.

Watts, A. W. (1957). *The way of Zen.* New York: Vintage Books.

Westen, D. (1998). The scientific legacy of Sigmund Freud: Toward a psychodynamically informed psychological science. *Psychological Bulletin, 124,* 333–371.

White, J. (Ed.) (1972). *The highest state of consciousness.* Garden City, NY: Anchor Books.

Wilhelm, R., & Jung, C. G. (1962). *The secret of the golden flower: A Chinese book of life.* New York: Harcourt, Brace, Jovanovich.

Winnicott, D. W. (1965). *The maturational process and the facilitating environment.* New York: International Universities Press.

Xinyue, Z., Saucier, G., Gao, D., & Liu, J. (2009). The factor structure of Chinese personality terms. *Journal of Personality, 77,* 363–400.

# 23

# East Meets West*
## *The Non-Self versus the Reified Self*

### Yozan Dirk Mosig

## Conceptions of the Self in Western and Eastern Psychology

To best understand psychological differences across cultures it is appropriate to focus on how individuals regard themselves, or rather, their *Selves*. What is the difference between the Western way of looking at the ego or the self, and the Eastern conception of the Self, especially the selfless Self of Buddhist psychology? In this chapter I will try to answer this question and examine the implications for psychotherapy and daily life.

Differences between West and East are not merely a matter of individualism versus collectivism, or the emphasis on the narcissistic ego as opposed to an over-evaluation of the harmony (*wah*) of the group. The complex social and cognitive dimensions underlying the variations in the concept of the self go much deeper and are rooted in fundamentally different views of reality.

## Western View

The concept of the self takes many forms in Western psychology, but invariably involves to some extent a dimension of "thingness," the reification of a homunculus assumed to reside within the individual, who is the thinker of thoughts, the doer of deeds, and the feeler of feelings. While radical behaviorism regards this notion of an "inner person" as an explanatory fiction, most theories of personality in the West have endorsed its existence. The psychology of Buddhism, on the other hand, rejects the notion of an inner self and proposes a radically different view, where thoughts exist without a thinker, deeds without a doer, and feelings without a feeler.

The origins of the notion of an inner self in Western psychology and philosophy are found in the idea of the soul in the Judeo-Christian tradition, which notion was actually derived in part from the writings of Philo, a Jewish theologian, and Plotinus, a pagan neo-Platonic philosopher. The theological dimensions of the concept of soul were elaborated by Augustine of Hippo as well as by Thomas Aquinas, from where it passed into the hands of René Descartes, and from there, almost unchanged, but referred to as "mind," into the realm of nineteenth- and twentieth-century psychology. Essentially the soul, mind, or self was viewed as an inner substance or entity, different from the body, in charge of volitional processes, essentially a "little man inside the head," ultimately responsible for the person's thoughts and actions.

Sigmund Freud (1940) offered a complex model of this inner self in his tripartite analysis of the human personality into id, ego, and superego, which became a distinguishing feature of his psychoanalytic theory. While the unconscious and non-rational id stood for the biological component of the personality, and the superego, another non-rational agency, for the internalized social dimensions of the individual, it was particularly the rational ego that functioned as the homuncular executor of the personality. The ego in turn served as the model for the self in a number of theories developed by those who wrote in the wake of Freud.

Alfred Adler (1927) proposed the notion of a "creative self" which interpreted both the innate abilities and the experiential components of the individual, developing a style of life to compensate for perceived inferiorities and achieve a degree of personal competence and superiority under the influence of an innate "social interest" or *Gemeinschaftsgefuehl*. Karen Horney (1950) distinguished between the "real self" and the "idealized self," the former being regarded as a unique central inner force common to all people and the latter as a fantasy resulting from social pressures and expectations. According to Horney, the congruence of the "real self" and the "idealized self" is the hallmark of a healthy personality.

Erich Fromm (1964) specified unique human needs that must be satisfied in order to achieve self-fulfillment, and argued that no human society had yet been developed that successfully met the needs of the self. Gordon Allport (1961) made an interesting distinction between the self-as-object and the self-as-knower, asserting that the former could be approached with the descriptive tools of psychology while the latter was to remain a subject for philosophical speculation, outside the realm of science. Because it is the self-as-knower that labels and classifies the characteristics of the self-as-object, it stands for a homunculus whose own inner self cannot be reached without infinite regression into absurdity. It was precisely this inner self that B. F. Skinner (1971) and the radical behaviorists rejected as "explanatory fiction."

Perhaps it was Carl Gustav Jung who provided the most significant expansion of the homuncular thesis in psychology (Jacobi, 1942). He did so by distinguishing between the ego as center of consciousness and the self as the emergent integration of the polarities of the personality. With Jung the self, transcending the ego, became ultimately identical with the whole psyche. The self-realization of Jung became the model for the concept of self-actualization in the humanistic psychologies of Abraham Maslow and Carl Rogers, and it was the latter who added a phenomenological dimension to the self. Rogers (1951) defined the self as "an organized, fluid, but consistent conceptual pattern of perceptions of characteristics and relationships of the 'I' or 'me,' together with values attached to these concepts" (p. 498). However, despite emphasizing a pattern-like notion of the self, his allusions to the "self-structure," as well as the suggestion that the self can actually revise or modify the structure of the self, retain a homuncular quality, albeit not as sharply drawn as that of his predecessors. The fuzzier Rogerian self does offer some points of commonality with the Eastern conception of the non-self, as will be clear from the discussion that follows.

## Eastern View

Although some Eastern conceptions of the self, most notably those derived from Hinduism, which center on the Vedic notion of the *atman* or soul, are similar to Western ideas of the self, Buddhist psychology provides a radically different interpretation. The Buddhist notions of the self are derived from the teachings of Siddhartha Gautama, better known as Shakyamuni Buddha, or simply Buddha ("the one who is awake"), after his experience of enlightenment under the *bodhi* tree over 2,500 years ago. The psychological commentaries of the Buddha, collected in the *Abhidharma Pitaka*, were further elaborated in India by Vasubandhu nine centuries later, providing the basis for the Yogacara or Vijnanavada conceptions of consciousness and the self.

Reification is the process by which the mind makes a thing (*res*), or a material object, out of a concept or an abstraction. By extension, it is making a thing out of a form, a shape, a configuration, a *Gestalt*, a perception, or an image. It is to "thing" an event or a phenomenon, to transform an ongoing, fluid process, into a frozen and static spatial or temporal cross-section of the same, endowing such construction with the qualities of reality and separateness. Vasubandhu understood that every single object differentiated by the mind out of its global and holistic experience is created by this process, including the concept of the individual self, the "I" or "me." Reifications are little more than delusions, and refer to momentary states remembered from the past experience of the person (whose concept of himself or herself as a separate individual is itself a reification). People constantly act, behave, and live out their lives as if reifications were actually real, separate entities, rather than the delusory constructions of the mind.

Language has developed as a system of communication for myriads of reified concepts, and consequently consists primarily of reified labels. These labels tend to perpetuate the illusion that reified concepts are actually real, existing objects, for their reality seems to be attested to by the very fact that labels exist for each of them. Language automatically fosters further reifications, in a vicious cycle which prevents the individual from effectively communicating in a non-reifying, non-dualistic manner. This is one of the reasons why "ultimate reality" is essentially "ineffable." As Lao Tze put it, "the tao that can be told is not the real Tao."

Buddhist training consists largely of short-circuiting the reification process, by using non-verbal, non-labeling experiential practice (such as meditation) to become "awakened" to the "as-it-is-ness" of inexpressible reality. Because of the delusory nature of any labeling process, with its consequent reifications, any attempt to offer a name for the unnamable Reality must always fall short, although sages have offered terms such as Thusness, *Tathagatagarba*, Buddha Nature, *Dharmakaya*, Suchness, the Big Self, the Absolute, or the *Tao*.

According to Walpola Rahula (1974)

> Buddhism stands unique in the history of human thought in denying the existence of a [separate] soul, self, or *atman*. According to the teaching of the Buddha, the idea of a [personal] self is an imaginary, false belief which has no corresponding reality, and it produces harmful thoughts of "me" and "mine," selfish desire, craving, attachment, hatred, ill-will, conceit, pride, egoism, and other defilements, impurities and problems. It is the source of all the troubles in the world, from personal conflicts to wars between nations. In short, to this false view can be traced all the evil in the world. (p. 51)

It is important to realize what is meant by the "self" rejected by the Buddha as illusory. Not only are human beings declared to lack a soul or self, but so is everything else: rivers, mountains, this book, your car, and your pen, all lack a separate self. What this means is that they cannot have any existence except in terms of the interconnected net of causal conditions that made their existence possible. All things (including human beings) are composites; in other words, they are composed of parts, and have no real existence other than as temporary (impermanent) collections of parts. They are essentially patterns, configurations, or *Gestalten* rather than objectively existing separate entities. They possess no separate essence, self, or soul that could exist by itself, apart from the component parts and conditions.

Consider, for example, an automobile. Does it have an essence or a "soul" when separated from its component parts? Does it have any real existence apart from its parts? One could try the following mental exercise. Removing one of the tires of the car, one could ask oneself, is this the car? Successively taking away the windshield, a door, a piston, a bolt, the radiator cap, and continuing until the last piece of metal, plastic, glass, or rubber has been removed, one would never find the part which, if removed, transforms what remains into a non-car. Such part, if found, would have represented the essence or the "soul" of the car, and yet it was nowhere to be found. Now all we have is a pile of parts. Where is the car? At which point did the car disappear? If we reflect carefully we are left with the realization that *there never was a car there*—all that was there was a conglomerate of parts temporarily connected in a certain way, so as to result in a particular mode of functioning, and "car" was just a convenient label to designate this working arrangement. The word "car" is nothing but a label for the *Gestalt* formed by the constituent parts, and although it is true (as realized by Wertheimer and the other Gestaltists) that the whole is more than the sum of the parts (one cannot drive sitting on any of the separate parts, or on a random heap of them, but driving is possible when one puts them together in a certain way), it is equally true that a *Gestalt* cannot continue to exist when separated from its parts. The *Gestalt*, the "whole," cannot exist by itself; it does not have a separate self or "soul."

## Implications for the Person

But what about a person? According to Buddhist psychology, what we call a "person" is the composite of five groups of elements or *skandhas*. The *skandhas* are form, feelings, perceptions, impulses, and consciousness. Just as an automobile is a temporary collection of car parts, a person is a temporary arrangement of these five aggregates or *skandhas*. There is no separate, independent self or soul that would be left if we removed form (which includes the body), feelings, perceptions, impulses, and consciousness. While these aggregates are together, the functioning *Gestalt* we call a person exists; if they are removed, the *Gestalt* ceases to be. For this reason, the self can be said to be "empty" of reality when separated from its component aggregates—a view of the self radically different from Western perspectives. But it is not only the self that is empty, and cannot exist by itself; the *skandhas* themselves are also empty.

The five *skandhas*, like everything else, are dependently arisen, and cannot exist by themselves. Take the form of one's body, for example. What would remain of it, if one removed one's perception of it, one's feelings about it, one's impulses to act on it or with it, and one's conscious awareness of it? Form is empty of reality when separated from perceptions, feelings, impulses, and consciousness. And what about feelings? They also cannot exist by themselves. Feelings are feelings about something, about one's body, one's perceptions, one's impulses, one's state of consciousness. The same is true of the remaining *skandhas*—each one is composed of the other four. They are in a state of interdependent co-origination, they inter-are (Hanh, 1988).

The teaching of "dependent origination" is at the core of the Buddha's teaching or *Dharma*. In its simplest expression, dependent origination is a law of causality that says *"this is, because that is; this is not, because that is not; when this arises, that arises; when this ceases, that ceases"* (Rahula, 1974, p. 53; my emphasis). Despite the apparent simplicity of this formulation, it is a far-reaching principle that leaves nothing untouched and, in fact, causally connects everything in the universe, for it implies that all phenomena, whether they be external objective events or internal subjective experiences, come into existence depending on causes and conditions without which they could not be. These causes and conditions can themselves be either internal mental states or external events.

Borrowing an example from Hanh (1988), consider a piece of paper: it can be, because a tree was, since the tree had to be in order to be cut down to make the paper. This same piece of paper is also because there was rain and sunshine, for without them the tree could not have grown. The same is true for the seed and the fertile soil, and for the logger who cut the tree down, for without them, the tree would not have been there for the paper to be. But for the logger to be, his parents had to be, and the food they consumed, and all the conditions that made their lives possible, and those lives upon which theirs in turn depended, and on, and on.

There is no end to this causal interconnectedness. Everything in the universe is connected to this piece of paper through a web of causal conditions. If the component conditions are regarded as elements, we can say that this piece of paper is composed of non-paper elements, or, in other words, that conditions other than the paper itself are necessary for the paper to exist. Stated differently, the paper cannot exist by itself; it lacks a separate self, soul, or essence. The same is true for anything else in the universe, including a person. It is also true of cognitive or mental states, because for every emotion, for every perception, for every thought, there are necessary causal conditions without which they would not have come into being. Everything is dependently arisen, everything exists only if the necessary conditions are there. This means that nothing is ever truly independent or separate from everything else.

The interconnectedness, or "interbeing," of everything in the universe, implied in the principle of dependent origination, finds an elegant expression in the metaphor of the jewel net of Indra, in the Buddha's "Flower Ornament" sermon (*Avatamsaka Sutra*). In this sutra, the universe is likened to an infinite net, stretching out in all directions, in which at every intersection of two strands is found a precious jewel. Each of these jewels reflects the whole net, so that the entire universe is contained in each part of it (Loy, 1993). The Buddha conceived of the universe as composed of an infinite number of *dharmas*, which are described as "point-instants" having infinitesimal extension and only momentary duration, somewhat analogous to the particle-waves of quantum physics (Soeng, 1991).

The following exercise makes the same point experientially. Close your hand into a fist and look at it. What do you see? A fist. Is it real? It certainly seems to be. Now open your fingers. What happened to the "real" thing called "fist" that was there a moment ago? Where did it go? Now consider your self, your ego. Is it real? Certainly. Or is it? What would remain of it if you removed form, feelings, perceptions, impulses, and consciousness? Just as the term "fist" is a convenient label to designate a particular (and transient) arrangement of the fingers, the term "self" or "I" is nothing but a label for an impermanent arrangement of the *skandhas*. There is no little man inside the head, no thinker of thoughts, no doer of deeds, no inner ego or self, other than the temporary *Gestalt* formed by the *skandhas*. This is the Buddha's concept of *anatta*, and this is why the Buddha declared the self an illusion.

But the concept of *anatta* does not negate the person, nor does it diminish it. On the contrary, it empowers the individual by erasing the boundaries of separateness that limit the personal ego or self. The person becomes transformed from an isolated and powerless individual struggling against the rest of the world, into an interconnected integral part of the universe. The person's boundaries dissolve, and the person becomes the universe. This is the realization known as enlightenment, the emergence of the Big Self, the Self with capital S, which is boundless. In the words of the Zen Master Sekito Kisen (700–790), *"a sage has no self, yet there is nothing that is not himself"* (Mosig, 1998; my emphasis).

This can be grasped best with another metaphor, often found in Buddhist literature. Consider a wave in the ocean. It has no reality separate from the water, and although its form seems to last as it continues to move on the surface of the ocean, it is composed each moment of different water particles. It seems so real, and yet, if we look deeply, we can see that there is no thing called "wave" there at all; all there is, is the movement of the water. The wave has no separate "self," no reality apart from the water. But now look again: where are the boundaries of the wave? Where does the wave end and the rest of the ocean start? In reality, it has no boundaries, the wave and the ocean are one, the wave is the ocean, and the ocean is the wave—the separation was just an illusion created by our perceptions and by the words we use to describe them. Now stretch your imagination, and assume for a moment that the collection of elements forming the wave had resulted in the phenomenon of consciousness. As long as the wave was unaware of the nature of the ocean, believing itself to be separate and independent of it, it might develop attachments and aversions, fears, jealousies, and worries about its size, its purpose, its importance, its possessions, or its destination. Clearly any such concerns would vanish instantly upon realizing the water-nature of the ocean, and its oneness with it. In the same way, all human problems and suffering disappear when the illusion of a separate self is eliminated.

The exhilarating and liberating effect of dissolving the illusion of the "I," "me," or "self" is reflected in these words by Achaan Chah:

> Hey, listen! There is no one here, just this. No owner, no one to be old, to be young, to be good or bad, weak or strong ... no one born, and no one to die ... When we carry a burden, it is heavy; when there is no one to carry it, there is not a problem in the world! (Kornfield & Breiter, 1985, p. 174)

Since upon realizing the universal oneness of all, the selfless Self, everyone and everything *is* oneself, this transcendent wisdom generates universal compassion and caring for everyone as oneself. To hurt another becomes to hurt oneself; to help another is to help oneself. True wisdom is automatically manifested as universal compassion, just as true compassion manifests itself as wisdom. Wisdom and compassion are dependently arisen, they "inter-are." In the final analysis, wisdom is compassion, and compassion is wisdom (Mosig, 1989).

## Consciousness and Thought

The psychological insights of the Buddha were explicated by a number of commentators after him. One of the most important ones was Vasubandhu, an oustanding Buddhist scholar living in the fourth century. He was a founder of the school known as the *Vijnanavada* ("path of knowledge") or *Yogacara* ("application of yoga"), and the author of one of the most important books of Buddhist psychology, the *Abhidharmakosa*.

According to Vasubandhu, all that can be experienced to exist is "mind only," or the mental processes of knowing. There is experience, but there is no subject (no *atman*) having the experience. *Vijnana*, or "consciousness," the last of the five *skandhas*, is a multilayered concept, including both conscious and unconscious aspects. There are eight consciousnesses, not just one. The first five correspond to the five basic sense fields, and share the same level of depth. They are the consciousnesses of seeing, hearing, smelling, tasting, and touching. Below is the *manovijnana*, the integrating basis of the five sense consciousnesses, which has functions such as knowing, evaluating, imagining, conceiving, and judging. It is essentially a perceptual and cognitive processing center.

Next comes *manas* ("mind"), where complex thinking and awareness takes place based on the information processed at the previous level. It is here where the illusion of a subjective "I" or "ego" arises. Being aware of the phenomenon of awareness results in the mistaken notion of an inner perceiver who is having the awareness and who is separate from it. This false sense of self or ego-individuality defiles the first six consciousnesses and is the source of all sort of psychological problems and delusions.

Finally comes the vast unconscious *alayavijnana*, or "storehouse consciousness," which is the passive or potential ground out of which emerge the other seven consciousnesses. It is the repository of all potential activities of the other consciousnesses. These potentials exist in the form of "seeds" (*bija*) (Epstein, 1995; Hanh, 1974). These "seeds," upon development, produce all sorts of mental phenomena. Furthermore, in the *alayavijnana*, the "seeds" affect each other in various ways. These "seeds" are "watered" by conscious activities, so that, for example, engaging in kind or compassionate thoughts makes the seeds of compassion ripen and grow (i.e., become more powerful), so that it will be easier to think compassionately next time. Allowing oneself to indulge in anger or hatred waters the corresponding seeds, so that it becomes easier to grow angry and to experience hate. This is why mindfulness of thoughts is so important, and why the "right effort" aspect of the Buddha's Eightfold Path of liberation from suffering deals with cutting off negative or destructive thoughts as soon as they appear, while nurturing positive ones. This develops positive mental habits rooted in the seeds of the *alayavijnana*, and has far-reaching effects on the life and well-being of the individual.

The *alayavijnana* is a vast unconscious realm, which is often compared to a stream, constantly flowing and renewing itself. If the individual is likened to a wave in the ocean, then the *alayavijnana* is the unconsciousness (or subconsciousness) of the ocean, providing the continuity of the karmic process. Jung's collective unconscious is the closest concept in Western psychology, with the archetypes being somewhat analogous to "seeds," but the Buddhist concept is vaster and more dynamic, allowing as it does for the "seeding" of the unconscious (Hanh, 1991). Although the archetypes in the Jungian collective unconscious manifest themselves in dreams and visions, the individual cannot modify their character. The "seeds" of the *alayavijnana*, on the other hand, can be made stronger or weaker through selective attentional and reactive phenomena. The Jungian model allows the ego to gain information from the unconscious but not to modify its nature, while the Buddhist concept of the *alayavijnana* is an interactive system which influences and at the same time is altered by actions and decisions unfolding in the present moment, moment after moment.

The eight consciousnesses should not be conceived as separate, but rather as eight manifestations or functions of an ongoing process. Think of a room illuminated by seven lightbulbs. The illumination is one ongoing phenomenon, integrating the contributions of the individual bulbs. In this example, the electricity that activates them is the equivalent of the *alayavijnana*. There are eight consciousnesses, and yet these are ultimately one (Epstein, 1995).

## Role in Therapy

The psychotherapeutic applications of Eastern and Western psychology have been examined by a number of authors (e.g., Goleman, 1981; Loy, 1992; Magid, 2005; Mruk & Hartzell, 2006; Watts, 1961; Zhang, 2006). Both aim at effecting a positive change in the mode of functioning and the lifestyle of the individual. However, Western psychotherapy is designed to effect such change in persons experiencing psychological or behavioral disorders, while Eastern disciplines affect primarily the practical everyday life of normal or healthy individuals. Buddhist psychology, although applicable in the treatment of psychopathology, is concerned primarily with the alleviation of the unnecessary suffering caused by the delusion of the separate self in human beings in general. The delusion of separateness results in cravings, grasping, clinging, greed, selfishness, hatred, fear, feelings of alienation, loneliness, helplessness, and anxiety, which afflict the "healthy" as well as the "unhealthy" (Brazier & Brazier 2001; Epstein, 2008; Rahula, 1974).

Western psychotherapy, in its efforts to heal the neurotic individual, attempts to strengthen the ego, or to foster the development of a stronger self, and yet it is this very notion of self which Buddhist psychology sees as the root cause of human suffering. Eastern psychotherapy attempts to dissolve the experience of the self-as-separate-entity and replace it with a feeling of interconnectedness, the non-self or selfless Self implied in the Buddhist concept of *anatta*. This radical change is seen as the key to liberation from *dukkha*, the dissatisfaction and suffering of human existence (Rahula, 1974).

Nevertheless, it is not enough for the healthy, liberated individual to eliminate the delusion of the separate self. While understanding universal interconnectedness and absolute reality—the emptiness or *no-thingness* of Buddhism—the person needs at the same time to experience reality in the relative sense, where individual identities exist. The integration of the two levels of awareness, the absolute and the relative, is essential for the normal functioning of the healthy human being in society. When crossing the street, it is not enough to contemplate an approaching car and to realize that we are one with it. It is true that the car, the road, our bodies, and everything else are nothing more than temporary collections of countless particles (or fluctuations of energy, at the quantum level of analysis) and that all there is, is an ocean of energy, where car, road, and person have no more reality than the transient shape of a wave on the surface of the ocean. Nevertheless, unless we act in the relative plane, and get out of the way of the car, the collection of *skandhas* that allows this awareness to occur will be promptly dissolved. What is needed is appropriate action in the relative world, while maintaining awareness of the big picture—this is the essence of wisdom (*prajna*). This larger awareness guides the individual in compassionate action, and eliminates unnecessary worries and suffering about impermanent events, which can now be accepted as the momentary and ever-changing contents of reality (Brazier & Brazier, 2001; Wegela, 2009).

Another area where the Buddhist approach to the elimination of unnecessary suffering created by the delusion of the homuncular self may be of particular benefit is in the training of mental health professionals. If it is true that it is not possible for a therapist to help a client reach a higher level of mental health than the therapist has accomplished, and if clinicians are to act as islands of safety and stability for those who seek their help, it is essential that the mental health practitioner develop a personal regimen establishing serenity, tranquility, and inner peace. Buddhist psychology offers such a path through the practice of meditation and the realization of the interconnectedness of the relative and absolute levels of reality (Brazier & Brazier, 2001; Epstein, 2008; Kaklauskas, Nimanheminda, Hoffman, & MacAndrew, 2008; Magid, 2005, Mruk & Hartzell, 2006; Wegela, 2009; Zhang, 2006).

## Conclusion

The different conceptions of the self in Western and Eastern psychology have clear implications for psychotherapy and everyday life. Despite their differences, an integration of Western and Eastern approaches may be possible or even necessary.

It could be argued that the self needs to be strengthened before it can be abandoned. Culture may play a critical role in this process. The delusion of the separate self is likely to be stronger in individuals raised in individualistic societies, such as those of Europe and America, and may be weaker in collectivistic societies, such as those of China or Japan, where the harmony (*wah*) of the group takes precedence over the needs of the individual. Western approaches may be extremely valuable in giving the person (primarily in individualistic societies, but to some extent also in collectivistic ones) sufficient self-confidence and maturity to discard ego-centeredness. This in turn can prepare the individual to transcend the isolation of the separate self through the realization of the universal interconnectedness stressed by Buddhist psychology as the gateway to wisdom and compassion.

## Note

\* This chapter contains work adapted from Y. Mosig (2006). Conceptions of the self in Western and Eastern psychology, *Journal of Theoretical and Philosophical Psychology, 26,* 39–50. Reprinted with permission, ©Yozan Mosig.

## References

Adler, A. (1927). *The practice and theory of individual psychology.* New York: Harcourt, Brace & World.

Allport, G. (1961). *Pattern and growth in personality.* New York: Holt, Rinehart, & Winston.

Brazier, D. & Brazier, C. (2001). *Zen therapy: A Buddhist approach to psychotherapy.* London: Constable & Robinson.

Epstein, M. (2008). *Psychotherapy without the self: A Buddhist perspective.* New Haven, CT: Yale University Press.

Epstein, M. (1995). *Thoughts without a thinker: Psychotherapy from a Buddhist perspective.* New York: Harper Collins.

Freud, S. (1940). An outline of psychoanalysis. In *The complete psychological works: Standard edition,* Vol. 23, J. Strachey (Ed.). London: Hogarth Press.

Fromm, E. (1964). *The heart of man.* New York: Harper & Row.

Goleman, D. (1981). Buddhist and Western psychology: Some commonalities and differences. *Journal of Transpersonal Psychology, 13,* 125–136.

Hanh, N. (1974). *Zen keys.* Garden City, NY: Doubleday.

Hanh, N. (1988). *The heart of understanding.* Berkeley, CA: Parallax Press.

Hanh, N. (1991). *Peace is every step: The path of mindfulness in everyday life.* New York: Bantam.

Horney, K. (1950). *Neurosis and human growth.* New York: Norton.

Jacobi, J. (1942). *The psychology of C. G. Jung.* London: Routledge & Kegan Paul.

Kaklauskas, F., Nimanheminda, S., Hoffman, L., & MacAndrew, J. (2008). *Brilliant sanity: Buddhist approaches to psychotherapy.* Colorado Springs, CO: Universities of the Rockies Press.

Kornfield, J. & Breiter, P. (1985). *A still forest pool: The insight meditation of Achaan Chah.* Wheaton, IL: Theosophical House.

Loy, D. (1992). Avoiding the void: The lack of self in psychotherapy and Buddhism. *Journal of Transpersonal Psychology, 24,* 151–180.

Loy, D. (1993). Indra's postmodern net. *Philosophy East and West, 43,* 481–510.

Magid, B. (2005). *Ordinary mind: Exploring the common ground of Zen and psychotherapy* (2nd ed.). Somerville, MA: Wisdom Publications.

Mosig, Y. (1989). Wisdom and compassion: What the Buddha taught. *Theoretical and Philosophical Psychology, 9:2,* 27–36.

Mosig, Y. (1998). Zen Buddhism. In Barbara Engler (Ed.), *Personality theories: An introduction* (5th ed., pp. 450–474). New York: Houghton Mifflin.

Mruk, C. J. & Hartzell, J. (2006). *Zen and psychotherapy: Integrating traditional and non-traditional approaches* (2nd ed.). New York: Springer.

Rahula, W. (1974). *What the Buddha taught.* New York: Grove.

Rogers, C. (1951). *Client-centered therapy: Its current practice, implications and theory.* Boston, MA: Houghton Mifflin.

Siegel, R. D. (2009). *The mindfulness solution: Everyday practices for everyday problems.* New York: Guilford.

Skinner, B. F. (1971). *Beyond freedom and dignity.* New York: Knopf.

Soeng Mu, S. (1991). *Heart sutra: Ancient Buddhist wisdom in the light of quantum reality.* Cumberland, RI: Primary Point.

Watts, A. (1961). *Psychotherapy East and West.* New York: Pantheon.

Wegela, K. (2009). *The courage to be present: Buddhism, psychotherapy, and the awakening of natural wisdom.* Boston: Shambhala.

Zhang, Y. (2006). *Zen and psychotherapy.* Victoria, BC (Canada): Trafford.

# Part X
# Social Psychology

Social psychology is a broad field encompassing aspects of diversity, cultural determinants of individual identity, cultural influences on the ways we draw conclusions about the causes of human behavior, and how attractiveness influences relationships in different cultures. Social psychology also attempts to describe and understand the role of cultural variables that underlie organizational behavior.

People are complex beings who think about themselves in varied ways, often possessing diverse cultural identities. The process of creating a cultural identity is stressful in the modern world—a world in which immigration and globalization contribute to socialization forces that may sometimes be in conflict. An important evolving area of study is the development of the skills that facilitate success in a multicultural world.

When individuals act, we invariably tend to draw conclusions about the reasons for their behavior. Much early research on these attributions studied Western samples, finding biases that investigators assumed were associated with characteristics of Western culture. More recent research, however, has shown that the connection between attributions and culture is both more complex and more mixed than early studies suggested.

Although much research has investigated differences in interpersonal attractiveness across cultures, current researchers seek to learn the extent to which personal relationships are grounded in the reality of particular cultures. Specifically, it is of interest to note that the role of attractiveness as a contributor to positive life outcomes may be quite different across differing types of cultures.

For a variety of reasons, researchers have often overlooked Africa and its richly varied cultural contributions to human behavior. In this section we will learn something of the role of intercontinental, cross-border, and interethnic cross-cultural interactions and their contributions to an understanding of cross-cultural psychology in Africa. The sub-Saharan cultures of Africa provide opportunity for enhanced illumination of cultural phenomena in settings with needs far greater than those of the so-called "developed" countries of the world.

# 24

# Multiple Dimensions of Human Diversity

## Loreto R. Prieto and Sara Schwatken

Cross-cultural research in psychology has, in most cases, been cross-national in its focus. However, numerous nations are ethnically and culturally diverse, with the United States being a prime example. Nagayama Hall and Maramba (2001) discussed the possible relationship between cross-cultural and ethnic minority psychology, and analyzed published work in the two fields. They found little overlap between the two, and suggested that one way to increase the focus on minority subcultures might be to combine the efforts of researchers in the two areas. This chapter is an effort to assist the reader to achieve that end.

The demography of the U.S. has been rapidly changing over the last several generations (U.S. Census Bureau, 2010). In particular, the number of persons who possess multiple dimensions of human diversity (e.g., permutations of sex, race/ ethnicity, sexual orientation, socioeconomic class) is increasing exponentially. For example, the United States Census Bureau more than a decade ago formally added the categories of "biracial" and "multiracial," along with the longstanding "Hispanic (any race)" in the collection of race/ethnicity data on its citizenry. No longer can we think about people as members of discrete, mutually exclusive categories in terms of demographic diversity. As Reynolds & Pope (1991) noted in irony as long as 20 years ago, affirmative action statements in employment advertisements encouraging women and minorities to apply can leave women of color wondering within which group they should be counted.

This rapidly changing mix of demography can also pose new challenges for conceptualizing and understanding individuals who possess multiple diverse demographic characteristics (e.g., Asian American lesbian woman), or a mix of majority and diverse cultural attributes (African American, middle-class, gay male). Which demographic characteristics take priority in how people perceive themselves? In how others perceive them?

# Nomenclature

A cogent place to start our discussion concerns how we define our labels and concepts. Important to clarify first is the concept of *cultural diversity*. The notion of cultural diversity itself suggests that there is a baseline culture, as well as culture(s) that differ from, or are diverse as compared with, that baseline culture. For our discussion we will rely on the commonly held concept of a *majority culture* in the U.S. that serves as the baseline.

We remind the reader that although the majority culture base reflects the demographic characteristics of those who hold societal and institutional power, members of the majority culture do not necessarily reflect a majority in the numerical sense (for example, there are more women than men in the U.S., but male-oriented standards and values define the majority culture and men more than women are the chief power holders in the U.S.). We also remind the reader that identifying a set of majority culture demography neither suggests that this demography is superior to other demography, nor that the institutional and societal power held by those with this set of demography defines the way things should be. We simply offer a description of the way things have evolved in the United States through centuries of European imperialism, the oppression and slavery of many non-European groups, the legal and social enforcement of racism, sexism, and heterosexism, as well as the long standing sociopolitical, legal, and economic positioning to power of a majority culture group with a particular set of demographic characteristics.

This set of majority culture demographic characteristics has by many scholars (see Iijima-Hall, 1997) long been purported to include: being male; being of young adult to middle adult age; having European national ancestry; having light skin color, possessing a heterosexual orientation; possessing a middle-class or higher socioeconomic status; being fully physically able; behaving in a rational and emotionally stable fashion, with rare demonstrations of strong emotion (especially publicly); adhering to the Christian faith; being a primary (and typically only) English speaker; and generally striving to think, act, hold values, and live in a way that adheres to a conservative male, Christian, European lifestyle.

As to cultural diversity, we reference and work from the general definition proffered by Iijima-Hall (1997). She defined diversity as "differences in age, color, ethnicity, gender, national origin, physical and mental ability, emotional ability, race, religion, language, sexual orientation, socioeconomic background, and individual unique style" (p. 646). Thus, although this is an extremely broad definition, basically any demographic or lifestyle characteristic that diverges from the above list of majority culture characteristics constitutes a culturally diverse characteristic.

With respect to multiple dimensions of human diversity, clearly there are ways in which many people will possess or exhibit differences along the continua of these demographic characteristics. For example, a primarily Spanish-speaking, Latina female will be diverse along three of these demographic axes (sex, race, language). This same Latina can also simultaneously hold majority culture axes as a 30-year-old, Catholic, heterosexual, fully physically able person. It is within this complex interweaving of human demography that we will discuss diversity issues, in lieu of a more traditional academic discussion of only one aspect of human cultural expression and identity. Furthermore, because certain demographic variables have historically engendered exceptionally longstanding social oppression in U.S. society, in this chapter we will limit our discussion to these variables. Specifically, we will use sex, race, sexual orientation, and socioeconomic class as frequent examples to highlight multiple dimensions of human diversity.

We wish to stress that this does not represent any kind of imposed hierarchy (on our part or otherwise) on the perceived or real importance of these demographic axes over others; rather, in this limited amount of space we have chosen to deal with those axes that have commonly been dealt with in texts, so as to help expand those presentations. Excellent chapters and texts exist that offer in-depth coverage of variables we will not touch on here (e.g., see Dunn, 2009 for an excellent discussion of diversity as it applies to disability issues). Finally, we believe that many of those diverse demographic axes we will not deal with or illustrate directly can nevertheless be conceptualized in the manner in which we will propose considering those variables we do present.

## An Overall Schema

Beyond the ways in which people can differ from one another in their demography, people also interact with, shape and are shaped by various environments and levels of environments within our society. Similar to the work of Abes, Jones, and McEwen (2007), we can conceptualize the diverse demography of people within the spheres of their intra-psychic, interpersonal, and socio-institutional domains of existence. Thus, the aforementioned Latina has a highly influential internal sense of awareness of and level of identity with her various demographic characteristics. Additionally, on a daily basis, her internal sense of self (derived in part from her demography) influences and is influenced by the people with whom she directly interacts (e.g., family, friends, co-workers, and service professionals). Finally, her intra- and interpersonal worlds are also influenced by the majority culture-based socio-institutional realm of the society within which she lives. She and the people with whom she directly interacts are all affected by the political, socioeconomic, religious, legal, educational, labor, and other social systems that are based upon the practices, values and perspectives that emanate from the majority culture base (e.g., male, European, heterosexual, Christian, middle-class).

These societal factors impinge on (and support) her demography in different ways, while simultaneously affecting the way others interact with her. For example, as a woman in the U.S., on average she will earn only 80 cents to a man's dollar.

Often she will be perceived as placing a (presumed and stereotyped) desire to be a mother as a higher priority than her desire to achieve success in a career. Moreover, she will be expected to abandon a career (or at the very least to significantly reduce her work hours) if she has children in order to be their primary caretaker, lest she be considered a bad mother. As a Spanish speaker, she will frequently encounter reactions ranging from confusion to anger when she attempts to speak with the majority of people living in the U.S., who have chosen to learn and speak only English. Others may view her accent and secondary use of English (even if it is fluent) as a sign that she is not a "real" American, or they may stereotype her as an "illegal alien" or recent immigrant, even though her family may have lived in the U.S. for several generations and have chosen simply to retain their fluency in Spanish. Finally, because of her darker skin and Latina cultural heritage, she may face racism and discrimination, both subtle and overt, both seen and unseen, and she will not enjoy the race-based cultural privileges that her more light skinned, European counterparts do (cf., Jensen, 2007; Rothenberg, 2007; Wise, 2007 on the concept of White privilege).

Yet, at the same time, she will enjoy some majority culture benefits and privileges because of the particular demographic characteristics she shares with the majority. As a heterosexual, she can walk down the street holding the hand of her boyfriend, even stopping to give him an intimate public kiss or display of affection, without fear of derision or assault, without being thought of as psychologically maladjusted or immoral (as most lesbian, gay, bisexual, and transgendered [LGBT] people are stereotyped), or without being advised to stop "flaunting" her sexuality publically or stop "forcing" it upon others. Ironically, we do not consider heterosexuals kissing in public as "flaunting" or "forcing" their sexuality upon us. She can place her boyfriend's picture on her desk at work and freely discuss her relationship with him with her friends, parents, and co-workers. She may even eventually choose to legally recognize her relationship in the form of a state marriage license that allows her a multitude of legal, economic, and political rights that her lesbian and gay counterparts do not have in all American states.

In sum, all of these factors simultaneously influence our Latina and her daily life (as they do each of us according to our own demography), and also to some extent have a reciprocal and interactive influence on the individuals in her social groups and in the institutions within which they all interact.

We believe that the two concept maps we have discussed here (intra-psychic and level of environmental context) interact to create the lived experience and public perception of moment-to-moment aspects of cultural diversity; especially the lived experience of multiple dimensions of diversity. We propose that rather than a cultural identity (singular), every human being possesses and manifests many cultural identities, according to their demography, culture-based experiences, and daily experiences in society at large, which itself favors its own cultural values, behavioral norms, and realities. In the remainder of this chapter, we will offer more detail on the factors we believe influence the waxing and waning of various cultural identifications and the salience each may possess dependent upon the intra-psychic and environmental context forces in play.

## The Intra-Psychic Realm

Prieto (2006) discussed various factors for persons with multiple dimensions of diversity that could influence the personal and environmental salience of a particular demographic characteristic. These intra-psychic factors included: the specific mix of majority and culturally diverse demography that people possess; differential identity development growth vectors surrounding these demographic characteristics (and their interaction); and, an individual's own shifting, internal weighting of her demographic characteristics as a function of salience perceptions. To these we now add: past experiences based on or attributed to demography; the effect of immediate learning and choice to alter cognitions or behavior; situational emotional reactions; learned coping strategies / ego defenses adapted as a function of life experiences (or those taught by others such as parents—see Kerwin, Ponterotto, Jackson, and Harris [1993] for strategies taught by parents to their biracial children to deal with potential future racism); and the impact of acculturative forces (the pressure from society to shape our being more toward the favored majority culture values, behavioral norms, and perceptions).

We suggest that these factors can be conceptualized by way of a regression equation of sorts; that is, each of these different intra-psychic factors (variables) has its own "beta weight" in a particular environmental or psychological context that can roughly explain individuals' manifestations and expressions of cultural identities. For example, we could write this as:

$$y = x_1 b_1 + x_2 b_2 + x_3 b_3 \ldots x_n b_n + e$$

where $y$ is an individual's moment-to-moment manifestations and expressions of cultural identities. Each $x$ (1 through $n$) is the intra-psychic factor of interest (e.g., impact of acculturative forces; effect of immediate learning and choice to alter cognitions or behavior; situational emotional reactions; and identity development surrounding demographic characteristics such as sex, race, sexual orientation and socioeconomic status). And each $b$ associated with each $x$ is the particular beta weight (salience) associated with that particular variable in a given situation or context (we will deal with how we include the interpersonal and institutional environmental variables in a later section). Error (or noise) in this equation would be conceptualized as $e$; we see this as a way of both providing "wiggle room" for the influence of additional variables not yet known theoretically or empirically, and to explain the sheer fuzziness of human (cultural) experience!

We recognize that we are making certain assumptions in using a linear, least squares regression model that might be limiting or might not match the reality of the phenomena we are describing. For example, a linear model does not account for moderation or mediation effects among the $x$ variables and ignores the possibility of various curvilinear relations among the $x$ variables or between the $x$ variables and the $y$ variable we wish to explain. However, we believe that a more parsimonious model is better to start with conceptually, and we look to future research to flesh out the shortcomings or unknowns in our present thinking on the matter. We also recognize that readers may balk at conceptualizing human experience via such a sterile and removed method as a statistical equation. However, this type of meta-structure allows for the modification of our schema in a tidy way and also allows for a relatively specific way of capturing a fluid, human event of lived experiences and social perception.

One way to think about this method of conceptualizing human culture-based experience is how one of us (Prieto) teaches applied psychology graduate students to conceptualize working with clients in psychotherapy. I often bring in a piece of moving classical music (the baroque composer Vivaldi is my favorite—specifically his *Four Seasons* concertos) and have my students listen to it while they note their visualizations, the emotion in the music, and the effects the changing melodies and mood of the music have upon them. I then show them the sheet music for the concertos, explaining that the same music they have subjectively experienced with their senses, that moved them emotionally, and that they connected with on a personal level (as they do with clients and their experiences in therapy), can also be written in the extremely structured and precise format of musical notation. The time, notes, key, and complex arpeggios of the music are all there; the structure and precision in the writing of the music does not detract from its phenomenological beauty and humanity. The sheet music and aural music are one and the same.

## The Interpersonal and Institutional Realms

In addition to the intra-psychic realm, we can identify two other important levels or spheres of environments within which individuals manifest and express their cultural identities. These are the interpersonal and the institutional levels. We will detail our conceptualizations of these levels below.

### The interpersonal realm

The easiest way to define this level is to say that the interpersonal realm encompasses all the human interactions we encounter on a daily basis within our more proximal networks. It is important to understand that by proximal we do not mean, necessarily, close to us with respect to physical distance. Rather, we mean proximal with respect to our ability to truly interact with people and experience direct reciprocal impact on personal manifestations and expressions of cultural identities. So, for example, our families, friends, co-workers, and colleagues, and those who offer us various services (waiters, transporters, educators, authorities) are all a part of our interpersonal realms. We can influence and affect their manifestation and expression of their cultural selves and identities about as much as they can influence ours. And that influence can come from across the world or just a cubicle away.

Within the interpersonal realm, there are several factors that can influence an individual's cultural identities. We conceptualize these as being: social power bases within the environment (e.g., authority hierarchies); the social formality and purpose of the environment (e.g., work, leisure, home); the similarity of the individual's demography to that of people in the environment; the level of acceptance and safety felt by the actor within the social environment; and the extent to which individuals in the environment enforce socially oppressive or culturally privileged aspects of the majority culture.

Additionally, the people with whom we interact also have their own intra-psychic factors bringing about the attitudes and behaviors they share with us. As noted above, these include: the specific mix of majority and culturally diverse demography that people possess; differential identity development growth vectors surrounding these demographic characteristics (and their interaction); an individual's own shifting, internal weighting of her demographic characteristics as a function of salience perceptions; past experiences based on or attributed to demography; the effect of immediate learning and choice to alter cognitions or behavior; situational emotional reactions; learned coping strategies / ego defenses adapted as a function of life experiences; and, the impact of acculturative forces.

### The socio-institutional realm

The institutional realm is the uppermost level of the socio-cultural milieu and context that we conceptualize. This level can be described as the more faceless, bureaucratic, codified systems in our society—like the legal, educational, and healthcare systems. Of course, these systems and institutions are nothing more than a collective of individuals, but because of their removed bureaucratic nature, the individuals who work within them generally have little personal vulnerability to those with whom they interact. And, except in the most egregious of situations (e.g., irrefutably clear instances of bias or harassment based on race, sex, sexual orientation, or socioeconomic status), workers in these systems can act with relative immunity. The people who make up these institutions in our society are the ones who create, maintain, and enforce both the socially oppressive policies and laws as well as the cultural privileges in operation in our society. They collectively create a monolithic force that sets the majority culture values, norms, mores, and guidelines for acceptable behavior toward others.

For example, although only a few federal legislators may personally sponsor, write, and publically advocate for a constitutional amendment to ban same-sex marriage (or restrict the legal use of a marriage contract to heterosexual couples only, either avenue has the same effect), no one lawmaker can ever be singled out for being personally responsible for the actual passage of such a law. The responsibility for such an oppressive law and its corresponding oppressive behavior is spread among several hundred lawmakers in Congress. Even after such a discriminatory law is passed, legislators who voted to approve it can attribute their behavior to the wishes of their constituencies; no one need take individual responsibility for their actions.

And, once an oppressive law is on the books, the attitudes and values it represents infiltrate the system and are enforced by those individuals who work in the system. They each now have the power to act in a discriminatory way toward LGBT persons, but they also have the ability to say to those LGBT persons (while in the process of discriminating against them) "It's not me—it's the law." In some fashion, the individuals within an institution can always hide behind or use the shield of bureaucracy, law, and policy. They can also hold themselves harmless and distance themselves from those they discriminate against and from the negative effects such discrimination brings into the lives of those who are oppressed. Likewise, these same individuals are able to extend cultural privileges without vulnerability to those who possess the demography favored by the majority culture base (in this case, heterosexuals). In fact, the policies and law often allow if not encourage this extension of these cultural privileges to those who have majority culture characteristics. As the old saying by cartoonist Walt Kelly goes: "We have met the enemy, and he is us."

One way in which this institutional oppression is commonly seen is the inability of many LGBT workers to find health insurance (or employers who offer health insurance) that will allow them to obtain coverage for their life partners. Often, LGBT partners are denied coverage because the couple remains unable to obtain a state marriage license, the document that legally confers the status of "marital spouse" and allows one to enjoy coverage on their partner's insurance policy.

In terms of an environmental realm within which individuals find themselves interacting as complex, multiply culturally identified beings, this socio-institutional realm can be thought of as a background that provides strong contextual elements suggesting how people should interact with one another. Recall that we conceptualize the institutional level as both the monolithic entity that legitimizes (by law and social policy) as well as enforces (by courts, money, and distribution of resources) our majority culture norms. The institutional level also serves as the vehicle within which individuals decide and create what our majority culture norms will be.

As an analogy, in clinical work and psychotherapy, we talk about both patients' mood and affect to describe their emotional states. As defined in the *Diagnostic and statistical manual—text revision* (4th ed., American Psychiatric Association, 2007), mood is "the pervasive and sustained emotion that colors the perception of the world" (p. 825). On the other hand, affect is defined as "the expression of a subjectively experienced feeling state (emotion)" (p. 819). Therefore, a person might feel and express a happy affect, even while in the midst of an overall depressed mood. Likewise, a person in a generally *euthymic* or good mood might feel and express a strong *dysthymic* or "down in the dumps" affect in reaction to a disappointing incident. So, in this analogy, we would use the concept of mood to describe the overarching socio-institutional realm (exerting a pervasive and sustained cultural influence) on the expression and manifestation of individuals' identities, and the concept of affect (transient experience) as the more proximal or immediate interpersonal and intra-psychic influences on the expression of identities.

In this way, we can see how the pervasive institutional realm can affect both the actions and reactions of individuals, as well as moderate the effects of more proximal interpersonal and intra-psychic experiences. For example, although a gay man might meet a supportive straight ally in a dorm and feel a good measure of acceptance and real friendship in that personal relationship, he will not forget that others in that same dorm might treat him badly if they knew he was gay. Similarly, he may know that the general public will not be accepting of him or his LGBT orientation because of the heterosexism and anti-LGBT oppressive values held and enforced by the majority culture society.

## Reciprocity among the Three Realms

We are conscious of the fact that we have presented the interactions of demographic and social psychological variables largely in an oppressive and biased-based perspective and framework. We also wish to point out the estimable nature of the reciprocal influence that individuals can have upon their environments. This is not only critical for the sake of accuracy in our theorizing, but also because this notion of reciprocity is utterly essential in the emergence of social justice and increasing acceptance of human diversity in our society. Just as individuals form the force behind oppressive values and attitudes that find their way into socio-institutional structures and policy, so too are those same individuals the agents of social change who can alter these policies and the society as a whole.

To continue with an above example, the behavior and values of the straight ally of the gay student may have an important effect on both the gay student and the dorm environment by acting against the majority norm value base and instead showing acceptance of LGBT persons. As time goes on and more instances of this acceptance occur, a sense of acceptance (knowledge and direct experience that not all people are anti-LGBT) will become a part of the daily experience of the gay student, and this sense will also become a part of the daily experience of other (gay and straight) individuals in the interpersonal (and socio-institutional) environments. When enough individuals begin to interact in an LGBT-accepting manner within the interpersonal realm, this new value and norm will begin to spread and take hold in the socio-institutional realm and eventually become a part of the codified systems reflecting the majority culture norms. Therefore, both oppression and social justice are born of the same teaching and learning pathway, and both lie essentially within the power of the individual to shape.

In terms of relating the more public realms (interpersonal and socio-institutional) to the more private realm of intra-psychic processes and experience, we are still struggling to make the best determination on how to conceptualize this bridge. We see at least two ways to do this: (1) add a variable (and beta weight) to the equation to stand for the single level of environment having the greatest influence on the manifestation and expression of multiple identities by individuals at a given time (easy to express but perhaps artificial); or (2) have the realms operate simultaneously (as in reality) on the individual and within interpersonal interactions with three distinct variables in the intra-psychic equation, each with its own beta weight (and the more complex algebraic relations that would bring into the equation). We will not seek to answer this conceptual question here, but will defer to investigators in the future to address it in a more empirical manner. However, we believe that our conceptualized model as is might help to spark critical discussion and further theory development in this area (see Figure 24.1).

The figure helps us to relay the notion that the individual is the center of our conceptualization concerning the manifestation and expression of multiple cultural identities, as well as relaying the notion that each larger environmental level emanating from the intra-psychic is inclusive of the content and factors in the one before it, yet also has additional elements unique to it. Finally, the figure relays the recursive nature among all of the levels, recapitulations that we conceptualize as an ongoing, shaping process.

## What Does It All Mean?

Our goal in this chapter was to introduce our conceptualization of persons with multiple dimensions of diversity so as to expand upon the more simplistic presentation in most text sources of humans evincing only single axes of diversity (e.g., "Here is the Latino culture," "Here is the gay culture," as opposed to "Here is a way to conceptualize the gay, male Latino culture"). As well, we wanted to present a model reflecting the various axes of cultural identities within and across individuals and how these can influence and interact with each other. Finally, we

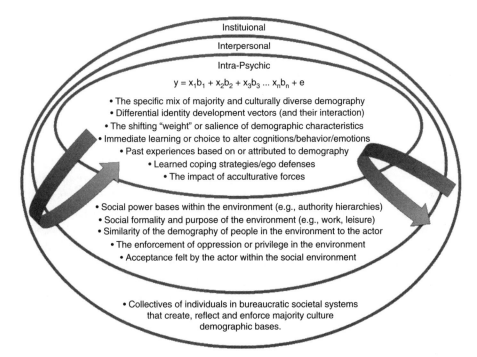

**Figure 24.1**  Multiple cultural identities across environmental contexts.

wished to place this model of multiple cultural identities within the realms of various environmental contexts to fully explicate the person-in-environment, recursive nature of how human cultural identities shape and are shaped by others within specific social arenas.

However, the model itself does not necessarily directly suggest specific strategies we can use to understand the everyday reality of interacting with the multiple cultures within each of us. To this end, we make the following suggestions that we hope are helpful to readers in understanding the real-world application of our model.

First, we agree with those who assert that that each individual is the best estimator of the particular identities that have the most salience for him or her in any given situation or environment (cf., Suzuki, Casas, Ponterotto & Alexander, 2001). So, when we interact with others, we must take care not to assume what particular cultural or demographic characteristic is most salient for them. For example, we may see a primarily Spanish-speaking, middle-class, Christian, Latino male sitting alone at a Catholic wedding ceremony for two European Americans, where the guests are largely European Americans. We might presume that among so many European Americans, this Latino looks worried, isolated, and unsure because he is of a different race/culture than most people there. Although this is a reasonable notion, we might be surprised to discover that he is most concerned about *being a gay man at a straight, Catholic wedding.* In reality, this type of event brings up many feelings for him, like the fact that where he lives he and his partner cannot be married even though they have been in a monogamous relationship for 15 years and love each other very deeply. Such events may also highlight for him the internal strain and conflict he wrestles with concerning his religious and sexual orientation identities. So, when we sense that this Latino man is not feeling comfortable or seems distant from others, we would do well to ask him what is on his mind, versus presuming his discomfort arises because he is Latino.

The importance of non-presumption (and respecting the self-definition of identity salience) becomes critical because certain kinds of diversity (e.g., sexual orientation, religion) can remain *invisible* if a person wishes. Some aspects of our demographic-cultural characteristics and identities are highly visible (e.g., our sex, skin color, race, language, physical ability), and it becomes easy for observers to make unfounded presumptions that these characteristics will be central to our identity. We often make the erroneous assumption that the demography we can see is the demography that is most salient to the person we are encountering.

Second, we must be aware that the salience of identities can shift, sometimes even moment-to-moment, depending upon environmental contexts and cues. Thus, even though we may ask for others to indicate for us the identities they feel are important and want to be recognized and respected in any given environment, this does not mean that their perceived salience of those identities will remain stable across time within that setting. For example, Prieto (2006) provided the example of a male professor of color whose female students of color might feel quite able to share race-based perspectives with him given that he is a person of color, but a moment later be a bit wary about discussing their perspectives as women with this same man if they are unsure of his personal and professional perspectives on feminism, womanhood, and male privilege. Likewise, this male Latino professor may feel a lessening in the salience he places on his racial/cultural identity (Latino) and a simultaneous increase in the salience of his sex-based identity (male) when the conversation with his female students shifts from race issues to issues of feminism.

Third, all of us, being multiply identified in our cultural identities, must learn to be aware of the interaction and differential development of those identities, and as well, must be interpersonally aware of the interaction and differential development of the demographic-cultural identities of others. For example, our aforementioned Latino wedding guest, with his mix of both majority and diverse cultural identities, may wrestle internally with accepting, balancing, and integrating his identities. He may be well aware of the challenges he faces as a homosexual and a Latino in our society, but simultaneously fail to realize that his sex (male) and socioeconomic class have allowed him to avoid many hardships that others without that demography encounter—in fact, that those majority cultural characteristics have actually provided him with privileges that others do not possess! This may be a hard reality for him to see, but it is nonetheless true. Finally, he may be at different stages of identity development with respect to his various demographic-cultural characteristics. For example, he may have personally grown to an advanced level of understanding and acceptance of racial issues in the U.S. and how he wishes to view himself and others in an accurate way. For example, although he clearly and accurately acknowledges that racism is present in our society, he does not think all European Americans are racists. Instead, he may go on a case-by-case basis when it comes to determining European Americans' motivations, attitudes, and sense of acceptance concerning people of color. However, even though advanced and open-minded in his understanding of racial issues, he may be simultaneously less well advanced (and even biased, stereotyped, and closed minded) in his view of non-Christian persons, of the homeless or economically disadvantaged, or of women and feminism. In short, we cannot expect that the level of personal growth, knowledge, understanding, and acceptance will be equivalent within any one individual in relation to his or her multiple cultural identities. There will be variance, both within and between their majority and diverse culture characteristics.

## A Few Suggestions for Future Research

Our proposed model is exactly that, a proposed model. To validate and more fully understand the interactions in the model, it will become necessary to conduct empirical research. Below we have suggested a few basic guidelines we think will help investigators test the model we have outlined.

### Start in the laboratory

The first step in beginning to empirically test our model is to examine its overall tenets. The idea is to first try to understand the big picture, examining whether the major components of our model relate to one another in the way we have proposed. To do this, it will be necessary to transpose our fuzzy, real-life based model into the more structured laboratory setting. Although we have streamlined our theory into a regression equation that fits nicely inside concentric intrapsychic, interpersonal, and socio-institutional realms, the reality of how we express our identities and humanity is not so easily delineated. For example, in our model we propose that the intra-psychic, interpersonal, and institutional realms are distinct contexts possessing the capacity to simultaneously and conjointly interact to influence the expression of identities in a given situation. In everyday experience, it is much more likely that these environmental levels will blur. Therefore, by initially testing the model in the laboratory we will be able to better control for extraneous "noise" in order to more accurately determine the reality of how contexts affect identities.

Although there are drawbacks to conducting laboratory studies to examine real-world experiences (e.g., internal validity versus external validity), testing in the lab allows for a more robust and experimentally sound way of evaluating our model. Laboratory study allows for better control of experimental conditions and better control over subject selection and assignment among experimental conditions. Once basic relations in the model have been validated, then investigators can move from exploratory, correlational designs to more confirmatory designs to test model elements and postulations. For now, exploratory designs examining relations within the expression of diverse identities in various situations will allow us to move forward in reaching an understanding of the complex nature of multiple dimensions of human diversity.

## Determine the interplay of cultural privilege, social oppression, and environmental contexts

As we have seen, an individual can simultaneously hold a number of demographic-cultural characteristics from both majority and non-majority cultures. And, depending upon the environmental contexts at play, people may alter their expression of cultural identities. What is not clear is how holding culturally dominant characteristics affects the negative effects and experiences that come along with possessing culturally diverse characteristics. Are there buffering effects against social oppression and discriminatory experience that arise from possessing majority culture characteristics? Do persons with both majority and non-majority characteristics tend to place greater salience on one group of these characteristics over the other? Do these characteristics play moderating or mediating roles for each other? Do relations change depending upon the environmental level settings? Many complex relational aspects of the model need to be examined.

## How can we best foster social acceptance of diverse characteristics?

As investigations progress toward uncovering and validating relations among key parts of the model, we should also examine how the model can inform us about increasing the acceptance of diverse cultural characteristics and reducing social oppression. We predict that interpersonal interaction among people who establish norms and values counter to those more oppressive ones in the majority culture can, with time, effort, and numbers, eventually spread a new perspective of acceptance into the socio-institutional realm. After all, institutions are simply collectives of individuals, and if enough individuals with a new and different perspective can form an institutional collective, change could be at hand. However, this aspect of the model requires empirical support and validation.

Last, many additional concepts and experimental approaches in social psychology (cf. Matsumoto & Juang, 2008) are directly applicable to human diversity, cross-cultural psychology, the psychology of prejudice and discrimination, and the psychology of persuasion and attitude change. These resources may be a fruitful place to begin to investigate our model as an avenue toward understanding possible interventions aimed at social justice, social change, and intercultural relations.

## Conclusion

We have tried to explicate our conceptualization of what we see as the baseline for all individuals; that is, human beings possess multiple dimensions of human diversity. Very few will possess purely majority culture characteristics (in the broad sense of Iijima-Hall, 1997), and even these individuals have varied investments of salience and expression of all the identities they possess. Thus, conceptualizing all of us as having multiple cultural identities simply makes good sense. We can no longer artificially pretend that our human demography and associated identities can be adequately discussed or scientifically examined in an isolated fashion as if only one aspect matters to us or others. We are multivariate, complex beings and we need to think about, interact with, and study ourselves in that way. This more complex view of human identity may help to broaden our understanding of ourselves, others, and those human potentials yet to be unlocked. We might also be better able to perceive and change ourselves and our society so that we can reduce social oppression and ills and build upon our strengths and the beauty of our widely diverse humanity.

## References

Abes, E., Jones, S. & McEwen, M. (2007). Reconceptualizing the model of multiple dimensions of identity: The role of meaning-making capacity in the construction of multiple identities. *Journal of College Student Development, 48*, 1–22.

American Psychiatric Association (2007). *Diagnostic and statistical manual of mental disorders—text revision* (4th ed.). Washington DC: Author.

Dunn, D. S. (2009). Teaching about the social psychology of disability: Issues of being, not becoming. In R. A. R. Gurung & L. Prieto (Eds.), *Getting culture: Best practices for incorporating culture into the curriculum* (pp. 120–127). New York: Stylus.

Iijima Hall, C. (1997). Cultural malpractice: The growing obsolescence of psychology with the changing U.S. population. *American Psychologist, 52*, 642–651.

Jensen, R. (2007). White privilege shapes the U.S. In P. S. Rothenberg (Ed.), *White privilege: Essential readings on the other side of racism* (2nd ed., pp. 129–132). New York: Worth.

Kerwin, C., Ponterotto, J. G., Jackson, B. L., & Harris, A. (1993). Racial identity in biracial children: A qualitative investigation. *Journal of Counseling Psychology, 40,* 221–231.

Matsumoto, D., & Juang, L. (2008). *Culture and psychology* (4th ed.). Florence, NY: Wadsworth Cengage Learning.

Nagayama Hall, G. C., & Maramba, G. G. (2001). In search of cultural diversity: Recent literature in cross-cultural and ethnic minority psychology. *Cultural Diversity and Ethnic Minority Psychology, 7,* 12–26.

Prieto, L. R (2006). Multiple cultural identities: Will the real student please stand up?. In W. Buskist & S. Davis (Eds), *The handbook of the teaching of psychology* (pp. 175–178). Malden, MA: Blackwell Publishing Ltd.

Reynolds, A. L., & Pope, R. L. (1991). The complexities of diversity: Exploring multiple oppressions. *Journal of Counseling and Development (Special Issue: Multiculturalism as a fourth force in counseling), 70,* 174–180.

Rothenberg, P. S. (2007). *White privilege: Essential readings on the other side of racism* (2nd ed.). New York: Worth.

Suzuki, L. Casas, M. J., Ponterotto, J., & Alexander, C. (Eds.) (2001). *Handbook of Multicultural Counseling* (3rd ed.). Thousand Oaks, CA: Sage.

United States Census Bureau (2010). *The 2006–2008 American Community Survey 3-Year Estimates.* Retreived from http://factfinder.census.gov/

Wise, T. (2007). Membership has its privileges: Thoughts on acknowledging and challenging whiteness. In P. S. Rothenberg (Ed.), *White privilege: Essential readings on the other side of racism* (2nd ed., pp. 133–136). New York: Worth.

# 25

# Cross-Cultural Differences and Similarities in Attribution

## Anne M. Koenig
## and Kristy K. Dean

Imagine you are sitting at a restaurant with some friends, enjoying a nice meal. A stranger at a different table makes eye contact with you and smiles at you briefly. Why do you think the stranger smiled at you? Now imagine the reverse scenario—you smile at a stranger while eating your meal. Why did you smile at the stranger? The answers to these questions are attributions. *Attributions* are inferences about the causes of events—why you or someone else acts the way they do (Heider, 1958). Did the stranger smile at you because he/she is attracted to you? Because he/she is following social norms of politeness? Because he/she thinks they know you? Because you have salad dressing on your face?

Attributions are often categorized as internal or external in nature (Heider, 1958). *Internal attributions* are dispositional causes for behavior, which place the cause of behavior in something about an individual (e.g., personality traits, attitudes, ability, effort). In the example above, causes such as "he thinks he knows me" or "she's attracted to me" are internal attributions because they suggest something about the internal, dispositional state of the actor. *External attributions* are situational causes for behavior which place the cause of behavior in the environment (e.g., some feature of the current social situation, other group members, luck). Causes such as "he's just following social norms of politeness" and "my face was messy with food" are external attributions because they suggest something about the external situation.

In this chapter we will discuss internal and external attributions with regard to several common biases people have when attributing the causes of others' behavior and our own behavior. We will also discuss how each of these biases is similar or different across cultures and explore why these cultural differences exist. Finally, we will apply what is known about cultural differences in attribution to group behavior and academic success across cultures.

As you will see, research studies on cultural differences in attribution are almost entirely based on comparisons between people from Eastern cultures (e.g., Japanese, Chinese, Koreans) and Western cultures (e.g., European Americans,

European Canadians, Western Europeans). Referring to "Eastern cultures" and "Western cultures" is indeed a broad categorization, and such categorizations admittedly gloss over the traditions, languages, history, religious beliefs, and political systems that differ across and even within the "East" and the "West." However, there is a great deal of theory and research that suggests Eastern cultures share similar cultural orientations—which differ from the shared cultural orientations of Western cultures—to warrant such broad categorizations (e.g., Hofstede, 1980; Triandis, 1995). On the one hand, Western cultures support an *individualistic* orientation or worldview, which prioritizes personal concerns (e.g., individual rights, autonomy, and distinctiveness from others) and a focus on the individual. On the other hand, Eastern cultures share a more *collectivistic* worldview, which prioritizes social concerns (e.g., familial duties and obligations, connectedness to others) and a focus on the social environment. There are also individual differences within cultures; someone from an Eastern culture could think, feel, and behave like someone from a Western culture, and vice versa. But living and participating in a particular culture inherently shapes a person's psychology, resulting in cultural differences between the average Easterner and the average Westerner (Kitayama, Markus, Matsumoto, & Norasakkunkit, 1997); this includes attributions. We will return to these cultural orientations when discussing possible causes for cross-cultural differences in attributions for behaviors by others and the self.

## Attributions of Others' Behavior: The Correspondence Bias

When attributing the causes of others' behavior, a common bias is to explain behavior in terms of internal, dispositional attributes of the target, even when that person's behavior is constrained by external, situational factors (see Gilbert & Malone, 1995; Jones, 1979; Ross, 1977). This bias is called the *correspondence bias* or the fundamental attribution error (for a discussion of the distinction between the correspondence bias and the fundamental attribution error, see Gawronski, 2004). There are two common paradigms in correspondence bias research.

In the classic example of the *attitude attribution paradigm*, Jones and Harris (1967) had participants read an essay either praising or derogating Fidel Castro, the then Prime Minister of Cuba, and then estimate the actual attitude of the essay writer. For some participants, this inference was a straightforward one, as the content of the writer's essay likely indicated their attitude as pro- or anti-Castro. The other half of the participants, however, were told that the essay writer was *forced* to write a pro- or anti-Castro essay—that they did not have a choice in the matter. In this condition, the content of the essay would not logically reflect the actual attitude of the writer. Jones and Harris' results indicated, however, that American participants in both the choice and no choice conditions rated writers of pro-Castro essays as more favorable toward Castro than writers of anti-Castro essays. That is, they attributed the content of the essay to the writer's disposition, even when the content of the essay was situationally constrained.

A second paradigm that displays the correspondent bias is the *quiz role paradigm* (Ross, Amabile, & Steinmetz, 1977). In this paradigm, three participants unfamiliar with each other are randomly assigned to be the quizmaster, contestant, or observer in a quiz show game. The questioner creates several trivia questions which the contestant attempts to answer (and gets several incorrect). Why does this paradigm show the correspondence bias? Observers rate the questioner as more intelligent than the contestant—an attribution that does not take into account the random assignment of roles. Questioners only *look* more intelligent because they get to write questions based on their own idiosyncratic knowledge, whereas contestants may likely not know the answers to such specific questions, making them look less intelligent. Thus, as represented by the correspondence bias, observers make internal, dispositional attributions about the intelligence of the two people in the quiz show, even though their behavior is situationally constrained (by the random drawing of who gets what role).

## Cultural differences and similarities in the correspondence bias

Do both Easterners and Westerners show the correspondence bias? Although the first cross-cultural research on the correspondence bias indicated that Easterners show a weaker correspondence bias than Westerners (Lee, Hallahan, & Herzog, 1996; Miller, 1984; Morris & Peng, 1994), more recent research shows that Easterners are also susceptible to the correspondence bias. Koreans, Japanese, and Chinese made similar dispositional attributions as Americans in the attitude attribution paradigm where participants make attributions for another's forced behavior (Choi & Nisbett, 1998; Kashima, Siegel, Tanaka, & Kashima, 1992; Krull et al., 1999; Masuda & Kitayama, 2004, see also van Boven, Kamada, & Gilovich, 1999). Chinese also show the same bias as Americans in the quiz show paradigm (Krull et al., 1999).

Although Easterners and Westerners show similar dispositional biases under the basic paradigms described above, there are situations in which Easterners reduce their bias. For one, East Asians show a weaker correspondence bias when social constraints are made salient. For example, when Korean participants were themselves forced to write an essay either supporting or opposing capital punishment, they more readily perceived the situational constraints inherent in this forced essay-writing procedure and displayed a weaker correspondence bias when rating the attitudes of other essay writers (Choi & Nisbett, 1998). In addition, East Asians show less bias when the person's behavior is deemed non-diagnostic of internal attitudes or dispositions. For example, when the essay written under forced conditions was short and not persuasive, suggesting that the writer was not writing about his or her true attitude (Geeraert & Yzerbyt, 2007; Miyamoto & Kitayama, 2002), or when the essay was written by someone else and randomly selected for the actor to read (Masuda & Kitayama, 2004), East Asian participants showed a reduced correspondence bias. American participants still showed the correspondence bias in all of these cases. Thus, these findings suggest that Easterners and Westerners both show the correspondence bias in some cases, but that, when the situational constraints are salient or the behavior is non-diagnostic of their disposition, Easterners show a reduced bias (see also Norenzayan, Choi, & Nisbett, 1998).

## Explanations for cultural differences and similarities in the correspondence bias

Generally, the correspondence bias is assumed to result from a failure in the second step of a two-step process (see Krull, 1993; Gilbert, Pelham, & Krull, 1988). First, an internal, dispositional attribution is made automatically (i.e., effortlessly, spontaneously). This automatic attribution is, in itself, not a problem unless it is not adjusted or corrected to account for external, situational causes of behavior within the second step of the process. This second step of correction is assumed to be an effortful process that takes motivation and cognitive effort. Thus, if people are distracted, busy, or do not care, they will not correct their initial dispositional attribution for situational constraints and make the correspondence bias.

Given the evidence of cross-cultural differences in the correspondence bias, this process cannot be assumed to be identical for Eastern and Western cultures. Importantly, the bias does not appear to result from a lack of knowledge about situational constraints on behavior. Indeed, Westerners *understand* that the situation can influence behavior; it is just that Westerners do not readily *apply* situational inferences to others' behavior (Gawronski, 2004). Easterners apply this situational information more often, by either (a) correcting their automatic dispositional attributions with situational information or (b) starting with an automatic situational attribution. Why do people from Eastern cultures appear to notice and use situational constraints within this process more often than people from Western cultures?

Recall that Eastern cultures encourage collectivistic orientations (i.e., worldviews) and Western cultures encourage individualistic orientations, and these orientations subsequently "get inside our heads" to create different cognitive, affective, motivational, and behavioral patterns in Eastern and Western cultures (Kitayama et al., 1997). These general orientations have resulted in several specific differences in the psychological cognitive processes of Easterners and Westerners that influence the attributions individuals from each culture make to explain others' behavior (Norenzayan et al., 1998; see Choi, Nisbett, & Norenzayan, 1999).

First, people in individualistic cultures place responsibility for behaviors within the individual's personality or disposition, whereas individuals in collectivistic cultures focus on the whole context of behavior, including the context or situation (see Markus & Kitayama, 1991; Triandis, 1995). Second, collectivists have a more holistic view of the world, which means they see personal dispositions as shaped by the surrounding context, whereas individualists have a more analytic view, perceiving objects as independent of their context and using a fixed set of rules to predict and explain the behavior of those objects (Nisbett, Peng, Choi, & Norenzayan, 2001). Thus collectivists tend to view objects as bound to their backgrounds (i.e., their context) and direct their attention to the central objects as well as their surroundings (called *field dependence*), whereas individualists separate objects from their background and focus on the central objects over their surroundings (*field independence*; see Kitayama, Duffy, Kawamura, & Larsen, 2003). This propensity to see objects as dependent on their context could create attributions that take into account the situational context. Third, collectivists' beliefs about the dispositions of others are more "incremental" in nature, whereas individualists are more often entity theorists (Norenzayan et al., 1998). Incremental theorists believe that peoples' dispositions are flexible, whereas entity theorists believe dispositions are stable and uncontrollable (Dweck, Hong, & Chiu, 1993). Because collectivists are more likely to hold incremental beliefs, they would be more wary of attributing people's behavior to dispositions, which they believe will change (see Chiu, Hong, & Dweck, 1997).

Because of all of these differences in psychological cognitive processes, Easterners, compared to Westerners, are more likely to take the context into account when making attributions about behavior within the two-step process of attribution. Specifically, Easterners may be more likely to correct an automatic dispositional attribution because the situational constraints are more salient to them and seen as more relevant to behavior, making it more likely situations will be factored into attributions (even when this information should be discounted as the cause of behavior, Lieberman, Jarcho, & Obayashi, 2005). In addition, Easterners appear not to require as much cognitive capacity as Westerners to apply situational factors to cognitive inferences, since reducing cognitive capacity increases the correspondence bias for Americans but not East Asians (Knowles, Morris, Chiu, & Hong, 2001; Miyamoto & Kitayama, 2002). Thus, Easterners appear to be able to automatically (and effortlessly) correct their dispositional attributions, without much cognitive effort, whereas correction takes cognitive effort for Westerners. Easterners may also be more likely to start the two-step attribution process with an automatic situational attribution (see Geeraert & Yzerbyt, 2007), especially when situational constraints are salient and they have a goal to focus on the situation. Westerners, on the other hand, appear to have a chronic goal to assess individuals' actions, which results in the correspondence bias. However, if you give Westerners the goal to learn about the situation, the correspondence bias is reduced (Krull, 1993), suggesting that having a situational goal does change the first step of the attribution process from an automatic dispositional attribution to an automatic situational one. A cultural difference in the salience of these goals and motivations could help to account for cultural differences in the correspondence bias.

In sum, Easterners are less likely to attribute others' behaviors to internal dispositions, especially when situational constraints on others' behaviors are salient. This cultural difference in the correspondence bias is likely the result of the cognitive orientations (e.g., focus on context, holistic versus analytic views, incremental versus entity views of personality) that are more encouraged in collectivistic versus individualistic cultures. A focus on the situation and other external causes of behaviors allows Easterners to correct their attributions for situational constraints and perhaps even automatically create situational attributions for others' behaviors, reducing the correspondence bias in some circumstances.

## Attributions for Our Behavior: The Self-serving Bias

When identifying the causes of our own behavior, the main error we face is the *self-serving bias*—a tendency to explain our desired outcomes as caused by internal attributes (e.g., ability) and our undesired outcomes as caused by situational factors (e.g., task difficulty, luck; Bradley, 1978; Miller & Ross, 1975). If you've ever credited a stellar exam grade to your diligent work ethic but dismissed a C or D as due to a tricky exam (or a mean professor!), then you are well-acquainted with the self-serving bias.

The self-serving bias is aptly named—it is a strategically motivated bias aimed at enhancing or protecting our sense of self-worth (Zuckerman, 1979). Attributing successes to our abilities boosts self-esteem and perceived control—we feel positively and we feel that we have ultimate control over the path our life takes. Attributing failures to luck or situational circumstances preserves our oh-so-positive sense of self and distances us from the negative feelings that come with failure. The self-serving bias is just one of many strategies people enact to enhance the self (for a full discussion of self-enhancement strategies see Heine & Hamamura, 2007; Heine, Lehman, Markus, & Kitayama, 1999; Sedikides, Gaertner, & Toguchi, 2003).

### Cultural differences and similarities in self-serving attributions

Do both Easterners and Westerners attribute their behaviors in a self-serving manner? Based on a review of 23 studies assessing the self-serving bias in Japan, Kitayama, Takagi, and Matsumoto (1995) concluded that the self-serving bias is relatively absent in Japan, and instead replaced by a self-critical bias, whereby successes are attributed to luck or effort (although effort is an internal attribution, it can change over time and in different situations) and failures are due to lack of ability.

For instance, Japanese participants named ability as the least important influence on success (Shikanai, 1978) and believed task feedback was a more accurate assessment of ability when the feedback was negative rather than positive (Heine et al., 2001). The self-critical bias even appears in Japan as early as second grade, with elementary school students de-emphasizing the role of ability when explaining successful outcomes (Yoshida, Kojo, & Kaku, 1982).

In stark contrast, a growing body of literature does display a self-serving bias among individuals from collectivistic cultures. People from China, Japan, Korea, and Southeast Asia attributed their successes more to internal than external causes, just as did people from the U.S. (Yan & Gaier, 1994). Additionally, Japanese participants explained their success feedback as due to their ability and effort, and attributed their failure to task difficulty and bad luck—a self-serving pattern (Kudo & Numazaki, 2003).

The research becomes even murkier because evidence for the self-serving and the self-critical biases are inconsistent within studies, with some researchers finding evidence of both self-serving and self-critical attributions (Kashima & Triandis, 1986) or self-critical attributions paired with other self-enhancement strategies (Muramoto, 2003). Inconsistencies have also been noted across studies. For example, one study with East Indians demonstrated a self-critical bias (Fry & Ghosh, 1980), whereas another study with an East Indian sample found evidence of a strong self-serving bias (Chandler, Shama, Wolf, & Planchard, 1981).

Taken altogether, the research sends a very mixed message regarding the universality of the self-serving bias. Although Eastern cultures may encourage self-critical attributional tendencies, it appears that the desire to maintain a positive sense of self remains and is—sometimes, at least—manifested in self-serving attributions for success and failure. A recent meta-analysis (Mezulis, Abramson, Hyde, & Hankin, 2004) confirms that the self-serving bias is stronger in the U.S. and other Western countries than in Asian countries, but also finds variations within collectivistic cultures. Although Japanese and Pacific Islanders show little evidence for a self-serving bias, Indians display a moderately strong self-serving bias, and Chinese and Koreans appear just as self-serving in their attributions as Americans. Interestingly, Asian Americans and Hispanic Americans were found to make self-serving attributions to the same degree as European Americans, suggesting that the attributional patterns encouraged by one's culture of residence trump those encouraged by one's ethnic culture.

## Explanations for cultural differences and similarities in self-serving attributions

Why do people from Eastern cultures often display a weaker self-serving bias than people from Western cultures? The literature provides two explanations—the self-serving bias is attenuated because of (a) cultural differences in how the self is construed and evaluated, and (b) cultural differences in the importance of modest self-presentation. These explanations differ in terms of "culture on the inside"—culturally encouraged ways of thinking about the self—and "culture on the outside"—cultural restrictions on behavior (Kitayama et al., 1997).

Because of the Western orientation toward individualism, people from American culture come to perceive themselves primarily in terms of their autonomy and distinctiveness from others, thus developing a strong *independent self-construal*. Individualistic cultures also emphasize enhancing or maintaining one's unique internal attributes and place importance on possessing high self-esteem (Heine et al., 1999). As a result, independent self-construals encourage self-enhancement motivations and likely increase self-serving attributions.

Because of the Eastern emphasis on collectivism, people from East Asian cultures come to perceive themselves as inherently socially connected to others, thus developing an *interdependent self-construal* (Markus & Kitayama, 1991). Collectivistic cultures also emphasize motives to enhance or maintain the social harmony experienced within social relationships. The emphasis is not on the positivity of internal attributes, but rather on the positivity of social relationships outside the self. Possessing an interdependent self-construal actually deters a person from displaying self-enhancing motivations—spouting off about our wonderfulness often results in negative evaluations from our peers, jealousy, and very few party invitations. Because self-serving attributions fail to foster social harmony, and may even jeopardize it, they are inconsistent with the interdependent sense of selfhood encouraged in collectivistic cultures and therefore less prevalent in these cultures.

Although theoretical perspectives imply that self-construals are causal factors influencing self-serving attributions (e.g., Kitayama et al., 1997), very little research has directly tested this notion. For instance, desire for social approval inhibits the self-serving bias for Japanese (Morinaga, 1984, as discussed in Kudo & Numazaki, 2003), and because this desire is highly characteristic of interdependent self-construals (which are especially encouraged within Japanese culture), one might conclude that interdependent self-construals "caused" this effect. However, causal claims can only be made when conducting an experiment, which would involve varying how people construe the self, at least temporarily. Luckily, research has accomplished this through priming (i.e., inducing a certain mindset). For example, priming an interdependent (vs. independent) self-construal led people to emphasize social obligations over self-interest (Gardner, Gabriel, & Lee, 1999) and display more field-dependent cognitive patterns (Kuhnen, Hannover, & Schubert, 2001). Presumably, priming an interdependent (vs. independent) self-construal would inhibit self-serving attributions, a hypothesis for future research.

A second explanation for the cross-cultural difference in the self-serving bias is based on cultural restrictions on behavior—to the extent that cultures encourage different self-presentational strategies, they may encourage (or discourage) self-serving attributions. Self-presentation constitutes behaviors enacted to control how others evaluate the self (e.g., Baumeister, 1982). In an individualistic culture, a person may solicit positive evaluations from others by presenting the self as favorably as possible; if I convey how friendly and smart I am, people will like me. Accepting responsibility for successes but not failures, therefore, would seem a reasonable self-presentational strategy. People from collectivistic cultures also want to be perceived positively, however they need to balance this motivation with cultural restrictions against "standing out." Indeed, Chinese participants rated a target person as less likeable when they made self-serving attributions for a success (Bond, Leung, & Wan, 1982), and even Japanese fifth graders evaluated a self-enhancing classmate more negatively than a modest classmate (Yoshida et al., 1982). These findings suggest that, in a collectivistic culture, presenting the self as modest is socially advantageous.

Evidence in support of the self-presentational perspective is also limited and indirect, but holds promise. Given that people from collectivistic cultures display less self-enhancement the more modesty is culturally encouraged (Kurman, 2003), it is likely that self-serving attributions are also attenuated when there is a strong proscription to behave modestly. Interestingly, the self-serving bias is also decreased when modesty concerns are salient to people from individualistic cultures, such as when people are aware that their attributions would be known to others (Miller & Schlenker, 1985). This suggests that experimental procedures could be created to vary the importance of modesty in a given situation, allowing for the causal role of modesty to be tested.

In sum, Easterners are sometimes less likely to show the self-serving bias and more likely to show a self-critical bias than Westerners. This cultural difference is likely the result of an interdependent self-construal (versus independent self-construal) and a greater importance of modest self-presentation in collectivistic compared to individualistic cultures. Cultural similarities in the self-serving bias may also be due to self-construals and modest self-presentation given that both can vary as a function of the situation (i.e., experimental primes).

## Applications of the Attribution Biases Across Cultures

We now wish to turn your attention to the implications of these biases to two social issues—group behavior and academic success. How do internal and external attributions, the correspondence bias, and the self-serving bias relate to group-level behavior and to success in academic domains and how do these implications vary across cultures?

### Attributions for group behavior

All of the attribution biases discussed above assess attributions toward individual actors. Sometimes, however, we behave as members of a group or within a group. Collectivist and individualist philosophies suggest differences in the treatment of groups and group action. Collectivist cultures emphasize groups: Easterners are expected to forgo individual interests to maintain social harmony and fit in with the group (Hofstede, 1980; Triandis, 1995), they incorporate group memberships into their self-concepts (Markus & Kitayama, 1991), and they see groups as more cohesive (Spencer-Rodgers, Williams, Hamilton, Peng, & Wang, 2007). Thus, group memberships, and knowing who is in your group (the in-group) and who is not (the out-group), appear more important in collectivist than individualist cultures. In addition, collectivistic cultures emphasize the autonomy of social collectives and give groups causal control of social outcomes, whereas individualistic cultures emphasize individual autonomy and give individuals causal control of social outcomes (Kashima et al., 2005; Menon, Morris, Chiu, & Hong, 1999; Morris, Menon & Ames, 2001). Therefore, in collectivist cultures, people more readily perceive groups as acting as a whole, rather than as individual members.

What are the implications of this differential focus on group and individual agency on attributions across cultures? For one, Easterners show a greater correspondence bias when making attributions for *group* behavior than for individuals. For example, when given information about either an individual or a workgroup who had to make salary decisions in the workplace, or a fireman or group of firemen who had to rescue a girl from a burning building, Chinese participants were more likely than Americans to make situational attributions about individuals (a weaker correspondence bias), but did not differ from Americans in situational attributions about groups. In fact, the Chinese used more dispositional attributions for a group's action than an individual's, while Americans used more dispositional attributions for an individual's action than for a group action (Menon et al., 1999; see also Chiu, Morris, Hong, & Menon, 2000; Friedman, Liu, Chen, & Chi, 2007; Morris & Peng, 1994). Collectivists see groups as causal agents and make internal attributions for a *group's* behavior, even as they attribute an individual's actions to the situation.

A second implication of this focus on groups in collectivist cultures is in the *group-serving bias*, or the self-serving bias at the group level. This bias involves in-group favoritism (internal attributions for positive events by in-group members and external attributions for negative events by in-group members) as well as out-group derogation (internal attributions for negative events by out-group members and external attributions for positive events by out-group members). As with the self-serving bias, group-serving biases enhances self-esteem (Tajfel & Turner, 1986), which may indicate that, similar to the self-serving bias, Easterners would show reduced biases because self-enhancement is not a strong, culturally encouraged motive for collectivistic cultures. However, because of collectivists' focus on groups, and their attempts to balance self-enhancement motives with modesty restrictions, Easterners may also show an increased group-serving bias because it may be more socially sanctioned to enhance group memberships. As with the research on self-serving bias, research on in-group favoritism is mixed. Although some studies find in-group bias in Western but not Eastern cultures (e.g., Heine &

Lehman, 1997; Snibbe, Kitayama, Markus, & Suzuki, 2003), other studies do find the biases in Eastern cultures (e.g., Taylor & Jaggi, 1974; Hewstone, Bond, & Wan, 1983). Importantly, Heine (2003) notes that this research does not indicate that East Asians show group-serving biases *more* than North Americans. Thus, more research will be required before making conclusions about the presence or absence of the bias in collectivistic cultures.

A third implication of this difference between individual and group agency is stereotyping. Stereotypes are beliefs about the characteristics of members of certain groups. Given East Asian's propensity to see groups as possessing agency and their higher levels of attributing groups' behavior to group dispositions, they may engage in more stereotyping. In fact, East Asians were found to stereotype fictional group members as well as members of national groups such as Kenyans, Chinese, and Americans more than Americans (Spencer-Rodgers et al., 2007). Easterners are also more likely to assume that individuals who are members of certain groups will act in accordance with group norms (i.e., actually behave in "stereotypical" ways), presumably because of cultural norms to maintain group harmony, because groups demand conformity, and because groups are readily included within the interdependent self-concept (Spencer-Rodgers et al., 2007). In addition, to the extent that groups are seen as cohesive, both Easterners and Westerners see them as more stereotypical (Spencer-Rodgers et al., 2007), but Easterners see groups as more cohesive than Westerners which helps to account for differences in the amount of stereotyping in different cultures. In sum, because of the collectivist tendency to see groups as cohesive and agentic, collectivists are more likely to stereotype individuals based on group membership and attribute behavior to group membership given that groups are a more useful cue to one's identity and behavior in collectivistic cultures than individualist ones.

## Attributions and cultural discrepancies in academic performance

East Asian students have been found to consistently outperform their American counterparts across a range of academic subjects and levels of education (e.g., Stevenson, Chen, & Lee, 1993; Stevenson et al., 1990). These discrepancies in academic achievement cannot be explained as due to national differences in the amount of time spent in school, the amount of money spent on education, or class size (Stigler, Lee, Lucker, & Stevenson, 1982), especially considering that discrepancies also arise within the U.S. between Asian American and European American students (Chen & Stevenson, 1995). Attention has thus turned to psychological explanations, and to effort attributions for success and failure in particular.

East Asian cultures have a long history of emphasizing scholarly effort as a means of doing well in education (and other settings), as evidenced by Confucianism teachings and current cultural practices. For instance, Confucianism and Asian proverbs often convey the need for self-improvement through effort (e.g., "Be not ashamed of mistakes and thus make them crimes") and the positive outcomes resulting from one's efforts (e.g. "Enough shovels of earth—a mountain. Enough pails of water—a river."). Japanese students are encouraged to engage in *hansei*, which involves reflecting on one's shortcomings (in this case, academic failures) so as to improve upon these in the future, and Japanese teachers praise *gambaru* (perseverance) and *gaman* (enduring hardships; Heine et al., 1999).

These cultural teachings and traditions mirror empirical research findings which demonstrate cultural differences in effort attributions. Chinese and Japanese students attributed success to "studying hard" more so than Asian American students, who made this attribution more than Caucasian American students (Chen & Stevenson, 1995; Holloway, 1988). Hong Kong Chinese students stated that effort is the most important contributor to academic success, career success, and being wealthy (Salili & Mak, 1988). Additionally, American mothers cited lack of ability as well as a lack of effort when their child underperformed academically, whereas Asian mothers cited lack of effort (Crystal & Stevenson, 1991; Hess, Chih-Mei, & McDevitt, 1987) and set higher academic standards in response to successes (Stevenson et al., 1990).

In sum, cultural differences in academic achievement may be due, in part, to Asian and Asian American students' (and parents') heightened emphasis on effort than their Caucasian American counterparts. This rationale, however, is dependent on the notion that effort attributions are beneficial—that they foster academic success. Theory and research both directly and indirectly provide support for this notion.

The idea that effort attributions foster academic success stems from Weiner's idea that effort is not only an internal attribution, but also that it is more unstable (susceptible to changes across time and situation) and more controllable (amenable to volitional control) than ability (Weiner, 1986; Weiner & Kukla, 1970). Importantly, an unstable and controllable cause can be changed and improved in the future (Weiner, 1986). Explaining success as due to one's ability may increase self-esteem (as suggested by the self-serving bias), but when one fails because of a lack of ability there is no hope for improvement. Instead, attributing academic successes to effort can indicate that similar performance can be attained in the future with similar effort, and attributing failures to lack of effort may strategically assert that performance can be improved; because effort is controllable, then one only has to increase effort in order to achieve success in future endeavors. Indeed, reinforcing the use of effort (vs. ability) attributions for failure experiences increased the time students devote to academically based tasks (Heine et al., 2001), which ultimately results in improved performance (Dweck, 1975). In sum, effort attributions convey a sense of improvement of and control over future outcomes that is likely missing for ability attributions.

Similar findings emerge for implicit theories of intelligence. People with incremental theories believe in the malleability of intelligence and commonly attribute academic setbacks to situational features (e.g., effort, problem-solving strategies). However, entity theorists believe intelligence is fixed and unchangeable, so they are somewhat restricted to attribute setbacks to faulty ability (Dweck et al., 1993). Incremental theories for intelligence, and not entity theories, are consistently associated with positive academic outcomes. When academic performance is subpar, incremental theorists take action (by expressing interest in a remediation course or completing tutorial exercises) more so than entity theorists, especially when they attributed their initial academic performance as due to lack of effort (Hong, Chiu, Dweck, Lin, & Wan, 1999).

Because people from collectivistic cultures are more likely to hold incremental theories (as mentioned earlier), they are the ones who often reap the educational benefits of such a mindset. For example, when failure feedback was received on a verbal task, Japanese participants persisted longer on a subsequent version of the task than did Americans, presumably in an attempt to improve their verbal skills (Heine et al., 2001). But, although cultures may differentially encourage ability vs. effort attributions, and entity vs. incremental theories of intelligence, attributions and implicit theories can still vary within cultures as well (Hong et al., 1999). This variation within cultures means that, while cultures differ in the value they give to effort, the benefits of encouraging effort in academic contexts likely transcend cultural boundaries, and may reduce national and ethnic discrepancies in educational achievement.

## Future Directions and Conclusions

The story of cross-cultural research in attribution should sound familiar by now: Research on attribution biases, such as the correspondence bias and the self-serving bias, started out using only Western samples. Given the differences between collectivistic and individualistic cultures—holistic versus analytic views, a focus on the context, incremental versus entity views, interdependent versus independent self-construals, and emphasis on modesty—psychologists hypothesized that these biases would be weaker or even absent in Eastern nations and many of the first studies assessing these biases in collectivistic cultures appeared to show this was the case. However, more recent research gives a more complete, if mixed, story. Easterners do show the correspondence bias and the self-serving bias just as strongly as Westerners in some circumstances, although in other circumstances these biases are reduced. A more precise definition of what circumstances create or reduce these biases is still being determined.

There are also other attributional biases that we did not discuss here which still need more cross-cultural research. For example, another important bias is the actor–observer bias, which occurs at the intersection of attributions of the self and others. People showing the actor–observer bias attribute their own behavior to situational factors but the same behavior by others to dispositional factors (Jones & Nisbett, 1972). Research indicates that the bias may be lessened in collectivistic compared to individualistic cultures (Choi & Nisbett, 1998, Study 2). However, because so little research has examined the actor–observer bias across cultures, more research will be needed before making final conclusions.

In addition, as alluded to when discussing self-construal and incremental versus entity theories, current research is moving in new directions in order to help figure out the causes of cross-cultural similarities and differences in these biases by priming the self-construals and cognitive mindsets that are associated with collectivistic and individualistic cultures within one sample (Gardner et al., 1999; Heine et al., 2001). In addition, researchers have started to examine bicultural individuals, who possess both individualistic and collectivistic mindsets and can easily shift between these when primed with cultural cues (e.g., Hong, Morris, Chiu, & Benet-Martinez, 2000). Thus, experimental procedures (like priming) are useful tools for future research studies that aim to go beyond describing cross-cultural differences (and similarities) and instead identify why these occur.

In addition, the implications of these cultural differences for many domains such as work life, the penal system, and close relationships have yet to be fully explored. How might effort attributions influence worker productivity, satisfaction, and turnover across cultures? How might cultural differences in the correspondence bias influence the legal system and punishments for those who break the law? How would the self-serving bias extend to close family members and other loved ones in different cultures? We look forward to the research on cross-cultural similarities and differences in attribution that is yet to come.

# References

Baumeister, R. F. (1982). A self-presentational view of social phenomena. *Psychological Bulletin, 91*, 3–26.

Bond, M. H., Leung, K., & Wan, K. C. (1982). The social impact of self-effacing attributions: The Chinese case. *Journal of Social Psychology, 118*, 157–166.

Bradley, G. W. (1978). Self-serving biases in the attribution process: A reexamination of the fact or fiction question. *Journal of Personality and Social Psychology, 36*, 56–71.

Chandler, T. A., Shama, D. D., Wolf, F. M., & Planchard, S. K. (1981). Multiattributional causality: A five cross-national samples study. *Journal of Cross-Cultural Psychology, 25*, 207–221.

Chen, C., & Stevenson, H. W. (1995). Motivation and mathematics achievement: A comparative study of Asian-American, Caucasian-American, and East Asian high school students. *Child Development, 66*, 1215–1234.

Chiu, C. Y., Hong, Y. Y., & Dweck, C. S. (1997). Lay dispositionism and implicit theories of personality. *Journal of Personality and Social Psychology, 73*, 19–30.

Chiu, C. Y., Morris, M. W., Hong, Y. Y., & Menon, T. (2000). Motivated cultural cognition: The impact of implicit theories on dispositional attribution varies as a function of need for closure. *Journal of Personality and Social Psychology, 78*, 247–259.

Choi, I., & Nisbett, R. E. (1998). Situational salience and cultural differences in the correspondence bias and in the actor-observer bias. *Personality and Social Psychology Bulletin, 24,* 949–960.

Choi, I., Nisbett, R. E., & Norenzayan, A. (1999). Causal attribution across cultures: Variation and universality. *Psychological Bulletin, 125,* 47–63.

Crystal, D. S., & Stevenson, H. W. (1991). What is a bad kid? Answers of adolescents and their mothers in three cultures. *Journal of Research on Adolescence, 5,* 71–91.

Dweck, C. S. (1975). The role of expectations and attributions in the alleviation of learned helplessness. *Journal of Personality and Social Psychology, 36,* 451–462.

Dweck, C. S., Hong, Y. Y., & Chiu, C. Y. (1993). Implicit theories and individual differences in the likelihood and meaning of dispositional inference. *Personality and Social Psychology Bulletin, 19,* 644–656.

Friedman, R., Liu, W., Chen, C. C., & Chi, S. S. (2007). Causal attribution for interfirm contract violation: A comparative study of Chinese and American commercial arbitrators. *Journal of Applied Psychology, 3,* 856–864.

Fry, P. S., & Ghosh, R. (1980). Attributions of success and failure: Comparison of cultural differences between Asian and Caucasian children. *Journal of Cross-Cultural Psychology, 11,* 342–363.

Gardner, W. L., Gabriel, S., & Lee, A. Y. (1999). "I" value freedom but "we" value relationships: Self-construal priming mirrors cultural differences in judgment. *Psychological Science, 10,* 321–326.

Gawronski, B. (2004). Theory-based bias correction in dispositional inference: The fundamental attribution error is dead, long live the correspondence bias. *European Review of Social Psychology, 15,* 183–217.

Geeraert, N., & Yzerbyt, V. Y. (2007). Cultural differences in the correction of social inferences: Does the dispositional rebound occur in an interdependent culture? *British Journal of Social Psychology, 46,* 423–435.

Gilbert, D. T., & Malone, P. S. (1995). The correspondence bias. *Psychological Bulletin, 117,* 21–38.

Gilbert, D. T., Pelham, B. W., & Krull, D. S. (1988). On cognitive busyness: When person perceivers meet persons perceived. *Journal of Personality and Social Psychology, 54,* 733–740.

Heider, F. (1958). *The psychology of interpersonal relations.* New York: Wiley.

Heine, S. J. (2003). Self-enhancement in Japan? A reply to Brown & Kobayashi. *Asian Journal of Social Psychology, 6,* 75–84.

Heine, S. J., & Hamamura, T. (2007). In search of East Asian self-enhancement. *Personality and Social Psychology Review, 11,* 1–24.

Heine, S. J., Kitayama, S., Lehman, D. R., Takata, T., Ide, E., Leung, C., & Matsumoto, H. (2001). Divergent consequences of success and failure in Japan and North America: An investigation of self-improving motivations and malleable selves. *Journal of Personality and Social Psychology, 81,* 599–615.

Heine, S. J., & Lehman, D. R. (1997).The cultural construction of self-enhancement: An examination of group-serving biases. *Journal of Personality and Social Psychology, 72,* 1268–1283.

Heine, S. J., Lehman, D. R., Markus, H. R., & Kitayama, S. (1999). Is there a universal need for positive self-regard? *Psychological Review, 106,* 766–794.

Hess, R. D., Chih-Mei, C., & McDevitt, T. M. (1987). Cultural variations in family beliefs about children's performance in mathematics: Comparisons among People's Republic of China, Chinese-American, and Caucasian-American families. *Journal of Educational Psychology, 79*, 179–188.

Hewstone, M., Bond, M. H., & Wan, K.-C. (1983). Social facts and social attributions: The explanation of intergroup differences in Hong Kong. *Social Cognition, 2*, 140–155.

Hofstede, G. (1980). *Culture's consequences: International differences in work-related values.* Beverly Hills, CA: Sage.

Holloway, S. D. (1988). Concepts of ability an effort in Japan and the United States. *Review of Educational Research, 58*, 327–345.

Hong, Y. Y., Chiu, C. Y., Dweck, C. S., Lin, D. M. S., & Wan, W. (1999). Implicit theories, attributions, and coping: A meaning system approach. *Journal of Personality and Social Psychology, 77*, 588–599.

Hong, Y. Y., Morris, M. W., Chiu, C. Y., & Benet-Martinez, V. (2000). Multicultural minds: A dynamic constructivist approach to culture and cognition. *American Psychologist, 55*, 709–720.

Jones, E. E. (1979). The rocky road from acts to disposition. *American Psychologist, 34*, 107–117.

Jones, E. E., & Harris, V. A. (1967). The attribution of attitudes. *Journal of Experimental Social Psychology, 3*, 1–24.

Jones, E. E., & Nisbett, R. E. (1972). The actor and the observer: Divergent perceptions of the causes of behavior. In E. E. Jones, D. E. Kanouse, H. H. Kelley, R. E. Nisbett, S. Valins, & B. Weiner (Eds.), *Attribution: Perceiving the causes of behavior* (pp. 79–94). Morristown, NJ: General Learning Press.

Kashima, Y., Kashima, E. S., Chiu, C., Farsides, T., Gelfand, M. J., Hong, Y., Kim, U., ... Yzerbyt, V. (2005). Culture, essentialism, and agency: Are individuals universally believed to be more real entities than groups? *European Journal of Social Psychology, 35*, 147–169.

Kashima, Y., Siegel, M., Tanaka, K., & Kashima, E. S. (1992). Do people believe behaviors are consistent with attitudes? Towards a cultural psychology of attribution processes. *British Journal of Social Psychology, 31*, 111–124.

Kashima, Y., & Triandis, H. C. (1986). The self-serving bias in the attributions as a coping strategy: A cross-cultural study. *Journal of Cross-Cultural Psychology, 17*, 83–97.

Kitayama, S., Duffy, S., Kawamura, T., & Larsen, J. (2003). Perceiving an object and its context in different cultures: A cultural look at New Look. *Psychological Science, 14*, 201–206.

Kitayama, S., Markus, H. R., Matsumoto, H., & Norasakkunkit, V. (1997). Individual and collective processes in the construction of the self: Self-enhancement in the United States and self-criticism in Japan. *Journal of Personality and Social Psychology, 72*, 1245–1267.

Kitayama, S., Takagi, H., & Matsumoto, H. (1995). Causal attribution of success and failure: Cultural psychology of the Japanese self. *Japanese Psychological Review, 38*, 247–280.

Knowles, E. D., Morris, M. W., Chiu, C.-Y., & Hong, Y.-Y. (2001). Culture and the process of person perception: Evidence for automaticity among East Asians in correcting for situational influences on behavior. *Personality and Social Psychology Bulletin, 27*, 1344–1356.

Krull, D. S. (1993). Does the grist change the mill? The effect of the perceiver's inferential goal on the process of social inference. *Personality and Social Psychology Bulletin, 19,* 340–348.

Krull, D. S., Loy, M. H., Lin, J., Wang, C. F., Chen, S., & Zhao, X. (1999). The fundamental attribution error: Correspondence bias in individualist and collectivist cultures. *Personality and Social Psychology Bulletin, 25,* 1208–1219.

Kudo, E., & Numazaki, M. (2003). Explicit and direct self-serving bias in Japan: Reexamination of self-serving bias for success and failure. *Journal of Cross-Cultural Psychology, 34,* 511–521.

Kuhnen, U., Hannover, B., & Schubert, B. (2001). The semantic–procedural interface model of the self: The role of self-knowledge for context-dependent versus context-independent modes of thinking. *Journal of Personality and Social Psychology, 80,* 397–409.

Kurman, J. (2003). Why is self-enhancement low in certain collectivistic cultures? An investigation of two competing explanations. *Journal of Cross-Cultural Psychology, 34,* 496–510.

Lee, F., Hallahan, M., & Herzog, T. (1996). Explaining real-life events: How culture and domain shape attributions. *Personality and Social Psychology Bulletin, 22,* 732–741.

Lieberman, M. D., Jarcho, J. M., & Obayashi, J. (2005). Attributional inference across cultures: Similar automatic attributions and different controlled corrections. *Personality and Social Psychology Bulletin, 31,* 889–901.

Markus, H. R., & Kitayama, S. (1991). Culture and the self: Implications for cognition, emotion, and motivation. *Psychological Review, 98,* 224–253.

Masuda, T., & Kitayama, S. (2004). Perceiver-induced constraint and attitude attribution in Japan and the U.S.: A case for the cultural dependence of the correspondence bias. *Journal of Experimental Social Psychology, 40,* 409–416.

Menon, T., Morris, M. W., Chiu, C. Y., & Hong, Y. Y. (1999). Culture and the construal of agency: Attribution to individual versus group dispositions. *Journal of Personality and Social Psychology, 76,* 701–717.

Mezulis, A. H., Abramson, L. Y., Hyde, J. S., & Hankin, B. J. (2004). Is there a universal positivity bias in attributions: A meta-analysis review of individual, developmental, and cultural differences in the self-serving attributional bias. *Psychological Bulletin, 130,* 711–747.

Miller, D. T., & Ross, M. (1975). Self-serving biases in the attribution of causality: Fact or fiction? *Psychological Bulletin, 82,* 213–225.

Miller, J. G. (1984). Culture and the development of everyday social explanation. *Journal of Personality and Social Psychology, 46,* 961–978.

Miller, R. S., & Schlenker, R. B. (1985). Egotism in group members: Public and private attributions of responsibility for group performance. *Social Psychology Quarterly, 48,* 85–89.

Miyamoto, Y., & Kitayama, S. (2002). Culture and correspondence bias: Is the road from act to disposition rockier in Japan? *Journal of Personality and Social Psychology, 83,* 1239–1248.

Morris, M. W., Menon, T., & Ames, D. R. (2001). Culturally conferred conceptions of agency: A key to social perception of persons, groups, and other actors. *Personality and Social Psychology Review, 5,* 169–182.

Morris, M. W., & Peng, K. (1994). Culture and cause: American and Chinese attributions for social and physical events. *Journal of Personality and Social Psychology, 67,* 949–971.

Muramoto, Y. (2003). An indirect self-enhancement in relationship among Japanese. *Journal of Cross-Cultural Psychology, 34*, 552–566.

Nisbett, R. E., Peng, K., Choi, I., & Norenzayan, A. (2001). Culture and systems of thought: Holistic vs. analytic cognition. *Psychological Review, 108*, 291–310.

Norenzayan, A., Choi, I., & Nisbett, R. E. (1998). Cultural similarities and differences in social inference: Evidence from behavioral predictions and lay theories of behavior. *Personality and Social Psychology Bulletin, 28*, 109–120.

Ross, L. (1977). The intuitive psychologist and his shortcomings: Distortions in the attribution process. In L. Berkowitz (Ed.), *Advances in experimental social psychology* (pp. 173–220). New York: Academic Press.

Ross, L., Amabile, T. M., & Steinmetz, J. L. (1977). Social roles, social control, and biases on social-perception processes. *Journal of Personality and Social Psychology, 35*, 485–494.

Salili, F., & Mak, P. H. T. (1988). Subjective meaning of success in high and low achievers. *International Journal of Intercultural Relations, 12*, 125–138.

Sedikides, C., Gaertner, L., & Toguchi, Y. (2003). Pancultural self-enhancement. *Journal of Personality and Social Psychology, 84*, 60–79.

Shikanai, K. (1978). Effects of self-esteem on attribution of success and failure. *Japanese Journal of Experimental Social Psychology, 18*, 35–46.

Snibbe, A. C., Kitayama, S., Markus, H. R., & Suzuki, T. (2003). They saw a game: A Japanese and American (football) field study. *Journal of Cross-Cultural Psychology, 34*, 581–595.

Spencer-Rodgers, J., Williams, M. J., Hamilton, D. L., Peng, K., & Wang, L. (2007). Culture and group perception: Dispositional and stereotypic inferences about novel and national groups. *Journal of Personality and Social Psychology, 93*, 525–543.

Stevenson, H. W., Chen, C., & Lee, S. Y. (1993). Mathematics achievement in Chinese, Japanese, and American children: Ten years later. *Science, 259*, 53–58.

Stevenson, H. W., Lee, S. Y., Chen, C., Lummis, M., Stigler, J., Fan, L., & Ge, F. (1990). Mathematics achievement of children in China and the United States. *Child Development, 61*, 1053–1066.

Stigler, J. W., Lee, S. Y., Lucker, G. W., & Stevenson, H. W. (1982). Curriculum and achievement in mathematics: A study of elementary school children in Japan, Taiwan, and the United States. *Journal of Educational Psychology, 74*, 315–322.

Tajfel, H., & Turner, J. C. (1986). The social identity theory of intergroup behavior. In S. Worchel & W. G. Nelson (Eds.), *Psychology of intergroup relations* (2nd ed., pp. 7–24). Chicago: Nelson-Hall.

Taylor, D. M., & Jaggi, V. (1974). Ethnocentrism and causal attribution in a South Indian context. *Journal of Cross-Cultural Psychology, 5*, 162–171.

Triandis, H. C. (1995). *Individualism and collectivism*. Boulder, CO: Westview Press.

van Boven, L., Kamada, A., & Gilovich, T. (1999). The perceiver as perceived: Everyday intuition about the correspondence bias. *Journal of Personality and Social Psychology, 77*, 1188–1199.

Weiner, B. (1986). *An attributional theory of motivation and emotion*. New York: Springer-Verlag.

Weiner, B., & Kukla, A. (1970). An attributional analysis of achievement motivation. *Journal of Personality and Social Psychology, 15*, 1–20.

Yan, W. & Gaier, E. L. (1994). Causal attributions for college success and failure: An Asian-American comparison. *Journal of Cross-Cultural Psychology, 25,* 146–158.

Yoshida, T., Kojo, K., & Kaku, H. (1982). A study on the development of self-presentation in children. *Japanese Journal of Educational Psychology, 30,* 120–127.

Zuckerman, M. (1979). Attribution of success and failure revisited, or: The motivational bias is alive and well in attribution theory. *The Journal of Personality, 47,* 245–287.

# 26

# The Importance of Attractiveness Across Cultures

## Stephanie L. Anderson

When Susan Boyle—a rather frumpy, middle-aged woman from Scotland—made her singing debut on the television program *Britain's Got Talent*, nobody expected such a lovely gift to be wrapped in such plain packaging: in fact, "[t]he eye-rolling public and the three jaded judges were waiting for her to squawk like a duck" (McManus, 2009, para. 4). However, when she began to sing, her voice stunned the audience and judges alike. (Ms. Boyle, whose story quickly generated international interest, went on to earn runner-up in the competition.) Why was Ms. Boyle's performance so surprising?

Despite reminders that one should "never judge a book by its cover," research documents the existence of a physical attractiveness stereotype, or the tendency to ascribe positive characteristics to attractive individuals. In addition to being perceived more favorably by others, studies indicate that good-looking people also experience better life outcomes, contrary to the notion that "beauty is only skin deep." Attractive adults receive more attention, positive social interaction, and help from others than do unattractive adults; in addition, they achieve greater occupational success, have more dating and sexual experience, are more popular, and—perhaps as a result of positive treatment—enjoy better physical and mental health (see Langlois et al., 2000, for a meta-analytic review). In sum, attractiveness matters.

In this chapter, I first consider the extent to which conceptions of attractiveness vary as a function of sociocultural setting. I will then discuss research that explains why beauty matters and the benefits that accrue to good-looking people. Finally, I will draw upon work that suggests the importance of attractiveness in everyday life is not just a natural, inevitable feature of human existence, but is instead a product of particular cultural worlds. Recent work in cultural psychology suggests that the importance of physical attractiveness in everyday life varies depending on the extent to which different cultures afford or require individual choice in the construction and maintenance of personal relationships (Adams, Anderson, & Adonu, 2004; Anderson, Adams, & Plaut, 2008; Plaut, Adams, & Anderson, 2009).

I will contrast two ways of understanding the nature of relationship construction—*voluntaristic-independent* and *embedded-interdependent*—and describe research that examines the importance of beauty across cultures to determine implications for the role of physical attractiveness in everyday life.

## Physical Attractiveness

Physical attractiveness is a highly sought-after quality in mainstream, contemporary American settings. People spend a great deal of time and money trying to improve their appearances, from rigorous diet and exercise programs to elaborate grooming practices. Some people even choose to permanently alter their looks through cosmetic surgery. Certainly, individuals may be motivated to engage in these activities for reasons other than appearance (e.g., to be more healthy), but the pursuit of physical attractiveness is probably not far from anyone's mind. What are the qualities that comprise physical attractiveness? And, is everyone who seeks beauty looking for the same thing?

People generally agree about who is and is not physically attractive, both within and across cultural and ethnic groups (Cunningham, Roberts, Barbee, Druen, & Wu, 1995; Zebrowitz, Montepare, & Lee, 1993). This suggests the existence of some universal standards by which beauty is measured. Indeed, research has identified attributes that are commonly considered attractive. For instance, female faces that possess expressive (e.g., dilated pupils, high eyebrows, and large smiles with a full lower lip), neonate (e.g., large eyes and a small nose), and sexually mature characteristics (e.g., prominent cheekbones, a narrow face and thin cheeks, and a small chin) are judged more attractive by participants from varied cultural backgrounds (Cunningham et al., 1995). Features associated with fertility (e.g., youthfulness, small waist-to-hip ratio in women) and health (e.g., facial averageness and symmetry) are broadly recognized as indicators of physical attractiveness, as well. These traits translate into reproductive success and are thus vital for sexual selection and the transmission of one's genes into future generations (see Berry, 2000, for a thorough review on this topic).

Some aspects of what is considered beautiful do seem to vary across time and place, however. This is especially true for malleable characteristics of appearance (e.g., body ornamentation and scarification). For instance, body weight and shape ideals in the West are markedly different now than they were in the past. An evaluation of *Playboy* centerfold models and Miss America Pageant contestants throughout the 1960s and 1970s revealed evidence of a gradual shift away from more voluptuous figures toward a thin, "tubular" body shape (Garner, Garfinkel, Schwartz, & Thompson, 1980). Research has confirmed this trend toward more slender centerfolds into the 1980s and 1990s, as well (Sypeck et al., 2006). Ethnic differences between European American, African American, and Asian American men and women exist for eating behaviors and attitudes and body dissatisfaction, with European American participants reporting more disordered eating and dieting behaviors and attitudes and greater body dissatisfaction than either African American or Asian American participants (Akan & Grilo, 1995). This finding suggests that ethnic differences in desired body type exist, too, leading European American participants to strive toward a thinner ideal. Indeed, when asked to rank female silhouettes of varying size, European American men preferred thinner figures than did African American men (Greenberg & LaPorte, 1996). Thus, even though many of the characteristics that constitute beauty hold universal appeal, some attractive qualities are culture-specific.

## The Benefits of Beauty

### "What is beautiful is good": Research on the physical attractiveness stereotype

Much of the research examining the benefits of attractiveness has emerged from a stereotyping perspective. Numerous studies have documented a physical attractiveness stereotype (PAS), or a tendency to evaluate physically attractive people more positively than physically unattractive people, especially for traits associated with social skills (Eagly, Ashmore, Makhijani & Longo, 1991; Feingold, 1992; Langlois et al., 2000). In a seminal study evaluating PAS, researchers presented undergraduate students with photographs of relatively attractive, average, and unattractive male and female faces (Dion, Berscheid, & Walster, 1972). The participants evaluated the stimulus photos on several personality traits (e.g., sociability, trustworthiness) and also indicated the likelihood of the targets experiencing happiness or success in various life domains (e.g., marriage, occupation). Participants judged attractive targets more positively on a composite measure of socially desirable personality traits; in addition, they also expected the attractive targets to experience more positive life outcomes (e.g., obtain more prestigious jobs, have better marriages, and lead more satisfying social and professional lives) than their less attractive peers, leading the researchers to dub PAS the "what is beautiful is good" effect. This tendency has been replicated for ratings of children (e.g., Dion, 1973) and even infants (e.g., Stephan & Langlois, 1984).

PAS effects are also evident in entertainment media. A random sample of popular American films across five decades revealed a beauty bias such that films in the sample portrayed attractive characters more positively than unattractive characters in terms of both moral goodness and subsequent happiness, regardless of production decade or character sex (Smith, McIntosh, & Bazzini, 1999). Moreover, merely viewing a film that portrayed attractive characters more positively increased the tendency of participants in a subsequent experiment to ascribe positive characteristics to attractive targets. This study demonstrated the existence of PAS in cultural representations; moreover, results suggest that the strength of such effects can vary with exposure to different representations.

## Cultural variation in the physical attractiveness stereotype

Some researchers have suggested that PAS effects might reflect sociocultural factors (see Dion, 1986). If physical attractiveness serves as a heuristic cue about a target's defining essence, then one can expect the tendency to ascribe positive attributes to attractive individuals to be stronger in settings that promote a focus on personal characteristics as the essence of identity (i.e., settings associated with individualism). In this context, attractiveness serves as a cue that a target's essential nature is good, a cue that extends to judgments about other traits. In contrast, the tendency to stereotype on the basis of attractiveness may be weaker in settings that promote a focus on ascribed social locations (e.g., roles, family connection, and group identities) as the essence of identity (i.e., settings associated with collectivism). In this context, attractiveness may provide little information about the target's essential nature, leading perceivers to ignore this (irrelevant) information when making judgments about other traits.

To test this idea, researchers examined the role of physical attractiveness in judgments of traits and life outcomes among samples of Chinese Canadian participants who varied in involvement with the local Chinese community and cultural life (Dion, Pak, & Dion, 1990). Highly involved participants (who presumably had greater exposure to collectivism) demonstrated less physical attractiveness stereotyping than did participants who were not as involved in their context. This was especially true for ratings of traits that reflected social morality (e.g., *kind* and *considerate*). Participants in both groups did show evidence of PAS effects on items concerning desirable life outcomes (e.g., *a happy life*), however.

An alternative account of cultural variation maintains that the tendency to ascribe positive characteristics to attractive people occurs to an equal extent across settings, but the traits that people consider valuable and therefore associate with physical attractiveness vary. Because people value different traits in different settings, the particular dimensions on which one will observe PAS effects will vary depending on context; in other words, "what is beautiful is *culturally* good." To test this idea, researchers exposed Korean participants to photos of Korean targets of varying attractiveness and asked them to judge the targets on traits reflecting domains of value in North American settings (e.g., *potency*) and Korean settings (e.g., *integrity* and *concern for others*; Wheeler & Kim, 1997). Korean participants did not show effects of physical attractiveness on ratings of *potency* (an American-valued trait), as North American participants do, but did show effects for *integrity* and *concern for others* (Korean-valued traits), as North American participants do not (Eagly et al., 1991; Feingold, 1992), thus leading the researchers to conclude that physical attractiveness stereotyping for judgments about traits is universal, but the particular traits on which stereotyping will occur are culturally specific (cf. Chen, Shaffer, & Wu, 1997; Shaffer, Crepaz, & Sun, 2000).

Work by my colleagues and myself may help shed some light on these differing accounts (Anderson et al., 2008). We exposed Ghanaian and American participants to photos of Black and White faces and asked them to judge the targets on Ghanaian-valued (e.g., *sensitive, modest*) and American-valued (e.g., *genuine, spontaneous*) traits. (These traits were derived from a pretest among an independent sample of Ghanaian and American students.) Consistent with PAS research, American participants rated attractive targets more positively than unattractive targets. This was especially true for American-valued traits, providing support for both the "what is beautiful is good" and the "what is beautiful is *culturally* good" versions of PAS. In contrast, there was no evidence that Ghanaian participants rated attractive targets more positively than unattractive targets, even for Ghanaian-valued traits. These results are inconsistent with the "what is beautiful is *culturally* good" effect (Wheeler & Kim, 1997), perhaps reflecting differences in research settings (i.e., East Asian and West African worlds). However, results for Ghanaian participants do align with the previously described research demonstrating cultural variation in the influence of attractiveness on judgments about traits (Dion et al., 1990). Dion and colleagues' (1990) assessment of cultural engagement resonates closely with our comparison of settings that varied in the extent to which implicit cultural patterns afford an experience of relationship as something embedded in the structure of everyday worlds. This suggests that future researchers may likewise observe small or non-existent PAS effects, even for culturally valued traits, when they conceptualize culture in terms of engagement with everyday worlds.

## A Cultural Perspective on Attraction

Contrary to popular understandings, the point of a cultural perspective is not simply to demonstrate that phenomena vary "across cultures"; instead, the goal is to illuminate a process that is typically invisible in mainstream accounts: the extent to which psychological phenomena are not "just natural," but reflect particular constructions of reality. In other words, the emphasis on physical attractiveness and the resulting benefits of beauty that are extensively documented by social psychologists are not a reflection of the default condition of humankind. Rather, the process of attraction takes on special significance precisely because of the specific characteristics of the social and cultural environment in which it has been studied.

Previous research (briefly described above) has framed attractiveness as a stereotyping phenomenon and has investigated its effects on trait ratings. In contrast, our research frames attractiveness as a relationship phenomenon and considers its implications for life outcomes. From this perspective, the importance of physical attractiveness depends upon the particular constructions of reality—voluntaristic-independent

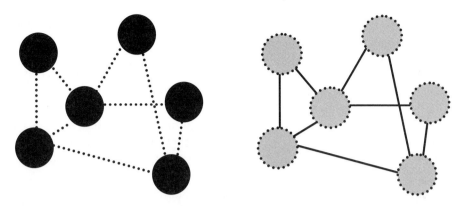

**Figure 26.1.**   Voluntaristic-independent and embedded-interdependent constructions of self and relationship reality.

*Note*: The left side of the diagram represents *voluntaristic-independent* constructions of self and relationship. These constructions locate psychological experience in the internal properties of individuals (represented by solid circles) and relationship (represented by dashed lines) as a relatively tenuous, secondary product of ontologically prior selves. They promote a thin, frictionless experience of relationship—characterized by relative freedom of entry and exit—as the unstable product of choice.

The right side of the diagram represents *embedded-interdependent* constructions of self and relationship. These constructions locate psychological experience in fields of relational connection (represented by solid lines) that are ontologically prior to the individual experience (represented by shaded circles). They promote a thick, sticky experience of relationship—characterized by more constraints on entry and exit—as an environmentally afforded fact.

*Source*: From G. Adams, S. L. Anderson, & J. K. Adonu (2004). The cultural grounding of closeness and intimacy. In D. J. Mashek & A. Aron (Eds.), *The handbook of closeness and intimacy* (pp. 321–339). Mahwah, NJ: Lawrence Erlbaum Associates. Adapted with permission.

or embedded-interdependent—that inform relationship experience. In the next section, I will elaborate on the theoretical framework that informs our research.

## Theoretical framework: construction of self and relationship

Human beings are intensely social creatures; in fact, some researchers even claim we have a fundamental need to belong (Baumeister & Leary, 1995). And, although virtually everyone on the planet can identify at least a handful of meaningful interpersonal relationships, our implicit understandings about relationship—specifically, how connections are formed and perhaps even the value we place on different forms of relationality—are not necessarily shared across time and space. Based on Markus and Kitayama's (1991) distinction between independent and interdependent selves, my colleagues and I have elaborated a theory that differentiates between two ways of explaining connection— *voluntaristic-independent* and *embedded-interdependent* constructions of relationship—that differ primarily in the affordance of choice in relationship construction (Adams et al., 2004; Anderson et al., 2008) (see Figure 26.1).

In mainstream, contemporary American settings, as well as other Western societies (e.g., Canada, Western Europe), *voluntaristic-independent* constructions of relationship prevail. In these settings, the self is viewed as an inherently separate entity, a unique being set apart from other persons and the social context at large. Thoughts, feelings, and actions originate from the internal properties of independent actors as expressions of individuality (Markus & Kitayama, 1991). When the self is construed as independent, relationship is framed as secondary in the sense that it must be voluntarily created: autonomous actors are free—and even compelled—to forge and dissolve connections with others (Adams et al., 2004; Anderson et al., 2008).

In many non-Western cultures (e.g., East Asia, Latin America, West Africa), *embedded-interdependent* constructions of relationship are prominent. In these settings, ideas about the self emphasize inherent connection. The individual exists in relation to other persons and the social context. A desire for appropriate action within one's proper role, which in turn satisfies individual desires, provides motivation for behavior and cognition (Markus & Kitayama, 1991). When the self is construed as interdependent, relationship is framed as primary in the sense that the larger social network exists even apart from the individual: connection is inescapable. Rather than an emphasis on contracting relationships based on personal choice, these settings emphasize management of connections in densely interconnected networks associated with situations of limited mobility (Adams et al., 2004; Anderson et al., 2008).

These terms—voluntaristic-independence and embedded-interdependence— refer to implicit understandings about the nature of connection, but they are more than mere ideas; the essence of these concepts is built into the structural realities of our everyday lives. For example, in settings where the self is construed as independent and relationship as voluntaristic-independent, normative behavior includes leaving home in young adulthood, living independently for a period of time, and marrying a partner of one's choice; in contrast, living with extended family from birth until death and entering into arranged marriages are commonplace practices in settings where the self is construed as interdependent and relationship as embedded-interdependent (Adams et al., 2004). To further illustrate this point, let us consider two of the research settings from which our work arises: North American and West African worlds.

Voluntaristic-independent constructions of relationship are inscribed in several patterns of mainstream American worlds. The notion of relationship as the product of personal choice figures prominently in linguistic practices. Despite the well-documented influence of environmental factors (e.g., propinquity) on relationship experience, lay people talk about *making* friends, and researchers study mate *selection* and friendship *choice*. The popularity of social networking websites (e.g., myspace.com and facebook.com), which allow users to "link" to relationship partners, and online dating services (e.g., match.com and e-harmony.com), which allow users to browse photographs and biographies for hundreds of potential mates, provides further evidence that relationship is one of many domains in mainstream American worlds where abundant opportunities for choice figure prominently in daily life. In contexts that privilege choice as a fundamental feature of human agency—where choice is valued, where many opportunities for choice exist, and where choice affects liking—selection of a relationship partner is essential to self-determination and personal expression (Iyengar & Lepper, 2002; Kim & Sherman, 2007; Snibbe & Markus, 2005).

Associated with embedded-interdependent constructions of relationship, the de-emphasis on personal choice in relationship experience is evident in many West African worlds. Perhaps the most important pattern is the centrality of kinship, manifest in such practices as arranged marriage, but this de-emphasis on choice extends to other forms of relationship. For instance, "friendship" in these settings suggests more constricting, less voluntary connections than are common in North American experience (see Carrier, 1999; Wierzbicka, 1997). Contrary to stereotypes about sociable collectivists, people in West African settings tend to report fewer friends and are more likely to claim enemies than people in North American settings (Adams, 2005; Adams & Plaut, 2003). People in North American settings report a large number of friends and few enemies in part because local constructions of relationship afford them freedom of choice both to create positive connections and to avoid negative connections. In contrast, people in West African settings report fewer friends and frequently report that they are the target of malicious enemies, in part because local constructions of relationship afford less choice or agency either to create positive connection or to avoid negative connection (Adams, 2005; Adams & Plaut, 2003).

## Implications for attraction

The study of attraction is one area in which divergent constructions of relationship have notable implications for psychological understanding. A cursory reading of the social psychological literature suggests that interpersonal attraction seems as natural and normal to human behavior as eating or sleeping. Attraction certainly seems to be a process of great consequence (just ask any undergraduate!). However, much of the weight interpersonal attraction assumes—in the scientific literature and in Western culture at large—is due to the aforementioned implicit understandings about the nature of self and relationship reality, specifically voluntaristic-independent constructions that are prominent in most of the settings where psychological research is conducted: mainstream, contemporary American university campuses in large cities across the U.S.A.

If (as in the case of embedded-interdependent constructions of relationship) social networks exist apart from the individual self, making connection the product of environmental affordance, the process of attraction is rendered somewhat meaningless. After all, if one has little choice in his or her relationship ties, beauty does not have much of an opportunity to matter. Attraction—and the qualities that might make one a more desirable relationship partner, such as physical attractiveness—assumes greater value when (as in the case of voluntaristic-independent constructions of relationship) the self is perceived as inherently separate from context and connection is framed as the product of choice. To the extent that people experience relationship as a discretionary product based on personal preference, personal preference (as a determinant of choice) and attraction (as a basis of preference) are important determinants in relationship formation (Rosenblatt & Cozby, 1972). Likewise, attractive attributes like beauty loom large. In such instances, physical attractiveness becomes an important commodity on the market of interpersonal relationship. People who possess attractive attributes (like physical beauty) will be in higher demand and are better able to contract satisfying connections (Sangrador & Yela, 2000). In this way, voluntaristic-independent constructions of relationship promote the expectation that attractive people will have more satisfying lives than unattractive people.

# Our Research

In the remainder of the chapter, I will discuss three studies that test the idea that the association between attractiveness and life outcomes varies across cultural worlds. In particular, I propose that attraction is especially important for life outcomes in worlds that promote constructions of relationship as the product of personal choice. To the extent that people experience relationship as an agentic creation and expression of personal preferences, attraction and other bases of preference loom large in relationship life. However, attraction may be less relevant in worlds that promote constructions of relationship as environmental affordance. To the extent that people experience less agency in the construction of relationship, attraction and other bases of personal preference have less impact on life outcomes.

## Attractiveness and actual outcomes:
## A cross-national comparison

In our first study on this topic, we focused on actual life outcomes, investigating the relationship between participants' satisfaction with their own life outcomes and judges' ratings of participants' attractiveness (Anderson et al., 2008). This study included a cross-national comparison between students at two North American universities (settings in which voluntaristic-independent constructions of relationship are prominent) and a West African university in the country of Ghana (where more embedded-interdependent constructions of relationship prevail). In addition, we included a comparison of relationship contexts. To the extent that friendship is the prototypical "chosen" relationship (Palisi & Ransford, 1987) and kinship is the prototypical "given" relationship, cross-national differences in the attractiveness–outcome relationship should be greater for the former than the latter. As mating relationship entails an intermediate degree of choice—specifically, it allows more personal discretion than kinship, but is more exclusive and therefore provides less opportunity for choice than friendship—we expected cross-national differences in the association between attractiveness and outcomes for mating relationship to be somewhere in between differences for friendship and kinship.

Participants first rated their satisfaction with various life outcomes (e.g., *I am satisfied with my achievements, I am happy overall, Other people like me*). In addition to the overall measure of general life outcomes, we also included measures of outcomes (*practical support, emotional support, quality, closeness/intimacy*) within three relationship types—friend, mating, and kin relationship. Finally, we took a head-and-shoulders photograph of each participant, which a separate sample of opposite-sex, same-nationality students later rated for attractiveness (Anderson et al., 2008).

We predicted that the positive association between attractiveness and life outcomes would be stronger or more evident in contexts characterized by constructions of relationship as the product of personal choice (i.e., in American settings and friendship, the prototypical "chosen" relationship) than the product of environmental affordance (i.e., in Ghanaian settings and kinship, the prototypical "given" relationship). Results provided support for our hypothesis for both general life outcomes and particular relationship contexts. For the measure of general life outcomes, the relationship between attractiveness and life outcomes was positive among American participants but negative among Ghanaian participants. Although attractive Americans reported more positive outcomes than unattractive Americans, the reverse pattern was true of Ghanaian participants. For the measure of particular relationship contexts, results revealed no association between attractiveness and relationship outcomes in either the non-voluntary context of kinship or the semi-voluntary context of mating relationship. In contrast, results did reveal a positive association between attractiveness and outcomes in the voluntary context of friendship, but only among participants in American settings (Anderson et al., 2008).

## Attractiveness and expected outcomes: A cross-national, cross-cultural, and experimental comparison

In our second study, we focused on judgments about the life outcomes of others, similar to much of the existing PAS research (Anderson et al., 2008). This study again included a cross-national comparison between students at a North American university and a West African university in the country of Ghana. We also included a cross-cultural comparison between students from urban and rural backgrounds. Extending research that examines differences in agency and relationship as a function of region (e.g., Markus, Ryff, Curhan, & Palmersheim, 2004; Plaut, Markus, & Lachman, 2002; Vandello & Cohen, 1999), we hypothesized that urban and rural settings differ in the extent to which they afford the experience of relationship as a product of choice. Urban settings typically foster greater relative social mobility (due to fewer constraints), anonymity, and a larger pool of potential interaction partners. This promotes a "free market" of relationship, in which personal choice—and the qualities, like attractiveness, that influence choice—can become important determinants of relationship outcomes. In contrast, the structure of life in rural settings—limited social and geographic mobility (due to greater constraints) and a circumscribed pool of potential interaction partners with whom one may have substantial duties or obligations (e.g., kin)—provides less opportunity for choice in relationship (Beggs, Haines, & Hurlbert, 1996). In these settings, attractiveness effects may be less evident as there is relatively little opportunity (or necessity) for personal preferences or qualities that constitute attractiveness to influence relationship outcomes. In addition to the cross-national and cross-cultural comparisons, we introduced an experimental manipulation of relationship constructions (Anderson et al., 2008).

Participants first described either their three most meaningful personal characteristics (to influence them to experience themselves as a decontextualized bundle of traits; voluntaristic-independent condition) or their three most meaningful personal relationships (to influence them to experience themselves as embedded in connection with others; embedded-interdependent condition). They then received photos of Black and White, male and female, attractive and unattractive faces. Participants rated the likelihood of each target experiencing various life outcomes (e.g., *be liked by others, have monetary success, get what he/she wants in life*) (Anderson et al., 2008).

We predicted that the divergence in expected outcomes of attractive and unattractive targets would be greater in settings associated with voluntaristic-independent constructions of relationship as discretionary product (i.e., among American participants, urban participants, and participants in the voluntaristic-independent condition) than in settings associated with embedded-interdependent constructions of relationship as environmental affordance (i.e., among Ghanaian participants, rural participants, and participants in the embedded-interdependent condition). Results provided support for our hypothesis along all three dimensions of variation in relationship construction. Attractiveness effects (i.e., the discrepancy between expected life outcomes of attractive and unattractive targets) were greater for American participants than for Ghanaian participants, for urban participants than for rural participants, and (though only among Ghanaian participants) for participants in the voluntaristic-independent condition than for participants in the embedded-interdependent condition (Anderson et al., 2008).

## Attractiveness and actual outcomes: A cross-cultural comparison

In our third study, we focused again on actual life outcomes, investigating the relationship between attractiveness, social connectedness, and well-being (Plaut et al, 2009). This study included a cross-cultural comparison between residents of urban settings (in which voluntaristic-independent constructions of relationship are prominent) and rural settings (where more embedded-interdependent constructions of relationship prevail).

We analyzed data from the National Survey of Midlife Development in the United States (MIDUS; MacArthur Research Network on Successful Midlife Development). Participants included female respondents who indicated rural or city residence. Based upon research suggesting waist-to-hip ratio (WHR) as an indicator of female attractiveness (Streeter & McBurney, 2003), we utilized this variable as our measure of physical attractiveness. Our composite measure of well-being included participants' responses to items concerning life satisfaction, positive affect, self-acceptance, and environmental mastery. Our composite measure of social connectedness included participants' responses to items concerning contact with friends, social integration, support from friends, and strain from friends. We controlled all analyses for age, household income, and marital status, as well as body mass index (Plaut et al., 2009).

We predicted that the positive association between attractiveness and well-being would be stronger or more evident in contexts characterized by constructions of relationship as the product of personal choice (i.e., urban settings) than the product of environmental affordance (i.e., rural settings). More specifically, we hypothesized that the positive relationship between attractiveness (low WHR) and well-being would be present in urban settings but absent in rural settings because attractiveness (low WHR) is also associated with better social connectedness in urban settings but not rural settings. Results confirmed our hypothesis. The relationship of WHR and well-being was negative among urban, but not rural, participants. The relationship of WHR and social connectedness was also negative among urban, but not rural, participants. More importantly, we observed support for our guiding hypothesis in the form of mediated moderation, such that social connectedness mediated the moderating effect of urban vs. rural background on the relationship between WHR and well-being. In other words, attractive individuals in urban settings experience better relationships which—at least in part—contribute to their greater well-being (Plaut et al., 2009).

## Conclusion

Together, results of these studies provide strong and consistent support that the well-documented association of attractiveness with positive life outcomes is not simply a natural or inevitable pattern, but rather a reflection of the particular cultural worlds—specifically, sociocultural settings (such as North American and urban worlds) that promote voluntaristic-independent constructions of relationship as the product of personal choice—in which much of the existing research has been conducted. Despite its importance in psychological theory and research, attractiveness appears to be less relevant in sociocultural settings (such as West African and rural worlds) that promote embedded-interdependent constructions of relationship as the product of environmental affordance.

In conclusion, our goal is not simply to document cross-national or cross-cultural differences, although that is a worthwhile pursuit; instead, we aim to provide an explanation for the status quo. The point of a cultural approach is to reveal how a phenomenon, like attraction, is grounded in particular constructions of reality—in this case, contemporary, mainstream North American worlds in which relationship is constructed in terms of personal choice. Our research illuminates the cultural grounding of personal relationship, a process that is typically overlooked. A comprehensive understanding of human behavior and cognition benefits through greater attention to this process not only when describing "others," but especially in the more typical case of mainstream research (conducted among North American undergraduates)—in which this process tends to remain invisible.

# References

Adams, G. (2005). The cultural grounding of personal relationship: Enemyship in North American and West African worlds. *Journal of Personality and Social Psychology, 88*, 948–968.

Adams, G., Anderson, S. L., & Adonu, J. K. (2004). The cultural grounding of closeness and intimacy. In D. J. Mashek & A. Aron (Eds.), *The handbook of closeness and intimacy* (pp. 321–339). Mahwah, NJ: Lawrence Erlbaum Associates.

Adams, G., & Plaut, V. C. (2003). The cultural grounding of personal relationship: Friendship in North American and West African worlds. *Personal Relationships, 10*, 333–347.

Akan, G. E. & Grilo, C. M. (1995). Socio-cultural influences on eating attitudes and behaviors, body image and psychological functioning: A comparison of African-American, Asian-American and Caucasian college women. *International Journal of Eating Disorders, 18*, 181–187.

Anderson, S. L., Adams, G., & Plaut, V. C. (2008). The cultural grounding of personal relationship: The importance of attractiveness in everyday life. *Journal of Personality and Social Psychology, 95*, 352–368.

Baumeister, R. F., & Leary, M. R. (1995). The need to belong: Desire for interpersonal attachments as a fundamental human motivation. *Psychological Bulletin, 117*, 497–529.

Beggs, J., Haines, V., & Hurlbert, J. (1996). Revisiting the rural–urban contrast: Personal networks in nonmetropolitan and metropolitan settings. *Rural Sociology, 61*, 306–325.

Berry, D. S. (2000). Attractiveness, attraction, and sexual selection: Evolutionary perspectives on the form and function of physical attractiveness. *Advances in Experimental Social Psychology, 32*, 273–342.

Carrier, J. G. (1999). People who can be friends: Selves and social relationships. In S. Bell & S. Coleman (Eds.), *The anthropology of friendship* (pp. 21–38). Oxford, UK: Berg.

Chen, N. Y., Shaffer, D. R., & Wu, C. (1997). On physical attractiveness stereotyping in Taiwan: A revised sociocultural perspective. *Journal of Social Psychology, 137*, 117–124.

Cunningham, M. R., Roberts, A. R., Barbee, A. P., Druen, P. B., & Wu, C.-H. (1995). "Their ideas of beauty are, on the whole, the same as ours": Consistency and variability in the cross-cultural perception of female physical attractiveness. *Journal of Personality and Social Psychology, 68*, 261–279.

Dion, K. K. (1973). Young children's stereotyping of facial attractiveness. *Developmental Psychology, 9*, 183–188.

Dion, K. K. (1986). Stereotyping based on physical attractiveness: Issues and conceptual perspectives. In C. P. Herman, M. P. Zanna, & E. T. Higgins (Eds.), *Physical appearance, stigma, and social behavior: The Ontario Symposium on Personality and Social Psychology* (Vol. 3, pp. 7–21), Hillsdale, NJ: Lawrence Erlbaum.

Dion, K., Berscheid, E., & Walster, E. (1972). What is beautiful is good. *Journal of Personality and Social Psychology, 24*, 285–290.

Dion, K. K., Pak, A. W.-P., & Dion, K. L. (1990). Stereotyping physical attractiveness: A sociocultural perspective. *Journal of Cross-Cultural Psychology, 21*, 158–179.

Eagly, A. H., Ashmore, R. D., Makhijani, M. G., & Longo, L. C. (1991). What is beautiful is good, but…: A meta-analytic review of research on the physical attractiveness stereotype. *Psychological Bulletin, 110*, 109–128.

Feingold, A. (1992). Good-looking people are not what we think. *Psychological Bulletin, 111*, 304–341.

Garner, D. M., Garfinkel, P. E., Schwartz, D., & Thompson, M. (1980). Cultural expectations of thinness in women. *Psychological Reports, 47*, 483–491.

Greenberg, D. R., & LaPorte, D. J. (1996). Racial differences in body type preferences of men for women. *International Journal of Eating Disorders, 19*, 275–278.

Iyengar, S. S., & Lepper, M. R. (2002). Choice and its consequences: On the costs and benefits of self-determination. In A. Tesser, D. A. Stapel, & J. V. Wood (Eds.), *Self and motivation: Emerging psychological perspectives* (pp. 71–96). Washington, DC: American Psychological Association.

Kim, H. S., and Sherman, D. K. (2007). "Express yourself": Culture and the effect of self-expression on choice. *Journal of Personality and Social Psychology, 92*, 1–11.

Langlois, J. H., Kalakanis, L., Rubenstein, A. J., Larson, A., Hallam, M., & Smoot, M. (2000). Maxims or myths of beauty? A meta-analytic and theoretical review. *Psychological Bulletin, 126*, 390–423.

Markus, H. R., & Kitayama, S. (1991). Culture and the self: Implications for cognition, emotion, and motivation. *Psychological Review, 98*, 224–253.

Markus, H. R., Ryff, C. D., Curhan, K. B., & Palmersheim, K. A. (2004). In their own words: Well-being at midlife among high school-educated and college-educated adults. In O. G. Brim, C. D. Ryff, & R. C. Kessler (Eds.), *How healthy are we? A national study of well-being at midlife* (pp. 273–319). Chicago: University of Chicago Press.

McManus, J. (2009, April 17). The dream she dreamed: Cheers for a voice to silence the cynics. *Washington Post*.

Palisi, B. J., & Ransford, H. E. (1987). Friendship as a voluntary relationship: Evidence from national surveys. *Journal of Social and Personal Relationships, 4*, 243–259.

Plaut, V. C., Adams, G., & Anderson, S. L. (2009). Does attractiveness buy happiness? "It depends on where you're from." *Personal Relationships, 16*, 619–630.

Plaut, V. C., Markus, H. R., & Lachman, M. E. (2002). Place matters: Consensual features and regional variation in American well-being and self. *Journal of Personality and Social Psychology, 83*, 160–184.

Rosenblatt, P. C., & Cozby, P. C. (1972). Courtship patterns associated with freedom of choice of spouse. *Journal of Marriage and the Family, 34*, 689–695.

Sangrador, J. L., & Yela, C. (2000). "What is beautiful is loved": Physical attractiveness in love relationships in a representative sample. *Social Behavior and Personality, 28*, 207–218.

Shaffer, D. R., Crepaz, N., & Sun, C. (2000). Physical attractiveness stereotyping in cross-cultural perspective: Similarities and differences between Americans and Taiwanese. *Journal of Cross-Cultural Psychology, 31*, 557–582.

Smith, S. M., McIntosh, W. D., & Bazzini, D. G. (1999). Are the beautiful good in Hollywood? An investigation of the beauty-and-goodness stereotype on film. *Basic and Applied Social Psychology, 21*, 69–80.

Snibbe, A. C., & Markus, H. R. (2005). You can't always get what you want: Educational attainment, agency, and choice. *Journal of Personality and Social Psychology, 88*, 703–720.

Stephan, C. W., & Langlois, J. H. (1984). Baby beautiful: Adult attributions of infant competence as a function of infant attractiveness. *Child Development, 55*, 576–585.

Streeter, S. A., & McBurney, D. (2003). Waist–hip ratio and attractiveness: New evidence and a critique for a "critical test." *Evolution and Human Behavior, 24*, 88–98.

Sypeck, M. F., Gray, J. J., Etu, S. F., Ahrens, A. H., Mosimann, J. E., & Wiseman, C. V. (2006). Cultural representations of thinness in women, redux: *Playboy* magazine's depiction of beauty from 1979 to 1999. *Body Image, 3*, 229–235.

Vandello, J. A., & Cohen, D. (1999). Patterns of individualism and collectivism across the United States. *Journal of Personality and Social Psychology, 77*, 279–292.

Wheeler, L., & Kim, Y. (1997). What is beautiful is culturally good: The physical attractiveness stereotype has different content in collectivistic cultures. *Personality and Social Psychology Bulletin, 23*, 795–800.

Wierzbicka, A. (1997). *Understanding cultures through their keywords. English, Russian, Polish, German, and Japanese.* New York: Oxford University Press.

Zebrowitz, L. A., Montepare, J. M., & Lee, H. K. (1993). They don't all look alike: Individuated impressions of other racial groups. *Journal of Personality and Social Psychology, 65*, 85–101.

# 27

# Multicultural Identity Development
## *Theory and Research*

### Richard L. Miller

Over the course of our lives, we inhabit several worlds, including the world that revolves around our family, the world of education, the job world and the world created by our culture. Our experiences in each of these several worlds influence our understanding of who we are and form the basis of our identity. As a result of globalization, assimilation, cross-cultural marriages, and immigration, we live in an increasingly interconnected world. Growing up in an independent, coherent, and stable culture has become less typical than it once was. The process of globalization alone, which includes the expansion of mass tourism, creation of multinational corporations, the emergence of multilateral governmental and non-governmental agencies, as well as the unprecedented availability of multicultural, media-based influences, has changed the processes by which individuals form a sense of identity. This chapter reviews the process of identity formation, especially the formation of a cultural identity, describes several factors that promote the development of a multicultural identity in today's world, and examines the positive and negative consequences of forming a multicultural identity.

## Theories of Identity Formation

How do we form a sense of who we are? Harry Stack Sullivan (1953) suggested that interactions with significant others was the primary source of a person's identity, while Hartman, in his book *Ego psychology* (1958), noted that a sense of identity prepares individuals for adaptation to both the biological and social environment.

Eric Erikson (1964, 1966, 1982, 1987) was one of the earliest and most influential theorists to examine the process of identity formation. Within the scope of his lifespan developmental stage theory, he conceptualized the process of achieving a stable identity as the most critical task of adolescence. Erikson suggested that individuals experience an identity crisis during adolescence and that the successful resolution of this crisis is dependent upon the extent to which individuals balance the various self-images they experience with the social roles that are available to them as they mature. Erikson's psychosocial theory takes into account both psychological and social factors in identity negotiation. Thus, the importance of cultural context is an integral part of the theory, for it is the balance between aspects of the individual and their cultural context that leads to the resolution of the identity crisis. Erikson (1964, 1966) made the point that an individual's culture provides people with an appropriate range of social roles from which to select who they will become and also a process by which they can validate their identity by providing a means for recognizing themselves in their chosen role. Similarly, in their book *Lives across cultures*, Gardiner and Kosmitzki (2008) point out that successful resolution of a crisis at any stage of development will depend on how the culture views the crisis and the chosen resolution. They note that while Erikson's ideas were based on models from Western society, they can be modified to be applicable to other cultural and ecological settings.

Erikson also suggested that situational changes such as immigration to a new country could cause an imbalance between the person and the cultural context in which they formed their identity. In his book *Insight and responsibility* (1966), Erikson suggested that those with strong identities are not likely to experience a renewed identity crisis but noted that even those with a strong sense of who they are, still respond to changes in cultural context: "Identity does not connote a closed inner system impervious to change, but rather a psychosocial process which preserves some essential features in the individual as well as his society" (p. 96).

Expanding on Erikson's ideas, Marcia (1966, 2002) suggested that the process of identity development is not limited to adolescence but continues throughout the lifespan as one's cultural context may change and develop. According to Marcia, a person's identity is influenced by personality, maturity, and cultural context. Marcia's identity status model (1966) proposed that identity is a result of two processes: exploration and commitment, which can result in one of four possible identity statuses. *Identity diffusion* occurs when there is a low level of exploration of identity options and little commitment to a particular identity role. *Identity foreclosure* occurs when individuals demonstrate a low level of exploration of what roles are available in their situation but demonstrate a high level of commitment to the role they may have prematurely chosen. *Identity moratorium* occurs when there is a high level of exploration with a low level of commitment. Going to college is a good example of this. *Identity achievement* combines a high level of exploration and a high level of commitment. Individuals with a strong sense of who they are (i.e., identity achievement) tend to be happier and healthier than those whose identity is diffused, foreclosed, or not yet fully formed. For more on the consequences of identity statuses see Chapter 5.

## Cultural Identity

What is a cultural identity? According to Richard Shweder and his colleagues (1998), cultural identity involves adopting the cultural worldview and behavioral practices that unite individuals within a community. The cultural worldview includes our conception of human nature, the relationship of the individual to society, and moral and religious values. Worldview beliefs are transmitted from generation to generation through everyday practices such as work, play, and meals, as well as culturally relevant rites of passage, including school graduation, marriage, and childbearing. Cultural identity includes a wide range of beliefs and practices and includes the key areas that Erikson (1968) considered to be central to the formation of a person's identity.

Erikson was not the only theorist to discuss the importance of cultural context in identity formation. Several researchers have noted the influence of contextual factors that are both immediate (one's present situation) and broad (the historical milieu) on the formation and experience of one's identity (Sellers, 1998). For example, if you are the only Hispanic person in a room of African Americans, you may become extremely aware of race, and that awareness will in turn affect your behavior and how you think of yourself. How situations can cause aspects of our identity to become more accessible has been demonstrated in several studies in which individuals were reminded of their cultural identity (e.g., Benet-Martinez, Leu, Lee, & Morris, 2002; Hong, Morris, Chui, & Benet-Martinez, 2000). Priming cultural identity can affect how people perceive and interpret a variety of stimuli.

James Côté's (1997) personality and social structure perspective model (PSSP) suggests that identity is a function of three factors: personality, interaction, and social structure. At the level of personality, an individual's identity formation is affected by self-perception and cognitive structure. Interaction refers to patterns of behavior that bring the individual into contact with family, friends, and the community. The social structure includes the prescribed roles available to the individual as well as the political, social, and economic conditions in their society. According to Côté, successful identity formation is more likely when individuals possess several elements of identity capital: the financial, academic, human, social, linguistic, and cultural resources readily available to the individual.

Other theories that suggest that membership in a cultural group or groups will influence how individuals define themselves include social identity theory (Tajfel, 1981; Tajfel & Turner, 1986) and self-categorization theory (Turner, Hogg, Oakes, Reicher, & Wetherell, 1987; Turner, Oakes, Haslam, & McGarty, 1994). These theories suggest that as membership in a cultural group becomes salient, individuals model their social beliefs and behavior on those they perceive to be prototypical of the group.

# Individualism and Collectivism

Cultural differences in how we understand ourselves in relationship to other people have received considerable attention from cross-cultural researchers. In cross-cultural research, the term self-construal is often used instead of identity. A self-construal is the awareness of our thoughts and feelings that provides an understanding of our private inner self: The theory of divergent self-construals (Markus & Kitayama, 1991) attempted to expand upon the limited "Western" view of the self held by many contemporary researchers. Drawing upon research delineating cross-cultural differences in the views of personhood, Markus & Kitayama (1991) proposed that self-construals could be divided into two distinct conceptual representations of the self: independent and interdependent. Although some aspects of the self may be universal, they asserted that the fundamental nature of the self-construal is inextricably bound to the culture in which the individual was reared. Independent self-construals are, according to Markus and Kitayama (1991), generally representative of individuals in Western cultures, while individuals in non-Western cultures are more likely to possess interdependent self-construals. Culturally shared assumptions about the relationship of the individual to others—the degree of separation or connectedness between individuals as perceived by people in a particular society—influence the view of self that characterizes an individual.

Markus and Kitayama (1991) and Singelis (1994) provided definitions of independent and interdependent self-construals. Persons of the Western world (e.g., the United States) generally subscribe to strongly individualistic beliefs, emphasizing the uniqueness of every individual and encouraging development of an independent self-construal. The independent self-construal views the self as an autonomous entity whose own thoughts, feelings, and actions are of utmost importance. Other people are important largely as a basis for social comparison, and the realization of internal attributes and accomplishment of personal goals are viewed as highly desirable states. In contrast, many cultures categorized as non-Western (e.g., China) are characterized as collectivist, focusing on the inherent connectedness of the individual to others. The interdependent construal of self is derived from this belief, viewing the self as an integral part of the social relationships in which one is engaged, and recognizing that thoughts, feelings, and actions are directly related to those of others with whom the person interacts. Relationships with others are integral to self-definition, as is the ability to maintain harmony in such social relationships (by engaging in appropriate actions, filling proper roles, and promoting the goals and needs of the group/others). In one representative study, Parkes, Schneider, and Bochner (1999) administered the twenty statements test (Kuhn & McPartland, 1954) to participants from nationalities classified as either individualist or collectivist (based upon Hofstede's individualism index, 1980). Their results clearly indicated that individualists are more likely to employ autonomous self-descriptions (referring to their own internal attributes), while collectivists are more likely to describe themselves with social references (referring to group membership or to other people). Markus and Kitayama (1991) posited that these divergent views of the self maintain a crucial role in the organization of one's self-regulatory schemata and the interpretation of one's experiences, leading to a variety of consequences. One's self-construal can affect cognitive, emotional, and motivational processes. Likewise, the self is also a product of the social experiences to which it is exposed, especially those of culture, which provides a continually evolving and dynamic presence (Cross & Madson, 1997).

The independent and interdependent self-construals, as described above, are closely related to the cultural syndromes of individualism and collectivism (Triandis, 1995). In fact, Triandis (1995) pointed out that Markus and Kitayama's (1991) terms independent and interdependent construal of self are more or less equivalent to the social patterns that he labels individualism and collectivism. According to Triandis (1996), a cultural syndrome can be defined as the following:

> A pattern of shared attitudes, beliefs, categorizations, *self-definitions*, norms, role definitions, and values that is organized around a theme that can be identified among those who speak a particular language, during a specific historic period, and in a definable geographic region. (p. 408)

Within a culture, variation exists in the extent to which one extreme of a cultural syndrome (in this case, individualism or collectivism) is emphasized above the other, but most members of a specific culture will tend toward the same view. In an individualistic culture, the definition of self is independent of the group; in a collectivistic culture, the definition of self is tied to the in-group. Triandis (1995) suggested additional attributes of individualism and collectivism that are helpful in clarifying the distinction between cultures that promote independent and interdependent self-construals. Individualists promote personal goals, while collectivists give priority to in-group goals. Individualists rely more heavily upon attitudes as determinants of social behavior rather than norms, which are a key influence upon collectivists' social behaviors. Individualists maintain relationships that are personally advantageous and eliminate those that are costly to the individual, but collectivists will often maintain individually taxing relationships if they are beneficial to the in-group. Triandis (1996) also identified factors that promote either individualism or collectivism within a particular culture. Heterogeneous societies that have a large number of role definitions but relatively fewer norms (complex and loose) promote individualism; homogeneous societies with fewer role definitions and a large number of norms foster the development of collectivism. High social class, migration, social mobility, and exposure to mass media also contribute to individualism.

# Sources of Multicultural Identity

Although the concepts of individualism and collectivism have received widespread attention, Hermans and Kempen (1998) have pointed out that in today's world, individuals are influenced by a much broader range of social processes than they were previously, and that cultural dichotomies suggesting we can categorize countries as individualist or collectivist are less useful than they once were for understanding identity formation. When Margaret Mead (1928/1961) wrote *Coming of age in Samoa*, she described a situation where a single cultural tradition led to "one girl's life being so much like another's" (p. 11). Growing up in a single cultural tradition is becoming more and more unusual today. In fact, in today's global world, it is more common for individuals to internalize more than one culture, speak more than one language, live in a multicultural community and have ties to individuals whose nationality is different from their own. Several factors contribute to our exposure to an increasingly broad range of cultural influences, including globalization, cross-cultural marriages, immigration, and the growing number of multicultural societies.

## Globalization

Globalization is an ongoing process of interaction and integration among the people and institutions of different nations. This process effects the environment, social and political systems, economic development, and human well-being in societies around the world. In recent years, international business, migration, and information technology have, in the words of journalist Thomas Friedman (2000), made globalization go "farther, faster, cheaper and deeper" (p. xviii). According to Wilkinson (1995) we live in a world in which there is a single, global civilization. By civilization, he proposes a transactional definition that suggests that the boundaries of a society are not defined spatially, but exist in terms of the connectedness between people.

Seen this way, globalization tends to "deterritorialize" the range of social influences on identity development and to diminish the significance of socioegographical location in regulating the flow of cultural experiences (Garcia-Canclini, 1995; Tomlinson, 1999). Although some theorists have expressed their concern that globalization will destroy localities and produce people who are homogenized and uniform, others have suggested that globalization removes the traditional anchoring of attitudes, beliefs, and behavior from their particular localities (Tomlinson, 2003). The latter view suggests that globalization is likely to promote the development of a multicultural identity that incorporates a broader based worldview.

## Cross-cultural marriages

As cultural boundaries become increasingly more flexible in today's world, the number of intercultural marriages and the children of such unions have increased. Rather than being instructed in the cultural expectations of one particular culture, children of these cross-cultural marriages are exposed to aspects of both cultures. When parents are of two distinctly different cultures—for example, one culture emphasizing an independent self-construal and one culture promoting an interdependent view of the self—children are likely to receive conflicting points of view. Matsumoto (2000) contended that under such circumstances, children develop multicultural identities, resulting in the existence of multiple psychocultural systems of representations in the minds of such individuals. Children of mixed marriages will incorporate this multicultural identity in one of three ways when developing a sense of self. Children of such marriages could draw upon aspects of both cultures, utilizing a mixture of independent and interdependent self-construals in which neither culture is represented in a robust manner. Alternatively, children may develop a strong sense of identification to both cultures, providing an exemplar of each. Another possibility is that children with multicultural identities will develop a sense of self that depends upon the context. These individuals may be encouraged to utilize aspects of either an independent or an interdependent self-construal, depending upon the social or cultural situation. A study by Oyserman (1993) suggested the final possibility, documenting the existence of both individualistic and collectivistic tendencies in response to differing aspects of the self among Arab and Israeli Jewish students in Israel, an area that, while traditionally considered collectivist, has been exposed to individualistic beliefs throughout its history of contact with cultures of the Western world. Oyserman (1993) asserted that individualism and collectivism are both culturally and situationally based.

If individuals with multicultural identities do indeed develop both independent and interdependent self-construals, which are then utilized differently based upon the situation, priming for one or the other should result in a shift in self-construal consistent with the prime. Gardner, Gabriel, and Lee (1999) found that such a shift does occur. They presented European Americans with both independent and interdependent primes. Primes consist of stimuli that influence responses to later stimuli. For example, an individual could be primed with the word *table* and then asked the meaning of the word *chair*. In that situation, they are unlikely to think of the chair of a committee and more likely to think of a kitchen chair. In the Gardiner et al. study, the participants who were primed with interdependence described themselves with a relatively greater proportion of interdependent statements than did those who were primed with independence. In addition, the participants primed with interdependence also made value endorsements and social judgments that were consistent with interdependent self-construals. They also found that the greatest shift in value endorsements occurred when participants were given a prime that contrasted with that encouraged by their own cultural context.

## Immigration

Because identity formation is a prime challenge for adolescents, children and adolescents who immigrate to a new country are likely to face some difficulty in integrating the culture of their parents and the culture of their new home. The degree to which this is a challenge is somewhat dependent on the age of the immigrant. Mena, Padilla, and Maldonado (1987) found that children under the age of 12 experienced less acculturative stress than did university students who had immigrated to the United States. Several factors may play a role in this difference, including the relative ease with which younger children acquire a second language.

Another important factor in the adjustment process is the type of support and assistance they receive from their primary caretakers while they make the transition to the new culture, as well as the peer and institutional supports in place to assist the newcomers. While peers and the educational system play an important role in transmitting the beliefs and values of the new culture, parents may continue to maintain the cultural practices of their home country. The socialization process for immigrants may also contain a role reversal when children provide their parents with information about the ways of the new country (Morales & Hanson, 2005). While the parents may benefit from learning what the children have discovered, it is often a burden for children to serve as cultural and linguistic brokers while still being socialized by their parents. For parents, the situation can be difficult, as they may have to surrender too much power to their children in coming to understand the ways of the new culture (Umana-Taylor & Fine, 2004; Weisskirch & Alatorre Alva, 2002). Finally, the degree to which the community in which a child lives accepts him or her as "one of their own" can have considerable effect on the child's psychological well-being and ability to achieve a stable multicultural identity.

Cross (1995) created a model that can be applied to the experience immigrants go through in developing a new identity. The model consists of four stages: *pre-encounter, encounter, immersion/emersion*, and *internalization*. In the pre-encounter stage individuals think of the world in terms defined by their cultural heritage. In the encounter stage, individuals experience attitudes, beliefs, and behaviors that are remarkably different from those to which they are accustomed. In the immersion/emersion stage, individuals often react to the culture shock of the encounter stage by idealizing the old ways. In the internalization stage they are able to embrace the best of what was and the best of what is new.

## Forming a Multicultural Identity: Gains and Losses

While a multicultural identity can provide feelings of pride and uniqueness, and a rich and varied sense of community and history, it can also lead to role confusion, values clashes, and competing cultural expectations. LaFromboise, Coleman and

Gerton (1993) described five models that can be used to illustrate different processes by which an individual may acquire a multicultural identity. They are *assimilation, acculturation, alternation, multiculturalism* and *fusion*.

Assimilation occurs when an individual living in a multicultural society attempts to fully embrace the culture that is perceived to be dominant. It often requires "culture shedding": the unlearning or rejection of aspects of the culture of one's parents. For example, Fordham (1988) found that academically successful African American students felt the need to reject the values of the African American community in order to achieve their academic goals. According to the assimilation model, an individual in transition between two cultures will feel isolated and alienated until accepted by the new chosen culture (Sung, 1985). In addition, the loss of support from the old culture and the initial inability to use assets of the new culture are likely to lead to social problems, academic underachievement, and anxiety-related disorders (Pasquali, 1985). According to Kerchoff and McCormick (1955) marginalization, leading to low self-esteem, poor social relationships, and negative emotional states, is more likely to occur when the individual's goal is assimilation but the barriers are manifest.

Acculturation occurs when an individual wants to become a fully competent member of the majority culture, but is still identified as a member of the minority culture. Such individuals may be considered to be bicultural and will often engage in a process called frame switching. Frame switching is a process by which individuals switch between two cultural orientations in response to cues from the environment. Bicultural individuals vary in their degree of bicultural identity integration. Those with a high degree of integration see their two cultural frames as complementary and compatible. According to Benet-Martinez and Hariatos (2005), individuals with a high degree of integration have better mainstream language proficiency, stronger mainstream cultural identity, and exhibit less anxiety and depression than those whose degree of integration is low. In addition, individuals with a high degree of bicultural integration are more responsive to cultural primes in ways that demonstrate a greater awareness of cultural context, while those who are low in bicultural integration are more likely to react to cultural primes in ways that demonstrate a reversal or contrast effect—exhibiting behavior that is opposite to the cultural prime (Benet-Martinez et al., 2002).

Alternation suggests that individuals may come to know and understand their original culture and the new culture and can then alter their behavior in ways appropriate to a given situation (Ogbu & Matute-Bianchi, 1986). Rashid (1984) suggested that this process allowed African Americans to function effectively within core American institutions while maintaining a sense of ethnic and cultural identity. He found that individuals who could effectively engage in alternation exhibited higher cognitive functioning and better mental health. A study by Sodowsky and Carey (1988) provides an example of the alternation model. They found that first-generation Indians who reported a high degree of proficiency in speaking English still preferred to think in an Indian language and that many preferred to eat Indian food and wear Indian clothing at home, but to eat American food and wear American dress when going out.

The multicultural model suggests that individuals can maintain a distinct and positive identity within the context of working and living in a multicultural society. Berry and his colleagues (Berry, 1984; Berry, Kim, Power, Young, & Bujaki, 1989; Berry, Poortinga, Segall, & Dasen, 1992) have argued that individuals who live in plural societies must face two challenges: how to maintain one's culture of origin and how to engage in intergroup contact. They have suggested that multicultural integration allows the individual to engage in the activities of one culture while maintaining identity and relationships in another. What makes integration possible in their model is the assumption that both the original and the new culture are tied together in a single social structure. Support for this type of integration comes from a study by Kelly (1971), who found that Native Americans in Tucson could occupy social roles in the local Native American community that were equal in status to those they occupied in the overall Tucson social structure.

Fusion suggests that cultures evolve and change as a result of multicultural influences and that a culture that shares social, political, economic, and geographic space will ultimately become a "melting pot." Gleason (1979) proposed that cultural pluralism would ultimately produce fusion. Unique to this process is the idea that both majority and minority cultures have an influence on the creation of the new culture. Support for this idea comes from studies by Weatherford (1988), who chronicled the influence that Native American culture has had on the social, political, economic, and cultural practices of non-Native Americans. In the fusion process, a multicultural identity is one that includes aspects of many contributing cultures. Thus, the answer to the question "Who am I?" becomes a composite derived from multiple influences transmitted through a variety of socialization processes and embraced by a host of individuals. How easy or difficult this process is depends on many factors. One factor is the degree of cultural distance between the cultures to which the individual has been exposed. Condon's (1988) research on Inuit adolescents' adjustment to becoming Canadian demonstrated that the greater the cultural distance between two cultures, the greater the psychological and social problems.

## Life in a Multicultural World

Ramirez (1999) coined the term multicultural personality to describe individuals who are able to function well in a multicultural society. His research focused on immigrants who successfully integrated aspects of their original worldview with the worldview prevalent in their new country. Other researchers have studied individuals who have developed a multicultural identity as expatriates working in international businesses (van der Zee & van Oudenhoven, 2000), as well as individuals who have responded to the increasing multiculturalism of their own country (Ponterotto, Costa, & Werner-Lin, 2002). In characterizing the multicultural personality, Ponterotto and colleagues have incorporated several theoretical perspectives that

**Table 27.1** Factors that contribute to multicultural identity development

| Model | Characteristics |
| --- | --- |
| Racial/ethnic identity (higher levels) | Connectedness to the individual's racial/ethnic heritage; openness to people of other cultural groups; cognitive flexibility; willingness to interact across cultures and a commitment to social justice for individuals from all cultural backgrounds |
| Coping with cultural diversity (balanced bicultural integration) | Ability to balance multiple roles; bicultural and multicultural interaction and coping skills |
| Tolerant personality | Empathic skills with a broad spectrum of people; self-aware, introspective, and self-analytic; cognitively sophisticated; sense of humor |
| Universal-diverse orientation | Appreciative of similarities and differences between self and others; sense of connectedness and shared experience with all people |
| Expansion of gender roles | Transcends multiple roles, thus enhancing social support and interpersonal anchoring; increased self-complexity; enhanced empathy skills |
| Collectivist values and mental health | Collectivist and spiritual essence to human interaction and self-growth |
| Expatriate multicultural personality | Empathic, open-minded, emotionally stable, action oriented, adventurous, curious |

*Source*: Adapted with permission from Ponterotto, Utsey, and Pedersen, 2006. Copyright © 2006 by Sage Publications

describe the components of a person with a strong multicultural identity. Table 27.1 summarizes these components. As can be seen in the table, a robust multicultural identity is based in a strong sense of personal identity, emotional stability, the ability to engage in self-reflection and to empathize with others, cognitive flexibility, and a sense of connectedness to others. In the aftermath of such natural disasters as hurricanes, earthquakes, and tsunamis, the outpouring of assistance from individuals far removed from the victims of those disasters suggests that more and more of the world's people may be developing a multicultural identity.

# Conclusion

In today's multicultural societies, adolescents are coming of age in a world where creating a cultural identity has become complex. In addition, globalization and immigration have created the need for adults as well as adolescents to integrate diverse cultural beliefs and behaviors provided for them by multiple agents of socialization. To further complicate the situation, many socialization agents are at times at odds with one another (e.g., parents and the Internet). The task of forming a coherent multicultural identity that allows individuals to become contributing members of society presents stressful challenges. However, the challenges of developing a multicultural identity can be met by developing the kinds of skills necessary for success in a multicultural world. These skills allow people to function well psychologically and to contribute to the society they have chosen to help mold.

Bicultural identity integration, the advance of cultural pluralism, and socialization processes that promote the factors described in Table 27.1 can assist in this developmental process. A multicultural identity has the potential to enhance our lives because it creates a sense of self-efficacy within the dominant institutions of a society along with a sense of pride and identification with one's heritage. As Bandura (1997) demonstrated, self-efficacy promotes effective performance. Thus, the individual with a multicultural identity is likely to believe he or she can live effectively and satisfyingly within a multicultural society. In the fast-paced changing world of today, that is a notable asset.

# References

Bandura, A. (1997). *Self-efficacy: The exercise of control.* New York: W. H. Freeman.

Benet-Martínez, V., & Hariatos, J. (2005). Bicultural identity integration (BII): Components and psychological antecedents. *Journal of Personality, 73*, 1015–1050.

Benet-Martinez, V., Leu, J., Lee, F., & Morris, M. (2002). Negotiating biculturalism: Cultural frame switching in biculturals with "oppositional" vs. "compatible" cultural identities. *Journal of Cross-Cultural Psychology, 33*, 492–516.

Berry, J. W. (1984). Cultural relations in plural societies: Alternatives to segregation and their socio-psychological implications. In N. Miller & M. Brewer (Eds.), *Groups in contact* (pp. 11–27). San Diego, CA: Academic Press.

Berry, J. W., Kim, U., Power, S., Young, M., & Bujaki, M. (1989). Acculturation attitudes in plural societies. *Applied Psychology: An International Review, 38*, 185–206.

Berry, J. W., Poortinga, Y. P., Segall, M. H., & Dasen, P. R. (1992). *Cross-cultural psychology: Research and applications.* New York: Cambridge University Press.

Condon, R. G. (1988). *Inuit youth: Growth and change in the Canadian Arctic.* New Brunswick, NJ: Rutgers University Press.

Côté, J. E. (1997). An empirical test of the identity capital model. *Journal of Adolescence, 20*, 421–437.

Cross, S. E., & Madson, L. (1997). Models of the self: Self-construals and gender. *Psychological Bulletin, 122*, 5–37.

Cross, W. E. (1995) The psychology of nigrescence: Revising the Cross model. In J. G. Ponterotto, J. M. Casas, L. A. Suzuki, & C. M. Alexander (Eds.), *Handbook of multicultural counseling* (pp. 93–122). Thousand Oaks, CA: Sage.

Erikson, E. H. (1964). *Childhood and society*. New York: Norton.

Erikson, E. H. (1966). *Insight and responsibility: Lectures on the ethical implications of psychoanalytic insight*. London: Faber and Faber.

Erikson, E. H. (1968). *Identity: Youth and crisis*. New York: Norton.

Erikson, E. H. (1982). *The life cycle completed*. New York: Norton.

Erikson, E. H. (1987). Remarks on the "wider identity." In S. Schlein (Ed.), *A way of looking at things: Selected papers from 1930 to 1980* (pp. 497–502). New York: Norton.

Fordham, S. (1988). Racelessness as a factor in Black students' school success: Pragmatic strategy or Pyrrhic victory. *Harvard Educational Review, 58*, 54–84.

Friedman, T. L. (2000). *The Lexus and the olive tree: Understanding globalization*. New York: Farrar, Straus and Giroux.

Garcia-Canclini, N. (1995) *Hybrid cultures: Strategies for entering and leaving modernity*. Minneapolis: University of Minnesota Press.

Gardiner, H. K., & Kosmitzki, C. (2008), *Lives across cultures: Cross-cultural human development*. Boston, MA: Pearson.

Gardner, W. L., Gabriel, S., & Lee, A. Y. (1999). "I" value freedom, but "we" value relationships: Self-construal priming mirrors cultural differences in judgment. *Psychological Science, 10*, 321–326.

Gleason, P. (1979). Confusion compounded: The melting pot in the 1960s and 1970s. *Ethnicity, 6*, 10–20.

Hartman, H. (1958). *Ego psychology and the problem of adaptation*. New York: International Universities Press.

Hermans, H. J. M., & Kempen, H. I. G. (1998). Moving cultures: The perilous problems of cultural dichotomies in a globalizing society. *American Psychologist, 53*, 1111–1120.

Hofstede, G. (1980). *Culture's consequences: International differences in work-related values*. Thousand Oaks, CA: Sage.

Hong, Y. Y., Morris, M., Chui, C. Y., & Benet-Martinez, V. (2000). Multicultural minds: A dynamic constructivist approach to culture and cognition. *American Psychologist, 55*, 709–720.

Kelly, M. C. (1971). Las fiestas como reflejo del order social: El caso de San Xavier del Bac. *America Indigena, 31*, 141–161.

Kerchoff, A. C., & McCormick, T. C. (1955). Marginal status and marginal personality. *Social Forces, 34*, 48–55.

Kuhn, M. H., & McPartland, T. (1954). An empirical investigation of self-attitudes. *American Sociological Review, 19*, 69–76.

LaFromboise, T., Coleman, H. L. K., & Gerton, J. (1993). Psychological impact of biculturalism: Evidence and theory. *Psychological Bulletin, 114*, 395–412.

Marcia, J. E. (1966). Development and validation of ego identity status. *Journal of Personality and Social Psychology, 3*, 551–559.

Marcia, J. E. (2002). Identity and psychosocial development in adulthood. *Identity: An International Journal of Theory and Research, 2*, 7–28.

Markus, H. R., & Kitayama, S. (1991). Culture and the self: Implications for cognition, emotion, and motivation. *Psychological Review, 98*, 224–253.

Matsumoto, D. (2000). *Culture and psychology: People around the world*. Belmont, CA: Wadsworth/Thomson Learning.

Mead, M. (1928/1961). *Coming of age in Samoa*. New York: Morrow Quill Paperbacks.

Mena, F. J., Padilla, A. M., & Maldonado, M. (1987). Acculturative stress and specific coping strategies among immigrant and later generation college students. *Hispanic Journal of Behavioral Sciences, 9*, 207–225.

Morales, A., & Hanson, W. E. (2005). Language brokering: An integrative review of the literature. *Hispanic Journal of Behavioral Sciences, 27*, 471–503.

Ogbu, J. U., & Matute-Bianchi, M. A. (1986). Understanding sociocultural factors: Knowledge, identity, and social adjustment. In California State Department of Education, Bilingual Education Office, *Beyond language: Social and cultural factors in schooling* (pp. 73–142). Sacramento, CA: California State University-Los Angeles, Evaluation, Dissemination and Assessment Center.

Oyserman, D. (1993). The lens of personhood: Viewing the self and others in a multicultural society. *Journal of Personality and Social Psychology, 65*, 993–1009.

Parkes, L. P., Schneider, S. K., & Bochner, S. (1999). Individualism-collectivism and self-concept: Social or contextual? *Asian Journal of Social Psychology, 2*, 367–383.

Pasquali, E. A. (1985). The impact of acculturation on the eating habits of elderly immigrants: A Cuban example. *Journal of Nutrition for the Elderly, 5*, 27–36.

Ponterotto, J. G., Costa, C. I., & Werner-Lin, A. (2002). Research perspectives in cross-cultural counseling. In P. B. Pedersen, J. G. Draguns, W. J. Lonner, & J. E. Trimble (Eds.), *Counseling across cultures* (5th ed., pp. 395–420). Thousand Oaks, CA: Sage.

Ponterotto, J. G., Utsey, S. O., & Pedersen, P. B. (2006). *Preventing prejudice: A guide for counselors, educators, and parents* (2nd ed.). Thousand Oaks, CA: Sage.

Ramirez, M. (1999). *Multicultural psychotherapy: An approach to individual and cultural differences* (2nd ed.). New York: Pergamon.

Rashid, H. M. (1984). Promoting biculturalism in young African-American children. *Young Children, 39*, 13–23.

Sellers, R. M. (1998). Multidimensional model of racial identity: A reconceptualization of African American racial identity. *Personality and Social Psychology Review, 2*, 18–39.

Shweder, R. A., Goodnow, J., Hatano, G., LeVine, H., Markus, H., & Miller, P. (1998). The cultural psychology of development: One mind, many mentalities. In W. Damon (Ed.), *Handbook of child development* (pp. 865–937). New York: Wiley.

Singelis, T. M. (1994). The measurement of independent and interdependent self-construals. *Personality and Social Psychology Bulletin, 20*, 580–591.

Sodowsky, G. R., & Carey, J. C. (1988). Relationship between acculturation-related demographics and cultural attitudes of an Asian-Indian immigrant group. *Journal of Multicultural Counseling and Development, 16*, 117–136.

Sullivan, H. S. (1953). *The interpersonal theory of psychiatry*. New York: Norton.

Sung, B. L. (1985). Bicultural conflicts in Chinese immigrant children. *Journal of Comparative Family Studies, 16*, 255–269.

Tajfel, H. (1981). *Human groups and social categories*. Cambridge: Cambridge University Press.

Tajfel, H., & Turner, J. C. (1986). The social identity theory of intergroup behavior. In S. Worchel, & W. G. Austin (Eds.), *Psychology of intergroup relations* (pp. 7–24). Chicago: Nelson-Hall.

Tomlinson, J. (1999) *Globalization and culture*. Cambridge, UK: Polity Press.

Tomlinson, J. (2003) Globalization and cultural identity. In D. Held and A. McGrew (Eds.), *The global transformations reader* (pp. 269–277). Cambridge, UK: Polity Press.

Triandis, H. C. (1995). *Individualism and collectivism*. Boulder, CO: Westview Press.

Triandis, H. C. (1996). The psychological measurement of cultural syndromes. *American Psychologist, 51*, 407–415.

Turner, J. C., Hogg, M. A., Oakes, P. J., Reicher, S. D., & Wetherell, M. S. (1987). *Rediscovering the social group: A self-categorization theory*. Oxford, UK: Blackwell.

Turner, J. C., Oakes, P. J., Haslam, S. A., & McGarty, C. (1994). Self and collective: Cognition and social context. *Personality and Social Psychology Bulletin, 20*, 454–463.

Umana-Taylor, A. J., & Fine, M. A. (2004). Examining ethnic identity among Mexican-origin adolescents living in the United States. *Hispanic Journal of Behavioral Sciences, 26*, 36–59.

van der Zee, K. I., & van Oudenhoven, J. P. (2000). The Multicultural Personality Questionnaire: A multidimensional instrument of multicultural effectiveness. *European Journal of Personality, 14*, 291–309.

Weatherford, J. (1988). *Indian givers: How the Indians of the Americas transformed the world*. New York: Fawcett Columbine.

Weisskirch, R. S., & Alatorre Alva, S. (2002). Language brokering and the acculturation of Latino children. *Hispanic Journal of Behavioral Sciences, 24*, 369–378.

Wilkinson, D. (1995). Central civilizations. In S. K. Sanderson (Ed.), *Civilizations and world systems: Studying world-historical change* (pp. 46–74). London: Altamira Press.

# 28

# Cross-Cultural Organizational Psychology
## An African Perspective

### Terence Jackson

Western organizational psychology scholars have ignored Africa for years, and it is often omitted even from cross-cultural texts. Aspects that impinge on the fundaments of human interaction, and that often take a back seat in organizational psychology, are highly evident when studying organizational behavior in Africa. Geopolitical dynamics cannot be ignored, and raise important questions concerning cross-cultural power dynamics, the nature of knowledge in organizations, and the process and ethicality of knowledge transfer. Similarly, questions of cultural identity are complex among processes of Westernization, cosmopolitanization, urbanization, intermarriage, biculturalism, and fundamentally the different levels of cross-cultural interaction involved. This chapter sets out to explore common issues in cross-cultural organizational psychology, such as leadership, management, decision-making, and motivation, drawing on what can be learned from studying organizations and human processes in Africa.

## Why Study Africa?

Much can be missed from organizational psychology if we overlook the 80% of the globe we call "developing." Africa, as part of this 80%, has long been ignored by behavioral scholars, and its study is still in its infancy. Its importance may primarily be understood through an appreciation of the cross-cultural dynamics operating on organizational factors south of the Sahara. Yet one of the difficulties lies in overcoming the pejorative and obstructive influences on scholarship of the "developing–developed" world paradigm (itself a cultural construct, defined by the "developed" world and also adopted by intellectuals and elite in the "developing" world) which still seems to persist, and certainly hampered research well into the 1990s (e.g., Blunt & Jones, 1992; Jaeger & Kanungo, 1990).

The developing–developed world dichotomy is perhaps indicative of the power relations existing on a global basis in Africa and influences the way we see organizational dynamics such as leadership and management effectiveness. When considering the cross-cultural dynamics of organizational psychology in Africa (most countries in sub-Saharan African countries are multicultural, all are subject to Western cultural influences, and many operate across borders in regional groupings), these power relations must be taken into consideration (e.g., see Human's (1996) view on this in the context of South Africa). The disparaging of African culture is but one example of such power relations, and the developing–developed world dichotomy is an articulation of this.

In addition to power dynamics, which must be considered a key element in the cross-cultural dynamics of organizational behavior in Africa, far too little systematic analysis of different cross-cultural levels of interaction has been undertaken. These levels at the very least include the following:

- *intercontinental*: interaction between Western (in its different varieties) and African cultural influences which can be pervasive in areas such as education and management practices;
- *intercountry*: interaction across borders, particularly as organizations increasingly do business in neighboring countries, encouraged through regional economic agreements (an interaction that was generally discouraged during colonial times); and,
- *interethnic*: intracountry, intercultural working within organizations where many African countries have a complexity of ethnic and language groupings, and where such cross-cultural working is commonplace.

These are the levels of analysis that impact daily lives, and affect the management of organizations and interaction within them. Yet the study of cross-cultural interaction in African organizations operating at these different levels and involving power relations has not yet been thoroughly undertaken. Concepts and theories which are now commonplace in the West, such as Hofstede's (1980) dimensions of culture, seem inadequate in explaining cultural interaction in Africa.

Africa's history, even before the slave trade, is one of cross-cultural interaction and often antagonistic dynamics (e.g., Reader, 1998), normally within systems of power relations (based on military, political, social, technological, and economic domination). Modern organizations in Africa still contain these diverse cultural elements: ideas and practices as well as people (Dia, 1996; Merrill-Sands & Holvino, 2000; Noorderhaven, Vunderink & Lincoln, 1996). Not only is an understanding of these dynamics necessary, but also a reconciling, integrating, and synergizing of disparities contained within these dynamics is essential to understanding behavior in organizations in Africa.

Much can be learned by studying these dynamics in Africa that can be applied and integrated into organizational psychology at a global level. However, a barrier to this is the view that African indigenous thought has little to offer. In some ways it is difficult to know, in a globalized world, what an "indigenous psychology" actually is. The convergence thesis suggests that world cultures are coming together, while the divergence thesis sees cultures as remaining distinct. The current author subscribes to the crossvergence view that different globalizing/localizing dynamics lead to hybrid forms of knowledge, organization, and action (cf. Priem, Love, & Shaffer, 2000). These dynamics can best be understood by focusing on three "ideal type" organizational systems that, through historical, modernizing, and localizing processes appear to represent the types of organization present in sub-Saharan Africa.

## Organizational Systems in Africa

These three types of organizational systems can be conceptualized as:

- *postcolonial systems*, arising through the historical and political legacy of colonial Africa, and representing a coercive-oriented form of organizational leadership;
- *post-instrumental systems*, arising from modernizing economic and structural influences, and represented by a results-oriented organizational leadership;
- Africa *"renaissance"* systems, arising from an embryonic cultural and political indigenous revival, focusing on humanistic values and represented by people-oriented leadership.

### Postcolonial organization

Descriptions of management in Africa have largely been informed by the developed–developing world dichotomy as noted above, and exemplified in the work of Blunt and Jones (1992), and that of Jaeger and Kanungo (1990), of management and organization in developing countries in general. Particularly important is the distinction between "Western" leadership styles (e.g., teamwork, empowerment) and "African" styles (e.g., centralized, bureaucratic, authoritarian) (Blunt & Jones, 1997).

However, systems of management identified in the literature as African (Blunt & Jones, 1992; 1997) or as developing (Jaeger & Kanungo, 1990) are mostly representative of a postcolonial heritage, reflecting a theory X style of management (McGregor, 1960) which generally mistrusts human nature, with a need to impose controls on workers, allowing little worker initiative, and rewarding a narrow set of skills simply by financial means. This system is identified in the literature as being "tacked on" to African society, originally by the colonial powers (Carlsson,

1998; Dia, 1996), and perpetuated after independence, perhaps as a result of vested political and economic interest, or purely because this was the way managers in the colonial era were trained.

Postcolonial organizational structures, in terms of their governance and decision-making, can be characterized as having top management that is overworked, and as having authoritarian and paternalistic decision styles with centralized control and decision-making (Kiggundu, 1989). This was also reflected in Blunt and Jones's (1997) view that leadership is highly centralized, hierarchical, and authoritarian. They also added that there is an emphasis on control mechanisms, rules and procedures rather than performance (and a high reluctance to judge performance), a bureaucratic resistance to change, a high level of conservatism, and importance of kinship networks.

The character of such organizations may well reflect public sector, state-owned enterprises or recently privatized organizations that are not foreign owned. Some of the inadequacies which Joergensen (1990) drew attention to, in relation to state-owned enterprises in East Africa, include lack of clear objectives, over-staffing, lack of job descriptions and job evaluation, lack of incentives, and political interference, as well as poor infrastructure and lack of systems. Part of the inefficiency of postcolonial organizational systems may be the levels of corruption and unethical behavior (e.g., de Sardan, 1999).

Internal policies may be discriminatory as a result of preferences given to in-group or family members. Kanungo and Jaeger (1990) suggested that because of the associative thinking in developing countries, there is a tendency for behavior in organizations to be context-dependent, rather than the developed country orientation toward context-independent behavior orientation. In the latter, explicit and universal rules apply to a situation rather than the situation and context determining responses to it. This may lead to decisions based on relationships rather than the application of universal rules, and may therefore be regarded as discriminatory. A reflection also of the theory X nature of management and general distrust of human nature, as well as a lack of organizational democracy may be revealed in employee policies aimed at duties of workers rather than of rights.

The internal climate of postcolonial organizations may be revealed in employee alienation. Accordingly, Kiggundu (1989) identified a number of features of such organizations: understaffing; poor motivation; risk aversion; unwillingness to take independent action; close supervision of subordinates with little delegation; high-cost, inefficient operations with low productivity; over-staffing; under-utilization; poor pay; and poor morale indicated by high turnover and absenteeism. Diversity, including ethnicity and gender, also seems to be an issue (Merrill-Sands & Holvino, 2000; although this is inadequately treated in the literature except that pertaining to South Africa). This may be a reflection of discriminatory policies based on context dependency, and promotion by ascription (who you are rather than what you have achieved; e.g., Trompenaars, 1993).

Given the coercive orientation of postcolonial systems, managers who fit in well could be expected to be motivated by control features of their jobs and by economic security. Although little research has been undertaken on management motivation in Africa, the few studies that exist (from Kenya and Malawi), although not recent, seem to support this supposition (Blunt, 1976; Blunt & Jones, 1992; Jones, 1986).

The direction of management commitment can also be derived from the above discussion. An indication of a commitment to "business" objectives involves the pursuit of end results at the expense of means, although not reflecting an achievement orientation. Montgomery (1987) for example, noted a regard for internal aspects of the organization rather than policy issues, development goals, or public welfare, remarking on an aloofness of managers in the public sector.

Management principles may be related to an external locus of control in developing countries, where events are considered beyond individual control, where creative potential is regarded as limited, and people are generally fixed in their ways and not malleable or changeable (Kanungo & Jaeger, 1990). This may also reflect a mistrust of human nature, and a belief in the undisciplined nature of African workers in industrial life (Abudu, 1986). I will return to this aspect later.

Decisions in postcolonial organizations are focused in the past and present rather than the future (Kanungo & Jaeger, 1990; Montgomery, 1987) and therefore may be deontological in nature rather than teleological. Action is focused on the short term, and success orientation may be moralistic rather than pragmatic as a result. This may reflect a lack of achievement orientation and status orientation as a management principle. A passive-reactive orientation (Kanungo & Jaeger, 1990) is assumed. This too may give rise to a theory X conception of management.

The way these principles are manifested in management practices is widely accepted in the existing literature as authoritarian management styles with reliance on hierarchy, use of rank, low egalitarianism, and a lack of openness in communication and information-sharing (Blunt & Jones, 1992; Blunt & Jones, 1997; Montgomery, 1987). This may lead to conclusions that the main organizational leadership orientations within postcolonial management systems are geared toward managing internal processes and power relations.

This conceptualization of African leadership within a developed–developing world creates perceptions of fatalism, resistance to change, reactivity, short-term vision, authoritarianism, risk reduction, and context dependency, among others, that may not seem useful when contrasted with management in the developed world. Implicit in this conceptualization is the notion that the developing world should be "developed," and thus become more like the developed world.

The developing–developed conceptualization often fails to recognize other (sometimes embryonic) management systems operating in Africa. It is also not sufficiently underpinned by cultural theory. The developing–developed world paradigm reflects a paucity of cultural analysis, and in management theory reflects the traditions of the convergence thesis (Kerr, Dunlop, Harbison & Myers, 1960).

Where this view of management in developing countries is explained by cross-cultural theory, reference is often made to Hofstede's (1980) value dimensions. Hence, Kanungo and Jaeger (1990) depicted the organizational situation in developing countries as relatively high in uncertainty avoidance (low tolerance for risk and ambiguity), low individualism, high power-distance (reflected in a lack of consultative or participatory management), and low in masculinity (a lack of competitiveness and achievement orientation, and a low centrality of work). Hofstede's (1980) data are not very helpful on African cultures, because he had low sample sizes from West and East African countries that he combined into two regional samples, and a Whites only sample from South Africa. The more current results from the GLOBE study (House, Hanges, Javidan & Dorfman, 2004) are more comprehensive but also somewhat limited in their analytical use.

The popular South African management literature supports a view that African cultures have a collectivist propensity (Koopman, 1991). Blunt and Jones (1992) indicated from the now somewhat dated literature that African societies are low on individualism. More recent studies that included African countries suggested lower levels of values associated with individualism (Munene, Schwartz, & Smith, 2000), and higher levels of those associated with collectivism (Noorderhaven & Tidjani, 2001; Smith, Dugan, & Trompenaars, 1996). Yet these say little about the nature of African collectivism, and provide little explanation of the "disconnect" thesis of Dia (1996), who postulated a separation between the individualist institutions of the colonizers (such as the firm) and the more communalistic local populations.

The concept of *locus of human value* in distinguishing an antithesis between an *instrumental* view of people in organizations, which perceives people as a means to an end, and a *humanistic* view of people, which sees them as having a value in their own right, and being an end in themselves, may be more useful in exploring the implications of this disconnect thesis (Jackson, 2002a). The Western concept of "human resources" typifies the former approach in its view of people as another "resource" to meet the objectives of the organization. It is likely that this concept would predominate in postcolonial African organizations to a certain extent. Blunt and Jones's (1992) assertion that African (postcolonial) organization is input- rather than output-dependent may lead to the conclusion that such organizational structure is not functional in the sense of objective seeking. Yet it is difficult to conceptualize such organizations as humanistic. Organizations in Japan and other East Asian countries may have been more successful in harnessing the latter (humanistic) approach in order to obtain employee commitment to the organization (Allinson, 1993), but organizations in Africa have largely not done this. Hence African workers see work organizations as instrumental toward providing a contribution to their own livelihood (Blunt & Jones, 1992) and that of their communal group.

The *instrumental-humanistic* construct may avoid some of the pitfalls of applying a developing–developed dichotomy (as in Jaeger & Kanungo, 1990), and of applying a simplistic individualism-collectivism model (Hofstede, 1980) to cultural analysis in explaining differences between indigenous and imported views of human relations. It may also explain the levels of inappropriateness of what is next termed post-instrumental management systems.

## Post-instrumental organization

A belief within the developing–developed world paradigm, reflecting the convergence theory of Kerr et al. (1960) and the contingency theory of Hickson and Pugh (1995; see also Cray and Mallory, 1998), is that the developing world, through industrialization, should become more like the developed world. This is reflected in the trend for Western management approaches to be imported into African countries through multinational companies, and Western approaches to be sought out by managers who are increasingly educated within Western or Western-style management courses, and trained in Western traditions. This may not only affect organizations in the private sector, but also those in the public sectors, including state-owned enterprises, and those recently privatized enterprises which are in the process of refocusing as a result of downsizing and other major organizational change. This may reflect also a disparaging of "African" (i.e. postcolonial) ways of organizing and managing. Much of the literature reviewed above reflects this disparagement.

Numerous authors (Beer & Spector, 1985; Hendry & Pettigrew, 1990; Storey, 1992; Tyson & Fell, 1986; Vaughan, 1994) have made a distinction, in the British and American human resource management (HRM) literature, between a "hard" organizational perspective, reflecting utilitarian instrumentalism which sees people in the organization as a mere resource to achieve the ends of the organization, and a "soft" developmental human relations approach which sees people more as valued assets capable of development, worthy of trust, and providing inputs through participation and informed choice. Tayeb (2000) quite rightly stated that the concept of HRM is itself a product of a particular Anglo-American culture. It is likely that both the hard and soft approaches taken within Western organizations are a reflection of an inherent cultural view of human beings in organizations as a means to an end (Blunt & Jones, 1997, used the term "functionalism"). If this is the case, it is likely that when Western companies, or managers educated in the Western tradition, try to implement Western human resource practices in cultures with a different concept of people, and a different regard for people in organizations, incompatibilities will be manifested through lack of motivation and alienation leading to low productivity and labor relations issues.

The extent to which such manifestations are the case in foreign-owned and Western management-oriented companies in Africa has been little researched. This remains at the moment a hypothesis ripe for testing. The Western ideal is seen as a concern for performance, a drive for efficiency and competitiveness, and a participative style, with relative equality of authority and status between manager and subordinate. This approach also features delegation of authority, decentraliza-tion, teamwork, and an emphasis on empowerment. This occurs within a context of acceptance of change and uncertainty, with high levels of trust and openness, and the support of followers being essential to commitment and high morale. Evidence over the last decade has suggested that organizations in Africa are mov-ing more toward this type of Western or post-instrumental approach (e.g., Kamoche, 2001). Yet some are struggling with the ideal of an African indigenous approach, and what this might look like.

## African renaissance organization

It may be somewhat idealistic to try to identify a particular African style or even philosophy of management and organization (Human, 1996), but it is worth point-ing to aspects that it may include, so that in empirical studies those aspects may be discerned where they do exist. Binet (1970) provided a useful framework on African economic psychology. Dia (1996) presented an account of this work, which can be supplemented and supported by popular African management texts (Boon, 1996; Mbigi, 1997; Mbigi & Maree, 1995), as well as specific anthropological work (such as that of Gelfand, 1973, which is used here to illustrate specific aspects of values of the Shona, a people indigenous to Zimbabwe, and comprising the largest ethnic group in that country). Key values can be summarized as follows.

*Sharing*
A need for security in the face of hardship has provided a commitment to helping one another. However, it is likely this value is not based on simple exchange, but is rather a result of a network of social obligations based predominantly on kinship. More recently the concept of *ubuntu* has been prominent in the South African popular management literature, a value built on the assumption that people are only people through other people. Mbigi (1997), for example, suggested that col-lective trust is a large part of this value that should be developed in organizations before participation and empowerment initiatives can succeed. Certainly Gelfand (1973) suggested that trust (*ruvimbo*) is seen as an important virtue in Shona cul-ture. Openness, sharing, and welcome together form important components of *ubuntu* (Boon, 1996). These aspects reflect a wider community orientation which also includes elements of family and other outside involvement, and a character that involves development and well-being of people, with a general people-orientation and sense of belongingness, trust and openness.

*Deference to rank*
Dia's (1996) assertion that this refers to power-distance (in Hofstede's 1980 con-ceptualization), particularly within the organizational context between employer and employee, is probably rather simplistic. Although traditional rulers were

such by virtue of their title to the senior lineage, they had to earn the respect of their followers and rule by consensus. Political decision-making occurred through obtaining consensus, and through a system of checks and balances against autocratic rule. People were free to express opinions and dissent (Mbigi, 1997). At the same time, taking one's proper place in the social scale (*kuzvipeta* in Shona) is an important aspect of the virtue of humility (*kuzvidukupisa*), and refers not only to deference to rank and seniority, but also to the senior person showing humility toward the younger person, and the educated person not looking down on those less educated (Gelfand, 1973). This is leadership control that involves benign rules of action, and promotion based on the legitimization of status.

### Sanctity of commitment

Commitment and mutual obligations stem from group pressures to meet one's promises, and to conform to social expectations. This involves both involvement within the group and loyalty to one's kinship and community group, as well as obligations and promises to external persons, for example within business dealings.

### Regard for compromise and consensus

This certainly involves the maintenance of harmony within the social context, but also qualifies the deference to rank discussed above. Boon (1996) summarized the main characteristics of traditional African leadership by saying that the chief personifies the unity of the tribe and must live the values of his community in an exemplary way; not being an autocrat, the chief must rely on representatives of the people, on councillors to assist him (chiefs were and are male), and must be guided by consensus. Failure to do so would result in his people ignoring his decisions and law. The people are strongly represented, with a duty to attend court hearings, and all have a responsibility to each other, collectively, to ensure the laws are upheld. As a result of this collective responsibility everyone has a right to question in open court. The concept of openness is an important value and implies that no one should receive retribution for anything said correctly in an open forum. If this is a latter-day idealization of consensual authority, it was also certainly a perception of early anthropologists working in Southern Africa (e.g., Gluckman, 1956). This is reflected in organizational structures that have flatter and more accessible hierarchies, consensus seeking decision-making, internal climates of participation and openness, and protection of rights. Management practices also reflect a participative, egalitarian, and open approach.

### Good social and personal relations

This stems from many of the aspects discussed above, particularly the commitment to social solidarity. Dia (1996) observed that the tensions of management–labor relations that have been a feature in Western and postcolonial organizations in Africa can be attributed largely to a lack of a human dimension, and to the adversarial attitudes of colonial employment relations. This is reflected in an internal organizational climate of interethnic harmony (although group solidarity may also act against this), other aspects of people orientation generally, and a humanistic orientation.

This presents a different picture to that of Blunt and Jones (1997) and other commentators on organizational management in African countries. Both this view, and an idealized view of what African management could have been (without colonial interference), is probably too simplistic, as I have stated above. With the increase in interest in African approaches to management, as indicated in the South African popular management press, and the general call for a renaissance of African thinking, values, education, and political transformation (Makgoba, 1999), any description of management systems within Africa should include a consideration of an indigenous African management.

This discussion has presented three systems of organization as "ideal types" that are purported to be operating in African countries. It is unlikely that these are operating in any pure form. The hybridization of management systems is an important consideration in Africa. Concepts of crossvergence have been operationalized and researched in other regions such as Hong Kong (Priem et al., 2000). These studies indicate that rather than a tendency of convergence (the coming together of value systems) in regions and countries with high levels of influence from other cultures, there is rather a tendency toward crossvergence (developing of hybrid value systems as a result of cultural interactions). The nature of change, and continued influences from different cultural sources in African countries, may indicate the development of hybrid systems of various forms.

## Leadership Styles in Africa

There has been little evidence of the nature of these hybrid forms of organization and how they are manifest in terms of organization and leadership in Africa. In a 15-country[1] management study the current author (Jackson, 2004) linked these organizational forms to leadership styles in order to gain empirical evidence of the nature of management and organization. In particular Etzioni's (1975) control styles were linked to the three "ideal" organizational types as follows:

- *postcolonial*: employing coercive control
- *post-instrumental*: employing remunerative control, or a results focus
- *African renaissance/humanistic*: employing normative control or a humanistic/ people focus.

The results of this survey of managers across 15 countries revealed a combination of coercive or controlling mechanisms indicative of postcolonial management systems, and results-oriented, remunerative control systems indicating the introduction of modern post-instrumental management systems. This appears to support the view of Kamoche (1992), whose case study research indicated an introduction of Western practices, yet still reflected the views of, for example, Kiggundu (1988) and Blunt and Jones (1992), who saw organizations in Africa as authoritarian and hierarchical—predominantly postcolonial—systems.

Yet despite a low people-orientation across the 15 countries, managers appear to have a strong desire to see a greater emphasis placed on a humanistic approach. With few exceptions, there appears to be a disparity between the perceived ideal situation, the current one, and that projected for the future. Nevertheless, with this particular orientation, by which managers express the way they would like things to be in their ideal form, there is greater variation among the countries than when they are expressing the way they see it at the moment, and the way it is going. If we make the logical assumption that the way managers see things at the moment and the way they are going reflects the perceived current organizational reality, their expression of an ideal can be seen as a value judgement of *what should be*, rather than *what is* of leadership and management styles. It is the way managers would wish it to be, and reflects their own values and attitudes (although not necessarily reflecting their behavior). This may explain why there is greater variance among the 15 countries for the *ideal*. Structures and systems may well be similar across a number of countries, yet values and management attitudes may be quite different. Managers from the Democratic Republic of Congo (DRC), for example, have a much lower desire for humanistic leadership than managers in Botswana, Kenya, or South Africa.

Some conclusions about leadership in African countries can be drawn from these findings:

- The values that managers hold of the ideal leadership and management style in organizations are out of line with the actual nature of organization in Africa. As this involves power relations that are enforced through control systems, and which tend to be low in consultation and consensus, this does not allow attitudes and values stemming from the cultural context of Africa to be converted to management actions. In other words, leadership in African organizations seems generally to be out of kilter with African cultures.
- Although there is some variation among African countries in what managers see as actual leadership and management styles in organizations, there appears to be greater variation in aspirations and ideals of managers among the countries. If this is a reflection of the cultural context in each country, we might assume that although the management influences on organizations in each country are similar, the cultural context is not. Generally speaking, it is unlikely that these differences are taken into account by organizations operating in different countries (e.g., multinational organizations).

- In order to take account of the expectations and ideals of managers, organizations should be moving toward a people- and results-orientation and away from a coercive controlling orientation (although with variation among the countries taken into consideration: e.g., DRC).

If organization and leadership style, *as is*, is out of kilter with African indigenous cultures, what are the implications for employee motivation and commitment?

## Staff commitment and motivation in Africa

Coupled with the difficulties of managing in Africa there may still be a legacy of the idea of the "lazy African" (Dumont, 1960), who lacks motivation (Blunt & Jones, 1992; Kiggundu, 1988) and has a high expectation of benefits to themselves and family, but low commitment and loyalty to the organization (Jones, 1986). Yet taken alongside the industriousness (Abudu, 1986; Ayittey, 1991) and entrepreneurial attitudes (Mbigi, 1997; Wild, 1997) noted outside the organized workplace, this assumption bears closer examination. Abudu (1986) proposed that attitudes of Europeans toward Africans in the colonial period could be explained by racial arrogance and a failure to appreciate the socioeconomic background.

One of the main challenges in the management of people in Africa, as elsewhere, is reconciling differences between home and community life, and the world of work. That is, organizations must reconcile societal culture with organizational culture (Jackson, 2004).

## Toward a conceptual model

Katz and Kahn (1978) used the term "control" to convey the styles of management used as "bases of compliance to produce the coordinated patterns of social behavior known as organizations" (p. 284). As we have seen, Etzioni (1975) posited three main forms of control: coercive, remunerative and normative. These have implications for employee motivation.

- *Coercive power* operates by being able to punish or compel through physical or other means, and would be related to authoritarian management styles.
- *Remunerative power* is based on an ability to reward people through monetary means or withholding or supplying other tangible resources, or intangible resources related to remuneration, such as promotion, and would be related to results-oriented management styles.
- *Normative power* relates to the ability to use moral and symbolic influence, and is more likely to be based on obligatory or reciprocal relations. This may need

more explanation beyond Etzioni's (1975) conceptualization, and must be placed within a cross-cultural frame of reference and linked with obligation and shared values (Jackson, 2002b). This is very much a humanistic and people-centered perspective that encompasses Etzioni's concept of normative control. Normative values have to be shared and internalized, and cannot be imposed. This suggests that people are involved in the organization as individuals with a value in their own right, and part of the corporate body, rather than as a means to an end as in an economic contractual relation, or a coercive relation with the organization. It would therefore be related to people-oriented management styles.

Etzioni (1975) suggested that these different forms of control influence the type of employee *involvement* with the organization. Hence:

- Coercive power would be associated with *alienative* involvement (or at best *compliant* involvement) with a corresponding lack of involvement in, or commitment to, the company.
- Remunerative power would be associated with *calculative* involvement where people are committed explicitly as far as they are rewarded appropriately, and as far as they lack alternative employment choices.
- Normative power would be associated with *moral* involvement where commitment is internalized and is implicit.

These three control types, and the type of employee involvement associated with them, can be linked directly to the three ideal organization types discussed above in the way employees are managed and the way employees are likely to respond:

- *Postcolonial management*: Derived from an historical colonial heritage, and including remnants of institutions tacked onto local communities (Dia, 1996), this is largely interpreted as "African" management (Blunt & Jones, 1992) or a management style of developing (as opposed to developed) countries (Kanungo & Jaeger, 1990). It is seen as autocratic, hierarchical, centralized, and bureaucratic. It is most linked with Etzioni's (1975) coercive control and management styles, and alienated or compliant employee commitment.
- *Post-instrumental (Western) management*: Evidence of the influence of Western HRM and management generally in sub-Saharan Africa was provided by Kamoche (2000) and Jackson (2004). This is essentially results-oriented, and seen as an alternative to "African" (or more accurately, "postcolonial") management in the sense of a modernization project within a developing–developed world paradigm. It is most linked to Etzioni's (1975) remunerative control and reflects results-oriented management styles and calculative employee commitment.

- *Humanistic or African renaissance management.* Embryonic indigenous approaches to management such as the *ubuntu* concept in South Africa (Mbigi, 1997) that reflect a cultural renaissance appear to distinguish humanistic management from other approaches. There is an emphasis on people as the major focus, together with a consensual approach to managing. It is more in line with Etzioni's (1975) normative control mechanism, as it appeals to people's community values and attempts to integrate the values of the work organization with those of community life. It reflects people-oriented management styles, and moral employee commitment may therefore follow.

Again, recognizing the absence of empirical evidence about employee commitment in organizations in Africa, the current author collected, with research collaborators, data from four countries: South Africa, Kenya, Cameroon, and Nigeria in approximately 10 organizations from different sectors in each country (Jackson, 2004). This replicated the questionnaire used in the management survey, focusing on employees' perceptions of *coercive-*, *results-* and *people-*oriented management styles, and sought perceptions on the *current* and *ideal* situations in their organizations. Within this study significant differences existed among country scores for current people- and results-oriented styles, but not ideal scores. This indicates a general desire among employees in the four countries that their organizations move more toward both people- and results-orientations. Employees shared a perception that these two orientations were lower than their ideals, and they saw their organizations as more results-oriented than people-oriented. Moreover, Nigerian employees saw their organizations' management styles as less people-oriented than employees from the other countries. Kenyan employees saw their organizations' management styles as more results-oriented than the other countries. Cameroonian employees saw their organizations' management styles as more coercive-oriented than employees from the other countries, but this was also represented in their ideal. Hence, Cameroonian employees appeared to favor coercive-oriented management significantly more than employees from the other countries.

Despite the fact that Cameroonian employees did not appear to associate coercive-oriented management directly with their work motivation, they did associate it with successful and ethical management as well as with high levels of management skills in their organizations. None of the groups favored low levels of coercive management, with all "ideal" scores falling above the mid-range score of 3. South Africans had the lowest ideal score and theirs was the only group of employees to negatively associate coercive management with work motivation, and to not associate it with successful organization.

Although further work needs to be undertaken to contextualize these results, it would appear that employees positively associate both people- and result-focused management styles with work motivation as well as with their organizations being ethical and successful, and having high levels of management competence. Nigeria is an exception in that no such connection appears to be made between people-oriented management styles and work motivation and successful organization. This could be because the vestiges of colonial, coercive management are still present, despite a move toward result-oriented, Western-style management. Certainly this is also reflected in the correlations between work motivation and result-oriented styles for Nigeria. Higher significant correlations between people-oriented management and work motivation for South African employees appear to reflect the strong articulation of empowerment and *ubuntu* in that country (Jackson, 2004). Yet Kenya also yields similar results without this kind of articulation in the popular management press.

Although employee motivation is under-researched in sub-Saharan Africa, the results from this study (Jackson, 2004) appear to support the assumption of a connection between management styles or the type of management control used in organizations, and work motivation. There is an assumption in the literature that coercive styles are in some way indigenous to Africa (e.g., Kiggundu, 1988), yet they appear not to be associated with work motivation. Although the appropriateness of Western-style results-oriented management appears to be supported by these results, there is a clear indication that management should be more people-oriented, or people-centered, perhaps reflecting a humanistic, indigenous African approach.

## Indigenous Psychology and Interethnic Level of Analysis

So far, much of this chapter has been concerned with the intercontinental level of cross-cultural interaction—that is, West–nonWest, or North–South dynamics. This is important because it provides the means of understanding power dynamics, and aspects such as the transferability of knowledge across continents, or indeed from one national cultural group to another. This is where Hofstede's (1980) work is useful as it provides the basis for a critique of the appropriateness of Western organizational and management systems in non-Western countries. Understanding the intercontinental level of cross-cultural interaction is important in Africa, because the colonial legacy permeates many aspects of organizational life. This includes interaction at the interethnic level.

An interesting finding from the 15-country study discussed above (Jackson, 2004) was the lack of significant differences among within-country ethnic groups, compared with the significant differences found among the African countries. The nations that constitute Africa were artificially created out of the power struggles of the colonial powers. In fact, these powers came together in Berlin in 1884 and divided up the continent of Africa between them. The accepted wisdom has appeared to be that, in view of the artificially created states, culturally ethnic groups are more important than national groups. Yet history has proved that these nation-states are stable. There are very few border disputes between African countries. Despite continual cross-border interaction within ethnic groups (as often the colonial powers split up ethnic groups between two or more national borders), the current author's findings (Jackson, 2004) appear to suggest that nations might be more important than ethnic groups in terms of cultural identity. There are a number of reasons for this, which are important for the study of indigenous psychology in Africa. These reasons, which we will now explore, consist of the colonial creation of ethnic groups, the shifting allegiances of ethnic identities, and migration and the identification of the "indigenous."

## Colonial creation of ethnic groups

Thomson (2000) argued that current ethnic groups are a creation of colonialism. Thus, the Hausa-Fulani, Yoruba, and Igbo of Nigeria, became the dominant groups in three regions of post-independence Nigeria (northern, western and eastern respectively), where "tribes" were encouraged to develop in order to work with the colonial authorities for distributing resources. Ethnic groups that had previously had only loose and changing affiliations came together as tribes; otherwise they had little power in dealing with the authorities and gaining resources.

Thomson described the example of the Yoruba, which he claimed is a modern social and political construct. Previous to colonial rule the term *Yoruba* did not exist. People of the region identified themselves as Oyo, Ketu, Egba, Ijebu, Ijesa, Ekiti, Ondon, or members of other smaller groupings, although they were aware of each other and had links through trade, social contacts, or war. They had a common language, but with different dialects that were not always mutually understandable. The colonial authorities wanted larger communities to deal with, as did the missionaries who consequently invented a standard Yoruba vernacular based on the Oyo dialect, and printed a Yoruba Bible. If people wanted access to Western education they had to adopt this common language.

## Shifting loyalties

This identification with a larger or more important group can be found in people's pursuit of better job opportunities. Nyambegera (2002), for example, pointed out the impact of ethnicity on areas such as recruitment and promotion opportunities. This is bound up with power relations within interethnic interactions in the workplace, where an ethnic group tends to predominate. Studies in the private sector in Cameroon found evidence of this particularly in the public sector, where national politics also becomes embroiled and can have a profound effect on how organizations and people are managed (Jackson & Nana Nzepa, 2004).

The role of political polarization by ethnicity and the resulting degree of political influence on HRM in Cameroon can be discerned first by the results of a survey undertaken in five ministerial departments, managed by three political parties. Three of these ministerial departments were managed by heads from the ruling party. Two departments were managed by two different opposition parties. An analysis of political affiliation according to appointment shows that for top-level managers (director to under-minister) 80% (of a total of 78 appointments made within the five ministries) were politically motivated. Top jobs in Finance, Post, and External Affairs were held by people from the ruling party; the Industry and Commerce Ministry was directed by the president of the ruling party; and the Scientific and Technical Research Ministry was headed by a member of the major opposition party.

It is normal for such managers to campaign for the ruling party during elections, rather than being at their posts, in order to maintain their positions. The implication of this may be the exclusion of talents of people not belonging to appropriate political parties and ethnic groups. The public service also experiences a relatively high turnover of managers, as people fall out of favor and others fall into favor. Being seen to be actively campaigning, and indeed returning the ruling party back to power, is a means of safeguarding one's job. Yet this situation also appears to give rise to inequity, frustrations, and low motivation at managerial levels. It also provides evidence of a dual system: a formal system put in place by French colonialism, and an informal system which has implications for power relations within interethnic interactions.

The informal system, generally established and used in preference to the formal system, has as its main function the dominance and preservation of power of the dominant group and its allies. Hence, formal power through the administrative influences of HRM systems (e.g., formal selection, appraisal and promotion procedures) is weak in terms of challenging the interests of the dominant group. This "tribalization" of the managerial workforce appears not to relate to any inherent ethnic antagonisms, but simply to political polarization along apparent ethnic lines (Jackson & Nana Nzepa, 2004).

At the level of recruitment and promotions, political patronage may not only affect who is favored. The process of ethnic phagocytosis (smaller groups being swallowed up by dominant groups) that this stimulates may actually be having an effect on the apparent ethnic composition of the country. It is therefore not unusual in the private sector of the economy, for Bakoko or Yabassi (both minority ethnic groupings) to present themselves as the more prestigious and influential Douala in the commercial city and port of the same name. Similarly, within the public sector, members of the various small minority groups around the Central Province may present themselves as the politically dominant Beti.

These aspects of politicization and tribalization affect the way people are managed in public sector organizations. This results in a lack of formal rules of recruitment and career progression: no promotion at the higher managerial levels in the public sector can be accepted if not approved within the informal system. The real decision-makers are not the leaders or managers of the formal system, but rather the king-makers of the informal system who appear to be motivated along political/ethnic lines. Apart from providing a better understanding of the fluid nature of ethnicity, and its relationship to power dynamics, this also enables the organizational psychologist to question the efficacy of any formal motivational system introduced in organizations where these informal processes may be in operation.

## Identifying the "indigenous"

It is very difficult, in the context of sub-Saharan African countries, to conceptualize and identify "the indigenous" or "an indigenous" people. For example, in the context of South Africa, the Khoisan peoples are generally regarded as the original occupants of the southern part of the continent, although now mostly obliterated by successive Dutch and British colonists (Beinart, 1994; Sparks, 1990). The Bantu people more recently moved into this part of the continent from much farther north and are now regarded as the "indigenes" (Reader, 1998). The extent to which Afrikaners established a "tribe" within South Africa, as quite distinct from their mostly Dutch origin, allowed them to be thought of equally as colonists and as indigenes some three centuries after the first settlements were established. If indigenous Blacks suffered under apartheid, so did the Afrikaners suffer under British rule. Yet to what extent can a White African "tribe" be thought of as indigenous? Clearly Afrikaners have no other home, other than in South Africa. These issues are well known and contested in South Africa (Beinart, 1994; Sparks, 1990). Similar issues could be raised within the context of the U.K. and U.S. in relation to successive waves of immigration and migration; who are the indigenes, and what constitutes the indigenous? This has implications also for what we consider indigenous knowledge, attitudes, and values, as well as organization and management, yet this also carries further issues of who identifies what is indigenous.

Within indigenous African institutions the chief is seen through Western eyes as an autocrat and his institutions reflect this high power-distance, in much the same way as we saw that the African organization is identified with a postcolonial construct. This is a view contested by Ayittey (1991), who described many African societies' chiefs as ruling by consensus. However, the view that African organizations can somehow revert back to indigenous values and structures is, as Human (1996) suggested, slightly naïve. Unravelling the indigenous from the long history of colonial occupation, intercontinental and intra-continental migration, and settlement is a complex project.

For example, Marsden (1991) described the use of the term "indigenous" in three ways. First is the reference to indigenous people. In this sense, the term as it is often applied to marginal peoples such as Native Americans or Australians, is difficult to apply to African countries. In colonial times, the whole Black population was often marginalized, and given second- or third-class status. The dispossessed today are a result of rapid urbanization and the breaking up of traditional agricultural rural communities and movement to the large cities. Marsden's second use of the word is in the context of "indigenization," for example following independence from colonial rule, and is not directly relevant here other than noting that this may have led to discrimination, for example against Asian groups in East Africa.

His third sense of the use of "indigenous" (Marsden, 1991) is in "insider knowledge": local approaches to management that reflect knowledge of the local context and local communities. Marsden (1991) gave the example of insider knowledge systems in farming. This therefore does not assume an indigenous people, but rather implies a distinction between what can be regarded as "local," as distinguished from "global." Global here could mean "Western," but could also be "Eastern"—the issue is imposition by, or adoption of, the "foreign." It is a knowledge of the local, by local people "who know what will and will not work" (Marsden, 1991, p. 31). Perhaps a way of linking these different concepts of "indigenous" may be to introduce a factor of social solidarity: that is, identifying oneself as part of a local community, having its own networks and insider knowledge and favoring one's fellow group members. In other words, one may take a lead from the literature on collectivism, where identity is based in belonging to a social group or network (Hofstede, 1980; Triandis, 1990) to the extent that the solidarity of collectivism is target specific: aimed at in-group members, and exhibiting different behaviors and attitudes toward out-group members (Hui, 1990). Here, insider knowledge may well be guarded and kept from out-group members, as Hui's (1990) discussion of Chinese family businesses suggested, and as the lack of knowledge on successful informal African micro-businesses suggests. An understanding of the indigenous as insider knowledge should therefore be qualified to reflect the multiple influences on the management of organizations in sub-Saharan Africa.

## Some Conclusions

It is important to understand that in order to do cross-cultural psychology in Africa, there is a need to pay attention to at least three levels of cross-cultural interaction: intercontinental, cross-border, and interethnic. The intercontinental is particularly important because it impacts the other levels substantially. National borders were defined by colonial powers. They also dictated the nature of interaction between them; the legacy of this still exists today in lines of transport and communication. Colonial powers also in some cases defined ethnic groups and influenced the nature of the indigenous.

At all these levels of cross-cultural interaction, power dynamics should therefore be given consideration. Cross-cultural psychology has not really provided good theories and tools for dealing with these power relationships other than at the interpersonal and organizational level. We may therefore have to look else-where—to, for example, postcolonial theory (Said, 1978/1995) to better under-stand the impact of geopolitical factors on cross-cultural psychological phenomena. A fertile region to do this is sub-Saharan Africa, where these issues are perhaps more manifest and in need of addressing than in the so called "developed" regions of the globe.

## Note

1   The 15 countries were Botswana, Burkina Faso, Cameroon, Côte d'Ivoire, Democratic Republic of Congo, Ghana, Kenya, Malawi, Mozambique, Namibia, Nigeria, Rwanda, South Africa, Zambia and Zimbabwe.

## References

Abudu, F. (1986). Work attitudes of Africans, with special reference to Nigeria. *International Studies of Management and Organization, 16*(2), 17–36.

Allinson, R (1993). *Global disasters: Inquiries into management ethics*, New York: Prentice Hall.

Ayittey, G. B. N. (1991). *Indigenous African institutions*, New York: Transnational Publishers.

Beer, M., & Spector, B. (1985). Corporate wide transformations in human resource man-agement. In R. E. Walton and P. R. Lawrence (Eds), *Human resource management: Trends and challenges* (pp. 219–253). Boston, MA: Harvard Business School Press.

Beinart, W. (1994). *Twentieth century South Africa*. Oxford: Oxford University Press.

Binet, J. (1970). *Psychologie economique africaine*. Paris: Payot.

Blunt, P., & Jones, M. L. (1992). *Managing organizations in Africa*. Berlin, Germany: Walter de Gruyter.

Blunt, P. (1976). Management motivation in Kenya: Some initial impressions, *Journal of Eastern African Research and Development, 6* (1), 11–21.

Blunt, P., & Jones, M. L. (1997). Exploring the limits of Western leadership theory in East Asia and Africa. *Personnel Review, 26*(1–2), 6–23.

Boon, M. (1996). *The African way: The power of interactive leadership*. Johannesburg, South Africa: Zebra Press.

Carlsson, J. (1998). Organization and leadership in Africa. In L. Wohlgemuth, J. Carlsson, & H. Kifle (Eds.), *Institution building and leadership in Africa* (pp. 13–32). Uppsala, Sweden: Nordiska Afrikainstitutet.

Cray, D., & Mallory, G. R. (1998). *Making sense of managing culture*. London: Thomson.

de Sardan, J. P. O. (1999). A moral economy of corruption in Africa? *Journal of Modern African Studies, 37*, 25–52.

Dia, M. (1996). *Africa's management in the 1990s and beyond*. Washington, DC: World Bank.

Dumont, R (1960). *False start in Africa*. London: André Deutsch.

Etzioni, A. (1975). *A comparative analysis of complex organizations*. New York, NY: The Free Press, 1975.

Gelfand, M. (1973). *The genuine Shona*. Harare, Zimbabwe: Mambo Press.

Gluckman, M. (1956). *Custom and conflict in Africa*. Oxford: Basil Blackwell.

Hendry, C., & Pettigrew, A. (1990). Human resource management: an agenda for the 1990s, *International Journal of Human Resource Management, 1*, 17–44.

Hickson, D. J., & Pugh, D. S. (1995). *Management worldwide*. London: Penguin.

Hofstede, G. (1980). *Culture's consequences: International differences in work related values*. Beverly Hills, CA: Sage.

House, R., Hanges P. J., Javidan, M., & Dorfman, P. W. (2004). *Leadership, culture and organizations: The GLOBE study of 62 societies*. Thousand Oaks, CA: Sage.

Hui, C. H. (1990). Work attitudes, leadership and managerial behavior in different cultures. In R. W. Brislin (Ed.), *Applied cross-cultural psychology* (pp. 186–209). Newbury Park, CA: Sage.

Human, L. (1996). *Contemporary conversations*. Dakar, Senegal: The Goree Institute.

Jackson, T. (1999). Managing change in South Africa: Developing people and organizations, *International Journal of Human Resource Management, 10*, 306–326.

Jackson, T. (2002a). The management of people across cultures: Valuing people differently, *Human Resource Management, 41*, 455–475.

Jackson, T. (2002b). *International HRM: A cross-cultural approach*. London: Sage.

Jackson, T. (2004). *Management and change in Africa: A cross-cultural perspective*. London: Routledge.

Jackson, T., & Nana Nzepa, O. (2004). Cameroon: Managing cultural complexity and power. In T. Jackson (Ed.), *Management and change in Africa* (pp. 203–233). London: Routledge.

Jaeger, A. M., & Kanungo, R. N. (1990). *Management in developing countries*. London: Routledge.

Joergensen, J. J. (1990). Organizational life-cycle and effectiveness criteria in state-owned enterprises: The case of East Africa. In A. M. Jaeger & R. N. Kanungo (Eds.), *Management in developing countries* (pp. 62–82). London: Routledge.

Jones, M. L. (1986). Management development: An African focus, *Management Education and Development, 17*, 302–16.

Kamoche, K. (1992). Human resource management: An assessment of the Kenyan case, *International Journal of Human Resource Management, 3*, 497–521.

Kamoche, K. (2000). *Sociological paradigms and human resources: An African context*. Aldershot, U.K.: Ashgate.

Kamoche, K. (2001). Human resource management in Kenya. In P. S. Budhwar & Y. A. Debrah (Eds.), *Human resource management in developing countries* (pp. 209–221). London: Routledge.

Kanungo, R. N., & Jaeger, A. M. (1990). Introduction: The need for indigenous management in developing countries. In A. M. Jaeger & R. N. Kanungo (Eds.), *Management in developing countries* (pp. 1–23). London: Routledge.

Katz, D., & Kahn, R. L. (1978) *The social psychology of organizations* (2nd ed.). New York: Wiley.

Kerr, C., Dunlop, J. T., Harbison, F. H., & Myers, C. A. (1960). *Industrialism and industrial man*. Cambridge, MA: Harvard University Press.

Kiggundu, M. N. (1988). Africa. In R. Nath (Ed.), *Comparative management: A regional View* (pp. 169–243). Cambridge, MA.: Ballinger.

Kiggundu, M. N. (1989). *Managing organizations in developing countries*. West Hartford, CT: Kumarian Press.

Koopman, A. (1991). *Transcultural management*. Oxford: Basil Blackwell.

Makgoba, M. W. (Ed.). (1999). *African renaissance*. Sandton, South Africa: Mafube/Cape Town, South Africa: Tafelberg.

Marsden, D. (1991). Indigenous management. *International Journal of Human Resource Management, 2*, 21–38.

Mbigi, L (1997). *Ubuntu: The African dream in management*. Randburg, South Africa: Knowledge Resources.

Mbigi, L., & Maree, J. (1995). *Ubuntu: The spirit of African transformational management*. Randburg, South Africa: Knowledge Resources.

McGregor, D. (1960). *The human side of enterprise*. New York: McGraw Hill.

Merrill-Sands, D., & Holvino, E. (2000). *Working with diversity: A framework for action*. Working Paper 24, CGIAR (Consultative Group on International Agricultural Research) Gender and Diversity Program, Nairobi, Kenya.

Montgomery, J. D. (1987). Probing managerial behaviour: image and reality in Southern Africa, *World Development, 15*, 911–29.

Munene, J. C., Schwartz, S. H., & Smith, P. B. (2000). Development in sub-Saharan Africa: Cultural influences and managers' decision behaviour, *Public Administration and Development, 20*, 339–351.

Noorderhaven, N, G., & Tidjani, B. (2001). Culture, governance, and economic performance: An exploratory study with a special focus on Africa. *International Journal of Cross Cultural Management, 1*, 31–52.

Noorderhaven, N. G., Vunderink, M., & Lincoln, P. (1996). African values and management: A research agenda, *IFE Psychologia, 4*, 13–50.

Nyambegera, S. M. (2002). Ethnicity and human resource management practices in sub-Saharan Africa: The relevance of managing diversity discourse, *International Journal of Human Resource Management, 13*, 1077–1090.

Priem, R. L., Love, L. G., & Shaffer, M. (2000) Industrialization and values evolution: The case of Hong Kong and Guangzhou, China, *Asia Pacific Journal of Management, 17*, 473–92.

Reader, J., (1998). *Africa: A biography of the continent*. London: Penguin.

Said, E. W., (1978/1995). *Orientalism*. London: Penguin.

Smith, P. B., Dugan, S., & Trompenaars, F. (1996). National cultures and values of organizational employees: A dimensional analysis across 43 nations, *Journal of Cross-Cultural Psychology, 27*, 231–264.

Sparks, A. (1990). *The mind of South Africa*. London: Mandarin.

Storey, J. (1992). *Developments in management of human resources*. Oxford: Blackwell.

Tayeb, M. H. (2000, November). The internationalisation of HRM policies and practices: The case of Japanese and French companies in Scotland. Presented at 11ème Congrès de l'AGRH, November 16–17, 2000, ESCP-EAP, Paris.

Thomson, A. (2000). *An introduction to African politics*. London: Routledge.

Triandis, H. C. (1990). Theoretical concepts that are applicable to the analysis of ethnocentrism. In R. W. Brislin (Ed.), *Applied cross-cultural psychology* (pp. 34–55). Newbury Park, CA: Sage.

Trompenaars, F. (1993). *Riding the waves of culture*. London: Brealey.

Tyson, S., & Fell, A. (1986). *Evaluating the personnel function*. London: Hutchinson.

Vaughan, E. (1994). The trial between sense and sentiment: A reflection on the language of HRM, *Journal of General Management, 19*, 20–32.

Wild, V. (1997). Profit not for profit's sake: History and business culture of African entrepreneurs in Zimbabwe. Harare, Zimbabwe: Baobab Books.

# Part XI

# Concluding Thoughts

We have seen in this book clear evidence of the advances the field of cross-cultural psychology has experienced over the past century. However, serious challenges remain. We see ongoing conflicts among the peoples of the world, often arising from political, religious, and ideological differences. Cross-cultural psychology has much to offer as we strive to understand others' feelings, cognitions, and needs.

As the world's population increases, we realize more than ever the impact of environmental limits and the inequalities existing in the distribution of the world's resources—in nutrition, education, and healthcare, among others. And advance of sophisticated technology has produced a mixed picture, improving communication, education, and access to information for many, but also contributing to the gap between the "haves" and the "have nots" in other cases. Cross-cultural psychology may well play a role in solving these complex problems, particularly to the extent that researchers can add to the data and knowledge base on needs of developing countries.

The teaching of cross-cultural psychology continues to grow, both in terms of the numbers of courses available, and the breadth and sophistication of material covered. This is as it should be, as cross-cultural studies find their way into the mainstream of psychological research and interest. However, we might also hope to see the day when all teaching in psychology will be sensitive to the importance of cultural influence on the science of the discipline. We could thus envision a future in which the teaching of cross-cultural psychology would no longer be necessary, a time when the term *psychology* will encompass not only the mainstream psychology of today, but also the role of culture.

# 29

# Cross-Cultural Psychology in Perspective

## What Does the Future Hold?

### Kenneth D. Keith

The field of cross-cultural psychology, as embodied in research and teaching, has come a long way since its modern era inception early in the twentieth century. From an early fascination with so-called primitive cultures, and how they differed from those researchers considered more advanced, investigators have moved toward a much more nuanced approach to the study not only of differences and similarities, but of the complex interplay between culture and behavior as well.

As the authors of the chapters in this volume have illustrated, cross-cultural researchers have explored a wide range of psychological processes, principles, and phenomena representing the spectrum of interests and subject matters of the discipline. From basic research methods to complex social interactions and organizations, cross-cultural researchers continue to advance our understanding. Yet there remain major issues for cross-cultural psychologists of the future. A host of serious challenges faces the world's cultures, and many of these challenges are candidates for psychological and behavioral understanding and solutions. Among these are the cultural conflicts engendered by political and governmental differences; major ecological and environmental problems; distribution of resources necessary for sustaining human communities; and the implications of technological change.

## World Conflict—Can Psychology Help?

### Political/governmental conflict

Violent conflict between cultural groups has existed throughout human history (Hofstede & Hofstede, 2005), and researchers have conducted studies aimed toward illuminating psychological principles that could aid understanding of international events and the kinds of decisions that lead to conflict. Bourne, Healy, and

Beer (2003), for example, used various priming strategies to establish cross-cultural conflict scenarios, including the existence of hypothetical peace treaties, and tested the level of conflict responses of young American adults. Although these researchers found that dominant individuals were more aggressive than others in the face of the conflict scenarios, and that there are differences in response for men and women, they acknowledged the need to take such research beyond the laboratory, to the international context in the real world. Despite its limitations, their work illustrates the potential contributions of psychology to cross-cultural relations in a world that is too often threatening and violent.

One form of violence that seems to cry out for cross-cultural understanding is the behavior of those individuals whom members of Western and Asian cultures have labeled terrorists. Several countries, including Bali, Israel, Japan, Saudi Arabia, Spain, Sri Lanka, and the U.S. have seen violent attacks in which the attacker deliberately dies (Locicero & Sinclair, 2008). Social scientists have offered explanations for such violent behavior, ranging from the individual level to the community or cultural level. However, psychological analyses are sometimes contradictory, prompting Locicero and Sinclair to develop a psychological model including recognition not only of politics, but also the religious and ideological backdrop of terrorism. In the context of such developmental and ecological approaches, cross-cultural knowledge of development, cognition, altruism, personality, and social processes will surely have a role to play.

Psychologists have long understood the importance of tolerance for differences, but acceptance of cultural difference is too often overcome by anger, hate, fear, ethnocentrism, and nationalism (Hatfield & Rapson, 2005). A key to effective relations and communication across cultures is the ability of individuals to control negative feelings and judgments about others—the ability researchers call emotional regulation (Matsumoto & Juang, 2008). In a related vein, Smith (2004) proposed that one of psychology's greatest contributions to international relations could be empathy—an understanding of the thoughts and feelings of others. Despite the fact that progress toward intercultural understanding sometimes may seem unattainable, well over a half century ago psychologists banded together to make a statement about peaceful relations among cultures (Smith, 1999). Signed by some of the most prominent psychologists of the time, *The psychologists' manifesto: Human nature and the peace: A statement by psychologists* (Allport et al., 1945) identified a number of tenets that remain timely today. They included:

- War can be avoided: War is not born in men; it is built into men.
- Racial, national, and group hatreds can, to a considerable degree, be controlled.
- Condescension toward "inferior" groups destroys our chances for a lasting peace.
- Liberated and enemy peoples must participate in planning their own destiny.

- The root desires of the common people of all lands are the safest guide to framing a peace.
- The trend of human relationships is toward ever wider units of collective security (Smith, 1999, p. 5).

World events of the six decades since they issued the *Manifesto* might seem to suggest these psychologists had little influence on cultural relations. Yet the possibility that psychology could contribute to understanding and reduction of conflict still might seem self-evident. However, Ratner (2006) observed that cultural psychologists have seemed disinclined to include political issues as a part of their studies of culture. And historically, out-group enemies have often served to preserve in-group cohesion (Hofstede & Hofstede, 2005). Nevertheless, psychologists have persisted, studying the psychosocial consequences of violence, terrorism, and disasters for children (Williams, 2007), the relation between international conflict and social identity (Kolbe, Boos, & Gurtner, 2005), and moral characteristics of rescuers, bystanders, and Nazis during the Holocaust (Monroe, 2008), among many other correlates of intercultural conflict. The need for continuing cross-cultural research and teaching seems clear.

## Environment/resource distribution

Further prospects for cultural conflict may be found in the connection between cultures and the environmental limits of the earth, and in the vast global inequalities that exist among the countries of the world—inequalities in, for example, income, nutrition, education, and healthcare. For instance, billions of people, about two thirds of the earth's population, have no safe sanitation facilities, more than a billion lack access to safe drinking water, and nearly two million children die each year as a result of these conditions (George, 2008). To those living in the industrial world, these resources are necessities, taken for granted by many—yet modern culture would not exist without them (see Johnson, 2006), and increasing world population will only bring the likelihood of more cultural competition for limited supplies of such natural resources as water. Life in the least affluent countries is especially difficult for people with disabilities, where no more than 10% of such individuals may receive any kind of human services (McConkey & O'Toole, 2000).

Similarly, while obesity has become a significant problem in some industrialized countries, at least a quarter of the world's population lacks adequate daily nutrition (Bryjak & Soroka, 1997). The increasing human population and the efforts of that population to develop the resources necessary to sustain it have resulted not only in conflict between cultures, but also in degradation of the natural environment. Thus, in developing countries, increasing population has produced massive deforestation, including destruction of millions of acres of rain forests each year (Bryjak & Soroka, 1997).

Cross-cultural researchers have begun to investigate behaviors and attitudes in the realm of environmental and ecological concerns. This work has included, for example, studies of motives concerning environmental issues (Milfont, Duckitt, & Cameron, 2006), water conservation (Corral-Verdugo, Carrus, Bonnes, Moser, & Sinha, 2008), and environmental values (Reser & Bentrupperbumer, 2005). Lest we assume that such environmental problems and conflicts exist only in developing countries, we need look only as far as heavily populated and industrialized regions of the U.S. to see major cultural conflicts over issues like availability of water and use of land (Walters, 2009). The time has surely come for a psychology that not only describes cultural differences, but also grapples in a serious way with the underlying causes of such differences as we move toward improved understanding of cultural and societal relations (Heine & Norenzayan, 2006).

## Technological change

I remember a fascinating conversation with my grandfather. He told me about his earliest recollections of the first locomotive when it arrived in his small town; the barnstorming airplanes that came to local fairs and festivals; driving to his wedding in a horse-drawn wagon; and the wonder he felt when, later in his life, he watched on television as the first humans landed on the surface of the moon. My grandfather's story reflects enormous cultural and technological change occurring within the lifetime of a single person. The lives of billions of people have changed in important ways as a result of changes in technology, transforming how we do business, how we educate our young, and even how we interact interpersonally.

For many of the world's people, technology, particularly as embodied in the computerized, digital realm of modern industrialized societies, has brought convenience, access to information, and greater affluence. On the other hand, according to Argyle (1999), heavy television watching is actually associated with reduced levels of happiness, perhaps suggesting that not all technology produces good outcomes for people, even in rich societies.

Many of the world's people, of course, lack access to technology. According to a report published by the International Monetary Fund (Jaumotte, Lall, & Papageorgiou, 2008), wider access to education is one key to a broader ability to take advantage of the opportunities associated with technology. But technology may be a double-edged sword; although income inequality (between "haves" and "have nots") has decreased somewhat in sub-Saharan Africa, in many other places around the world, including most industrialized nations, it has increased in the past two decades (Chen & Ravallion, 2004, 2007). This increasing inequality in income, Jaumotte et al. (2008) reported, has come as a result of the impact of technological change. And, although inequality of resources may not lead inevitably to cultural conflict, there is a need, especially in developing countries, for reliable, high-quality data from researchers studying the issue (Cramer, 2005).

## Summary

The issues I have mentioned in this section represent only a few of the pressing challenges facing the people of planet Earth in the twenty-first century. As long as we continue to exhibit the universal tendency to elevate in-groups and denigrate out-groups, humans will experience cultural conflict. Although today we would see many of his views as outmoded, Sumner (1906), writing more than a century ago, discussed these issues, and others—war, land, inequality, racial divides, women's roles, economy, and more—that continue to trouble us today. It is no doubt true, as Cole (2006) concluded, that psychologists cannot solve all the world's problems, but, Cole pointed out, if they work with others—from different cultures and different disciplines—psychologists can certainly be contributors to solutions for the common problems of humanity. There is no lack of opportunity, no dearth of challenges, for the budding psychologist with an interest in culture.

## Where Have We Been?

The authors of the earlier chapters in this book have provided a variety of cultural perspectives from which to view many of the subject matters of twenty-first-century psychology. These have included such broad concepts as universal ethnocentric tendencies, basic research methods underlying cross-cultural research, the wide scope of human development, the culture–cognition connection, the roles of women across cultures, culture and emotion, and human health and well-being. Some other chapters have a more specific or focused emphasis: educational assessment, the teaching of mathematics, historical aspects of research in perception, sexual minorities, psychotherapy, disabilities, conceptions of self, attribution theory, attractiveness, and African organizational styles. The authors of chapters on these topics, and more, have demonstrated that cross-cultural psychology spans a fascinating range of theoretical, empirical, and applied interests.

Although we have used the term *cross-cultural psychology* as an inclusive label, these chapters contain ideas consistent with the perspectives identified by previous writers as cross-cultural (Segall, Dasen, Berry, & Poortinga, 1999), cultural (Heine, 2008), and indigenous (Shams, 2002). And they touch upon aspects of all the domains that Kagitçibaşi and Berry (1989) suggested cross-cultural psychology should encompass: theory and method, biology and evolution, perception and cognition, social psychology, values and attitudes, personality, gender, human development, mental health and therapy, ethnic psychology and acculturation, and work and organizational psychology. Further, the authors of this volume share at least three core values:

1   They couch their work in research-based findings arising from empirical investigation.
2   They assign culture a central role in their research and their interpretations.
3   They are committed to broadening cultural understanding, and to strengthening cross-cultural psychology, through teaching.

The last of these, teaching, holds promise not only for development and communication of the content of cross-cultural psychology, but also for cultivation of the next generation of psychologists who will place culture at the fore in their own future work. What can we learn from psychologists who have made the teaching of cross-cultural psychology their central emphasis?

## Teaching Cross-Cultural Psychology

As you have seen in Chapter 1 of this volume, teaching in American psychology has too often been limited in its scope, with its focus placed largely on white European Americans. Western psychologists have too often assumed that their findings were universally valid (e.g., Arnett, 2009), leading critics to argue that mainstream psychology has been mechanistic, individualistic, and acultural (Misra & Gergen, 1993). The cultural limitations of Western psychology are not new; Albee (1988), for example, pointed out the ethnocentrism and prejudice present in the work of early leaders in the field, including Francis Galton, G. Stanley Hall, and Robert Yerkes, among others. Despite longstanding neglect of culture in the teaching of undergraduate psychology, Segall, Lonner, and Berry (1998) argued that cross-cultural psychology is a scholarly field that should find its place in the curriculum.

A number of teachers of psychology have worked to develop pedagogical approaches to effectively teach cross-cultural psychology. As early as 1975, Brislin wrote about teaching the subject, and Cushner (1987) characterized cross-cultural psychology as the "missing link" in teaching, suggesting that students' understanding of culture may be impaired by their lack of experience, and that, conversely students who have traveled abroad may lack the conceptual foundation to properly appreciate the experience. At about the same time, Cole (1984) observed that cross-cultural psychology was "often treated as a slightly miscreant stepchild, or perhaps as just a specialized method" (p. 1000). Cushner described the use of scenarios presenting students with depictions of incidents involving people from different cultures. This is a technique that Brislin, Cushner, Cherrie, and Yong

(1986) called culture-assimilator training. Participants chose from among possible alternative responses to the incidents, and received feedback about their choices—resulting in improved knowledge and empathy.

Goldstein (1995) offered guidelines to psychology teachers for integration of culture and diversity into the curriculum. Specifically, she recommended:

1  avoiding the marginalization of cross-cultural materials and perspectives
2  raising awareness about bias within the cross-cultural literature
3  avoiding the creation or reinforcement of stereotypes
4  using accurate terminology to make cross-cultural comparisons
5  distinguishing between etics and emics
6  creating a classroom environment in which diversity is valued. (pp. 228–231)

Cross-cultural teachers, Goldstein argued, could be transformative agents in moving the field of psychology toward recognition of human diversity and preparing students to more effectively combat bias and stereotyping in research and practice.

Hill (2002) further emphasized the importance of integration of cross-cultural perspectives in the teaching of psychology, not only noting the limitations of an ethnocentric American psychology, but also suggesting that the field would suffer the loss of multicultural and international students who might choose not to enter a field they perceived lacking in ethnic and cultural diversity. Hill's message echoed that of Albert (1988), who described the neglect of the concept of culture, and Romero (1988), who advocated for teaching emphasizing ethnic psychology.

More recently, Abrahamson (2009) described a variety of assignments designed to increase student awareness of culture and to bring students into contact with people of other cultures in meaningful ways. Abrahamson concluded that students gained heightened awareness and that faculty members reported improvement in students' ability to interpret research across cultures. Goldstein (2008) presented a large collection of teaching activities, demonstrations, and assignments similarly intended to aid student understanding and application of cultural concepts in psychology courses, and Phan (2009) reported the use of a variety of games and simulations to engage students with cultural issues.

Clearly, teachers of psychology are increasingly making culture an integral part of their courses, and courses in cross-cultural psychology seem to be increasing in number in curricula (Hill, 2002). And, in addition to the aforementioned teaching activities and resources, such groups as the Society for the Teaching of Psychology (http://teachpsych.org) and the Center for Cross-Cultural Research (http://www.ac.wwu.edu/~culture/) offer a variety of materials to support the teaching of culture and diversity. Cross-cultural psychology has indeed become a field meriting a place in the curriculum of the discipline (Segall et al., 1998).

# Summing Up

In an article prepared for an undergraduate student audience, Lonner (2000), a pioneering figure in cross-cultural psychology, emphasized the availability of resources, and the exciting promise yet to come in twenty-first-century psychology. He highlighted the vibrancy of the field, and the opportunities that lie ahead for students contemplating careers in psychology.

Increasingly, we live in a world made smaller by electronic communications, international travel, and multinational business. As I write this chapter, people have serious concerns about the H1N1 influenza virus—a pathogen that can spread easily from country to country as air travel facilitates rapid movement of people around the world. The people of Africa have more than 280 million mobile phones—vastly changing access of poor people to medical care, market information, and distant relatives (McPhee, 2008). The availability of information has, of course, become mind-boggling; for example, a recent Google® search using "culture" as a search term returned 187 million entries! And the interconnected components of the multinational financial system nearly collapsed in the financial crisis of 2008. These examples, as well as the ease with which international commerce has both created and displaced industrial and commercial interests, illustrate the importance of cross-cultural communication, negotiation, and understanding in the twenty-first century.

In addition to the potential for conflict at the level of governments, religions, or economies, individuals increasingly face the need to communicate and interact in their work and their travel (Brislin, 2000), with all the possibilities for misunderstanding and uncertainty inherent in such exchanges. Cross-cultural psychology is a discipline that will be important to the future of today's students, and researchers will continue to refine and develop more useful and effective methodologies (Heine & Norenzayan, 2006; Matsumoto & Yoo, 2006).

For the near term, advocates for the teaching and development of cross-cultural psychology (e.g., Hill, 2002) are likely to continue to seek more cross-cultural courses in the curricula of psychology programs. This seems destined to be both useful and necessary. But, as we come to the conclusion of this volume, we might imagine a future in which culture would be an integral part of all teaching and research in psychology. In such a future, we would not need specialized courses to ensure consideration of cultural variables, and our psychology would be a psychology of *all* people, not an ethnocentric European American discipline. This is the future Segall et al. (1998) dreamed of when they wrote that

> cross-cultural psychology will be shown to have succeeded when it disappears. For, when the whole field of psychology becomes truly international and genuinely

intercultural—in other words, when it becomes truly a science of human behavior—cross-cultural psychology will have achieved its aims and become redundant. (p. 1108)

I hope that you, the student reader, will be a contributor to this goal.

# References

Abrahamson, C. (2009). Infusing cross-cultural experiences into the classroom. In R. A. R. Gurung & L. R. Prieto (Eds.), *Getting culture: Incorporating diversity across the curriculum* (pp. 91–99). Sterling, VA: Stylus Publishing, LLC.

Albee, G. W. (1988). Foreword. In P. Bronstein & K. Quina (Eds.), *Teaching a psychology of people: Resources for gender and sociocultural awareness* (pp. vii–x). Washington, DC: American Psychological Association.

Albert, R. D. (1988). The place of culture in modern psychology. In P. Bronstein & K. Quina (Eds.), *Teaching a psychology of people: Resources for gender and sociocultural awareness* (pp. 12–18). Washington, DC: American Psychological Association.

Allport, G., Murphy, G., Crutchfield, R. S., English, H. B., Heidbreder, E., Hilgard, E., Klineberg, O. ... Tolman, E.C. (1945, March). The psychologists' manifesto: Human nature and peace: A statement by psychologists. *Newsletter of the Society for the Psychological Study of Social Issues.*

Argyle, M. (1999). Causes and correlates of happiness. In D. Kahneman, E. Diener, & N. Schwarz (Eds.), *Well-being: The foundations of hedonic psychology* (pp. 353–373). New York: Russell Sage Foundation.

Arnett, J. J. (2008). The neglected 95%: Why American psychology needs to become less American. *American Psychologist, 63,* 602–614.

Arnett, J. J. (2009). The neglected 95%: A challenge to psychology's philosophy of science. *American Psychologist, 64,* 571–574.

Bourne, L. E., Healy, A. F., & Beer, F. A. (2003). Military conflict and terrorism: General psychology informs international relations. *Review of General Psychology, 7,* 189–202.

Brislin, R. W. (1975). Teaching cross-cultural psychology: The United States, Asia and the Pacific. In J. Berry & W. Lonner (Eds.), *Applied cross-cultural psychology: Selected papers from the Second International Conference, International Association for Cross-Cultural Psychology* (pp. 277–282). Amsterdam, The Netherlands: Swets and Zeitlinger B.V.

Brislin, R. (2000). *Understanding culture's influence on behavior* (2nd ed.). Fort Worth, TX: Harcourt College Publishers.

Brislin, R., Cushner, K., Cherrie, C., & Yong, M. (1986). *Intercultural interaction: A practical guide.* Beverly Hills, CA: Sage.

Bryjak, G. J., & Soroka, M. P. (1997). *Sociology: Cultural diversity in a changing world* (3rd ed.). Needham Heights, MA: Allyn and Bacon.

Chen, S., & Ravallion, M. (2004). How have the world's poorest fared since the early 1980s? *World Bank Research Observer, 19,* 141–169.

Chen, S., & Ravallion, M. (2007). *Absolute poverty measures for the developing world, 1981–2004.* Policy Research Working Paper No. 4211. Washington, DC: World Bank.

Cole, M. (1984). The world beyond our borders: What might our students need to know about it? *American Psychologist, 39,* 998–1005.

Cole, M. (2006). Internationalism in psychology: We need it now more than ever. *American Psychologist, 61,* 904–917.

Corral-Verdugo, V., Carrus, G., Bonnes, M., Moser, G., & Sinha, J. B. P. (2008). Sustainable development principles in water conservation. *Environment and Behavior, 40,* 703–725.

Cramer, C. (2005). *Inequality and conflict: A review of an age-old concern.* Geneva: United Nations Research Institute for Social Development.

Cushner, K. H. (1987). Teaching cross-cultural psychology: Providing the missing link. *Teaching of Psychology, 14,* 220–224.

George, R. (2008). *The big necessity: The unmentionable world of human waste and why it matters.* New York: Metropolitan Books.

Goldstein, S. B. (1995). Cross-cultural psychology as a curriculum transformation resource. *Teaching of Psychology, 22,* 228–232.

Goldstein, S. B. (2008). *Cross-cultural explorations: Activities in culture and psychology* (2nd ed.). Boston, MA: Allyn and Bacon.

Hatfield, E., & Rapson, R. L. (2005). Social justice and the clash of cultures. *Psychological Inquiry, 16,* 172–175.

Heine, S. J. (2008). *Cultural psychology.* New York: W. W. Norton.

Heine, S. J., & Norenzayan, A. (2006). Toward a psychological science for a cultural species. *Perspectives on Psychological Science, 1,* 251–269.

Hill, G. W., IV (2002). Incorporating cross-cultural perspectives into the psychology curriculum: Challenges and strategies. In S. F. Davis & W. Buskist (Eds.), *The teaching of psychology: Essays in honor of Wilbert J. McKeachie and Charles L. Brewer* (pp. 431–443). Mahwah, NJ: Lawrence Erlbaum Associates.

Hofstede, G., & Hofstede, G. J. (2005). *Cultures and organizations: Software of the mind* (2nd ed.). New York: McGraw Hill.

Jaumotte, F., Lall, S., & Papageorgiou, C. (2008). *Rising income inequality: Technology, or trade and financial globalization?* Washington, DC: International Monetary Fund.

Johnson, S. (2006). *The ghost map: The story of London's most terrifying epidemic—and how it changed science, cities, and the modern world.* New York: Riverhead Books.

Kagitçibaşi, Ç., & Berry, J. W. (1989). Cross-cultural psychology: Current research and trends. *Annual Review of Psychology, 40,* 493–531.

Kolbe, M., Boos, M., & Gurtner, A. (2005). Social identity in times of international conflict. *Peace and Conflict: Journal of Peace Psychology, 11,* 313–336.

Locicero, A., & Sinclair, S. J. (2008). Terrorism and terrorist leaders: Insights from developmental and ecological psychology. *Studies in Conflict and Terrorism, 31,* 227–250.

Lonner, W. J. (2000). On the growth and continuing importance of cross-cultural psychology. *Eye on Psi Chi, 4*(3), 22–26.

Matsumoto, D., & Juang, L. (2008). *Culture and psychology* (4th ed.). Belmont, CA: Thomson/ Wadsworth.

Matsumoto, D., & Yoo, S. H. (2006). Toward a new generation of cross-cultural research. *Perspectives on Psychological Science, 1,* 234–250.

McConkey, R., & O'Toole, B. (2000). Improving the quality of life of people with disabilities in least affluent countries: Insights from Guyana. In K. D. Keith & R. L. Schalock

(Eds.), *Cross-cultural perspectives on quality of life* (pp. 281–289). Washington, DC: American Association on Mental Retardation.

McPhee, J. (2008). *Cell phone revolution.* World Vision Canada, retrieved from http://www.worldvision.ca/ContentArchives/content-stories/pages/CellularAid.aspx

Milfont, T. L., Duckitt, J., & Cameron, L. D. (2006). A cross-cultural study of environmental motive concerns and their implications for proenvironmental behavior. *Environment and Behavior, 38*, 745–767.

Misra, G., & Gergen, K. J. (1993). On the place of culture in psychological science. *International Journal of Psychology, 28*, 225–243.

Monroe, K. R. (2008). Cracking the code of genocide: The moral psychology of rescuers, bystanders, and Nazis during the Holocaust. *Political Psychology, 29*, 699–736.

Phan, L. U. (2009). Intercultural simulations and games. In R. A. R. Gurung & L. R. Prieto (Eds.), *Getting culture: Incorporating diversity across the curriculum* (pp. 269–279). Sterling, VA: Stylus Publishing, LLC.

Ratner, C. (2006). *Cultural psychology: A perspective on psychological functioning and social reform.* Mahwah, NJ: Lawrence Erlbaum Associates.

Reser, J. B., & Bentrupperbumer, J. M. (2005). What and where are environmental values? Assessing the impacts of current diversity of use of environmental and World Heritage values. *Journal of Environmental Psychology, 25*, 125–146.

Romero, D. (1988). Teaching ethnic psychology to undergraduates: A specialized course. In P. Bronstein & K. Quina (Eds.), *Teaching a psychology of people: Resources for gender and sociocultural awareness* (pp. 120–124). Washington, DC: American Psychological Association.

Segall, M. H., Dasen, P. R., Berry, J. W., & Poortinga, Y. H. (1999). *Human behavior in global perspective: An introduction to cross-cultural psychology* (2nd ed.). Boston, MA: Allyn and Bacon.

Segall, M. H., Lonner, W. J., & Berry, J. W. (1998). Cross-cultural psychology as a scholarly discipline: On the flowering of culture in behavioral research. *American Psychologist, 53*, 1101–1110.

Shams, M. (2002). Issues in the study of indigenous psychologies: Historical perspectives, cultural interdependence and institutional regulations. *Asian Journal of Social Psychology, 5*, 79–91.

Smith, M. B. (1999). Political psychology and peace: A half-century perspective. *Peace and Conflict: Journal of Peace Psychology, 5*, 1–16.

Smith, M. B. (2004). Realistic empathy: A key to sensible international relations. *Peace and Conflict: Journal of Peace Psychology, 10*, 335–339.

Sumner, W. G. (1906). *Folkways: A study of the sociological importance of usages, manners, customs, mores, and morals.* New York: Ginn and Company.

Walters, D. (2009, October 30). Fighting over water and land. *San Diego Union-Tribune*, B6.

Williams, R. (2007). The psychosocial consequences for children of mass violence, terrorism and disasters. *International Review of Psychiatry, 19*, 263–277.

# Index